WITHDRAWN

MANAGEMENT PRINCIPLES
and
PRACTICE

MANAGEMENT
INFORMATION
GUIDE : : 32

MANAGEMENT PRINCIPLES
and
PRACTICE.

A GUIDE TO
INFORMATION SOURCES

K. G. B. Bakewell

Senior Lecturer
Department of Library and Information Studies
Liverpool Polytechnic

GALE RESEARCH COMPANY · BOOK TOWER · DETROIT, MICHIGAN

OTHER BOOKS IN THE
MANAGEMENT INFORMATION GUIDE SERIES
Write for Complete List

INVESTMENT INFORMATION—Edited by James B. Woy, 1970 (MIG No. 19)

RESEARCH IN TRANSPORTATION—Edited by Kenneth U. Flood, 1970 (MIG No. 20)

ETHICS IN BUSINESS CONDUCT—Edited by Portia Christian with Richard Hicks, 1970 (MIG No. 21)

PUBLIC RELATIONS INFORMATION SOURCES—Edited by Alice Norton, 1970 (MIG No. 22)

AMERICAN ECONOMIC AND BUSINESS HISTORY INFORMATION SOURCES—Edited by Robert W. Lovett, 1971 (MIG No. 23)

INSURANCE INFORMATION SOURCES—Edited by Roy Edwin Thomas, 1971 (MIG No. 24)

COMMUNICATION IN ORGANIZATIONS—Edited by Robert M. Carter, 1972 (MIG No. 25)

PUBLIC AND BUSINESS PLANNING IN THE UNITED STATES—Edited by Martha B. Lightwood, 1972 (MIG No. 26)

NATIONAL SECURITY AFFAIRS—Edited by Arthur D. Larson, 1973 (MIG No. 27)

OCCUPATIONAL SAFETY AND HEALTH—Edited by Theodore P. Peck, 1974 (MIG No. 28)

CHEMICAL INDUSTRIES INFORMATION SOURCES—Edited by Theodore P. Peck, 1977* (MIG No. 29)

PURCHASING INFORMATION SOURCES—Edited by Douglas C. Basil, Emma Jean Gillis, and Walter R. Davis, 1977 (MIG No. 30)

EXECUTIVE AND MANAGEMENT DEVELOPMENT FOR BUSINESS AND GOVERNMENT—Edited by Agnes O. Hanson, 1976 (MIG No. 31)

MANAGEMENT AND ECONOMICS JOURNALS—Edited by Vasile Tega, 1977 (MIG No. 33)

AGRICULTURAL ENTERPRISES MANAGEMENT IN AN URBAN-INDUSTRIAL SOCIETY—Edited by Portia Christian, 1977* (MIG No. 34)

DEVELOPING ORGANIZATIONS—Edited by Jerome L. Franklin, 1977* (MIG No. 35)

*In preparation

Library of Congress Cataloging in Publication Data

Bakewell, K   G   B
    Management principles and practice.

    (Management information guide ; v. 32)
    Includes indexes.
    1. Management-Bibliography. 2. Industrial
management-Bibliography. I. Title. II. Series.
Z7164.07B25   [HD31]   016.6584   76-16127
ISBN 0-8103-0832-0

VITA

Kenneth Bakewell is a Senior Lecturer, Department of Library and Information Studies, Liverpool Polytechnic, Liverpool, England. He has held senior posts in a number of British public and special libraries and has been particularly interested in the problems of management documentation since holding the post of librarian at the British Institute of Management between 1961 and 1964. He is the author of the Pergamon Press publication HOW TO FIND OUT: MANAGEMENT AND PRODUCTIVITY, now in its second edition, and has contributed articles on management documentation to several periodicals including MANAGEMENT DECISION, INTERNATIONAL LIBRARY REVIEW, and ASLIP PROCEEDINGS.

CONTENTS

Contents

Contents

Contents

Contents

Contents

PREFACE

There is a tremendous amount of information available on management, and if we are to make effective use of this information to improve our performance as managers, we need to be adequately guided through the jungle. In this guide, Ken Bakewell has pinpointed the most important printed sources on all aspects of management, while drawing our attention to material other than printed books and periodicals where appropriate.

Ken Bakewell gained considerable experience in assessing the literature of management between 1961 and 1964 when he was in charge of the British Institute of Management's very busy library, the largest management library in Europe. Since that time he has lectured to various groups and has produced many publications on the problems of management documentation. In 1972 he was awarded the degree of Master of Arts by the Queen's University of Belfast for a thesis on the development of management documentation services in the United Kingdom.

I am very happy to commend this practical but broadly based guide, and I hope it will be put to good use by librarians and managers throughout the world.

John Marsh, C.B.E., D.Sc.
Assistant Chairman and
    Counsellor
The British Institute of
    Management
London, England

INTRODUCTION

Management is a vast subject, and it follows that any guide to its literature must necessarily be very selective. In making my selections I have almost certainly omitted items which some of my readers would have included, and listed items which some would have omitted. I hope, however, that I have presented a reasonably balanced approach.

The sections on the functional areas of management are particularly selective. These could themselves be the subjects of major bibliographies--some indeed have been covered in this series--so that I have attempted to record only major works of reference and works which make a special contribution.

In addition to books and periodicals, I have pointed out significant periodical articles, organizations, and films and other audiovisual materials. We must cease to think only in terms of the printed word when seeking information.

While compiling this guide I was disturbed by the number of publications lacking indexes. Such publications must have a limited value for people seeking specific items of information, and I have drawn attention to this serious omission in my annotations.

In the arrangement of this guide I have used THE LONDON CLASSIFICATION OF BUSINESS STUDIES (see item 2065), with some amendments. This classification scheme may be new to American readers, but it is used in approximately fifty libraries in Britain and a number of other countries, and has been translated into French.

Many titles listed in the guide deal, of course, with multifaceted subjects such as management by objectives in local government. To have listed each such subject as it appeared (in some cases three or four times) would have bulked the guide excessively. I have provided some cross-references, but the surest way of locating every item relating to a topic is to use the alphabetical subject index. I have indicated which items are available in a paperback edition.

Introduction

I am pleased to acknowledge the help of many people, beginning with those who kindly supplied information at some stage: Phyllis Cutting, Lorna M. Daniells, Gillian Dare, Bridget Howard, Julia Juttke, Kathleen Morris, Doreen Mortimer, Josephine Salond, and Julia Seaton. I am grateful to the librarians of the British Institute of Management, the Central Management Library of the British Civil Service Department, the London Graduate School of Business Studies, the Manchester Business School, and the Urwick Management Center for allowing me to use their resources. Teresa Buckley gave me valuable help with bibliographic checking and my wife, Agnes, was a tower of strength in many ways, notably in the compilation of the indexes. Last but by no means least I am very grateful to Paul Wasserman, general editor of the MIG series, and Margaret Fisk, former MIG Coordinator at the Gale Research Company, not only for their help and encouragement but also for entrusting the compilation of this guide to me, a foreigner. I like to think that this is some acknowledgment of the increased contribution made to management literature by British writers during recent years, following the excellent examples set by our American friends.

I alone, of course, remain responsible for any errors or omissions.

K.G.B. Bakewell
Liverpool, England

ABBREVIATIONS USED IN THIS GUIDE

AMA	American Management Association
BIM	British Institute of Management
CPM	critical path method
EDP	electronic data processing
MBO	management by objectives
MD	management development
MIS	management information systems
MTM	methods-time-measurement
O & M	organization and methods (British term for systems and procedures)
OD	organization development or organization design
OR	operations research
PDM	physical distribution management
PERT	program evaluation and review technique
PMTS	predetermined motion time systems
PPBS	planning-program-budgeting system
R & D	research and development

Section 1

MANAGEMENT IN GENERAL

Few managers would agree with one of the definitions of "management," given in THE CONCISE OXFORD DICTIONARY (5th ed., 1964), "trickery, deceitful connivance," although devotees of musicals who recall HOW TO SUCCEED IN BUSINESS WITHOUT REALLY TRYING might feel there is something in this definition. More acceptable is the definition offered by Dalton E. McFarland in MANAGEMENT: PRINCIPLES AND PRACTICES (item 186 below): "the basic, integrating process of the organizational activity that surrounds our daily life." McFarland points out that management is a process universal to all organized living and is not confined to factory, store, or office. True though this undoubtedly is, the emphasis in this guide is on management in business and industrial enterprises.

This first section begins with works on the history and development of management ideas and a selection of the classics of management, followed by bibliographies and other reference works, textbooks, and other materials dealing with the broad area of management rather than some particular aspect.

THE HISTORY OF MANAGEMENT

1   Aitken, Hugh G.J. TAYLORISM AT WATERTOWN ARSENAL: SCIEN-
     TIFIC MANAGEMENT IN ACTION 1908-1915. Cambridge, Mass.: Har-
     vard University Press, 1960. 269 p. Bibliography.

     This is a detailed case study of the application of scientific
     management at Watertown Arsenal, near Boston, and its results.

2   American Society of Mechanical Engineers. FIFTY YEARS' PROGRESS IN
     MANAGEMENT, 1910-1960. New York: 1960. 329 p. Illustrations,
     diagrams, tables.

     This book traces the development of the art and science of
     management as reflected in the cumulative TEN YEARS PROG-
     RESS IN MANAGEMENT reports sponsored by the Manage-
     ment Division of ASME and published in the transactions of
     the society. It contains an index of names (authors and sub-
     jects) but no topic index.

1

3   Bursk, Edward C.; Clark, Donald T.; and Hidy, Ralph W., eds. THE
    WORLD OF BUSINESS: A SELECTED LIBRARY OF THE LITERATURE OF
    BUSINESS FROM THE ACCOUNTING CODE OF HAMMURABI TO THE
    20TH CENTURY 'ADMINISTRATOR'S PRAYER.' 4 vols. New York:
    Simon & Schuster, 1962. xii, 2,655 p. Illustrations, portraits.

    Each volume has a separate index, with a comprehensive one
    in volume 4.

4   George, Claude S., Jr. THE HISTORY OF MANAGEMENT THOUGHT.
    2d ed. Englewood Cliffs, N.J.: Prentice-Hall, 1972. xvi, 223 p. Bib-
    liography. Paperback.

    The author traces the development of management ideas from
    prehistory to the present day, with a chronology (5000 B.C.
    to 1955), pp. vii-xiii. Selected chronological bibliography
    of management literature (500 B.C. to 1971), pp. 189-216.

5   Tillett, Anthony; Kempner, Thomas; and Wills, Gordon, eds. MANAGE-
    MENT THINKERS. Harmondsworth, Eng.: Penguin, 1970; Magnolia,
    Mass.: Peter Smith, 1970. 363 p. Diagrams, tables, bibliographies.
    Paperback.

    The editors present the development of management techniques
    in four sections: a historical perspective of industry and man-
    agement; the criterion of efficiency as seen in the work of
    Taylor, Gilbreth, and Fayol, and the development of opera-
    tional research; the criterion of welfare with particular refer-
    ence to the work of B. Seebohm Rowntree; the criterion of
    cooperation, including the work of Mary Parker Follett, Elton
    Mayo, and Chester Barnard.

6   Urwick, Lyndall Fownes. "The Development of Scientific Management in
    Great Britain." BRITISH MANAGEMENT REVIEW 3 (1938): 18-96.

    Urwick's article is an outstanding review of the evolution of
    modern management practice in Britain, including the develop-
    ment of management literature.

7   Urwick, Lyndall Fownes, and Brech, E.F.L. THE MAKING OF SCIEN-
    TIFIC MANAGEMENT. 3 vols. London: Management Publications Trust
    and Pitman, 1946-48.

    Volume 1 (Pitman, 1946. 196 p. Portraits, tables, bibliog-
    raphies), entitled THIRTEEN PIONEERS, contains biographies
    of Babbage, Taylor, Fayol, Follett, Rowntree, Gantt, Walter
    Rathenau, Henry Le Chatelier, Charles de Freminville, Henry
    S. Dennison, F.B. Gilbreth, and Edward Tregaskiss Elbourne,
    with chapters on scientific management and society, scientific
    management, and government. Volume 2 (Management Publi-
    cations Trust, 1946. 241 p. Illustrations, diagrams [2 folding],

2

portraits, bibliographies) is entitled MANAGEMENT IN BRIT-
ISH INDUSTRY. Volume 3 (Management Publications Trust,
1948. 225 p. Illustrations, diagrams, tables) is entitled THE
HAWTHORNE INVESTIGATIONS.

8   Wren, Daniel A. THE EVOLUTION OF MANAGEMENT THOUGHT.
New York: Ronald Press, 1972. xii, 556 p. Diagrams, bibliography.

This is a scholarly study that reviews the development of management ideas, from prehistory through the scientific management movement and "social man" eras to the present day. Indexes of names and subjects.

Bibliography

9   Larsen, Henrietta M. GUIDE TO BUSINESS HISTORY: MATERIALS FOR
THE STUDY OF AMERICAN BUSINESS HISTORY AND SUGGESTIONS
FOR THEIR USE. Cambridge, Mass.: Harvard University Press, 1948.
xxvi, 1,181 p.

This useful bibliography lists 4,904 items, classified under
seven broad headings and annotated. It includes biographies,
histories of industries, and histories of individual firms.

Periodicals

10   BUSINESS HISTORY. London: Cass, 1958- . Twice yearly.

11   BUSINESS HISTORY REVIEW. Boston: Harvard University Graduate School
of Business Administration, 1926- . Quarterly.

CLASSICS

12   American Society of Mechanical Engineers. THE FRANK GILBRETH CEN-
TENNIAL. Winter Annual Meeting, New York, December 1968. New
York: 1969. 116 p. Illustrations, bibliography. Paperback.

Published in celebration of the centennial of Frank Gilbreth's
birth, this book contains papers given at the winter annual
meeting of ASME, including personal reminiscences of Gilbreth
as a pioneer, philosopher, and human being, together with papers on current applications of motion study. A bibliography
of Gilbreth's works appears on pp. 63-67.

13   Babbage, Charles. ON THE ECONOMY OF MACHINERY AND MANU-
FACTURES. London: Charles Knight, 1832. xvi, 320 p. Reprint.
Clifton, N.J.: Kelley, 1974.

This work is based on visits by the author to "a considerable number of workshops and factories, both in England and on the Continent, for the purpose of endeavouring to make himself acquainted with the various resources of mechanical art."

14   Babcock, George D., and Trautschold, Reginald. THE TAYLOR SYSTEM IN FRANKLIN MANAGEMENT: APPLICATION AND RESULT. New York: Engineering Magazine Co., 1917. xx, 245 p. Illustrations, diagrams, tables. 2d ed., 1918. Reprint. Easton, Pa.: Hive Publ ' ˙ˌg Co., 1972, as Management History Series no. 7.

This book is an account of the introduction and effects of the Taylor system of scientific management at the H.H. Franklin Manufacturing Company between 1908 and 1917.

15   Brodie, M.B. FAYOL ON ADMINISTRATION. An Administrative Staff College Monograph. London: Lyon, Grant & Green, 1967. xii, 46 p. Portraits, tables, bibliography. Paperback.

16   Burnham, James. THE MANAGERIAL REVOLUTION; OR, WHAT IS HAPPENING IN THE WORLD NOW. New York: John Day, 1941; London: Putnam, 1942. 271 p. Reprint. Westport, Conn.: Greenwood Press, 1972.

Burnham argues that the Second World War resulted in a social revolution in which managers strove to become the ruling class. "The war of 1914 was the last great war of capitalist society; the war of 1939 is the first great war of managerial society."

17   Clark, Wallace. THE GANTT CHART: A WORKING TOOL FOR MANAGEMENT 3d ed. London: Pitman, 1952. xvi, 168 p. Diagrams, forms (1 folding).

This is a useful description of the chart developed by Henry Laurence Gantt (see item 22) for use in production planning and control.

18   Elbourne, Edward Tregaskiss. FUNDAMENTALS OF INDUSTRIAL ADMINISTRATION: AN INTRODUCTION TO MANAGEMENT. 2 vols. 4th ed., revised by H. McFarland Davis. London: Macdonald & Evans, 1947-49. Bibliographies.

Volume 1 (1947. xxix, 299 p. Diagrams, tables) is concerned particularly with commercial aspects of management, with an introductory section on management as a profession. Volume 2 (1949. xxv, 417 p. Diagrams, tables) covers industrial management, personnel and training, technological developments, and industrial legislation. The first edition of this British classic was published in 1934.

19   Emerson, Harrington. THE TWELVE PRINCIPLES OF EFFICIENCY. 5th
      ed. New York: Engineering Magazine Co., 1917. xviii, 423 p. Ann
      Arbor, Mich.: University Microfilms, 1971.

      First published in 1912, alas without an index, this work de-
      scribes Emerson's twelve principles for an efficient organiza-
      tion: clearly defined ideals; common sense; competent counsel;
      discipline; the fair deal; reliable, immediately available, and
      adequate records; dispatching; standards and schedules; standard-
      ized conditions; standardized operations; written standard prac-
      tice instructions; and efficiency reward.

20   Fayol, Henri. GENERAL AND INDUSTRIAL MANAGEMENT. Translated
      by Constance Storrs. London: Pitman, 1949. xxvii, 110 p. Tables.

      The absence of an index is regrettable in this presentation of
      Fayol's five elements of management: planning, organizing,
      command, coordination, and control.

21   Follett, Mary Parker. DYNAMIC ADMINISTRATION: THE COLLECTED
      PAPERS OF MARY PARKER FOLLETT. 2d ed., edited by Elliot M. Fox
      and Lyndall Fownes Urwick. London: Pitman, 1973. xxxii, 331 p.
      Bibliography. Paperback.

      This volume, the first edition of which was published in 1941,
      contains seventeen lectures by the distinguished advocate of
      the application of psychology to industrial problems. There is
      a bibliography of the known publications and papers of Mary
      Parker Follett, pp. 325-28. No index.

22   Gantt, Henry Laurence. GANTT ON MANAGEMENT: GUIDELINES FOR
      TODAY'S EXECUTIVE. Edited by Alex W. Rathe. New York: American
      Management Association and American Society of Mechanical Engineers,
      1961. 288 p. Portraits, diagrams, tables, bibliographies.

      Selections from Gantt's writings are grouped under four head-
      ings: (1) scientific approach to management, (2) human ef-
      fort: key results, (3) operating effectively, and (4) manage-
      ment and society. There is a biography of Gantt by Leon
      Pratt Alford on pp. 239-81. A bibliography of Gantt's writ-
      ings is found on pp. 285-88.

      Three of Gantt's major works were reprinted in 1973 by Hive
      Publishing Co. of Easton, Pennsylvania, as numbers 41-43 of
      their Management History Series. They are: INDUSTRIAL
      LEADERSHIP (1921); ORGANIZING FOR WORK (1919); and
      WORK, WAGES AND PROFITS (1916).

      Gantt is particularly remembered for the Gantt Chart, a tool
      widely used in production planning and control. This has been
      described by Wallace Clark (see item 17).

23   Gilbreth, Frank Bunker, and Gilbreth, Lillian. THE WRITINGS OF THE
      GILBRETHS. Edited by William R. Spriegel and Clark E. Myers. Irwin
      Series in Industrial Engineering and Management. Homewood, Ill.: Irwin,
      1953. 513 p. Diagrams, tables.

      This volume contains FIELD SYSTEM, CONCRETE SYSTEM,
      BRICKLAYING SYSTEM, PRIMER OF SCIENTIFIC MANAGE-
      MENT, MOTION STUDY, MOTION STUDY FOR THE HANDI-
      CAPPED (all by Frank B. Gilbreth), APPLIED MOTION STUDY
      and FATIGUE STUDY (both by Frank B. and Lillian Gilbreth),
      and THE PSYCHOLOGY OF MANAGEMENT (by Lillian Gil-
      breth).

      A number of the Gilbreths' works have been reprinted by Hive
      Publishing Co. of Easton, Pennsylvania, as numbers 12, 14,
      and 28-32, respectively, of their Management History Series.
      They are: PRIMER OF SCIENTIFIC MANAGEMENT (1973),
      MOTION STUDY (1972), APPLIED MOTION STUDY (1973),
      FATIGUE STUDY (1973), FIELD SYSTEM (1973), BRICKLAY-
      ING SYSTEM, and THE PSYCHOLOGY OF MANAGEMENT
      (1973).

24   Gulick, Luther, and Urwick, Lyndall Fownes, eds. PAPERS ON THE
      SCIENCE OF ADMINISTRATION. New York: Institute of Public Admin-
      istration, 1937. 195 p. Reprint. Clifton, N.J.: Kelley, 1969, in
      Reprints of Economic Classics Series. Diagrams, tables.

      Contains eleven major papers by Gulick, Urwick, James D.
      Mooney, Henri Fayol, Henry S. Dennison, L.J. Henderson,
      T.N. Whitehead and Elton Mayo, Mary Parker Follett, John
      Lee, and V.A. Graicunas. No index.

25   Hoxie, Robert Franklin. SCIENTIFIC MANAGEMENT AND LABOR. Re-
      prints of Economic Classics. Clifton, N.J.: Kelley, 1966. 302 p.

      This is a study of the attitude of the labor movement to the
      scientific management movement, carried out for the U.S.
      Commission on Industrial Relations and first published in 1915.
      No index.

26   Kakar, Sudhir. FREDERICK TAYLOR: A STUDY IN PERSONALITY AND
      INNOVATION. Cambridge, Mass.: M.I.T. Press, 1970. xiii, 221 p.
      Hardcover and paperback.

      The author uses psychoanalytic techniques to show how Taylor's
      introduction of scientific management was directly related to
      his own mental problems emanating from family and school cri-
      ses, as well as to the needs of his era.

27   Merrill, Harwood F., ed. CLASSICS IN MANAGEMENT. Rev. ed.
      New York: American Management Association, 1970. xiv, 495 p. Bib-
      liography.

This volume has extracts from the writings of Robert Owen, Charles Babbage, Henry Metcalfe, Henry Robinson Towne, Frederick Winslow Taylor, Henry Laurence Gantt, Russell Robb, Harrington Emerson, Alexander Hamilton Church and Leon Pratt Alford, Henri Fayol, Frank Bunker Gilbreth, Oliver Sheldon, Mary Parker Follett, Henry Arthur Hopf, Elton Mayo, Chester Barnard, and Douglas McGregor. Each selection is preceded by a brief study of the writer. Selected bibliography, pp. 485-95. No index.

28 Owen, Robert. THE LIFE OF ROBERT OWEN: WRITTEN BY HIMSELF, WITH SELECTIONS FROM HIS WRITINGS AND CORRESPONDENCE. Reprints of Economic Classics. 2 vols. Clifton, N.J.: Kelley; London: Cass, 1967. Portraits.

Volume 1 (xliv, 390 p.) contains selections from Owen's writings and correspondence. Volume 1A (xxxvii, 358 p.) contains a supplementary index to volume 1 with a series of reports, addresses, memorials, and other documents referred to in that volume and published between 1803 and 1820. The first edition of this work was published in 1857-58.

29 _____. A NEW VIEW OF SOCIETY; OR, ESSAYS ON THE FORMATION OF THE HUMAN CHARACTER PREPARATORY TO THE DEVELOPMENT OF A PLAN FOR GRADUALLY AMELIORATING THE CONDITION OF MANKIND. With an introduction by John Saville. Reprints of Economic Classics. Clifton, N.J.: Kelley, 1972. xvii, 184 p.

This is a facsimile reprint of the second edition of 1816.

30 Sheldon, Oliver. THE PHILOSOPHY OF MANAGEMENT. London and New York: Pitman, 1924. Reprint 1965. xix, 296 p. Diagrams.

The 1965 reprint of this classic British study includes an introduction by Alex W. Rathe of New York University Graduate School of Business Administration. He sets Sheldon's work in its historical context and assesses its relevance to current problems.

31 Taylor, Frederick Winslow. SCIENTIFIC MANAGEMENT. New York: Harper, 1964. Reprint. Westport, Conn.: Greenwood Press, 1972. Var. pag. Illustrations, forms.

The book comprises a foreword on Taylor by Harlow S. Person (pp. v-xvi); SHOP MANAGEMENT (1911; 207 p.); THE PRINCIPLES OF SCIENTIFIC MANAGEMENT (1911; 144 p.); and Taylor's evidence before the Special House Committee investigating the Taylor and other systems of shop management (1912). Only SHOP MANAGEMENT has an index. THE PRINCIPLES OF SCIENTIFIC MANAGEMENT is also published in paperback (New York: Norton, 1967).

32 Urwick, Lyndall Fownes. THE ELEMENTS OF ADMINISTRATION. 2d
ed. London: Pitman, 1947. 132 p. Diagrams, tables.

An analysis of the management principles enunciated by Fayol,
Mooney and Reiley, Taylor, Follett, and Graicunas, the book
includes the exception principle, the scalar process, and the
span of control. Tabular summary of principles, pp. 119-29.

33 _____, ed. THE GOLDEN BOOK OF MANAGEMENT: AN HISTOR-
ICAL RECORD OF THE LIFE AND WORK OF SEVENTY PIONEERS.
London: Newman Neame, 1956. xix, 298 p. Portraits, bibliogra-
phies.

This volume was edited for the International Council for Scientific Management (CIOS), and contains brief biographies of
seventy major influences on the management movement, with
select bibliographies. Appendix 1 (pp. 287-88) is a chronolo-
gical list of the key management books and papers mentioned
in the introductory sections of the outlines. Appendix 2 (pp.
289-95) consists of a select bibliography of publications dealing wholly or partially with the history of management.

BIBLIOGRAPHIES

In this section are listed not only bibliographies covering the whole area of
management but also some general lists, notably items 68 and 71, which are
useful sources for reference works of interest to the manager (such as directories and general dictionaries) but do not deal specifically with management and
would otherwise be outside the scope of this guide.

34 Allen, David E., Jr. BUSINESS BOOKS TRANSLATED FROM ENGLISH:
1950-1965. Reading, Mass.: Addison-Wesley, 1966. xiv, 414 p.

This classified, unannotated bibliography has sections on business administration, administration, finance, accounting, production, industry, labor, personnel, marketing, and public relations. Indexes of authors, languages, and subjects.

35 American Management Association. TEN-YEAR INDEX OF AMA PUBLI-
CATIONS 1957-1966. New York: 1967. xii, 186 p.

This is supplemented by annual lists.

36 ANBAR MANAGEMENT SERVICES BIBLIOGRAPHY. London: Anbar Publications, 1961- . Twice yearly.

This classified list includes books, pamphlets, and films reviewed in journals covered by the Anbar abstracting services
(see items 105, 1279, 1597, 1785, and 1858), with references
to reviews. The second annual issue is a cumulated volume.

37   Bakewell, K.G.B. HOW TO FIND OUT: MANAGEMENT AND PRO-
DUCTIVITY. A GUIDE TO SOURCES OF INFORMATION ARRANGED
ACCORDING TO THE UNIVERSAL DECIMAL CLASSIFICATION. 2d ed.
Commonwealth and International Library, Libraries and Technical Informa-
tion Division. Oxford, Eng.: Pergamon Press, 1970. 389 p. Illustra-
tions.

38   Bennett, John B., and Weiher, Ronald L. "The Well-Read Manager."
HARVARD BUSINESS REVIEW 50 (July-August 1972): 134-46.

The authors present a definition of management literature and
suggest how it, and other information on management, may be
obtained. They give a list of recommended books, periodicals,
and literature guides that is somewhat superficial, especially
in its listing of periodicals.

39   Berg, R.M., comp. BIBLIOGRAPHY OF MANAGEMENT LITERATURE
(UP TO JANUARY 1931). New York: American Society of Mechanical
Engineers, 1931. 142 p. SUPPLEMENT: A MANAGEMENT BIBLIOG-
RAPHY COVERING 1931-1935. 1937. 88 p.

40   Besterman, Theodore. COMMERCE, MANUFACTURES AND LABOR: A
BIBLIOGRAPHY OF BIBLIOGRAPHIES. 2 vols. Besterman World Bibliographies. Totowa, N.J.: Rowman and Littlefield, 1971.

This volume lists those items from Besterman's WORLD BIBLIOG-
RAPHY OF BIBLIOGRAPHIES (4th edition, 1965-66) which are
concerned with labor, productivity, trade unions, unemployment, wages and salaries, industrial administration, and related
subjects.

41   BIBLIOGRAPHY OF PUBLICATIONS OF UNIVERSITY BUREAUS OF BUSI-
NESS AND ECONOMIC RESEARCH. Boulder: University of Colorado
Business Research Division, 1957- . Annual.

Listed are each year's output of American business schools under institution, subject, and author. This was entitled INDEX
TO PUBLICATIONS OF UNIVERSITY BUREAUS OF BUSINESS
AND ECONOMIC RESEARCH and was published by University
of Oregon Bureau of Business and Economic Research, Eugene,
from 1950 to 1962.

42   British Institute of Management. A BASIC LIBRARY OF MANAGEMENT.
Rev. ed. London: 1974. 48 p. Paperback.

This is a classified, unannotated list, with no indexes.

43   Burger, Ruth. "The Media of Management." SCIENCE AND TECHNOL-
OGY, February 1968, pp. 72-77.

Burger's article provides a guide to books, films, and organizations on management.

44   BUSINESS BOOKS IN PRINT. New York: Bowker, 1973. 934 p.

This book contains separate listings of books on all aspects of business by subject, author, and title.

45   BUSINESS SERVICE CHECKLIST. Washington, D.C.: U.S. Department of Commerce, 1946- . Weekly.

This weekly guide to Department of Commerce publications also gives key business indicators.

46   Coman, Edwin T., Jr. SOURCES OF BUSINESS INFORMATION. Rev. ed. Berkeley and Los Angeles: University of California Press, 1964. xii, 330 p.

This work, the first edition of which was published in 1949, includes chapters on methods of finding information as well as descriptions of basic books and periodicals. Particularly relevant chapters are 8 "The Literature of Accounting," pp. 133-50; 9 "Automation," pp. 151-58; 10 "Management," pp. 159-75; 11 "Personnel and Industrial Relations," pp. 176-202; 12 "Marketing, Sales Management, and Advertising," pp. 203-29. A successor to this book compiled by Lorna M. Daniells was published by the University of California Press in September 1976.

47   Danak, Jagdish T., and Keown, William H. ADMINISTRATION AND MANAGEMENT: A SELECTED AND ANNOTATED BIBLIOGRAPHY. Norman: University of Oklahoma Regional Rehabilitation Research Institute, 1969. 60 p. Paperback.

Listing 116 items in five main sections, this work was supported in part by a research grant from the Social and Rehabilitation Service of the Department of Health, Education, and Welfare. Author index.

48   Daniells, Lorna M., ed. BUSINESS LITERATURE: AN ANNOTATED LIST FOR STUDENTS AND BUSINESSMEN. Reference List, no. 25. Boston: Harvard University Graduate School of Business Administration, Baker Library, 1968. 139 p. Paperback.

A very useful list, this work is arranged under fourteen subject headings and has three appendixes (general bibliographies and periodicals, published case histories, and publishers) and an index of authors, titles, and subjects. It is generally restricted to items in print by December 1967.

49 _____. BUSINESS REFERENCE SOURCES: AN ANNOTATED GUIDE FOR HARVARD BUSINESS SCHOOL STUDENTS. Reference List, no. 27. Boston: Harvard University Graduate School of Business Administration, Baker Library, 1971. 108 p. Paperback.

This is a revision of Reference List, no. 24, originally published in 1963, whose aim is "to introduce Harvard Business School students to the reference resources of Baker Library so that they may make more effective use of the wealth of published information in business and economics," but its usefulness extends far beyond the Harvard Business School. It has a systematic arrangement, with an index of authors, titles, and subjects. Although some management items are included, emphasis is on items _for_ management (such as directories, statistical sources, financial sources, etc.) rather than items _on_ management.

50 ENCYCLOPEDIA OF BUSINESS INFORMATION SOURCES: A DETAILED LISTING OF PRIMARY SUBJECTS OF INTEREST TO MANAGERIAL PERSONNEL WITH A RECORD OF SOURCEBOOKS, PERIODICALS, ORGANIZATIONS, DIRECTORIES, HANDBOOKS, BIBLIOGRAPHIES, AND OTHER SOURCES OF INFORMATION ON EACH TOPIC. Edited by Paul Wasserman et al. 2 vols. Detroit: Gale Research Co., 1970.

This is the second edition of EXECUTIVE'S GUIDE TO INFORMATION SOURCES (1965). Volume 1 covers general subjects, arranged alphabetically by subject headings, and volume 2 covers geographic sources.

51 European Foundation for Management Development. DOCUMENTATION ON BOOKS. Delft, Netherlands: EFMD Literature Service, Poortweg 6-8. Monthly.

This annotated monthly bibliography is arranged by the Universal Decimal Classification.

52 Fletcher, John, ed. THE USE OF ECONOMICS LITERATURE. Information Sources for Research and Development. London: Butterworth; Hamden, Conn.: Shoe String Press, 1971. 310 p.

This book contains twenty-four contributions, and is of fringe interest to management. However, it does provide useful information on publications of government and international organizations, statistics, and sources of information on such topics as business cycles, industrial economics, labor economics, and industrial relations.

53 Gee, Kenneth P. "Searching the Literature of Management." MANAGEMENT EDUCATION AND DEVELOPMENT 4 (1973): 49-55.

This is a not-altogether-reliable guide to books, periodicals, abstracts, and other information sources. See also the reply by Cemach and Bakewell (4 [1973]: 167-69).

54   Georgi, Charlotte; Allen, Eleanor B.; Daniells, Lorna M.; Kalis, Esther
      S.; Malkin, Audree; Margolis, Sarah R.; Smith, Marion M.; and Woods,
      William R., eds. LITERATURE OF EXECUTIVE MANAGEMENT. SLA
      Bibliography, no. 5. New York: Special Libraries Association, 1963.
      124 p. Paperback.

      A classified and annotated list of 470 items, this volume was
      compiled in connection with the 13th International Management
      Congress, held in New York in 1963. Index of authors and
      titles of journals (and newspapers).

55   Harvard University Graduate School of Business Administration, Baker Li-
      brary. AUTHOR-TITLE AND SUBJECT CATALOGS OF THE BAKER
      LIBRARY. 32 vols. Boston: G.K. Hall, 1971.

      In this most comprehensive bibliography of management in exis-
      tence, the author-title catalog consists of approximately 388,000
      cards in twenty-two volumes, while the subject catalog contains
      approximately 228,000 cards in ten volumes. It does not include
      entries for corporate records, current journals, or manuscripts.

56   _____. CORE COLLECTION: AN AUTHOR AND SUBJECT GUIDE.
      Boston: Baker Library, 1969/70- . Annual. Paperback.

      Each annual issue lists 4,000 titles in the Baker Library's open
      shelf browsing collection, with emphasis on recent, represen-
      tative books on business and related fields.

57   _____. NEW BOOKS IN BUSINESS AND ECONOMICS: RECENT AD-
      DITIONS TO BAKER LIBRARY. Boston: Baker Library. 10 issues yearly.

      This listing is a subject guide.

58   Institute of Chartered Accountants in England and Wales. CURRENT AC-
      COUNTING LITERATURE: A CATALOGUE OF BOOKS, PAMPHLETS AND
      PERIODICALS OF CURRENT INTEREST IN THE MEMBERS' LIBRARY OF THE
      INSTITUTE OF CHARTERED ACCOUNTANTS IN ENGLAND AND WALES
      AS AT 31 AUGUST 1971. Edited by M.G.J. Harvey. London: Mansell,
      1971. 586 p.

      This volume is classified by the Universal Decimal Classifica-
      tion with author and subject indexes and is supplemented by:

      CURRENT ACCOUNTING LITERATURE 1972: A SUPPLEMENT
      TO CURRENT ACCOUNTING LITERATURE 1971. Compiled at
      the library of the Institute of Chartered Accountants in England
      and Wales under the editorial supervision of Kathleen Bolton.
      London: Mansell, 1973. xiii, 242 p.

          This union list covers the stocks of the Institute of
          Chartered Accountants in England and Wales, the
          Institute of Chartered Accountants of Scotland (Ed-
          inburgh), the Institute of Chartered Accountants of

Scotland (Glasgow), the Association of Certified
Accountants, the Institute of Cost and Management
Accounts, and the Liverpool Society of Chartered
Accountants. A second supplement is CURRENT
ACCOUNTING LITERATURE 1973 (London: Man-
sell, 1974. 292 p.).

59   INTERNATIONAL BIBLIOGRAPHY OF THE SOCIAL SCIENCES. Chicago:
      Aldine; London: Tavistock, 1954- . Annual.

      Published for the International Committee for Social Sciences
      Documentation in four volumes (economics, sociology, politi-
      cal science, social and cultural anthropology), this work has
      a classified arrangement with author and subject indexes. Man-
      agement books and journal articles are indexed in the econom-
      ics and sociology volumes. This very comprehensive work
      covers approximately 2,000 journals from most countries of the
      world, but there is a two-year time lag between their original
      publication and indexing.

60   International University Contact for Management Education. Library and
      Documentation Centre. LIST OF DOCUMENTATION. Rotterdam, Nether-
      lands: 1967. 55 leaves. Paperback.

      This publication lists 500 articles, brochures, etc., in the IUC
      library and documentation center, classified under twenty-one
      broad subject headings. No annotations and no index.

61   Johnson, H. Webster. HOW TO USE THE BUSINESS LIBRARY, WITH
      SOURCES OF BUSINESS INFORMATION. 4th ed. Cincinnati, Ohio,
      and Brighton, Eng.: South-Western Publishing Co., 1972. 182 p. Paper-
      back.

      This is a useful guide with descriptions of some major informa-
      tion sources.

62   Kipp, Laurence J. "Management Literature for Librarians." LIBRARY
      JOURNAL 97 (January 15, 1972): 158-60.

      The author claims that "appallingly bad management practices"
      are common in American libraries and suggests several books
      from which librarians might benefit.

63   A LONDON BIBLIOGRAPHY OF THE SOCIAL SCIENCES. 32 vols. Lon-
      don: London School of Economics and Political Science, 1931-68 (vols.
      1-14); London: Mansell, 1970-75 (vols. 15-32). (Distributed by Interna-
      tional Publications Service, New York.)

      This major bibliography, recording the stock of the British Li-
      brary of Political and Economic Science at the London School
      of Economics and other British libraries to 1974, includes sev-

eral items on management and associated subjects. It consists
of a main sequence (vols. 1-4, published 1931-32) followed
by ten supplements covering June 1929 to May 1931 (vol.
5, 1934), June 1931 to May 1936 (vol. 6, 1937), June 1936
to May 1950 (vols. 7-9, 1952-55), 1950 to 1955 (vols. 10-11,
1958-60), 1956 to 1962 (vols. 12-14, 1966-68), 1962 to 1968
(vols. 15-21, 1970), 1969 to 1972 (vols. 22-28, 1973), 1972
to 1973 (vols. 29-31, 1974), 1974 (vol. 32, 1975), and 1975
(vol. 33, 1976). Arrangement is alphabetical by subject, with
author indexes in early volumes only.

64   Maltby, Arthur. ECONOMICS AND COMMERCE: THE SOURCES OF
INFORMATION AND THEIR ORGANISATION. London: Bingley; Hamden, Conn.: Shoe String Press, Archon Books, 1968. 239 p. Tables.

A very useful and carefully prepared guide, Maltby's work is
aimed primarily at students of librarianship and information
science.

65   Olive, Betsy Ann. MANAGEMENT: A SUBJECT LISTING OF RECOM-
MENDED BOOKS, PAMPHLETS AND JOURNALS. Ithaca, N.Y.: Cornell University Graduate School of Business and Public Administration,
1965. 222 p. Paperback.

Intended as a basis for management libraries in developing
countries, this book lists 4,281 books and pamphlets under fifteen subject headings, without annotations, followed by an
alphabetical list of journals and an author index.

66   U.S. Civil Service Commission Library. SELF-DEVELOPMENT AIDS FOR
SUPERVISORS AND MIDDLE MANAGERS. Personnel Bibliography Series,
no. 34. Washington, D.C.: 1970. Var. pag. Paperback.

This volume is a collection of annotated lists on identification
and development of managerial skills, career planning, improving leadership skills, human relations skills, managing health
and tension, followership (communication and relations with
supervisors), completed staff work, developing creative ability
and innovative skills, management of time, decision-making
and problem-solving skills, communications skills, delegation
and order giving, effective speaking (including telephone us-
age), effective listening, writing improvement, conference
leadership and participation, and reading improvement. No
index.

67   THE UNIVERSAL REFERENCE SYSTEM: POLITICAL SCIENCE, GOVERN-
MENT, AND PUBLIC POLICY SERIES. Vol. 4: ADMINISTRATIVE MAN-
AGEMENT: PUBLIC AND PRIVATE BUREAUCRACY. Edited by Alfred
de Grazia et al. Princeton, N.J.: Universal Reference System, 1968.
xx, 888 p. Distributed by Pergamon Press, New York and Oxford.

The publisher describes this work as an "annotated and intensively indexed compilation of significant books, pamphlets and articles, selected and processed by the Universal Reference System—a computerized information retrieval service in the social and behavioral sciences." This volume, one of ten, lists 2,407 items according to the "Grazian classification and indexing system," which consists basically of about 351 standard descriptors. Indexing is intensive, with each item having ten to twenty entries. There are, however, some surprising omissions from the list.

68   Walford, A.J., ed. GUIDE TO REFERENCE MATERIAL. 3 vols. London: Library Association, 1968-75. Vol. 1: SCIENCE AND TECHNOLOGY. 3d ed. 1973. 615 p. Vol. 2: SOCIAL AND HISTORICAL SCIENCES, PHILOSOPHY AND RELIGION. 3d ed. 1975. 647 p. Vol. 3: GENERALITIES, LANGUAGES, THE ARTS AND LITERATURE. 2d ed. 1970. 585 p. Distributed by Bowker, New York.

This work is the outstanding British guide to general works of reference.

69   Wasserman, Paul. INFORMATION FOR ADMINISTRATORS: A GUIDE TO PUBLICATIONS AND SERVICES FOR MANAGEMENT IN BUSINESS AND GOVERNMENT. Ithaca, N.Y.: Cornell University Press, 1956. xiv, 375 p. Diagrams.

Although obviously dated now, this well-written and well-annotated guide remains useful reading.

70   White, Carl M., et al. SOURCES OF INFORMATION IN THE SOCIAL SCIENCES: A GUIDE TO THE LITERATURE. 2d ed. Chicago: American Library Association, 1973. xviii, 702 p.

Section 4 (pp. 181-242) covers economics and business administration, with seven books on management listed on pp. 201-2 and some guides to the literature, abstracting, and indexing services and reference material on pp. 209-42. This very thorough and well-indexed guide is also valuable for its coverage of such fringe topics as education, psychology, and sociology.

71   Winchell, Constance M., comp. GUIDE TO REFERENCE BOOKS. 9th ed., revised by Eugene P. Sheehy. Chicago: American Library Association, 1976. 1,040 p.

BIBLIOGRAPHIES OF THESES AND DISSERTATIONS

72   DISSERTATION ABSTRACTS INTERNATIONAL: A. THE HUMANITIES

AND SOCIAL SCIENCES. Ann Arbor, Mich.: University Microfilms, 1938- . Monthly。

Listed are abstracts of doctoral dissertations from about 270 U.S. and Canadian universities and colleges and a few Australian and European universities which are available on microfilm or as xerox reproductions. Arrangement is by subject category, including accounting and business administration, with author and keyword title indexes. It is supplemented by AMERICAN DOCTORAL DISSERTATIONS, a complete listing of doctoral dissertations accepted by U.S. and Canadian universities.

73   The European Institute for Advanced Studies in Management has a data bank of more than 800 doctoral theses on management and associated subjects from more than seventy-five European universities. It plans to publish a bibliography of theses written after 1960, followed by quarterly supplements. Further information from Harald Stiehler, Librarian, European Institute for Advanced Studies in Management, Place Stephanie 20, B-1050 Brussels, Belgium.

74   INDEX TO THESES ACCEPTED FOR HIGHER DEGREES IN THE UNIVERSITIES OF GREAT BRITAIN AND IRELAND AND THE COUNCIL FOR NATIONAL ACADEMIC AWARDS. London: Aslib, 1950/51- . Annual.

The chief disadvantage of this work is delay in publication. Not until 1964-65 were any theses on management listed, but since then the number has grown steadily.

BIBLIOGRAPHIES OF CASES

The case study method of teaching management, in which students are given written descriptions of actual situations to consider individually and in groups before suggesting appropriate action, is used widely in business schools throughout the world and most notably at the Harvard University Graduate School of Business Administration. This school has combined with the American Association of Collegiate Schools of Business to form the Intercollegiate Case Clearing House, a number of whose bibliographies are listed below. In Britain there is a Case Clearinghouse of Great Britain and Ireland at Cranfield Institute of Technology.

75   BIBLIOGRAPHY: CASES AND OTHER MATERIALS FOR THE TEACHING OF BUSINESS ADMINISTRATION IN DEVELOPING COUNTRIES: AFRICA AND THE MIDDLE EAST. Andrew R. Towl, director of project; Grace V. Lindfors, editor. Boston: Intercollegiate Case Clearing House, Harvard University Graduate School of Business Administration, 1969. 456 p. Paperback.

This work includes a glossary of geographic and political terms, pp. 359-65. See annotation for item 77.

76   BIBLIOGRAPHY: CASES AND OTHER MATERIALS FOR THE TEACHING OF BUSINESS ADMINISTRATION IN DEVELOPING COUNTRIES: LATIN AMERICA. Andrew R. Towl, director of project; Ruth C. Hetherston, editor. Boston: Intercollegiate Case Clearing House, Harvard University Graduate School of Business Administration, 1966. xv, 366 p. Paperback.

      See annotation for item 77.

77   BIBLIOGRAPHY: CASES AND OTHER MATERIALS FOR THE TEACHING OF BUSINESS ADMINISTRATION IN DEVELOPING COUNTRIES: SOUTH AND SOUTHEAST ASIA. Andrew R. Towl, director of project; Grace V. Lindfors, editor. Boston: Intercollegiate Case Clearing House, Harvard University Graduate School of Business Administration, 1968. 408 p. Paperback.

      These three bibliographies (items 75-77) are arranged systematically with indexes of authors (personal and institutional), titles, and subjects. There is a combined index in the following work.

78   BIBLIOGRAPHY: CASES AND OTHER MATERIALS FOR THE TEACHING OF BUSINESS ADMINISTRATION IN DEVELOPING COUNTRIES: COMPARATIVE INDEX. Grace V. Lindfors, editor; Charles N. Gebhard, computer analyst; Andrew R. Towl, director of project. Boston: Intercollegiate Case Clearing House, Harvard University Graduate School of Business Administration, 1969. xxi, 328 p.

      In this volume are indexes by topic, title, and author of the 1,889 cases and 1,725 books, articles, and pamphlets listed in the three bibliographies of cases and other materials for the teaching of business administration in developing countries (items 75-77).

79   Burleson, Jean, ed. CASE BIBLIOGRAPHY AND INDEX: MANAGEMENT OF ORGANIZATIONS: EUROPE. Boston: Intercollegiate Case Clearing House, Harvard University Graduate School of Business Administration, 1972. xxiv, 1,157 p. Paperback.

      This annotated list of cases, with indexes, was produced in cooperation with the European Institute of Business Administration (INSEAD) and the European Foundation for Management Development.

80   Institut pour l'Etude des Methodes de Direction de l'Entreprise (IMEDE). "Bibliography of Selected Cases and Technical Notes." Lausanne, Switzerland: 1972. 97 p. Mimeographed.

International in scope, this volume lists classified and annotated cases, all available from the Intercollegiate Case Clearing House. No index.

81   INTERCOLLEGIATE BIBLIOGRAPHY: CASES IN BUSINESS ADMINISTRATION. Vol. 14 with supplementary lists. Edited by Grace V. Lindfors. Boston: Intercollegiate Case Clearing House, Harvard University Graduate School of Business Administration, 1971. 148 p. Paperback.

This bibliography was first published in 1956 and has been issued at approximately annual intervals since then. Volumes 11-13 were published together in 1970 and included a cumulative index to volumes 1-13 (by topic, title, and author) covering more than 2,800 cases.

82   Simmons, Donald D., ed. CASES IN MANAGEMENT: A SELECT BIBLIOGRAPHY. Cranfield, Eng.: Case Clearinghouse of Great Britain and Ireland, Cranfield Institute of Technology, 1974. Var. pag. Looseleaf.

This annotated list is arranged under seven broad headings with indexes of authors and titles but no specific subject index.

BIBLIOGRAPHIES OF PERIODICALS

83   Dews, J.D. "Core Periodicals in Business Studies: A European List." MANAGEMENT EDUCATION AND DEVELOPMENT 4 (December 1973): 170-77.

Listed are the principal journals (not solely European in origin) compiled as a joint project by members of an informal group of librarians of European business schools.

84   Harvard University Graduate School of Business Administration, Baker Library. CURRENT PERIODICAL PUBLICATIONS IN BAKER LIBRARY. Boston: 1971/72- . Annual. Paperback.

Three sequences, under title, subject, and geographic region, are contained in this source, which includes journals, bulletins, statistical and other yearbooks, proceedings of conferences, directories, government annual reports, and looseleaf services. This is a very useful list.

BIBLIOGRAPHIES OF ABSTRACTING AND INDEXING SERVICES

85   Dews, J.D., and Ford, Monica M. AN INVESTIGATION INTO EXISTING DOCUMENTATION SERVICES IN BUSINESS STUDIES: A REPORT SUBMITTED TO THE OFFICE FOR SCIENTIFIC AND TECHNICAL INFOR-

MATION. Manchester, Eng.: Manchester Business School, 1969. 143 leaves. Tables. Paperback.

The authors report on a detailed examination of fifty-one documentation services (thirty-two abstracting services, ten indexing services, and nine other services such as digests, book lists, and contents lists). The work examines coverage, time lag, cost, indexing facilities, etc.

86   International Federation for Documentation (FID). ABSTRACTING SERVICES. VOL. 2: SOCIAL SCIENCES AND HUMANITIES. 2d ed. FID Publication no. 456. The Hague, Netherlands: 1969. 92 p. Paperback.

The authors report on a detailed examination of fifty-one documentation services (thirty-two abstracting services, ten indexing services, and nine other services such as digests, book lists, and contents lists). The work examines coverage, time lag, cost, indexing facilities, etc.

Listed herein are approximately 200 services, including thirty titles in the field of management, but with some omissions. This does not include indexing services.

BIBLIOGRAPHIES OF FILMS

87   FILMS FOR MANAGERS: A GUIDE TO MANAGEMENT AND SUPERVISORY TRAINING FILMS AVAILABLE IN THE U.K. Edited by Marilyn J. Jacobs. Consultant editor, B.M. Platt. Rev. ed. London: Management Publications, 1971. 200 p.

This annotated guide to films covers all aspects of management and is preceded by advice on obtaining and using films.

88   HIGHER EDUCATION LEARNING PROGRAMMES INFORMATION SERVICE CATALOGUE (HELPIS). Edited by James Ballantyne. 4th ed. London: British Universities Film Council, 1976. xiv, 133 p. Paperback.

This is a catalog of teaching materials produced in British universities, polytechnics, and other institutions of higher education, including videotapes, films, slides, and audiotapes. It is arranged by the Universal Decimal Classification with indexes of titles, names, and subjects. The first edition was published by the National Council for Educational Technology in 1971.

89   Wachs, William, ed. FILM GUIDE FOR MARKETING EXECUTIVES. New York: Sales and Marketing Executives-International, 1966. xiii, 71 p. Bibliography. Paperback.

An annotated classified list, this work has useful introductory sections on the conduct of meetings using films, suggestions for getting films produced, and a checklist of applications.

ABSTRACTING AND INDEXING SERVICES

90 ANBAR MANAGEMENT SERVICES JOINT INDEX. London: Anbar Publications, 1971- . Annual.

A comprehensive index to the five abstracting journals pub-
lished by this organization: ACCOUNTING + DATA PROCESS-
ING ABSTRACTS (item 1785), MARKETING + DISTRIBUTION
ABSTRACTS (item 1597), PERSONNEL + TRAINING ABSTRACTS
(item 1858), TOP MANAGEMENT ABSTRACTS (item 105) and
WORK STUDY + O AND M ABSTRACTS (item 1279).

91 BUSINESS PERIODICALS INDEX. New York: H.W. Wilson, 1958- .
Monthly with quarterly and annual cumulations.

This outstanding indexing service covers the whole field of
business studies, including management. Until 1957 it formed
a part of the INDUSTRIAL ARTS INDEX.

92 CONTENTS PAGES IN MANAGEMENT. Manchester, Eng.: Manchester
Business School, 1972- . Weekly.

Originally entitled CURRENT CONTENTS IN MANAGEMENT,
this publication contains photocopies of contents pages of periodicals received in the Manchester Business School Library.
Quarterly author index, cumulating annually.

93 CURRENT CONTENTS: BEHAVIORAL, SOCIAL AND MANAGEMENT
SCIENCES. Philadelphia: Institute for Scientific Information, 1969- .
Weekly.

This is part of the CURRENT CONTENTS service containing
contents pages of journals.

94 ECONOMIC ABSTRACTS. The Hague, Netherlands: Martinis Nijhoff,
1953- . Biweekly.

The abstracts are compiled by the library of the Economic Information Service, Dutch Ministry of Economic Affairs. Normally in the language of the original article, they are classified according to the Universal Decimal Classification. It
contains annual author and subject indexes, but the latter are
sometimes difficult to use.

95 INDEX OF ECONOMIC ARTICLES IN JOURNALS AND COLLECTIVE
VOLUMES. 10 vols. Homewood, Ill.: Irwin, 1961-71.

This comprehensive index to English-language articles includes
some management items. It is prepared by the American Economic Association and covers so far the period 1886-1968.
Volumes 1-7 were entitled INDEX OF ECONOMIC JOURNALS

and covered the period 1886-1965. Volume 7A is an index of
articles in collective volumes (conference proceedings, readings, etc.) published in 1964 and 1965.

96   Institut pour l'Etude des Methodes de Direction de l'Enterprise (IMEDE).
      MONTHLY BULLETIN. Lausanne, Switzerland: IMEDE, Management
      Development Institute, 1957- .

      This is a current awareness service of systematically arranged
      abstracts from the major management and business periodicals.
      It also lists new books added to the IMEDE library. No in-
      dexes.

97   INTERNATIONAL MANAGEMENT INFORMATION. EDITION B. Hoerby,
      Sweden: AB Information, 1950- . Quarterly.

      These lengthy digests of management articles have illustrations
      and are arranged under broad subject headings. No indexes.

98   JOURNAL OF ECONOMIC LITERATURE. Nashville, Tenn.: American
      Economic Association, 1963- . Quarterly.

      Each issue contains review articles, long signed book reviews,
      and a classified sequence of abstracts. There is also a useful
      listing of the contents of some other economic journals. It
      was entitled JOURNAL OF ECONOMIC ABSTRACTS until 1968.

99   MANAGEMENT REVIEW AND DIGEST. London: British Institute of Man-
      agement, 1974- . Quarterly.

      Each issue includes book and film reviews, news of research
      activities, and a section of abstracts previously published sepa-
      rately as MANAGEMENT ABSTRACTS, DIGESTS AND REVIEWS.

100   PUBLIC AFFAIRS INFORMATION SERVICE BULLETIN. New York: 1915- .
      Weekly with regular cumulations.

      A very useful alphabetical subject index of books, pamphlets,
      reports, and periodical articles on all aspects of public af-
      fairs, including management. The bulletin was started in 1913
      by a group of special librarians.

101   RESEARCH INDEX. Wallington, Surrey, Eng.: Business Surveys, 1965- .
      Fortnightly.

      This indexes articles and news items in about 100 newspapers
      and journals.

102   SELECTED RAND ABSTRACTS. Santa Monica, Calif.: Rand Corp.,
      1963- . Quarterly.

This is a guide to the Rand Corporation's unclassified publications (books, articles, reports, and papers), which are mainly
scientific and technical but which also include management,
the social sciences, economics, and quantitative methods. It
is cumulated throughout the year with annual author and subject indexes.

103 SOCIAL SCIENCES CITATION INDEX. Philadelphia and Uxbridge, Eng.:
Institute for Scientific Information, 1973- . Three issues annually.

The index covers a wide range of subjects, including management. It uses the principles of citation indexing whereby all
papers which cite an author are listed together under that
author's name. Each issue also includes a "permuterm" subject index produced from the title input to the main index.
The final issue for each year is a cumulative one. Approximately 1,000 journals are covered.

104 SOCIOLOGICAL ABSTRACTS. New York: American Sociological Association, 1952- . Six issues annually.

This covers approximately 800 journals, including a number
in the management area. Annual index.

105 TOP MANAGEMENT ABSTRACTS. London: Anbar Publications, 1971- .
Eight issues annually.

One of five abstracting journals in the excellent Anbar series,
this one is published in association with the British Institute of
Management. Each issue contains 70-100 abstracts of articles
selected from more than 200 journals. Critical comments are
occasionally included, distinguished from the factual summaries
by being printed in italics. Annual index. Incorporated in
ANBAR MANAGEMENT SERVICES ABSTRACTS 1961-71.

DIRECTORIES OF ORGANIZATIONS

106 Anderson, I.G., ed. MARKETING AND MANAGEMENT: A WORLD
REGISTER OF ORGANIZATIONS. Beckenham, Eng.: CBD Research,
1969. xii, 228 p. Paperback. (Distributed by International Publications
Services, New York.)

An alphabetical list of international organizations is followed
by similar lists for individual countries, giving such information as the aims of the organization, publications, frequency
of meetings, etc. Indexes of publications and organizations.
The activities of the organizations fall into ten main groups:
industry, trade, and commerce in general; management; marketing and sales management; market research; advertising; public

relations; purchasing; consumer protection; industrial design and packaging; productivity. It was compiled in collaboration with the Institute of Marketing.

107 ENCYCLOPEDIA OF ASSOCIATIONS. 11th ed. 3 vols. Edited by Margaret Fisk. Detroit: Gale Research Co., 1977.

> Volume 1 (1,456 p.) lists national organizations of the United States; volume 2 (729 p.) is a geographic-executive index; volume 3 is a quarterly looseleaf register of new associations. More than 14,000 associations are listed in volume 1, including many in the management area. Arrangement is by broad subject with a keyword index. Information given about each organization includes address, telephone number, date of foundation, previous names, aims and publications, details of committees, divisions, and regular meetings. There is a separate list of inactive or defunct organizations and former names of existing organizations.

ENCYCLOPEDIAS, HANDBOOKS, AND GLOSSARIES

This section lists dictionaries or glossaries giving brief definitions of management terms; encyclopedias containing lengthier articles on such terms, sometimes with reading lists; and major handbooks covering the whole spectrum of management.

108 Alexander Hamilton Institute. 2001 BUSINESS TERMS AND WHAT THEY MEAN: A DESK DICTIONARY. New York: 1963. 303 p. (Distributed by Doubleday, New York.)

109 Argenti, John. MANAGEMENT TECHNIQUES: A PRACTICAL GUIDE. International Business Management Series, no. 5. London: Allen & Unwin, 1969. Diagrams, tables. Hardbound and paperback. (Distributed by Davlin Publications, Beverly Hills, Calif.)

> The first 62 pages consist of a discussion of management techniques, which the author defines as "a recognized method of analyzing or solving a recognized type of management problem in a detailed, systematic way." Pages 63-274 are a glossary of more than 100 techniques with the comments on each technique arranged under six headings: class of technique; type of problem which it is designed to solve; brief description of technique; training in the use of the technique; cost/effect of using the technique; comment.

110 Argenti, John, and Rope, Crispin. A NEW GLOSSARY OF MANAGEMENT TECHNIQUES. Rev. ed. London: Management Publications, 1971. 32 p. Bibliographies. Paperback.

> Given are brief definitions of eighty-three techniques, grouped

under six headings; company problems, marketing and sales problems; production problems; personnel problems; purchasing problems, and research problems. Recommended readings are appended to many of the definitions, although these are not always accurate and are sometimes dated. Each technique is graded as "essential aid to good management," "useful technique," "needs highly trained expert knowledge or specialized equipment," or "best left to the specialist."

111   Brech, E.F.L., ed. THE PRINCIPLES AND PRACTICE OF MANAGE-MENT. 3d ed. London: Longman, 1975. 1,081 p. Diagrams, bibliography. (Distributed by Fernhill House, New York.)

This standard British handbook, the first edition of which was published in 1953, is arranged in seven sections: "Management in Principle," "Manufacturing Supply and Technical Development," "Personnel," "The Finance and Control Function," "Computer Management," "Organizational Planning," and "Management Development." The section on management in principle includes an outline history of management literature (pp. 132-46).

112   COMPANY ADMINISTRATION HANDBOOK. Rev. 2d ed. Epping, Eng.: Gower Press, 1973. 799 p. Illustrations, diagrams, tables, bibliographies. (Distributed by Beekman Publishers, New York.)

Thirty-two contributions are presented in six sections: constitution and conduct of companies, accounting and finance (including the management of mergers and acquisitions), commercial functions, office administration, the company and its employers, and management of physical assets.

113   DIRECTORS' GUIDE TO MANAGEMENT TECHNIQUES, WITH GLOSSARY OF MANAGEMENT TERMS. Edited by Dennis Lock. Advisory Editor, George Bull. Rev. ed. London: Directors Bookshelf, Gower Press, 1972. xvi, 482 p. Diagrams, tables, bibliographies.

In covering thirty-two techniques, this book summarizes each and then gives a detailed account. Most articles lack reading lists. A glossary of managment terms on pp. 455-82 provides brief definitions of some 150 terms and serves as a partial index to the work, although a more detailed index would improve the reference value of the book.

114   Fiddes, D.W., ed. BUSINESS TERMS, PHRASES AND ABBREVIATIONS. 14th ed. London and New York: Pitman, 1971. 230 p. Paperback.

115   Great Britain. Civil Service Department. "The Meaning of Some Management Terms." O & M BULLETIN 27 (May 1972): supplement, 12 p.

Though not a definitive glossary, this article outlines meanings and possible misuses of frequently used terms.

116   Great Britain. Treasury. GLOSSARY OF MANAGEMENT TECHNIQUES. London: H.M. Stationery Office, 1967. 26 p. Diagrams, tables, bibliographies. Paperback.

Definitions of ninety-four terms are often supported by bibliographical references. Later impressions were issued by the Civil Service Department.

117   Hamburger, Edward. A BUSINESS DICTIONARY OF REPRESENTATIVE TERMS USED IN ACCOUNTING, ADVERTISING, BANKING, CREDIT, DATA PROCESSING, EXPORT, FINANCE, INSURANCE, INVESTMENTS, LABOR, LAW, MERCHANDISING, PERSONNEL, PURCHASING, RETAILING, REAL ESTATE, SELLING, SHIPPING, STATISTICS, STOCK MARKET, TRAFFIC, WAREHOUSING. Englewood Cliffs, N.J.: Prentice-Hall, 1967. 198 p. Paperback.

118   HANDBOOK FOR MANAGERS. 3 vols. London: Kluwer-Harrap, 1972- . Diagrams, forms, bibliographies. Looseleaf.

Revised pages for this work are dispatched twice yearly. Articles, originally published in journals and elsewhere, are presented in eight sections: views on management problems, management activities, the manager and his development, the manager at work, management problems, methods and techniques, the manager and automation, and advice and help for managers. There is a detailed index.

119   Heyel, Carl, ed. THE ENCYCLOPEDIA OF MANAGEMENT. 2d ed. New York: Van Nostrand-Reinhold, 1973. xxvii, 1,161 p. Illustrations, diagrams, tables, bibliographies.

If you could afford to buy only one book on management, this would probably be the best. The first edition of this outstandingly important reference work was published in 1963. The articles, by 199 contributors, are arranged alphabetically with a guide to core-subject reading classified under twenty-six headings on pp. xxiii-xxvii. A specific alphabetical subject index assists in the location of information. Valuable reading lists are appended to many articles, and there are three appendixes listing associations and publishers mentioned in the text, periodicals mentioned in the text, and universities and colleges offering programs in business administration.

120   Horton, Forest W., Jr. REFERENCE GUIDE TO ADVANCED MANAGEMENT METHODS. New York: American Management Association, 1972. xii, 333 p. Diagrams, tables, bibliographies.

Descriptions of sixty-one management techniques, arranged alphabetically, are followed by bibliographical references. Glossary, pp. 306-20. A helpful alphabetical subject index is included.

121 INTERNATIONAL ENCYCLOPEDIA OF THE SOCIAL SCIENCES. Edited by David L. Sills. 17 vols. New York: Macmillan and Free Press, 1968. Bibliographies.

Relevant articles include "Accounting" by Sidney Davidson (vol. 1, pp. 14-20); "Administration" by Herbert Kaufman, Norton Lang, and Herbert A. Simon (vol. 1, pp. 61-79); "Automation" by Joseph N. Fromkin (vol. 1, pp. 480-88); "Business Management" by Richard M. Cyert (vol. 2, pp. 249-56); "Productivity" by Solomon Fabricant (vol. 12, pp. 523-35). Bibliographical references are appended to all articles. Scattered references to topics can easily be traced in the alphabetical subject index under such headings as "Business Management," "Management," and "Scientific Management."

122 Johannsen, Hano, and Page, G. Terry. INTERNATIONAL DICTIONARY OF MANAGEMENT: A PRACTICAL GUIDE. London: Kogan Page, 1974. 416 p. Diagrams, tables.

This outstanding work of reference defines terms on all aspects of management and related subjects in current use in the United States, Britain, and Europe. It also contains addresses and descriptions of many associations and government bodies.

123 Johannsen, Hano, and Robertson, Andrew B. MANAGEMENT GLOSSARY. Management Studies Series. London: Longman; New York: American Elsevier, 1968. 146 p. Diagram, bibliography.

Taking to heart a comment in BRITISH MANAGEMENT REVIEW 7 (1948) that "one of the roots of our lack of organization of management knowledge is the absence of any standardized and agreed terminology," the compilers have provided brief definitions of approximately 700 terms in the following areas: fundamental management terms; the more significant and commonly used terms from the specialist areas of management such as marketing, finance, production, and personnel; terms describing management techniques, without attempting to cater for the specialist; terms from allied subjects such as economics, law, statistics, and sociology insofar as they are closely associated with management. Names of organizations are included, and there are useful cross-references from abbreviations. There is on pp. 142-46 a classified bibliography of glossaries, handbooks, and standard works which will be helpful in locating management terms.

124 Kempner, Thomas, ed. A HANDBOOK OF MANAGEMENT. London:

Weidenfeld & Nicholson; New York: Hastings House Publishers, 1971.
xxvi, 416 p. Bibliographies.

Written "to provide a handy reference book on the main concepts and ideas which underpin the work of management" and
"to help managers survive in an increasingly complex and jar-
gon-obsessed society," this work includes contributions by
twelve authors, all British. Arrangement is under alphabetical
subject headings, individuals, and organizations, and the articles are brief and readable. Each is followed by select reading lists. There are some surprising omissions, particularly from
the organizations. A useful synoptic index groups all the subjects under eleven headings; the contributors claim that by
looking up the entries on these headings the reader can get an
overview of the field of management.

125 Lasser, Jacob K. J.K. LASSER'S BUSINESS MANAGEMENT HANDBOOK.
Edited by Bernard Greisman. 3d ed. New York and London: McGraw-
Hill, 1968. xiii, 770 p. Diagrams, tables.

This handbook contains twenty-two contributions by twenty-
four American authorities: financing a business, starting a business, organizing for more efficient management, facing the
risks in business, buying and selling a business, finding the
best location for a business, using electronic data processing,
installing productive accounting systems, increasing marketing
productivity, using cost accounting systems, utilizing budgets
as a managerial decision-making tool, controlling business
paper work, designing systems for internal control of a business,
avoiding business fraud, marketing products and services, using
corporate house counsel, establishing good employee relations,
building better relations with shareholders, buying business
insurance, doing business abroad, understanding laws pertaining to competitive relationships of a business, and advertising
and the law.

126 THE MCGRAW-HILL DICTIONARY OF MODERN ECONOMICS: A HAND-
BOOK OF TERMS AND ORGANIZATIONS. Edited by Douglas Greenwald
et al. 2d ed. New York and London: McGraw-Hill, 1973. xii, 792 p.
Diagrams, tables.

Definitions are given for approximately 1,400 terms, including
a few management terms, pp. 3-639. Approximately 225 or-
organizations are described, pp. 643-792. Though the dictionary's editors claim to cover important agencies and organizations outside the United States, a major omission is the British
Institute of Management.

127 Maynard, Harold B., ed. HANDBOOK OF BUSINESS ADMINISTRATION.
New York and London: McGraw-Hill, 1967. Var. pag. Illustrations,
diagrams, tables, bibliographies.

This work contains 166 contributions arranged in seventeen sections: introduction to business administration, organization, general management, common concerns of all managers, research and development management, materials management, manufacturing management, marketing management, financial management, accounting and control, management of human resources, managing external relations, secretarial and legal activities, office administration, systems and data processing, management of international operations, and tools and techniques of management decision making and control.

128 _____. TOP MANAGEMENT HANDBOOK. New York and London: McGraw-Hill, 1960. 1,236 p. Diagrams, tables.

The fifty-nine contributions making up the handbook are arranged in seven sections: the managing function, management by objectives, management of people, measurement and control, management of the future, activity area management, and other aspects of top management.

129 Moore, Russell F., ed. AMA MANAGEMENT HANDBOOK. New York: American Management Association, 1970. Var. pag. Illustrations, diagrams, tables.

More than 100 experts have contributed portions, which are presented in eleven sections: general management, administrative services, personnel, finance, marketing, manufacturing, research and development, international management, risk and insurance management, purchasing, and public relations. These are based on AMA seminars, courses, and briefings.

130 Standingford, Oliver, comp. and ed. NEWNES ENCYCLOPAEDIA OF BUSINESS MANAGEMENT. London: Newnes, 1967. 637 p. Illustrations, diagrams, tables.

Within a classified arrangement are found seven major sections: the background to business; accounting, economics, and finance; communication; business calculations; business policy and practice; personnel management; and office administration.

BILINGUAL GLOSSARIES

English-speaking managers are becoming aware that it sometimes is necessary to read material in languages other than English and to speak to colleagues overseas. This is particularly important in these days of the large multinational corporation. The glossaries listed below will help.

131 Anderla, Georges, and Schmidt-Anderla, Georgette. BUSINESS DICTIONARY: ENGLISH-FRENCH, FRENCH-ENGLISH. Paris: J. Delmas & Co.;

London: Harrap, 1972. 587 p. Tables. (Distributed by International
Publications Service, New York.)

This volume contains some 70,000 terms and acts as a thesaurus
as well as a bilingual dictionary. It includes a list of basic
weights, measures, and conversion coefficients.

132 Coveney, James, and Moore, Sheila J., comps. GLOSSARY OF FRENCH
AND ENGLISH MANAGEMENT TERMS. London: Longman, 1972. xii,
146 p. Paperback.

This pocket-sized glossary has two sequences, English-French
and French-English.

133 Eichborn, Reinhart von. BUSINESS DICTIONARY. Rev. ed. 2 vols.
Englewood Cliffs, N.J.: Prentice-Hall, 1961. Vol. 1 (xvi, 923 p.),
English-German; vol. 2 (xx, 1,080 p.), German-English.

This work was originally published by Econ-Verlag GMBH,
Duesseldorf, Germany, in collaboration with Prentice-Hall.

134 Gunston, C.A., and Corner, C.M. GERMAN-ENGLISH GLOSSARY OF
FINANCIAL AND ECONOMIC TERMS. 6th ed. Frankfurt-am-Main,
Ger.: Fritz Knapp Verlag; London: English Universities Press, 1972.
xxiii, 1,203 p.

135 Herbst, Robert. DICTIONARY OF COMMERCIAL, FINANCIAL AND
LEGAL TERMS PERTAINING TO TRADE AND INDUSTRY. . . . 3 vols.
Lucerne, Switzerland: Thali Publishers; New York: Heinman, 1955-66.
Vol. 1 (1955. 1,150 p.), English-German-French; vol. 2 (1959. 985 p.),
German-English-French; vol. 3 (1966. 979 p.), French-German-English.

136 International Council for Scientific Management (CIOS). LIST OF PUBLI-
CATIONS CONCERNING MANAGEMENT TERMINOLOGY. Wiesbaden,
Ger.: Betriebswirtschaftlicher Verlag Dr. Th. Gabler, 1963. 96 p. Pa-
perback.

This is a useful bibliography of glossaries.

137 Sommer, Werner, and Schonfeld, Hanns-Martin. MANAGEMENT DIC-
TIONARY: FACHWOERTERBUCH FUER BETRIEBSWIRTSCHAFT, WIRTSCHAFTS-
UND STEUERRECHT UND LOCHKARTENWESEN. ENGLISCH-DEUTSCH,
DEUTSCH-ENGLISCH. 2 vols. Berlin and New York: Walter de Gruyter.
Vol. 1, 4th ed. (1972), English-German; vol. 2, 3d ed. (1968), Ger-
man-English.

138 Zahn, Hans E. EURO WIRTSCHAFTS-WOERTERBUCH. DICTIONARY OF
ECONOMICS AND BUSINESS: GERMAN-ENGLISH-FRENCH. Frankfurt-
am-Main, Ger.: Fritz Knapp Verlag, 1973. xiii, 702 p.

GENERAL TEXTBOOKS AND MONOGRAPHS

139 Albers, Henry H. MANAGEMENT: THE BASIC CONCEPTS. New York and London: Wiley, 1972. 328 p. Diagrams, tables.

This textbook for undergraduates employs the process framework originally formulated by Fayol, with planning, organizing, directing, and controlling regarded as the elements of managerial action. It includes an introductory section on "management: past and present" and a final part on the responsibility of management.

140 _____. PRINCIPLES OF MANAGEMENT: A MODERN APPROACH. 4th ed. Wiley Series in Management and Administration. New York and London: Wiley, 1974. xii, 579 p. Diagrams, tables, bibliographies.

Concerned with the basic elements of managerial action-- planning, communication, motivation--within an organized managerial structure, this book has six parts which deal with the management problem past and present, organization for management, behavioral aspects of managerial organization, communication and control, decision making, and leadership and motivation. Each part concludes with descriptions of several cases. Indexes of names and subjects.

141 Allen, Louis A. THE MANAGEMENT PROFESSION. McGraw-Hill Series in Management. New York and London: McGraw-Hill, 1964. xii, 375 p. Diagrams, bibliography.

According to its preface, this book aims "to present a fully validated statement of the concepts and principles of modern, professional management." It is based on twelve years of research involving 12,000 managers in 385 organizations throughout the world. It is arranged in five sections: leaders and managers; management planning; management organizing; management leading (including decision making, motivation, communication, and selection); and management controlling. Glossary, "The Louis A. Allen Common Vocabulary of Professional Management," pp. 351-56.

142 _____. PROFESSIONAL MANAGEMENT: NEW CONCEPTS AND PROVEN PRACTICES. McGraw-Hill European Series in Management. London and New York: McGraw-Hill, 1973. 236 p. Diagrams, tables, bibliography.

This is an excellent approach by an American management consultant to the problem of matching new concepts to old principles. It includes chapters on the work of the professional manager, planning and delegating work, better decision making, motivating, building a stronger team, and controlling for results.

143 Appleby, Robert C. MODERN BUSINESS ADMINISTRATION. London and New York: Pitman, 1969. 275 p. Diagrams, table, bibliographies. Hardbound and paperback.

Appleby has written a practical textbook for students of British professional examinations. Part one deals with management principles (the nature of management, planning, organization, direction, and control). Part two covers management in action (marketing and sales management, production, personnel, office management, and current developments). Review questions, problems, and bibliography are found at the end of each chapter.

144 Argenti, John. A MANAGEMENT SYSTEM FOR THE SEVENTIES. London: Allen & Unwin, 1972. 254 p. Diagrams, bibliography. (Distributed by Davlin Publications, Beverly Hills, Calif.)

The author attempts to design "a completely new system of management that is specifically tailored to the conditions in which managers will be working during the 1970's" (p. 1). He argues that too many management books seem to offer solutions to yesterday's problems rather than tomorrow's.

145 Basil, Douglas C. MANAGERIAL SKILLS FOR EXECUTIVE ACTION. New York: American Management Association, 1970. 282 p. Diagrams, tables, bibliography.

The author believes that managerial skills (including long-range planning and management by objectives) are more valuable than a set of abstract principles, although he concludes with a chapter on the philosophy of management. He provides practical advice on such topics as line-staff relationships, organization structure, delegation, decision making, management information systems, and management control and performance standards, with brief case histories. There is an appendix on decision theory and operations research, pp. 259-72.

146 Batten, Joe D. DEVELOPING A TOUGH-MINDED CLIMATE . . . FOR RESULTS. New York: American Management Association, 1965. 250 p.

Batten identifies a climate that encourages individual productivity, accomplishment, and pride with a view to enabling managers to obtain the best results from their employees through the employee's involvement and acceptance of responsibility. Glossary of tough-minded terms, pp. 247-50. No index.

147 _____. TOUGH-MINDED MANAGEMENT. Rev. ed. New York: American Management Association, 1969. 218 p. Diagrams.

The author wrote this stimulating guide to and critique of modern management in response to questions received as a manager and consultant and in AMA seminars.   No index.

148   Beckett, John A.   MANAGEMENT DYNAMICS: THE NEW SYNTHESIS.
McGraw-Hill Management Series.   New York and London: McGraw-Hill,
1971.   234 p.   Diagrams, tables.

Beckett presents a systems approach to management, arguing
that new developments in science and society demand a new
approach to management thinking and practice.   Indexes of
authors and subjects.   An instructor's manual is also available.

149   Bethel, Lawrence L.; Atwater, Franklin S.; Smith, George H.E; Stack-
man, Harvey A., Jr.   INDUSTRIAL ORGANIZATION AND MANAGE-
MENT.   5th ed.   Revised by James L. Riggs.   New York and London:
McGraw-Hill, 1971.   xiv, 682 p.   Illustrations, diagrams, forms, tables,
bibliography.

This is a comprehensive textbook on the organization of U.S.
industry and the management process.   It includes chapters on
managerial controls and international expansion of American
enterprises.   This edition pays special attention to management
philosophies and policies as the foundation for management
direction consistent with the purposes of each company.   Many
case problems are included.   A solutions manual, by Riggs, is
available.

150   Bittel, Lester R.   THE NINE MASTER KEYS OF MANAGEMENT.   New
York and London: McGraw-Hill, 1972.   303 p.   Illustrations, diagrams,
tables.

McGraw-Hill's director of information services, formerly an
executive with Western Electric Company and the Keppers Company, identifies nine keys to managerial success under three
areas: keys for the analysis of management problems (the situation analyzer wheel, the vital target selector, and the judgment stabilizer for "preparing for the probable"); keys for effective managerial action (managerial performance alliance,
five-point planning guide, and action-indicator chart for managing by exception); and keys for successful human relations
(the confidence meter for developing confidence in others,
the improvement cycle for "employing the power of training,"
and the self-knowledge tree for "knowing your true self").

151   Bower, Marvin.   THE WILL TO MANAGE: CORPORATE SUCCESS
THROUGH PROGRAMMED MANAGEMENT.   New York and London:
McGraw-Hill, 1966.   276 p.   Bibliography.

This is an American consultant's guide to the philosophy of
management; strategic planning; policies, standards, and procedures; organization; personnel administration; operational
planning and control; and activating people.   Annotated bibliography, pp. 266-71.

152 Brech, E.F.L. MANAGEMENT: ITS NATURE AND SIGNIFICANCE. 4th ed. London and New York: Pitman, 1967. 238 p.

After asking "what is this management?" Brech provides chapters on general management, delegation, policy, managers at work, management development, and performance and profitability, with an appendix summarizing the principles of management. This volume is a readable, practical introduction. The absence of an index is unfortunate, although the author attempts to justify this in his preface by arguing that the book is an essay rather than a textbook.

153 _____. MANAGING FOR REVIVAL. London: Management Publications, 1972. 292 p. Tables, bibliography.

One of Britain's leading management writers explains market orientation in what he describes as an "annotated agenda" for the deliberations of the directors and managers of Britain's industrial and commercial enterprises. No index.

154 Clay, Michael J., and Walley, B.H. PERFORMANCE AND PROFITABILITY: A MANUAL OF PRODUCTIVITY AND COST REDUCTION TECHNIQUES FOR INDUSTRY AND COMMERCE. Management Studies Series. London: Longman, 1965. xvi, 610 p. Illustrations, diagrams, tables, bibliography. (Distributed by Fernhill House, New York.)

This very valuable guide to modern management techniques is divided into five sections: diagnosis and measurement, planning and control, operations research, specialist applications, and aids to implementation.

155 Dale, Ernest. MANAGEMENT: THEORY AND PRACTICE. 3d ed. McGraw-Hill Series in Management. New York and London: McGraw-Hill, 1973. xiii, 800 p. Diagrams, tables, bibliographies.

The first edition (1965) of this important book by a distinguished American consultant and professor won the McKinsey Foundation Book award. Part one deals with management and its environment, part two with the beginnings of modern management, part three with the management functions, and part four with the management of foreign operations. The fifth and final part covers current trends and the future, with special reference to management sciences, the computer, and social responsibility. There are appendixes on management in Japan and on the applications of operations research. The book is rich in case studies, and the chapter references are annotated. Glossary, pp. 767-84. Indexes of names and subjects.

156 Dale, Ernest, and Michelon, L.C. MODERN MANAGEMENT METHODS. London: Foulsham, 1966. 211 p. Diagrams, tables.

The authors deal with such subjects as management by objectives, long-range planning, decision trees, critical path analysis, management and the computer.

157 Drucker, Peter F. DRUCKER ON MANAGEMENT. London: Management Publications, 1972. 165 p.

Ten essays focus on the central theme of the changing role of the manager in a society whose future depends less on the old style industries and more on the new knowledge-based industries, such as computer sciences and advertising. All the papers were previously published elsewhere.

158 _____. MANAGEMENT: TASKS, RESPONSIBILITIES, PRACTICES. New York: Harper and Row, 1973. xvi, 839 p. Bibliography.

In this latest contribution of the most distinguished contemporary writer on management, Drucker emphasizes that the essence of management is performance. He then presents his proposals for effective performance in three sections: the tasks; the manager--work, jobs, skills, and organization; top management--tasks, organizations, strategies. These major sections are preceded by an introductory section entitled "From Management Boom to Management Performance." There are several case studies, including references to Sears, Roebuck and Company, IBM Corporation, General Motors, Bell Telephone Company, Zeiss, and Georg Siemens and the Deutsche Bank.

159 _____. MANAGING FOR RESULTS: ECONOMIC TASKS AND RISK-TAKING DECISIONS. New York: Harper and Row; London: Heinemann, 1964. 224 p. Bibliography.

Described by the author as a "what to do" book, this work attempts to organize the economic tasks which any business must discharge for economic results so that executives can perform them systematically, purposefully, with understanding, and with reasonable probability of accomplishment. Drucker includes many case studies.

160 _____. THE PRACTICE OF MANAGEMENT. New York: Harper and Row, 1954; London: Heinemann, 1955. 399 p. Bibliography.

Perhaps the most influential management book of modern times, this volume contains sections on the nature of management, managing a business, managing managers, the structure of management, the management of worker and work, what it means to be a manager, and the responsibilities of management. The author introduces his theory of management by objectives and provides several references to management practices at Sears, Roebuck and Company, Ford Motor Company, and IBM Corporation.

161 Duerr, Carl. MANAGEMENT KINETICS: CARL DUERR ON COMMUNI-
CATION. McGraw-Hill European Series in Management. London: Mc-
Graw-Hill, 1971. xvii, 215 p. Illustrations, tables.

> A highly readable account of management principles, this work
> unfortunately lacks an index. Management, says Duerr, is
> communication, taking the form of a continuous dialogue between
> the manager and those around him. Part four, pp. 183-215,
> is an account of the author's approach to management at Jen-
> sen Motors Ltd. after he took charge of the company in 1967.

162 Dunn, J.D.; Stephens, Elvis; and Kelley, J. Roland. MANAGEMENT
ESSENTIALS: PRACTICUM. New York: McGraw-Hill, 1973. 199 p.
Diagrams, forms, bibliography.

> This work is designed to help the student grasp more quickly
> the central ideas in MANAGEMENT ESSENTIALS: RESOURCE
> (see below, item 163). It includes "key concepts," self-check
> questions, true/false questions, and bibliographical references,
> but no index.

163 _____. MANAGEMENT ESSENTIALS: RESOURCE. New York: McGraw-
Hill, 1973. xvii, 382 p. Diagrams, forms, tables.

> Dunn defines the role of the manager as it is practiced in
> simple and complex organizations; examines the results of
> managerial performance in terms of employee productivity, em-
> ployee satisfaction, and organizational effectiveness; and sharp-
> ens the reader's managerial skills in leading, planning, deci-
> sion making, organizing, and controlling. He includes a num-
> ber of case studies.

164 Falk, Sir Roger. THE BUSINESS OF MANAGEMENT: ART OR CRAFT?
4th ed. London: Management Publications, 1970. 267 p.

> Penguin Books published the first edition of this stimulating
> work by a British consultant in 1961. It includes a number of
> case histories.

165 Foster, Douglas W. MANAGING FOR PROFIT. Practical Management
Series, no. 1. London: Longman, 1972. xv, 307 p. Diagrams, tables,
bibliographies. Paperback.

> This practical guide first defines management and then provides
> chapters on organization, objectives, corporate policy and
> planning, marketing, product planning, profit planning, and
> pricing.

166 George, Claude S., Jr. MANAGEMENT FOR BUSINESS AND INDUS-
TRY. 3d ed. Englewood Cliffs, N.J.: Prentice-Hall, 1970. xiii, 642 p.
Illustrations, diagrams, forms, tables, bibliographies.

This is a revised edition of MANAGEMENT IN INDUSTRY, first published in 1959. It is a comprehensive study in seven parts: management as a total system, organizing, product analysis and development, the production system, the human system, work standards and wages, and the control system. Each chapter concludes with study questions and bibliographical references.

167 Haimann, Theo, and Scott, William G. MANAGEMENT IN THE MODERN ORGANIZATION. 2d ed. Boston: Houghton Mifflin, 1974. 583 p. Bibliography.

The authors attempt to integrate the older, functional approach to management with more recent ideas from systems theory and the behavioral sciences. The text is supported by reading lists and case studies.

168 Haynes, W. Warren, and Massie, Joseph L. MANAGEMENT: ANALYSIS, CONCEPTS AND CASES. 2d ed. Englewood Cliffs, N.J.: Prentice-Hall, 1969.

This work contains text, readings, and cases presented in six parts: the setting of management, the behavioral side of management, planning and control, analytical tools for decision making, management systems, and broader horizons in management.

169 Heller, Robert. THE NAKED MANAGER. London: Barrie & Jenkins, 1972. 246 p.

A leading British authority--editor of MANAGEMENT TODAY and first winner of the John Player Award for management journalism--writes with humor and frankness about the myths surrounding modern management and "recipes" for success. The book includes many case histories but, unfortunately, no index.

170 Heyel, Carl. MANAGEMENT FOR MODERN SUPERVISORS. New York: American Management Association, 1962. 255 p. Diagrams, tables.

This book describes what the supervisor should know about automation, job definition, budgets and cost control, planning, quality control, maintenance, training, work simplification, motivation, communication, and several other aspects of management.

171 Hicks, Herbert G. THE MANAGEMENT OF ORGANIZATIONS: A SYSTEMS AND HUMAN RESOURCES APPROACH. 2d ed. New York: McGraw-Hill, 1972. 513 p. Diagrams, tables, bibliographies.

Hicks blends the classical, behavioral, scientific, and systems

approaches to management into a unified presentation in four
sections: organizations--an overview; human behavior--the
basic resource in organization; functions of management (creating, planning, organizing, motivating, communicating, and
controlling); and management thought and practice. Review
and discussion questions, cases, and annotated bibliographies
conclude each chapter. A softcover study guide is available
and a 35-mm slide set may be obtained from the author.

172 Hicks, Herbert G., and Gullett, C. Ray. MODERN BUSINESS MAN-
AGEMENT: A SYSTEMS AND ENVIRONMENTAL APPROACH. McGraw-
Hill Series in Management. New York: McGraw-Hill, 1974. xxiv,
536 p. Illustrations, diagrams, tables.

A practical explanation for the student who does not intend
taking further courses in management, this work is presented
in seven parts: the formation of business organizations, the resources of business organizations, managing the activities of
business organizations, the results of business organizations,
business organizations and the world around them, special issues in managing organizations, and summary and conclusions.
Cases and simulation exercises are included.

173 Holden, Paul E.; Pederson, Carlton A.; and Germane, Gayton E. TOP MAN-
AGEMENT: A RESEARCH STUDY OF THE MANAGEMENT POLICIES
AND PRACTICES OF FIFTEEN LEADING INDUSTRIAL CORPORATIONS.
New York: McGraw-Hill, 1968. xviii, 263 p. Diagrams, tables.

This research project, conducted under the auspices of the
Graduate School of Business, Stanford University, pays particular attention to the following: overall control; management
of the corporate income; long-range planning; organization
structure; centralization vs. decentralization; committees;
boards of directors; management of research and development;
product-line direction and control; mergers and acquisitions;
international operations; management information systems; external relations; employee relations; and development of executive personnel. The research objectives were to determine the
current top management policies and practices of the fifteen
chosen companies; to identify major changes since an earlier
study (TOP MANAGEMENT ORGANIZATION AND CONTROL
by Holden, Lounsberry Fish, and Hubert L. Smith. Stanford,
Calif.: Stanford University Press, 1941); and to assess trends
in future policies in top management organization, direction,
and control. The companies are unnamed, but the author says
that their annual contribution to the U.S. gross national product during recent years has been approximately 8 percent.

174 Hurst, Ronald. INDUSTRIAL MANAGEMENT METHODS: A GUIDE TO
TECHNIQUES AND THEIR APPLICATIONS. London: Hutchinson, 1970.
254 p. Diagrams, tables, bibliographies. Paperback. (Distributed by

International Publications Service, New York.)

This is a practical guide to company organization, the use of management consultants, discounted cash flow (by Brian Whitworth), critical path analysis, value analysis/value engineering, operations research, zero defects, work study, personnel problems, communications, marketing research, and the computer. It includes a case study of production control by computer using the PROMPT (Production Reviewing, Organizing and Monitoring of Performance Techniques) method, a software package developed by International Computers Ltd.

175   Jay, Antony. MANAGEMENT AND MACHIAVELLI. London: Hodder & Stoughton, 1967; New York: Holt, Rinehart & Winston, 1968. 224 p. Hardcover and paperback.

In this fascinating book Jay compares modern management methods with the organization of societies in feudal and Tudor Britain, Renaissance Europe, and other historical eras. Royal marriages have their counterpart in modern mergers, the baronial wars in top management feuds. Jay suggests that most discussion of management has been conducted at too low a level --the level of systems analysis, work study, and cost accountancy.

176   Jervis, F.R.J., and Frank, W.F. AN INTRODUCTION TO INDUSTRIAL ADMINISTRATION. 2d ed. London: Harrap, 1970. 603 p. Tables, bibliographies.

This useful British textbook is arranged in six sections: background to modern industry, economic aspects of industrial organization, theory of management, legal aspects of industrial administration, industrial organization, and personnel management. The book includes some case studies.

177   Kast, Fremont E., and Rosenzweig, James E. ORGANIZATION AND MANAGEMENT: A SYSTEMS APPROACH. 2d ed. McGraw-Hill Series in Management. New York: McGraw-Hill, 1974. 655 p. Illustrations, diagrams, tables, bibliographies.

Through the use of systems concepts, the authors integrate traditional principles of management and more recent developments in organization theory. Indexes of names and subjects.

178   Katz, Robert L. MANAGEMENT OF THE TOTAL ENTERPRISE: CASES AND CONCEPTS IN BUSINESS POLICY. Englewood Cliffs, N.J.: Prentice-Hall, 1970. xiv, 657 p. Diagrams, tables.

This work is arranged in four sections: analysis of the total enterprise (including a study of the general management functions and the concept of corporate strategy), industry analysis --establishing a competitive advantage, planning corporate strategy and deploying resources, and organizing for corporate

growth. Included are fourteen case studies and an analysis
of the competitive strategy of five major airlines--United Air
Lines, American Airlines, Eastern Airlines, Trans World Airlines, and Pan American Airways. No index.

179 Killian, Ray A. MANAGING BY DESIGN . . . FOR MAXIMUM EXEC-
UTIVE EFFECTIVENESS. New York: American Management Association,
1968. xiii, 370. Bibliography.

Killian deals with the skills of professional management (management by objectives, planning, organizing, controlling, evaluating, and improving performance), maximizing managerial performance, human relations, and the challenge to management
of the modern world.

180 Koontz, Harold, and O'Donnell, Cyril. ESSENTIALS OF MANAGEMENT.
McGraw-Hill Series in Management. New York: McGraw-Hill, 1974.
482 p. Diagrams, tables. Paperback.

This concise version of PRINCIPLES OF MANAGEMENT (see
below, item 181) omits some chapters not required to understand the basics of management, some more advanced concepts,
and many references to research in the field. Many case incidents are included.

181 _____. PRINCIPLES OF MANAGEMENT: AN ANALYSIS OF MANA-
GERIAL FUNCTIONS. 5th ed. McGraw-Hill Series in Management.
New York: McGraw-Hill, 1972. 748 p. Diagrams, tables, bibliogra-
phies.

Six sections are included in this standard comprehensive text:
the basis of management, planning, organizing, staffing, directing, and controlling. The book contains forty-five case incidents, pp. 678-711. Indexes of names/places and subjects.
A study guide, with solutions to case incidents by John F.
Halff, is available.

182 Light, H.R. THE NATURE OF MANAGEMENT: AN INTRODUCTION
TO BUSINESS AND MANAGEMENT STUDIES. 3d ed. London: Pitman,
1968. xiii, 167 p. Diagrams, forms, tables.

A very practical guide for British students, this book has chapters on the purpose of management, organization, purchasing,
production, marketing, development, personnel, control, coordination and communication, and the responsibilities of managers.

183 Longenecker, Justin G. PRINCIPLES OF MANAGEMENT AND ORGANI-
ZATIONAL BEHAVIOR. 3d ed. Columbus, Ohio: Merrill, 1973. 709 p.
Diagrams, tables, bibliographies.

The author attempts to blend recent developments in management thought with older concepts of classical theory to provide a strong conceptual foundation for successful managerial
performance. He includes several case studies.

184 Louden, J. Keith. MAKING IT HAPPEN: THE UNIT PRESIDENT CON-
CEPT. New York: American Management Association, 1971. xii, 178 p.
Diagrams.

Louden uses a running case history to discuss the qualities of
a professional manager, techniques of planning and organization, performance standards, and control. If decentralization
of responsibility, authority, and accountability is to be effective, each manager must "think and act like a president."
Glossary, pp. 165-71.

185 McConkey, Dale D. UPDATING THE MANAGEMENT PROCESS. New
York: American Management Association, 1971. 181 p. Diagrams,
tables.

This book argues that traditional approaches to management
need to be reconsidered in the light of modern circumstances
with chapters on delegation, planning, controlling, management by exception, evaluation and development of managers,
compensation, communication, relationships with unions, and
prevention of management obsolescence. No index.

186 McFarland, Dalton E. MANAGEMENT: PRINCIPLES AND PRACTICES.
4th ed. New York: Macmillan; London: Collier-Macmillan, 1974. 688 p.
Diagrams, tables, bibliographies.

This standard guide to the elements of the managerial process
is presented in five parts: management, managers, and organizations; organization structure and processes; managerial functions and processes; organization development and managerial
behavior; and trends, prospects, and perspectives. Each chapter concludes with a summary, questions for study, and a list
of bibliographical references. There are appendixes on the
analysis of management cases and descriptions of twenty-one
cases. Indexes of names and subjects.

187 Marvin, Philip. MULTIPLYING MANAGEMENT EFFECTIVENESS. New
York: American Management Association, 1971. 211 p. Diagrams,
tables.

Marvin presents nine "guidelines for the 70's" dealing with
motivation, avoiding operational obsolescence, job definition,
alignment of AIM (Achievement-oriented action, Identified incentives, Management-defined targets), development of team
men, developing decision makers, managing time, delegation,
and capitalizing on change.

188   Massie, Joseph L. ESSENTIALS OF MANAGEMENT. 2d ed. Engle-
       wood Cliffs, N.J.: Prentice-Hall, 1971. 257 p. Diagrams, tables.
       Hardcover and paperback.

       A summary of the essential features of modern management pre-
       sented in five sections: background of modern management,
       functions in the managerial process, disciplinary foundations
       for managers, applications in operational activities of a busi-
       ness firm, and dynamics of management.

189   Massie, Joseph L., and Douglas, John. MANAGING: A CONTEM-
       PORARY INTRODUCTION. Englewood Cliffs, N.J.: Prentice-Hall,
       1973. xii, 436 p. Diagrams, tables.

       This book consists of five parts: the manager in the modern
       world, management fundamentals--the knowledge base, manage-
       ment fundamentals--the process for managing, management funda-
       mentals--the reality of managing, and the manager in a changing
       world. Review questions are at the end of each chapter.

190   Mescon, Michael H.; Hammond, William Rogers; Byars, Lloyd L.; and
       Forest, Joseph R., Jr. THE MANAGEMENT OF ENTERPRISE. New
       York: Macmillan; London: Collier-Macmillan, 1973. 245 p. Bibliog-
       raphy. Paperback.

       Four sections make up this practical guide to the management
       process: aspects of organization (including conformity and or-
       ganizations, security and sectionalism, and patterns of con-
       flict), leadership and management, human relations, and im-
       provement of the organization (including a final chapter on
       "the seven sins of management"--poor treatment of profit, the
       myth of professional management, the failure to recognize in-
       dividual differences, the lack of training, too legalistic an
       approach to labor relations, poor communication, and the ten-
       dency to look upon work as being of low status).

191   Michelon, L.C. THE MYTHS AND REALITIES OF MANAGEMENT. Re-
       public Education Institute Series. Cleveland: Republic Education Insti-
       tute, 1972. 199 p. Bibliography. Paperback.

       This book attempts to distill from the literature the prevailing
       management myths and to compare these with management re-
       alities by a series of alphabetically arranged chapters. It con-
       cludes with some reflections on management organization and
       a thirteen-page classified bibliography.

192   Moore, Franklin G. MANAGEMENT ORGANIZATION AND PRACTICE.
       New York: Harper & Row, 1964. 625 p. Diagrams, tables, bibliog-
       raphies.

       This comprehensive text has many case studies and bibliogra-
       phies at end of each chapter. It focuses particularly on man-

agerial activities, organization structure, line-staff relationships, and delegation.

193 Mueller, Robert Kirk. RISK, SURVIVAL AND POWER: AXIOMS MAN-
AGERS LIVE BY. New York: American Management Association, 1970.
223 p. Bibliographies.

Mueller explains some of the axioms of management: the anatomy of risk, managerial instinct, management as a combination of scientific discipline with artistic freedom, the "man-
agementality gap," survival of the fittest, executive authority,
profit as the catalyst, the social profile, an understanding of
behavioral science, intelligent use of power, ability to adjust
to colleagues' styles and moods, and the executive way of life.

194 Mundel, Marvin E. A CONCEPTUAL FRAMEWORK FOR THE MANAGE-
MENT SCIENCES. McGraw-Hill Series in Management. New York:
McGraw-Hill, 1967. 310 p. Diagrams, tables, bibliographies.

Seven introductory chapters on the range of managerial activities are followed by four chapters on designing the components
of an industrial enterprise, nine chapters on control, and a
final chapter on decision making.

195 Newman, William H. ADMINISTRATIVE ACTION: THE TECHNIQUES
OF ORGANIZATION AND MANAGEMENT. 2d ed. Englewood Cliffs,
N.J.: Prentice-Hall, 1963; London: Pitman, 1965. 486 p. Diagrams,
tables.

Standard work on planning, organizing, assembling resources,
supervising, and controlling. The first edition was published
in 1950 as PRINCIPLES OF ADMINISTRATION.

196 Newman, William H., and Warren, E. Kirby. THE PROCESS OF MAN-
AGEMENT: CONCEPTS, BEHAVIOR AND PRACTICE. 4th ed. Englewood Cliffs, N.J.: Prentice-Hall, 1976. xv, 670 p. Diagrams,
tables, bibliographies.

An introductory chapter on the social role of managers is followed by twenty-eight chapters arranged in six parts: organizing, human factors in organizing, planning (two parts), controlling, and activating. There are many case studies, problem questions, and annotated bibliographical references.

197 Owens, Richard N. MANAGEMENT OF INDUSTRIAL ENTERPRISES. 6th
ed. Homewood, Ill.: Irwin; Georgetown, Ont.: Irwin-Dorsey, 1969.
xvi, 636 p. Diagrams, tables.

The first edition of this comprehensive standard text was published in 1949. A historical survey is followed by sections on
organizational problems; equipment and working conditions;
product research, design, and quality; motion and time study;
wages and incentives; personnel relations; materials management; planning and control of quantities; and general planning
and control. Each chapter concludes with study questions and
one or more cases. Appendix on the use of computers in production management.

198   Perrigo, A.E.B.   MODERN MANAGERIAL TECHNIQUES.   Princeton,
N.J.: Van Nostrand, 1968. xiii, 392 p. Diagrams, tables.

This clear and comprehensive guide has a chapter on the chief
executive and his team followed by chapters on the application
of techniques in specific areas (marketing, production, control,
personnel, accounting), the use of management consultants,
international business, the workings and use of the computer,
operations research and cybernetics.

199   Richardson, Keith.   DO IT THE HARD WAY: A QUIZZICAL GUIDE TO
THE BRITISH WAY OF MISMANAGEMENT.   London: Weidenfeld &
Nicholson, 1972. 191 p.

Richardson's frank guide to what is wrong with British management is illustrated by a semifictitious boss called "Donovan."

200   Scanlan, Burt K.   PRINCIPLES OF MANAGEMENT AND ORGANIZA-
TIONAL BEHAVIOR.   Wiley Series in Management and Administration.
New York: Wiley, 1973. xv, 512 p. Diagrams, tables, bibliographies.

Scanlan combines the traditional and behavioral approaches to
management with sections on the historical development of
management thought, planning and decision making, organization, the behavioral science view of management, managerial
direction, and leadership. Each chapter concludes with a
summary, definitions of key concepts, discussion questions,
and bibliographical references.

201   Shilt, Bernard Abdil; Everard, Kenneth E.; and Johns, John M.   BUSI-
NESS PRINCIPLES AND MANAGEMENT.   6th ed. Cincinnati: South-
Western Publishing Co., 1973. 664 p. Illustrations, diagrams, forms,
tables.

This book provides instructional materials which will enable
students planning a career in business to gain an understanding
of the characteristics, organization, and operations of business.

202   Taylor, W.J., and Watling, T.F.   THE BASIC ARTS OF MANAGEMENT.
London: Business Books, 1972. xvi, 207 p. Illustrations, diagrams,

tables, bibliography. (Distributed by Cahners Publishing Co., Boston.)

The authors, experienced managers with International Computers Ltd. who have lectured on management topics in Britain and Europe, give a "straightforward introduction to management" (introduction). The book has four parts: managing yourself; managing people; managing money; and being in front and keeping in front.

203   Terry, George R. PRINCIPLES OF MANAGEMENT. 6th ed. Irwin Series in Management. Homewood, Ill.: Irwin, 1972. xvii, 817 p. Illustrations, diagrams, forms, tables, bibliography.

This standard work has been regularly revised since its first edition in 1953. Terry provides a detailed and practical exposition of management theory, schools of management thought, managerial activities, and the management functions, with many case studies and problem questions and an annotated bibliography.

204   Uris, Auren. THE EXECUTIVE DESKBOOK. New York: Van Nostrand Reinhold, 1970. xii, 269 p. Diagrams, forms, tables.

This is a guide to good management practice in the form of brief notes presented in four sections: areas of management action (time saving and self-scheduling, communication, decision making, planning, delegation, building group effectiveness, leadership and motivation, dealing with problem people, dealing with interpersonal problems, and improving one's own effectiveness); reviews and appraisals; key management concepts; and management tool kit (checklists, charts, forms, etc.).

205   _____. MASTERY OF MANAGEMENT: HOW TO AVOID OBSOLESCENCE BY PREPARING FOR TOMORROW'S MANAGEMENT TODAY. Homewood, Ill.: Dow Jones-Irwin, 1968. xiii, 265 p. Diagrams, tables. Paperback ed. New York: Playboy Press, 1971.

Uris identifies key areas and concepts of the managerial revolution under three broad areas (dynamics, environment, and tools) with a final chapter on the twenty-first-century executive.

MORE LIGHTHEARTED APPROACHES

The approach of these works may be lighthearted, but the message is serious.

206   Parkinson, C. Northcote. PARKINSON'S LAW; OR, THE PURSUIT OF PROGRESS. Boston: Houghton Mifflin, 1957; London: John Murray, 1958. 122 p. Illustrations, tables. Hardcover and paperback.

This classic humorous approach to management develops the author's thesis that work expands so as to fill the time available for its completion. The book also includes amusing comments on selection methods, meetings, and other topics.

207 Smith, Martin R. I HATE TO SEE A MANAGER CRY; OR, HOW TO PREVENT THE LITANY OF MANAGEMENT FROM FOULING UP YOUR CAREER. Reading, Mass.: Addison-Wesley, 1973. xviii, 209 p.

In his efforts to expose "the sham and hypocrisy of the litany of management" the author, an American consultant, comments on such topics as business ethics, democratic management, Theory Y, management training, management by objectives, recruitment, and dismissal. Part one is concerned with "recognizing management diseases." An index would be useful.

208 Townsend, Robert. UP THE ORGANIZATION: HOW TO STOP THE CORPORATION FROM STIFLING PEOPLE AND STRANGLING PROFITS. New York: Knopf; London: Michael Joseph, 1970. 188 p. Paperback ed. New York: Fawcett World Library, 1970.

This is a humorous presentation of the ABC's of good (and bad) management practice by a former president and chairman of the Avis Rent-a-Car Corporation.

PROGRAMMED TEXTS

A programmed text presents material in a systematic series of steps or frames. After each frame the student is normally asked a question, which he must answer satisfactorily before proceeding to the next frame. He can thus work through a subject at his own pace.

There are a number of useful programmed texts on aspects of management, with the American Management Association's PRIME (Programmed Instruction for Management Education) Series being particularly valuable. Items 209-11 cover the whole field of management and are especially recommended.

209 American Management Association. HOW TO PLAN AND ORGANIZE WORK. PRIME 9. New York: 1968. Var. pag. Looseleaf.

This programmed guide covers planning, scheduling, organizing and delegating, employee development, and managing change. It was produced jointly by the American Management Association and the Training Branch of Federal Electric Corporation.

210 Kazmier, Leonard J. PRINCIPLES OF MANAGEMENT: A PROGRAMMED-INSTRUCTIONAL APPROACH. 3d ed. New York: McGraw-Hill, 1974. xxii, 519 p. Diagrams, tables, bibliographies.

This very useful text reflects the increased emphasis and integration of the behavioral sciences, quantitative methods, and systems theory. It covers the development of management concepts, the functions of the manager, organizing, directing, controlling, and systems concepts. Each "unit" concludes with a review, case studies, and bibliography. Earlier editions (1964 and 1969) were subtitled A PROGRAM FOR SELF–INSTRUCTION.

211 Strohmer, Arthur F., Jr. THE SKILLS OF MANAGING. Reading, Mass.: Addison-Wesley, 1970. 149 p. Paperback.

A practical introduction, this work is mainly in the form of a scrambled programmed text. It includes two hypothetical case studies. No index.

READINGS

In recent years there have been numerous collections of readings on management topics. Although it is obviously useful to have major contributions on a theme collected in one volume, many publishers detract from the value of such collections by failing to provide an index which would allow speedy retrieval of information on specific subjects.

Included in this section are general collections of readings covering the whole or a major area of management, together with a few collections from the work of a single author.

212 Appley, Lawrence A. THE MANAGEMENT EVOLUTION. New York: American Management Association, 1963. 304 p.

This collection of writings by the chairman of the board of AMA centers on the general theme of what the manager can do to make things happen, such as determining objectives, assigning responsibility, and keeping the organization dynamic. No index.

213 _____. VALUE IN MANAGEMENT. New York: American Management Association, 1969. 269 p.

The chairman and former president of AMA reveals thoughts on management. No index.

214 Bass, Bernard M., and Deep, Samuel D., eds. CURRENT PERSPECTIVES FOR MANAGING ORGANIZATIONS. Englewood Cliffs, N.J.: Prentice-Hall, 1970. xii, 594 p. Diagrams, tables, bibliographies.

This volume contains forty-three readings on setting and achieving objectives, compensation, developing management and the

organization, motivation, communication, supervision, developing teamwork, decision making, resolving conflict, managing
in the future, and managing multinationally.

215 Bonaparte, Tony H., and Flaherty, John E., eds. PETER DRUCKER:
CONTRIBUTIONS TO BUSINESS ENTERPRISE. New York: New York
University Press, 1970. 373 p. Bibliography.

The contents include twenty-three critical essays on Drucker
and his work presented in five parts: background, the practice
and theory of management, entrepreneurship: the economic
dimension, international environment, and corporation and
society. Bibliography of Drucker's writings, pp. 366-68. No
index.

216 Carroll, Stephen J., et al., eds. THE MANAGEMENT PROCESS: CASES
AND READINGS. New York: Macmillan; London: Collier-Macmillan,
1973. xii, 435 p. Diagrams.

This work contains twenty-eight readings and twenty-four good,
short case studies grouped in six sections: management theory;
policy planning; organization planning; directing, coordinating,
and controlling; perspectives on management; and secondary
management functions. No index.

217 Dale, Ernest, ed. READINGS IN MANAGEMENT: LANDMARKS AND
NEW FRONTIERS. 2d ed. McGraw-Hill Series in Management. New
York: McGraw-Hill, 1970. xiii, 557 p. Tables. Paperback.

Approximately 150 articles are arranged under five broad headings: management and its environment, the beginnings of modern management, the management organizations, management
of foreign operations, and current trends and the future. About
one-third of the articles did not appear in the first edition
(1965). The plan of the book is similar to that of Dale's
MANAGEMENT: THEORY AND PRACTICE (item 155). No
index.

218 Dartnell Corporation. FOR EXECUTIVES ONLY: AN ANTHOLOGY OF
THE BEST MANAGEMENT THOUGHT. Chicago: 1967. 480 p.

Contained are thirty-five readings.

219 Doktor, Robert H., and Moses, Michael A., eds. MANAGERIAL IN-
SIGHTS: ANALYSIS, DECISIONS AND IMPLEMENTATION. Englewood
Cliffs, N.J.: Prentice-Hall, 1973. 437 p. Illustrations, bibliographies.

An introductory section on the conceptual framework of management is followed by twenty-two readings on managerial problem analysis, decision making, solution implementation, and
alternative futures. Some more bibliographical references would
be useful.

220 Donnelly, James H.; Gibson, James L.; and Ivancevich, John M., eds.
     FUNDAMENTALS OF MANAGEMENT: SELECTED READINGS. Austin,
     Tex.: Business Publications; Georgetown, Ont.: Irwin-Dorsey, 1971.
     357 p. Diagrams, tables. Paperback.

> This work contains twenty-nine readings in five sections: an
> introduction to management; classical school of management;
> behavioral school of management; management science school
> of management; and the future of management. No index.

221 Drucker, Peter F. THE NEW MARKETS . . . AND OTHER ESSAYS. Lon-
     don: Heinemann, 1971. 226 p.

> Twelve essays cover a variety of topics, including "The New
> Markets and the New Entrepreneurs" (the longest essay, on
> changes in industrial economics), "Henry Ford," and "What
> We Can Learn from Japanese Management." Many of the es-
> says were originally published as journal articles.

222 _____. TECHNOLOGY, MANAGEMENT AND SOCIETY. New York:
     Harper & Row; London: Heinemann, 1970. 182 p.

> These twelve essays were originally published, mainly as jour-
> nal articles, between 1958 and 1970. The topics range from
> "the technological revolution" and its implications for manage-
> ment to long-range planning, "Can Management Ever Be a
> Science?" and "The Manager and the Moron" (i.e., the com-
> puter).

223 Hampton, David R., ed. MODERN MANAGEMENT: ISSUES AND
     IDEAS. Belmont, Calif.: Dickenson, 1969. xii, 493 p. Diagrams.

> Included are contributions by thirty-nine experts on a number
> of management topics, including organization structure, organi-
> zation theory, planning, decision making, human resources
> management, leadership, and control. No index.

224 Hutchinson, John G., ed. READINGS IN MANAGEMENT STRATEGY
     AND TACTICS. New York: Holt, Rinehart & Winston, 1971. 562 p.
     Diagrams, tables.

> Forty-nine readings are arranged in seven parts: perspectives on
> management, recognition of problems and opportunities, deci-
> sion making, strategy and organizational design, evaluation and
> review of contribution, developing superior performance, man-
> agement of critical areas of operation, and management in
> the future. Index of authors, but no subject index.

225 Koontz, Harold, and O'Donnell, Cyril, eds. MANAGEMENT: A BOOK
     OF READINGS. 3d ed. McGraw-Hill Series in Management. New York:
     McGraw-Hill, 1972. 818 p. Diagrams, tables.

Approximately 100 readings on management theory, planning,
organizing, staffing, directing, controlling, and managers and
the changing environment make up this volume.

226   Lazarus, Harold; Warren E. Kirby; and Schnee, Jerome E., eds. THE PROG-
RESS OF MANAGEMENT: PROCESS AND BEHAVIOR IN A CHANGING
ENVIRONMENT. 2d ed. Englewood Cliffs, N.J.: Prentice-Hall, 1972.
500 p. Diagrams, tables, bibliographies. Paperback.

This volume contains forty-nine readings on the social role of
managers, organizing, human factors in organizing, planning
and decision making, leading, measuring and controlling, and
management as an adaptive process. No index.

227   McGuire, Joseph W., ed. CONTEMPORARY MANAGEMENT: ISSUES
AND VIEWPOINTS. Englewood Cliffs, N.J.: Prentice-Hall, 1974.
662 p. Diagrams, tables, bibliographies.

Twenty contributions are organized into three parts: the disci-
plinary foundations of management; the environment of management, internal and external; and the management "core."
Questions and bibliographies are found at the end of each
chapter.

228   Mann, Roland, ed. THE ARTS OF TOP MANAGEMENT: A MCKINSEY
ANTHOLOGY. McGraw-Hill European Series in Management and Marketing. London: McGraw-Hill, 1970. 404 p. Diagrams, tables.

Contributions by twenty-five consultants with the international
McKinsey Company discuss the shaping of corporate strategy,
organizing for effectiveness, profit improvement, managing
executive manpower, marketing and distribution strategy, har-
nessing the technological explosion, management sciences, and
the computer. Unlike so many collections of readings, this
one includes a reasonably detailed index. There are slight
differences in the British and U.S. editions.

229   Massie, Joseph L.; and Luytjes, Jan; with Hazen, N. William, eds.
MANAGEMENT IN AN INTERNATIONAL CONTEXT. New York: Harper & Row, 1972. xviii, 386 p. Bibliographies. Paperback.

This volume contains seventeen papers on the study of management in an international context; the international transfer of
management skills through consulting; management and its environment in Great Britain, France, Belgium, Germany, Czechoslovakia, Yugoslavia, Romania, India, Korea, Singapore and
Malaysia, South Africa, Nigeria, and Argentina; cultural assumptions underlying U.S. management concepts; and environmental influences on managerial approaches.

230 Moore, Franklin G., ed. A MANAGEMENT SOURCEBOOK. New York: Harper & Row, 1964. 474 p. Diagrams, tables. Paperback.

Fifty-six readings consider the managerial job, objectives and policies, management fundamentals, decision making, planning, control, staffing, delegation, decentralization, supervision, committees, departments, line-staff relationships, organization structures, and executive compensation. No index.

231 Revans, Reginald W. SCIENCE AND THE MANAGER. London: Macdonald, 1965. 160 p. Diagrams, tables.

Eight stimulating papers on industrial relations, automation, management control, the nature of operations research, and the general application of science to management. No index.

232 _____. THE THEORY OF PRACTICE IN MANAGEMENT. London: Macdonald, 1966. 167 p. Diagrams, tables.

This is a further collection of papers by the British management expert, now a research fellow with the European Association of Management Training Centres. Topics include management education, the elements of organization, the manager's job, and the development of research into management and its problems. No index.

233 Richards, Max D., and Nielander, William A., eds. READINGS IN MANAGEMENT. 3d ed. Cincinnati: South-Western Publishing Co., 1969. 972 p. Diagrams, tables, bibliographies.

This compilation contains seventy-five readings in six sections: basic elements in management, planning, controlling, directing, organizing, and staffing. Author index, but no subject index.

234 Urwick, Lyndall Fownes. THE PATTERN OF MANAGEMENT. London: Pitman, 1957. 100 p. Diagrams.

Five papers comprise this volume: management in an adaptive society, the marriage of theory and practice, the main outline of knowledge, the principles of government and of leadership, and the principles of government and of management. It was originally published by University of Minnesota Press, Minneapolis.

235 Wild, Ray, and Lowes, Bryan, eds. THE PRINCIPLES OF MODERN MANAGEMENT. London: Holt, Rinehart & Winston, 1972. 356 p. Diagrams, tables. Paperback.

The twenty papers included here are mainly, though not exclusively, by members of the staff of the University of Bradford Management Centre. Part one contains ten papers on the

background to management, while part two contains ten contributions on the major management functions. Indexes of authors
and subjects.

236   Wills, Gordon, and Yearsley, Ronald B., eds. HANDBOOK OF MAN-
AGEMENT TECHNOLOGY. London: Heinemann, 1967; New York: Funk
& Wagnall, 1968. xx, 228 p. Diagrams, tables, bibliographies.

This handbook contains eleven papers on numeracy in business,
human environments, business data, communication and control,
project planning, operations research, design, financial control,
quality control, marketing research, manpower planning, and
development. There are indexes to text and references.

CONFERENCE PROCEEDINGS

237   ACADEMY OF MANAGEMENT PROCEEDINGS. Tampa, Fla.: University of Tampa. Annual.

These are the proceedings of the annual meetings of the Academy of Management.

238   Institute of Management Sciences. International Meeting, 6th, Paris,
1959. MANAGEMENT SCIENCES: MODELS AND TECHNIQUES. PRO-
CEEDINGS OF THE SIXTH INTERNATIONAL MEETING OF THE INSTI-
TUTE OF MANAGEMENT SCIENCES, CONSERVATOIRE NATIONAL DES
ARTS ET METIERS, PARIS, 7-11 SEPTEMBER 1959. Edited by C. West
Churchman and Michel Verhulst. 2 vols. New York: Pergamon Press,
1960. Diagrams, forms, tables, bibliographies.

Although now obviously dated, this is a very important work
with contributions in English and French on management economics, simulation, management games, decision processes, computer systems, management education, production and inventory
management, measurements in management, behavioral sciences,
organization theory, management communications, research and
development management, and long-range planning. The final
sections contain case histories and discussions of methodology.
Separate name indexes and French and English subject indexes
are found in each volume.

239   International Management Congress, 14th, Rotterdam, 1966. MANAGE-
MENT AND GROWTH: MANAGEMENT'S CREATIVE TASK IN A WORLD
OF INCREASING COMPLEXITY AND ACCELERATED GROWTH. PRO-
CEEDINGS OF THE FOURTEENTH INTERNATIONAL MANAGEMENT
CONGRESS OF CIOS (CONSEIL INTERNATIONAL POUR L'ORGANISA-
TION SCIENTIFIQUE), ROTTERDAM, SEPTEMBER 19-23 1967 (i.e.
1966), ORGANIZED BY THE NEDERLANDS INSTITUUT VOOR EFFICI-
ENCY. Rotterdam: Rotterdam University Press, 1967. 463 p. Diagrams,
portraits, tables. Paperback.

The proceedings of one of the triennial congresses organized by the International Council for Scientific Management contain an international set of contributions on three themes: growth--an element of today's business environment; the organization as a whole meets the challenges of growth; and management and its functions meet the challenges of growth. No index.

240   International Management Congress, 15th, Tokyo, 1969. THE NEW ROLE OF MANAGEMENT: INNOVATION, INTEGRATION AND INTERNA-TIONALIZATION: PROCEEDINGS OF THE FIFTEENTH CIOS INTERNA-TIONAL MANAGEMENT CONGRESS. Tokyo: Kogakusha Co., 1969. xii, 489 p. Diagrams, portraits, tables. Paperback.

Contained are more than fifty papers by well-known writers on management on such themes as management in the developing countries, management in the USSR, and management in Japan. A more detailed subject index would be useful.

241   Koontz, Harold, ed. TOWARD A UNIFIED THEORY OF MANAGEMENT. McGraw-Hill Series in Management. New York: McGraw-Hill, 1964. xiv, 273 p.

The papers and discussions at a symposium held at the Graduate School of Business Administration, University of California, Los Angeles, November 8 and 9, 1962, make up this volume. There are thirteen contributions, presented in six sections: making sense of management theory; approaching a theory of manage-ment; synthesizing of terms, methods, and contributions; the practicing of management theory and research; assessing the role of the university in management theory and research; and conclusions by Harold Koontz.

242   North American Conference of Management Consultants, 3d, New York, 1974. MEETING THE CHALLENGES FOR GROWTH IN THE SEVENTIES: PROCEEDINGS OF THE NORTH AMERICAN CONFERENCE OF MAN-AGEMENT CONSULTANTS, JANUARY 22, 1974, THE PLAZA, NEW YORK. New York: The Conference?, 1974. 157 p. Illustrations. Paperback.

Among this volume's thirteen papers is one by Pieter Kuin, professor of management at the Netherlands School of Eco-nomics and formerly executive director of Unilever N.V., on trends in management around the world. Also included are reports on ten workshops. No index.

243   World Management Congress, 16th, Munich, 1972. PROCEEDINGS. Geneva: CIOS (International Council for Scientific Management), 1972? Var. pag. Illustrations. Paperback.

These papers survey a variety of topics, including the chal-lenge of youth to management, the effects on management of world cooperation and merger trends, the possibilities and constraints of management in East and West, and in the developing countries, management of multinational operations, motivation and behavior, women in management, the role of managers' wives, evaluation of the performance of managers, management information and decision systems, forecasting and futurology, and development and training.

CASE STUDIES

Case studies dealing with a particular subject are listed under that subject.

244   Champion, John M., and Bridges, Francis J. CRITICAL INCIDENTS IN MANAGEMENT. Rev. ed. Irwin Series in Management. Homewood, Ill.: Irwin, 1969. xxxviii, 206 p. Bibliographies. Paperback.

This book describes fifty "incidents" which illustrate situations which have developed from managerial efforts to plan, organize, control, and direct others in organizational situations. Many have critiques and reading lists. No index.

245   Eilon, Samuel; Hall, Roger I.; and King, John R. EXERCISES IN INDUSTRIAL MANAGEMENT: A SERIES OF CASE STUDIES. Studies in Management. London: Macmillan; New York: St. Martin's Press, 1966. 207 p. Diagrams, tables.

Eighteen case studies, with solutions, concern mainly the area of production management, but one relates to pricing.

246   Greenwood, Frank. CASEBOOK FOR MANAGEMENT AND BUSINESS POLICY: A SYSTEMS APPROACH. Scranton, Pa.: International Textbook Co., 1968. xii, 481 p. Diagrams, tables.

The forty-two cases described focus on general management, data processing, planning and control, organizing, and directing. There is an author index but no subject index.

247   Ivens, Michael, and Broadway, Frank. CASE STUDIES IN MANAGEMENT. London: Business Publications; New York: Beekman, 1964. xxiv, 387 p. Illustrations, diagrams, maps, tables, bibliographies.

A collection of ninety cases on all aspects of management, this work contains chapters on the functions and problems of the case study leader, some responsibilities of managers, the incident process method, and problems for discussion.

248   Kempner, Thomas, and Wills, Gordon, eds. BRADFORD EXERCISES IN MANAGEMENT, 1-12. London: Nelson, 1967. 339 p. Diagrams, tables.

The authors discuss twelve cases developed at the University
of Bradford Management Centre which deal with marketing,
joint consultation, world trade, stock control, production
planning, takeover opportunities in the textile industry, an
in-tray exercise in human and organizational problems, tariff
pricing, redundancy negotiations, organization, board-level
decision making, and product management. No index.

249 Learned, Edmund P.; Aguilar, Francis Joseph; and Valtz, Robert C.K.
EUROPEAN PROBLEMS IN GENERAL MANAGEMENT. Homewood, Ill.:
Irwin, 1963. xvi, 810 p. Diagrams, map, tables.

This excellent collection is arranged in eight parts: business
policy and general management; business objectives, strategy,
and policy; objectives, strategy, and policy in the European
chemical industry; forward planning; building an organization;
mergers and joint ventures; executive control and executive
leadership; and the total management process. The book includes case studies of Alfred Herbert Ltd. (Coventry, England);
the abortive Imperical Chemical Industries-Courtaulds takeover
bid; Jaquier S.A. (Geneva); KLM Royal Dutch Airlines; Rugby
Portland Cement Company; Selenia Elettroniche S.p.A. (Italy);
Société NORMACEM (France); Solartron Electronics Group;
and several other companies whose names have been disguised.
Index of cases, but no subject index.

COMPARATIVE MANAGEMENT

250 Davis, Stanley M. COMPARATIVE MANAGEMENT: ORGANIZATIONAL
AND CULTURAL PERSPECTIVES. Englewood Cliffs, N.J.: Prentice-Hall,
1971. xii, 593 p. Tables, bibliographies.

Text, readings, and cases are arranged in sections on Africa,
Latin America, Asia, Europe, and North America. No index.

251 Granick, David. MANAGERIAL COMPARISONS OF FOUR DEVELOPED
COUNTRIES: FRANCE, BRITAIN, UNITED STATES AND RUSSIA. Cambridge, Mass.: M.I.T. Press, 1972. 394 p. Tables.

Case studies of corporate structure and managerial behavior in
Britain and France are examined against the background of
U.S. and Russian managerial behavior. The book provides detailed information on the education, career structure, and remuneration of managers in four companies and examines two
major problems of managerial decision making--investment behavior and pricing methods. Glossary, pp. 383-84.

252 Grosset, Serge. MANAGEMENT: EUROPEAN AND AMERICAN STYLES.
Belmont, Calif.: Wadsworth Publishing Co., 1970. 153 p. Tables.
Paperback.

This is a comparative study of perspectives on the concept of managing, environmental factors, the social background of managers, management training and development, the relationship of the environment to the manager's work, and managers as a power group.

MANAGEMENT IN JAPAN

Japan's economic recovery after the long war years has become one of the wonders of the industrial world. Items 253-56 explain some of the background to this recovery.

253 Drucker, Peter F. "Drucker on Japan." MANAGEMENT TODAY, June 1974, pp. 89-92, 138, 140, 142. Illustrations.

The international management expert comments on management methods in Japan, including continuous training at all levels, the paternalistic approach to management, and the Japanese system of decision making, which concentrates on analyzing the question rather than finding the answer.

254 Kobayashi, Shigeru. CREATIVE MANAGEMENT. New York: American Management Association, 1971. 259 p.

The author describes the revolutionary management changes he introduced in the Atsuzi plant of the Sony Corporation. These center on greater job satisfaction and the development of the teamwork concept. The English-language edition was planned and translated under the auspices of the Japanese Management Center and was developed from two books published in 1966 and 1967.

255 MODERN JAPANESE MANAGEMENT. London: Management Publications, 1970. 141 p. Tables.

Included are introductory chapters by Rex Winsbury on "The Managers of Japan" and Nobuo Noda on "How Japan Absorbed American Management Methods," followed by five papers given at the fifteenth CIOS (International Council for Scientific Management) International Management Congress in Tokyo in 1969 (see item 240). No index.

256 Yoshino, M.Y. JAPAN'S MANAGERIAL SYSTEM: TRADITION AND INNOVATION. Cambridge, Mass.: M.I.T. Press, 1968. xvi, 292 p. Diagrams, tables, bibliography.

Yoshino considers the factors contributing to Japan's postwar managerial success and argues that the most significant is the ideology of continual adaptation and innovation in terms of the

socioeconomic and political environment. Bibliography of
books and articles in English and Japanese, pp. 276–83.

AUDIOVISUAL MATERIALS

Books and periodicals remain the major sources of information, but other media
such as films, tapes, cassettes, and videocassettes are becoming increasingly
important and are particularly valuable for training and demonstration purposes.
Six such items covering the whole area of management are:

257   Batten, Joe D. TOUGH-MINDED MANAGEMENT. New York: Time-
Life Video; Rockville, Md.: BNA Communications; Peterborough, Eng.:
Guild Sound & Vision, 1969.

In these five twenty-five-minute 16-mm color films or videotapes
(Time-Life Video) Batten dramatizes his principle of "tough-
minded management" (see items 146–47). The five films are
"Management by Example"; "The Man in the Mirror," which
dramatizes the behavior of the manager off the job as well as on
the job; "The Fully Functioning Individual"; "The Fully Functioning Organization"; and "The Fully Functioning Society."

258   Drucker, Peter F. MANAGING DISCONTINUITY. Rockville, Md.:
BNA Communications; Peterborough, Eng.: Guild Sound & Vision, 1971.

In these nine 16-mm color films Drucker and Elizabeth Hall,
managing editor of PSYCHOLOGY TODAY, appear with various business leaders. The films are "Tomorrow's Customers,"
in which Vermont Royster discusses the importance of innovative marketing as a means of reaching tomorrow's customers
(30 minutes); "The Future of Technology," in which Charles
DeCarlo points out the new areas where technology must direct
its attention during the next ten years (30 minutes); "Coping
with Technological Change," with further advice from DeCarlo
(30 minutes); "Who's Gonna Collect the Garbage?", in which
Richard Hexter, Roy Lee, and Jerry Wurf join Elizabeth Hall
in a panel discussion of various segments of the work force
(45 minutes); "Pollution Control: the Hard Decisions," in
which Robert V. Hansberger discusses the responsibilities of
business in relation to the environment (30 minutes); "Social
Needs as Business Opportunities," a further discussion with
Hansberger (30 minutes); "The Multinational Corporation," a
discussion with Dan Seymour (30 minutes); "The Innovative Organization," in which John W. Humble comments on vital issues in today's organizations (30 minutes); and "The Manager
as Entrepreneur," in which Drucker and Humble discuss the
managerial staffing required by today's and tomorrow's organization (30 minutes). The sound tracks of the films are available separately on nine cassette tapes.

259 THE EFFECTIVE MANAGEMENT PROGRAM. Rockville, Md.: BNA
Communications.

This series consists of four integrated programs, each containing ten cassettes, ten booklets, and guide sheets. Series one
deals with "Managing Individuals Effectively" and contains cassettes and booklets on the employment interview, getting an
employee off to a good start, getting responsibility into the
job, developing standards of performance, helping an employee
learn his job, the performance appraisal interview, the salary
interview, managing discipline, the handling of personal problems, and employee development. Series two, "Achieving
Group Effectiveness," covers concepts of group effectiveness,
development of an achieving team, development of departmental
goals, organization for getting things done, the conducting of
an effective meeting, the handling of conflict in a group,
brainstorming, the think-tanking approach to new solutions,
organizational renewal, and management of change. Series
three, "Developing Personal Effectiveness," deals with the
achiever's profile, becoming an achiever, developing career
goals, management of time, relating to the boss, improving
communication skills, preparing for promotion, understanding
Theory Y, achieving continuous growth, and developing life-
style goals. Series four, "The Leadership Guide," covers the
new motivations, the management process, the universal human
characteristics, understanding differences in people, the generation gap, understanding how adults learn, identifying learning
needs, becoming a trainer, devising a training program, and
measuring training results.

260 Gellerman, Saul W. GELLERMAN ON PRODUCTIVITY. New York:
AMACOM, 1973.

In this sixty-minute cassette Gellerman discusses aspects of management with successful managers. Also included is a ques-
tion-and-answer session with young people who are trying to
understand managers and management. There is a contribution
on how it feels to be a woman manager.

261 Hayes, James L. HOW TO IMPROVE MANAGEMENT PERFORMANCE.
Rev. ed. Brussels: Management Centre Europe, 1969.

This series consists of four thirty-minute 16-mm color films of
lectures by the president of the American Management Association, with three five-minute case studies. Topics covered are
concepts of management, management organization and position
descriptions, standards of performance, and performance appraisal.

262 Townsend, Robert. UP THE ORGANIZATION. New York: Time-Life
Video, 1972.

The author of UP THE ORGANIZATION (item 208) gives his views on management in a thirty-minute color 16-mm film or videotape.

PERIODICALS

Listed below are the best of the many periodicals covering the whole or a major area of management.

263 ACADEMY OF MANAGEMENT JOURNAL. Tampa, Fla.: University cf Tampa, 1958- . Quarterly.

This contains scholarly articles, research notes, and communications.

264 ACROSS THE BOARD. New York: Conference Board, 1939- . Monthly.

This focuses on practical articles on management and economic trends, with occasional book reviews. Formerly CONFERENCE BOARD RECORD, in 1976 it was changed to ACROSS THE BOARD.

265 ADMINISTRATIVE SCIENCE QUARTERLY. Ithaca, N.Y.: Cornell University, Graduate School of Business Administration, 1956- .

Long scholarly articles, notes, signed book reviews, and lists of books received are included.

266 BUSINESS HORIZONS. Bloomington: Indiana University Graduate School of Business Administration, 1958- . Bimonthly.

Scholarly articles, research reports, and book reviews make up this publication.

267 BUSINESS QUARTERLY: CANADA'S MANAGEMENT JOURNAL. London, Ont.: University of Western Ontario School of Business Administration, 1934- .

Book reviews and a taxation section are included.

268 BUSINESS WEEK. New York: McGraw-Hill, 1929- . Weekly.

This review of the business and management world also has book reviews.

269 CALIFORNIA MANAGEMENT REVIEW. Berkeley, Calif.: University of California Graduate School of Business Administration, 1958- . Quarterly.

The review includes long signed book reviews.

270 COLUMBIA JOURNAL OF WORLD BUSINESS. New York: Columbia University Graduate School of Business Administration, 1965- . Quarterly.

> This consists of scholarly articles on business and management, with signed book reviews.

271 DUN'S REVIEW. New York: Dun & Bradstreet Publications Corp., 1893- . Monthly.

> Formerly DUN'S, this publication covers the U.S. business and industrial scene.

272 EUROPEAN BUSINESS. Paris: Société Européenne d'Edition et de Diffusion, 1964- . Quarterly.

> This publication is sponsored by a number of European business schools and industrial and commercial organizations.

273 FORBES. New York, 1917- . Twice monthly.

> This is a well-known review of business and industry.

274 FORTUNE. Chicago: Time, 1930- . Monthly.

> This well known "glossy" contains general interest articles, articles on business and management including many detailed studies of the organization of individual companies, biographies of prominent industrialists, and occasional directories of top U.S. companies.

275 HARVARD BUSINESS REVIEW. Boston, Mass.: Harvard University Graduate School of Business Administration, 1922- . Bimonthly.

> This is generally regarded as the outstanding management journal. Many of its more significant articles on particular themes are collected and issued in reprint series.

276 INDUSTRIAL MANAGEMENT. London: Embankment Press, 1928- . Monthly.

> This publication, which incorporates BUSINESS MANAGEMENT, contains brief, practical articles with book notes.

277 INDUSTRIAL SOCIETY. London: Industrial Society, 1918- . Monthly.

> This journal concentrates on developments in five industrial fields: leadership, union/management relations, communications, terms and conditions of employment, and development of young employees. It includes signed book reviews and a legal page.

278 JOURNAL OF BUSINESS. Chicago: University of Chicago Press, 1928- . Quarterly.

> Devoted to "professional and academic thinking in business," the journal includes scholarly articles, signed book reviews, and lists of books received. It is edited by the faculty of the Graduate School of Business at Chicago University.

279 JOURNAL OF BUSINESS ADMINISTRATION. Vancouver: University of British Columbia, Faculty of Commerce and Business Administration, 1969- . Quarterly.

280 JOURNAL OF BUSINESS RESEARCH. Athens: University of Georgia College of Business Administration, 1966- . Quarterly.

> The journal is sponsored by the Southern Finance Association, the Southern Management Association, the Southern Marketing Association, the Mills B. Lane Foundation, and the University of Georgia. Emphasis is on empirical investigation, but the journal also includes conceptual and theoretical studies.

281 JOURNAL OF CONTEMPORARY BUSINESS. Seattle: University of Washington Graduate School of Business Administration, 1970- . Quarterly.

282 JOURNAL OF GENERAL MANAGEMENT. London: Mercury House Business Publications, 1973- . Quarterly.

283 JOURNAL OF MANAGEMENT STUDIES. Oxford: Basil Blackwell, 1961- . Quarterly.

> Edited from Manchester Business School, this journal combines an academic and practical approach. It includes signed book reviews.

284 LONDON BUSINESS SCHOOL JOURNAL. London: 1973- . Three issues annually.

> This contains short articles on management topics and news of London Business School activities.

285 McKINSEY QUARTERLY: A REVIEW OF TRENDS AND PROBLEMS OF CURRENT CONCERN TO TOP MANAGEMENT. New York: McKinsey & Co., 1964- .

> This controlled circulation journal is issued by the well-known consultant firm.

286 MANAGEMENT CHECKLISTS. London: British Institute of Management, 1969- . Published irregularly.

These very useful brief notes on management topics highlight
questions to be considered when contemplating a new management technique or problem area. Most checklists are supported
by brief reading lists.

287 MANAGEMENT DECISION: THE EUROPEAN REVIEW OF MANAGEMENT
TECHNOLOGY. Bradford: MCB (Management Decision), 1963- . Six
issues annually.

Three journals each year alternate with three monographs. The
journals contain practical articles, approximately 4,000 words
in length, and book reviews.

288 MANAGEMENT IN ACTION. Coulsdon, Surrey, Eng.: J.P. Harvey,
1969-76. Monthly.

This replaced OFFICE METHODS AND MACHINES (1953-69)
and incorporates the journal of the (British) Organization and
Methods Society. It includes short articles on management
sciences, methods and techniques, reviews of trends in business equipment applications, reports of conferences and seminars, brief book reviews, and lists of books received. Ceased
publication in 1976.

289 MANAGEMENT INFORMATION SHEETS. London: British Institute of
Management, 1969- . Published irregularly.

These are brief notes on management topics.

290 MANAGEMENT INTERNATIONAL REVIEW. Wiesbaden: Betriebswirtschaftlicher Verlag Dr. Th. Gabler GmbH for European Foundation for
Management Development, 1961- . Bimonthly.

Published in cooperation with other international associations,
the review contains scholarly articles in English, French, or
German (summaries in other languages) with classified and annotated bibliographies in each issue.

291 MANAGEMENT REVIEW. New York: AMACOM, 1923- . Monthly.

Contained are original articles, digests, abstracts, and book reviews.

292 MANAGEMENT TODAY. London: Haymarket Publishing, 1966- . Monthly.

This publication is composed of brief, practical articles on industry and management, with many case studies. One or two
book reviews appear in each issue, and a few pages are de-
voted to British Institute of Management activities.

293 MICHIGAN BUSINESS REVIEW. Ann Arbor: University of Michigan
Graduate School of Business Administration, 1949- . Bimonthly.

The review includes signed book reviews.

294 M.S.U. BUSINESS TOPICS. East Lansing: Michigan State University
Graduate School of Business Administration, 1953- . Quarterly.

295 RYDGE'S. Sydney: Rydge Publications Pty. 1928- . Monthly.

Contained are articles on industrial affairs and management,
with book notes.

296 S.A.M. ADVANCED MANAGEMENT JOURNAL. New York: Society
for the Advancement of Management, 1935- . Quarterly.

297 SLOAN MANAGEMENT REVIEW. Cambridge, Mass.: M.I.T., 1961- .
Three issues annually.

Scholarly articles on all aspects of management, together with
signed book reviews and lists of recent publications, are found
in this review, which was formerly the INDUSTRIAL MANAGE-
MENT REVIEW.

ORGANIZATIONS

Required information may not always be available in the form of a book or periodical article, and it is here that the professional associations and similar organizations may be able to help. As well as often having their own publications program, such organizations have access to experts on their own staff and
among members of the organization who may be able to assist with a particularly
knotty problem; normally they also arrange training courses, seminars, conven-
tions, and other meetings. Some of the more important organizations concerned
with the whole area of management are listed below as items 298-316.

298 Academy of Management. Secretary-Treasurer (1976), Rosemary Pledger,
University of Houston at Clear Lake City, 2700 Bay Area Boulevard,
Houston, Tex. 77058.

Founded 1947 as an association of professors who teach management subjects, the academy publishes ACADEMY OF MANAGE-
MENT JOURNAL and (from 1976) ACADEMY OF MANAGE-
MENT REVIEW. It has divisions concerned with business policy and planning, international management, managerial consultation, management education and development, management
history, manpower management, organizational behavior, organization and management theory, organization development,
production and operations management, social issues in management, and organizational communication.

299 American Foundation for Management Research.

Founded in 1960, this organization's concern was research

into management topics. It was absorbed by the American Management Association (item 300) in 1973.

300 American Management Association, 135 West 50th Street, New York, N.Y. 10020.

Founded 1923, this is the largest American management organization. It has a strong educational and research program, holds numerous seminars, workshops, and courses, and has a vast number of publications (books, reports, and periodicals) to its credit, many of which are listed in this bibliography. It maintains management centers in various parts of the United States and South and Central America and also in Canada (see item 303) and Europe (see item 314). Its divisions correspond to the major management functions. It also maintains a large library of books, periodicals, and audiovisual materials.

301 British Institute of Management (BIM), Management House, Parker Street, London, WC2B 5PT, England.

Founded 1947, this very active organization has an excellent library and information service and a heavy program of publications, courses, seminars, and conferences. Its Management Education Information Unit provides information about courses and its Management Consulting Services Information Bureau provides a similar service about consultant firms. It also maintains a Centre for Physical Distribution Management and a Small Business Information Bureau, and in 1959 helped to establish, as an independent body, the Centre for Interfirm Comparison. In 1975 Management Research Groups, formed in 1926, became part of BIM.

302 Canadian Institute of Management, 51 Eglinton Street East, Toronto, Ontario, Canada.

Founded in 1942 as the Society of Industrial Methods Engineers, this later became the Canadian Industrial Management Association. It aims to promote the advancement of industrial organization and technological efficiency by the application of scientific principles and the cumulative experience of its members.

303 Canadian Management Centre of the American Management Association, CIL House, Suite 1635, 630 Dorchester Boulevard West, Montreal, Quebec, Canada.

304 CIOS - World Council of Management, 1 rue de Varembé, CH-1211 Geneva 20, Switzerland.

The chief aim of this organization is to promote internationally the art and science of management, to improve the standards of living in all nations through the more effective release, and to utilize human and natural resources. Its membership consists of representatives of management societies in many countries. The organization holds triennial congresses, the proceedings of which are published by the national member responsible for the organization of the congress. Founded in 1926 as the International Council for Scientific Management in 1975 it became CIOS - World Council of Management.

305 The Conference Board, 845 Third Avenue, New York, N.Y. 10022.

This was founded 1916 as the National Industrial Conference Board. It conducts research and holds courses, seminars, and conferences on business economics and management. Its large library provides an intensive information service. It publishes a wide range of reports and other documents, many of which are listed in this bibliography, and also maintains a Canadian office (see item 306).

306 The Conference Board in Canada, 615 Dorchester Boulevard West, Montreal, Quebec, Canada.

This is the Canadian office of the organization described above.

307 Council for International Progress in Management, 135 West 50th Street, New York, N.Y. 10020.

The council was founded in 1933 "to stimulate abroad the development of management and related philosophies, techniques, accomplishments and attitudes which have developed in the U.S. by transmitting the thinking and achievements of management movements in other countries." It is the U.S. member of CIOS (World Council of Management). See item 304.

308 Industrial Management Society, 570 Northwest Highway, Des Plaines, Ill. 60016.

This group was founded 1935 with the objects of advancing the profession of management, promoting research in the various·fields of management activity, and studying the problems of social sciences as related to industry. It publishes a monthly journal, INDUSTRIAL MANAGEMENT.

309 The Industrial Society, Robert Hyde House, 48 Bryanston Square, London, W.1, England.

Founded 1918 as the Industrial Welfare Society, this group sought to anticipate legislation covering working conditions by means of voluntary action. It has since broadened its activi-

ties to cover the whole sphere of management with particular
reference to encouragement of good leadership, improvement
in management-union relationships, review of conditions of
work, development of adequate communication, and training.
It publishes INDUSTRIAL SOCIETY monthly.

310 Institute of Directors, 10 Belgrave Square, London, SW1X 8PW, England.

The institute was founded 1903 to raise the status and responsibilities of company directors. It provides information and
other services to directors of all types of companies and publishes THE DIRECTOR monthly.

311 Institute of Scientific Business, 200 Keighley Road, Bradford, BD9, 4JZ,
Yorkshire, England.

The institute, founded in 1963, is concerned with the development of management as a recognized profession with scientific
foundation and accepted standards of qualifications and ethics,
improvement of management standards, the helping of managers
to understand and apply new ideas and techniques, and the
development of sound management teaching. Members receive
MANAGEMENT DECISION (see item 287) and other publications.

312 International Academy of Management, 100 Pacific Highway, North Sydney, NSW 2060, Australia.

This was founded in 1958. A section of CIOS (World Council of Management), its members consist of leaders in management from six continents and twenty-eight countries. Its main
aim is to provide members of CIOS with a consultative organ
at international level for fundamental research in theories of
practical and philosophical management.

313 International Management Association, 135 West 50th Street, New York,
N.Y. 10020.

Founded in 1956 and affiliated with the American Management
Association, this group has special responsibility for international activities.

314 Management Centre Europe, avenue des Arts 3/4, Brussels, Belgium.

This was founded in 1964 as the European office of the American Management Association.

315 National Management Association, 2210 Arbor Boulevard, Dayton,
Ohio 45439.

Founded 1925 as the National Association of Foremen, the association is concerned particularly with the development of management as a profession and draws its membership from the supervisory level and above.

316 Society for the Advancement of Management, 135 West 50th Street, New York, N.Y. 10020.

This was founded in 1936 by a merger of the Taylor Society and the Society of Industrial Engineers, dating originally to 1912. It is affiliated with the American Management Association and has many publications, notably the quarterly S.A.M. ADVANCED MANAGEMENT JOURNAL.

Section 2

THE MANAGEMENT AUDIT

The management or operations audit involves the study and appraisal, by an internal or external team, of management standards and techniques throughout an organization. Any aspect of management may be examined in a management audit, including financial policies, personnel problems, organization, corporate planning, and use of modern management techniques. In this section only works concerned with the overall approach to the management audit or management services are listed; works dealing with specific techniques, such as work study or systems and procedures, are listed in section 10.

317 Arnstein, William E., and Burstein, Herman. MANAGEMENT SERVICES BY ACCOUNTING FIRMS. New York: Ronald Press, 1967. 444 p. Diagrams, tables.

> This is a guide to the services which accountants can provide in the areas of top management, sales and marketing services, manufacturing services, data processing, and office services.

318 Baker, John K., and Schaffer, Robert H. "Making Staff Consulting More Effective." HARVARD BUSINESS REVIEW 47 (January–February 1969): 62-71.

> The internal consultancy in the Union Carbide Corporation is reviewed.

319 Baldwin, Andrew L. "A Case for Management of Management Services." WORK STUDY AND MANAGEMENT SERVICES 14 (May 1970): 389-93. Bibliography.

> This case study examines the centralized management services in the Booker Group of Companies, Guyana, with emphasis on communication within the team, setting objectives, and measuring performance.

320 Barkdull, Charles W. "Periodic Operations Audit: Management Tool." MICHIGAN BUSINESS REVIEW 18 (July 1966): 19-25. Forms.

> Barkdull defines periodic operations audit as "a systematic and

periodic review of the various phases of a business by someone outside the immediate departments being reviewed to determine their individual and collective effectiveness." He emphasizes the financial and control aspects.

321   Blake, Robert R., and Mouton, Jane Srygley. CORPORATE EXCELLENCE DIAGNOSIS. Austin, Tex.: Scientific Methods, 1968. 441 p.

Believing that "diagnosis of the health of the organization corpus is as essential to the identification and correction of corporate maladies as it is to the correction of problems or to the improvement or maintenance of good physical health," the authors propose an instrument for the diagnosis and cure of problems in human resources, financial management, operations, marketing, research and development, and the corporation generally. No index.

322   Boyce, R.O., and Eisen, H. MANAGEMENT DIAGNOSIS: A PRACTICAL GUIDE. Management Studies Series. London: Longman, 1972. 274 p. Diagrams, tables.

Two management consultants give advice on the observation and diagnosis of "the symptoms of inefficiencies or of potential troubles." The value of formalized periodic reviews is stressed.

323   British Institute of Management. KNOW YOUR BUSINESS ACTION PROGRAMME. 2 vols. London: 1973. Diagrams, tables, bibliography. Looseleaf.

Volume 1: BUSINESS ANALYSIS. Volume 2: MANAGING THE SMALLER COMPANY: GUIDELINES AND INFORMATION. This set is described as "a relatively simple do-it-yourself method of analysing an organization's activities in logical stages." It is based in part on material originally published by the Swedish Employers' Confederation and is aimed particularly at smaller firms. The program is in four stages: collection and analysis of basic financial information, a general management audit consisting of fifteen checklists, collection of all the figures assembled during the first two stages, and planning for the future. Volume 2 includes several bibliographical references and addresses of sources of information.

324   _____. A MANAGEMENT CHECKLIST. BIM Occasional Paper, n.s., OPN 2. London: 1968. 18 p. Paperback.

This checklist of questions enables top management to examine the extent to which accepted management practices and techniques are used in their organization. It was produced in collaboration with the Institute of Management Consultants.

325 Clay, Michael J. "Diagnosing Company Ailments." BUSINESS MAN-
AGEMENT 100 (February 1970): 32-33, 35. Bibliography.

This brief survey is useful as a literature review. It was continued by the same author's "Company Ailments: A Cure" in
BUSINESS MANAGEMENT 100 (March 1970): 36-39. Bibliography.

326 Dekom, Anton K. THE INTERNAL CONSULTANT. AMA Research Study,
no. 101. New York: American Management Association, 1969. 102 p.
Forms, tables, bibliography. Paperback.

This work reviews U.S. practices on internal consultant departments, including structure of departments, pay, initiation of
projects, and evaluation of internal consultancy. It includes
detailed comments on internal consultancy in more than twenty
named companies. Annotated reading list, pp. 100-101.

327 Dodwell, Joseph W. "Operational Auditing: A Part of the Basic Audit."
JOURNAL OF ACCOUNTANCY 121 (June 1966): 31-39.

Reviewed are approaches to the operational or management
audit, defined as "a bridge between a basic traditional financial audit and a management services approach to a client's
program."

328 Eisenberg, Joseph, ed. TURNAROUND MANAGEMENT: A MANUAL
FOR PROFIT IMPROVEMENT AND GROWTH. New York: McGraw-Hill,
1972. 288 p. Tables.

This volume contains twelve contributions by members of Profit-
Improvement Inc., management consultants, on "turning around"
an area in which results have been less than satisfactory. Topics covered include more effective use of computers, executive
development, and executive compensation.

329 Faucett, Philip M. MANAGEMENT AUDIT FOR SMALL MANUFACTUR-
ERS. Small Business Management Series, no. 29. Washington, D.C.:
Small Business Administration, 1963. 58 p. Paperback.

An introduction to the management audit is followed by 144
questions to be asked when auditing sixteen specific areas of
management, with comments.

330 Greenwood, William T. BUSINESS POLICY: A MANAGEMENT AUDIT
APPROACH. New York: Macmillan; London: Collier-Macmillan, 1967.
xiv, 656 p. Diagrams, maps, tables.

This collection of readings and cases is aimed at helping students apply analytically the theories, methods, and techniques
learned in the business administration curriculum. Part two
consists of eleven contributions on aspects of the management

audit, followed by case studies of management audits in Kargl Instruments Inc., ACME Brass Manufacturing Company, Kentucky Food Stores Inc., and E.W. Walton Company.

331 Howard, Leslie R. "The Management Audit." ACCOUNTANCY 80 (October 1969): 772-74; 80 (November 1969): 835-38; 81 (January 1970): 33-36.

This three-part survey defines areas which might be investigated under a management audit and some of the failings which might be uncovered.

332 Jenkins, S.R. "The Case for the Management Audit." THE ACCOUNTANT 168 (March 2, 1972): 272-74.

Jenkins defines management audit as "a systematic procedure for analyzing and appraising the overall performance of the management of a business." He suggests that the audit should include evaluation of executives and points out that the need for a regular audit is not universally accepted.

333 Keating, Stephen F. "How Honeywell Management Views Operational Auditing." THE INTERNAL AUDITOR 26 (September/October 1969): 43-51.

The former president, now chairman of Honeywell Inc. gives his views on internal operational auditing and its value to management.

334 Leonard, William P. THE MANAGEMENT AUDIT: AN APPRAISAL OF MANAGEMENT METHODS AND PERFORMANCE. Englewood Cliffs, N.J.: Prentice-Hall, 1962. 238 p. Bibliography.

Introductory sections on the basic elements of management are followed by sections dealing with the purpose and practice of the management audit; organizing and initiating an audit; analysis, interpretation, and synthesis; gathering and recording information; measuring performance; difficulties often encountered; evaluating executive effectiveness; developing and recommending improvements; preparing and writing the management audit report; reviewing audit findings with those concerned; the audit follow-up; and the future. A shorter version appears in Lazzaro, Victor, ed. SYSTEMS AND PROCEDURES: A HANDBOOK FOR BUSINESS AND INDUSTRY. 2d ed. Englewood Cliffs, N.J.: Prentice-Hall, 1968. Pp. 90-121. Form (see item 1310).

335 Lindberg, Roy A., and Cohn, Theodore. OPERATIONS AUDITING. New York: AMACOM, 1972. 317 p. Diagram, tables, bibliography.

This work is described by the publishers as "a definitive guidebook to the entire operations auditing function." Part one (pp. 3-44) deals with the nature and role of operations audit, setting up the operations audit department, and performing the audit; part two (pp. 47-209) provides advice on applying the audit to specific management functions; and part three (pp. 213-94) describes the use of questionnaires in the audit with specimen questionnaires for each of the functions dealt with in part two. The general questionnaire used by Honeywell Inc. is reproduced in an appendix.

336 Lines, A.H., and Metz, C.K.C. "Managing Management Services." London: Industrial and Commercial Techniques, 1972. 51 leaves. Diagrams, forms, tables. Mimeographed, spiral binding.

These are notes from a seminar aimed at provoking management services managers, or the directors to whom they report, into reviewing their patterns of operations; suggesting ways in which the terms of reference, organization, and objectives of the management services unit might be amended; and suggesting techniques which might help the manager sell his services more successfully or improve the effectiveness of his staff.

337 MANAGEMENT ADVISER. New York: American Institute of Certified Public Accountants, 1964-76. Bimonthly.

This journal contains articles and book reviews on the management audit and other topics. It formerly was MANAGEMENT SERVICES. Ceased publication in 1976.

338 Martindell, Jackson. THE APPRAISAL OF MANAGEMENT FOR EXECUTIVES AND INVESTORS. New York: Harper & Brothers, 1962. xviii, 204 p. Tables.

Though not a book on management audit, this work focuses on the evaluation of management. Believing that the investor should only consider companies where superior management is present, the chairman of the American Institute of Management presents a guide to the evaluation of management systems and lists (on pp. 185-94) seventy-three "excellently managed companies" to which his theory is particularly applicable.

339 Michael, Stephen R. APPRAISING MANAGEMENT PRACTICES AND PERFORMANCE. Englewood Cliffs, N.J.: Prentice-Hall, 1963. 217 p. Diagrams, portrait, tables.

This step-by-step guide to the conduct of a management audit is defined by the author as "the objective, comprehensive study of the business organization or some part of it, for the purpose of successfully adapting it to changes in its environment and to resolve specific internal problems that have occurred because of these changes, as well as to enable the organization to take advantage of special opportunities for change."

340 Rose, T.G. THE MANAGEMENT AUDIT. 3d ed. London: Gee, 1961. 40 p. Diagrams.

> One of the earliest statements of the case for a systematic review of the whole management process, originally given as a paper to the (British) Institute of Industrial Administration and first published in 1932.

341 Santocki, J. "Management Audit: Chance, Challenge or Lost Opportunity?" THE ACCOUNTANT 170 (January 3, 1974): 14-18.

> Santocki reviews the first stages of research in the United Kingdom aimed at establishing the scope and application of management audit and considers the arguments for and against it.

342 Scantlebury, D.L. "The Structure of a Management Audit Finding." THE INTERNAL AUDITOR 29 (March/April 1972): 10-22. Tables.

> This article suggests a framework for a management audit report covering its aims, procedures, and the conclusions and recommendations of the investigation.

343 Smith, Brian P. "The Development of Management Services Groups." O & M BULLETIN 25 (May 1970): 89-96.

> Smith explains the value of management services groups, the requirements of a management services department, and the services it should provide, and the priorities to which it should attend.

344 Snellgrove, Olin C. "The Management Audit: Organizational Guidance System." JOURNAL OF SYSTEMS MANAGEMENT 22 (December 1971): 10-12.

> The author considers the functions of management audits and the problems of performing these functions.

345 Walley, B.H. MANAGEMENT SERVICES HANDBOOK. London: Business Books, 1973. 452 p. Diagrams, forms, tables. (Distributed by Cahners Publishing Co., Boston.)

> This comprehensive handbook is in seven parts: the role of management services; diagnosis and appraisal techniques; measurement techniques; planning, strategy, formulation, and general management methods; control of performance; motivation and communication; and aids to decision making and profit improvement.

346 Wilde, Frazar B., and Vancil, Richard F. "Performance Audit by Outside Directors." HARVARD BUSINESS REVIEW 50 (July/August 1972): 112-16.

The authors review the ways in which outside directors may become more involved in company affairs by conducting audits of performance.

347 Wingate, John W. MANAGEMENT AUDIT FOR SMALL RETAILERS. Small Business Management Series, no. 31. Washington, D.C.: Small Business Administration, 1964. 51 p. Paperback. (Distributed by Government Printing Office.)

An introduction to the management audit is followed by 149 questions to be asked when auditing seventeen specific functions, with comments.

ORGANIZATIONS

The following organizations are particularly concerned with management auditing or the evaluation of management.

348 American Institute of Management, 125 East 38th Street, New York, N.Y. 10016.

Founded in 1948, this is a research organization of executives interested in management efficiency and appraisal of management performance. It issues numerous publications, including MANUAL OF EXCELLENT MANAGEMENTS (biennially), THE MANAGEMENT AUDIT (irregularly), and Management Audit Monographs.

349 Association of Internal Management Consultants, c/o Albert Aiello, Jr., Sperry and Hutchinson Company, 330 Madison Avenue, New York, N.Y. 10017.

This group was founded in 1971 to encourage the professional practice of internal management consultants, establish high standards of professional performance, and act as a forum for the exchange of information and the sharing of professional expertise.

350 Institute of Internal Auditors, 5500 Diplomat Circle, Suite 104, Orlando, Fla. 32810.

This professional organization of auditors and others in internal auditing positions in industry, commerce, and government was established in 1941. It has local chapters in the United States, Canada, and other countries. Its publications include the bimonthly INTERNAL AUDITOR.

Section 3

THE BEHAVIORAL SCIENCE APPROACH TO MANAGEMENT

The behavioral science approach to management, emphasizing the importance of individual and group relations in the working environment, has exercised the minds of many writers since the now classic Hawthorne Experiments carried out by Elton Mayo and his associates at the Hawthorne Works of the Western Electric Company (see items 401-2 and 415). These showed that the major pressures on the individual were exerted by the group with which he worked, and stressed that managers must realize they were dealing with groups rather than with individuals.

Included in this section are works on organization theory (though more traditional approaches to organization structure are covered in section 4), industrial psychology, management styles, leadership and motivation, and participative management. More specific applications are dealt with in appropriate sections, notably section 19 (Personnel Management). See also item 1019.

GENERAL STUDIES

351 Argyris, Chris. THE APPLICABILITY OF ORGANIZATIONAL SOCIOL-OGY. Cambridge, Eng.: Cambridge University Press, 1972. 138 p. Bibliography.

> Argyris offers a critique of recent contributions by sociologists and psychologists to the problem of organizational structure and behavior, with particular reference to the work of Peter Blau, James D. Thompson, Charles Perrow, John Goldthorpe, and David Lockwood.

352 _____. INTEGRATING THE INDIVIDUAL AND THE ORGANIZATION. New York: Wiley, 1964. xii, 330 p. Tables.

> After analyzing the causes of human relations problems within organizations, the author offers suggestions for their improvement. He examines such topics as organizational structures, job design, rewards and penalties, incentive systems, recruitment, and dismissal. He suggests a "mix model" for integrat-

ing individuals and organizations by constructing an organization through the interrelationships of all its parts. Indexes of names and subjects.

353 _____. INTERPERSONAL COMPETENCE AND ORGANIZATIONAL EFFECTIVENESS. New York: Irwin; London: Tavistock, 1962. 292 p. Tables.

The author shows how a successful change was brought about in the behavior of top executives through laboratory training and includes examples of T-Group exercises. He includes a chapter by Roger Harrison on research carried out to evaluate the impact of the program. Indexes of authors and subjects.

354 _____. ORGANIZATION AND INNOVATION. Irwin-Dorsey Series in Behavioral Science. Homewood, Ill.: Irwin and Dorsey Press, 1965. xii, 274 p. Tables.

This classic work is based on studies in three organizations: a physical science industrial laboratory with about 150 employees; the executive committee and department directors of a large research and engineering laboratory with about 3,000 employees; and the board of directors of a firm of management consultants. Indexes of names and subjects.

355 _____. PERSONALITY AND ORGANIZATION: THE CONFLICT BETWEEN THE SYSTEM AND THE INDIVIDUAL. New York: Harper & Row, 1957. xiii, 291 p.

Argyris attempts to integrate the research literature relevant to understanding human behavior in organizations. He concludes with a 12-page appendix presenting some basic categories of a theory of organization.

356 Athos, Anthony G., and Coffey, Robert E. BEHAVIOR IN ORGANIZATIONS: A MULTI-DIMENSIONAL VIEW. Prentice-Hall International Series in Management. Englewood Cliffs, N.J.: Prentice-Hall, 1968. xx, 549 p. Illustrations, diagrams, tables.

This study of complete organizations is followed by a systematic study of their integral parts, including group behavior, leadership, and decision making. The text is supported by fourteen readings and thirty-one cases.

357 Berkley, George E. THE ADMINISTRATIVE REVOLUTION: NOTES ON THE PASSING OF ORGANIZATION MAN. Englewood Cliffs, N.J.: Prentice-Hall, 1971. 181 p. Bibliography. Hardcover and paperback.

Drawing on experiences of government and business administration in Europe, Japan, Israel, and the United States, the author traces the collapse of bureaucracy, the demise of organization man,

the growth of employee participation in decision making, and
the development of the administrative state. The bibliography
surprisingly omits William H. Whyte's ORGANIZATION MAN,
although there are several references to this in the text.

358 Blau, Peter M., and Scott, W. Richard. FORMAL ORGANIZATIONS:
A COMPARATIVE APPROACH. Introduction and additional bibliography
by J.H. Smith. New York: Chandler, 1962; London: Routledge, 1963.
xiv, 312 p. Bibliography.

This work considers the effect of organizations on the structure
of society and their significance as a work environment for a
major part of the labor force.

359 Cartwright, Dorwin, and Zander, Alvin, eds. GROUP DYNAMICS: RE-
SEARCH AND THEORY. 3d ed. New York: Harper & Row; London:
Tavistock, 1968. 580 p. Diagrams, tables. Hardcover and paperback.

This book contains forty-two papers on group dynamics research
and its application to various social problems, including management problems, presented in seven sections: introduction
to group dynamics, groups and group membership, pressures to
uniformity in groups, power and influence in groups, leadership and performance of group functions, motivational pressures
in groups, and structural properties of groups. Indexes of
names and subjects.

360 Cherns, Albert Bernard. "Can Behavioral Scientists Help Managers Improve Their Organizations?" ORGANIZATIONAL DYNAMICS 1 (Winter
1973): 51-67. Diagrams, bibliography.

Cherns argues that social scientists can help managers most
effectively by providing them with new ways of looking at
their world rather than by selling packages, conducting surveys,
or discovering facts. He suggests areas where they might be
of greatest value.

361 Child, John. "More Myths of Management Organisation?" JOURNAL
OF MANAGEMENT STUDIES 7 (October 1970): 376-90. Diagram, table.

This is a critique of various organizational theories from Urwick and Fayol to Argyris and Herzberg. The author stresses
the advantages of research which treats the key areas of operating situation, management structure, and organizational development as interdependent within a systems analysis.

362 Cyert, Richard M., and March, James G. A BEHAVIORAL THEORY OF
THE FIRM. Prentice-Hall Behavioral Sciences in Business Series and
Prentice-Hall International Series in Management. Englewood Cliffs,
N.J.: Prentice-Hall, 1963. 332 p. Diagrams, tables.

Behavioral studies of the internal operation of the firm, such as organization structure and goals, are as important for effective decision making as are studies of market factors, the authors contend. The authors develop a theory for decision making based on this argument, placing great stress on the use of computer simulation for the construction of models of organizational behavior. The work also includes contributions by G.P.E. Clarkson, K.J. Cohen, William R. Dill, E.A. Feigenbaum, E. Grunberg, C.G. Moore, P.O. Soelberg, W.H. Starbuck, and Oliver E. Williamson.

363 Dalton, Gene W.; and Lawrence, Paul R.; with Lorsch, Jay W., eds. ORGANIZATIONAL STRUCTURE AND DESIGN. Irwin-Dorsey Series in Behavioral Science. Homewood, Ill.: Irwin and Dorsey Press, 1970. 309 p. Diagrams, tables, bibliography. Paperback.

Included are eighteen case studies with readings on the influence of technical change on organization structure, organizing for product innovation, and automation and technical change. No subject index.

364 Drake, Richard I., and Smith, Peter J. BEHAVIOURAL SCIENCE IN INDUSTRY. London: McGraw-Hill, 1973. 134 p. Diagrams, tables, bibliographies. Paperback.

This book contains six chapters on the meaning, methods, and concepts of behavioral research and five on its applications, including leadership, group relations training, job design, and organizational development.

365 Flippo, Edwin B. MANAGEMENT: A BEHAVIORAL APPROACH. 2d ed. Boston: Allyn & Bacon, 1970. xiv, 573 p. Diagrams, tables.

Flippo believes both the traditional and behavioral approaches can contribute to more effective management and that the task is one of diagnosing situations to determine the optimum mix. Chapters are arranged in groups reflecting the traditional functions: planning (including the human element), organizing (formal and informal), directing (including motivation), and control (including integration of interests). Name and subject indexes.

366 Frank, H. Eric, ed. ORGANIZATION STRUCTURING. London: McGraw-Hill, 1971. 351 p. Diagrams, tables, bibliographies.

This contains twenty contributions by eighteen writers arranged in six parts: understanding the structure, the organization as a system, the influence of objectives, the human element, the changing organization, and what works best? No index.

367 Goldberg, Walter, ed. BEHAVIORAL APPROACHES TO MODERN MAN-

AGEMENT. Gothenburg Studies in Business Administration. 2 vols. Goeteborg, Sweden: Graduate School of Economics and Business Administration, 1970. Diagrams, tables, bibliographies.

These are papers given at a symposium held in 1968. Volume 1 (338 p.) deals with "Information Systems and Decision Making"; volume 2 (365 p.) with "Applications of Marketing, Production, and Finance." No index.

368 Graves, Desmond, ed. MANAGEMENT RESEARCH: A CROSS-CULTURAL PERSPECTIVE. Amsterdam: Elsevier, 1973. xiv, 349 p. Diagrams, tables. (Distributed by Jossey-Bass, Inc., San Francisco.)

Fourteen papers deal with research into organization behavior and organizational change. They were originally given at a symposium sponsored by Philips N.V. and held at Eersal, Holland, in 1970. Topics include a comparison of managerial behavior in Japan, Korea, and the United States; Japanese organization behavior; workers' participation in managerial decision making; attitudes to work in the chemical industry; organizational size; organization development in the multinational enterprise; and managerial attitudes and behavior in England and France. Indexes of authors and subjects.

369 Greenwood, William T. MANAGEMENT AND ORGANIZATIONAL BE-HAVIOR THEORIES: AN INTERDISCIPLINARY APPROACH. Cincinnati: South-Western Publishing Co., 1965. xii, 890 p. Diagrams, tables, bibliographies.

The text and fifty-two readings are divided into seven parts: management theories and philosophies, planning, decision making, organizing, staffing, direction and leadership, and controlling. Indexes of names and subjects.

370 Hacon, Richard, ed. PERSONAL AND ORGANIZATIONAL EFFECTIVE-NESS. London: McGraw-Hill, 1972. 304 p. Diagrams, tables, bibliographies.

Contained are twenty-two contributions on methods and phases of development, systematic task development, learning and motivation, and improving the organization. Included are case studies of Command Group Training (CGT), a method of improving an organized unit by training together all the people who manage it in relation to their current opportunities and problems, and organization development in the British-American Tobacco Company Ltd. No index.

371 Haire, Mason, ed. MODERN ORGANIZATION THEORY: A SYMPO-SIUM OF THE FOUNDATION FOR RESEARCH ON HUMAN BEHAVIOR. New York: Wiley, 1959. 324 p. Diagrams.

This work contains ten contributions by Haire, Richard M.

Cyert and J.G. Marsh, Anatole Rapoport, Chris Argyris, William Foote Whyte, Rensis Likert, Robert Dubin, Dorwin Cartwright, and Jacob Marschak.

372 _____. ORGANIZATION THEORY IN INDUSTRIAL PRACTICE. New York: Wiley, 1962. 173 p. Diagrams, tables.

These eleven papers, mainly by industrial executives, were given at a symposium on modern approaches to organizational theory organized by the Foundation for Research on Human Behavior, Institute of Industrial Relations, University of California. Included are case studies of Genesco Incorporated and the Maytag Company. This complements MODERN ORGANIZATION THEORY (item 371), which presents the views of academics.

373 Heald, Gordon, ed. APPROACHES TO THE STUDY OF ORGANIZATIONAL BEHAVIOR: OPERATIONAL RESEARCH AND THE BEHAVIORAL SCIENCES. London: Tavistock, 1970. 161 p. Diagrams, tables, bibliographies. (Distributed by Barnes & Noble, Scranton, Pa.)

The eleven contributions include papers on manpower planning, a management information system using subjective probability estimates, and ergonomics and organizational behavior. No index.

374 Hersey, Paul, and Blanchard, Kenneth H. MANAGEMENT OF ORGANIZATIONAL BEHAVIOR: UTILIZING HUMAN RESOURCES. 2d ed. Englewood Cliffs, N.J.: Prentice-Hall, 1972. xii, 209 p. Diagrams, tables, bibliography. Hardcover and paperback.

This is a concise approach to the interaction of people, motivation, and leadership.

375 Huse, Edgar F., and Bowditch, James L. BEHAVIOR IN ORGANIZATIONS: A SYSTEMS APPROACH TO MANAGING. Reading, Mass.: Addison-Wesley, 1973. 500 p. Illustrations, diagrams, tables.

A very readable guide, this work is profusely illustrated and has many case studies. Indexes of authors and subjects.

376 Hutchinson, John G. MANAGEMENT STRATEGY AND TACTICS. New York: Holt, Rinehart & Winston, 1971. 536 p. Diagrams, tables, bibliographies.

Hutchinson combines behavioral and quantitative approaches to management. Part one deals with general perspectives on management strategy and tactics; part two with strategies and tactics in the areas of decision making, organizational design, control, and motivation; and part three with tactical areas for tomorrow's managers (government-business relations, union relations, research and development, and multinational operations). There are many case studies.

377   Hutton, Geoffrey. THINKING ABOUT ORGANIZATIONS. 2d ed. London: Tavistock in association with Bath University Press, 1972. 180 p. Diagrams, tables, bibliography. Hardcover and paperback. (Distributed by Barnes & Noble, Scranton, Pa.)

This work examines, in the light of contemporary research and theory, the nature of organization and the effects of organization on human behavior. Part one, "The Field and the Nature of the System," begins with a literature review. Part two, "Organizational Design," includes studies of organizational design in a hospital, a school, and a research laboratory. Part three, "Design and the Social System," is concerned with the role of managers and individuals within the enterprise. Indexes of authors and subjects.

378   Jaques, Elliott. WORK, CREATIVITY AND SOCIAL JUSTICE. London: Heinemann; New York: International Universities Press, 1970. 262 p.

This collection of fourteen essays, some previously published elsewhere, has the underlying theme that analysis of the social and psychological conditions for work and creativity can offer valuable insights into almost every human activity. Topics include "The Human Consequences of Industrialization," "Disturbances in the Capacity to Work," and "On Being a Manager."

379   Jay, Antony. CORPORATION MAN. New York: Random House, 1971; London: Cape, 1972. 269 p. Bibliography.

Jay considers the evolution and present role of corporation man in an effort to explain the central reality of the modern corporation.

380   Joyce, Robert D. ENCOUNTERS IN ORGANIZATIONAL BEHAVIOR: PROBLEM SITUATIONS. Pergamon Management & Business Series, vol. 2. New York: Pergamon Press, 1972. 263 p. Diagrams, tables, bibliographies. Hardcover and paperback.

These case studies in various aspects of group behavior at work include communication; leadership; styles; decision making; recruitment, selection, and development; motivation; team development; and problems of new technologies. The book includes many discussion questions. No index.

381   Kahn, Robert L., and Boulding, Elise, eds. POWER AND CONFLICT IN ORGANIZATIONS. London: Tavistock, 1964. xvi, 173 p. Diagrams, tables.

These are proceedings of a seminar published as part of the

program of the Foundation for Research on Human Behavior,
Ann Arbor, Michigan. The book contains four papers on power
and nine on conflict and its resolution.

382 Kahn, Robert L.; Wolfe, Donald M.; Quinn, Robert P.; and Snoek, J.
Diedrick; with Rosenthal, Robert A. ORGANIZATIONAL STRESS: STUDIES
IN ROLE CONFLICT AND AMBIGUITY. New York: Wiley, 1964. xii,
470 p. Diagrams, tables, bibliography.

The authors examine the nature, causes, and consequences of
pressures occurring in large-scale organizations as a result of
role conflict and role ambiguity.

383 Katz, Daniel, and Kahn, Robert L. THE SOCIAL PSYCHOLOGY OF
ORGANIZATIONS. New York: Wiley, 1966. 498 p. Bibliography.

This is partly an effort to provide a general treatment of some
of the issues discussed by Likert in NEW PATTERNS OF MAN-
AGEMENT (item 392). It includes chapters on the characteristics
of social organizations, the development of organizational structures, organizational effectiveness, organizational roles, power
and authority, communication, decision making, and organizational change.

384 Kelly, Joe. ORGANIZATIONAL BEHAVIOR. Irwin-Dorsey Series in
Behavioral Science. Homewood, Ill.: Irwin and Dorsey Press, 1969.
xvi, 664 p. Diagrams, tables, bibliography.

A comprehensive introduction to organizational psychology, this
book contains many readings and cases. It includes sections
on executive behavior, executive recruitment and selection,
and sensitivity training. Indexes of names and subjects.

385 Lawless, David J. EFFECTIVE MANAGEMENT: SOCIAL PSYCHOLOGI-
CAL APPROACH. Englewood Cliffs, N.J.: Prentice-Hall, 1972. 422 p.
Diagrams, table, bibliography.

Lawless demonstrates the applicability to management of social
psychological theory, with many references to the literature.
The book is arranged in five parts: social behavior, harmony
among groups, group dynamics, leadership, and the science of
organizational behavior.

386 Lawrence, Paul R., and Lorsch, Jay W. "Differentiation and Integration
in Complex Organizations." ADMINISTRATIVE SCIENCE QUARTERLY 12
(June 1967): 1-47. Tables.

This is a comparative study of six organizations operating in
the same industrial environment.

387 _____. "New Management Job: The Integrator." HARVARD BUSINESS

REVIEW 45 (November–December 1967): 142-51. Diagrams.

This article reviews a comparative study of ten organizations, which suggests how integration may be achieved in complex R & D-intensive organizations.

388 _____. ORGANIZATION AND ENVIRONMENT: MANAGING DIF-FERENTIATION AND INTEGRATION. Boston: Harvard University Graduate School of Business Administration, Division of Research, 1967. xv, 279 p. Diagrams, tables. Paperback ed. Homewood, Ill.: Irwin, 1969.

Organizational characteristics which allow firms to deal effectively with different kinds and rates of environment change, especially technological and market changes, are explored. The book includes chapters on traditional organization theories, environmental demands and organizational states, and the resolution of interdepartmental conflict. Indexes of names and subjects.

389 Leavitt, Harold J.; Dill, William R.; and Eyring, Henry B. THE ORGANIZATIONAL WORLD. New York: Harcourt Brace Jovanovich, 1973. xvi, 335 p. Diagrams. Paperback.

This study of relationships within organizations and the organization's relationships with the outside world includes many references to the literature. Indexes of names and subjects.

390 Levinson, Harry; with Molinari, Janice; and Spohn, Andrew G. ORGANIZATIONAL DIAGNOSIS. Cambridge, Mass.: Harvard University Press, 1972. xviii, 557 p. Bibliography.

Levinson and associates present a psychoanalytic approach to the diagnosis of organizational effectiveness, with a detailed case history on pp. 369-492 and several other references to cases. No index.

391 Likert, Rensis. THE HUMAN ORGANIZATION: ITS MANAGEMENT AND VALUE. New York: McGraw-Hill, 1967. 258 p. Diagrams, tables, bibliography.

This guide to the application of the results of quantitative research to the management of human resources gives profiles of organizational characteristics pp. 196-211. Table of organizational variables, pp. 231-35. Indexes of names and subjects.

392 _____. NEW PATTERNS OF MANAGEMENT. New York: McGraw-Hill, 1961. 279 p. Diagrams, tables, bibliography.

Although no longer new, this remains a stimulating guide to the problem of human relations in industrial and other organizations. Indexes of names and subjects.

393 Litterer, Joseph A. THE ANALYSIS OF ORGANIZATIONS. 2d ed.
Wiley Series in Management and Administration. New York: Wiley,
1973. 757 p. Diagrams, tables, bibliographies.

A major work on organizational functions, structures and behavior, this book is aimed at students and managers.

394 _____, comp. ORGANIZATIONS: STRUCTURE AND BEHAVIOR. 2d
ed. 2 vols. Wiley Series in Management and Administration. New
York: Wiley, 1969. Diagrams, tables.

According to its preface this book's aim is "to bring together
the most important writings on organizations" with particular
reference to "the organizational processes about which the
manager, actual or potential, will have to make decisions
in developing or operating an organization." Volume 1:
STRUCTURE AND BEHAVIOR, contains forty-nine contributions;
volume 2: SYSTEMS, CONTROL AND ADAPTATION, contains thirty-one contributions. Separate author and subject
indexes are contained in each volume.

395 Lupton, Tom. MANAGEMENT AND THE SOCIAL SCIENCES: AN ES-
SAY. An Administrative Staff College Publication. 2d ed. London:
Lyon, Grant & Green, 1970. xii, 123 p. Tables.

The deputy director of Manchester Business School (England)
writes on the relevance to managers of social science research
with particular reference to developments in the theory of organizations. He includes useful comments on the scientific
value of case studies, the Glacier management system, the
Hawthorne experiments, job enrichment, management by objectives, the managerial grid, Theory X and Theory Y, participative management, and the writings of such people as
Argyris, Cyert, Likert, March, McGregor, and Woodward.
Name and subject indexes.

396 Luthans, Fred, ed. CONTEMPORARY READINGS IN ORGANIZATIONAL
BEHAVIOR. McGraw-Hill Series in Management. New York: McGraw-
Hill, 1972. xvii, 460 p. Diagrams, tables, bibliographies. Paperback.

Thirty-six readings are arranged in five sections: foundations
for organizational behavior, modern organizational environment,
basic understanding of behavior, dynamics of organizational behavior, and applications and future dimensions.

397 Maier, Norman R.F., and Hayes, John J. CREATIVE MANAGEMENT.
New York: Wiley, 1962. 226 p. Diagrams, tables.

A study of conflicts between individuals and the organizations
in which they are employed, and approaches to their solution,
by a noted psychologist and behavioral scientist (Maier) and
the superintendent of management training at United Airlines
Inc., Chicago (Hayes).

398   March, James G., ed. HANDBOOK OF ORGANIZATIONS. Rand-
      McNally Sociology Series. Chicago: Rand-McNally, 1965. xvi,
      1,247 p. Diagrams, tables.

      This book contains twenty-eight contributions on foundations,
      methodology, theoretical-substantive areas (including communi-
      cations, interpersonal relations, organizational decision making,
      and studies of organization in unions, political parties, public
      bureaucracies, military service, English county government
      1558-1640, schools, hospitals, prisons, and business communi-
      ties), and applications (including organization design and or-
      ganizational change). Indexes of authors and subjects.

399   March, James G.; and Simon, Herbert A.; with Guetzkow, Harold. OR-
      GANIZATIONS. New York: Wiley, 1958. 262 p. Diagrams, bib-
      liography.

      This important work is based on research at the Graduate
      School of Industrial Administration, Carnegie Institute of Tech-
      nology, on organizational behavior, classical organization
      theory, motivational constraints, conflict in organizations,
      and planning and innovation in organizations. Bibliography,
      pp. 213-48.

400   Maslow, Abraham H. EUPSYCHIAN MANAGEMENT: A JOURNAL. Ir-
      win-Dorsey Series in Behavioral Science. Homewood, Ill.: Irwin and
      Dorsey Press, 1965. xvi, 277 p. Bibliography. Paperback.

      These journal notes were made by the author in 1962 during
      a period spent at the plant of Non-Linear Systems Inc., Del
      Mar, California, at the invitation of the company's president.
      "Eupsychian" is defined as "the culture that would be gener-
      ated by 1,000 self-actualizing people on some sheltered is-
      land where they would not be interfered with" or as "moving
      toward psychological health," and the author describes the
      interrelations between psychological theory and an enlightened
      modern management. It contains a chronological bibliography
      of Maslow's writings (104 items) pp. 267-77. No index.

401   Mayo, Elton. THE HUMAN PROBLEMS OF AN INDUSTRIAL CIVILIZA-
      TION. 2d ed. Boston: Harvard University Graduate School of Business
      Administration, Division of Research, 1946. 187 p. Diagrams.

      An important study of fatigue, monotony, morale and other
      human problems of industry, with special reference to the
      Hawthorne Investigations at the Western Electric Company.
      Indexes of authors and topics.

402   _____. THE SOCIAL PROBLEMS OF AN INDUSTRIAL CIVILIZATION;
      WITH AN APPENDIX ON THE POLITICAL PROBLEM. Boston: Harvard
      University Graduate School of Business Administration, Division of Re-

search, 1945; London: Routledge & Kegan Paul, 1949. xvi, 148 p. Diagrams.

A significant study of the importance of adequate group relations in industrial society, this work includes pertinent comments on the Hawthorne Investigations, absenteeism, and labor turnover.

403 Miller, E.J., and Rice, A.K. SYSTEMS OF ORGANIZATION: THE CONTROL OF TASK AND SENTIENT BOUNDARIES. London: Tavistock, 1967. xviii, 286 p. Diagrams, bibliography. Paperback.

This well-researched study argues that activity systems geared to task performance (task systems) and relationship systems making for the satisfaction of human needs (sentient systems) rarely have common boundaries. They suggest that a tripartite system of organization is needed for controlling task performance, ensuring commitment of members to enterprise objectives, and regulating relations between task and sentient systems. The arguments are supported by case studies, notably from airline management, research organizations, and the building of a new steel works.

404 Miner, John B. THE MANAGEMENT PROCESS: THEORY, RESEARCH AND PRACTICE. New York: Macmillan; London: Collier-Macmillan, 1973. 559 p. Diagrams, tables, bibliographies.

Miner considers the various schools of management thought (e.g., the classical management approach and the behavioral science approach), with particular emphasis on the findings of scientific research and on problems related to human resources. The discussion is presented in five parts: management theory; planning; directing; coordinating and controlling; and secondary management functions (e.g., management recruitment, selection, appraisal and compensation, public relations). Indexes of authors and subjects.

405 Mott, Paul E. THE CHARACTERISTICS OF EFFECTIVE ORGANIZATIONS. New York: Harper & Row, 1972. 227 p. Tables. Paperback.

This summary of fourteen years' research seeks to develop measures of organizational effectiveness and determine some of the characteristics of organizations which influence this effectiveness.

406 Mouzelis, Nicos P. ORGANIZATION AND BUREAUCRACY: AN ANALYSIS OF MODERN THEORIES. International Library of Sociology and Social Reconstruction. London: Routledge & Kegan Paul; Chicago: Aldine Publishing Co., 1967. 230 p.

Part one discusses classical studies of bureaucracy, including the writings of Marx, Max Weber, and Robert Michels. Part two deals with the managerial tradition including Taylorism, the Hawthorne experiments, and more recent approaches to organizational theory and decision making. Part three analyzes recent theoretical trends pointing to a convergence of the bureaucracy and managerial lines of thought.

407 Paterson, Thomas Thomson. MANAGEMENT THEORY. London: Business Publications, 1966. xiv, 212 p. Diagrams, bibliography.

Paterson counters arguments that business management can be learned only through experience and shows that management can be based on scientific and philosophical principles. It consists of four sections on the theory of organization, the theory of administration, general systems theory, and personal and social authority. A survey of the author's writings on the theories of organization and administration is found on p. 206.

408 Perrow, Charles. ORGANIZATIONAL ANALYSIS: A SOCIOLOGICAL VIEW. Belmont, Calif.: Wadsworth; London: Tavistock, 1970. xii, 192 p. Diagrams, tables, bibliography.

A sociological approach to organizational structure, this work emphasizes the diverse requirements of different organizations, the need for clear goals, and environmental influences.

409 Porter, Donald E.; Applewhite, Philip B.; and Misshauk, Michael J., eds. STUDIES IN ORGANIZATIONAL BEHAVIOR AND MANAGEMENT. 2d ed. Scranton, Pa.: Intext Educational Publishers, 1971. xii, 859 p. Diagrams, tables. Paperback.

This volume contains fifty-seven readings on work behavior and attitudes, supervisory behavior, work group behavior, leadership and motivation, communication and decision making, effect of organizational structure on behavior, effect of change on behavior, and effect of new technology on behavior. No index.

410 Pugh, D.S., ed. ORGANIZATION THEORY: SELECTED READINGS. Penguin Modern Management Readings. Harmondsworth, Eng. and Baltimore: Penguin, 1971. 382 p. Bibliography. Paperback.

Five readings deal with the structure of organizations, six on the management of organizations, and seven on behavior in organizations. Indexes of authors and subjects.

411 Pugh, D.S.; Hickson, D.J.; and Hinings, C.R. WRITERS ON ORGANIZATIONS: AN INTRODUCTION. 2d ed. Penguin Modern Management Texts. Harmondsworth, Eng. and Baltimore: Penguin, 1971. 183 p. Paperback.

This is a study of the work of thirty-two writers, arranged under five headings: the structure of organizations; the functioning of organizations; the management of organizations; people in organizations; the organization in society. The first edition was published in London by Hutchinson, 1964.

412   Pugh, D.S.; Hickson, D.J.; Hinings, C.R.; and Turner, C. "The Context of Organization Structures." ADMINISTRATIVE SCIENCE QUARTERLY 14 (March 1969): 91-114. Tables, bibliography.

This article examines seven aspects of organizational context held to be relevant to organizational structure: origin and history, ownership and control, size, charter, technology, location, and dependence on other organizations.

413   Reeves, Elton T. THE DYNAMICS OF GROUP BEHAVIOR. New York: American Management Association, 1970. 399 p.

Reeves covers such topics as motivation, properties of group leadership and followership, and the social deviant. Glossary, pp. 380-85.

414   Roethlisberger, F.J. MAN-IN-ORGANIZATION: ESSAYS OF F.J. ROETHLISBERGER. Cambridge, Mass.: Harvard University Press, 1968. 322 p.

Twenty-six essays written by a distinguished professor between 1928 and 1968 consider the human aspects of management.

415   Roethlisberger, F.J.; and Dickson, William J.; with Wright, Harold A. MANAGEMENT AND THE WORKER: AN ACCOUNT OF THE RESEARCH PROGRAM CONDUCTED BY THE WESTERN ELECTRIC COMPANY, HAWTHORNE WORKS, CHICAGO. New York: Wiley, 1964. xxiv, 615 p. Diagrams, tables.

The authors give a detailed account of the Hawthorne Investigations into the human effects of work and working conditions, described in PERSONNEL JOURNAL as "the most outstanding study of industrial relations that has been published anywhere, any time." The twenty-six chapters are grouped in five parts: working conditions and employee efficiency; improvement of employee relations; the understanding of employee dissatisfaction; social organization of employees; and application of research results. The original edition was published by Harvard University Press in 1939.

416   Rush, Harold M.F. BEHAVIORAL SCIENCE: CONCEPTS AND MANAGEMENT APPLICATIONS. Studies in Personnel Policy, no. 216. New York: National Industrial Conference Board, 1969. 178 p. Illustrations, tables, bibliography. Paperback.

Rush examines theories of behavioral scientists and their relevance to management, with particular reference to the work of McGregor, Maslow, Herzberg, Argyris, and Likert. He includes case studies of the behavioral science approach in American Airlines, Armstrong Cork Company, Corning Glass Works, Genesco Incorporated, Hotel Corporation of America, Raymond Corporation, Steinbergs Ltd., Syntex Corporation, Texas Instruments Inc., and the Systems Group of TRW Inc.

417 Sayles, Leonard R. BEHAVIOR OF INDUSTRIAL WORK GROUPS: PREDICTION AND CONTROL. New York: Wiley; London: Chapman & Hall, 1958. 182 p.

After completing a two-year study of 300 work groups in thirty firms, the author suggests a method of predicting behavior of work groups based on their structural characteristics. He identifies four work group types, which he calls the "apathetic," "erratic," "strategic," and "conservative" groups.

418 _____. INDIVIDUALISM AND BIG BUSINESS. New York: McGraw-Hill, 1963. xiv, 200 p.

Drawing on his own research and on the views of twelve other distinguished writers on organizational problems, Sayles analyzes life in large industrial organizations and its implications for individual personnel, with case studies. He concludes that the "organization man" syndrome is in fact an exciting challenge and that the maintenance of effective human relations in large-scale organizations is one of the marvels of our age.

419 Schroeter, Louis C. ORGANIZATIONAL ELAN. New York: American Management Association, 1970. 181 p.

Elan is defined by the author as "the zest that humanizes organizational life." Four essays show managers how to develop an organizational spirit which will help their company meet present and future challenges. The essays cover entente (mutual understanding of that which is vital to the individual and the organization); leadership (the human qualities of honor, integrity, and personal commitment that inspire each individual to realize his full potential within the organization); adaptation (the continuing survival of the vital spirit of achievement); and nexus (the motivation and linking together of individuals in the achievement of organizational goals).

420 Scott, W.E., Jr., and Cummings, L.L., eds. READINGS IN ORGANIZATIONAL BEHAVIOR AND HUMAN PERFORMANCE. Rev. ed. Homewood, Ill.: Irwin; London: Irwin-Dorsey International, 1973. xii, 611 p. Diagrams, tables, bibliographies. Paperback.

This volume contains fifty-six readings in five sections: theoretical and empirical foundations of organizational behavior and human performance; dependent variables in organizational behavior and human performance; structural and environmental determinants of behavior in organizations; interpersonal processes as determinants of behavior in organizations; and behavioral direction and change strategies. No index.

421 Shepard, Jon M., ed. ORGANIZATIONAL ISSUES IN INDUSTRIAL SOCIETY. Prentice-Hall Sociology Series. Englewood Cliffs, N.J.: Prentice-Hall, 1972. xiii, 449 p. Diagrams, tables. Hardcover and paperback.

This work includes thirty-three readings grouped in eight sections: the impact of industrialization: are industrial societies becoming alike?; occupational mobility: a cross-national similarity in pattern?; bureaucracy: is there an alternative?; informal organization in industry: functional or dysfunctional?; union organization: can labor unions be democractic?; human relations in industry: will participative management really work?; work incentives: what role does money play in motivation and productivity?; and job enlargement: do workers really want larger jobs? No index.

422 Sofer, Cyril. ORGANIZATIONS IN THEORY AND PRACTICE. London: Heinemann; New York: Basic Books, 1972. xxviii, 419 p. Bibliographies.

This well-documented study of organizational theory and practice was developed from a series of lectures given at Cambridge which drew on nine years of research into organizations at the Tavistock Institute and fifteen years of academic study.

423 Stewart, Rosemary. THE REALITY OF MANAGEMENT. Heinemann Studies in Management. London: Heinemann, 1963. 196 p. Bibliography.

Stewart reviews what has been written about management theory against what has been learned about management in practice during twelve years' research involving interviews with 1,500 managers about their work and problems. Part one describes the organization within which the manager has to work, part two outlines the nature of the manager's job, and part three analyzes the diversity of the manager's task and management styles in different countries and environments.

424 _____. THE REALITY OF ORGANIZATIONS: A GUIDE FOR MANAGERS. London: Macmillan, 1970; Garden City, N.Y.: Doubleday, 1972. 157 p. Diagrams, tables, bibliography.

A companion volume to THE REALITY OF MANAGEMENT, this work describes the ways in which different writers have looked at organizations; examines organizational tasks including coordination and grouping of activities; and considers or-

ganizational problems of relationships, balance, and change
and their solution.

425 Taylor, Jack W. "What the Behaviorists Haven't Told Us." PERSONNEL
JOURNAL 52 (1973): 874–78.

Taylor offers a criticism of such behavioral "packages" as the
managerial grid and Theories X and Y.

426 Thompson, James D. ORGANIZATIONS IN ACTION: SOCIAL SCIENCE
BASES OF ADMINISTRATIVE THEORY. New York: McGraw-Hill, 1967.
192 p. Bibliography.

Part one deals with the behavior of organizations rather than
behavior within organizations. Part two considers the behavior
of people in and around organizations and their effect on organizational behavior. Indexes of names and subjects.

427 Thompson, Victor A. MODERN ORGANIZATION: A GENERAL THEORY.
New York: Knopf, 1961. 197 p.

The author regards modern organization as a system of human
behavior comprising several subsystems: the authority subsystem,
the status subsystem, and the technical subsystem. He argues
that the impact of these three upon face-to-face communication creates a fourth subsystem or "informal organization," and
he analyzes each subsystem.

428 Turner, Arthur N., and Lombard, George F.F. INTERPERSONAL BEHA-
VIOR AND ADMINISTRATION. New York: Free Press; London: Collier-Macmillan, 1969. xx, 683 p. Bibliography.

The authors examine why one person fails or succeeds in understanding another person when there is shared responsibility between them for accomplishing a task within an organization.
The book is arranged in five parts: communication in an organizational relationship; sources of misunderstanding; the understanding of another person's behavior; helping of another person in understanding his behavior; and organizational relations
and interpersonal skill. The book includes case studies and
readings, but has no subject index.

429 Ullrich, Robert A. A THEORETICAL MODEL OF HUMAN BEHAVIOR
IN ORGANIZATIONS: AN ECLECTIC APPROACH. Morristown, N.J.:
General Learning Corporation, 1972. xiii, 249 p. Diagrams, tables,
bibliography.

Ullrich assesses major theories on the way people behave in
organizations and includes a sample questionnaire on the individual's attitude to his organization.

430   Wadia, Maneck S. MANAGEMENT AND THE BEHAVIORAL SCIENCES:
       TEXT AND READINGS. Boston: Allyn & Bacon, 1968. xii, 543 p.
       Diagrams, tables, bibliographies.

       The first three parts define management and the behavioral
       sciences and suggest a scheme for their integration. Parts four
       to ten present forty-one readings on the applications of the
       behavioral sciences to management. The work has an index
       of authors but no subject index.

431   Wegner, Robert E.C., and Sayles, Leonard R. CASES IN ORGANIZA-
       TIONAL AND ADMINISTRATIVE BEHAVIOR. Englewood Cliffs, N.J.:
       Prentice-Hall, 1972. xviii, 204 p. Diagrams, forms. Paperback.

       Contained are thirty-two cases designed for use with standard
       texts on organizational and administrative behavior, each fol-
       lowed by discussion questions. No index.

432   Whyte, William Foote. ORGANIZATIONAL BEHAVIOR: THEORY AND
       APPLICATION. Irwin-Dorsey Series in Behavioral Science. Homewood,
       Ill.: Irwin and Dorsey Press, 1969. 807 p. Bibliographies.

       Originally intended as a revision of the author's MEN AT
       WORK, this eventually became a new book. It includes ma-
       jor sections on intergroup relations, vertical relations, lateral
       and diagonal relations, union-management relations, and in-
       troduction of change, with a chapter comparing organizational
       behavior in the United States, Japan, and Peru. There are
       annotated chapter references and indexes of cases and subjects.

433   Williamson, Oliver E. CORPORATE CONTROL AND BUSINESS BEHAV-
       IOR: AN INQUIRY INTO THE EFFECTS OF ORGANIZATION FORM
       ON ENTERPRISE BEHAVIOR. Englewood Cliffs, N.J.: Prentice-Hall,
       1970. xii, 196 p. Diagrams, bibliography.

       Williamson argues, with supporting examples, that successful
       management control owes much to organizational innovation
       and organization structure.

434   Woodward, Joan, ed. INDUSTRIAL ORGANIZATION: BEHAVIOR AND
       CONTROL. London: Oxford University Press, 1970. xiii, 262 p. Pa-
       perback.

       Eleven papers by members of a research team at Imperial Col-
       lege, London, investigate the relationship between technology
       and organizational behavior. The first three deal with the
       general problem of technology and organizational behavior,
       the measurement of technical variables, and the study of man-
       agerial control. The others are case studies of various as-
       pects of management control. Name and subject indexes.

435 _____. INDUSTRIAL ORGANIZATION: THEORY AND PRACTICE. London: Oxford University Press, 1965. xii, 281 p. Diagrams, tables. Paperback.

> The results of ten years' empirical study of management organization in British industry, beginning with a survey of management organization in 100 firms in South Essex, are given. These are followed by more detailed investigations into organization structure. The book is particularly concerned with the effects of technological change on organization.

436 _____. MANAGEMENT AND TECHNOLOGY. Problems of Progress in Industry, no. 5. London: H.M. Stationery Office, 1958. 40 p. Diagrams, maps, tables. Paperback.

> This is a concise version of the research into the organization of 100 firms in South-East Essex, England, which is reported more fully in the author's INDUSTRIAL ORGANIZATION: THEORY AND PRACTICE (item 435).

437 Zwerman, William L. NEW PERSPECTIVES ON ORGANIZATION THEORY: AN EMPIRICAL RECONSIDERATION OF MARXIAN AND CLASSICAL ANALYSES. Contributions in Sociology. Westport, Conn.: Greenwood Press, 1970. xx, 219 p. Tables, bibliography.

> Zwerman extends Joan Woodward's theories (see items 434-36) to American industry, using data obtained from fifty-five firms in the St. Paul-Minneapolis area.

Audiovisual Materials

438 EFFECTIVE ORGANIZATION. Rockville, Md.: BNA Communications; New York: Time-Life Video; Brentford, Eng.: Rank Audio Visual, 1971.

> Six thirty-minute 16-mm color films or videotapes (Time-Life Video) were coordinated by Saul W. Gellerman: ASSESSING MANAGEMENT POTENTIAL, in which Douglas W. Bray advocates a management progression program entailing early identification of managerial potential, career planning, and estimating the number of future managers needed at each level; MANAGEMENT BY PARTICIPATION, in which Alfred J. Marrow explains the application of the behavioral sciences to management problems at the Marion, Virginia, plant of the Harwood Companies; PAY FOR PERFORMANCE, in which Emanuel Kay examines the behavioral effects of pay and goal setting; MAKING HUMAN RESOURCES PRODUCTIVE, a discussion of job enrichment by M. Scott Myers; TEAM BUILDING, in which Sheldon Davis explains the concept of managerial work groups working as a team; and CONFRONTING CONFLICT, a continuation of TEAM BUILDING, which shows a team-building session.

Periodicals

The following journals contain regular contributions on organizational behavior:

439   AMERICAN BEHAVIORAL SCIENTIST. Beverly Hills, Calif.: Sage Publications, 1957- . Bimonthly.

440   HUMAN RELATIONS. London: Plenum Press, 1947- . Quarterly.

This journal contains scholarly articles on all aspects of human
relations, including human relations in industry.

441   JOURNAL OF APPLIED BEHAVIORAL SCIENCE. Washington, D.C.: NTL
Institute for Applied Behavioral Science, 1965- . Bimonthly.

This includes lengthy articles, sometimes dealing with organizational problems at work, and briefer notes.

442   ORGANIZATIONAL BEHAVIOR AND HUMAN PERFORMANCE: A JOUR-
NAL OF FUNDAMENTAL RESEARCH AND THEORY IN APPLIED PSY-
CHOLOGY. New York: Academic Press, 1966- . Bimonthly.

Contained are papers describing "original empirical research
and theoretical developments in all areas of human performance
theory and organizational psychology."

443   ORGANIZATIONAL DYNAMICS. New York: AMACOM, 1973- .
Quarterly.

This reviews the application of organizational behavior studies
to management problems.

ORGANIZATIONAL CHANGE AND DEVELOPMENT

An organization cannot remain static if it is to cater adequately to the needs
of its members and is to remain a dynamic force. Behavioral scientists have
contributed much to the theories underlying organizational change and development, even though their contributions have occasionally been criticized. See
also items 486, 521-22, 693, 695, 1428, 1430, 1511, 1537.

444   Argyris, Chris. INTERVENTION THEORY AND METHOD: A BEHAVIOR-
AL SCIENCE VIEW. Reading, Mass.: Addison-Wesley, 1970. 374 p.
Diagrams, tables.

Argyris evaluates the role of the consultant in helping managers introduce successful organizational change. Part one
(pp. 12-216) deals with theory and method; part two (pp. 218-369)
provides case illustrations. Indexes of authors and subjects.

445 Beckhard, Richard. ORGANIZATION DEVELOPMENT: STRATEGIES AND MODELS. Organization Development Series. Reading, Mass.: Addison-Wesley, 1969. 119 p. Tables. Paperback.

Beckhard attempts a systematic description of the state of the art. Part one deals with the what, why, and how of Organizational Development, part two with OD strategies at work (five case studies, each with a summary of conditions for failure and success), and part three with managing change. No index.

446 Bennis, Warren G. CHANGING ORGANIZATIONS: ESSAYS ON THE DEVELOPMENT AND EVOLUTION OF HUMAN ORGANIZATION. McGraw-Hill Series in Management. New York: McGraw-Hill, 1966. 223 p. Diagrams, tables, bibliographies.

Part one traces the evolution of organizational development, resulting in democratic society, scientific management, and changing patterns of leadership; part two deals with planned and controlled organizational change and, in particular, with the role of behavioral scientists in influencing such change. An epilogue, which concerns the work of behavioral scientists in organizational studies, was originally presented at the seminar on behavioral sciences in Management Education, Indian Institute of Management, Calcutta, 1965.

447 _____. ORGANIZATION DEVELOPMENT: ITS NATURE, ORIGINS AND PROSPECTS. Organization Development Series. Reading, Mass.: Addison-Wesley, 1969. 87 p. Diagrams, tables, bibliography. Paperback.

This is an introductory primer, with a chapter on the problem of sensitivity training analyzing three cases of failure. No index.

448 Bennis, Warren G.; Benne, Kenneth D.; and Chin, Robert, eds. THE PLANNING OF CHANGE. 2d ed. New York: Holt, Rinehart & Winston, 1969. 627 p. Diagrams, tables. Paperback.

This volume has forty-three papers on the evolution, dynamics, and application of planned change in organizations, with particular reference to social psychological aspects.

449 Burke, W. Warner. "Organization Development: Current Prospects." INDUSTRIAL TRAINING INTERNATIONAL 7 (February 1972): 49-52. Bibliography.

The director of the Center for Organization Studies, Washington, D.C., defines OD as a planned process of organizational change. He considers its problems, its future, as well as its relationship with such techniques as management by objectives, job evaluation, and management development.

450   Clark, Peter A. ORGANIZATIONAL DESIGN: THEORY AND PRAC-
      TICE. Organizations, People, Society Series. London: Tavistock, 1972.
      xiv, 290 p. Bibliography.

      Part one describes the principles and application of organiza-
      tional development; parts two to five consider the implications
      of case studies of the use of organizational design in two com-
      panies. Particular attention is paid to the "Alternatives and
      Differences Approach" (ADA)--the development of alternative
      designs and the identification of major organizational differ-
      ences and the social and political issues which they imply.
      Name and subject indexes.

451   Dalton, Gene W.; and Lawrence, Paul R.; with Greiner, Larry E., eds.
      ORGANIZATIONAL CHANGE AND DEVELOPMENT. Irwin-Dorsey Series
      in Behavioral Science. Homewood, Ill.: Irwin and Dorsey Press, 1970.
      393 p. Diagrams, tables, bibliography. Paperback.

      This book contains sixteen case studies and eleven readings.
      There is an index to cases by company but no subject index.

452   Davey, Neil G. THE EXTERNAL CONSULTANT'S ROLE IN ORGANI-
      ZATIONAL CHANGE. MSU Business Studies. East Lansing: Michigan
      State University Graduate School of Business Administration, 1971. xiv,
      202 p. Forms, tables, bibliography. Paperback.

      This research on organization-consultant relationships used a
      sample of 1,700 organizations, including manufacturing, mer-
      chandising, financial, transportation and public utility institu-
      tions, and 120 federal government departments and agencies.
      No index.

453   Fordyce, Jack K., and Weil, Raymond. MANAGING WITH PEOPLE:
      A HANDBOOK OF ORGANIZATION DEVELOPMENT METHODS. Read-
      ing, Mass.: Addison-Wesley, 1971. xv, 192 p. Diagrams, tables,
      bibliography. Paperback.

      Included are four case studies.

454   French, Wendell L., and Bell, Cecil H., Jr. ORGANIZATION DE-
      VELOPMENT: BEHAVIORAL SCIENCE INTERVENTIONS FOR ORGANI-
      ZATION IMPROVEMENT. Englewood Cliffs, N.J.: Prentice-Hall, 1973.
      xvi, 207 p. Diagrams, tables. Paperback.

      Part one defines organization development, traces its develop-
      ment, and gives examples of its use; part two provides a de-
      tailed assessment of the theory and practice of OD; part three
      discusses job design, management by objectives, consultant-
      client relationships, and the future of OD.

455   Galbraith, Jay. DESIGNING COMPLEX ORGANIZATIONS. Organiza-

tion Development Series. Reading, Mass.: Addison-Wesley, 1973. xii, 150 p. Diagrams, bibliographies. Paperback.

Galbraith presents a framework for designing and analyzing matrix forms of organization and shows how different forms of organizational structure evolve in response to increasingly difficult problems of information processing. He includes several illustrations of applications of matrix designs and analyses of lateral decision processes. No index.

456　Herman, Stanley M. "What Is This Thing Called Organization Development?" PERSONNEL JOURNAL 50 (1971): 595-603. Diagram.

This article includes a useful checklist of preconditions for embarking on an OD program.

457　Huse, Edgar F., and Beer, Michael. "Eclectic Approach to Organizational Development." HARVARD BUSINESS REVIEW 49 (September-October 1971): 103-12. Diagrams.

In describing a successful application of an OD program in one plant of a multiplant organization the authors emphasize that no single OD technique can be completely effective by itself and that operating managers use multiple techniques and approaches.

458　Kaufman, Herbert. THE LIMITS OF ORGANIZATIONAL CHANGE. University: University of Alabama Press, 1971. 124 p.

Kaufman considers the bases and theoretical implications of organizational change. An introductory section discusses why organizations tend not to change and thus why many die.

459　Kegan, Daniel L. "Organizational Development: Description, Issues and Research Results." ACADEMY OF MANAGEMENT JOURNAL 14 (December 1971): 453-64. Table, bibliography.

Kegan discusses the growth of OD from sensitivity training and presents research emphasizing the importance of making participants in an OD program aware that other members of the organization may be hostile to the program. He urges that the program reflect an awareness of the current organizational climate.

460　Kingdon, Donald Ralph. MATRIX ORGANIZATION: MANAGING INFORMATION TECHNIQUES. Organizations, People, Society Series. London: Tavistock, 1973. xx, 227 p. Diagrams, tables, bibliography.

The problem of organizational development in relation to information technologies is considered. Name and subject indexes.

461 Kuriloff, Arthur H. ORGANIZATIONAL DEVELOPMENT FOR SURVI-
VAL. New York: American Management Association, 1972. 275 p.
Diagrams.

Kuriloff views the organization as an integrated system of different subsystems of people and processes. The book contains
sections on the background and definition of OD, behavioral
science in OD, management by objectives in OD, and the
management of human resources.

462 Lawrence, Paul R., and Lorsch, Jay W. DEVELOPING ORGANIZA-
TIONS: DIAGNOSIS AND ACTIONS. Organization Development Series.
Reading, Mass.: Addison-Wesley, 1969. 101 p. Diagrams. Paperback.

Three critical aspects of organizational problems are examined:
the organization-environment interface, the group-group interface, and the individual-organization interface. The book
derives from seven years research into the work of developing
organizations.

463 Lievegoed, B.C.J. THE DEVELOPING ORGANIZATION. Translated
by J. Collis. Organizations, People, Society Series. London: Tavistock, 1973. 271 p. Diagrams, tables, bibliographies.

Originally published in Dutch as ORGANISATIES IN ONT-
WIKKELING (Rotterdam: Lemniscaat, 1969), this work applies
systems thinking to the need to create flexible organizations
which are responsive both to the demands of a constantly
changing environment and the human needs of the individuals
and groups involved. The book includes a chapter on organizational development by C.J. Zwart and an appendix on the
use of quantitative models by A.F.G. Hanken.

464 Lippit, Gordon. ORGANIZATION RENEWAL. Rockville, Md.: BNA
Communications; Peterborough, Eng.: Guild Sound & Vision, 1969.

Five twenty-five-minute 16-mm color films deal with the growth
stages of organizations, confrontation, individuality and teamwork,
coping with change, and organization renewal.

465 Lorsch, Jay W., and Lawrence, Paul R., eds. STUDIES IN ORGANI-
ZATION DESIGN. Irwin-Dorsey Series in Behavioral Science. Homewood, Ill.: Irwin and Dorsey Press, 1970. 196 p. Diagrams, tables.

There are eleven contributions, many of them based on doctoral
theses at the Harvard Business School. No index.

466 McFeely, Wilbur M. ORGANIZATION CHANGE: PERCEPTIONS AND
REALITIES. Conference Board Report, n.s., no 561. New York: Conference Board, 1972. 56 p. Paperback.

This analysis of the dynamics of organizational change is based

on in-depth interviews with executives at different levels in
fifteen companies.

467 Mangham, I.L.; Shaw, D.; and Wilson, B. MANAGING CHANGE: A
PRACTICAL GUIDE TO ORGANIZATION DEVELOPMENT WITH EXAMPLES
DRAWN FROM I.C.I. (PETROCHEMICALS DIVISION). Management
Guide, no. 3. London: British Institute of Management, 1971. 48 p.
Diagrams, tables, bibliography. Paperback.

The authors present a practical, integrated approach to organization development. The work is based largely on work carried
out within the Petrochemicals Division of Imperial Chemical
Industries Ltd., much of it in association with the Organization Development Unit of Leeds University.

468 Margerison, Charles J. "Organizational Development: A Managerial
Problem Solving Approach." MANAGEMENT DECISION 11 (Autumn
1973): 205-36. Management Decision Monograph. Diagrams, tables,
bibliography.

This is a useful review of the OD process, the manager's role
in it, and organizational change strategy.

469 Margulies, Newton. "The Myth and Magic in OD." BUSINESS HORI-
ZONS 14 (August 1972): 77-82.

Margulies argues that organization development is a magical,
spiritual process, and he suggests certain myths which support
the magical qualities of OD.

470 Margulies, Newton, and Raia, Anthony P. ORGANIZATIONAL DEVEL-
OPMENT: VALUES, PROCESS AND TECHNOLOGY. McGraw-Hill
Series in Management. New York: McGraw-Hill, 1972. 640 p. Dia-
grams, bibliographies.

Arranged in five sections, this work considers organizational
development in perspective, the components of organizational
development, the process and technology of organizational
development, emerging issues in organizational development,
and case studies in organizational development. No index.

471 Mogensen, Allan H. PEOPLE DON'T RESIST CHANGE. Rockville, Md.:
BNA Communications; Peterborough, Eng.: Guild Sound & Vision, 1965.

This twenty-two-minute 16-mm color film considers the introduction of change, in the form of new and improved work methods,
into an organization.

472 Mouton, Jane Srygley, and Blake, Robert R. "Behavioral Science Theories underlying Organization Development." JOURNAL OF CONTEM-
PORARY BUSINESS 1 (Summer 1972): 9-22.

473 Parker, Treadway C. THE ANATOMY OF ORGANIZATION DEVELOP-
MENT: AN EXPLORATORY STUDY OF A PLANNED CHANGE IN OR-
GANIZATIONAL CLIMATE WITHIN A LARGE COMPANY. New York:
American Foundation for Management Research, 1968. xiii, 163 p. Dia-
grams.

Parker describes an exploratory study of a planned OD program
conducted within a large food products company, with comments on its effects on organizational performance and organizational climate.

474 Rice, A.K. THE ENTERPRISE AND ITS ENVIRONMENT: A SYSTEM
THEORY OF MANAGEMENT ORGANIZATION. London: Tavistock,
1963. xiv, 364 p. Diagrams, tables, bibliography. Hardcover and
paperback. (Distributed by Barnes & Noble, Scranton, Pa.)

This study of organizational problems, especially the management of change and resistance to change, is illustrated by a
number of case studies, notably from the Ahmedabad Manufacturing and Calico Printing Company Ltd. (Calico Mills),
manufacturers of finished cloth from raw cotton, Sarabhai
Chemicals, and Sarabhai Industries, concerned with glass making, machinery manufacturing, building and plant installation,
and fine chemicals.

475 Roeber, Richard J.C. THE ORGANIZATION IN A CHANGING EN-
VIRONMENT. Organization Development Series. Reading, Mass.: Addison-Wesley, 1973. xv, 158 p. Paperback.

This practical guide to value changes which influence organizational functioning and managerial thought shows how large
organizations (including governments, oil companies, and General Motors) are adapting to individual demands and how they
must continue to change if they are to survive. No index.

476 Rush, Harold M.F. ORGANIZATION DEVELOPMENT: A RECONNAIS-
SANCE. Conference Board Report, n.s., no. 605. New York: Conference Board, 1973. 74 p. Diagrams, tables. Paperback.

Rush covers the evolution of OD, compares some OD and
non-OD companies, and gives case studies of OD in Donnelly
Mirrors Inc. (Holland, Mich.) Saga Administrative Corporation
(Menlo Park, Calif.) and the Humble Oil and Refining Company (now Exxon Company). Brief glossary of OD terms, pp.
64-68.

477 Schein, Edgar H. PROCESS CONSULTATION: ITS ROLE IN ORGANI-
ZATION DEVELOPMENT. Organization Development Series. Reading,
Mass.: Addison-Wesley, 1969. 147 p. Diagrams, tables, bibliography.
Paperback.

Schein defines organizational process consultation as a system which involves manager and consultant in a period of joint diagnosis. No index.

478 Starbuck, W.H., ed. ORGANIZATIONAL GROWTH AND DEVELOP-MENT. Penguin Modern Management Readings. Harmondsworth, Eng.: Penguin, 1971. 384 p. Diagrams, tables, bibliography. Paperback.

Included are nine contributions with indexes of names and subjects.

479 Thomas, John M., and Bennis, Warren G., eds MANAGEMENT OF CHANGE AND CONFLICT: SELECTED READINGS. Penguin Modern Management Readings. Harmondsworth, Eng.: Penguin, 1972. 507 p. Diagrams, bibliographies. Paperback.

Eighteen readings are presented in six sections: the future context of organizational change and conflict, new perspectives from organization theory and practice, issues and concepts in organizational change and innovation, the practice of planned organizational change, issues and concepts in organizational conflict, and the management of conflict. Indexes of authors and subjects.

480 Walton, Richard E. INTERPERSONAL PEACEMAKING: CONFRONTA-TIONS AND THIRD PARTY CONSULTATION. Organization Development Series. Reading, Mass.: Addison-Wesley, 1969. 151 p. Diagrams. Paperback.

Third-party consultation is considered as an integral part of organizational programs to resolve the industrial conflicts which are now so prevalent. No index.

481 Wilcock, Stephen. "Personnel Strategy and Organization Development: A Case Study." MANAGEMENT DECISION 9 (1971): 39-49. Diagram.

Wilcock describes the use of OD in an electronic company in Britain, the subsidiary of an American parent.

Bibliographies

482 Franklin, Jerome L. "Organization Development: An Annotated Bibliography." Ann Arbor: University of Michigan, Institute for Social Research, Center for Research on Utilization of Scientific Knowledge, 1973. 104 p. Mimeographed.

483 Frohman, Mark A., and Sashkin, Marshall. THE PRACTICE OF ORGA-NIZATION DEVELOPMENT: A SELECTIVE REVIEW. Report no. AD 714 261. Washington, D.C.: U.S. Dept. of Commerce, 1970. 64 p. Paperback.

This is a literature review carried out at the Institute for Social Research of University of Michigan under contract to the
U.S. Office of Naval Research, covering the managerial grid,
survey feedback procedures, sensitivity training, and socio-
technical systems approach.

INDUSTRIAL AND MANAGERIAL PSYCHOLOGY

Organizational change is one area in which the psychologist can make a major
contribution, but there are many others, including recruitment, training, motivation, control, and indeed the whole management process. A number of works
dealing in general terms with industrial and managerial psychology are listed below.

484 Argyle, Michael. THE SOCIAL PSYCHOLOGY OF WORK. London:
     Allen Lane, Penguin Press; New York: Taplinger, 1972. xii, 291 p.
     Diagrams, bibliography.

     This is a comprehensive study of the social problems of work
     including the effects of technology, motivation, working in
     groups, job satisfaction, and comparison of working conditions
     in Israel, Yugoslavia, Japan, and Britain. Indexes of names
     and subjects.

485 Dempsey, Peter J.R. PSYCHOLOGY AND THE MANAGER. Pan Man-
     agement Series. London: Pan, 1973. 293 p. Diagrams, bibliography.
     Paperback.

     Part one deals with the nature of human activities and part
     two with the application of psychology to such management
     problems as planning and organization, selection and place-
     ment, training and development, coordination and control, and
     conciliation and communication.

486 Dubrin, Andrew J. THE PRACTICE OF MANAGERIAL PSYCHOLOGY:
     CONCEPTS AND METHODS FOR THE MANAGER AND ORGANIZATION
     DEVELOPMENT. Pergamon Management and Business Series, vol. 1. New
     York: Pergamon Press, 1972. xv, 326 p. Diagrams, tables, bibliog-
     raphy.

     The author, associate professor of behavioral sciences at Ro-
     chester Institute of Technology's College of Business, defines
     managerial psychology as "the application of psychological
     concepts, techniques, approaches, and methods toward increas-
     ing the effectiveness of managers and organizations." There
     are chapters on the application of psychology to management
     development, personnel systems, managerial obsolescence, or-
     ganizational analysis, motivation, and conflict resolution, and
     the author presents a unique "conflict matrix" to provide a
     simple, tabular technique for identifying conflict patterns in

any organization or group. The final chapter deals with some manager and organization needs of the future, and an appendix is provided on the profession of managerial psychology. Chapter 10 is a case history of organization development at the Syntax Corporation.

487 Fraser, John Munro. PSYCHOLOGY: GENERAL, INDUSTRIAL, SOCIAL. 3d ed. London: Pitman, 1971. 383 p. Diagrams, bibliography. Hardcover and paperback.

This is a standard British work.

488 Gellerman, Saul W. THE USES OF PSYCHOLOGY IN MANAGEMENT. Collier Books. New York: Macmillan; London: Collier-Macmillan, 1970. xvii, 268 p. Paperback.

Originally published by McGraw-Hill in 1960 as PEOPLE, PROBLEMS AND PROFITS, this work discusses recruitment and selection, promotion, communications, human relations, and a philosophy for mature management.

489 Gilmer, B. von Haller; with Crissy, W.J.E.; Glasser, Robert; Gregg, Lee W.; Hilton, Thomas L.; Joseph, Myron L.; Lewis, Richard J.; Miller, Robert B.; and Short, Jerry. INDUSTRIAL AND ORGANIZATIONAL PSYCHOLOGY. 3d ed. McGraw-Hill Series in Psychology. New York: McGraw-Hill, 1971. xiii, 682 p. Diagrams, tables, bibliographies.

Previous editions were entitled INDUSTRIAL PSYCHOLOGY. This work is presented in five parts: psychology in organizations; organizational structures and management; motivation and human needs; personnel psychology; and men and machines. Annotated chapter bibliographies with a complete bibliography, pp. 603-47. Indexes of names and subjects.

490 Haire, Mason. PSYCHOLOGY IN MANAGEMENT. 2d ed. McGraw-Hill Series in Psychology. New York: McGraw-Hill, 1964. xiv, 238 p. Diagrams, tables.

This overview is aimed at the student and the practicing manager. It includes chapters on the nature of people, leadership and supervision, communication, training, productivity and wage payment plans, and organizations.

491 Hayden, Spencer. "Psychology on the Business Scene: A Survey of Company Practices." ORGANIZATIONAL DYNAMICS 1 (Summer 1972): 43-55. Tables.

Summary of the views of 367 U.S. top managers on the applications and value of industrial psychology.

492 Holding, D.H., ed. EXPERIMENTAL PSYCHOLOGY IN INDUSTRY:

SELECTED READINGS. Penguin Education, Penguin Modern Psychology Readings. Harmondsworth, Eng.: Penguin, 1969. 445 p. Illustrations, diagrams, tables, bibliography.

This work contains twenty-three readings, presented in seven sections: human engineering, maintenance, monitoring and inspection, technological skills, training, aging, and noise. Indexes of authors and subjects.

493 Leavitt, Harold J. MANAGERIAL PSYCHOLOGY: AN INTRODUCTION TO INDIVIDUALS, PAIRS, AND GROUPS IN ORGANIZATION. 3d ed. Chicago: University of Chicago Press, 1972. 366 p. Diagrams, bibliography.

Leavitt deals with managerial psychology in four sections: people one at a time, people two at a time, people in threes to twenties, and people in hundreds and thousands.

494 Leavitt, Harold J., and Pondy, Louis R., eds. READINGS IN MANAGERIAL PSYCHOLOGY. Chicago: University of Chicago Press, 1964. xii, 641 p. Diagrams, tables. Hardcover and paperback.

This book contains thirty-eight readings with indexes of names and subjects.

495 Maier, Norman R.F. PSYCHOLOGY IN INDUSTRY: A PSYCHOLOGICAL APPROACH TO INDUSTRIAL PROBLEMS. 3d ed. Boston: Houghton Mifflin; London: Harrap, 1965. xiv, 718 p. Illustrations, diagrams, tables, bibliography.

Maier discusses twenty applications of psychology in industry, each chapter concluding with a case problem and suggested readings. Indexes of names and subjects.

496 Sayles, Leonard R., and Strauss, George. HUMAN BEHAVIOR IN ORGANIZATIONS. Englewood Cliffs, N.J.: Prentice-Hall, 1966. xii, 500 p. Diagrams.

The authors describe and evaluate behavior patterns among all levels of personnel in many types of organizations. Part one deals with individuals, jobs, and groups (including unions and labor relations); part two with leadership and motivation (including delegation); part three with managerial skills; part four with organization; and part five with management's responsibilities. Each chapter concludes with case problems. Indexes of names and subjects.

497 Schein, Edgar H. ORGANIZATIONAL PSYCHOLOGY. 2d ed. Foundations of Modern Psychology. Englewood Cliffs, N.J.: Prentice-Hall, 1970. xiv, 138 p. Diagrams, tables, bibliography. Hardcover and paperback.

This book includes chapters on recruitment, selection, training and allocation (with a case study of training in the International Harvester Company); organizational man and the process of management; groups and intergroup relationships; the organization as a complex system; and organizational effectiveness.

498   Scott, Donald. THE PSYCHOLOGY OF WORK. London: Duckworth, 1970. 256 p. Bibliography.

This discussion of recent British and U.S. research into the nature of and attitudes to work includes chapters on industrial relations; job dissatisfaction; automation; retirement problems; women, marriage, and work; leisure; and the author's own work in a London teaching hospital.

499   Super, Donald E., and Bohn, Martin J., Jr. OCCUPATIONAL PSYCHOLOGY. Behavioral Science in Industry Series. London: Tavistock, 1971. 209 p. Diagrams, tables, bibliography. Paperback ed. Belmont, Calif.: Brooks/Cole Publishing Co., 1971.

This is particularly concerned with the study of career patterns and the applications of occupational psychology in selection and placement and in vocational guidance and counseling.

500   Tannenbaum, Arnold S. SOCIAL PSYCHOLOGY OF THE WORK ORGANIZATION. Belmont, Calif.: Wadsworth; London: Tavistock, 1966. 136 p. Diagrams, tables, bibliography.

This is an introductory text.

501   Tiffin, Joseph, and McCormick, Ernest J. INDUSTRIAL PSYCHOLOGY. 6th ed. Englewood Cliffs, N.J.: Prentice-Hall, 1975. xii, 625 p. Diagrams, tables.

The book is a comprehensive text with sections on personnel selection and evaluation (including personnel tests), the organizational and social context of human work, the job and work situation, human errors and accidents, and psychological aspects of consumer behavior. List of representative personnel tests, pp. 605-8.

502   Warr, Peter B., ed. PSYCHOLOGY AT WORK. Penguin Education Series. Harmondsworth, Eng.: Penguin, 1971. 460 p. Diagrams, bibliography. Paperback.

Contained are seventeen contributions on aspects of industrial psychology including stress, aging, selection methods, decision making since the computer, management effectiveness and training, motivation, employee participation, group relations, and organizations as psychological environments. Bibliographical references, pp. 403–44. Indexes of names and subjects.

Periodicals

The following journals regularly contain articles on industrial psychology:

503   INTERNATIONAL REVIEW OF APPLIED PSYCHOLOGY. Liverpool, Eng.: Liverpool University Press for the International Association of Applied Psychology, 1952– . Twice yearly.

504   JOURNAL OF APPLIED PSYCHOLOGY. Washington, D.C.: American Psychological Association, 1917– . Bimonthly.

505   JOURNAL OF PERSONALITY AND SOCIAL PSYCHOLOGY. Washington, D.C.: American Psychological Association, 1965– . Monthly.

506   OCCUPATIONAL PSYCHOLOGY. London: British Psychological Society for the National Institute of Industrial Psychology, 1922– . Quarterly.

       This contains scholarly articles and signed book reviews and also reproduces contents pages of other psychological and related journals.

507   PERSONNEL PSYCHOLOGY. Durham, N.C.: 1948– . Quarterly.

       This journal includes signed book reviews.

Abstracting and Indexing Service

508   PSYCHOLOGICAL ABSTRACTS. Washington, D.C.: American Psychological Association, 1927– . Monthly, with semiannual author and subject indexes.

       Literature on all aspects of psychology, including industrial psychology, can be traced through these. They cover approximately 500 periodicals and abstract approximately 17,000 items a year.

MANAGEMENT STYLES

The behavioral scientist is concerned with the various styles and attitudes adopted by managers.

509   Bassett, Glenn A. MANAGEMENT STYLES IN TRANSITION. New York:

American Management Association, 1966. 208 p.

This is a guide for the manager who wishes to adapt to changing styles, with sections on leadership, human relations, delegation, appraisal, conflict management, and management selection and development.

510 Dively, George S. THE POWER OF PROFESSIONAL MANAGEMENT. New York: American Management Association, 1971. xv, 176 p. Diagrams, forms, tables.

The author suggests that, in order to cope with the era of social change through which we are passing, managers must develop new foresight, learn how to involve people more deeply in their actions, learn how to manage change rapidly yet well, and must have the will to manage and the ability to lead.

511 Fox, Alan. "Organizational Design and Management Style." PERSONNEL REVIEW 1 (Autumn 1971): 12-20. Bibliography.

This excellent review of the concept of management style considers its interaction with job design, decision-making systems, and other aspects of organization structure.

512 Hersey, Paul, and Blanchard, Kenneth H. "So You Want to Know Your Leadership Style?" TRAINING AND DEVELOPMENT JOURNAL 28 (February 1974): 22-37. Diagrams, tables, bibliography.

The authors analyze twelve organizational situations and suggest alternative approaches for dealing with them.

513 Mitton, Daryl G. "The Dimensions of Leadership Style." MANAGEMENT OF PERSONNEL QUARTERLY 10 (Winter 1971): 9-12. Tables.

Included is a chart to enable managers to make an assessment of their own style, with explanation.

514 _____. "Management in 3-D." INDUSTRIAL SOCIETY 51 (July 1969): 139-41. Diagrams, tables.

515 Reddin, William J. MANAGERIAL EFFECTIVENESS. McGraw-Hill Series in Management. London: McGraw-Hill, 1970. xiv, 352 p. Diagrams, tables, bibliography.

This guide to management principles and styles is based on Reddin's 3-D theory of managerial effectiveness: a conceptual framework which develops three essential management skills--diagnostic skill (the ability to evaluate a situation); style flexibility (the ability to match managerial approach to a situation once it is analyzed); and situational management (the ability to change a situation needing to be changed). There is a 3-D concept dictionary, pp. 331-39.

516 _____. "The 3-D Management Style Theory: A Typology Based on Task and Relationship Orientations." TRAINING AND DEVELOPMENT JOURNAL 21 (April 1967): 8-17. Tables, bibliography.

517 Rhenman, Eric. INDUSTRIAL DEMOCRACY AND INDUSTRIAL MANAGEMENT: A CRITICAL ESSAY ON THE POSSIBLE MEANINGS AND IMPLICATIONS OF INDUSTRIAL DEMOCRACY. Technology and Democratic Society Series. London: Tavistock, 1968. 174 p. Diagrams, tables, bibliography.

Rhenman analyzes the roots of success and failure in industrial enterprises, with particular reference to the influence of leadership style and job satisfaction. He suggests that better planning, clearer company policies, more sophisticated management training, and greater attention to wage and productivity systems will result in increased productivity and efficiency.

518 Sampson, Robert C. MANAGING THE MANAGERS: A REALISTIC APPROACH TO THE BEHAVIORAL SCIENCES. New York: McGraw-Hill, 1965. 272 p. Tables, bibliography.

The author shows how the manager can benefit by using the power of his subordinates rather than imposing his power on them.

519 Stessin, Lawrence, ed. MANAGERIAL STYLES OF FOREIGN BUSINESSMEN. Hofstra University Yearbook of Business, ser. 9, vol. 1. Hempstead, N.Y.: Hofstra University, 1972. 283 p. Bibliographies. Paperback.

This work explores management styles in the USSR, Italy, France, Japan, England, and West Germany. No index.

520 Swope, George S. INTERPRETING EXECUTIVE BEHAVIOR. New York: American Management Association, 1970. 335 p.

Swope challenges executives to examine and improve their management style. The final chapters cover five characteristic executive styles and management during the period 1970-2000.

THE MANAGERIAL GRID

The grid theory, developed by Robert Blake and Jane Srygley Mouton, enables the manager to identify his style by indicating on a nine-point scale the range of possible interactions between the key areas of concern for people and concern for production. See also item 1068.

521 Blake, Robert R., and Mouton, Jane Srygley. BUILDING A DYNAMIC CORPORATION THROUGH GRID ORGANIZATION DEVELOPMENT. Or-

ganization Development Series. Reading, Mass.: Addison-Wesley, 1969. 120 p. Diagrams, bibliography.

The authors explain the grid theory in organization development and planned change.

522 _____. CORPORATE EXCELLENCE THROUGH GRID ORGANIZATION DEVELOPMENT. Houston, Tex.: Gulf Publishing, 1968. xv, 374 p. Diagrams, tables.

This work applies the grid theory to organization development, with cases. The authors identify six phases in the application: phases one to three are concerned with communication (seminars to explain and discuss the approach, teamwork development, and intergroup development); phases four to six are concerned with planning (design of an ideal strategic model, implementation, and systematic critique, including selecting the OD coordinator).

523 _____. THE MANAGERIAL GRID. Rockville, Md.: BNA Communications, 1965.

These are two thirty-minute 16-mm color films on the grid theory. The first deals with "The Managerial Grid in Action" and the second with "The Grid Approach to Problem Solving."

524 _____. THE MANAGERIAL GRID: KEY ORIENTATIONS FOR ACHIEVING PRODUCTION THROUGH PEOPLE. Houston, Tex.: Gulf Publishing, 1964. 340 p. Tables, bibliographies.

A detailed account of the various managerial styles identified by the grid theory, this work also has indexes of authors and subjects.

525 Brianas, James G. "Behavioral Technology: A Challenge to Modern Management." PUBLIC PERSONNEL MANAGEMENT 2 (July-August 1973): 290-98. Diagram, table.

Brianas presents the "managerial matrix," based on the concept of participative management, as an alternative to the managerial grid for use as a diagnostic tool in organizational change.

526 "Using the Managerial Grid to Ensure MbO." ORGANIZATIONAL DYNAMICS 2 (Spring 1974): 54-65. Bibliography.

This article explains the use of the grid theory to ensure full commitment to the goals of management by objectives at the Union Mutual Life Insurance Company, Portland, Maine.

527 Williams, A.P.O. "The Managerial Grid: Phase 2. Case Study of a Top Management Team." OCCUPATIONAL PSYCHOLOGY 45 (1971): 253-72. Diagrams, tables, bibliography.

An in-depth evaluation study by a business school observer in
a manufacturing unit of the British-American Tobacco Company
is described.

LEADERSHIP AND MOTIVATION

An important aspect of the manager's style is the method used to lead and motivate his subordinates.

528 Adair, John. ACTION-CENTRED LEADERSHIP. London: McGraw-Hill,
1973. 186 p. Diagrams, tables, bibliography.

This is an explanation and evaluation of Action-Centred Leadership (ACL), developed at the Royal Military Academy, Sand-
hurst, England, with case studies of its application at Fisons
Ltd., the National Westminster Bank Ltd., the South-East
Metropolitan Hospital Board, and the British armed forces. A
list of British organizations employing the ACL approach to
leadership training is given on pp. 181-82.

529 _____. TRAINING FOR LEADERSHIP. London: Macdonald, 1968. 157 p.
Diagrams, tables, bibliography.

Based particularly on the author's military experience, this
book contains nine chapters on the nature of leadership and
its development in industry, particularly among junior managers. No index.

530 Argyris, Chris. EXECUTIVE LEADERSHIP: AN APPRAISAL OF THE MAN-
AGER IN ACTION. New York: Harper & Row, 1953. xv, 139 p.
Tables. Reprint. Hamden, Conn.: Shoe String Press, Archon Books,
1967.

Argyris describes the actions of a leader in a deteriorating organization and discusses what other managers may learn from
these actions.

531 Basil, Douglas C. LEADERSHIP SKILLS FOR EXECUTIVE ACTION. New
York: American Management Association, 1971. 198 p. Diagrams, bibliography.

This is a guide to successful motivation through leadership
skills, satisfactory organization structure, delegation, management controls, and communication.

532 Bass, Bernard M. LEADERSHIP, PSYCHOLOGY AND ORGANIZATIONAL
BEHAVIOR. New York: Harper Brothers, 1960. xiii, 548 p. Diagrams,
tables, bibliography. Reprint. Westport, Conn.: Greenwood Press,
1973.

Bass organizes research into leadership problems into "a set of generalizations held together by reason as well as experiment." Arranged in seven sections, the book has two introductory chapters on studying behavior in groups and the nature and purpose of group theory, followed by sections on attractiveness and effectiveness; leadership and interaction; ability to lead; coercive and permissive leadership; status and esteem; and situations, individuals, and interaction potential, including leadership during emergencies. Bibliography of 1,155 items, pp. 463-529. Indexes of names and subjects.

533 Cribbin, James J. EFFECTIVE MANAGERIAL LEADERSHIP. New York: American Management Association, 1972. 264 p. Bibliography.

Practical guide with chapters on motivation, communication, coping with tensions, business ethics, etc. Chapter two deals with "57 varieties of leader."

534 Dalton, Gene W., and Lawrence, Paul R. MOTIVATION AND CONTROL IN ORGANIZATIONS. Irwin-Dorsey Series in Behavioral Science. Homewood, Ill.: Irwin and Dorsey Press, 1971. 417 p. Illustrations, diagrams, tables.

An introductory section by the editor is followed by twenty-four case studies and nine readings. No index.

535 Dowling, William F., Jr., and Sayles, Leonard R. HOW MANAGERS MOTIVATE: THE IMPERATIVES OF SUPERVISION. New York: McGraw-Hill, 1971. 436 p. Illustrations, diagrams, forms, bibliographies.

Each of the twelve chapters in this book contains a selection from the ideas of a classical management writer, selected bibliographical references, and questions. The book is geared to a continuing case study which records the development of a typical new supervisor.

536 Gellerman, Saul W. MANAGEMENT BY MOTIVATION. New York: American Management Association, 1968. 286 p. Diagrams.

The sequel to MOTIVATION AND PRODUCTIVITY (item 537), this book examines the role of the behavioral scientist in selecting, assessing managerial performance, individual growth and development, and organization development, with three chapters analyzing the effect of money on motivation.

537 _____. MOTIVATION AND PRODUCTIVITY. New York: American Management Association, 1963. 304 p. Bibliography.

A McKinsey Foundation award-winning book for excellence in management literature, this work traces the development of motivation theories from Mayo through Whyte, Argyris, McGregor, and others, and considers the impact of motivation on leadership, recruitment, morale, change, and the labor unions.

538   Gellerman, Saul W., and Kay, Emanuel. GELLERMAN ON MOTIVA-
TION. New York: AMACOM, 1971.

An eighty-minute cassette, tape, or record has six manuals and
covers such matters as building psychological challenges and
rewards into a job and capitalizing on the motivational potential of selecting, training, and appraising employees.

539   Goble, Frank. EXCELLENCE IN LEADERSHIP. New York: American
Management Association, 1972. xii, 222 p. Diagrams.

This is a guide to proven practices in leadership, emphasizing
the human aspects with two chapters on motivation and one
on leadership by participation. Includes several case studies,
an organization checklist, and the Hewlett-Packard Company's
statement of corporate objectives.

540   Guilford, Joan S., and Gray, David E. MOTIVATION AND MODERN
MANAGEMENT. Addison-Wesley Business Series. Reading, Mass.: Addison-Wesley, 1969. 204 p. Bibliography.

This is a programmed text designed to provide students and managers with guidance on human motivation from a behavioral
point of view. Glossary, pp. 199-204. No index.

541   Herzberg, Frederick. JUMPING FOR THE JELLYBEANS: HERZBERG ON
MOTIVATION. New York: Time-Life Video, 1973.

In this twenty-five-minute 16-mm color film or videotape Herzberg discusses the two distinct needs of people at work: the "hy-
giene" needs, concerned with the working environment, and the
"motivators," concerned with the job itself and including job
enrichment, job design, and adequate communication.

542   _____. WORK AND THE NATURE OF MAN. Cleveland: World Publishing, 1966; London: Staples Press, 1967. xx, 203 p. Diagrams,
tables, bibliography.

This volume develops the author's "motivation-hygiene" theory,
based on experiences and discussions with managers in thirty-four
American and European companies. No index.

543   Herzberg, Frederick; Mausner, Bernard; and Snyderman, Barbara Bloch.
THE MOTIVATION TO WORK. 2d ed. New York: Wiley, 1959. xv,
156 p. Tables, bibliography.

This research study is based on interviews with more than 200
employees.

544 _____. THE MOTIVATION TO WORK. Rockville, Md.: BNA Communications; New York: Time-Life Video; Peterborough, Eng.: Guild Sound & Vision, 1969.

> These are five twenty-five-minute 16-mm color films or videotapes (Time-Life Video): THE MODERN MEANING OF EFFICIENCY; KITA, OR, WHAT HAVE YOU DONE FOR ME LATELY? (an analysis of the "hygiene" part of the motivation-hygiene theory); JOB ENRICHMENT IN ACTION; BUILDING A CLIMATE FOR INDIVIDUAL GROWTH; and THE ABC MAN: THE MANAGER IN MID-CAREER.

545 Hill, Paul. TOWARDS A NEW PHILOSOPHY OF MANAGEMENT: THE COMPANY DEVELOPMENT PROGRAMME OF SHELL UK LTD. Epping, Essex, Eng.: Gower Press, 1971; Scranton, Pa.: Barnes & Noble, 1972. xiv, 255 p. Tables, bibliography.

> This is a description of a long-term staff development program begun at Shell UK in 1965 with assistance from the Tavistock Institute of Human Relations.

546 Killian, Ray A. MANAGERS MUST LEAD! A SUPERVISOR'S ROADMAP TO ADVANCEMENT. New York: American Management Association, 1966. 284 p. Illustrations.

> Killian discusses human attitudes, motivation, and relationships in training, counseling, performance evaluation, and methods improvement.

547 Levinson, Harry. THE EXCEPTIONAL EXECUTIVE: A PSYCHOLOGICAL CONCEPTION. Cambridge, Mass.: Harvard University Press, 1968. 297 p. Bibliographies.

> This is a well-documented study of the behavioral science approach to leadership and motivation.

548 McGregor, Douglas. LEADERSHIP AND MOTIVATION: ESSAYS OF DOUGLAS MCGREGOR. Edited by Warren G. Bennis and Edgar H. Schein with the collaboration of Caroline McGregor. Cambridge, Mass.: M.I.T. Press, 1966. xxiii, 286 p. Bibliography.

> A collection of essays by the noted industrial psychologist, this was published to mark his death in 1964. It is presented in five sections: managerial philosophy; leadership; union-management relations; growth and development of individuals and groups; and the manager and the human sciences. A bibliography of McGregor, prepared by Patricia McPherson, is on pp. 277-80.

549 Maslow, Abraham H. MOTIVATION AND PERSONALITY. 2d ed. New York: Harper & Row, 1970. xxx, 369 p. Bibliography. Paperback.

Though not a management book, this is an important psychological study of the problem of human motivation. Most of the chapters were previously published. Indexes of names and subjects.

550 Morrison, James H. THE HUMAN SIDE OF MANAGEMENT. Reading, Mass.: Addison-Wesley, 1971. 115 p. Illustrations. Paperback.

The author defines a concept of personality to clarify and develop understanding of human behavior as a base for leadership training. Much of the material was originally developed for training programs in the Western Auto Supply Company. No index.

551 MOTIVATION AND PRODUCTIVITY. Rockville, Md.: BNA Communications; New York: Time-Life Video; Peterborough, Eng.: Guild Sound & Vision, 1967-69.

These nine 16-mm color films or videotapes (Time-Life Video) were coordinated by Saul W. Gellerman: STRATEGY FOR PRODUCTIVE BEHAVIOR (1969, 20 minutes), in which Gellerman provides background information to help managers become familiar with the behavioral science approach to motivation; MOTIVATION THROUGH JOB ENRICHMENT (1967, 28 minutes), in which Frederick Herzberg discusses his "motivation-hygiene" theory; THE SELF-MOTIVATED ACHIEVER (1967, 28 minutes), which demonstrates David C. McClelland's theory that, although most people have some degree of achievement motivation, not more than 10 percent of the U.S. population are high in it; UNDERSTANDING MOTIVATION (1967, 28 minutes), in which Gellerman explains the theories of behavioral science; THEORY X AND THEORY Y (1969), two 25-minute films in which Warren Bennis, Richard Beckhard, and John Paul Jones interpret and explain Douglas McGregor's theories (see items 557-62); HUMAN NATURE AND ORGANIZATIONAL REALITIES (1967, 28 minutes), in which Chris Argyris demonstrates the need for a change in top management attitude and behavior if employee motivation and productivity are to be improved; THE MANAGEMENT OF HUMAN ASSETS (1967, 28 minutes), in which Rensis Likert explains how to rate an organization to describe its prevailing management system; and MOTIVATION IN PERSPECTIVE (1967, 20 minutes), in which Gellerman summarizes the ideas expressed in the series.

552 Rosen, Ned A. LEADERSHIP CHANGE AND WORK-GROUP DYNAMICS: AN EXPERIMENT. Ithaca, N.Y.: Cornell University Press, 1969; London: Staples Press, 1970. xviii, 261 p. Diagrams, tables, bibliography.

This account of a research project carried out in a furniture factory for more than a four-year period sought to ascertain whether foremen had a causal impact on the productivity of their work groups under highly structured technical conditions.

553 Sutermeister, Robert A. PEOPLE AND PRODUCTIVITY. 2d ed. McGraw-Hill, 1969. 511 p. Diagrams, tables, bibliography. Hardcover and paperback.

Contents include 65 pages of textual material on the motivation of employees for increased productivity, followed by a bibliography and thirty-five readings.

554 Tannenbaum, Robert, and Schmidt, Warren H. "How to Choose a Leadership Pattern." HARVARD BUSINESS REVIEW 51 (May–June 1973): 162-80. Diagram.

This classic HBR article was originally published in volume 36 (March–April 1958): 95-101. The authors discuss the factors which a manager should consider when choosing his leadership style, and they emphasize the need for his subordinates to be aware of the style chosen. This issue includes a commentary in which the authors view their article from a fifteen-year perspective, pp. 166-68.

555 Tannenbaum, Robert; Weschler, Irving R.; and Massarik, Fred. LEADERSHIP AND ORGANIZATION: A BEHAVIORAL SCIENCE APPROACH. McGraw-Hill Series in Management. New York: McGraw-Hill, 1961. xiv, 456 p. Diagrams, tables, bibliography.

A collection of articles written between 1950 and 1966 by members of the Human Relations Research Group at the University of California, Los Angeles, these papers are grouped under the headings of leadership, training, and organization. Contributions are included by nine other writers, and there are commentaries on the group's ideas by George R. Bach, Robert Dubin, and Lyndall Fownes Urwick. Annotated bibliography, pp. 436-46. Indexes of names and subjects.

Bibliography

556 U.S. Civil Service Commission. Library. "Improving Employee Performance." Personnel Bibliography Series, no. 45. Washington, D.C.: 1972. 95 p. Mimeographed.

This classified, annotated list of books and articles covers individual-organizational relationships, organizational change and development, improvement of morale and job satisfaction, attitude surveys, improvement of motivation and productivity, job enlargement as a motivating device, the fostering of cre-

ativity and innovative behavior, and use of incentive awards.
No index.

THEORY X AND THEORY Y

Douglas McGregor developed his X and Y Theory at Massachusetts Institute of
Technology and presented it to a wider audience in THE HUMAN SIDE OF
ENTERPRISE (item 560). Theory X assumes that individuals need and expect
to be directed if they are to produce satisfactory work; Theory Y suggests that
individuals take pride in their work and welcome responsibility within the work
group. See also item 551.

557   Allen, Louis A. "M for Management: Theory Y Updated." PERSON-
      NEL JOURNAL 52 (1973): 1061-67. Tables.

      Allen suggests that the basic assumptions on which McGregor
      founded his X and Y Theories were no longer valid in 1973.
      He formulates "Theory M" as a realistic theory reflecting man-
      agers' assumptions about people.

558   Argyris, Chris. MANAGEMENT AND ORGANIZATIONAL DEVELOP-
      MENT: THE PATH FROM XA TO YB. New York: McGraw-Hill, 1971.
      xv, 211 p. Diagrams, tables, bibliography.

      Pattern A represents Argyris's findings on the interpersonal be-
      havior, group dynamics, and organizational norms associated
      with McGregor's Theory X, the idea that people cannot be
      trusted and prefer to be controlled by and dependent upon
      management for all their actions. Pattern B represents the
      interpersonal norms, group dynamics, and organizational norms
      associated by Argyris with McGregor's Theory Y, the assump-
      tion that management ideas are more consistent with man's
      potentialities as described by recent research and that man
      can be an active contributor to his and the organization's
      well being. The book provides case histories of three organi-
      zations which decided to begin to travel the road from XA
      to YB.

559   Johnson, Leroy. "Towards a Y System." CALIFORNIA MANAGEMENT
      REVIEW 15 (Fall 1972): 22-29.

      Johnson outlines the results of "X" and "Y" policies in the
      areas of production, workers' attitudes, supervisory behavior,
      and motivation.

560   McGregor, Douglas. THE HUMAN SIDE OF ENTERPRISE. New York:
      McGraw-Hill, 1960. 246 p. Bibliographies.

      This work introduces the concepts of Theory X and Theory Y,
      with sections on management by integration, performance ap-

praisal, salary administration, promotion, the Scanlon plan,
participative management, staff-line relationships, and management development. No index.

561 _____. THE PROFESSIONAL MANAGER. Edited by Caroline McGregor
and Warren G. Bennis. New York: McGraw-Hill, 1967. xvi, 202 p.
Tables.

McGregor's final work, a follow-up to THE HUMAN SIDE OF
ENTERPRISE (item 560), shows how a Theory Y organization
may be developed through managerial intervention and understanding. The book contains eleven chapters, presented in
five sections: the manager and the human sciences, managerial
behavior, improving organizational effectiveness, power and
control, and teamwork and tension.

562 THEORY X AND THEORY Y. Rockville, Md.: BNA Communications;
Peterborough, Eng.: Guild Sound & Vision, 1969.

In these two twenty-five-minute 16-mm color films Warren G.
Bennis, Richard Beckhard, and John Paul Jones explain Douglas
McGregor's findings on the assumptions which management is
prone to make about its employees. The first film describes
the theory, with a comparison of the two sets of assumptions;
the second film shows why a "Theory Y" manager will be more
likely to obtain better results from his employees. The films
are two of a series of nine on motivation and productivity (see
item 551).

THE GLACIER PROJECT

In 1948 the Tavistock Institute of Human Relations and the Glacier Metal Company, an engineering factory in London employing some 1,500 people, began
research studying the psychological and social forces affecting the group life,
morale, and industrial productivity of an industrial community; development of
more effective ways of resolving social stresses; and the facilitating of agreed-
upon social change. See also items 1918-20, 1924.

563 Brown, Wilfred. EXPLORATION IN MANAGEMENT. Glacier Project
Series. London: Heinemann; Carbondale: Southern Illinois University
Press, 1960. xxii, 326 p. Diagrams, tables, bibliography.

This classic account of the Glacier Metal Company's approach
to organization and management was written by the company's
chairman. Glossary of technical terms, pp. 283-92. Company
policy document, pp. 293-319.

564 _____. ORGANIZATION. London: Heinemann, 1971. xv, 400 p.
Illustrations, diagrams, bibliography. (Distributed by International Publications Service, New York.)

The former chairman and chief executive of the Glacier Metal Company held government office in the United Kingdom between 1965 and 1970, and the lack of organizational clarity in government departments urged him to define organization. The book is in four parts: the anatomy of employment systems; power groups, participation, and wage differentials; operational work and techniques; and personnel work and techniques. Glossary of terms used, pp. 380-89.

565 Brown, Wilfred, and Jaques, Elliott. GLACIER PROJECT PAPERS: SOME ESSAYS ON ORGANIZATION AND MANAGEMENT FROM THE GLACIER PROJECT RESEARCH. Glacier Project Series. London: Heinemann; Carbondale: Southern Illinois University Press, 1965. xvii, 277 p. Diagrams, tables, bibliography.

These sixteen essays by the Glacier Metal Company's chairman and consultant social analyst were prepared mainly for teaching at the Glacier Institute of Management. Topics covered include the nature and etymology of work; performance appraisal; organization; management teaching; boards, committees, and executive meetings; negotiation between managers and representatives; legislation; and a national incomes policy.

566 Jaques, Elliott. THE CHANGING CULTURE OF A FACTORY. London: Tavistock; Boston: Routledge & Kegan Paul, 1951. xvii, 341 p. Diagrams, tables, bibliography.

This account of the beginnings of the Glacier Project (April 1948 to November 1950) outlines the history of the Glacier Metal Company from 1898 to 1949.

567 Kelly, Joe. IS SCIENTIFIC MANAGEMENT POSSIBLE? A CRITICAL EXAMINATION OF GLACIER'S THEORY OF ORGANIZATION. Society Today and Tomorrow Series. London: Faber; New York: Humanities Press, 1968. 332 p. Bibliography.

A writer from the School of Business Studies at McGill University, Montreal, Kelly uses the tools of social psychology to examine organization, industrial relations, and executive behavior at the Glacier Metal Company. He concludes that the Glacier system is consistent, but not always valid. It provides a model which allows executives to make dynamic adjustments to organizational events and has considerable utilitarian value.

568 Newman, A.D., and Rowbottom, R.W. ORGANIZATION ANALYSIS: A GUIDE TO THE BETTER UNDERSTANDING OF THE STRUCTURAL PROBLEMS OF ORGANIZATIONS. Glacier Project Series. London: Heinemann; Carbondale: Southern Illinois University Press, 1968. 139 p. Diagrams, bibliography.

This study of the executive system and the organizational environment looks at manager/subordinate relationships, communication and meetings, group relations, and control. It is based on research at the Glacier Metal Company.

PARTICIPATIVE MANAGEMENT

The ultimate in the human relations approach to management is the full participation of employees in the decision-making process, perhaps by representation on the board of directors or perhaps through workers' councils. Peter Drucker has warned that worker participation is going to be "a horrible let-down, a horrible delusion" (MANAGEMENT TODAY [July 1974], p. 82). He suggests that in Germany it has made managers more autocratic, because they no longer have to worry about the reaction of the shop floor. Worker participation, says Drucker, is really union participation and is a conspiracy against the consumer--the idea that the enterprise exists for the sake of the worker. However, the Institute for Labour Studies, which has undertaken a survey of participative management in fifteen countries throughout the world (see item 597), believes that workers' participation in management may be a significant feature of the future of industrial relations in all countries. Both views are represented in the items listed below.

569 Albrook, Robert C. "Participative Management: Time for a Second Look." FORTUNE 75 (May 1967): 166-70, 197, 198, 200. Diagram.

> Albrook explains the advantages and limitations of participative management in areas of change.

570 Appleyard, J.R., and Coates, J.A.G. "Workers' Participation in Western Europe." IPM Information Report, n.s., no. 10. London: Institute of Personnel Management, 1971. 103 p. Tables, bibliography. Mimeographed.

> A brief survey of current practices, this work has a twenty-page bibliography, pp. 83-103.

571 Balfour, Campbell, ed. PARTICIPATION IN INDUSTRY. London: Croom Helm, 1973. Paperback ed. Totowa, N.J.: Rowman & Littlefield, 1973. 217 p. Diagrams, tables, bibliography.

> This volume includes case studies of the National Coal Board, the British Steel Corporation, and the shipbuilding industry, with a section on workers' participation in private enterprise organizations. The editor's introduction defines participation and links the various contributions. A concluding section covers workers' participation in Western Europe.

572 Blumberg, Paul. INDUSTRIAL DEMOCRACY: THE SOCIOLOGY OF PARTICIPATION. Sociology and Social Welfare Series. London: Con-

stable, 1968; New York: Schocken Books, 1969. 278 p. Tables, bibliography.

This well-documented survey traces the development of participative management from the "forgotten lessons" of Elton Mayo and has two chapters on worker participation in Yugoslavia and one on criticisms of workers' management by Hugh Clegg and others.

573   British Institute of Management. INDUSTRIAL DEMOCRACY: SOME IM-PLICATIONS FOR MANAGEMENT. AN EXPLORATORY STUDY. BIM Occasional Paper, n.s., OPN 1. London, 1968. 52 p. Bibliography. Paperback.

Some of the major management issues involved in industrial democracy are examined. Arguments advanced for and against industrial democracy by the three major British political parties are presented, as well as extracts from the literature on the subject. Definitions of industrial democracy are given on page 43.

574   Broekmeyer, M.J., ed. YUGOSLAV WORKERS' SELF-MANAGEMENT: PROCEEDINGS OF A SYMPOSIUM HELD IN AMSTERDAM, 7-9 JANUARY 1970. Dordrecht, Holland; Boston: D. Reidel Publishing Co., 1970. 259 p. Diagrams, tables, bibliographies.

This book contains twelve papers with reports of discussions. No index.

575   Butteriss, Margaret. JOB ENRICHMENT AND EMPLOYEE PARTICIPA-TION: A STUDY. London: Institute of Personnel Management, 1971. 71 p. Diagrams. Paperback. (Distributed by International Publications Service, New York.)

This is a discussion of various methods of job enrichment and em-ployee participation in relation to management theories. It has case studies of Joseph Newsome and Sons, Dunlop Footwear, Vencel Limited, Avon Rubber Company, ENV, Imperial Chemical Industries Ltd., and other companies.

576   Chaney, Frederick B., and Teel, Kenneth S. "Participative Management: A Practical Experience." PERSONNEL 49 (November-December 1972): 8-19.

This case study documents the successful introduction of partic-ipative management at Autometics, a division of North Ameri-can Rockwell.

577   Clarke, R.O.; Fatchett, D.J.; and Roberts, B.C. WORKERS' PARTICI-PATION IN MANAGEMENT IN BRITAIN. London School of Economics Industrial Relations Series. London: Heinemann Educational, 1972. 214 p. Tables, bibliography.

This book traces the development of workers' participation in British management, various forms of participation, and the pattern of workers' influence upon managerial decision making. It emphasizes the importance of participation if industrial efficiency is to increase.

578 Clegg, H.A. A NEW APPROACH TO INDUSTRIAL DEMOCRACY. Oxford: Blackwell, 1960. 140 p.

Clegg reflects on a congress on workers' participation in management organized by the Congress for Cultural Freedom in Vienna in 1958. The book surveys postwar developments in Britain, France, Germany, Yugoslavia, and Israel.

579 Daniel, Bill, and McIntosh, Neil. THE RIGHT TO MANAGE? A STUDY OF LEADERSHIP AND REFORM IN EMPLOYEE RELATIONS. London: Macdonald for Political and Economic Planning, 1972. 217 p. Bibliography. Hardcover and paperback.

Reports of research by the authors are presented in three parts: job enrichment, worker involvement in decision making and representation, and the reform of systems of payment and job evaluation. This is an important work.

580 Emery, F.E.; and Thorsrud, Einar; with Trist, Eric L. FORM AND CONTENT IN INDUSTRIAL DEMOCRACY: SOME EXPERIENCES FROM NORWAY AND OTHER EUROPEAN COUNTRIES. Technology and Democratic Society Series. London: Tavistock, 1969. 116 p. Diagrams, tables, bibliography. (Distributed by Barnes & Noble, New York.)

Originally published in Norwegian by Oslo University Press, 1964, this work provides examples of worker participation in Norway, Yugoslavia, West Germany, and Great Britain.

581 Greiner, Larry E. "What Managers Think of Participative Leadership." HARVARD BUSINESS REVIEW 51 (March-April 1973): 111-17. Tables.

Greiner suggests that there is more agreement about how participative management operates than about how (or whether) it gets results.

582 Industrial Democracy in the Netherlands Seminar, The Hague, Oct. 1969. INDUSTRIAL DEMOCRACY IN THE NETHERLANDS. Meppel: J.A. Boom en Zoon, 1969. 122 p. Diagrams, tables, bibliography. Paperback.

These papers were presented at a seminar organized under the auspices of the European Association of National Productivity Centres by the Commissie Opvoering Produktiveit van de Sociaal-Economische Raad. Contents: "Industrial Democracy at the Level of the Enterprise," by P.H. van Gorkum; "The Works' Councils in the Netherlands," by P.J.D. Dreath; "Integration of White and Blue Collar Workers and Case Study," by Ch. J. de Wolff; "Responsibility on the Job," by J.J. Ramondt; "Job Design Within the Organization," by M.R. van Gils; "Sociological Research as an Instrument for Social Policy," by H. Verwey-Jonker. Annotated bibliography, pp. 107-22. No index.

583 INDUSTRIAL PARTICIPATION: A JOURNAL OF INFORMATION AND COMMENT ON CURRENT TRENDS AND PRACTICE, NEW THINKING AND RESEARCH. London: Industrial Participation Association, 1894- . Three issues a year.

Each issue contains articles and case studies.

584 Klein, S.M., and Schaupp, D. "Participative Management in the United States: A Corporate Experience." MANAGEMENT INTERNATIONAL REVIEW 12 (1972): 17-22. Tables.

This article reviews participative management in the IBM Corporation.

585 Leidecker, Joel K., and Hall, James L. "A New Justification for Participative Management." HUMAN RESOURCE MANAGEMENT 13 (Spring 1974): 28-31. Diagrams.

The authors cite research indicating that the most effective managers are those who spend a considerable amount of their time in "lateral relations" (i.e., contacts with their peers). They see a direct link between these findings and the adoption of a participative style of management.

586 McLeod, Ian H., and Bennett, J.E. "When Participative Management Doesn't Work." MCKINSEY QUARTERLY 8 (Winter 1972): 54-62.

587 _____. "Why Participative Management Doesn't Work." BUSINESS QUARTERLY 36 (Winter 1971): 81-87.

McLeod and Bennett examine conditions that hamper the use of participative management, supporting their arguments with comments from Canadian industrialists.

588 Mandry, W.J. "Participative Management: the CIL Experience." BUSINESS QUARTERLY 36 (Winter 1971): 73-79.

Participative management at Canadian Industries Ltd. is explored.

589 Marrow, Alfred J.; Bowers, David G.; and Seashore, Stanley E. MANAGEMENT BY PARTICIPATION: CREATING A CLIMATE FOR PERSONAL AND ORGANIZATIONAL DEVELOPMENT. New York: Harper & Row, 1967. xv, 264 p. Diagrams, tables.

A well-documented study, this is particularly concerned with

the Weldon Manufacturing Company, which was taken over by
the Harwood Manufacturing Company in 1962. It is a classic
case study of participative management and organizational development.

590 Roach, John M. WORKER PARTICIPATION: NEW VOICES IN MAN-
AGEMENT. Conference Board Report, n.s., no. 594. New York: Conference Board, 1973. 45 p. Paperback.

Roach summarizes the views of 143 top executives from fifty
countries.

591 Rush, Harold M.F. "A Non-Partisan View of Participative Management."
CONFERENCE BOARD RECORD 10 (April 1973): 34-39.

Research findings indicate that participative management is
used far more in companies employing organizational development than in those which do not.

592 Sheaf, Robert. "Industrial Democracy: The Draft Fifth Directive."
EUROPEAN COMMUNITY, May 1974, pp. 10-11. Diagrams.

This is a summary of the European Community Commission's
directive, based on the German pattern of worker participation which proposes a Board of Managers to manage and rep-
resent the company and a Supervisory Board responsible for
controlling the managers.

593 Tabb, J. Yanai, and Goldfarb, Amira. WORKERS' PARTICIPATION
IN MANAGEMENT: EXPECTATIONS AND EXPERIENCE. Commonwealth
and International Library: Industrial Relations. Oxford, Eng.: Pergamon
Press, 1970. xv, 302 p. Diagrams, tables.

The results of a survey carried out among members of the His-
tadruth (Israel Federation of Labor), covering sixteen enterprises, are included. There is also a case study of the Israel
Electric Corporation, which has used worker participation since
1957. Indexes of names and subjects.

594 Towers, Brian. "Worker Participation in Management: An Appraisal and
Some Comment." INDUSTRIAL RELATIONS JOURNAL 4 (Winter 1973):
4-12. Table.

An editorial review of the meaning of worker participation and
its implications for the United Kingdom is presented. There is
a tabular assessment of the degree of worker influence upon
managerial decision making in the United Kingdom.

595 Vanek, Jan. THE ECONOMICS OF WORKERS' MANAGEMENT: A
YUGOSLAV CASE STUDY. London: Allen & Unwin, 1972. 315 p.
Tables, bibliography.

Vanek offers a detailed study of participative management in Yugoslav industry and its implications for management generally.

596   "Workers' Participation in Management." MANAGEMENT AND PRODUC-
      TIVITY, no. 38 (1973), pp. 1-66. Diagrams, tables.

      Summary of findings of studies carried out by the International Institute for Labour Studies in France, the Federal Republic of Germany, Yugoslavia, and India.

597   "Workers' Participation in Management in. . . ."

      This series of country studies was carried out by the International Institute for Labour Studies and published in the Institute's BULLETIN as follows: "A Review of Indian Experience." INTERNATIONAL INSTITUTE FOR LABOUR STUDIES BULLETIN no. 5, (November 1968), pp. 153-87 (Country Studies, no. 1); "Poland." Ibid.: 188-220 (Countries Studies, no. 2); "France." Ibid.: no. 6, (June 1969), pp. 54-93 (Country Studies, no. 3); "Federal Republic of Germany." Ibid.: 94-148 (Country Studies, no. 4); "A Review of United States Experience." Ibid.: 149-86 (Country Studies, no. 5); "Israel." Ibid.: no. 8 (June 1970), pp. 153-99 (Country Studies, no. 6); "Japan." Ibid.: 200-251 (Country Studies, no. 7); "Spain." Ibid.: 252-85 (Country Studies, no. 8); "Yugoslavia." Ibid.: no. 9 (1972), pp. 129-72 (Country Studies, no. 9); "Great Britain." Ibid.: 173-207 (Country Studies, no. 10).

Section 4

MANAGEMENT ORGANIZATION STRUCTURE

In this small section are listed works dealing in a very practical manner with organization structures and notably with the line-staff approach to organization. The line managers are those responsible for direct executive control of the organization's operations. Works dealing with the organization of specific management functions (e.g., personnel or marketing) are listed in the appropriate sections. See also items 1424-27, 1429, 1431-34.

598   Allen, Louis A. CHARTING THE COMPANY ORGANIZATION STRUC-
      TURE. Studies in Personnel Policy, no. 168. New York: National
      Industrial Conference Board, 1959. 60 p. Diagrams, tables. Paperback.

      Practices in 375 companies are summarized. Detailed instruc-
      tions for preparation of organization charts in the Boeing Com-
      pany are given on page 60.

599   AMERICAN BUSINESS SYSTEM: THE CHALLENGE OF MANAGEMENT.
      Brooklyn, N.Y.: Business Education Films.

      A twenty-nine-minute, 16-mm black-and-white film shows three
      different types of managerial structure: a laundry operated as a
      proprietorship, a filling station run as a partnership, and the
      Minnesota Mining and Manufacturing Company, a large cor-
      poration.

600   Barnes, M.C.; Fogg, A.H.; Stephens, C.N.; and Titman, L.G. COM-
      PANY ORGANISATION: THEORY AND PRACTICE. Professional Man-
      agement Library. London: Allen & Unwin, 1970. 235 p. Diagrams,
      bibliography.

      This valuable guide, written by members of the training depart-
      ment of the British firm of P.A. Management Consultants, is
      presented in four sections: history, theory, people, and prac-
      tice. It includes case studies of the reorganization of an
      electricity board, marketing and product innovation in a manu-
      facturer of heating equipment, decentralization in a public
      body, growth and diversification in confectionery, reorganiza-
      tion of committees in a local authority, and organization in

a newspaper office. Glossary, pp. 217-31.

601   Bergen, Garret L., and Haney, William V. ORGANIZATIONAL RELA-
TIONS AND MANAGEMENT ACTION: CASES AND ISSUES. McGraw-
Hill Series in Management. New York: McGraw-Hill, 1966. 756 p.
Diagrams, bibliographies.

This book contains introductory chapters on organizational problems, the use of cases, and an organization sampler, followed
by eighty-six cases. No index.

602   Brech, E.F.L. ORGANIZATION: THE FRAMEWORK OF MANAGE-
MENT. 2d ed. Management Studies Series. London: Longman; New
York: Fernhill House, 1965. xii, 561 p. Illustrations, diagrams
(1 folding).

A major British work on organization theory and practice, this
volume has chapters on such topics as creating the organization structure, the responsibilities of top management, centralization vs. decentralization, organization charts, organization
planning, and management development. It includes an outline history of thought on organization, pp. 497-547, and
thirty-six specimen job descriptions.

603   Dale, Ernest. THE GREAT ORGANIZERS. New York: McGraw-Hill,
1960. xiii, 277 p. Diagrams, tables, bibliographies. Hardcover and
paperback.

Dale examines approaches to organization in the Du Pont Company, General Motors (with particular reference to the work of
Alfred P. Sloan, Jr.), the National Steel Corporation (with
particular reference to the work of E.T. Weir), and the Westinghouse Electric Corporation. He also includes some of his
own views on organizational theory and practice and on management accountability.

604   _____. ORGANIZATION. New York: American Management Association, 1967. 368 p. Diagrams, forms, tables, bibliography.

This important work is based on the author's experiences as a
management consultant and on an in-depth study of organization practices in 166 companies. The five sections deal with
the bases of organization, the division of the work, coordination (including the use of committees), reorganization, and
factors such as international operations and the impact of the
computer. Dale includes many specimen forms and organization charts. Classified bibliography, pp. 343-60.

605   _____. PLANNING AND DEVELOPING THE COMPANY ORGANIZA-
TION STRUCTURE. AMA Research Report, no. 20. New York: American Management Association, 1952. 232 p. Diagrams, forms, bibliography.

Part one, "The Dynamics of Organization," analyzes the major organizational problems as they arise at various stages of a company's growth. Part two, "The Mechanics of Organization," offers guidance for analyzing the existing structure and modifying it, in the light of the best established practice, to conform to the needs of the individual company. Specimen job descriptions are included. Bibliography, pp. 213-25.

606   Dale, Ernest, and Urwick, Lyndall Fownes. STAFF IN ORGANIZATION. New York: McGraw-Hill, 1960. 241 p. Diagrams, tables.

An American and British expert present views on the load on top management, the effect of overload on executive health, how executives spend their time, methods of reducing executive burdens, the military use of staff, a comparison of military and business staffs, the U.S. presidency and the staff system, a profile of the assistant in business, and the practical use of general staff positions in business, with case studies of unsuccessful "assistants-to." Appendixes include some definitions and/or descriptions of staff in typical books on management, a comparative glossary of U.S. and British military terms, a work description sheet analyzed by functions of leadership, a specimen job description, and the functions of the control section of the Koppers Company.

607   Famularo, Joseph J. ORGANIZATION PLANNING MANUAL. New York: American Management Association, 1971. xiv, 288 p. Diagrams, tables.

This work contains sample organization charts, position descriptions, and policy statements from numerous companies. Glossary, pp. 277-88. No index.

608   Golembiewski, Robert T. ORGANIZING MEN AND POWER: PATTERNS OF BEHAVIOR AND LINE-STAFF MODELS. Chicago: Rand-McNally, 1967. 277 p. Diagrams, tables. Paperback.

Drawing on both practical operations and current research, the author challenges the notion that "staff" in enterprises should be outside the chain of command. Indexes of authors and subjects.

609   Hulme, Robert D., and Maydew, John C. "A View of the Top: A Study of Collective Management Organization." BUSINESS HORIZONS 15 (October 1972): 19-30.

This review of research into top management organization, especially in large multinational corporations, stresses the trend toward the multiple top executive or "office-of-the-president." The authors examine other forms of top management organization which resemble the "office-of-the-president" concept and explore possible developments in this field.

610   Johannsen, Hano. COMPANY ORGANIZATION STRUCTURE. London: British Institute of Management, 1970. 93 p. Diagrams, tables, bibliography. Paperback.

        Organization charts for nineteen British companies are presented.

611   Kemball-Cook, R.B. THE ORGANIZATION GAP: DESIGNING PRACTICAL ORGANIZATION STRUCTURES AND MANAGEMENT INFORMATION SYSTEMS BY THE USE OF DECISION CENTRE ANALYSIS. Unwin Professional Management Library. London: Allen & Unwin; Beverly Hills, Calif.: Davlin Publications, 1972. 200 p. Diagrams, tables.

        The author describes the study and design of organization structures with the P-E Consulting Group, with particular reference to the development and application of Decision Centre Analysis (DCA), a procedure which takes account not only of the valid principles of organization but also of the multiplicity of activities taking place in a modern business. A decision center is defined as "a role in an organization holding responsibility for performing certain tasks in pursuit of certain objectives, with the authority to make decisions to commit certain of the resources of the enterprise" (p. 189). Glossary, pp. 188-90.

612   McFeely, Wilbur M. STAFF SERVICES IN SMALLER COMPANIES: THE VIEW FROM THE TOP. Conference Board Report, n.s., no. 592. New York: Conference Board, 1973. 31 p. Diagrams, tables. Paperback.

        The staffing needs and problems of moderate-sized manufacturing companies, based on data supplied by ninety firms all employing less than 2,000 employees, are discussed. Staff-type work is defined as "those activities which, although contributing to the growth, character, and renewal or perpetuation of a company, do not of themselves make a direct contribution to the fulfillment of the economic objectives of the organization"; a staff person is defined as "a professional whose principal activities are providing advice and counsel."

613   Mooney, James D. THE PRINCIPLES OF ORGANIZATION. Rev. ed. New York: Harper & Row, 1947. 223 p. Tables.

        Mooney considers the relationship of organization in history, the church, and the armed forces to contemporary industrial organization. He describes the "coordinative," "scalar," and "functional" approaches to organization; i.e., systems based on coordinating the activities of groups of personnel, strict hierarchy or grading of duties, and clear distinctions between functions or kinds of jobs.

614   Newman, Derek. ORGANIZATION DESIGN: AN ANALYTICAL AP-
       PROACH TO THE STRUCTURING OF ORGANIZATIONS. London: Ed-
       ward Arnold, 1973. 136 p. Diagrams, bibliography. (Distributed by
       St. Martin's Press, New York.)

       Part one examines the current situation in real organizations,
       while in part two the author explores broader questions of or-
       ganization design and the various design options which are
       available. Glossary, pp. 131-33.

615   P.A. Management Consultants. RENEWING THE MANAGEMENT STRUC-
       TURE: RESPONDING TO THE PROBLEMS OF THE 70'S. London: British
       Institute of Management, 1972. 66 p. Bibliographies. Paperback.

       Seven edited papers given at a BIM conference in April 1972
       deal with the changing needs of individuals, the changing re-
       wards and conditions for managers, society's new demands on
       companies, the demands of the market, the impact of technol-
       ogy, and current trends in management structure.

616   Phillips, Victor F., Jr. THE ORGANIZATIONAL ROLE OF THE ASSIST-
       ANT-TO. New York: American Management Association, 1971. 96 p.
       Tables, bibliography. Paperback.

       This survey is based partly on the author's doctoral thesis. No
       index.

617   Sokolik, Stanley L. THE PERSONNEL PROCESS: LINE AND STAFF DI-
       MENSIONS IN MANAGING PEOPLE AT WORK. Scranton, Pa.: Inter-
       national Textbook Co., 1970. 726 p. Illustrations, diagrams, forms,
       tables, bibliography.

       Sokalik attempts to clarify the separate though complementary
       roles of line and staff managers.

618   Stieglitz, Harold. "On Concepts of Corporate Structure: Economic De-
       terminants of Organization." CONFERENCE BOARD RECORD 11 (Febru-
       ary 1974): 7-13. Table.

       The author argues that economic characteristics within com-
       panies can influence their organization structure requirements.
       He discusses types of company and their structural elements,
       including such factors as degree of delegation and the roles
       of corporate staff.

619   Stieglitz, Harold, and Wilkerson, C. David. CORPORATE ORGANIZA-
       TION STRUCTURES. Studies in Personnel Policy, no. 210. New York:
       National Industrial Conference Board, 1968. 173 p. Diagrams, tables.
       Paperback.

       This work contains charts showing the organization of divisions
       and subunits of fifty-nine divisionalized companies, preceded

by an analysis of the patterns to be distinguished in these corporate structures.

620   White, K.K. UNDERSTANDING THE COMPANY ORGANIZATION
CHART. AMA Research Study, no. 56. New York: American Management Association, 1963. 224 p. Diagrams.

This study of the practices of 118 firms has forty-five detailed case studies. Indexes of subjects and companies.

THE ORGANIZATION DEPARTMENT

621   Glueck, William F. ORGANIZATION PLANNING AND DEVELOPMENT.
AMA Research Study, no. 106. New York: American Management Association, 1971. 165 p. Tables, bibliography. Paperback.

Glueck studies the evolution of organization planning and development departments in American industry since the late 1950s. He includes examples from Stanley Works, Lockheed Aircraft Corporation, Standard Oil Company of California, Kaiser Aluminum and Chemical Corporation, Standard Oil Company (Ohio), and other companies. Appendix A outlines the historical antecedents of the organization function. No index.

622   _____. "Who Needs an Organization Department?" CALIFORNIA
MANAGEMENT REVIEW 15 (Winter 1972): 77-82.

After assessing the results of research into the organization of 1,500 U.S. companies, Glueck suggests broad criteria for deciding whether or not particular firms need organization departments.

THE PETER PRINCIPLE

In propounding his theory that work is accomplished by those employees who have not yet reached their level of incompetence (see item 625), Laurence J. Peter also drew attention to "the salutary science of hierarchiology," the study of hierarchies and their structures and functions.

623   Healey, James H. "Why Not a Paul Principle?" BUSINESS HORIZONS
16 (December 1973): 51-54.

Healey presents the Paul Principle--that for every employee who rises above his level of competence, there are several whose full talents are not utilized. He examines factors which lead to this situation and suggests how to avoid it.

624   Peter, Laurence J. THE PETER PRESCRIPTION: HOW TO BE CREATIVE,

CONFIDENT, AND COMPETENT. New York: Morrow, 1972. 224 p. Illustrations.

This continuation of THE PETER PRINCIPLE (see below) presents sixty-four "prescriptions" for the achievement of competence. No index.

625 Peter, Laurence J., and Hull, Raymond. THE PETER PRINCIPLE. New York: Morrow, 1969. 179 p. Illustrations.

A satirical and penetrating analysis of the reasons for ineffici- ency, this book develops the theory that "work is accomplished by those employees who have not yet reached their level of incompetence" (p. 27). It is dedicated to "all those who, working, playing, loving, living, and dying at their level of incompetence, provided the data for the founding and develop- ment of the salutary science of hierarchiology." This impor- tant book deserves, but does not have, an index.

626 Tracy, Lane. "Postscript to the Peter Principle." HARVARD BUSINESS REVIEW 50 (July-August 1972): 65-67. Diagrams.

Tracy considers why, if the Peter Principle that every employee rises to his level of incompetence is valid, organizations con- tinue to function. He suggests that the void is filled by sec- retaries and that a more efficient, horizontal hierarchical struc- ture is needed.

THE MANAGERS

Who are the managers, and what makes them "tick"? How are they recruited, selected, trained, and paid? What are their working conditions? How do they spend their time? What are their relations with their family and with the rest of society? These and other questions are answered by the items listed in this section. See also items 1435-42 for managers in multinationals.

GENERAL STUDIES

627   Barnard, Chester. THE FUNCTIONS OF THE EXECUTIVE. Cambridge, Mass.: Harvard University Press, 1938. xvi, 334 p. Hardcover and paperback.

>   This is a classic account of industrial organization theory and structure and the role of the executive within this structure.

628   Battalia, O. William, and Tarrant, John J. THE CORPORATE EUNUCH. New York: Crowell; London: Abelard-Schuman, 1973. xii, 180 p. Hardcover and paperback.

>   This work is a guide to the achievement of success in management. No index.

629   Burger, Chester. EXECUTIVES UNDER FIRE: PERSONAL CASE HISTORIES FROM THE EXECUTIVE JUNGLE. New York: Macmillan; London: Collier-Macmillan, 1966. 224 p.

>   This study of executive problems is based on tape-recorded interviews collected by the author during his career as a management consultant.

630   _____. SURVIVAL IN THE EXECUTIVE JUNGLE. New York: Macmillan, 1964. 274 p.

>   Burger gives advice on how to deal with one's superiors and subordinates, including a chapter on "Living with Your Secretary."

631　Campbell, John P.; Dunnette, Marvin D.; Lawler, Edward E. III; and Weick, Karl E. MANAGERIAL BEHAVIOR, PERFORMANCE AND EFFECTIVENESS. McGraw-Hill Series in Psychology; McGraw-Hill Series in Management. New York: McGraw-Hill, 1970. xiv, 546 p. Diagrams, forms, tables, bibliography.

Reported are results of a research study set up to examine the practices used in government and industry to develop effective managers. The extent to which these practices are related to the results of behavioral science research is also examined. Indexes of names and subjects.

632　Dalton, Melville. MEN WHO MANAGE: FUSIONS OF FEELING AND THEORY IN ADMINISTRATION. New York: Wiley, 1959. 318 p. Diagrams (1 folding), tables, bibliography.

Dalton analyzes the formal behavior and unofficial actions of managers. He identifies and investigates the collaborative struggles between two types of executive--those to whom method and procedure are paramount and those who adapt and reorganize official directives by stressing ends rather than means. Bibliography, pp. 287-99. Indexes of names and subjects.

633　Dill, William R.; Hilton, Thomas L.; and Reitman, Walter R. THE NEW MANAGERS: PATTERNS OF BEHAVIOR AND DEVELOPMENT. Englewood Cliffs, N.J.: Prentice-Hall, 1962. 258 p. Diagrams, tables.

The behavior of executives in three different organizations is studied. Indexes of names and subjects.

634　Drucker, Peter F. THE EFFECTIVE EXECUTIVE. New York: Harper & Row; London: Heinemann, 1967. 148 p.

Drucker argues that the first task of the executive is to be effective and that effectiveness can and must be learned. He shows how effectiveness can be improved by proper management of time, knowledge of what to contribute to an organization, knowledge of where and how to apply company strengths for the best effect, establishment of the right priorities, and effective decision making.

635　_____. THE EFFECTIVE EXECUTIVE. Rockville, Md.: BNA Communications; New York: Time-Life Video; Peterborough, Eng.: Guild Sound & Vision, 1968.

Five twenty-five-minute 16-mm color films or videotapes (Time-Life Video) are based on Drucker's book (item 634). Drucker appears in the role of management consultant to the mythical Hudson-Lansing Corporation. The five films are: "Managing Time," "What Can I Contribute?" "Focus on Tomorrow," "Effective Decision," and "Staffing for Strength."

636   Emery, David A. THE COMPLEAT MANAGER: COMBINING THE HU-
      MANISTIC AND THE SCIENTIFIC APPROACHES TO THE MANAGEMENT
      JOB. New York: McGraw-Hill, 1970. 201 p. Diagrams, bibliography.

      Several case studies are included in this systematic guide to
      executive self-diagnosis and self-improvement.

637   Ewing, David W. THE MANAGERIAL MIND. New York: Free Press of
      Glencoe; London: Collier-Macmillan, 1964. 218 p.

      The intellectual processes of managers when dealing with their
      daily problems are examined.

638   Feinberg, Mortimer R. SELF-DISCOVERY FOR THE MANAGER. New
      York: AMACOM, 1973.

      Three forty-minute cassettes cover "The Person Called You,"
      "Clues to Maturity and Emotional Health," "Life Goals: How
      Do You Stand?"

639   Getty, J. Paul. HOW TO BE A SUCCESSFUL EXECUTIVE. Chicago:
      Playboy Press, 1971. 208 p.

      The American multibillionaire, founder of the Playboy empire,
      presents his guide to becoming a good businessman. No index.

640   Ghiselli, Edwin E. EXPLORATIONS IN MANAGERIAL TALENT. Pacific
      Palisades, Calif.: Goodyear, 1971. 166 p. Diagrams, tables.

      This survey, based on twenty years research, deals with the ac-
      tivities, personalities, and motivation of managers and the extent
      to which managers are differentiated from supervisors and line
      workers.

641   Granick, David. THE EUROPEAN EXECUTIVE. New York: Doubleday;
      London: Weidenfeld & Nicholson, 1962. 384 p. Tables, bibliography.

      Granick compares managerial methods in Britain, Belgium,
      France, and Germany, with an epilogue on American firms and
      managerial behavior. Glossary, pp. 368-70.

642   Guzzardi, Walter. THE YOUNG EXECUTIVES. New York: New Ameri-
      can Library; London: New English Library, 1964. xxi, 228 p. Dia-
      grams, tables, bibliography.

      This guide to executive success is based on interviews, with
      chapters on executive attitudes and behavior, managerial styles,
      managers and computers, and other topics. No index.

643   Haire, Mason; Ghiselli, Edwin E.; and Porter, Lyman W. MANAGERIAL

THINKING: AN INTERNATIONAL STUDY. New York: Wiley, 1966. 298 p. Diagrams, map, tables.

The attitudes of 3,600 managers in fourteen countries are surveyed.

644 Hall, David; de Bettignies, H.-Cl.; and Amado-Fischgrund, G. "The European Business Elite." EUROPEAN BUSINESS, no. 23 (October 1969), pp. 45-55. Diagrams, bibliography.

This paper discusses the backgrounds, remuneration, and linguistic abilities of managers in Britain, France, Germany, Italy, Belgium, and the Netherlands.

645 Jennings, Eugene Emerson. THE EXECUTIVE: AUTOCRAT, BUREAUCRAT, DEMOCRAT. New York: Harper & Row, 1962. xiv, 272 p.

Jennings outlines the executive's role and essential qualities, with a detailed account of three common types and a briefer discussion of the "neurocrat," whose neurotic needs help him to become an effective executive.

646 _____. THE EXECUTIVE IN CRISIS. MSU Business Studies. East Lansing: Michigan State University Graduate School of Business Administration, 1965. xiii, 218 p. Diagrams, bibliography. Paperback ed. New York: McGraw-Hill, 1972.

This study of executives who reached "the top of the corporate ladder and then stumbled" is based on fifteen cases of presidents and vice-presidents who went to the author for professional counseling. Jennings suggests reasons and remedies for failure in an effort to initiate discussion of administrative anxiety. He identifies three basic crisis patterns: the authority-centered pattern, the organization-centered pattern, and the self-centered pattern. No index.

647 _____. EXECUTIVE SUCCESS: STRESSES, PROBLEMS, AND ADJUST-MENT. New York: Appleton-Century-Crofts, 1967. 205 p. Diagrams.

This revision and enlargement of THE EXECUTIVE IN CRISIS (item 646) deletes the theoretical language and references to scholarly studies. It details and more systematically analyzes the fifteen cases provided, and it adds four new cases. Still no index.

648 Juran, Joseph M. MANAGERIAL BREAKTHROUGH: A NEW CONCEPT OF THE MANAGER'S JOB. New York: McGraw-Hill, 1964. 396 p. Diagrams, tables.

Juran urges the manager to synthesize the two major elements of his activities: (1) breaking through into new levels, or creating change as required, and (2) holding the resulting gains through control, or preventing change.

649   Kreider, Leonard Emil. THE DEVELOPMENT AND UTILIZATION OF
MANAGERIAL TALENT: A CASE STUDY OF MANUFACTURING MAN-
AGERS IN COLUMBUS, OHIO. Ann Arbor, Mich.: University Micro-
films, 1970. xiii, 316 p. 87 tables. Bibliography. Paperback.

This doctoral thesis, prepared at Ohio State University in 1968,
covers the tasks of managers, mobility patterns of managers,
and educational patterns of managers in fifty-one Columbus
firms. No index.

650   Livingston, Robert Teviot, and Waite, William W. THE MANAGER'S
JOB. New York: Columbia University Press, 1960. xiii, 459 p. Diagrams, tables.

These papers were given at Columbia University Utility Management Workshop between 1956 and 1959. They are here
divided into six parts: the job of the top manager, the job of
any manager, the manager and human relations, communication
and management, development of managers, and decision making. No index.

651   Mintzberg, Henry. THE NATURE OF MANAGERIAL WORK. New York:
Harper & Row, 1973. xiii, 298 p. Diagrams, tables, bibliography.
Hardcover and paperback.

This fascinating account of what managers do is based on empirical studies in Sweden, the United Kingdom, and the United
States. A chapter summarizing eight contemporary views of
the manager's job is followed by an assessment of management
as a science and the role of the manager in this science, with
observations on the future of managerial work. A literature
review of major studies of the manager's job is on pp. 199-
220. A description of seven research methods used to study
managerial work is on pp. 221-29. A study of the work of
five chief executives is on pp. 230-77.

652   Mitchell, William Norman. THE BUSINESS EXECUTIVE IN A CHANG-
ING WORLD. New York: American Management Association, 1965.
208 p.

Mitchell appraises the executive's job in terms of functions,
effort, motivation, adjustment to environment, and development. The book won the McKinsey Foundation Award for excellence in management literature, but it has no index.

653   Moonman, Eric. THE MANAGER AND THE ORGANIZATION. London:
Tavistock, 1961. 221 p. Diagrams, tables, bibliography. Reprint.
London: Pan Books, 1965. Paperback. (Distributed by Barnes & Noble,
Scranton, Pa.)

The manager's role within an organization is examined in terms
of coordination and communication. Moonman suggests that
the higher an executive moves up the management ladder, the
less he depends on his technical knowledge and ability and
the more he depends on his administrative and social skills.

654   Rapoport, Robert N.; with Brodie, M.B.; and Life, E.A. MID-CAREER
DEVELOPMENT: RESEARCH PERSPECTIVES ON A DEVELOPED COMMU-
NITY FOR SENIOR ADMINISTRATORS. London: Tavistock, 1970. xii,
290 p. Diagrams, tables, bibliography. (Distributed by Barnes & Noble,
Scranton, Pa.)

This research on the midlife crisis among managers was carried
out at the Administrative Staff College, Henley-on-Thames,
England, and involved 600 managers. Indexes of names and
subjects.

655   Sayles, Leonard R. MANAGERIAL BEHAVIOR: ADMINISTRATION IN
COMPLEX ORGANIZATIONS. New York: McGraw-Hill, 1964. 269 p.
Diagrams.

Several years' research underlie this analysis of the manager's
job in one division of a large American corporation.

656   Sofer, Cyril. MEN IN MID-CAREER: A STUDY OF BRITISH MANAGERS
AND TECHNICAL SPECIALISTS. Studies in Sociology, no. 4. Cam-
bridge, Eng.: Cambridge University Press, 1970. xxii, 376 p. Tables.
Hardcover and paperback.

This study of managers between the ages of thirty-five and
forty is based on a comprehensive review of British and American
literature and interviews with eighty-one managers from two
companies. Indexes of names and subjects.

657   Uris, Auren. DEVELOPING YOUR EXECUTIVE SKILLS. New York:
McGraw-Hill, 1955. 270 p.

A guide to self-development, this work has sections on the
executive approach, administrative skills, desk discipline,
working with people, and raising overall efficiency.

658   _____. THE FRUSTRATED TITAN: EMASCULATION OF THE EXECU-
TIVE. New York: Van Nostrand Reinhold, 1972. xii, 201 p.

Uris describes eleven major ways in which executive talent
is wasted and frustration is created. He then suggests solutions.

659   Uris, Auren, and Noppel, Marjorie. THE TURNED-ON EXECUTIVE:
BUILDING YOUR SKILLS FOR THE MANAGEMENT REVOLUTION. New
York: McGraw-Hill, 1970. xiv, 236 p.

The executive is offered advice on how to cope with the stresses of modern life. Included are chapters on "reving up" for better ideas, improving one's memory, dictation at 300 words a minute, efficient use of speech, and the psychology of meetings, as well as on "the turned-on secretary" and "the turned-on wife."

THE EXECUTIVE'S USE OF TIME

660 Copeman, George; Luijk, H.; and Hanika, F. de P. HOW THE EXECUTIVE SPENDS HIS TIME. London: Business Publications, 1963. 149 p. Diagrams, tables. (Distributed by International Publications Service, New York.)

Analyses by George Copeman and Joy Larkcom consider how British executives spend their day, and one by H. Luijk concerns how Dutch executives spend their day. F. de P. Hanika advises on how to study the executive day, and Copeman presents conclusions.

661 Heyel, Carl. ORGANIZING YOUR JOB IN MANAGEMENT. New York: American Management Association, 1960. 208 p. Diagrams, forms, tables.

Practical suggestions on how the manager can make effective use of the limited time available to him are given. Chapters on delegation, conference organization, communication, and improvement of speed and comprehension in reading are included.

662 Stewart, Rosemary. MANAGERS AND THEIR JOBS: A STUDY OF THE SIMILARITIES AND DIFFERENCES IN THE WAYS MANAGERS SPEND THEIR TIME. London: Macmillan; New York: St. Martin's Press, 1967. xii, 186 p. Diagrams, tables.

This research, financed by the Nuffield Foundation, involved use of especially designed diaries by 160 managers from more than 100 companies who represented all major management functions.

663 Webber, Ross A. TIME AND MANAGEMENT. Frontiers in Management Series. New York: Van Nostrand Reinhold, 1972. 166 p. Diagrams, tables.

Webber examines the attitudes and behaviors of managers in different cultures, suggests why time is wasted, and offers help in managing personal time. He also discusses how time affects and distorts organizational decisions and compares individual and group decision making.

WOMEN AS MANAGERS

664   Basil, Douglas C.; with Traver, Edna. WOMEN IN MANAGEMENT.
New York: Dunellen, 1972. xvi, 124 p. Illustrations, bibliography.

This book presents the results of a mail survey, organized by
the University of Southern California, of the attitudes of some
2,000 organizations towards women in management. There was
only a 16 percent response to the survey, consisting of 102 female executives and 214 male executives.

665   Business and Professional Women's Foundation. WOMEN EXECUTIVES:
A SELECTED ANNOTATED BIBLIOGRAPHY. Washington, D.C.: 1970.
26 p. Paperback.

This useful bibliography is available from the Foundation, 2012
Massachusetts Avenue N.W., Washington, D.C. 20036.

666   Hackamack, Laurence C., and Solid, Alan B. "The Woman Executive:
There is Still Ample Room for Progress." BUSINESS HORIZONS 15 (April
1972): 89-93. Table.

The authors trace the development of the woman manager,
examine qualities which fit women for executive responsibility,
and explore obstacles in their way.

667   Hartmann, Heinz. "The Enterprising Woman: A German Model." CO-
LUMBIA JOURNAL OF WORLD BUSINESS 5 (March-April 1970): 61-66.
Bibliography.

An examination by a German sociologist of the role of women
in German business indicates that many women owners or managers do not consider themselves to be disadvantaged.

668   Kealiher, Carolyn L. "Women: The Wasted Resource?" PERSONNEL
ADMINISTRATOR 18 (July-August 1973): 15-18.

Kealiher reports that equal promotion opportunities are being
encouraged by the First National Bank of Denver. Other articles on women in management in this issue are "Women in
Management: Fable or Fact?" by T.A. Duckworth (pp. 19-
22); "Formula for Successful Women Managers," by Lois Ann
Koff (pp. 23-25); and "Middle Management: Key to the Femi-
nist Drive," by John K. Mills, Jr. (pp. 28-31).

669   Loring, Rosalind, and Wells, Theodore. BREAKTHROUGH: WOMEN IN-
TO MANAGEMENT. New York: Van Nostrand Reinhold, 1973. 202 p.
Diagrams.

The authors argue that there are too few women in managerial
positions, especially as more than one-third of the U.S. work

force is female. They also suggest that they could not have written this book without the examples of the women executives "who have aspired, who have achieved, who have clearly demonstrated their abilities and won recognition." No index.

670 Macdonald, Eleanor. "Women in Management." WORK STUDY 19 (April 1970): 27-30, 32-35.

Macdonald stresses the lack of management opportunities for women in British industry, where only 3 percent of the female work force holds managerial posts. She suggests that lack of training and development programs is the major reason for this.

671 Political and Economic Planning. WOMEN IN TOP JOBS: FOUR STUDIES IN ACHIEVEMENT. London: Allen & Unwin, 1971. 328 p. Tables.

These studies were sponsored by the Leverhulme Trust and were undertaken by Political and Economic Planning in collaboration with the Tavistock Institute under the direction of Michael P. Fogarty, Robert Rapoport, and Rhona Rapoport. There are four parts: "Women in Two Large Companies," by Isobel Allen; "The Woman Director," by A.J. Allen; "Women in the British Broadcasting Corporation," by Isobel Allen; "Women in the Administrative Class of the Civil Service," by Patricia A. Walters.

BIOGRAPHIES OF MANAGERS

See also items 7, 33.

672 Appley, Laurence A. A MANAGER'S HERITAGE. New York: American Management Association, 1970. 222 p.

The chairman and former president of AMA presents brief portraits of thirty-two people who have influenced him. No index.

673 THE BUSINESS WHO'S WHO 1974/5. London: Leviathan House, 1974. 551 p.

This biographical dictionary of chairmen, chief executives, and managing directors of British registered companies includes an alphabetical index of companies.

674 WHO'S WHO IN FINANCE AND INDUSTRY. Chicago: Marquis Who's Who, 1936- . Annual.

This has had various titles and began as WHO'S WHO IN COMMERCE AND INDUSTRY.

RECRUITMENT AND SELECTION OF MANAGERS

675 Dooher, M. Joseph, and Marting, Elizabeth, eds. SELECTION OF MAN-
AGEMENT PERSONNEL. 2 vols. New York: American Management
Association, 1957. Illustrations, diagrams, tables, bibliography.

Volume 1 (542 p.) contains contributions by specialists on the
selection of supervisors, the selection of executives, and the
practical aspects of executive and supervisory selection. Volume 2 (364 p.) deals with company practices in management
selection, giving nineteen examples, and contains a list of
supplementary reading and an index.

676 Kingston, N. SELECTING MANAGERS: A SURVEY OF CURRENT PRAC-
TICE IN 200 COMPANIES. Management Survey Report, no. 4. London:
British Institute of Management, 1971. 77 p. Diagrams, forms, tables,
bibliography.

677 Lamb, Warren, and Turner, David. MANAGEMENT BEHAVIOUR. London:
Duckworth; New York: International University Press, 1969. 177 p.
Diagrams.

A guide to the recognition and assessment of management potential, this book contains cases and specimen job descriptions.

678 Lopez, Felix M. THE MAKING OF A MANAGER: GUIDELINES TO
HIS SELECTION AND PROMOTION. New York: American Management
Association, 1970. xii, 291 p. Diagrams.

Lopez assesses the role, selection, motivation, and rewarding
of managers during the last thirty years. He argues that there
is a managerial crisis and that there is an urgent need for today's managers to create the conditions for tomorrow and to
prepare their organizations to move into the future.

679 Miner, John B. "The Real Crunch in Managerial Manpower." HARVARD
BUSINESS REVIEW 51 (November–December 1973): 146–58. Tables.

Miner discusses recruitment strategies to conquer the serious
shortage of managerial talent which he foresees over the next
decade.

680 Packard, Vance. THE PYRAMID CLIMBERS. New York: Fawcett World
Library; London: Longman, 1963. 339 p. Bibliography. Paperback.

This is a critical study of the selection, promotion, and manipulation of the modern executive.

681 Sands, Edith. HOW TO SELECT EXECUTIVE PERSONNEL. Reinhold
Management Reference Series. New York: Reinhold; London: Chapman

& Hall, 1963. xvi, 215 p. Illustrations, forms.

> Sands's book is based on research involving eighty-two of the largest U.S. corporations. It contains a list of psychological tests, pp. 203-8.

682 Shaeffer, Ruth G. STAFFING SYSTEMS: MANAGERIAL AND PROFES-
SIONAL JOBS. Conference Board Report, n.s., no. 558. New York:
Conference Board, 1972. 121 p. Illustrations, diagrams, forms, tables.
Paperback.

> This book deals with systems for staffing lower and middle-
level managerial and professional posts and suggests that the
hiring, transfer, and promotion of executives within an organization should be managed as an integrated total process.
It includes case studies of R.H. Macy & Co., Inc., Uniroyal
Inc., First National City Bank, and the American Telphone
and Telegraph Company (A.T. & T.).

683 Taylor, Jack W. HOW TO SELECT AND DEVELOP LEADERS. New
York: McGraw-Hill, 1962. 262 p. Diagrams, forms, tables.

> This is a practical guide to the setting up of an effective
SDL (Selecting and Developing Leaders) program.

EDUCATION, DEVELOPMENT, AND TRAINING OF MANAGERS

General studies of management development, education, and training are listed
here. Items on training techniques are listed under Personnel Management in
section 19.

684 Bursk, Edward C., and Blodgett, Timothy R., eds. DEVELOPING EX-
ECUTIVE LEADERS. Cambridge, Mass.: Harvard University Press, 1971.
191 p. Diagrams.

> Reprints of sixteen articles from HARVARD BUSINESS REVIEW
are presented in three sections: personal growth, coping with
the job, and motivation for growth.

685 Crawford, Merle. "Management Education: The Nature of Things to
Come." HUMAN RESOURCE MANAGEMENT 12 (Fall 1973): 2-6.

> The author outlines trends he believes will change current
ideas on management education, including changes in university courses and the recruitment of more women as top managers.

686 Desatnick, Robert L. A CONCISE GUIDE TO MANAGEMENT DEVELOP-
MENT. New York: American Management Association, 1970. 175 p.
Forms, tables.

Management development as a way of life within an organization is stressed. The book includes several appendixes: job
descriptions, appraisal rating guides, management by objectives
goals, and inventory forms, for example.

687   Duerr, Michael G. ARE TODAY'S SCHOOLS PREPARING TOMORROW'S
       BUSINESS LEADERS? A WORLDWIDE SURVEY OF CHIEF EXECUTIVES.
       Conference Board Report, n.s., no. 622. New York: Conference Board,
       1974. 30 p. Paperback.

       The views of ninety-eight business leaders from forty-one coun-
       tries on the adequacy of formal education at school and uni-
       versity as a preparation for business leadership are summarized.
       A final section concerns changes in management style influ-
       enced by younger managers, including greater emphasis on
       training and communication, more delegation of authority,
       and more participative management.

688   Goodstein, Leonard D. "Management Development and Organizational
       Development: A Critical Difference in Focus." BUSINESS QUARTERLY
       36 (Winter 1971): 30-37. Bibliography.

       After considering the nature of OD and MD and some confu-
       sions about the two techniques, Goodstein concludes that MD
       may be useful for improving the effectiveness of the individual
       manager but that OD is more useful if organizational effective-
       ness is sought.

689   Haire, Mason. "Managing Management Manpower: A Model for Human
       Resource Development." BUSINESS HORIZONS 10 (Winter 1967): 23-
       28. Diagrams.

       This article contains a matrix, representing the problem of
       managerial career development, which can be used by manage-
       ment to establish a centralized overview of the manpower situ-
       ation.

690   House, Robert J. MANAGEMENT DEVELOPMENT: DESIGN, EVALUA-
       TION AND IMPLEMENTATION. Ann Arbor: University of Michigan
       Graduate School of Business Administration, Bureau of Industrial Relations,
       1967. 138 p. Diagrams, tables, bibliography.

       Included are contributions by Henry L. Tosi, John R. Rizzo,
       and Richard C. Dunnock. Bibliography, pp. 125-38. No in-
       dex.

691   Humble, John W., ed. IMPROVING THE PERFORMANCE OF THE EX-
       PERIENCED MANAGER. McGraw-Hill European Series in Management.
       London: McGraw-Hill, 1973. xx, 346 p. Diagrams, forms, tables,
       bibliography.

These papers concern management development and training, including contributions on how to train, management training centers, seminars, audiovisual aids, in-company courses, and social responsibilities of management.

692   Livingston, J. Sterling. "Myth of the Well Educated Manager." Mc-KINSEY QUARTERLY 9 (Summer 1972): 33-49. Bibliography.

Livingston suggests that many managers do not learn from experience and discusses three important characteristics of men who learn to manage effectively.

693   Lundberg, Craig C. "Planning the Executive Development Program." CALIFORNIA MANAGEMENT REVIEW 15 (Fall 1972): 10-15. Diagram, tables, bibliography.

Lundberg traces the history of formalized management development and notes the current emphasis on the management of organizational change. He discusses the content of a training program aimed at developing the required skills.

694   Markwell, D.S., and Roberts, T.J. ORGANIZATION OF MANAGE-MENT DEVELOPMENT PROGRAMMES. Epping, Essex, Eng.: Gower Press, 1969. xv, 182 p. Illustrations, diagrams, tables. (Distributed by Beekman Publishers, New York.)

Part one deals with the design of training programs, with sections on management career planning, sensitivity training, mathematics and management, technology of management development, and evaluation of training. Part two contains case studies of management development in International Printers Ltd., Tetley Walker Ltd., Churchill Gear Machines Ltd., Glaxo Laboratories Ltd., Stone-Platt Industries Ltd., and Pilkington Brothers Ltd.

695   Miner, John B. "The OD-Management Development Conflict." BUSINESS HORIZONS 16 (December 1973): 31-36.

Discussed are organization development and management development approaches as they relate to each other, to company problems, to training needs, and to the objectives of the organization.

696   Morris, John, and Burgoyne, John. DEVELOPING RESOURCEFUL MANAGERS. London: Institute of Personnel Management, 1973. 86 p. Diagrams, bibliography. Paperback.

This practical guide has case studies of management development in a public utility, the Administrative Staff College (Henley-on-Thames), and an international company. The need

for managers to develop themselves is discussed. Brief annotated guide to further reading, pp. 82-83.

697 Odiorne, George S. TRAINING BY OBJECTIVES: AN ECONOMIC AP-
PROACH TO MANAGEMENT TRAINING. New York: Macmillan; London: Collier-Macmillan, 1970. 354 p. Diagrams, bibliographies.

Odiorne examines the management by objectives approach to
management training, using a systems approach. Case studies,
questions, and bibliographies are given with each chapter.

698 Torrington, Derek P., and Sutton, David F., eds. HANDBOOK OF
MANAGEMENT DEVELOPMENT. Epping, Eng.: Gower Press, 1973.
xxv, 402 p. Diagrams, forms, tables. (Distributed by Beekman Publishers, New York.)

This volume's twenty-one papers are arranged in three parts:
the setting of management development (its nature, manpower
planning, recruitment and selection of potential managers,
motivation, salaries, etc.); the management development activity (including management training, performance appraisal,
the management by objectives approach); and management development in action (case studies of Wall Paper Manufacturers
Ltd., a division of Reed International; the Taylor Woodrow
Group; the Manchester Regional Hospital Board; the Legal and
General Assurance Society Ltd., and organizations in the field
of agriculture and distribution).

699 Wikstrom, Walter S. DEVELOPING BETTER MANAGERS: AN EIGHT
NATION STUDY. Studies in Personnel Policy. New York: National
Industrial Conference Board, 1961. 189 p. Diagrams, tables. Paper-
back.

This work studies management development procedures in Chile,
France, Germany, Great Britain, India, Italy, Japan, and
the United States.

Periodicals

700 AACSB BULLETIN. St. Louis: American Assembly of Collegiate Schools
of Business, 1964- . Three issues a year.

701 BUSINESS GRADUATE: JOURNAL OF THE BUSINESS GRADUATES AS-
SOCIATION IN BRITAIN. London: 1974?- . Quarterly.

702 MANAGEMENT EDUCATION AND DEVELOPMENT. Southport, Eng.:
Association of Teachers of Management, 1970- . Three issues a year.

The organ of the Association of Teachers of Management, a

group of specialists in universities, other academic institutions, and industry, this journal was founded in 1960 with the object of appraising management education and raising the professional standard of its members. This useful journal replaces ATM NEWS-LETTER (1961–62) and ATM BULLETIN (1963–69).

703 STANFORD BUSINESS SCHOOL ALUMNI BULLETIN. Stanford, Calif.: Stanford Business School Alumni Association, 1931- . Quarterly.

704 TRAINING AND DEVELOPMENT JOURNAL. Madison, Wis.: American Society for Training and Development, 1947- . Monthly.

This contains articles, signed book reviews, reviews of films and other training tools, and abstracts of articles and reports. It is a very useful source of information on all aspects of training and development, including management training and the evaluation of training and development schemes.

Directories

705 BRICKER'S INTERNATIONAL DIRECTORY OF UNIVERSITY-SPONSORED EXECUTIVE DEVELOPMENT PROGRAMS PLUS MARKETING MANAGE-MENT PROGRAMS. 1975 ed. Compiled by George W. Bricker. South Chatham, Mass.: Bricker Publications, 1974. xix, 345 p.

The directory describes programs in the United States, United Kingdom, Australia, and the continent of Europe. All programs are at least two weeks in length, use the English language, and require fulltime attendance. Section one (pp. 3-282) deals with executive development programs, and section two (pp. 283-335) covers marketing management programs.

706 McNulty, Nancy G., comp. TRAINING MANAGERS: THE INTERNA-TIONAL GUIDE. New York: Harper & Row, 1969. 572 p.

Obviously dated now, this remains a useful guide. A general introduction giving brief comments on a number of teaching methods is followed by sections dealing with programs in general management, programs in functional management, programs at productivity centers sponsored by the International Labor Organization, and graduate programs in modern management and administration, with a tabular index by country and sponsoring organization. To qualify for inclusion a course must last at least five days. Within this limitation the aim is to include all courses outside the United States, but within the United States only the seventy-eight schools which are accredited by the American Association of Collegiate Schools of Business are included.

MANAGEMENT EDUCATION, DEVELOPMENT, AND TRAINING
IN THE UNITED STATES AND CANADA

707   American Association of Collegiate Schools of Business. THE AMERICAN
ASSOCIATION OF COLLEGIATE SCHOOLS OF BUSINESS, 1916-1966.
Homewood, Ill.: Irwin, 1966. 296 p. Tables.

The development of formal academic training for business administration is described from the establishment of AACSB by
the deans of seventeen business schools in 1916 until its gold-
en jubilee year.

708   Bridenne, Alain, and Tejtel, Marc. "The Cultural Revolution in Business
Schools." EUROPEAN BUSINESS, no. 36 (Winter 1973), pp. 37-46. Table.

The authors include a tabular summary of the programs of three
innovative schools--Case Western Reserve University, Southern
Methodist University, and Vanderbilt University.

709   Cone, Paul R., and McKinney, Richard N. "Management Development
Can Be More Effective." CALIFORNIA MANAGEMENT REVIEW 14
(Spring 1972): 13-19. Bibliography.

This article outlines the need for systematic management development within the firm and critically surveys the current
management development situation in the United States.

710   Drucker, Peter F., ed. PREPARING TOMORROW'S BUSINESS LEADERS
TODAY. Englewood Cliffs, N.J.: Prentice-Hall, 1969. xiv, 290 p.

These thirty papers were read at a symposium to celebrate the
fiftieth anniversary of the Graduate School of Business Administration, New York University. A historical survey of the
school by Hermann E. Kross and Peter F. Drucker is followed
by papers arranged under four subject headings: the changing
environment; new dimensions of business; international business;
and the mission of the business school.

711   Finkle, Robert B., and Jones, William S. ASSESSING CORPORATE TAL-
ENT: A KEY TO MANAGERIAL MANPOWER PLANNING. New York:
Wiley-Interscience, 1970. 248 p. Tables.

Procedures in the Standard Oil Company (Ohio) are described.

712   Gordon, Robert Aaron, and Howell, James Edwin. HIGHER EDUCATION
FOR BUSINESS. New York: Columbia University Press, 1959. 491 p.
Tables. Paperback.

This stimulating, though now dated, survey suggests several
areas which need improvement if the U.S. business community
is to be adequately served.

713 GRADUATE STUDY IN MANAGEMENT: A GUIDE FOR PROSPECTIVE
     STUDENTS 1974-75. Princeton, N.J.: Graduate Business Admissions
     Council, 1974. 399 p. Diagrams, maps, tables. Paperback.

> Introductory sections on careers in management, application
> for admission, finance, etc., are followed by details of courses
> offered at 288 business schools, mainly in the United States.
> A sample of an admission test for graduate study in business,
> with solutions, is included. No index.

714 Kelley, James W. "Management Grades the Graduate Business School."
     PERSONNEL 46 (September-October 1969): 16-26. Table.

> The results of a continuing dialogue between Boston University
> and 500 leading companies on the university's graduate pro-
> gram are presented.

715 Laporte, Lowell. DEVELOPING MANAGERS IN THE SMALLER COM-
     PANY. Managing the Moderate-Sized Company, no. 8. New York:
     National Industrial Conference Board, 1968. 33 p. Paperback.

> Laporte reviews practices in sixty companies, which use a
> variety of techniques for management development, including
> performance appraisal, project work, and the outside resources.

716 West, Jude P., and Sheriff, Don R. EXECUTIVE DEVELOPMENT PRO-
     GRAMS IN UNIVERSITIES. Studies in Personnel Policy, no. 215. New
     York: National Industrial Conference Board, 1969. 97 p. Tables, bib-
     liography. Paperback.

> The authors analyze forty-five executive development programs
> concerned with general management which were then being
> sponsored by universities, with a summary of company attitudes
> and practices. Annotated bibliography, pp. 92-94.

717 Wikstrom, Walter S. DEVELOPING MANAGERIAL COMPETENCE:
     CHANGING CONCEPTS, EMERGING PRACTICES. Studies in Personnel
     Policy, no. 189. New York: National Industrial Conference Board,
     1964. 128 p. Illustrations, tables. Paperback.

> Based partially on a survey of 167 companies, this work in-
> cludes case studies of Armco Steel Corporation, Standard Oil
> Company (Ohio), Eastman Kodak Company, Equitable Life As-
> surance Society of the United States, and Stone Container
> Corporation.

MANAGEMENT EDUCATION, DEVELOPMENT, AND TRAINING IN EUROPE

718 European Association of Management Training Centres. "A Handbook
     of the Association and Its Member Centres." Brussels: The As-

sociation, rue de la Concorde 53, 1050 Brussels, Belgium, 1970? 91 p. Paperback. Mimeographed.

Notes on the origins, objectives, and organization of the association are followed by descriptions of its centers in Belgium, Czechoslovakia, France, Germany, Ireland, Italy, the Netherlands, Scandinavia, Spain, Switzerland, and the United Kingdom.

719   Kubr, Milan. "The Systems Building Approach to Management Education in Eastern Europe." EUROPEAN TRAINING 2 (1973): 198-211.

Kubr reviews the nationwide management education system developed in the Socialist countries of Eastern Europe during the past ten years.

720   Revans, Reginald W. DEVELOPING EFFECTIVE MANAGERS: A NEW APPROACH TO BUSINESS EDUCATION. London: Longman, 1971. xix, 201 p. Diagrams, tables.

The Belgian interuniversity management development program and its implications are considered. No index.

721   Teresi, Salvatore. "The European Centre for Permanent Education (CEDEP): A Concrete Example of Continuing Education." EUROPEAN TRAINING 1 (Summer 1972): 145-50.

Review of the work of a management education center sponsored jointly by INSEAD (the European Institute of Business Administration) and a number of European companies, which began its activities in Fontainebleau, France, in May 1971.

MANAGEMENT EDUCATION, DEVELOPMENT, AND TRAINING IN BRITAIN

722   Advisory Panel on Management Education. BUSINESS SCHOOL PROGRAMMES: THE REQUIREMENTS OF BRITISH MANUFACTURING INDUSTRY. London: British Institute of Management, 1971. 31 p. Paperback.

The Advisory Panel on Management Education, set up jointly by the British Institute of Management and the Confederation of British Industry in 1969 to review major issues in education as they affect industry, commerce, and management, here reports on a survey conducted on behalf of the Council of Industry for Management Education and summarizing the views of fifty-three enterprises. The general consensus is that, while British business schools have made excellent progress, they still need to catch up with the much older American schools. Suggestions include the development of specializations within schools, greater coordination of schools' activities, and closer links between industry and the schools.

723 Black, Stephen. "Thoughts on Management Education." INDUSTRIAL RELATIONS JOURNAL 2 (Winter 1971): 34-62. Table, bibliography.

> Black summarizes the growth of management education in Britain and considers its effectiveness.

724 British Institute of Management. MANAGEMENT DEVELOPMENT AND TRAINING: A SURVEY OF SCHEMES USED BY 278 COMPANIES. Information Summary, no. 144. London: 1969. 20 p. Tables. Paperback.

725 THE DIRECTORY OF MANAGEMENT EDUCATION 1974. London: Careers Consultants, 20 Foubert Place, W1V 1HH, 1974. 237 p. Hardcover and paperback.

> This guide to postexperience courses is organized by academic institutions, professional associations, and industrial training boards.

726 Leggatt, T.W. THE TRAINING OF BRITISH MANAGERS: A STUDY OF NEED AND DEMAND. London: H.M. Stationery Office, 1972. 209 p. Tables. Paperback.

> Written for the Institute of Manpower Studies, this report sets out the views of employers, managers, and the industrial training boards on the present state of management training and future requirements.

727 MANAGEMENT EDUCATION YEARBOOK 1975-76. Epping, Essex, Eng.: Gower Press, 1975. 288 p.

> This is the first edition of a planned annual series providing a comprehensive review of management education resources and opportunities in Britain.

728 Mant, Alistair. THE EXPERIENCED MANAGER: A MAJOR RESOURCE. London: British Institute of Management, 1969. 48 p. Tables, bibliography. Paperback.

> British management education as it relates to experienced managers is examined. The contents are derived from meetings, interviews, correspondence, and questionnaires.

729 Rose, Harold B.; with Clark, D.G.; and Newbigging, E. MANAGEMENT EDUCATION IN THE 1970'S: GROWTH AND ISSUES. For the Management Education Training and Development Committee of the National Economic Development Office. London: H.M. Stationery Office, 1970. xii, 160 p. Forms, tables. Paperback.

> Rose surveys management education in the United Kingdom.

730   Wheatcroft, Mildred. THE REVOLUTION IN BRITISH MANAGEMENT
       EDUCATION. London: Pitman, 1970. xiv, 158 p. Tables.

       This is a stimulating survey of the development of management
       education in Britain.

EVALUATION OF MANAGEMENT DEVELOPMENT AND TRAINING PROGRAMS

731   Catalanello, Ralph F., and Kirkpatrick, Donald L. "Evaluating Training
       Programs: The State of the Art." TRAINING AND DEVELOPMENT
       JOURNAL 22 (May 1968): 2-9. Tables.

       Training programs in 154 companies are discussed and evaluated.
       The authors conclude that such evaluation was in its infancy
       in 1968.

732   Denova, Charles C. "Is This Any Way to Evaluate a Training Activity?
       You Bet It Is." PERSONNEL JOURNAL 47 (July 1968): 488-93.

       Denova suggests different types of tests to evaluate training
       programs, particularly with regard to employee behavior and
       achievement of organizational goals.

733   Dubin, Samuel S.; Mezack, M.; and Neidig, R. "Improving the Evalua-
       tion of Management Development Programs via a Training Design System."
       TRAINING AND DEVELOPMENT JOURNAL 28 (June 1974): 42-46.
       Diagram, table, bibliography.

       The authors review studies between 1971 and 1973 with a sug-
       gested design system for management development programs and
       their evaluation.

734   Hand, Herbert H. "The Mystery of Executive Education: Effectiveness
       Requires Evaluation." BUSINESS HORIZONS 14 (June 1971): 35-38.
       Diagram.

       Stresses the importance of evaluating executive development
       programs and suggests an approach to evaluation with experi-
       mental results.

735   House, Robert J. "Managerial Reactions to Two Methods of Management
       Training." PERSONNEL PSYCHOLOGY 18 (1965): 311-19. Tables,
       bibliography.

       House discusses a study of the reactions of forty-three managers
       to leader-centered and student-centered methods of training in
       a four-week management development program. The results
       showed no clear superiority of either method in gaining partici-
       pants' enthusiasm or holding their attention.

736 House, Robert J., and Tosi, Henry L. "An Experimental Evaluation of a Management Training Program." ACADEMY OF MANAGEMENT JOURNAL 6 (December 1963): 303-15. Diagrams, tables.

> The authors report on a study designed to test the importance of "climate" and pretraining on a training program's results, with analysis of data for twenty-four trained and thirty-three untrained personnel.

737 Jerkedal, Ake. TOP MANAGEMENT EDUCATION: AN EVALUATION STUDY. Stockholm: Personaladministrativa Radet [Swedish Council for Personnel Administration], Sturegaten 58, Box 5157, Stockholm 5, Sweden, 1967. 237 p. Diagrams, tables, bibliography.

> The author evaluates external courses in terms of such criteria as content, teaching methods, applicability to job requirements. He suggests that management training should concentrate on objectives and evaluation rather than instruction. No index.

738 Kohn, Vera. AN ASSESSMENT OF PARTICIPANTS' REACTIONS TO MANAGEMENT DEVELOPMENT MEETINGS. New York: American Foundation for Management Research, 1968. 67 p.

> Kohn discusses the views of 1,000 participants at each of two types of American Management Association meetings--a workshop seminar, emphasizing discussion, and an orientation seminar, emphasizing lectures.

739 _____, comp. A SELECTED BIBLIOGRAPHY ON EVALUATION OF MANAGEMENT TRAINING AND DEVELOPMENT PROGRAMS. New York: American Foundation for Management Research, 1969. 24 leaves. Paperback.

740 Kohn, Vera, and Parker, Treadway C. MANAGEMENT DEVELOPMENT AND PROGRAM EVALUATION: PARTNERS IN PROMOTING MANAGERIAL EFFECTIVENESS. New York: American Foundation for Management Research, 1969. 124 p. Diagrams, tables, bibliography. Paperback.

> The authors study the impact of a course in the principles of management on participants from a large company, summarizing the views of thirty-seven participants in American Management Association four-week management courses. No index.

741 _____. "Some Guidelines for Evaluating Management Development Seminars." TRAINING AND DEVELOPMENT JOURNAL 22 (July 1969): 18-23. Diagrams, bibliography.

> The authors report on the methodology of two evaluation studies of American Management Association seminars, illustrating the use of various measuring devices and analytical techniques.

742 Mansfield, R. "A Case Study in the Evaluation of Management Education." MANAGEMENT EDUCATION AND DEVELOPMENT 5 (April 1974): 7-16. Table, bibliography.

> Described is an evaluation study carried out at the London Graduate School of Business Studies, in which the criteria were attitude change, development of self-confidence, and subjective assessment by students.

743 Moffie, Dannie J.; Calhoon, Richard; and O'Brien, James K. "Evaluation of a Management Development Program." PERSONNEL PSYCHOLOGY 17 (1964): 431-40.

> The study outlined in this article was designed to evaluate a training course in problem solving and decision making given to three levels of management at a large paper mill.

744 Schwarz, Fred C.; Stilwell, William P.; and Scanlan, Burt K. "Effects of Management Development on Manager Behavior and Subordinate Perception." TRAINING AND DEVELOPMENT JOURNAL 22 (April 1968): 38-40, 42-44, 46-48, 50; and 22 (May 1968): 24-26, 27-30. Tables, bibliography.

> The authors describe a research project designed to assess the impact of a series of management development seminars at a large insurance company on the behavior of fifty-seven participants and to identify subordinates' reactions to any changes that did occur.

745 Tracey, William R. EVALUATING TRAINING AND DEVELOPMENT SYSTEMS. New York: American Management Association, 1968. 304 p. Tables.

> This is a comprehensive guide to the philosophy, principles, and methodology of evaluation.

746 Warr, Peter B.; Bird, Michael; and Rackman, Neil. EVALUATION OF MANAGEMENT TRAINING: A PRACTICAL FRAMEWORK, WITH CASES, FOR EVALUATING TRAINING NEEDS AND RESULTS. Gower Press Special Studies. London: Gower Press, 1971. 111 p. Diagrams, tables. (Distributed by Cahners Publishing Co., Boston.)

747 Whitelaw, Matt. THE EVALUATION OF MANAGEMENT TRAINING: A REVIEW. London: Institute of Personnel Management, 1972. 63 p. Diagrams, tables, bibliography. Paperback.

> Whitelaw reviews methods developed so far for evaluating management training, based on an extensive study of the literature, with recommendations and conclusions.

748 Williams, R., and Berger, M. "The Evaluation of Management Develop-

ment: Its Possible Relevance to a Levy/Grant System." MANAGEMENT EDUCATION AND DEVELOPMENT 3 (May 1972): 37-48. Tables, bibliography.

> The authors describe research being carried out to evaluate management development, based on three major stages identified in the Mant Report (item 728): the precourse climate, the learning experience in the course, and the subsequent performance on the job.

EXECUTIVE CAREER PLANNING

749 Lorsch, Jay W., and Barnes, Louis B., eds. MANAGERS AND THEIR CAREERS: CASES AND READINGS. Irwin-Dorsey Series in Behavioral Science. Homewood, Ill.: Irwin and Dorsey Press, 1972. 278 p. Diagrams. Paperback.

> This work contains seventeen cases and eight readings arranged in three sections: managers and their career dilemmas; career dilemmas and personal development; personal development and interpersonal difficulties. It tries to show "how managers in our pluralistic multiverse cope with their career dilemmas, development, and difficulties." Index of cases but no subject index.

750 Miller, Martin R. CLIMBING THE CORPORATE PYRAMID. New York: AMACOM, 1973. 136 p.

> Miller covers such topics as handling stress, working with peers, building and keeping an image, developing an executive personality, avoiding "plateauing out" in midcareer, and patterning oneself on executives who have reached the top and stayed there.

751 Moment, David, and Fisher, Dalmar. "Managerial Career Development and the Generation Confrontation." CALIFORNIA MANAGEMENT REVIEW 15 (Spring 1973): 46-55. Bibliography.

> Current approaches to managerial career development are criticized, and the importance of planned change of role is stressed.

752 Reeves, Elton T. SO YOU WANT TO BE A MANAGER! New York: American Management Association, 1971. 262 p.

> Reeves gives practical advice for the supervisor on how to implement a development program which will help him become a candidate for promotion to middle management.

753 Scheinfeld, Aaron. GET AHEAD IN BUSINESS! New York: Hawthorn

Books, 1969. 256 p. Paperback ed. New York: Universal Publishing & Distribution Corporation, 1970.

This advice by the chairman of Manpower Inc. on how to reach the top stresses communication and the stimulation of creative powers.

754 Schoonmaker, A. EXECUTIVE CAREER STRATEGY. New York: American Management Association, 1972. 214 p. Forms.

Practical advice on analyzing and implementing career goals is given.

MANAGERIAL JOBS: CLASSIFICATION AND DESCRIPTION

It is important for the manager to know exactly what the responsibilities of his job are. Apart from other considerations, the success which he achieves in carrying out these responsibilities and the value placed on the jobs he holds will be major factors in determining the executive's salary.

755 Bennet, C.L. DEFINING THE MANAGER'S JOB: THE AMA MANUAL OF POSITION DESCRIPTIONS. AMA Research Study, no. 33. New York: American Management Association, 1958. 447 p. Tables.

This work is based on a survey of practices in 140 companies. Part one consists of a description of these practices with advice on establishing a job description plan and preparing descriptions. Part two contains more than 150 job descriptions. Indexes by positions and company.

756 Evans, Gordon H. MANAGERIAL JOB DESCRIPTIONS IN MANUFAC-TURING. AMA Research Study, no. 65. New York: American Management Association, 1964. 366 p. Tables.

Evans includes 120 job descriptions used for managerial and supervisory positions from twenty named companies and others. Indexes by job and company.

757 Hemphill, John K. DIMENSIONS OF EXECUTIVE POSITIONS: A STUDY OF THE POSITIONS OF NINETY-THREE BUSINESS EXECUTIVES. Monograph no. 98. Columbus: Ohio State University College of Commerce and Administration, Bureau of Business Research, 1960. xiv, 103 p. Forms, tables.

758 Sauer, Robert L. "Measuring Relative Worth of Managerial Positions." COMPENSATION REVIEW 4 (First Quarter 1972): 9-18. Diagrams, tables.

Sauer surveys the use of formal evaluation of managerial posts. He examines problems in the application of traditional job clas-

sification systems to executive posts and introduces a new
technique called the Factor Analysis Chart Technique.

759   Stewart, Rosemary. "A Behavioural Classification of Managerial Jobs."
      OMEGA 1 (1973): 297-303. Bibliography.

      Stewart describes the aims, hypotheses, and first stage of a re-
      search project which seeks to compare the behavioral char-
      acteristics of managerial jobs and to develop a topology on
      this basis.

EXECUTIVE COMPENSATION

How are executives paid and rewarded for the work which they do?

760   Andrews, Robert, ed. MANAGERIAL COMPENSATION. Ann Arbor,
      Mich.: Foundation for Research on Human Behavior, 1965. 65 p. Dia-
      grams, tables. Paperback.

      Seven papers given at a seminar in 1964 are included.

761   Bivens, Karen Kraus, and Greene, James. COMPENSATION OF OVER-
      SEAS MANAGERS: TRENDS AND GUIDELINES: A REVIEW. Managing
      International Business, no. 5. New York: National Industrial Conference
      Board, 1969. 62 p. Paperback.

      The authors discuss a survey of 104 executives.

762   Carvalho, Gerard F. "Executive Salary Compression." PERSONNEL AD-
      MINISTRATION AND PUBLIC PERSONNEL REVIEW 1 (July-August 1972):
      16-24. Diagram, tables.

      The author examines published opinion that the absence of
      adequate salary differential between management and executive
      grades is a cause of executive stress. He then suggests solu-
      tions.

763   Crystal, Graef F. COMPENSATING U.S. EXECUTIVES ABROAD. Man-
      agement Briefing. New York: American Management Association, 1972.
      50 p. Tables. Paperback.

      This summary of current practice is based on an analysis of the
      expatriate policies of twenty-eight companies, interviews with
      the corporate compensation directors of seventeen of these com-
      panies, and interviews with thirty-two expatriate executives
      employed by one of the twenty-eight companies in London,
      Brussels, Paris, Geneva, Zurich, or Rome.

764   _____. FINANCIAL MOTIVATION FOR EXECUTIVES. New York:

American Management Association, 1970. 255 p.

Crystal examines the theories of behavioral scientists against the practical aspects of executive compensation. Chapters cover a philosophy of executive compensation, executive position evaluation, executive performance appraisal, payment for performance, the executive bonus, deferred compensation, and stock options.

765 _____. "Paying U.S. Executives Abroad: The Role of Premiums." COMPENSATION REVIEW 3 (Third Quarter 1971): 26-33.

Crystal discusses the use of foreign service premiums--additions to salary used as an inducement to accept overseas assignments --and gives results of a survey of practices in twenty-eight companies.

766 Fox, Harland. TOP EXECUTIVE COMPENSATION. 1974 ed. Conference Board Report, n.s., no. 640. New York: Conference Board, 1974. 64 p. Diagrams, tables. Paperback.

Fox analyzes the compensation in 1973 of the three highest-paid executives in 1,294 corporations, including bonus awards, stock options, and other extra-compensation plans.

767 Golightly, Henry O., and White, William L. "Pros and Cons of Tailor-Made Executive Compensation." COMPENSATION REVIEW 4 (Fourth Quarter 1972): 27-35.

The authors explore the advantages and disadvantages of individualized executive compensation programs and note the drawbacks of traditional policies.

768 Husband, T.M. "Developing a General Model of Executive Pay." COMPENSATION REVIEW 4 (Second Quarter 1972): 8-14. Diagrams, table.

The author claims that, in spite of the many variables for determining executive pay, it is possible to develop a general model. He presents such a model which can be refined to allow for type of management function, management ideology, number of employees, and other factors.

769 McBeath, Gordon. MANAGEMENT REMUNERATION POLICY. London: Business Books, 1969. 189 p. Diagrams, tables. (Distributed by International Publications Service, New York.)

The psychological and economic factors affecting management remuneration policy are studied. Included are sections on motivation and capacity, market value theory, grading, position guides and objectives, performance appraisal, bonus plans, taxation, and fringe benefits.

770 Moore, Russell F., ed. COMPENSATING EXECUTIVE WORTH. New York: American Management Association, 1968. 280 p. Diagrams, tables. Paperback.

> These thirteen papers on all aspects of executive compensation cover incentives, stock options, deferred compensation, legal problems, and problems of international executive compensation.

771 Patton, Arch. MEN, MONEY AND MOTIVATION: EXECUTIVE COMPENSATION AS AN INSTRUMENT OF LEADERSHIP. New York: McGraw-Hill, 1961. 233 p. Diagrams, tables.

> Patton draws on national surveys of compensation to discuss the theory and administration of compensation structures and the value of incentives, fringe benefits, and performance appraisal. He emphasizes the importance of promotion as the greatest incentive. No index.

772 Salter, Malcolm S. "What Is 'Fair Pay'?" HARVARD BUSINESS REVIEW 50 (May–June 1972): 6–8, 10, 12–13, 144, 146.

> Salter writes that executive compensation should not only be equitable but should be seen as equitable by employees and managers. He reviews three theoretical approaches to equity.

773 Wallace, Marc J., Jr. "Executive Compensation: Two Determinants." COMPENSATION REVIEW 5 (Fourth Quarter 1973): 18–23. Tables.

> The relative importance of firm size and profitability as factors influencing the bases for executive compensation are considered in this review of research.

INCENTIVES FOR EXECUTIVES

To what extent should executives be given payments over and above a basic salary, such as sharing in the company's profits or the option to purchase company stock or shares at a special rate?

774 Burdon, S.W.R. SHARE INCENTIVE SCHEMES FOR EXECUTIVES: A SURVEY OF CURRENT PRACTICES. Management Survey Report, no. 6. London: British Institute of Management, 1971. 40 p. Diagrams, tables, bibliography. Paperback.

> Burdon covers practices in 173 companies.

775 Foote, George H. "Performance Shares Revitalize Executive Stock Plans." HARVARD BUSINESS REVIEW 51 (November–December 1973): 121–30. Diagrams, tables.

> Foote describes an alternative to stock option plans for long-

term executive compensation--a share plan linked with company profit performance.

776   Fox, Harland. QUALIFIED STOCK OPTIONS FOR EXECUTIVES. Conference Board Report, n.s., no. 505. New York: Conference Board, 1970. 48 p. Tables. Paperback.

Fox examines company schemes and gives details of 1964 tax changes, executives eligible, size and restrictions of options, and the retention of purchased shares.

777   Harvard Business School Association. Annual National Business Conference, 31st, 1961. INCENTIVES FOR EXECUTIVES. Edited by David W. Ewing and Dan H. Fenn, Jr. New York: McGraw-Hill, 1962. 224 p.

Ten papers discuss stock options, business ethics and incentives, mergers and incentives, incentives for Soviet managers, and a case study of incentives at Texas Instruments Inc.

778   Merrett, A.J., and White, M.R.M. INCENTIVE PAYMENT SYSTEMS FOR MANAGERS. Epping, Eng.: Gower Press, 1968. xiii, 209 p. Diagrams, tables.

This critical review of practices in Britain also includes eight case studies.

779   Patton, Arch. "Why Incentive Plans Fail." HARVARD BUSINESS REVIEW 50 (May-June 1972): 58-66.

Patton suggests three reasons for the failure of many executive incentive plans: poor mathematics, administrative flaws, and industry characteristics.

780   Shwayder, Keith R.; Carr, Julian L.; and Schmieder, Frank J. "Financial Considerations of an Executive Incentive Compensation Program." FINANCIAL EXECUTIVE 39 (September 1971): 18-26. Diagrams.

The authors explain the contribution which the financial executive should make to an executive compensation plan if it is to be successful.

781   Smyth, Richard C. FINANCIAL INCENTIVES FOR MANAGEMENT. New York: McGraw-Hill, 1960. 309 p. Diagrams, forms, table.

A comprehensive text with five case studies, this work includes specimen incentive bonus plans, stock option plans, and stock purchase plans.

782   Striker, Allan M., and Carr, Julian L. "Executive Incentive Compensation." MANAGEMENT ADVISER 9 (September-October 1972): 21-28. Diagram, tables, bibliography.

Suggestions are offered for developing an executive incentive plan to motivate, improve the quality of planning, and (by relating incentives to return on investment) more effectively use assets.

783 Wilson, Sidney R. "The Incentive Approach to Executive Development." BUSINESS HORIZONS 15 (April 1972): 15-24.

Wilson outlines an incentive program that makes it possible to influence results by managing systematically factors which shape executive performance. He suggests that executives respond to incentives in the same way that machinists and salesmen do.

784 _____. "Motivating Managers with Money: How to Assess and Reward Performance." BUSINESS HORIZONS 16 (April 1973): 37-43. Tables.

Wilson suggests a method of linking management performance with rewards and gives examples of performance criteria and their relationship to annual salary value to arrive at a "performance base salary."

APPRAISAL OF MANAGERS

What criteria exist for assessing an executive's performance and helping him to improve it?

785 Enell, John W., and Haas, George H. SETTING STANDARDS FOR EXECUTIVE PERFORMANCE. AMA Research Study. New York: American Management Association, 1960. 120 p. Paperback.

This review of company practices contains case studies, including Snap On Tools Corporation, National Bank of Detroit, American Enka Corporation, Ethyl Corporation, and Canadian National Railways.

786 Heyel, Carl. APPRAISING EXECUTIVE PERFORMANCE. New York: American Management Association, 1958. 189 p. Tables.

Heyel outlines methods of executive appraisal, with case studies of General Electric Company (Missile and Ordnance Systems Department), Detroit Edison Company, Atlantic Refining Company, and New York Central System. It is a useful work, though obviously dated now. No index.

787 Howard, Ann. "An Assessment of Assessment Centers." ACADEMY OF MANAGEMENT JOURNAL 17 (March 1974): 115-34. Tables, bibliography.

Howard examines reliability and validity studies of assessment

centers used for the prediction of job success. She concludes
that the centers compare favorably with other methods of selecting and appraising higher level managers, but that there is
need for more research in this area.

788 Koontz, Harold. APPRAISING MANAGERS AS MANAGERS. New York:
McGraw-Hill, 1971. xii, 239 p. Diagrams, tables, bibliography.

Koontz shows how to appraise managers by measuring their
ability to plan, organize, staff, direct, and control by using
many case studies. He summarizes the pros and cons of management by objectives.

789 _____. "Making Management Appraisal Effective." CALIFORNIA MAN-
AGEMENT REVIEW 15 (Winter 1972): 46-55. Diagrams, table, bibliography.

The author includes a list of requirements for an appraisal system and examines the deficiencies of traditional systems. He
considers the value of a management by objectives approach to
appraisal.

790 Myers, John A., ed. PREDICTING MANAGERIAL SUCCESS. Ann Arbor, Mich.: Foundation for Research on Human Behavior, 1968. 173 p.
Diagrams (1 folding), forms, tables. Paperback.

The four papers contained here were given at two seminars:
"Research on the Identification of Management Potential," by
Harry Laurent; "The Administrative Use of Data for Early Iden-
tification of Management Potential," by Harry D. Kolb; "The
Sears (Sears, Roebuck & Company) Experience in the Investi-
gation, Description, and Prediction of Executive Behavior,"
by V. Jon Bentz; and "Choosing Good Managers," by Douglas
W. Bray. No index.

791 Rowland, Virgil K. EVALUATING AND IMPROVING MANAGERIAL
PERFORMANCE. New York: McGraw-Hill, 1970. xiv, 335 p.

An experienced writer, lecturer, and manager has attempted
to "pull together the management practices of many thousands
of successful managers and to classify, explain, and illustrate
these practices so that they may be used by other managers
who desire to improve their own managerial skills." The book
is in six sections: introduction (including a definition of management and comments on the effects of poor management);
major segments of a manager's job; responsibilities and authorities of the manager; standards of managerial performance;
evaluation of managerial performance; and concluding analysis.

792 Valentine, Raymond F. PERFORMANCE OBJECTIVES FOR MANAGERS.
New York: American Management Association, 1966. 208 p.

This book is aimed at second-line (and higher) managers who have to create and use performance measurement programs for their subordinate managers. No index.

793   Wickert, Frederic R., and McFarland, Dalton E., eds. MEASURING EXECUTIVE EFFECTIVENESS. Administration Series. New York: Appleton-Century-Crofts, 1967. 242 p. Diagrams, tables, bibliographies.

This discussion covers modern theories of executive success, criteria for evaluating executive effectiveness, and effective executive leadership style. A prediction of executive behavior in Sears, Roebuck and Company is included.

794   Williams, M.R. PERFORMANCE APPRAISAL IN MANAGEMENT. London: Heinemann; New York: Crane, Russak & Co., 1972. xii, 180 p. Diagrams, forms, tables, bibliographies.

Williams stresses the management by objectives or accountability management approach. Appendixes include a management job guide, a management performance review form, a self-appraisal exercise, analyses of the contents of 236 appraisal forms in eight companies, the Hay MSL management job description form, and an individual performance review and planning form.

MANAGERS' HOLIDAYS AND SABBATICALS

795   Birch, S. MANAGEMENT HOLIDAYS: A SURVEY OF CURRENT PRACTICE IN 200 COMPANIES. Management Survey Report, no. 11. London: British Institute of Management, 1972. 19 p. Tables. Paperback.

796   Goldston, Eli. "Executive Sabbaticals: About to Take Off?" HARVARD BUSINESS REVIEW 51 (September–October 1973): 57-68. Diagrams.

This is a survey of sabbaticals in American companies (extent, forms, pay arrangements, and service qualifications). The author recounts his experience of taking a sabbatical as a visiting fellow at the London Business School.

797   Tsaklanganos, Angelos A. "Sabbaticals for Executives." PERSONNEL JOURNAL 52 (May 1973): 363-66, 372. Bibliography.

The trend toward executive sabbaticals in the United States is reviewed.

MANAGEMENT OBSOLESCENCE AND REDUNDANCY

This is an increasingly important topic in these days of economic problems and technological change.

798   British Institute of Management. GUIDELINES FOR THE REDUNDANT
       MANAGER. London: 1972. 28 p. Tables, bibliography. Paperback.

       Advice is given on financial benefits, the problem of finding
       another job, and organizations and agencies which may be able
       to help.

799   Burack, Elmer H. "Meeting the Threat of Managerial Obsolescence."
       CALIFORNIA MANAGEMENT REVIEW 15 (Winter 1972): 83-90. Dia-
       gram, bibliography.

       Burack defines managerial obsolescence as the discrepancy be-
       tween the individual manager's expertise and the demands of
       work structures. He discusses factors affecting managers'
       adaptability to change and suggests ways of coping with obso-
       lescent situations.

800   Burger, Chester. WALKING THE EXECUTIVE PLANK: WHY MANAGE-
       MENT FIRINGS HAPPEN--AND HOW TO REDUCE THEM. New York:
       Van Nostrand Reinhold, 1972. 105 p.

       A consultant's view of reasons for executive dismissals, this
       work has many case studies. No index.

801   Connor, Samuel R., and Fielden, John S. "Rx for Managerial 'Shelf-
       Sitters.'" HARVARD BUSINESS REVIEW 51 (November-December 1973):
       113-20.

       The authors suggest that, in view of the increasing number of
       managers being passed over for promotion, companies should
       help young managers prepare for second careers in other orga-
       nizations, thus easing the corporate conscience if early retire-
       ment or demotion comes.

802   Cuddihy, Basil Robert. "How to Give Phased-Out Managers a New
       Start." HARVARD BUSINESS REVIEW 52 (July-August 1974): 61-69.
       Table.

       Described are the methods used by a Canadian company, Al-
       can Aluminum, to help 200 redundant professional and mana-
       gerial staff through the dismissal process and the finding of
       new jobs.

803   Dubin, Samuel S., ed. PROFESSIONAL OBSOLESCENCE. London:
       English Universities Press, 1971; Lexington, Mass.: Lexington Books,
       1972. 121 p. Diagrams, tables.

       These are the proceedings of a symposium held in Cambridge,
       England, in June 1970 and sponsored by the NATO Scientific

Affairs Division. The book contains twelve papers on the problem of professional and technical obsolescence (or failure to keep abreast of current developments in one's field of interest) and suggests solutions, such as reeducation and updating courses. Two of the papers are in French; the others are in English and present views from the United Kingdom, United States, Italy, and the Netherlands. No index.

804   Haas, Frederick C. EXECUTIVE OBSOLESCENCE. AMA Research Study, no. 90. New York: American Management Association, 1968. 72 p. Diagrams, forms, tables, bibliography. Paperback.

This survey of the causes of management obsolescence and methods which the company or the individual can use to overcome the problem has case studies. It includes a section on development programs in companies and academic institutions.

805   Harrison, Roger. "Towards A Strategy for Helping Redundant and Retiring Managers." MANAGEMENT EDUCATION AND DEVELOPMENT 4 (August 1973): 77-85. Bibliography.

Harrison offers a group program to minimize the stresses caused by redundancy or retirement and to help the transition to another life style.

806   Hodgson, Richard C. "Recycling the Middle-Aged Executive." BUSINESS QUARTERLY 37 (Spring 1972): 22-24, 26-27.

Hodgson examines reasons for the redundancy of middle-aged executives and shows, with the aid of a fictitious case study, how such a person can prepare for a new career.

807   Keeny, John. "Terminations: Bowing Out a Manager." PERSONNEL 48 (May-June 1971): 45-54.

Keeny emphasizes the importance of followup meetings for helping the redundant manager to find another job.

808   Kinzel, Robert. "Resolving Executives' Early Retirement Problems." PERSONNEL 51 (May-June 1974): 55-63.

Kinzel describes a vocational counseling approach to early retirement for executives.

809   Paget-Brown, Dudley. "The Complete Redundancy Guide." MANAGEMENT TODAY, February 1973, pp. 35, 38, 42, 45, 49.

Helpful advice is given for the executive faced with redundancy.

MANAGERIAL MOBILITY

How often does an executive change his job and why?

810   Birch, S., and Macmillan, B.   MANAGERS ON THE MOVE: A STUDY
      OF BRITISH MANAGERIAL MOBILITY.   Management Survey Report, no.
      7.   London: British Institute of Management, 1971. 20 p. Diagrams,
      tables, bibliography. Paperback.

      A survey carried out among 1,000 members of the British Insti-
      tute of Management indicates that a British manager changes
      his employer on average 2.7 times during his career; that 17
      percent of managers have never changed employers; and that
      nearly 20 percent of managers have changed employers five
      times or more. Factors influencing managerial mobility include
      education and type of industry.

811   British Institute of Management.   MANAGERIAL MOBILITY AND REDUN-
      DANCY. London: 1972. 31 p. Tables, bibliography. Paperback.

      This report of a BIM working party set up in 1971 gives the
      results of a survey in organizations employing, in total, half
      a million people and which have had significant experience
      of redundancy problems.

812   Jennings, Eugene Emerson.   THE MOBILE MANAGER: A STUDY OF THE
      NEW GENERATION OF TOP EXECUTIVES.   East Lansing: Michigan State
      University Graduate School of Business Administration, Bureau of Industrial
      Relations, 1967. 135 p. Tables. Paperback ed. New York: McGraw-
      Hill, 1971.

      Jennings describes the new technique of "mobilography," or
      the study of the mobility patterns of managers. He claims
      that application of the technique brings greater precision to
      managerial development and personnel selection. No index.

813   _____ .   ROUTES TO THE EXECUTIVE SUITE. New York: McGraw-Hill,
      1971. xii, 334 p.

      Jennings examines the strategies and successes of mobile execu-
      tives, arguing that the route taken to the top greatly deter-
      mines how the executive will behave. He includes many case
      studies.

814   Kimball, Patrick.   "The Journeyman Executive: The Demise of the Life-
      time Contract." BUSINESS HORIZONS 16 (April 1973): 47-52.

      Kimball traces the development of managerial mobility in the
      United States, including the benefits (to individual and organi-
      zation) and disadvantages of mobility.

MANAGERS AND SOCIETY

How do managers relate to their immediate family circle and to the environment in which they live?

815   Batten, Joe D., and Batten, Gail. THE CONFIDENCE CHASM. New York: American Management Association, 1972. 185 p. Bibliographies.

> The authors, father and daughter, claim that there is a "confidence chasm" implicit in the whole milieu of our society and that too many people underrate themselves and others. They suggest ways of overcoming this social problem in a book aimed not only at managers but at all in society who wish to make full use of their capabilities to achieve a more rewarding life. No index.

816   De Maria, Alfred T.; Tarnowieski, Dale; and Gurman, Richard.   MANAGER UNIONS? AMA Research Report. New York: American Management Association, 1972. 31 p. Diagrams, tables. Paperback.

> Summarized are the views of more than 1,000 executives on managerial unrest and discontent and attitudes towards unionization.   There was strong agreement that managerial discontent with corporate life was increasing, and there was strong support for some form of unionization.   However, the questionnaire was sent to 6,000 people, of whom only 1,108 replied.

817   Fendrock, John J.   GOALS IN CONFLICT: PERSONAL VS. BUSINESS SUCCESS.   New York: American Management Association, 1969. 239 p.

> Fendrock advises the manager on how to resolve the conflicting requirements of his family, his work, and his civic life.

818   Pahl, J.M., and Pahl, R.E.   MANAGERS AND THEIR WIVES: A STUDY OF CAREER AND FAMILY RELATIONSHIPS IN THE MIDDLE CLASS. London: Allen Lane, 1971. 326 p.   Tables, bibliography.

> This work is based on interviews with 172 men and women in different British regions and different occupations.   The authors question the assumption that the central focus of a manager's life is his career, and they point to the tension generated by the conflicting demands of work and family.   Some comparisons with the United States are included.

819   Whyte, William H., Jr.   THE ORGANIZATION MAN.   New York: Simon & Schuster, 1956; London: Cape, 1957.   429 p.   Diagrams.

> This very important work contains chapters on the ideology of organization man, the training of organization man, the neuro-

ses of organization man, the testing of organization man, the
organization scientist, the organization man in fiction, and
the organization man at home. An appendix discusses how to
cheat in personality tests. Whyte's work is based on observation
of management problems and research in Park Forest, a Chicago suburb for organization men and their families. Organization man is the middle-class, white-collar worker who staffs
executive levels in industrial, commercial, and public service
undertakings.

820 _____. "The Wives of Managers." FORTUNE 44 (October 1951): 86-
88, 204, 206-8, 210, 213.

Whyte surveys the "executive-corporation-wife" triangle from
the point of view of the wife, based on 230 interviews over
a three-month period. The article is continued from the point
of view of the corporation in "The Corporation and the Wife."
FORTUNE 44 (November 1951): 109-11, 150, 152, 155-56,
158.

EXECUTIVE HEALTH PROBLEMS

821 Kingston, N. EXECUTIVE HEALTH CARE: A SURVEY OF CURRENT
PRACTICE IN 193 COMPANIES. Management Survey Report, no. 9.
London: British Institute of Management, 1972. 20 p. Bibliography.
Paperback.

This book includes a section on the alcoholic in industry.

822 Levinson, Harry. EMOTIONAL HEALTH IN THE WORLD OF WORK.
Executive Policy and Leadership Series. New York: Harper & Row,
1964. xii, 300 p. Bibliographies.

Levinson considers psychological problems which can affect
executives, particularly in their relations with others. Topics
considered include fear and depressive reactions, suicide, with-
drawal, hostility, passive aggression, immaturity, and alcohol-
ism.

823 _____. EXECUTIVE STRESS. New York: Harper & Row, 1970. xiii,
289 p.

This collection of articles on the stresses and strains of executive life covers such topics as promotion, leadership and supervision, management of women, and social and community life.

824 McMurry, Robert N. "The Executive Neurosis." HARVARD BUSINESS
REVIEW 30 (November-December 1952): 33-47.

The author analyzes failure by executives because of forms of neurosis and gives clues for recognizing such neurosis and taking corrective action.

825 Pettigrew, Andrew. "Managing under Stress." MANAGEMENT TODAY, April 1972, pp. 99-100, 102.

Suggesting that executive stress is a neglected problem in British industry, Pettigrew discusses its causes. He then considers its diagnosis and cure, including the redesign of jobs to reduce the stress content.

826 Schoonmaker, Alan N. ANXIETY AND THE EXECUTIVE. New York: American Management Association, 1969. 285 p.

A psychologist with much experience of counseling executives gives his views on the causes and effects of anxiety and how to solve the problem.

827 Steiner, Jerome. "What Price Success?" HARVARD BUSINESS REVIEW 50 (March-April 1972): 69-74.

Steiner examines the physical ailments and personality stresses which frequently affect the top executive. He then suggests depth therapy or group experience as means for overcoming them.

BOARDS OF DIRECTORS

Having examined problems relating to executives in general, we now look at literature on specific levels of management, beginning with boards of directors. Works on specialist managers, such as production managers or personnel managers, are listed in the sections dealing with their specialization.

828 Bacon, Jeremy. CORPORATE DIRECTORSHIP PRACTICES: COMPENSA-TION. Conference Board Report, n.s., no. 596. New York: Conference Board and American Society of Corporate Secretaries, 1973. 60 p. Tables. Paperback.

This partial revision of CORPORATE DIRECTORSHIP PRACTICES (1967) deals primarily with fees and retainers for regular board service and for service on board committees, but it also includes fringe benefits, reimbursement of travel and other meeting expenses, and use of directors' and officers' liability insurance to provide protection for board members. The practices of 833 companies are reviewed.

829 _____. CORPORATE DIRECTORSHIP PRACTICES: MEMBERSHIP AND COMMITTEES OF THE BOARD. Conference Board Report, n.s., no. 588. New York: Conference Board and American Society of Corporate Secre-

taries, 1973. 73 p. Diagrams, tables. Paperback.

This companion volume to the previous item covers practices in 855 companies with regard to size of board; balance among employees, retired employees, and outside directors in membership; intervals at which directors are elected; policies on tenure and retirement; and incidence and makeup of board committees.

830   Bacon, Jeremy, and Brown, James K. CORPORATE DIRECTORSHIP PRACTICES: ROLE, SELECTION AND LEGAL STATUS OF THE BOARD. Conference Board Report, n.s., no. 646. New York: Conference Board and American Society of Corporate Secretaries, 1975. 161 p. Tables. Paperback.

A companion volume to the two previous items, this work considers such matters as responsibilities, legal and substantive, of directors; work routine of the board; relationships with managers and stockholders; functions of board committees; and exposure of directors to liability and measures to protect them from it.

831   THE BOARD OF DIRECTORS: NEW CHALLENGES, NEW DIRECTIONS. Conference Board Report, n.s., no. 547. New York: Conference Board, 1972. 73 p. Paperback.

These proceedings of a conference held in November 1971 consist of four papers dealing with pressures on today's board of directors and a discussion of the essential board function.

832   Cabot, Louis W. "Management and the Director." CONFERENCE BOARD RECORD 11 (April 1974): 50-55.

Cabot examines the immediate pressures on boards of directors, the need for collaboration rather than confrontation between management and board, the pros and cons of inside and outside directors, and the use of the board as a top-level audit committee. He includes a checklist of the demands a director should make before accepting a seat on the board.

833   Foster, Eric, and Bull, George, eds. THE DIRECTOR, HIS MONEY AND HIS JOB. London: McGraw-Hill, 1970. xv, 397 p. Illustrations, tables.

A selection of forty-nine articles from THE DIRECTOR on the work, attitudes, pay, and health and leisure activities of British directors. No index.

834   Garrett, Ray, Jr. "The SEC Study of Directors' Guidelines." CONFERENCE BOARD RECORD 11 (July 1974): 57-61.

The chairman of the Securities and Exchange Commission outlines the responsibilities of boards of directors.

835 Gibson, P.B.R. BOARDS OF DIRECTORS IN SMALL/MEDIUM SIZED PRI-
VATE COMPANIES: A SURVEY OF THE COMPOSITION OF THE BOARDS
OF DIRECTORS IN 289 COMPANIES. Information Summary, no. 149.
London: British Institute of Management, 1970. 20 p. Diagrams, tables,
bibliography. Paperback.

836 Heller, Milton F., Jr. "The Board: Legalistic Anachronism or Vital Force?"
CALIFORNIA MANAGEMENT REVIEW 14 (Spring 1972): 24-30.

Heller discusses the ineffectiveness of some boards of directors
and makes proposals for restructuring and reconstituting them.

837 Juran, Joseph M., and Louden, J. Keith. THE CORPORATE DIRECTOR.
New York: American Management Association, 1966. 400 p. Diagrams,
tables.

This comprehensive treatise on duties and functions has specimen job descriptions.

838 Koontz, Harold. THE BOARD OF DIRECTORS AND EFFECTIVE MAN-
AGEMENT. New York: McGraw-Hill, 1967. 275 p. Tables, bibliography.

This is a critical survey of the role of the board of directors
in the management hierarchy. Koontz includes examples of
position descriptions for the chairman of the board and president in Borg-Warner Corporation and Koppers Company (pp.
253-68), taken from C.L. Bennet's DEFINING THE MAN-
AGER'S JOB (item 755).

839 Lewis, Ralph F. "Choosing and Using Outside Directors." HARVARD
BUSINESS REVIEW 52 (July-August 1974): 70-78.

840 Littlefield, Edmund W. "New Realities for Corporate Directors." CON-
FERENCE BOARD RECORD 11 (July 1974): 51-54.

Littlefield offers a critical discussion of changes in company
direction and reasons for them and gives suggestions on the
constitution of boards.

841 Mace, Myles L. DIRECTORS: MYTH AND REALITY. Boston: Harvard
University Graduate School of Business Administration, Division of Research, 1971. 207 p.

The function of boards of directors are researched. No index.

842 Parker, Hugh, et al. EFFECTIVE BOARDROOM MANAGEMENT. London: British Institute of Management, 1971. 87 p. Tables. Paperback.

This is an edited version of four papers given by consultants from McKinsey and Company at a one-day forum organized by the British Institute of Management: "The Basic Role and Functions of Boards," by Hugh Parker; "Trends in U.S. Top Management Structure and Leadership Style," by Marvin Bower; "New Directions for Directors," by E. Everett Smith; and "Information Needed for Board Decision Making," by J. Roger Morrison.

843 Read, Alfred. THE COMPANY DIRECTOR: HIS FUNCTIONS, POWERS AND DUTIES. 4th ed. London: Jordan, 1971. xxxi, 231 p. Forms.

This standard British text was prepared under the auspices of the Council of the Institute of Directors. It emphasizes legal aspects, with many court cases as examples.

844 Shenfield, Barbara. COMPANY BOARDS: THEIR RESPONSIBILITIES TO SHAREHOLDERS, EMPLOYERS AND THE COMMUNITY. London: Allen & Unwin; Mystic, Conn.: Verry, Lawrence, 1971. 175 p. Tables.

This work is the product of a three-year study carried out as part of a wider program of research by Political and Economic Planning into the nature of the modern corporation. It includes case studies of participative management, security of employment in the construction industry, company giving, and government intervention.

845 Smith, E. Everett. "New Directions for Directors." McKINSEY QUARTERLY 7 (Spring 1971): 39-51.

Smith reviews trends in redefining the role of the director and suggests a portfolio of responsibilities which would enable the board to make a more significant contribution to the changing business environment.

846 Thomas, Michael, and Perry, Jane. THE BOARD OF DIRECTORS: A SURVEY OF ITS STRUCTURE, COMPOSITION AND ROLE. Management Survey Report, no. 10. London: British Institute of Management, 1972. 28 p. Tables, bibliography. Paperback.

The survey, carried out by members of the staff of Political and Economic Planning under the direction of John Pinder, covers 200 British companies.

847 Vance, Stanley C. THE CORPORATE DIRECTOR: A CRITICAL EVALUATION. Homewood, Ill.: Dow Jones-Irwin, 1968. 261 p. Diagrams, tables, bibliography.

Based on interviews with more than 200 top managers and directors, this book includes case studies of the Ford Motor Company, the E.I. Du Pont Company, Union Carbide Corporation, General Aniline & Film Corporation, Great Atlantic & Pacific Tea Company, Montgomery Ward & Company, the Hoover Company, General Dynamics Corporation, Philadelphia Contributionship & Mutual Assurance Companies, Standard Oil Company (New Jersey), and the New York Stock Exchange. Indexes of names and topics.

THE CHIEF EXECUTIVE AND TOP MANAGEMENT

848   American Management Association. ONLY A PRESIDENT. . . . New York: 1969. 319 p.

> The views of thirty-five company presidents on their responsibilities and problems are presented. The essays were originally published in THE PRESIDENT'S FORUM, a magazine distributed exclusively to members of the Presidents' Association, an affiliate of the American Management Association.

849   Argyris, Chris. "The CEO's Behavior: Key to Organizational Development." HARVARD BUSINESS REVIEW 51 (March-April 1973): 55-64. Diagram, table.

> Argyris discusses the effect which the behavior of the chief executive officer can have on the successful application of organizational development.

850   Bacon, Jeremy, and Laporte, Lowell. THE CHIEF EXECUTIVE AND HIS TENURE. Managing the Moderate Sized Company Series, no. 12. New York: Conference Board, 1969. 24 p. Tables. Paperback.

> The authors present the views of seventy-five chief executives with a median age of fifty-five. The average period served as chief executive was ten years, and the average expected tenure was seventeen years.

851   Carlson, Sune. EXECUTIVE BEHAVIOUR: A STUDY OF THE WORK LOAD AND THE WORKING METHODS OF MANAGING DIRECTORS. Stockholm: Strombergs, 1951. 122 p. Illustrations, diagrams, tables.

> This is a classic work by a professor of Business Administration in the Stockholm School of Economics on the background, social environment, and behavior patterns of top executives. It arose from the formation in 1944 of the Administrative Problems Study Group, an informal organization devoted exclusively to research and discussion of top management questions.

852   Copeman, George. THE CHIEF EXECUTIVE AND BUSINESS GROWTH: A COMPARATIVE STUDY IN THE UNITED STATES, BRITAIN AND GERMANY. London: Leviathan House, 1971. 362 p. Diagrams, tables. (Distributed by International Publications Service, New York.)

Copeman analyzes the career patterns, attitudes, and management methods of fifty-six British chief executives, thirty-one in the United States and sixteen in Germany. He tries to discover whether chief executives behave differently in different countries and, if so, whether this is a factor in differing rates of economic growth. The analysis is grouped into four broad areas: the means by which the chief executive acquired his skills; a detailed account of his methods of planning, organization, motivation, and control; personal work methods; and chief executive attitude and characteristics. A "problem-solving" index is included, but there is no alphabetical subject index.

853 Lohmann, M.R. TOP MANAGEMENT COMMITTEES: THEIR FUNCTIONS AND AUTHORITY. AMA Research Study, no. 48. New York: American Management Association, 1961. 63 p. Tables. Paperback.

This is a summary of facts gathered from ninety-three firms which maintain, between them, 319 management committees.

854 Mitchell, Don G. TOP MAN: REFLECTIONS OF A CHIEF EXECUTIVE. New York: American Management Association, 1970. 192 p.

The reflections of the vice-chairman of the Marriott Corporation, former chairman of General Time Corporation and Sylvania Electric Products Inc., former president of General Telephone and Electronics Corporation, and a board member of several companies are presented.

855 Ramsden, Pamela. TOP TEAM PLANNING: A STUDY OF THE POWER OF INDIVIDUAL MOTIVATION IN MANAGEMENT. London: Associated Business Programmes; New York: Halsted Press, 1973. 262 p. Illustration, diagrams, tables, bibliography. (Distributed in the U.K. by Cassell, London.)

Ramsden outlines a systematic way of describing the behavior of top managers both as individuals and as members of a team, based on the Action Profile method of assessment developed by Warren Lamb Associates. It includes several case studies of top team planning assignments in companies.

856 Stieglitz, Harold. THE CHIEF EXECUTIVE--AND HIS JOB. Studies in Personnel Policy, no. 214. New York: National Industrial Conference Board, 1969. 70 p. Diagrams, tables. Paperback.

Stieglitz reports on interviews with 300 executives on the organization of their job, their priorities, time allocation, pattern of delegation, and work hours. He includes thirteen specimen position guides.

857 Stieglitz, Harold, and Janger, Allen R. TOP MANAGEMENT ORGANI-

ZATION IN DIVISIONALIZED COMPANIES. Studies in Personnel Policy, no. 195. New York: National Industrial Conference Board, 1965. 198 p. Diagrams, tables. Paperback.

> Part one analyzes the nature of decentralized division; parts two to four cover the functions of chief executives and other general executives, operating executives, and staff executives. Summaries of position guides in fifty-six companies are on pp. 113-88. List of executive titles and unit designations in seventy-six divisionalized companies is on pp. 188-94.

858 Taylor, Bernard, and Macmillan, Keith, eds. TOP MANAGEMENT. London: Longman, 1973. xvi, 448 p. Diagrams, tables.

> This book contains twenty-five contributions by an international team of managers and academics on the role of top management, who are the top managers, top managers and the organization, top management's role in planning, international top management (including a chapter on top management in Japan), and wider business objectives.

ENTREPRENEURS

What are the special problems met by entrepreneurs--those who own their businesses and take their own risks as opposed to those professional managers who are paid to look after other people's businesses?

859 Dailey, Charles A. ENTREPRENEURIAL MANAGEMENT: GOING ALL OUT FOR RESULTS. New York: McGraw-Hill, 1971. xiii, 208 p. Diagrams, bibliography.

> Dailey argues that entrepreneurial management is the most essential type of management but also the least documented. He considers "managerial courage" with special reference to the stresses of entrepreneurs and how they can be put to positive benefit. He explores the impact of entrepreneurial management on the training, selection, and improvement of managerial performance.

860 Fogarty, Michael P. IRISH ENTREPRENEURS SPEAK FOR THEMSELVES. Broadsheet no. 8. Dublin 4, Ireland: Economic & Social Research Institute, 1973. 141 p. Bibliography. Paperback.

> Irish entrepreneurs discuss themselves and their work.

861 Komives, John L. "Characteristics of Entrepreneurs, with Emphasis on the Organizational Entrepreneur." BUSINESS QUARTERLY 37 (Summer 1972): 76-79. Table, bibliography.

> Komives profiles the "typical" entrepreneur.

862 Litt, B. "Why Entrepreneurs Succeed." JOURNAL OF GENERAL MAN-
AGEMENT 1 (1974): 77-93. Diagrams, tables, bibliography.

863 Lynn, Richard, ed. THE ENTREPRENEUR: EIGHT CASE STUDIES. London: Allen & Unwin, 1974. 175 p. Tables.

> The book includes case studies of Hilton Transport Services,
> Land Pyrometers, Horizon Holidays, Ryans Tourist Holdings,
> Bernard Matthews Ltd. (turkey culture), Fidelity Radio, Lotus
> Cars, and Plastic Coatings. No index.

864 Smith, Norman Raymond. THE ENTREPRENEUR AND HIS FIRM: THE
RELATIONSHIP BETWEEN TYPE OF MAN AND TYPE OF COMPANY.
East Lansing: Michigan State University Graduate School of Business Administration, Division of Research, Bureau of Business & Economic Research, 1967. 109 p. Diagrams, bibliography.

> Using data from fifty-two interviews in six Michigan cities,
> the author identifies different kinds of entrepreneurs, which he
> groups as "the constructed craftsman-entrepreneur" and "the
> constructed opportunistic-entrepreneur." He traces the life
> histories, career patterns, and characteristics of each type
> and relates them to their company.

865 Swayne, Charles B., and Tucker, William R. THE EFFECTIVE ENTRE-
PRENEUR. Morristown, N.J.: General Learning Corporation, 1973.
xv, 181 p. Diagrams, bibliographies. Paperback.

> The authors survey the alternative management styles, policies,
> and procedures available to the entrepreneur and the environ-
> ment within which he has to work.

MANAGEMENT CONSULTANTS

What are the characteristics of the people who help managers to diagnose the
faults of their organizations and advise on how they should set about curing
them?

866 Armand, Richard; Lattes, Robert; and Lesourne, Jacques. THE MAN-
AGEMENT REVOLUTION: MANAGEMENT CONSULTANCY AND COM-
PUTER-AIDED DECISION MAKING. Translated by George Ordish and
Caron Shipton. London: Macdonald, 1972. xvi, 319 p. Diagrams,
tables, bibliography. (Distributed by International Publications Service,
New York.)

> This was first published in France by Editions Denviel in 1970
> as MATIERE GRISE, ANNEE ZERO. It is an account by
> three members of the management consultancy firm Metra In-
> ternational of the development and role of consultancy in
> Europe, with particular reference to the impact of the com-

puter. "An ABC of Computers" is given as appendix 2, pp. 298-308.

867 Davidson, Frank. MANAGEMENT CONSULTANTS. London: Nelson, 1972. 138 p. Diagrams, bibliography.

This is a practical guide to the development and role of consultancy in Britain.

868 Egerton, Henry C., and Bacon, Jeremy. CONSULTANTS: SELECTION, USE AND APPRAISAL. Managing the Moderate Sized Company Series, no. 13. New York: Conference Board, 1970. 26 p. Paperback.

Included are comments from 103 companies, 70 percent of which use consultants at least occasionally.

869 Higdon, Hal. THE BUSINESS HEALERS. New York: Random House, 1969. 337 p.

Higdon examines the U.S. management consulting profession, based on six years of research.

870 Hollander, Stanley C., and Flaster, Stephen, comps. MANAGEMENT CONSULTANTS AND CLIENTS. MSU Business Studies. East Lansing: Michigan State University, Graduate School of Business Administration, Division of Research, 1972. xxii, 541 p.

This annotated list contains 1,212 books, papers, and articles, arranged systematically with author index but no subject index.

871 Hyman, Stanley. ASSOCIATIONS AND CONSULTANTS: EXTERNAL AIDS TO MANAGEMENT. London: Allen & Unwin, 1970. 309 p. Tables, bibliography.

Hyman reports results of a survey involving approximately 1,000 suppliers and users of aid and 216 organizations.

872 Tomer, John Frank. MANAGEMENT CONSULTING FOR PRIVATE ENTERPRISE: A THEORETICAL AND EMPIRICAL ANALYSIS OF THE CONTRIBUTION OF MANAGEMENT CONSULTANTS TO ECONOMIC GROWTH IN THE UNITED STATES. Ph.D. thesis, Rutgers University, New Brunswick, N.J., 1973. xiii, 424 p. Diagrams, tables, bibliography. Paperback.

Based partly on interviews with employees of thirty-two firms of management consultants, this paper includes a survey of management consulting roles, activities, types of firms, standards, and ethics. An authorized facsimile was produced by microfilm-xerography in 1974 by Xerox University Microfilms, Ann Arbor, Michigan.

873   United Nations. Industrial Development Organization. THE DEVELOP-
       MENT OF MANAGEMENT CONSULTANCY WITH SPECIAL REFERENCE
       TO LATIN AMERICA: A DIGEST OF PAPERS PRESENTED TO THE UNIDO
       MEETING HELD AT SANTIAGO, CHILE, JULY 1971. New York: Unit-
       ed Nations, 1973. 132 p. Diagrams, tables. Paperback.

       Sixteen papers discuss training personnel for management con-
       sultancy, building management consulting services in develop-
       ing countries, and management consultancy in Latin America.
       No index.

874   _____. MANUAL ON THE USE OF CONSULTANTS IN DEVELOPING
       COUNTRIES. New York: 1972. 158 p. Tables, bibliography. Paper-
       back.

       Included are several case studies, specimen contracts and fee
       scales, and excerpts from codes of ethics of the European
       Federation of Management Consultants Associations and the
       American Institute of Consulting Engineers. No index.

Directories

875   REGISTER OF MANAGEMENT CONSULTANTS AND ADVISORY SERVICES
       TO INDUSTRY IN BRITAIN. Rev. ed. Director's Bookshelf. London:
       Gower Press; New York: British Book Center, 1972. xv, 388 p. Illus-
       tration, tables.

       An alphabetical register of consultants, pp. 80-285, is pre-
       ceded by articles on the selection and use of consultants, the
       consultant's approach to problem solving, and the presentation
       and layout of a consultant's report; notes on the professional
       management consulting bodies; and a visual selector. Part
       two, pp. 286-323, contains a register of advisory services,
       which unfortunately lacks an index, although the consultancy
       firms are indexed by geographical location, expertise classifi-
       cation, size, and special industries. A bibliography would
       be useful.

876   Wasserman, Paul, and McLean, Janice, eds. CONSULTANTS AND
       CONSULTING ORGANIZATIONS DIRECTORY: A REFERENCE GUIDE
       TO CONCERNS AND INDIVIDUALS ENGAGED IN CONSULTATION FOR
       BUSINESS AND INDUSTRY. 3d ed. Detroit: Gale Research Co., 1976.
       1,034 p.

       Details of more than 5,000 firms and individuals are contained.

877   _____. WHO'S WHO IN CONSULTING: A REFERENCE GUIDE
       TO PROFESSIONAL PERSONNEL ENGAGED IN CONSULTATION FOR
       BUSINESS, INDUSTRY AND GOVERNMENT. 2d ed. Detroit: Gale
       Research Co., 1973. 1,011 p.

Organizations

878   Association of Consulting Management Engineers, 347 Madison Avenue, New York, N.Y. 10017.

> This is concerned with the maintenance of recognized standards of consultancy for the benefit of prospective clients. It acts as a clearing house for the collection and exchange of information about trends in consulting, operating problems and practices in consulting firms, and consulting organizations throughout the world.

879   Association of Management Consultants, 811 East Wisconsin Avenue, Milwaukee, Wis. 53202.

> This organization of professional management consulting firms and individual consultants was formed in 1959.

880   Management Consultants Association, 23/4 Cromwell Place, London SW7 2LG, England.

> Founded in 1956, this body is concerned with maintaining standards of ethical conduct and technical competence in management consulting.

881   Management Consulting Services Information Bureau, The British Institute of Management, Management House, Parker Street, London, WC2B 5PT, England.

> This group helps those seeking the advice of consultants in finding firms whose experience and style of operation will make them effective, using its records of more than 1,000 professional consultancy firms and individual practitioners.

882   Society of Professional Management Consultants, 205 West 89th Street, New York, N.Y. 10024.

> Founded in 1959, this organization offers a broad spectrum of management services in both the private and the public sector.

Section 6

CORPORATE PLANNING AND FORECASTING

Adequate planning is an essential prerequisite to good management. Although there are frequent needs for "one-off" plans for special projects, the planning process must be continuous if the organization is to prosper. The executive will be concerned with short-term planning for immediate action, but his greater problem will be in the evaluation and control of long-range plans for the organization's development over a number of years. A more hazardous area is that of forecasting: M.F. Elliott-Jones (item 900) has defined forecasting as "an attempt to foretell what is likely to happen" and planning as "an attempt to specify and control what will happen."

GENERAL STUDIES

883   Ackoff, Russell L. A CONCEPT OF CORPORATE PLANNING. New York: Wiley-Interscience, 1970. 158 p. Diagrams, tables, bibliography.

> Ackoff concentrates on the manager's planning needs with emphasis on "the objectives and logic of the planning process rather than the specific techniques and tools that can be used in this process." Useful annotated bibliography, pp. 146-54.

884   Andrews, Kenneth R. THE CONCEPT OF CORPORATE STRATEGY. Homewood, III.: Dow Jones-Irwin, 1971. xviii, 245 p.

> Andrews deals with the broad theme of business policy in relation to the company's environment, social responsibilities, and organizational structure and processes.

885   Ansoff, H. Igor. CORPORATE STRATEGY: AN ANALYTIC APPROACH TO BUSINESS POLICY FOR GROWTH AND EXPANSION. New York: McGraw-Hill, 1965. xiv, 241 p. Diagrams, tables, bibliography.

> This book covers the steps involved in strategy formulation

from the definition of company objectives through the structure
of business decisions to the final action plan. Indexes of
names and subjects.

886　Anthony, Robert N. PLANNING AND CONTROL SYSTEMS: A FRAME-
WORK FOR ANALYSIS. Studies in Management Control. Boston: Har-
vard University Graduate School of Business Administration, Division of
Research, 1965. xii, 180 p. Tables, bibliography.

Anthony offers a framework to guide research in the broad
area of planning and control systems. Notes on the terminology of management, by Marian V. Sears, pp. 117-29, and
of planning and control, by Mabel T. Cragg, pp. 129-56.

887　Argenti, John. CORPORATE PLANNING: A PRACTICAL GUIDE.
Studies in Management. London: Allen & Unwin, 1968; Homewood, Ill.:
Dow Jones-Irwin, 1969. 272 p. Diagrams, tables.

A practical, five-step process for corporate planning is detailed.
Glossary, pp. 264-69.

888　_____. SYSTEMATIC CORPORATE PLANNING. London: Nelson; New
York: Halsted Press, 1974. 316 p. Diagrams, tables, bibliography.

Part one outlines objectives and the need for a systematic approach in developing company strategy. Part two deals with
target setting, forecasting and planning techniques, and education and training. The book contains several case studies,
including detailed ones of an engineering company and a wine
distillery. It has been criticized for occasional lack of clarity.

889　Bacon, Jeremy. PLANNING AND FORECASTING IN THE SMALLER
COMPANY. Conference Board Report, n.s., no 524. New York: Conference Board, 1971. 30 p. Paperback.

This study is based on practices in ninety-three companies.

890　Beerschin, H.H. "Participation in Planning." LONG RANGE PLAN-
NING 6 (December 1973): 25-30. Diagrams.

Beerschin defines participative planning and control as an approach in which all levels of management are involved and
discusses its introduction in a large company.

891　Bonge, John W., and Coleman, Bruce P. CONCEPTS FOR CORPORATE
STRATEGY: READINGS IN BUSINESS POLICY. New York: Macmillan; London: Collier-Macmillan, 1972. xii, 603 p. Diagrams, tables,
bibliographies.

Forty-eight readings are presented in four sections: perspectives for strategy formulation; corporate strategy formulation; strategy implementation; and new dimensions for corporate strategy. Each section is preceded by a list of references for further study. Indexes of names and subjects.

892   Branch, Melville C. THE CORPORATE PLANNING PROCESS. New York: American Management Association, 1963. 253 p. Illustrations, diagrams, tables (1 folding).

This practical guide is based particularly on the author's seven years of experience as corporate associate for planning in a large company. No index.

893   _____. PLANNING: ASPECTS AND APPLICATIONS. New York: Wiley, 1966. 333 p. Illustrations, diagrams (2 folding), maps, bibliographies.

A survey of the context and present state of planning is followed by sections dealing with project planning for research and development, city planning, corporate planning, military planning, and suggestions for a comprehensive planning process in which the author identifies characteristics common to different forms of planning.

894   Brown, James K., and O'Connor, Rochelle. PLANNING AND THE CORPORATE PLANNING DIRECTOR. Conference Board Report, n.s., no. 627. New York: Conference Board, 1974. 94 p. Diagrams, forms, tables.

A review of the planning process and the corporate planning director's role in it, this work is based on answers to questionnaires by more than 100 chief corporate planners representing a wide variety of industries. The authors also interviewed thirty-five of the respondents and twelve planning assistants, divisional planners, planning consultants, or former heads of corporate planning. They include a case study of a new approach to planning in a diversified manufacturing company and several position descriptions.

895   Chamberlain, Neil W. THE FIRM: MICRO-ECONOMIC PLANNING AND ACTION. New York: McGraw-Hill, 1962. 428 p. Tables.

Chamberlain emphasizes budgeting as the integrating device in the planned manipulation of all the variables within a firm's control to achieve its objectives.

896   Cooper-Jones, Dennis. BUSINESS PLANNING AND FORECASTING. London: Business Books; New York: Halsted Press, 1974. xii, 265 p. Diagrams, tables, bibliography.

A practical guide to planning for lecturers, students, and

managers, this book illustrates all procedures by examples
based on a hypothetical light engineering business.

897   Dean, Joel. MANAGERIAL ECONOMICS. Englewood Cliffs, N.J.:
Prentice-Hall, 1951. xiv, 621 p. Diagrams, tables.

Dean aims to show "how economic analysis can be used in
formulating business policies." The ten chapters deal with
profits, competition, multiple products, demand analysis, cost,
advertising, basic price, product-line pricing, price differentials, and capital budgeting. Indexes of authors and subjects. Though now obviously dated, it is an important book.

898   Denning, Basil W., ed. CORPORATE PLANNING: SELECTED CON-
CEPTS. London: McGraw-Hill, 1971. 373 p. Diagrams, tables, bibliographies.

This book contains nineteen contributions on the concept of
corporate planning, strategic planning, planning tasks and
techniques, and corporate planning in different industries and
companies, together with case histories of corporate planning
systems in the IBM Corporation, International Minerals and
Chemical Corporation (IMC), and Pilkington Brothers' Ltd.
No index.

899   Egerton, Henry C., and Brown, James K. PLANNING AND THE CHIEF
EXECUTIVE. Conference Board Report, n.s., no. 571. New York: Conference Board, 1972. 62 p. Paperback.

The authors summarize the chief executive's role in the planning process, based on interviews with fifty chief executives
and twelve corporate planning officers in a variety of manufacturing and service industries.

900   Elliott-Jones, M.F. ECONOMIC FORECASTING AND CORPORATE
PLANNING. Conference Board Report, n.s., no. 585. New York: Conference Board, 1973. 75 p. Diagrams, bibliography. Paperback.

This is an economist's view of the relationship between corporate planning and economic forecasting. He considers the extent to which corporate planners can make use of economic
forecasts.

901   EUROPEAN DIRECTORY OF ECONOMIC AND CORPORATE PLANNING,
1976-77. Epping, Eng.: Gower Press, 1976. 317 p. (Distributed by
Beekman Publishers, New York.)

This directory, whose first edition was published in 1973, includes details of long-range planning units in the United Kingdom and Europe; a list of journals covering long-range planning; and information about seminars and courses on long-range

planning. A list of indexing and abstracting services would
be a useful addition.

902 Ewing, David W., ed. LONG-RANGE PLANNING FOR MANAGE-
MENT. 3d ed. New York: Harper & Row, 1972. xii, 464 p. Diagrams, tables.

The thirty-seven contributions in this work deal with corporate
planning concepts, policies, functions, goals, and the motivation for and introduction of corporate planning systems.

903 Ferrell, Robert W. MANAGING OPPORTUNITY. New York: American
Management Association, 1972. 230 p. Diagrams, tables.

A management consultant advises on early recognition of opportunities to assist in satisfactory managerial planning.

904 FOCUS THE FUTURE: INTRODUCING LONG RANGE PLANNING.
London: EMI Special Films Unit; Rockville, Md.: BNA Communications;
New York: Time-Life Video, 1971.

This twenty-four-minute 16-mm color film or videotape (Time-Life
Video) uses one imaginary and one real company to recommend
a simple framework for management in introducing long-range
planning on a formal basis. It was produced with cooperation from
the Society for Long Range Planning and with technical advice
from H.F. Robert Perrin as part of a series on management by
objectives. The series adviser is John Humble. (See also item
920.)

905 Fulmer, Robert M., and Rue, Leslie W. THE PRACTICE AND PROFIT-
ABILITY OF LONG-RANGE PLANNING. Oxford, Ohio: Planning
Executives Institute, 1973. 48 p. Diagrams. Paperback.

The authors compare the success of long-range planning applications in companies in terms of sales and earnings growth and
return on sales and capital. They suggest that planning is
still in a formative stage and has not yet yielded the returns
of which it is capable. This work is summarized in MAN-
AGERIAL PLANNING 22 (May-June 1974): 1-7. Tables,
bibliography.

906 Gerstner, Louis V., Jr. "Can Strategic Planning Pay Off?" BUSINESS
HORIZONS 15 (December 1972): 5-16. Diagram, tables.

Gerstner distinguishes strategic planning from forecasting and
suggests that much of the strategic planning in U.S. industry
may be ineffective. He stresses the need for top management
involvement in the planning process.

907 Glueck, William F. BUSINESS POLICY: STRATEGY FORMATION AND
MANAGEMENT ACTION. McGraw-Hill Series in Management. New
York: McGraw-Hill, 1972. xii, 896 p. Illustrations, diagrams, forms,
tables, bibliographies.

> Part one (pp. 3-363) consists of text and seventeen readings on
> objectives and goals in business policy, appraising the com-
> pany's status, corporate strategy, and implementing and evalu-
> ating strategy. Part two contains twenty-six detailed case
> histories. No index.

908 Hake, Bruno. HAZARDS OF GROWTH: HOW TO SUCCEED THROUGH
COMPANY PLANNING. English version by Peter Gray Lucas. Business
Strategy and Planning Series. London: Longman, 1974. 156 p. Dia-
grams, tables.

> This is a translation of WACHSTUM SINNVOLL PLANEN.
> Duesseldorf: Econ Verlag, 1971. It includes a number of case
> studies and twelve checklists. Indexes of names and products,
> but no subject index.

909 Higginson, M. Valliant. MANAGEMENT POLICIES: SOURCEBOOK OF
STATEMENTS. AMA Research Study, no. 78. New York: American
Management Association, 1966. 111 p.

> A companion volume to the entry below, this work contains fifty-
> two statements from sixteen companies.

910 _____. MANAGEMENT POLICIES: THEIR DEVELOPMENT AS COR-
PORATE GUIDES. AMA Research Study, no. 76. New York: American
Management Association, 1966. 127 p. Tables, bibliography.

> Material from more than seventy-five companies is covered.
> Indexes of subjects and company names.

911 Humble, John W., and Steiner, George A. WHAT EVERY MANAGER
NEEDS TO KNOW ABOUT LONG-RANGE PLANNING. Rockville,
Md.: BNA Communications; London: EMI Special Films Unit, 1973.

> These two thirty-minute color films are also available on a sixty-
> minute cassette.

912 Hussey, D.E. INTRODUCING CORPORATE PLANNING. Oxford, Eng.:
Pergamon Press, 1971. 210 p. Diagrams, tables, bibliography.

> Hussey provides a practical, concise guide to the introduction
> of corporate planning into an enterprise and the improvement
> of existing systems.

913 Katz, Robert L. CASES AND CONCEPTS IN CORPORATE STRATEGY.
Englewood Cliffs, N.J.: Prentice-Hall, 1970. xii, 820 p. Illustrations, tables.

Katz gives case studies of five major U.S. airlines, eight selected companies in the U.S. forest products industry, and fourteen other companies. The lack of an index is regrettable, particularly in view of errors in the contents table.

914 Learned, Edmund P.; Christensen, C. Roland; Andrews, Kenneth R.; and Guth, William D. BUSINESS POLICY: TEXT AND CASES. Rev. ed. Homewood, Ill.: Irwin, 1969. xii, 1,045 p. Illustrations, diagrams, tables.

This work is arranged in two sections: determining corporate strategy and implementing corporate strategy. Index of cases (twenty-six in all) but no subject index.

915 LONG RANGE PLANNING: INTERNATIONAL SYMPOSIUM, PARIS, 1965. New York: Gordon & Breach, 1967. xix, 531 p. Illustrations, diagrams, tables.

Contained are proceedings of a symposium sponsored jointly by UNESCO and the International Computation Center, Rome. Forty papers consider such matters as criteria for planning, organization for planning, evaluation of projects, planning for research and development and for new products, financial aspects of planning, use of network planning and similar techniques, the computer in planning, transport problems, and risk in planning. The papers are in English with French summaries, or vice versa. No index.

916 McNichols, Thomas J. POLICY MAKING AND EXECUTIVE ACTION: CASES ON BUSINESS POLICY. McGraw-Hill Series in Management. 4th ed. New York: McGraw-Hill, 1972. xvii, 978 p. Diagrams, tables.

This volume contains thirty-six cases presented in eight sections: the role of the policy maker; business as a system; the decision-making process; the strategy of acquisitions, mergers, and expansion; the implementation phase; management responsibilities and their limits; the human factor in administration; and the formulation phase. Case notes available in a separate volume, 292 p.

917 Miller, Ernest C. ADVANCED TECHNIQUES FOR STRATEGIC PLANNING. AMA Research Study, no. 104. New York: American Management Association, 1971. 174 p. Diagrams, tables, bibliography. Paperback.

This survey of applications of operations research and similar techniques to the planning process in U.S. industry is based on questionnaires received from forty companies, interviews with forty-one individuals in thirty-two companies, and a literature search. Annotated bibliography, pp. 169-74. No index.

918   Mockler, Robert J. BUSINESS PLANNING AND POLICY FORMULATION. New York: Appleton-Century-Crofts, 1972. xiii, 424 p. Illustrations, diagrams, tables, bibliography.

Mockler gives a comprehensive outline of planning and policy development systems and their applications. He includes chapters on quantitative and graphic techniques used in planning, information systems for planning, and planning for a small company. He also provides case studies of planning procedures in five companies.

919   _____. "The Theory and Practice of Planning." HARVARD BUSINESS REVIEW 48 (March-April 1970): 148-59. Bibliography.

The significant literature since 1958 is reviewed.

920   Perrin, H.F. Robert, and Long, Richard P. FOCUS THE FUTURE: AN INTRODUCTION TO LONG RANGE CORPORATE PLANNING. London: Management Publications, 1971. 109 p. Bibliography. Paperback.

This is an introduction to long-range planning, mainly in checklist form, and a guide to the film FOCUS THE FUTURE, (see also item 904). No index.

921   Rhenman, Eric. ORGANISATION THEORY FOR LONG-RANGE PLANNING. Translated by Nancy Adler. London: Wiley, 1973. xii, 208 p. Diagrams, tables, bibliography.

A Swedish professor's research into long-range planning and organizational change in more than twenty organizations is described. It was published by Albert Bonniers Forlag AB, Stockholm, 1969.

922   Rue, Leslie W. "The How and Who of Long-Range Planning." BUSINESS HORIZONS 16 (December 1973): 23-30. Diagrams, tables.

This article outlines "[a] specific, practical model for long range planning, plus empirical data gathered in a survey of U.S. industry, comparing long range planning's current state with an ideal progressive model."

923   Schaffir, Walter B. "What Have We Learned about Corporate Planning?" MANAGEMENT REVIEW 62 (August 1973): 19-26.

Schaffir considers the role and impact of planning, paying particular attention to new techniques in planning, the job of the planner, and the results to be expected from planning.

924   Scott, Brian W. LONG-RANGE PLANNING IN AMERICAN INDUSTRY. New York: American Management Association, 1965. 288 p. Forms, tables, bibliography.

This well documented survey is drawn from interviews with
executives in twelve companies and includes detailed case
studies of two divisions at the General Electric Company.

925 Society for Long Range Planning. CASE STUDIES IN CORPORATE
PLANNING. Edited by Peter Baynes. Times Management Library. London: Pitman, 1973. 187 p. Diagrams (1 folding), tables.

This book provides case studies of long-range planning in
Geigy (UK) Ltd., Irvin Great Britain Ltd., J. Bibby & Sons,
Rockware Glass Ltd., A. Wander Ltd., Astra Group, CPC
Europe, Fyffes Groups Ltd., and Simon Engineering Ltd.

926 Steiner, George A. TOP MANAGEMENT PLANNING. Studies of the
Modern Corporation. New York: Macmillan; London: Collier-Macmillan, 1969. xxiv, 795 p. Diagrams, tables, bibliography.

Believing that the major requisites for successful management
are "a first-rate planning system, charisma, and a sense of
competitive urgency," the author provides a detailed exposition of business planning, the process of developing plans,
tools for more rational planning, and planning in selected
functional areas (especially marketing, product planning, finance, diversification, and research and development). There
are indexes of authors and subjects. Retrieval of specific
items of information is also assisted by the inclusion of an
analytical contents table and synopses at the beginning of
each chapter.

927 _____, ed. MANAGERIAL LONG-RANGE PLANNING. McGraw-Hill
Series in Management. New York: McGraw-Hill, 1963. xii, 324 p.
Diagrams, tables.

This book contains twenty papers given at a two-day research
seminar conducted at the University of California, Los Angeles.
Case studies of long-range planning in eighteen organizations
are included.

928 Taylor, Bernard, and Hawkins, Kevin, eds. A HANDBOOK OF STRA-
TEGIC PLANNING. Business Strategy & Planning Series. London:
Longman, 1972. xxii, 456 p. Diagrams, tables, bibliography.

Thirty-five papers discuss formulation and development of corporate strategy, planning and the social environment, corporate
strategy and the use of resources (man management, financial
management, and the management of technology), corporate
strategy and the small firm, corporate strategy in a multinational perspective, and quantitative and analytical aids to
strategic planning. The papers were presented at conferences
at the University of Bradford Management Centre (England)
between 1967 and 1970. They are supplemented by reprints
of journal articles.

929 Uyterhoeven, Hugo E.R.; Ackerman, Robert W.; and Rosenblum, John W.
STRATEGY AND ORGANIZATION: TEXT AND CASES IN GENERAL
MANAGEMENT. Homewood, Ill.: Irwin; London: Irwin-Dorsey Inter-
national, 1973. xii, 856 p. Diagrams, tables.

> Part one deals with the general manager as strategist, includ-
> ing chapters on strategic forecasting and the research audit.
> Part two considers the general manager as organization builder.
> Index of cases, but no subject index.

Periodicals

930 LONG RANGE PLANNING. Oxford, Eng.: Pergamon Press, 1968- .
Bimonthly.

931 MANAGERIAL PLANNING. Oxford, Ohio: Planning Executives Institute, 1952- . Bimonthly.

> The former title was BUDGETING.

Bibliographies

932 Branch, Melville C., and Deacon, Amos R.L. SELECTED REFERENCES
FOR CORPORATE PLANNING: ANNOTATED, WITH A PARTIAL LIST
OF COMPANIES IN THE UNITED STATES AND CANADA WITH COR-
PORATE OR DIVISIONAL PLANNING ACTUALLY OR POTENTIALLY
COMPREHENSIVE IN NATURE. New York: American Management As-
sociation, 1966. 191 p. Paperback.

> This is a classified list of 500 books, pamphlets, and articles
> with an index of authors. On pp. 157-72 there is a list of
> 252 American and Canadian companies known to have corporate
> or divisional planning which is comprehensive or potentially
> comprehensive.

933 Daniells, Lorna M., comp. BUSINESS FORECASTING FOR THE 1970'S:
A SELECTED ANNOTATED BIBLIOGRAPHY. Reference List, no. 26.
Boston: Harvard University Graduate School of Business Administration,
Baker Library, 1970. 48 p. Paperback.

> This list of books and articles is classified under three headings:
> general forecasts; forecasts on specific subjects; and forecast-
> ing methods and long-range planning. The lists are followed
> by a list of bibliographies, periodicals dealing specifically
> with forecasting, organizations and institutes, and conferences.

934 Kettlewell, P.J. A EUROPEAN BIBLIOGRAPHY OF CORPORATE PLAN-
NING, 1961-1971. Oxford, Eng.: Pergamon Press, 1972. 22 p. Paperback. (Supplement to LONG RANGE PLANNING, June 1972).

This is a classified and annotated list of 363 items.

935 _____. "A European Bibliography of Corporate Planning, 1972." LONG RANGE PLANNING 7 (February 1974): 72-78.

This is a classified and annotated list of eighty-eight items.

936 Lightwood, Martha B., ed. PUBLIC AND BUSINESS PLANNING IN THE UNITED STATES: A BIBLIOGRAPHY. Management Information Guide, no. 26. Detroit: Gale Research Co., 1972. 314 p.

Part one (public planning) includes manpower planning. Part two (business planning) has sections on strategic planning and planning theory, managerial and organizational planning, planning business decisions, financial planning, research and development planning, planning manufacturing production, and business forecasts. Part three (planning information sources) lists general reference works, indexing and abstracting services, bibliographies, statistical sources, and associations.

937 Woy, J.B., ed. BUSINESS TRENDS AND FORECASTING: INFORMATION SOURCES. Management Information Guide, no. 9. Detroit: Gale Research Co., 1965. 152 p.

This work includes a glossary on pp. 105-34.

Organizations

938 North American Society for Corporate Planning, P.O. Box 3114, Grand Central Station, New York, N.Y. 10017.

Founded 1966 as a forum for executive and planning officers and others with a particular interest in planning the future of a business enterprise, this group seeks to emphasize the contributions which planning can make to the business enterprise.

939 Planning Executives Institute, 5500 College Corner Pike, Oxford, Ohio 45056.

This is a professional society of corporate planners, budget directors, controllers, accountants, etc., which was formed in 1951. It publishes MANAGERIAL PLANNING bimonthly.

940 Society for Long Range Planning, 8th Floor, Terminal House, Grosvenor Gardens, London, SW1W 0AR, England.

Formed in 1967 to help further the development of long range planning in Britain, this organization publishes LONG RANGE PLANNING bimonthly.

THE COMPUTER IN PLANNING

941   Benton, William K. THE USE OF THE COMPUTER IN PLANNING.
      Reading, Mass.: Addison-Wesley, 1971. 168 p. Diagrams, tables.

      Early chapters explain the nature of planning and the role and
      use of the computer. Later chapters discuss the use of the
      computer in several areas such as investment planning, simula-
      tions, and heuristic programming. Case studies are examined.

942   Higgins, J.C., and Whitaker, D. "Computer Aids to Corporate Plan-
      ning." COMPUTER BULLETIN 16 (September 1972): 434-39. Tables.

      This article describes the basic steps in the planning process
      and explains the value of the computer in considering alterna-
      tive plans. The authors examine five computer systems and
      include a comparative table which covers eleven packages.

943   Morris, E. Deigan. "Models, Computers: Why Should I Use Them in
      My Corporate Planning?" EUROPEAN BUSINESS, no. 40 (Winter/Spring
      1974), pp. 60-69. Diagrams.

      Morris analyzes the problems of integrating sales, production,
      and financial forecasts into planning processes and notes the
      value of the computer in solving problems of sales/production
      mix.

PLANNING-PROGRAMMING-BUDGETING SYSTEM (PPBS)

PPBS, or program budgeting, whereby budgets are linked to corporate plans
rather than being allocated to input headings such as staff, buildings, equipment, etc., has been widely used in the public service. It aroused a great
deal of interest in the 1960s, but in the 1970s its usefulness was questioned
(see item 957).

944   Bagley, J.G. "Planning, Programming, Budgeting in DES." O & M
      BULLETIN 27 (May 1972): 74-84. Tables, bibliography.

      The use of PPBS for planning expenditure and projects in the
      British Department of Education and Science is described.

945   Balls, Herbert R. "Planning, Programming and Budgeting in Canada."
      PUBLIC ADMINISTRATION 48 (Autumn 1970): 289-305. Bibliography.

      The use of PPBS in the Canadian government service is reviewed.

946   Bridgeman, J.M. "Planning, Programming, Budgeting Systems." O & M
      BULLETIN 24 (November 1969): 167-77. Bibliography.

      Bridgeman gives a historical introduction to PPBS.

947 Gorham, William. "Sharpening the Knife That Cuts the Public Pie."
PUBLIC ADMINISTRATION REVIEW 28 (May-June 1968): 236-41.

> Gorham provides a description of the U.S. Department of
> Health, Education, and Welfare's planning-programming-budget-
> ing system.

948 Harper, Edwin L.; Kramer, Fred A.; and Rouse, Andrew M. "Implementation and Use of PPB in Sixteen Federal Agencies." PUBLIC ADMINIS-
TRATION REVIEW 29 (November-December 1969): 623-32. Tables, bibliography.

> This article gives an account of a research study implemented
> by the U.S. Bureau of the Budget. The authors suggest that
> PPB has had limited influence on major resource allocation
> decisions in domestic agencies of the federal government,
> largely because PPB fails to give attention to political bar-
> gaining, a major feature of traditional budgeting.

949 Hinrichs, Harley H., and Taylor, Graeme M. PROGRAM BUDGETING
AND BENEFIT-COST ANALYSIS: CASES, TEXT AND READINGS. Pacific Palisades, Calif.: Goodyear, 1969. 420 p. Diagrams, tables, bibliography. Paperback.

> This book contains fifteen cases and seventeen readings grouped
> in four sections: the resource allocation framework, objectives
> criteria and output measures, program analysis, and the con-
> clusion. Annotated bibliography, pp. 379-420. No index.

950 Lyden, Fremont J., and Miller, Ernest G. PLANNING PROGRAMMING
BUDGETING: A SYSTEMS APPROACH TO MANAGEMENT. 2d ed.
Markham Political Science Series. Chicago: Markham Publishing Co.,
1972. 423 p. Diagrams, tables. Hardcover and paperback.

> The twenty-one readings are divided into eight sections: PPB
> in perspective, budgeting and the political process, the pro-
> gram planning-evaluation base of PPB, program design: PPB
> structure and information requirements, program design: ana-
> lytic techniques, relating goals to systems, implementing PPB,
> and critiques and prospects of PPB. No index.

951 Merewitz, Leonard, and Sosnick, Stephen H. THE BUDGET'S NEW
CLOTHES: A CRITIQUE OF PLANNING-PROGRAMMING-BUDGETING
AND BENEFIT-COST ANALYSIS. Markham Series in Public Policy Analysis. Chicago: Markham Publishing Co., 1971. 318 p. Diagrams,
tables. Hardcover and paperback.

> This detailed exposition and critique surveys several areas of
> public spending.

952   Novick, David. "The Origin and History of Program Budgeting." CALI-
       FORNIA MANAGEMENT REVIEW 11 (Fall 1968): 7-12. Bibliography.

       A pioneer of PPBS briefly describes its development, its early
       use in General Motors, the Weapons Systems Analysis of the
       Rand Corporation and the federal government, and its introduc-
       tion into the U.S. Department of Defense in 1961.

953   _____, ed. CURRENT PRACTICE IN PROGRAM BUDGETING (PPBS):
       ANALYSIS AND CASE STUDIES COVERING GOVERNMENT AND BUSI-
       NESS. New York: Crane, Russak & Co.; London: Heinemann, 1973.
       242 p. Diagrams.

       The twenty-six contributions in this book include case studies
       of PPBS in Australia, Austria, Belgium, Canada, the United
       Kingdom, France, Ireland, Japan, New Zealand, and the
       United States.

954   _____. PROGRAM BUDGETING: PROGRAM ANALYSIS AND THE
       FEDERAL BUDGET. 2d ed. Cambridge, Mass.: Harvard University Press,
       1967. xxiv, 382 p. Diagrams, tables.

       This was sponsored by the Rand Corporation of which the edi-
       tor is head of cost analysis. It contains twelve papers on the
       government decision-making process and the role of program
       budgeting; the evolution of program budgeting in the U.S.
       Department of Defense and its possible applications to the
       space program, transportation, education, federal health, and
       natural resources programs; and the implementation and opera-
       tion of program budgeting systems.

955   "Planning-Programming-Budgeting System Re-examined: Development,
       Analysis and Criticism." PUBLIC ADMINISTRATION REVIEW 29 (March-
       April 1969): 111-202.

       Eight papers consider the application of PPBS in American politi-
       cal and governmental life.

956   "Planning, Programming, Budgeting Systems: A Symposium." PUBLIC AD-
       MINISTRATION REVIEW 26 (December 1966): 243-310. Tables.

       Six papers on PPBS including its development; its implications
       for the federal government; its ideas, rationale, and language;
       and its possibilities for integrating the processes of planning,
       programming, budgeting, and accounting.

957   Schick, Allen. "A Death in the Bureaucracy: The Demise of Federal
       PPB." PUBLIC ADMINISTRATION REVIEW 33 (March-April 1973): 146-
       56.

       Schick provides the background to the announcement that "agen-
       cies are no longer required to submit with their budget sub-

missions the multi-year program and financing plans, program memoranda and special analytical studies . . . or the schedules . . . that reconcile information classified according to their program and appropriation structures," by which "PPB became an unthing."

958 State-Local Finances Project. PLANNING PROGRAMMING BUDGETING FOR CITY, STATE, COUNTY OBJECTIVES. 2 vols. PPB Notes 1-8. Washington, D.C.: State-Local Finances Project, George Washington University, 1968. Var. pag. Diagrams, tables. Paperback.

This is perhaps the most useful manual on PPBS. Notes 1-4 deal with organizational and staffing problems. Notes 5-8 cover the development of an objective-oriented governmental program structure, the role and nature of cost analysis in a PPB system, output measures for a multiyear program and financial plan, and details of the multiyear program and financial plan.

959 Taylor, Graeme M. PLANNING PROGRAMMING BUDGETING SYSTEM. Bradford, Eng.: University of Bradford Management Centre, 1970? 211 p. Diagrams, tables. Paperback.

These papers were prepared and assembled for the use of participants at a seminar on PPBS organized by the University of Bradford Management Centre as part of its corporate long-range planning program. It was led by the Management Analysis Center Inc. (U.S.A.). Included are papers by Allen Schick, Arthur Smithies, and Graeme M. Taylor. Case studies examine the application of PPBS in the U.S. Post Office, the Department of the Interior, the Bureau of Mines and the Bureau of National Capital Airports, and in disease control programs.

FUTURE STUDIES: FORECASTING

960 Benton, William K. FORECASTING FOR MANAGEMENT. Reading, Mass.: Addison-Wesley, 1972. 209 p. Diagrams, tables, bibliography.

This work, intended for the reader with a minimum knowledge of mathematics, includes several case studies.

961 Bright, James R., ed. TECHNOLOGICAL FORECASTING FOR INDUSTRY AND GOVERNMENT: METHODS AND APPLICATIONS. Englewood Cliffs, N.J.: Prentice-Hall, 1968. xxi, 483 p. Illustrations, diagrams, tables, bibliographies.

The twenty-four contributions in this volume are arranged in five sections: lessons from the past, techniques of technological forecasting, integrating technological and environmental forecasting, and organizing the technological forecasting effort. A technical forecasting bibliography, partially annotated, prepared by Marvin J. Cetron, is on pp. 451-63. Bibliography of appraisal techniques for research, development, and technological planning, also prepared by Cetron, is on pp. 464-74.

962 Council of Europe. Long-Term Planning and Policy Division. LONG-TERM FORECASTING IN EUROPE. 2 vols. Strasbourg, Ger.: Council of Europe, 1970. Paperback.

This is a directory of long-term forecasting projects being carried out in Belgium, Denmark, Federal Republic of Germany, France, Italy, the Netherlands, Norway, Sweden, Switzerland, the United Kingdom, and by international organizations. Descriptions are given in French or English.

963 FUTURES: THE JOURNAL OF FORECASTING AND PLANNING. Guildford, Eng.: IPC, 1968- . Bimonthly.

This journal is published bimonthly for the Institute for the Future and contains articles on all aspects of forecasting, in all fields, with news and reports and some signed book reviews.

964 Martino, Joseph P. TECHNOLOGICAL FORECASTING FOR DECISION MAKING. Policy Sciences Book Series. New York: American Elsevier, 1972. xviii, 750 p. Diagrams, tables, bibliographies.

An introductory chapter defining technological forecasting is followed by chapters dealing with (inter alia) Delphi, forecasting by analogy, trend extrapolation, analytical models, planning and decision making, research and development planning, product development, evaluating forecasts, and the future of technological forecasting. The book is illustrated with many examples of actual forecasts, and each chapter concludes with problems and bibliographical references.

965 Thurston, Philip H. "Make TF Serve Corporate Planning." HARVARD BUSINESS REVIEW 49 (September-October 1971): 98-102. Diagrams.

Thurston discusses links between technological forecasting and corporate planning and shows how the two techniques can be complementary.

966 Wills, Gordon; Ashton, David; and Taylor, Bernard, eds. TECHNOLOGICAL FORECASTING AND CORPORATE STRATEGY. London: Crosby Lockwood; New York: American Elsevier, 1969. xviii, 273 p. Illustrations, diagrams, tables, bibliographies.

Contributions by nineteen experts are arranged in two parts. Part one includes chapters on general aspects of technological forecasting. Part two considers the future for forecasting in the fields of polymers, metals, energy, transport and distribution, communications, computer systems, and food. A final chapter presents four case studies of technological forecasting techniques in British industry.

THE DELPHI TECHNIQUE

Delphi is a technique developed in the 1960s by Olaf Helmer, a mathematician with the Rand Corporation, for establishing a consensus of expert opinion about the future by pooling individual opinions in the hope of developing accurate forecasts. Its features include anonymous responses, repeated rounds of questionnaires, and systematic statistical processing of replies. See also item 1639.

967 Dalkley, Norman C. THE DELPHI METHOD: AN EXPERIMENTAL STUDY OF GROUP OPINION. Report no. RM-5888-PR. Santa Monica, Calif.: Rand Corp., 1969. 79 p. Diagrams, tables, bibliography. Paperback.

This is a report on the effectiveness of Delphi for formulating group judgments, based on ten experiments involving fourteen groups ranging in size from eleven to thirty members.

968 Derian, Jean-Claude, and Morize, Francoise. "Delphi in the Assessment of Research and Development Projects." FUTURES 5 (October 1973): 469-83. Diagrams, bibliography.

The authors conclude that Delphi is particularly useful for highly controversial or multiple dimension subjects, i.e., subjects with consequences which are not only technological but also economic, sociological, or medical. This, the authors suggest, makes it indispensable for the technological assessment of R and D projects.

969 Fusfield, Alan R., and Foster, Richard N. "The Delphi Technique: Survey and Comment." BUSINESS HORIZONS 14 (June 1971): 63-74. Diagrams, tables.

This article describes the Delphi technique, offers suggestions for its use in corporate forecasting, and provides four brief case studies.

970 Lachmann, Ole. "Personnel Administration in 1980: A Delphi Study." LONG RANGE PLANNING 5 (June 1972): 21-31. Diagrams, bibliography.

Described is the use of Delphi by the Management Training Division of the Danish Institute for Graduate Engineers for forecasting trends in the personnel field over the next decade. The author briefly discusses the adequacy of Delphi as a tool for defining planning objectives.

971   Nanus, Burt, and Adelman, Harvey M. "Work and Leisure, 1980."
       BUSINESS HORIZONS 14 (August 1971): 5-10. Tables.

       The authors discuss research, obtained by using a modification
       of Delphi, into the probable patterns of work and leisure in
       the 1980s. They tabulate the findings in terms of composition
       and location of the labor force; patterns of work, leisure,
       and education; federal manpower policies; and objectives in
       the total manpower system.

972   Pyke, Donald L. "A Practical Approach to Delphi." FUTURES 2 (June
       1970): 143-52. Diagrams, table.

       The use of Delphi in the Technical Liaison and Forecasting
       Group of TRW Inc. is examined.

973   Wills, Gordon. "The Preparation and Deployment of Technological Fore-
       casts." LONG RANGE PLANNING 2 (March 1970): 44-54. Diagrams,
       forms, tables.

       Wills stresses the importance of technological forecasting, in-
       cluding Delphi, and provides advice on its implementation.
       He includes an example of a Delphi questionnaire.

MANAGERIAL ACTIVITIES

Having decided upon its plans and set them in motion, managers must engage in a number of activities to ensure that these plans are executed satisfactorily. THE LONDON CLASSIFICATION OF BUSINESS STUDIES isolates various managerial activities, including control, delegation of authority, decision making, appraisal, and goal setting (including management by objectives).

MANAGEMENT CONTROL

The activities of planning and control are closely related. The control mechanism is the process by which managers ensure that an organization's resources are used effectively to accomplish the agreed objectives. In addition to control of specific functions (financial control, budgetary control, production control, etc.), it is also important to have an integrated control system as Mockler points out (item 979).

974 Anthony, Robert N.; Dearden, John; and Vancil, Richard F. MANAGEMENT CONTROL SYSTEMS: TEXT, CASES AND READINGS. Rev. ed. Willard J. Graham Series in Accounting. Homewood, Ill.: Irwin, 1972. xii, 857 p. Diagrams, forms, tables, bibliography.

This comprehensive review includes sixty-three cases and nine readings.

975 De Paula, F. Clive, and Willsmore, A.Q. THE TECHNIQUES OF BUSINESS CONTROL. London: Pitman, 1973. xiv, 110 p. Diagrams (1 folding), bibliography. Hardcover and paperback.

This glossary of techniques used in business control is arranged by functional area with cross-references where necessary.

976 Dew, R. Beresford, and Gee, Kenneth P. MANAGEMENT CONTROL AND INFORMATION: STUDIES IN THE USE OF CONTROL INFORMATION BY MIDDLE MANAGEMENT IN MANUFACTURING COMPANIES. London: Macmillan; New York: Halsted Press, 1973. 120 p. Diagrams, tables, bibliography.

These suggestions on how middle managers can make more effective use of the information provided to assist them in exer-
cising control are based on interviews with 279 managers. No
index.

977 Eilon, Samuel. MANAGEMENT CONTROL. Studies in Management.
London: Macmillan, 1971; New York: Wiley, 1972. 207 p. Diagrams,
tables, bibliographies.

Eilon identifies the management task as a control system and
shows how to provide effective control through management
information systems.

978 Jones, Reginald L., and Trentin, H. George. MANAGEMENT CON-
TROLS FOR PROFESSIONAL FIRMS. New York: American Management
Association, 1968. 207 p. Diagrams, tables.

Practical techniques are offered to help professionals define
the structure of their organization and tighten managerial controls.

979 Mockler, Robert J. THE MANAGEMENT CONTROL PROCESS. New
York: Appleton-Century-Crofts, 1972. xv, 357 p. Illustrations, diagrams, tables, bibliography.

Mockler defines management control as "an integrated scientific discipline, which encompasses all control activities within
a company (including financial control) and which has its own
systematically organized set of principles and processes to guide
the manager in handling all types of business control situations."
He pays special attention to the nonfinancial and accounting
aspects of control and includes chapters on the use of graphic
and mathematical tools and data processing techniques in control systems.

980 _____, ed. READINGS IN MANAGEMENT CONTROL. New York:
Appleton-Century-Crofts, 1970. 532 p. Diagrams, tables. Paperback.

This book contains thirty-nine readings grouped in three sections: the nature of management control; management control
tools and techniques; and applications of management control
principles and techniques to marketing, manufacturing, organizing, finance, and accounting.

981 Rose, T.G. HIGHER CONTROL IN MANAGEMENT. 7th ed. London:
Pitman, 1967. 281 p. Diagrams, tables (3 folding).

This is the standard British work on "the higher control method
of presenting the facts and figures of undertakings of all types
as a guide to their general management." The first edition
was published in 1934.

982 Vardaman, George T., and Halterman, Carroll C. MANAGERIAL CONTROL THROUGH COMMUNICATION: SYSTEMS FOR ORGANIZATIONAL DIAGNOSIS AND DESIGN. Wiley Series in Human Communication. New York: Wiley, 1968. xii, 496 p. Diagrams, tables.

   The authors attempt to provide middle managers and troubleshooting management consultants with a new model of managerial activity built on an integration of three elements: communication, the manager, and the control dimension. A text of 142 pages is followed by twenty-eight readings on communication, control, and the organization. Indexes of authors and subjects.

DELEGATION OF AUTHORITY

Knowing how, what, and when to delegate to his subordinates is an important part of the manager's job.

983 Bittel, Lester R. MANAGEMENT BY EXCEPTION: SYSTEMATIZING AND SIMPLIFYING THE MANAGERIAL JOB. New York: McGraw-Hill, 1964. xiv, 320 p. Diagrams, tables, bibliography.

   The author believes that management by exception, where only exceptional issues are referred to management and others are dealt with according to precise instructions or general principles in accordance with the organization's objectives, is "the foundation upon which most modern management practices are based." He notes that "without a clear understanding of its principles, most executives will have difficulty in planning wisely or in acting or controlling effectively."

984 Borgerding, Charles W., Jr. "Delegate! Delegate!" PERSONNEL JOURNAL 51 (May 1972): 327-29, 363.

   The author summarizes the dos and don'ts of delegation.

985 Bursk, Edward C., ed. THE MANAGEMENT TEAM. Cambridge, Mass.: Harvard University Press, 1954. 221 p.

   This book contains eleven papers on aspects of delegation and control, based on the proceedings of the 24th National Business Conference, sponsored by the Harvard Business School Association, 12 June 1954. No index.

986 Forrest, Andrew. DELEGATION. Rev. ed. Notes for Managers, no. 19. London: Industrial Society, 1972. 24 p. Tables, bibliography. Paperback.

   This useful, brief guide has a list of further reading and films.

987 Laird, Donald A., and Laird, Eleanor C. THE TECHNIQUES OF DELE-
GATING: HOW TO GET THINGS DONE THROUGH OTHERS. New
York: McGraw-Hill, 1957. 195 p. Diagrams, tables, bibliography.

This work includes many case studies, self-analysis tests,
quizzes, etc., as well as advice on how not to delegate and
to whom not to delegate.

988 McConkey, Dale D. HOW TO MANAGE BY RESULTS. Rev. ed. New
York: American Management Association, 1967. 160 p. Illustrations,
diagrams.

Management by results is defined as "an approach to management planning and evaluation in which specific targets for a
year, or for some other length of time, are established for
each manager on the basis of the results which each must
achieve if the overall objectives of the company are to be real-
ized. At the end of this period, the actual results achieved
are measured against the original goals--that is, against
the expected results which each manager knows he is responsible for achieving." The author includes case studies of Mon-
santo Company (Plastic Products & Resins Division), United Air
Lines, State Farm Insurance Companies, and a large brewing
company. No index.

989 PRACTICING THE ART OF DELEGATION. New York: American Management Association, 1969? 72 p. Illustrations, tables. Paperback.

Nineteen articles reprinted from AMA journals make up this
volume.

990 Schleh, Edward C. MANAGEMENT BY RESULTS: THE DYNAMICS OF
PROFITABLE MANAGEMENT. New York: McGraw-Hill, 1961. 266 p.
Diagrams.

Schleh focuses on the results to be expected from individuals
at the "bottom level" of an enterprise through delegation,
encouragement of supervisory decision making, and development of an individual's freedom to act on his own initiative.

991 Tracey, William R. "The Empty In-Basket Trick." PERSONNEL JOUR-
NAL 52 (January 1973): 36-40.

Tracey provides a concise guide to delegation and work organization.

DECISION MAKING

Perhaps the most difficult task facing the manager is that of making the right
decision, having identified and analyzed the available alternatives. Only works

dealing in a general manner with the decision-making process are listed here; works emphasizing the mathematical tools of decision making are listed in section 8.

992 Alexis, Marcus, and Wilson, Charles Z. ORGANIZATIONAL DECISION MAKING. Behavioral Sciences in Business Series. Englewood Cliffs, N.J.: Prentice-Hall, 1967. 447 p. Diagrams, tables.

Seven chapters consider the behavioral foundations of decision making; decision models; and planning, coordination, and control. Selected readings on the topic are appended to each chapter.

993 Amey, Lloyd R., ed. READINGS IN MANAGEMENT DECISION. Longman Business Series. London: Longman, 1973. 272 p. Diagrams, tables.

This work consists of twelve readings on the costs of decision, the goals of decision, particular decisions (production planning, capital budgeting, and replacement theory). It was sponsored by the Association of Teachers of Accounting in the United Kingdom. No index.

994 Bennett, Earl D.; Brandt, Floyd S.; and Klasson, Charles R. BUSINESS POLICY: CASES IN MANAGERIAL DECISION MAKING. Columbus, Ohio: Merrill, 1970. 757 p. Illustrations, diagrams, maps, tables.

The authors present forty-six case studies in seven sections: major decision problems confronting management, development of competitive and administrative policies, implementation of competitive and administrative policy decisions, implementation of policy decisions--operational problems, reappraisal of competitive prices and strategies, reappraisal of operational policies, and public and private enterprise. No index.

995 Brinkers, Henry S., ed. DECISION-MAKING: CREATIVITY, JUDGEMENT, AND SYSTEMS. Columbus: Ohio State University Press, 1972. 276 p. Illustrations, diagrams, tables, bibliographies.

These fourteen papers, originally presented at a conference at Ohio State University, are here arranged in five parts: decision-making strategies, decision-making aids, decision aid applications, human creativity and judgment, and implications.

996 DECISION-MAKING IN A CHANGING WORLD. Edited by the editors of INNOVATION. Princeton, N.J.: Auerbach, 1971. 189 p. Illustrations, diagrams.

Included are selected essays from INNOVATION, "the magazine about managing in an environment dominated by rapid change and advancing technology." They are arranged in

three sections: the new managerial environment; some tools for
decision making; and the framework for decision making.

997 Eccles, A.J., and Wood, D. "How Do Managers Decide?" JOURNAL
OF MANAGEMENT STUDIES 9 (October 1972): 291-302. Diagrams,
table.

The decision-making process is examined under laboratory conditions by using a business game as a research tool. The forty
participants were divided into five groups.

998 Gillis, Floyd E., Jr. MANAGERIAL ECONOMICS: DECISION MAKING
UNDER UNCERTAINTY FOR BUSINESS AND ENGINEERING. Reading,
Mass.: Addison-Wesley, 1969. 296 p. Diagrams, tables.

Gillis provides a guide to the application of economic theory
to such problems as capital decisions, replacement policy,
and pricing.

999 Gore, William J. ADMINISTRATIVE DECISION-MAKING: A HEURISTIC
MODEL. New York: Wiley, 1964. 190 p. Diagrams.

Gore distinguishes between (1) "rational" decision systems
which are logical and planned but presuppose an understanding
of causes and effects, and (2) "heuristic" decision systems
which are largely unconscious, intuitive, and unplanned, and
are more applicable to intangible and qualitative problems.
The author's theoretical analysis of the decision-making process
is supported by case materials from an eighteen-month study of
the Lawrence, Kansas, fire department. Glossary, pp. 184-87.

1000 Heller, Frank A. MANAGERIAL DECISION-MAKING: A STUDY OF
LEADERSHIP STYLES AND POWER SHARING AMONG SENIOR MAN-
AGERS. Organizations, People, Society Series. London: Tavistock,
1971. xxv, 140 p. Diagrams, tables, bibliography. (Distributed by
Barnes & Noble, Scranton, Pa.)

Heller uses a field research technique called group feedback
analysis to examine patterns of decision making and leadership
styles. His material is derived from a study of 260 managers
in fifteen large, successful, and progressive U.S. companies.
Glossary, pp. xxiv-xxv. Indexes of authors and subjects.

1001 Jones, Manley Howe. EXECUTIVE DECISION MAKING. Rev. ed. Irwin
Series in Management. Homewood, Ill.: Irwin, 1962. xvi, 560 p.
Tables.

Jones suggests improvements for executive effectiveness in three
areas: decision making, gaining acceptance for decisions, and
putting plans into effect. A checklist for writing business reports is on pp. 542-44. Glossary, pp. 545-50.

1002 Kepner, Charles H., and Tregoe, Benjamin B. THE RATIONAL MAN-AGER: A SYSTEMATIC APPROACH TO PROBLEM SOLVING AND DECISION MAKING. Edited by Perrin Stryker. New York: McGraw-Hill, 1965. 275 p. Diagrams, forms, bibliography.

> This work shows how the manager can develop his abilities in problem solving and decision making by using information more effectively. More than forty case histories are included. Annotated bibliography, pp. 243-52.

1003 Mack, Ruth P. PLANNING ON UNCERTAINTY: DECISION MAKING IN BUSINESS AND GOVERNMENT ADMINISTRATION. New York: Wiley-Interscience, 1971. 233 p. Tables.

> Mack suggests ways in which the cost of uncertainty in the decision-making process can be kept to a minimum, concluding with a checklist of fifty ways to reduce this uncertainty cost.

1004 Maier, Norman R.F. THE NEW TRUCK DILEMMA. Rockville, Md.: BNA Communications; Peterborough, Eng.: Guild Sound & Vision, 1967.

> In this twenty-five-minute 16-mm color film on group decision making, teams of managers participate in the process.

1005 _____. PROBLEM-SOLVING DISCUSSIONS AND CONFERENCES: LEADERSHIP METHODS AND SKILLS. McGraw-Hill Series in Management. New York: McGraw-Hill, 1963. 261 p. Diagrams, tables.

> The conference is considered as a decision-making tool.

1006 Mantel, Samuel J., Jr. CASES IN MANAGERIAL DECISIONS. Englewood Cliffs, N.J.: Prentice-Hall, 1964. 201 p. Diagrams, forms, maps, tables.

> The twenty case studies of decision making included here assume some knowledge of accounting and elementary statistics on the part of the reader. No index.

1007 Marvin, Philip. DEVELOPING DECISIONS FOR ACTION. Homewood, Ill.: Dow Jones-Irwin, 1971. 216 p. Diagrams.

> This guide by the University of Cincinnati's Dean of Professional Development concerns decision-making skills and the conversion of decisions into action.

1008 Melman, Seymour. DECISION MAKING AND PRODUCTIVITY. New York: Wiley; Oxford, Eng.: Blackwell, 1958. xii, 260 p. Illustrations, tables.

> This is an important, if somewhat dated, study by an American professor of the link between decision making by unions and

management and high productivity. It is based on his observations at the Standard Motor Company, Coventry, England.

1009 Morris, William T. THE ANALYSIS OF MANAGEMENT DECISIONS. Rev. ed. Irwin Series in Management. Homewood, Ill.: Irwin, 1964. 551 p. Diagrams, tables, bibliography.

The author shows how to apply mathematical analysis to a variety of decision-making problems. The reader will need an elementary knowledge of economics, accounting, and probability theory. Each chapter concludes with case problems and suggestions for further reading.

1010 _____ . MANAGEMENT FOR ACTION: PSYCHOTECHNICAL DECISION MAKING. Reston, Va.: Reston Publishing Co., 1972. 223 p. Diagrams, tables, bibliographies.

"Psychotechnical" refers to the practical or technical use of psychology in the decision-making process.

1011 Morrison, J. Roger; Hertz, David B.; and Gerstner, Louis V. DECISION-MAKING: THE CHIEF EXECUTIVE'S CHALLENGE. London: British Institute of Management, 1972. 44 p. Diagrams, tables. Paperback.

The book consists of three papers by consultants from the McKinsey Company, originally presented at a BIM top management seminar: "The Chief Executive's Decision-Making Dilemmas," by J. Roger Morrison; "Management Science and the Chief Executive," by David B. Hertz; and "Can Strategic Planning Pay Off?" by Louis V. Gerstner, Jr.

1012 Morton, Michael S. Scott. MANAGEMENT DECISION SYSTEMS: COMPUTER-BASED SUPPORT FOR DECISION MAKING. Boston: Harvard University Graduate School of Business Administration, Division of Research, 1971. xv, 216 p. Diagrams, tables, bibliography.

No index.

1013 Odiorne, George S. MANAGEMENT DECISIONS BY OBJECTIVES. Englewood Cliffs, N.J.: Prentice-Hall, 1969. xvi, 252 p. Diagrams, bibliography.

Odiorne explains how to apply management by objectives to the decision-making process. He includes chapters on group decision making, controlling the effects of decisions, and the tools of decision making. Annotated bibliography, pp. 238-42.

1014 Raymond, Thomas Cicchino. PROBLEMS IN BUSINESS ADMINISTRATION: ANALYSIS BY THE CASE METHOD. 2d ed. New York: McGraw-Hill, 1964. 331 p. Diagrams, maps, tables.

Part one describes the case study approach to management decision making; part two contains twenty cases for analysis. There is an alphabetical list of cases but no subject index.

1015 Richards, Max D., and Greenlaw, Paul S. MANAGEMENT DECISIONS AND BEHAVIOR. Irwin Series in Management. Homewood, Ill.: Irwin, 1972. xv, 655 p. Diagrams, tables.

This is a revised edition of MANAGEMENT DECISION MAK- ING (1966). Chapters 1-4 summarize the major historical and current trends in management thinking and provide an introduction to the decision-making process. Chapters 5-11 deal with individual and group behavior, leadership, and or- ganizational design. Chapters 12-19 cover organizational planning and control. The final chapter provides a tentative conditional theory of management. Indexes of names and sub- jects.

1016 Shull, Fremont A., Jr.; Delbecq, Andre L.; and Cummings, L.L. OR- GANIZATIONAL DECISION MAKING. New York: McGraw-Hill, 1970. xvi, 320 p. Diagrams, tables.

Three professors study the decision-making process in the indi- vidual, his interpersonal situations, and the larger, more com- plex organization.

1017 Simon, Herbert A. ADMINISTRATIVE BEHAVIOR: A STUDY OF DECI- SION MAKING PROCESSES IN ADMINISTRATIVE ORGANIZATIONS. New York: Macmillan; London: Collier-Macmillan, 1957. xlviii, 259 p. Paperback.

Simon's book is a classic work on organization theory and the psychology of decision making. The first edition was published in 1945.

1018 _____. THE NEW SCIENCE OF MANAGEMENT DECISION. The Ford Distinguished Lectures, vol. 3. New York: Harper & Row, 1960. xii, 50 p. Table.

Three lectures given at the School of Commerce, Accounts, and Finance of New York University have been rewritten as five chapters: "The Executive as Decision-Maker," "Tradi- tional Decision-Making Methods," "New Techniques for Pro- grammed Decision Making," "Heuristic Problem-Solving," and "Organization Design: Man-Machine Systems for Decision Making."

1019 Summer, Charles E.; and O'Connell, Jeremiah J.; with Yavitz, Bori. THE MANAGERIAL MIND: SCIENCE AND THEORY IN POLICY DECI- SIONS. Rev. ed. Homewood, Ill.: Irwin, 1968. xxiii, 872 p. Il- lustrations, diagrams, tables.

The text and twenty-eight case studies/readings stress the application of social and behavioral sciences to management problems. Index of authors but no subject index.

1020 Weber, C. Edward, and Peters, Gerald, eds. MANAGEMENT ACTION: MODELS OF ADMINISTRATIVE DECISIONS. Scranton, Pa.: International Textbook Co., 1969. 324 p. Diagrams, tables. Paperback.

This work contains ten studies of the use of models for decision making in the areas of sales planning, purchase planning, administrative budgeting, and program budgeting. A final section presents three studies which emphasize the decision process itself rather than its manifestation in a particular setting. Indexes of authors and subjects.

1021 Young, Stanley, ed. MANAGEMENT: A DECISION-MAKING APPROACH. Dickenson Series on Contemporary Thought in Management. Belmont, Calif.: Dickenson, 1968. 146 p. Diagrams, bibliography. Paperback.

Nine papers concern various aspects of decision making, including the application of operations research to managerial decision making and the ethics of rational decision. No index.

Brainstorming as a Decision-Making Tool

Brainstorming, or creative thinking, is a decision-making technique involving a group of people who pool and discuss their ideas, however unlikely they may seem. While some regard brainstorming as a powerful tool, others are skeptical: Bernard Benson (item 1022) regards it as "potluck thinking." Each manager must make his own choice.

1022 Benson, Bernard S. "Let's Toss This Idea Up." FORTUNE 56 (October 1957): 145-46.

This is a critique of brainstorming as a decision-making process. Systematic logic cannot, suggests Benson, be replaced by "potluck group-think" or "cerebral poppycorn."

1023 Bosticco, Mary. CREATIVE TECHNIQUES FOR MANAGEMENT. London: Business Books, 1971. xii, 146 p. (Distributed by Cahners Publishing Co., Boston.)

This is an account, with case studies, of Systematized Direct Induction, a problem-solving technique used by the author in the United States. Other techniques of creativity are also discussed.

1024 De Bono, Edward. LATERAL THINKING FOR MANAGEMENT: A HAND-
BOOK OF CREATIVITY. European Series in Management. New York:
American Management Association; London: McGraw-Hill, 1971.
225 p. Diagrams, tables.

> This is a practical guide to the development of creativity in
> management. No index.

1025 Gabriel, H.W. TECHNIQUES OF CREATIVE THINKING FOR MAN-
AGEMENT. Englewood Cliffs, N.J.: Prentice-Hall, 1961. xiii, 199 p.
Tables.

> Defines creative thinking as "the multiple-mind technique," a
> group of minds being "gathered together and caused to function
> simultaneously and collectively but as parts of a unit mind in-
> stead of as independent minds." No index.

1026 Osborn, Alex F. APPLIED IMAGINATION: PRINCIPLES AND PROCE-
DURES OF CREATIVE PROBLEM-SOLVING. 3d ed. New York: Scribner,
1963. xxviii, 417 p. Tables, bibliographies.

> This work describes the advantages and possible applications
> of brainstorming, with case studies. Discussion problems, exer-
> cises, and bibliographical references are found at the end of
> each chapter.

1027 Rawlinson, J. Geoffrey. CREATIVE THINKING AND BRAINSTORMING.
BIM Occasional Papers, n.s., OPN 7. London: British Institute of
Management, 1970. 15 p. Diagrams, tables, bibliography. Paper-
back.

1028 _____. CREATIVE THINKING AND BRAINSTORMING. London: Management Training, 1971.

> This tape-slide presentation is based on seminars conducted by
> Rawlinson for the British Institute of Management. It consists
> of sound tape, seventy-two color 35-mm slides, a leader's
> guide, and a display card designed to act as a visual remin-
> der of the guidelines to brainstorming.

1029 Whiting, Charles S. CREATIVE THINKING. Reinhold Management
Science Series. New York: Reinhold; London: Chapman & Hall, 1958.
xiii, 168 p. Diagrams.

> This is a survey of the possibilities of creative thinking and
> brainstorming as training and decision tools, with descriptions
> of the General Electric Company creative engineering pro-
> gram, the McCann-Erickson marketing communications work-
> shop, and the creative training programs of the A.C. Spark
> Plug Division of General Motors and the Gary works of the
> U.S. Steel Corporation.

209

Bibliographies

1030 Dumas, Neil W. THE DECISION MAKER'S GUIDE TO APPLIED PLAN-
NING, ORGANIZATION, ADMINISTRATION, RESEARCH, EVALUA-
TION, INFORMATION PROCESSING AND ANALYSIS TECHNIQUES.
Gainesville: University of Florida, Regional Rehabilitation Research In-
stitute, 1970. 191 p.

This is a computer-produced collection of 1,210 abstracts, all
published between 1964 and 1968. They are arranged numeri-
cally with an author index and a detailed subject index.

1031 Wasserman, Paul, and Silander, Fred S. DECISION-MAKING: AN AN-
NOTATED BIBLIOGRAPHY. Ithaca, N.Y.: Cornell University Graduate
School of Business and Public Administration, 1958. 111 p. Paperback.
SUPPLEMENT, 1958-1963. 1964. 179 p. Paperback.

Each volume is classified under eight broad headings, with indexes of authors and titles. The work covers books and journal articles.

APPRAISAL

Systematic appraisal of personnel and methods is obviously an important managerial activity.

1032 British Institute of Management. MANAGEMENT APPRAISAL PRACTICES.
Information Summary, no. 133. London: 1967. 61 leaves, diagrams,
tables, bibliography. Paperback.

A detailed analysis of appraisal systems in 100 British companies is presented.

1033 _____. SUCCESSFUL STAFF APPRAISAL. London: Management Training, 1971.

This consists of a twenty-seven-minute 16-mm color film, tape,
and a leader's guide. The appraisal interview and the involvement of top management are emphasized.

1034 Haeri, F.H. PERFORMANCE APPRAISALS: WHAT MANAGERS THINK.
A DETAILED SURVEY OF MANAGEMENT APPRAISAL SYSTEMS AND
PROCEDURES IN FOUR LARGE U.K. ORGANISATIONS. Information
Summary, no. 136. London: British Institute of Management, 1969.
53 p. Forms, bibliography. Paperback.

Haeri investigates in depth the appraisal systems of four companies which were covered in Information Summary no. 133
(item 1032).

1035 Kellogg, Marion S. WHAT TO DO ABOUT PERFORMANCE APPRAISAL. New York: American Management Association, 1965. 223 p. Forms, tables.

> Kellogg covers the ethics of employee appraisal, the coaching appraisal, work planning, the salary appraisal, termination appraisal, appraisal of potential, appraisal of candidates for promotion, and organization of the appraisal system. No index.

1036 McGregor, Douglas. "An Uneasy Look at Performance Appraisal." HARVARD BUSINESS REVIEW 50 (September–October 1972): 133–39.

> This reprint of an article originally published in 1957 examines the faults of conventional performance appraisal and suggests an alternative approach. An appreciation of McGregor's work by Warren G. Bennis follows on pp. 140–49.

1037 Sloan, Stanley, and Johnson, Alton C. "New Context of Personnel Appraisal." HARVARD BUSINESS REVIEW 46 (November–December 1968): 14–30, 194. Table, bibliography.

> The authors review the literature on personnel appraisal.

1038 Whisler, Thomas L., and Harper, Shirley F., eds. PERFORMANCE APPRAISAL: RESEARCH AND PRACTICE. New York: Holt, Rinehart & Winston, 1962. xiii, 593 p. Diagrams, tables.

> This four-part book covers the nature of performance appraisal, techniques of appraisal, appraisal in perspective, and case report and organization studies. It contains several case studies, including the joint employee rating plan of the P.J. Ritter Company and Local 56, Meat & Cannery Workers Union, AFL. Indexes of authors and subjects. The book was published in association with the A.G. Bush Library of Management, Organization and Industrial Relations, University of Chicago.

1039 Wilson, Vivian. SETTING PRECISE PERFORMANCE OBJECTIVES. Philadelphia: Auerbach, 1969. 222 p. Paperback.

> This is a programmed guide. No index.

Bibliography

1040 Wasserman, Paul. MEASUREMENT AND EVALUATION OF ORGANIZATIONAL PERFORMANCE: AN ANNOTATED BIBLIOGRAPHY. A McKinsey Foundation Annotated Bibliography. Ithaca, N.Y.: Cornell University Graduate School of Business Administration, 1959. 110 p. Paperback.

> Books and articles are listed under four headings: measurement and evaluation (general), measurement of the total enterprise,

measurement of functional units of organization, and measurement of individual performance. Indexes of authors and titles.

GOAL SETTING AND MANAGEMENT BY OBJECTIVES

Management by objectives is a technique involving agreement on realistic targets (or objectives) for particular tasks, identification and removal of any obstacles to achieving these objectives, and regular and systematic review of the objectives. See also items 697, 1013, 1563, 1838.

1041 Barrett, F.D. "The MBO Time Trip." BUSINESS QUARTERLY 37 (Autumn 1972): 42-51.

Barrett suggests that managers are not very good at managing their own time and that MBO can help here, although it means spending more time on management.

1042 Batten, Joe D. BEYOND MANAGEMENT BY OBJECTIVES. New York: American Management Association, 1966. 107 p. Diagrams.

Batten argues that MBO can achieve nothing without motivation and provides guidelines for the establishment of a motivational climate.

1043 Beck, Arthur C., Jr., and Hillmar, Ellis D., eds. A PRACTICAL APPROACH TO ORGANIZATION DEVELOPMENT THROUGH MBO: SELECTED READINGS. Reading, Mass.: Addison-Wesley, 1972. xii, 356 p. Diagrams, bibliography. Paperback.

This book contains twenty-eight readings on management by objectives and results (MBO/R). No index.

1044 Brady, Rodney H. "MBO Goes to Work in the Public Sector." HARVARD BUSINESS REVIEW 51 (March-April 1973): 65-74. Diagrams.

The successful application of MBO at the U.S. Department of Health, Education, and Welfare is described.

1045 Byrd, Richard E., and Cowan, John. "MBO: A Behavioral Science Approach." PERSONNEL 51 (March-April 1974): 42-50.

By using examples the authors demonstrate that a more flexible approach by behavioral scientists can overcome excessive rigidity by managers. They favor the team approach and periodical evaluation as part of a successful MBO program.

1046 Carroll, Stephen J., and Tosi, Henry L., Jr. MANAGEMENT BY OBJECTIVES: APPLICATIONS AND RESEARCH. New York: Macmillan; London: Collier-Macmillan, 1973. 216 p. Diagrams, tables, bibliographies. Paperback.

This practical guide, based on the author's experiences at the Black & Decker Manufacturing Company, is supported by research through interviews and questionnaires, literature surveys, and an exchange program. Indexes of authors and subjects.

1047 Goddard, E.E., and Bridle, G.W. "Management by Objectives: Two Case Studies." O & M BULLETIN 26 (February 1971) Supplement. 31 p. Tables. Paperback.

The authors examine case studies of the application of MBO in the Greater London Council and H.M.S. Collingwood, the Weapon & Electrical School of the Royal Navy.

1048 Hughes, Charles L. GOAL SETTING: KEY TO INDIVIDUAL AND ORGANIZATIONAL EFFECTIVENESS. New York: American Management Association, 1965. 157 p. Diagrams, tables.

Hughes explains ways of synchronizing company goals and those of the individual employee, the goal being the employee's recognition that by working for company goals he can reach his own.

1049 Humble, John W. HOW TO MANAGE BY OBJECTIVES. New York: AMACOM; London: Management Publications, 1972. 150 p. Illustrations, tables, bibliography. Paperback.

This is a new edition of a booklet originally entitled IMPROVING MANAGEMENT PERFORMANCE. The text of the original booklet is now revised as part two ("An Introduction to MBO"). Part one ("The Pitfalls of MBO") summarizes the mistakes which have been made in attempting to apply MBO. The British edition of this book is entitled MANAGEMENT BY OBJECTIVES.

1050 _____. IMPROVING BUSINESS RESULTS. London: McGraw-Hill for Management Centre Europe, 1968. 193 p. Diagrams, tables, bibliography.

This guide offers a "positive approach to improving company profit and growth through the efforts of a competent and purposeful team" developed by the author at Urwick, Orr & Partners Ltd., management consultants. Included are checklists for setting company objectives and case studies of K.L.M. Royal Dutch Airlines, Laporte Industries Ltd., and Smith Industries Ltd.

1051 _____. MANAGEMENT BY OBJECTIVES. Rockville, Md.: BNA Communications; New York: Time-Life Video; London: EMI Special Films Unit, 1970.

This twenty-seven-minute 16-mm color film or videotape (Time-

Life Video) introduces the basic philosophy of MBO as a total system of management and demonstrates the board of director's responsibility for setting clearly defined objectives and supporting them with a practical management development plan. This is one of six films in a series, the others being FOCUS THE FUTURE (on planning), DEFINING THE MANAGER'S JOB, PERFORMANCE AND POTENTIAL REVIEW, MANAGEMENT TRAINING, and COLT: A CASE HISTORY (a twenty-four-minute study of the application of MBO in a company, showing why it was introduced, the launching sequence, and the reactions of managers).

1052 _____, ed. MANAGEMENT BY OBJECTIVES IN ACTION. McGraw-Hill European Series in Management and Marketing. London: McGraw-Hill, 1970. 294 p. Diagrams, tables, bibliography.

Intended to complement IMPROVING BUSINESS RESULTS (item 1050), this book contains twenty contributions. There are five sections: management by objectives: basic concepts, MBO in practice, problem areas (setting objectives, training MBO advisers, management development), MBO in perspective, and an action program. This book includes case studies of Colt Heating & Ventilation Ltd., John Player & Sons, the Royal Naval Supply & Transport Service, Viners Ltd., and the use of MBO in marketing and in research and development. A list of books, articles, and films on MBO appears on pp. 287-90.

1053 Kieber, Thomas P. "Forty Common Goal-Setting Errors." HUMAN RESOURCE MANAGEMENT 11 (Fall 1972): 10-13.

Kieber offers a checklist of errors which can affect the use of MBO in an organization.

1054 McConkey, Dale D. "Applying Management by Objectives to Non-Profit Organizations." S.A.M. ADVANCED MANAGEMENT JOURNAL 28 (January 1973): 10-20.

This article includes a definition of MBO and a summary of its advantages and limitations, with brief accounts of its use in schools, hospitals, the U.S. Forest Products Laboratory, the Canadian Post Office, volunteer organizations, and municipal organizations.

1055 _____. "MBO: Twenty Years Later." BUSINESS HORIZONS 16 (August 1973): 25-36. Diagrams, tables.

McConkey reviews the background to MBO in the United States, its impact on management and managers, and its future viability.

1056 _____. "Twenty Ways to Kill Management by Objectives." MAN-
AGEMENT REVIEW 61 (October 1972): 4-13.

> The author outlines twenty "problem areas" of MBO, which,
> if overcome, increase its effectiveness and value. McConkey
> describes MBO as "a tough, demanding management system
> that requires highly competent managers to operate it."

1057 Mali, Paul. MANAGING BY OBJECTIVES: AN OPERATING GUIDE TO
FASTER AND MORE PROFITABLE RESULTS. New York: Wiley-Interscience,
1972. xiii, 314 p. Diagrams (1 folding), tables, bibliographies.

> This is a detailed and practical exposition of MBO, defined
> by the author as "a strategy of planning and getting results in
> the direction that management wishes and needs to take while
> meeting the goals and satisfaction of its participants." Each
> chapter includes a summary of its contents, guide questions,
> bibliographical references, and notes. There is a useful list
> of sample objectives on pp. 118-23: twelve for overall organi-
> zations, fifteen for finance, fifteen for marketing, thirteen
> for research and engineering, fifteen for production, and fif-
> teen for personnel.

1058 MANAGEMENT BY OBJECTIVES. Addlestone, Eng.: Classified Media,
1971- . Quarterly.

> This is a quarterly review of management by objectives and
> related methods of improving management performance.

1059 Miller, Ernest C. OBJECTIVES AND STANDARDS: AN APPROACH TO
PLANNING AND CONTROL. AMA Research Study, no. 74. New
York: American Management Association, 1966. 120 p. Diagrams,
forms, tables, bibliography. Paperback.

> This guide to MBO has case studies of more than fifty com-
> panies. There is an annotated reading list on p. 117. Index
> of companies, but no subject index.

1060 Molander, C.F. "Management by Objectives in Perspective." JOURNAL
OF MANAGEMENT STUDIES 9 (February 1972): 74-81.

> Molander outlines the philosophy of MBO, discusses the ways
> in which it may fail through lack of a basic underlying philos-
> ophy, and explores its relationship to sensitivity training and
> organization development.

1061 Morrisey, George L. MANAGEMENT BY OBJECTIVES AND RESULTS.
Reading, Mass.: Addison-Wesley, 1970. xii, 164 p. Diagrams, tables,
bibliography. Paperback.

> This book introduces another group of initials to the world of
> management techniques--MOR or Management by Objectives

and Results. It involves "a clear and precise identification of objectives or desired results, the establishment of a realistic program for their achievement, and an evaluation of performance in terms of measured results in attaining them." No index.

1062 Odiorne, George S. MANAGEMENT BY OBJECTIVES: A SYSTEM OF MANAGERIAL LEADERSHIP. New York: Pitman, 1965. 204 p. Diagrams, tables.

One of the best accounts of MBO, this book is based on the author's considerable experience in a variety of organizations. It outlines four major kinds of objective which should be included in each manager's targets: routine duties, emergency or problem-solving goals, creative goals, and personal development goals.

1063 O'Hea, Jerome. QUESTIONS AND ANSWERS ON MBO. London: Management Publications, 1971. 98 p. Illustrations, tables (1 folding), bibliography. Paperback.

The fifty-six questions and answers in this book are intended both as a guide to MBO and as background study for the film COLT: A CASE HISTORY (see item 1051). Annotated bibliography, pp. 73-75. Glossary, pp. 70-72. No index.

1064 Olsson, David E. MANAGEMENT BY OBJECTIVES. Palo Alto, Calif.: Pacific Books, 1968. 112 p. Diagrams, forms, tables, bibliography.

This is a brief, practical, and readable guide.

1065 Reddin, William J. EFFECTIVE MBO. London: Management Publications, 1971. 289 p. Diagrams, tables, bibliography.

This useful guide was prepared in collaboration with a team of consultants from AIC Management Consultants. Glossary, pp. 262-70.

1066 Schuster, Fred E., and Kindall, Alva F. "Management by Objectives: Where We Stand. A Survey of the Fortune 500." HUMAN RESOURCE MANAGEMENT 13 (Spring 1974): 8-11.

This article reports on the extent of use of MBO in the 500 largest U.S. companies. Almost half claimed to have adopted MBO, but far fewer had applied it in a meaningful sense and fewer still have had successful applications.

1067 Tosi, Henry L., and Carroll, Stephen J., Jr. "Improving Management by Objectives: A Diagnostic Change Program." CALIFORNIA MANAGEMENT REVIEW 16 (Fall 1973): 57-66. Diagrams, tables, bibliography.

The authors describe a diagnostic research project to evaluate the effects of MBO and to provide data for improving the program. They examine the introduction of the revised program and its results.

1068 "Using the Managerial Grid to Ensure MBO." ORGANIZATIONAL DY-NAMICS 2 (Spring 1974): 54-65. Bibliography.

This is a detailed account of the introduction by Union Mutual Life Insurance Company, Portland, Maine, of the managerial grid technique to improve teamwork, decision making, and managerial effectiveness as a basis for achieving commitment to MBO goals.

1069 Valentine, Raymond F. THE GOAL-SETTING SESSION. New York: AMACOM, 1967.

This forty-five-minute cassette, reel-to-reel tape, or record contains four dramatized situations which demonstrate target setting and the harmonization of individual targets with company goals.

1070 Villarreal, John J. "Management by Objectives Revisited." S.A.M. ADVANCED MANAGEMENT JOURNAL 39 (April 1974): 28-33.

The author discusses reasons for disillusionment with MBO and makes suggestions for improvement.

1071 Vine, K.W. "MBO in the DOE." O & M BULLETIN 27 (May 1972): 85-98. Diagrams, tables.

Vine discusses the introduction of MBO into the Accounts Division of the British Department of the Environment.

1072 Wikstrom, Walter S. MANAGING BY--AND WITH--OBJECTIVES. Studies in Personnel Policy, no. 212. New York: National Industrial Conference Board, 1968. 77 p. Illustrations. Paperback.

The concept and application of MBO are considered with case studies of its use in Honeywell Inc., General Mills Incorporated, St. Regis Paper Company, 3M Company, and Kimberly-Clark Corporation.

PROJECT MANAGEMENT

Dennis Lock (item 1079) defines project management as "a specialized branch of management which has evolved in order to co-ordinate and control some of the complex activities of modern industry." A group of people are asked to complete a specific task within a fixed period of time; the task is then examined, appraised, and frequently reported upon. Project management often involves the use of network planning techniques, such as PERT and CPM. Works which emphasize these techniques are listed in section 8.

1073 Avots, Ivars. "Making Project Management Work." DATAMATION 19 (January 1973): 42-45.

Avots considers why project management is more successful in some environments than in others. He identifies three key areas, each of which is discussed in some detail: organizational compatability, technical adequacy, and method of operation.

1074 Baumgartner, John Stanley. PROJECT MANAGEMENT. Homewood, Ill.: Irwin, 1963. 185 p. Diagrams, tables.

This book is particularly concerned with defense and space projects. Appendixes include a description of PERT and a glossary, pp. 181-85. No index.

1075 Brandon, Dick H., and Gray, Max. PROJECT CONTROL STANDARDS. Princeton, N.J.: Brandon/Systems, 1970. 204 p. Diagrams, forms, tables, bibliography.

This work is arranged in four sections: introduction and general principles, procedures, project control documentation, and setting up a project control system. Appendix on software packages for project control. The bibliography is divided into PERT and CPM sections, pp. 195-200, and a project control section, pp. 200-204. No index.

1076 Butler, Arthur G., Jr. "Project Management: A Study in Organizational Conflict." ACADEMY OF MANAGEMENT JOURNAL 16 (March 1973): 84-101. Bibliography.

The problem of integrating people of different professional disciplines into the project team is discussed.

1077 Cleland, David I., and King, William R. SYSTEMS ANALYSIS AND PROJECT MANAGEMENT. McGraw-Hill Series in Management. New York: McGraw-Hill, 1968. xvi, 315 p. Diagrams, tables, bibliography.

1078 Gullett, C. Ray. "Personnel Management in the Project Organization." PERSONNEL ADMINISTRATION AND PUBLIC PERSONNEL REVIEW 1 (November-December 1972): 17-22.

Gullett considers the impact of the project management concept on such activities as manpower planning, performance appraisal, wage and salary administration, and training and development.

1079 Lock, Dennis. PROJECT MANAGEMENT. Epping, Eng.: Gower Press, 1968. 210 p. Diagrams, forms, tables.

> This is a very practical guide to project management, which is defined as "a specialized branch of management which has evolved in order to co-ordinate and control some of the complex activities of modern industry" (p. 1). It covers defining the project, planning the timescale, scheduling resources, materials control, maintaining the program, modifications, and the relation of achievement to expenditure.

1080 Peart, A.T. DESIGN OF PROJECT MANAGEMENT SYSTEMS AND RECORDS. Epping, Eng.: Gower Press, 1971. xiii, 189 p. Diagrams, forms, tables, bibliography.

> An introductory section is followed by sections dealing with preparing the network, estimating and tendering, executing the project, coordinating materials, analyzing resources, and analyzing and controlling cost. Glossary, pp. 169-81.

1081 Taylor, Lynda King. "The Project Management Group as the Major Force for Change." INDUSTRIAL AND COMMERCIAL TRAINING 5 (April 1973): 170-74.

> Taylor describes how a project management group at Vosper-Thorneycroft, shipbuilders, have overcome key problems facing the company.

1082 Taylor, W.J., and Watling, T.F. PRACTICAL PROJECT MANAGEMENT. London: Business Books, 1973. xii, 198 p. Diagrams, bibliography.

> The emphasis in this book is on people, including the project manager and his team, personnel policies, and communication. A detailed case study forms the appendix.

1083 _____. SUCCESSFUL PROJECT MANAGEMENT. London: Business Books, 1970. 255 p. Diagrams, forms, tables. (Distributed by Beekman Publishers, New York.)

> This very practical guide has chapters on the need for and benefits of project management, choice of a project manager, communication, subcontracting, PERT, financial problems, and use of a computer.

1084 Thamhain, Hans J., and Gemmill, Gary R. "Influence Styles of Project Managers: Some Project Performance Correlates." ACADEMY OF MANAGEMENT JOURNAL 17 (June 1974): 216-24. Tables, bibliography.

> The authors report on an investigation into methods used by project managers to obtain support, involvement, and good performance.

Organization

1085 Project Management Institute, P.O. Box 43, Drexel Hill, Pa. 19026.

This group was formed in 1969 to provide a forum for project managers, defined as "persons engaged in efforts to weld or coordinate various disciplines so as to accomplish any desired project aim." It publishes PMI QUARTERLY.

Section 8

THE QUANTITATIVE APPROACH TO MANAGEMENT:
MANAGEMENT SCIENCES

Listed in this section are works emphasizing a mathematical or statistical approach to management, including items on operations research. Items on automation and computers in management are listed in section 9.

GENERAL STUDIES

1086 Aigner, Dennis J. PRINCIPLES OF STATISTICAL DECISION MAKING.
Macmillan Decision Series. New York: Macmillan; London: Collier-
Macmillan, 1968. xii, 148 p. Diagrams, tables, bibliographies.

> Aigner enumerates the principles of statistical decision making
> or inference without treating the subject in depth.

1087 Bierman, Harold, Jr.; Bonini, Charles P.; and Hausman, Warren H. QUAN-
TITATIVE ANALYSIS FOR BUSINESS DECISIONS. 4th ed. Irwin Series in
Quantitative Analysis for Business. Homewood, Ill.: Irwin; London: Irwin-
Dorsey, 1973. xii, 527 p. Diagrams, tables, bibliographies.

> The authors attempt to provide simplified accounts of sophisti-
> cated techniques for dealing with difficult problems. Each
> of the twenty-four chapters concludes with case problems.

1088 Brabb, George J. INTRODUCTION TO QUANTITATIVE MANAGE-
MENT. New York: Holt, Rinehart & Winston, 1968. xv, 576 p. Diagrams, tables. Paperback.

> Intended for students with no more than a knowledge of al-
> gebra, this work includes many examples, case problems, and
> exercises.

1089 Broster, E.J. GLOSSARY OF APPLIED MANAGEMENT AND FINAN-
CIAL STATISTICS. Epping, Eng.: Gower Press, 1974. 243 p. Diagrams, tables, bibliography.

> This book is arranged alphabetically by techniques, with an
> index of applications. Annotated bibliography, pp. 233-40.

1090 _____ . MANAGEMENT STATISTICS. Management Studies Series. London: Longman, 1972. xv, 333 p. Diagrams, tables.

> Broster provides a practical guide to statistical techniques with demonstrations of their application to various kinds of management problems, including production, costing, pricing, forecasting, business ratios, stock control, and break-even analysis.

1091 Brown, Rex V. "Do Managers Find Decision Theory Useful?" HARVARD BUSINESS REVIEW 48 (May-June 1970): 78-89. Illustrations, diagrams.

> Brown discusses a survey sponsored by the Marketing Science Institute on the experiences of such companies as the Du Pont Company, the General Electric Company, the Ford Motor Company, the Pillsbury Company, and Inmont Corporation with Decision Tree Analysis. He considers such matters as the impact of DTA on companies, its benefits, its organizational implications, and its potential for the future.

1092 Bursk, Edward C., and Chapman, John F., eds. NEW DECISION-MAKING TOOLS FOR MANAGERS: MATHEMATICAL PROGRAMMING AS AN AID IN SOLVING BUSINESS PROBLEMS. Cambridge, Mass.: Harvard University Press, 1963. xv, 413 p. Illustrations, diagrams, tables. Paperback ed. New York: New American Library; London: New English Library, Mentor Executive Library, 1971.

> This work contains seventeen contributions grouped under five headings: general, finance, marketing, product strategy, and production.

1093 Byrnes, W.G., and Chesterton, B.K. DECISIONS, STRATEGIES AND NEW VENTURES: MODERN TOOLS FOR TOP MANAGEMENT. Unwin Professional Management Library. London: Allen & Unwin, 1973. 195 p. Diagrams, tables, bibliography. (Distributed by International Publications Service, New York.)

> The author describes techniques for use in strategic planning, acquisitions, risk management, investment, diversification and new product management, product evaluation, and corporate development, with nine case studies. Annotated reading list, pp. 189-90.

1094 Chance, William A. STATISTICAL METHODS FOR DECISION MAKING. Irwin Series in Quantitative Analysis for Business. Homewood, Ill.: Irwin, 1969. 442 p. Tables.

1095 Clark, Charles T., and Schkade, Lawrence L. STATISTICAL METHODS FOR BUSINESS DECISIONS. Cincinnati: South-Western Publishing Co.; London: Edward Arnold, 1969. xii, 750, 95 p. Diagrams, tables, bibliographies. Paperback.

A review of descriptive statistics is followed by sections dealing with the computer and statistical analysis, probability and
probability distribution, sampling, inference, regression and
correlation, time series, and index numbers. An annotated
selected reading list appears at the end of each chapter. The
index section contains a glossary of symbols, and a glossary
of formulas.

1096 Cyert, Richard M., and Welsch, Lawrence A., eds. MANAGEMENT
DECISION MAKING: SELECTED READINGS. Penguin Modern Management Readings. Harmondsworth, Eng.: Penguin, 1970. 359 p. Diagrams, bibliography. Paperback.

This book's thirteen readings are grouped in five sections:
theory, nonprogrammed decision making, programmed decision
making, heuristic models, and algorithmic models. The aims
of the readings are to illustrate how decision-making processes
in the firm have been described and to present some of the
optimum decision rules which have been prescribed for managers.

1097 Darden, Bill R., and Lucas, William H. THE DECISION-MAKING
GAME: AN INTEGRATED OPERATIONS MANAGEMENT SIMULATION.
New York: Appleton-Century-Crofts, 1969. 190 p. Diagrams, tables,
bibliography. Paperback.

The authors outline a decision-making game designed to provide students with an overall understanding of the flows of
cash, materials, labor, capital, and information through a
manufacturing firm. No index.

1098 Emory, William, and Niland, Powell. MAKING MANAGEMENT DECI-
SIONS. Boston: Houghton Mifflin, 1968. 306 p. Diagrams, tables,
bibliographies.

The use of quantitative methods is emphasized.

1099 Forrester, Jay W. INDUSTRIAL DYNAMICS. Cambridge, Mass.: M.I.T.
Press, 1961. xv, 464 p. Diagrams, tables, bibliography. Paperback.

This important work is designed to introduce the student of
management to industrial dynamics, which the author defines
as "a way of studying the behavior of industrial systems to
show how policies, decisions, structure, and delays are in-
terrelated to influence growth and stability." A detailed
customer-producer-employment case study is included.

1100 Goetz, Billy E. QUANTITATIVE METHODS: A SURVEY AND GUIDE
FOR MANAGERS. New York: McGraw-Hill, 1965. xxix, 541 p.
Diagrams, tables, bibliographies.

This introduction to the mathematical approach to managerial problems seeks to improve cooperation between specialists and nonspecialists in the field. An annotated guide to recommended reading appears at the end of each chapter. Glossary of selected technical terms, pp. 501-8; glossary of symbols and Greek alphabet, pp. 509-12.

1101 Greenwood, William T. DECISION THEORY AND INFORMATION SYSTEMS: AN INTRODUCTION TO MANAGEMENT DECISION MAKING. Cincinnati: South-Western Publishing Co., 1969. xiii, 818 p. Diagrams, tables, bibliographies.

Text and forty-seven readings are contained in seven sections: decision theory, practice, and structure; business-management problem solving; decision information systems; information decision models; decision environment systems; organizational decision behavior; and computer information control systems. Indexes of authors and subjects.

1102 Haley, K. Brian. MATHEMATICAL PROGRAMMING FOR BUSINESS AND INDUSTRY. Studies in Management. London: Macmillan; New York: St. Martin's Press, 1967. 156 p. Diagrams, tables (1 folding), bibliography.

1103 Hein, Leonard W. THE QUANTITATIVE APPROACH TO MANAGERIAL DECISIONS. Englewood Cliffs, N.J.: Prentice-Hall, 1967. xxv, 386 p. Diagrams, tables, bibliographies.

An approach to basic probability for the nonmathematician. Topics covered include the computer and decision making; linear programming; the simplex method; the learning curve; the Bisson, Gamma, and Normal distributions; the Monte Carlo method; waiting lines; quality control charts; work sampling; PACE (Performance and Cost Evaluation); PERT; CPM; and line of balance.

1104 Heward, James H., and Steele, Peter M. BUSINESS CONTROL THROUGH MULTIPLE REGRESSION ANALYSIS: A TECHNIQUE FOR THE NUMERATE MANAGER. Epping, Eng.: Gower Press, 1972; New York: Halsted Press, 1973. 116 p. Illustrations, diagrams, forms, tables.

1105 Horowitz, Ira. DECISION MAKING AND THE THEORY OF THE FIRM. New York: Holt, Rinehart & Winston, 1970. xii, 468 p. Diagrams, tables.

Horowitz presents decision-making tools which economics and operations research can offer to management, with many mathematical illustrations and exercises.

1106 Hough, Louis. MODERN RESEARCH FOR ADMINISTRATIVE DECISIONS.

Englewood Cliffs, N.J.: Prentice-Hall, 1970. xix, 609 p. Diagrams, tables, bibliographies.

This is a critical study of modern business research techniques, based on the author's experience as senior economist with Dunlap and Associates, Stamford, Connecticut. The author emphasizes modern decision theory and includes chapters on computerization in administrative research, queueing theory, PERT, linear programming research, simplex and Monte Carlo techniques, and an appendix on Bayesian probability theory.

1107 Levin, Richard I., and Kirkpatrick, Charles A. QUANTITATIVE AP-
PROACHES TO MANAGEMENT. 3d ed. New York: McGraw-Hill,
1975. 544 p. Diagrams, tables, bibliography.

This is designed for students with a limited background in
quantitative techniques.

1108 Levin, Richard I., and Lamone, Rudolph P. LINEAR PROGRAMMING
FOR MANAGEMENT DECISIONS. Irwin Series in Quantitative Analysis
for Business. Homewood, Ill.: Irwin, 1969. 308 p. Diagrams, tables,
bibliography.

1109 Lim, Robin, ed. QUANTITATIVE METHODS IN MANAGEMENT: READ-
INGS FROM MANAGEMENT TODAY. London: Management Publications, 1972. 260 p. Diagrams, tables.

Twenty-three readings, including six case studies, make up
this book. No index.

1110 McRae, T.W. ANALYTICAL MANAGEMENT. London: Wiley-Interscience, 1970. xxi, 580 p. Diagrams, tables, bibliography.

A lecturer in economics at Manchester Business School, England,
introduces the practicing manager to a wide range of quantitative techniques useful to decision makers. Summaries and
review questions follow each chapter. Indexes of authors and
subjects.

1111 Magee, John F. "Decision Trees for Decision-Making." HARVARD BUSI-
NESS REVIEW 42 (July-August 1964): 126-38. Diagrams, tables.

Magee explains the role of decision trees in identifying the
choices, risks, objectives, monetary gains, and information
needs of investment problems. (See also item 1800).

1112 Miller, David W., and Starr, Martin K. EXECUTIVE DECISIONS AND
OPERATIONS RESEARCH. 2d ed. Prentice-Hall International Series in
Management. Englewood Cliffs, N.J.: Prentice-Hall, 1969. xvi, 607 p.
Diagrams, tables, bibliography.

Presented in five parts: organizations and decisions, the theory of decision, the nature of models, decision-problem paradigms, and the executive and operations research.

1113 Moore, Peter G. RISK IN BUSINESS DECISION. London Business School Series. London: Longman, 1972; New York: Halsted Press, 1973. 365 p. Diagrams, tables, bibliography.

The deputy director of the London Graduate School of Business Studies describes a statistical approach to decision making and the handling of uncertainty. Glossary of symbols, pp. 343-44; glossary of statistical terms, pp. 345-50.

1114 Newman, Joseph W. MANAGEMENT APPLICATIONS OF DECISION THEORY. New York: Harper & Row, 1971. xiv, 210 p. Diagrams, tables. Paperback.

This is a description of the Bayesian approach to decision making and its application.

1115 Paik, C.M. QUANTITATIVE METHODS FOR MANAGERIAL DECISIONS. New York: McGraw-Hill, 1973. xiii, 403 p. Diagrams, tables.

This basic introduction for the nonmathematician has questions and problems at end of each chapter.

1116 Schellenberger, Robert E. MANAGERIAL ANALYSIS. Irwin Series in Quantitative Analysis for Business. Homewood, Ill.: Irwin, 1969. xv, 461 p. Diagrams, tables.

This book is arranged in six sections: an overview; the process; analytical tools, mathematics, and statistics; models of common processes; models of complex systems; and validity.

1117 Schlaifer, Robert. ANALYSIS OF DECISIONS UNDER UNCERTAINTY. New York: McGraw-Hill, 1969. xvi, 729 p. Diagrams, tables.

This is an introduction to logical analysis of the problems of decision under uncertainty for undergraduate and graduate business school students. Part one deals with the basic principles. Part two covers basic quantitative methods for expressing preferences and judgments. Part three includes topics of interest to students and practitioners of management, such as the Monte Carlo method, simulation, sampling, and inventory control.

1118 Thomas, Howard. DECISION THEORY AND THE MANAGER. Times Management Library. London: Pitman, 1972. 137 p. Diagrams, bibliography.

This nontechnical account of decision-theory analysis by a lecturer at the London Graduate School of Business Studies is aimed at practicing managers and business school students. A useful annotated reading list is on pp. 132-33.

1119 Vazsonyi, Andrew. SCIENTIFIC PROGRAMMING IN BUSINESS AND IN-
DUSTRY. New York: Wiley, 1958. xix, 474 p. Diagrams, tables.

Although this book is intended for "management personnel
without advanced training in mathematics or science" it contains a fair amount of mathematics. Three sections are included: the fundamentals, mathematical programming, and programming in production and inventory control.

1120 Wagner, Harvey M. PRINCIPLES OF MANAGEMENT SCIENCE, WITH
APPLICATIONS TO EXECUTIVE DECISIONS. Prentice-Hall International
Series in Management. Englewood Cliffs, N.J.: Prentice-Hall, 1970.
xx, 562 p. Diagrams, tables, bibliography.

This is primarily a textbook for college students who intend
careers in management, but it may also be useful to practicing
managers who require a knowledge of management science.
It contains some mathematics.

1121 Weisselberg, Robert C., and Cowley, J. THE EXECUTIVE STRATEGIST:
AN ARMCHAIR GUIDE TO SCIENTIFIC DECISION MAKING. New York:
McGraw-Hill, 1969. xii, 249 p. Illustrations, diagrams, tables, bib-
liography.

This popular introduction guides executives through the analytical techniques and terminology employed by specialists. A
number of checklists and problems are included.

1122 Wiest, J.D. "Heuristic Programs for Decision Making." HARVARD BUS-
INESS REVIEW 44 (September-October 1966): 129-43. Diagrams.

The author defines heuristic programs and considers their role
in decision making, with examples from chess playing, inventory control, engineering design, and scheduling. He considers their effect on management.

Periodicals

1123 BELL JOURNAL OF ECONOMICS AND MANAGEMENT SCIENCE. New
York: American Telephone & Telegraph Company, 1970- . Twice yearly.

Published to "support and encourage research in the behavior
of regulated industries and the operations of large corporations,"
this journal includes long articles, symposia, and shorter notes.

1124 DECISION SCIENCES: THE JOURNAL FOR THE AMERICAN INSTITUTE
FOR DECISION SCIENCES. Atlanta: The Institute, 1970- . Quarterly.

This publication is concerned with the application of the
methods of science to the solution of decision problems of or-

ganized groups. Papers are normally arranged in three sections: concepts, theory, and techniques; applications and implementation; and education. A fourth section, communications, allows comments on previously published papers.

1125 MANAGEMENT SCIENCE: JOURNAL OF THE INSTITUTE OF MANAGEMENT SCIENCES. Providence, R.I.: The Institute, 1954- . Monthly.

This is published in alternate sections: theory and application.

1126 OMEGA: THE INTERNATIONAL JOURNAL OF MANAGEMENT SCIENCE. Oxford, Eng.: Pergamon Press, 1973- . Bimonthly.

This journal includes abstracts of research reports and theses.

Organizations

1127 American Institute for Decision Sciences, University Plaza, Atlanta, Ga. 30303.

Formed in 1969 to promote the application of quantitative methodology to functional and behavioral problems of administration, this organization publishes DECISION SCIENCES (item 1124).

1128 The Institute of Management Sciences (TIMS), 146 Westminster Street, Providence, R.I. 02903.

Formed in 1953 to identify, extend and unify scientific knowledge that contributes to the understanding and practice of management, this group has members in more than fifty countries. It publishes MANAGEMENT SCIENCE (item 1125) and BEHAVIORAL SCIENCE.

Bibliography

1129 IBM Corporation. MANAGEMENT SCIENCE AT WORK: A BIBLIOGRAPHY COVERING ALL ENTERPRISES, ALL FUNCTIONS AND ALL TECHNIQUES. White Plains, N.Y.: 1971. 107 p. Paperback.

This work lists approximately 5,000 journal articles, which are indexed by industry, function, and technique. No author index.

OPERATIONS RESEARCH

Operations research involves the application of scientific methods to a review of operational problems within an organization, with a view to making more effective use of known facts and reducing the use of subjective judgments in making management decisions.

1130 Ackoff, Russell L., and Sasieni, Maurice W. FUNDAMENTALS OF OPERATIONS RESEARCH. New York: Wiley, 1968. 455 p. Diagrams, tables, bibliographies.

> Included are many case studies, discussion topics, and exercises.

1131 Beer, Stafford. DECISION AND CONTROL: THE MEANING OF OPERATIONAL RESEARCH AND MANAGEMENT CYBERNETICS. New York: Wiley, 1966. xii, 556 p. Diagrams.

> Beer details how management can use scientific methods to solve problems of decision and control. He deals with the nature of operations research, the activity of operations research, the relevance of cybernetics, and the implications of the new techniques for industry, government, and management science.

1132 Brennan, J., ed. OPERATIONAL RESEARCH IN INDUSTRIAL SYSTEMS. London: English Universities Press; New York: American Elsevier, 1972. 325 p. Diagrams.

> This volume contains twenty-one papers, some in English and some in French, given at a conference held in St. Louis, France, in July 1970 under the aegis of the NATO Scientific Affairs Committee. Topics covered include corporate planning models, market research, evaluation and selection of research projects, technological forecasting for product development planning, costing, information handling, factory scheduling, inventory control, depot location, and materials handling. An index would have been useful.

1133 Chedzey, C.S., ed. SCIENCE IN MANAGEMENT: SOME IMPLICATIONS OF OPERATIONAL RESEARCH AND COMPUTER SCIENCE. British Library of Business Studies. London: Routledge & Kegan Paul, 1970. xv, 357 p. Illustrations, diagrams, tables, bibliographies.

> Contained are descriptions by twenty management consultants from Inbucon Ltd. and its subsidiary, Management Sciences Ltd., an organization specializing in operations research, of the methods used in their assignments. Many case studies are included.

1134 Cook, S.L. "Operational Research, Social Well-Being and the Zero Growth Concept." OMEGA 1 (1973): 647-67. Bibliography.

> Cook traces the history of OR and suggests that it no longer functions as a science helping society but as one helping the

establishment. He argues that OR must reexamine its social
role in the new world climate if it is to survive. Cook also
includes a detailed literature review.

1135 Eddison, R.T.; Pennycuick, K.; and Rivett, B.H. Patrick, eds. OPERA-
TIONAL RESEARCH IN MANAGEMENT. Management Science Series.
London: English Universities Press, 1962. 330 p. Diagrams, tables.

These sixteen contributions are aimed specifically at managers,
with mathematics kept to a minimum.

1136 Enrick, Norbert Lloyd. MANAGEMENT OPERATIONS RESEARCH. Modern Management Series. New York: Holt, Rinehart & Winston, 1965.
320 p. Diagrams, tables.

This simplified, nonmathematical approach is in four parts: the
nature of operations research; planning, programming, and program review; management of inventories and waiting lines; and
sampling and statistical analyses. The book includes an epilogue
on management in the 1970s and an appendix of cases and
problems.

1137 International Conference on Operational Research. PROCEEDINGS.

The proceedings of five conferences, organized by the International Federation of Operational Research Societies:

First, Oxford, Eng., 1957. Edited by Max Davies, R.T. Eddison, and Thornton Page. London: English Universities Press,
1957. 526 p. Diagrams, tables.

Second, Aix-en-Provence, 1960. Edited by J. Banbury and
J. Maitland. London: English Universities Press, 1961. xx,
810 p. Diagrams, tables.

Third, Oslo, 1963. Edited by G. Kreweras and G. Morlat.
London: English Universities Press, 1964. xiv, 952 p. Diagrams, tables.

Fourth, Massachusetts Institute of Technology, 1966. Edited
by David B. Hertz and Jacques Melesse. Publications in
Operations Research. New York: Wiley-Interscience, 1966.
xxxvi, 1,092 p. Diagrams (2 folding), tables.

Fifth, Venice, 1969. Edited by John Lawrence. London:
Tavistock, 1970. cxxvi, 855 p. Diagrams, tables. (Distributed by Barnes & Noble, Scranton, Pa.)

1138 Kaufmann, A., and Faure, R. INTRODUCTION TO OPERATIONS RE-
SEARCH. Translated by Henry C. Sneyd. Mathematics in Science and
Engineering Series, vol. 47. New York: Academic Press, 1968. 300 p.
Diagrams, tables, bibliography.

This practical guide for the decision maker is presented in the framework of eighteen short studies of simplified problems. It was originally published in 1965 by Dunod, Paris, as INVITA- TION A LA RECHERCHE OPERATIONELLE.

1139 Mansfield, Edwin, ed. MANAGERIAL ECONOMICS AND OPERATIONS RESEARCH: A NONMATHEMATICAL INTRODUCTION. Rev. ed. New York: Norton, 1970; London: Macmillan, 1971. xii, 396 p. Diagrams, tables.

This book contains thirty-nine contributions from various sources, arranged in seven sections: the decision-making process, cost and demand, capital budgeting and forecasting, linear programming and related techniques, and operations research in the public sector. No index.

1140 Martin, Michael J.C., and Denison, Raymond A., eds. CASE EXERCISES IN OPERATIONS RESEARCH. London: Wiley-Interscience, 1971. xvii, 210 p. Diagrams, map, tables.

This book contains fifteen cases from the University of Bradford collection, edited by the Head of the Management Science program at Bradford (Martin) and an assistant professor in Iowa State University's Department of Industrial Engineering (Denison). No index.

1141 Richmond, Samuel B. OPERATIONS RESEARCH FOR MANAGEMENT DECISIONS. New York: Ronald Press, 1968. xvi, 615 p. Diagrams, tables.

In six sections Richmond covers optimization problems, probability theory and applications, allocation problems, stochastic models, scheduling models, and decision theory.

1142 Rivett, B.H. Patrick, and Ackoff, Russell L. A MANAGER'S GUIDE TO OPERATIONAL RESEARCH. London: Wiley, 1963. 107 p. Bibliography.

The authors provide a brief literature review on pp. 99-101.

1143 Siemens, Nicolai; Marting, C.H.; and Greenwood, Frank. OPERATIONS RESEARCH: PLANNING, OPERATING AND INFORMATION SYSTEMS. New York: Free Press; London: Collier-Macmillan, 1973. 450 p. Diagrams, tables, bibliographies.

According to the authors, this book will provide "a sound foundation of basic OR concepts (including management information systems) for students, administrators, executives, etc. and assumes no prior exposure to OR or MIS" (preface). Part one deals with the application of OR to planning systems; part two with operating systems; and part three with management information systems. Practical problems are given at the end of chapters in parts one and two.

1144 Tomlinson, Rolfe C., ed. OR COMES OF AGE: A REVIEW OF THE WORK OF THE OPERATIONAL RESEARCH BRANCH OF THE NATIONAL COAL BOARD, 1968-1969. London: Tavistock, 1971. xii, 217 p. Diagrams, tables. (Distributed by Barnes & Noble, Scranton, Pa.)

> This book deals with the history and present organization of OR in the National Coal Board, including its relationship with other specializations like work study. Some specific achievements in the areas of production, marketing, planning, and man management are considered.

1145 Vollman, Thomas E. OPERATIONS MANAGEMENT: A SYSTEMS MODEL-BUILDING APPROACH. Reading, Mass.: Addison-Wesley, 1973. xx, 716 p. Illustrations, diagrams, tables.

> Designed to provide the reader with a basic understanding of the systems approach to the design of operations procedures, with a minimum of mathematics.

1146 Wagner, Harvey M. PRINCIPLES OF OPERATIONS RESEARCH, WITH APPLICATION TO MANAGERIAL DECISIONS. Englewood Cliffs, N.J.: Prentice-Hall, 1969. xxii, 1,164 p. Diagrams, tables, bibliography.

> This is a comprehensive text for students with no previous background in OR who plan management careers. Each chapter concludes with review exercises, computational and formulation exercises, and mind-expanding exercises.

Periodicals

1147 BULLETIN OF THE OPERATIONS RESEARCH SOCIETY OF AMERICA. Baltimore: 1959- . Twice yearly.

> Abstracts of papers given at national meetings of the society are included.

1148 INFOR: CANADIAN JOURNAL OF OPERATIONAL RESEARCH AND INFORMATION PROCESSING. Ottawa: 1963- . Three issues yearly.

1149 OPERATIONAL RESEARCH QUARTERLY. Oxford: Pergamon Press, 1950- .

> This journal is published for the Operational Research Society.

1150 OPERATIONS RESEARCH: THE JOURNAL OF THE OPERATIONS RESEARCH SOCIETY OF AMERICA. Baltimore: 1952- . Bimonthly.

Bibliographies

1151 Batchelor, James H. "Operations Research: An Annotated Bibliography."

2d ed. 4 vols. St. Louis: St. Louis University Press, 1959–64. Mimeographed.

> Vol. 1 (865 p.), 1959; vol. 2 (628 p.), 1962; vol. 3 (xvi, 384 p.), 1963; vol. 4 (477 p.), 1964. Each volume is arranged by author, with index of authors, titles, and subjects.

1152 Case Institute of Technology. Engineering Administration Dept. Operations Research Group. A COMPREHENSIVE BIBLIOGRAPHY ON OPERATIONS RESEARCH THROUGH 1956, WITH SUPPLEMENT FOR 1957. Operations Research Society of America. Publications in Operations Research, no. 4. New York: Wiley; London: Chapman & Hall, 1958. 188 p. Tables.

> This alphabetical author list contains approximately 3,000 articles, books, reports, proceedings, etc., and has a classified index. It covers all articles from JOURNAL OF THE OPERATIONS RESEARCH SOCIETY OF AMERICA, OPERATIONAL RESEARCH QUARTERLY, MANAGEMENT SCIENCE and NAVAL RESEARCH LOGISTICS QUARTERLY, and selected articles from ECONOMETRICA, JOURNAL OF INDUSTRIAL ENGINEERING, and some other titles.

1153 _____. A COMPREHENSIVE BIBLIOGRAPHY ON OPERATIONS RESEARCH, 1957-1958. Operations Research Society of America. Publications in Operations Research, no. 8. New York: Wiley, 1963. xiii, 403 p.

> This supplements item 1152.

1154 Great Britain. Government Communications Headquarters. OPERATIONAL RESEARCH. 2d ed. Compiled by W.F. Greenhalgh and edited by J. Dudley. Library Booklist, no. 21. Cheltenham, Eng.: 1969. 120 p. Paperback.

> This classified and annotated list of 592 books and articles has a name index. It includes a useful introductory guide to the literature, with annotated list of periodicals and abstracting journals. Classification of OR techniques, pp. 23-24.

1155 Townsend, Michael. OPERATIONAL RESEARCH ON ACTIVE SERVICE. ANBAR Monograph, no. 17. London: Anbar Publications, 1970. 32 p. Paperback.

> This volume contains abstracts of fifty articles and papers on the application of operations research to planning and scheduling, stock control, purchasing, investment, accounting, transport, distribution, and marketing culled from thirteen journals. It is preceded by a small glossary.

Abstracting and Indexing Services

1156 INTERNATIONAL ABSTRACTS IN OPERATIONS RESEARCH. Amsterdam, Netherlands: Elsevier/North-Holland Journal Division, 1961- . Bimonthly with annual author and subject indexes.

> This classified list, covering books, reports, and articles, is published for the International Federation of Operational Research Societies.

1157 OPERATIONS RESEARCH/MANAGEMENT SCIENCE. Whippany, N.J.: Executive Sciences Institute, 1961- .

> This looseleaf service consists of sheets which may be filed by page number, by an alphabetical code representing methodology subject-matter, or by a numerical classification permitting precise specification of function. Author and subject indexes are provided as each annual volume is completed.

Organizations

1158 Institute for Operational Research, 56-60 Hallam Street, London, WlN 5LH, England.

> This organization was formed in 1963 to carry out OR studies and to extend the field to which OR can be applied.

1159 Operational Research Society, 6th Floor, Neville House, Waterloo Street, Birmingham, B2 5TX, England.

> Founded in 1954, the society publishes OPERATIONAL RESEARCH QUARTERLY.

1160 Operations Research Society of America, 428 East Preston Street, Baltimore, Md. 21202.

> The publications of this organization, which was formed in 1952, include OPERATIONS RESEARCH and a twice-yearly BULLETIN.

SYSTEMS ANALYSIS

This section covers the analysis of organizational requirements and the design of new procedures, often involving the use of computers.

1161 Fitzgerald, John M., and Fitzgerald, Ardra F. THE FUNDAMENTALS OF SYSTEMS ANALYSIS. New York: Wiley, 1973. xii, 531 p. Illustrations, diagrams, forms, tables.

This book is suitable for a first course for college students, with "situation cases" at the end of each chapter. It is presented in three parts: the preliminaries, the system study itself, and the tools of systems analysis (charting, forms design, records retention, report analysis, and procedure writing). Glossary, pp. 443-67.

1162 Greenwood, Frank. MANAGING THE SYSTEMS ANALYSIS FUNCTION. New York: American Management Association, 1968. 137 p. Tables.

Greenwood discusses the selection, education, training, and motivation of analysts. The book includes a chapter on management and motivation by Richard W. French and one on day-to-day systems management by John C. Froelich. No index.

1163 Hanika, F. de P. NEW THINKING IN MANAGEMENT: A GUIDE FOR MANAGERS. London: Heinemann, 1972. xvi, 160 p. Diagrams, tables, bibliographies.

This was published for the Administrative Staff College, Henley-on-Thames, England. Part one ("The Systems Analysis Approach") explains systems analysis and its possibilities for management. Part two ("Some Advances in Management Technology") describes developments in decision theory, information theory, simulation and management games, programming and queueing and heuristic method. Part three ("New Thinking in Practice") shows how the new thinking is being applied in organization research, economic analysis, and operations analysis.

1164 Johnson, Richard A.; Kast, Fremont E.; and Rosenzweig, James E. THE THEORY AND MANAGEMENT OF SYSTEMS. McGraw-Hill Series in Management. 3d ed. New York: McGraw-Hill, 1973. xvii, 539 p. Diagrams, tables, bibliography.

This is arranged in three parts: systems theory and concepts, design and analysis, and managerial implications. It includes case studies of the Weyerhaeuser Company, Petersen General Contractors, Acme Aircraft Corporation, O-Nut Incorporated, the Hitonic Machine Corporation, Atlas Electronics Corporation, New York State (planning, programming, and budgeting system), and Consolidated Producers. Indexes of names and subjects.

1165 Optner, Stanford L. SYSTEMS ANALYSIS FOR BUSINESS MANAGE-MENT. 2d ed. Englewood Cliffs, N.J.: Prentice-Hall, 1968. 277 p. Illustrations, diagrams, tables, bibliography.

Part one provides a guide to the applications of systems analysis, with chapters on electronic data processing, characteristics of computer equipment, and costing. Part two consists of nine case studies.

1166 Siegert, Paul P. SYSTEMS AND GENERAL MANAGEMENT: A RATION-
ALE. New York: American Management Association, 1972. 181 p.
Tables.

> Siegert defines systems analysis, discusses the computer and
> the relationship between systems analysis and computer pro-
> gramming, illustrates systems problems, and explains the place
> of the systems staff in the corporate structure.

1167 SYSTEMS ANALYSIS AND DESIGN. New York: Time-Life Video.

> These are four color videotapes. THE SYSTEMS APPROACH
> (6 min.) defines a working system and provides a case study
> of a man who cannot get what he wants because he does not
> employ a system. DEFINING SYSTEMS OBJECTIVES (10 min.)
> uses a fifteenth-century town as a case study. INFORMA-
> TION SYSTEMS PLANNING (7 min.) demonstrates the need
> for alternative plans to be considered. In INFORMATION
> SYSTEMS ANALYSIS (10 1/2 min.) a team is given the task
> of designing a system to protect against famine on a new
> planet.

Bibliographies

1168 National Aeronautics and Space Administration. Scientific and Technical
Information Division. THE SYSTEMS APPROACH TO MANAGEMENT:
AN ANNOTATED BIBLIOGRAPHY WITH INDEXES. Washington, D.C.:
1969. 62 p. Paperback. (Distributed by Clearing House for Federal
Scientific and Technical Information, Springfield, Va.)

> This bibliography lists 527 books and articles under nine head-
> ings including multinational organization (eight items), public
> administration (ninety-seven items), manpower management
> (twenty-six items), and impact on management (seventy-two
> items).

1169 Organization for Economic Co-operation and Development. SYSTEMS
ANALYSIS FOR EDUCATIONAL PLANNING: SELECTED ANNOTATED
BIBLIOGRAPHY. Paris: 1969. 219 p. Paperback.

> This is a classified list of more than 300 items on the appli-
> cation of systems analysis to education, including items on
> operations research and the quantitative approach in general.
> No subject index.

NETWORK ANALYSIS

This is the generic name for a group of related techniques used in the planning
and control of complex projects. The time required for the activities and the

sequence in which they should be performed are analyzed and represented in
the form of a diagram known as a network. The two major network analysis
techniques are Program Evaluation and Review Technique (PERT) and Critical
Path Method (CPM).

1170 Archibald, Russell D., and Villoria, Richard L. NETWORK-BASED MAN-
AGEMENT SYSTEMS (PERT/CPM). Information Science Series. New
York: Wiley, 1968. xiv, 508 p. Diagrams, tables, bibliography.

Part one deals with network planning--what it is, how it works.
Part two is concerned with implementing the system. Part three
contains case studies. Part four covers pitfalls and potentials
of such systems.

1171 Battersby, Albert. NETWORK ANALYSIS FOR PLANNING AND SCHED-
ULING. 3d ed. London: Macmillan; New York: Wiley, 1970. 332 p.
Diagrams, tables, bibliography.

A standard, easy-to-follow book with case studies of the construction of twelve liquid oxygen tankers for British Oxygen
Co. Ltd., the launching of a new confectionery product, and
the prevention and detection of crime. Fifty-six exercises
and solutions are included.

1172 Hoare, H.R. PROJECT MANAGEMENT USING NETWORK ANALYSIS.
London: McGraw-Hill, 1973. 109 p. Diagrams, tables, bibliography.
Paperback.

This is intended to provide nontechnical managers with suffi-
cient knowledge to allow them to question networks and to
provide constructive criticism of the development of project
plans and controls. Glossary, pp. 104-6.

1173 Holden, Ian R., and McIlroy, P.K. NETWORK PLANNING IN MAN-
AGEMENT CONTROL SYSTEMS. London: Hutchinson, 1970. xvi, 119 p.
Diagrams, tables. Hardcover and paperback.

The authors consider preplanning, the mechanics of network
planning, the link between operational and financial control,
management control, budgetary control, and profitability control. There is a list of computer software available in Britain
for network planning, pp. 109-14.

1174 International Congress on Project Planning by Network Techniques, 3d,
Stockholm, 1972. THE PRACTICAL APPLICATION OF PROJECT PLAN-
NING BY NETWORK TECHNIQUES. Edited by Mats Ogander. 3 vols.
Stockholm: Alquist & Wiksell; New York: Halsted Press, 1972. Illus-
trations, diagrams, tables.

Volume 1: INTRODUCTION AND NETWORK PLANNING IN
ACTION (411 p.); volume 2: PRACTICAL APPLICATION OF
NETWORK PLANNING IN BRANCHES/AREAS (658 p.); volume

3: COMPUTER PROGRAMS FOR INTEGRATED NETWORK PLAN-
NING; PROJECT MANAGEMENT AND INFORMATION SYSTEMS
USING NETWORK TECHNIQUES (596 p.). This work contains
110 papers, international in scope, including several case studies.
Index of authors, but no subject index.

1175 Levin, Richard I., and Kirkpatrick, Charles A. PLANNING AND CON-
TROL WITH PERT/CPM. New York: McGraw-Hill, 1966. 179 p. Diagrams, tables, bibliography. Hardcover and paperback.

1176 Lockyer, K.G. AN INTRODUCTION TO CRITICAL PATH ANALYSIS.
3d ed. London: Pitman, 1969. 219 p. Diagrams, tables, bibliography.

This is a standard British text. Annotated reading list, pp.
203-8. Glossary, pp. 209-14.

1177 McLaren, K.G., and Buesnel, E.L. NETWORK ANALYSIS IN PROJECT
MANAGEMENT: AN INTRODUCTORY MANUAL BASED ON UNILEVER
EXPERIENCE. London: Cassell, 1969. Diagrams, forms, tables, bib-
liography.

This is a manual for self-instruction or for use in training
courses, with material from twelve companies in the Unilever
group and exercises. Glossary, pp. 192-94.

1178 Martino, R.L. CRITICAL PATH NETWORKS. New York: McGraw-Hill,
1970. 157 p. Diagrams, tables.

A basic primer, this work includes a list of computer programs
available. It was originally published by Management Development Institute, Wayne, Pennsylvania, 1967. No index.

1179 _____. PROJECT MANAGEMENT AND CONTROL. 3 vols. New
York: American Management Association, 1964-65.

Volume 1: FINDING THE CRITICAL PATH, 1964 (144 p.);
volume 2: APPLIED OPERATIONAL PLANNING, 1964 (184 p.,
diagrams, tables, bibliography); volume 3: ALLOCATING
AND SCHEDULING RESOURCES, 1965 (143 p., diagrams,
forms, tables). No index.

1180 Miller, Robert W. SCHEDULE, COST AND PROFIT CONTROL WITH
PERT: A COMPREHENSIVE GUIDE FOR PROGRAM MANAGEMENT.
New York: McGraw-Hill, 1963. xvi, 227 p. Diagrams, tables, bib-
liography.

This work is one of the earliest texts to consider the application of PERT, a network planning system originally evolved
for government projects, to management systems. Glossary
of some representative management systems terms, pp. 207-15;
glossary of PERT terminology, pp. 217-22.

1181 Moder, Joseph J., and Phillips, Cecil R. PROJECT MANAGEMENT WITH CPM AND PERT. 2d ed. New York: Van Nostrand Reinhold, 1970. xviii, 360 p. Diagrams, tables, bibliographies.

Many exercises with solutions are included.

1182 O'Brien, James J. CPM IN CONSTRUCTION MANAGEMENT: PROJECT MANAGEMENT WITH CPM. 2d ed. New York: McGraw-Hill, 1971. 321 p. Diagrams, tables.

O'Brien gives a comprehensive account of the application of the critical path method and other network planning techniques, with several case histories. Glossary, pp. 291-93.

1183 Smith, K.M. CRITICAL PATH PLANNING: A PRACTICAL GUIDE. 2d ed. London: Management Publications, 1971. xiii, 151 p. Diagrams, tables, bibliography.

This readable and practical guide has several appendixes, including a list of selected bureaus offering computer facilities for network analysis, examples of computer input forms and printed output, and details of the two original network planning systems (PERT and CPM).

1184 Stilian, Gabriel N., et al. PERT: A NEW MANAGEMENT PLANNING AND CONTROL TECHNIQUE. New York: American Management Association, 1962. 192 p. Diagrams, forms, bibliography.

The technique is no longer new, but this remains a useful collection of contributions by thirteen authors in four sections: PERT and the manager; PERT theory; practical experience with PERT (four case studies); and allied techniques.

1185 Stires, David M., and Murphy, Maurice R. MODERN MANAGEMENT METHODS: PROGRAM EVALUATION REVIEW TECHNIQUE AND CRITICAL PATH METHOD. Boston: Materials Management Institute, 1962. 294 p. Diagrams, forms, tables, bibliography.

Numerous case studies are included. Glossary, pp. 108-15. No index.

1186 Thornley, Gail, ed. CRITICAL PATH ANALYSIS IN PRACTICE: COLLECTED PAPERS ON PROJECT CONTROL. London: Tavistock, 1968. xii, 152 p. Diagrams, tables, bibliography. Hardcover and paperback. (Distributed by Barnes & Noble, Scranton, Pa.)

This is a collection of eighteen contributions by thirteen authorities. Glossary of terms and symbols, pp. 137-39. Selective annotated reading list, pp. 140-42. List of computer programs available in Britain, pp. 145-47.

1187 Woodgate, Harry Samuel. PLANNING BY NETWORKS: PROJECT PLAN-
NING AND CONTROL USING NETWORK TECHNIQUES. 2d ed. Lon-
don: Business Publications; Philadelphia: Auerbach, 1967. xx, 385 p.
Diagrams, tables.

Glossary, pp. 368-73.

Section 9

AUTOMATION AND COMPUTERS

There are a great number of works on automation and computers, but many are technical in approach. Those listed here emphasize the management problems and the implications for society. The section is very selective and readers are referred to the bibliographies and abstracting services listed as items 1224-33 for further guidance, particularly the companion volume in this series by Chester Morrill, Jr. (item 1227).

GENERAL STUDIES

1188 American Management Association. MAKING THE COMPUTER WORK FOR MANAGEMENT. PRIME 100 Series. New York: American Management Association, 1967.

> This programmed instruction course is designed to last for six study hours. Its four sections show how computer capabilities can help in planning, scheduling, executing, and controlling. It also considers how the manager can determine whether computerization will solve his problems. Eight typical problems are analyzed for practice.

1189 Birch, S., and Johannsen, Hano. ACHIEVING COMPUTER PROFITABILITY: A SURVEY OF CURRENT PRACTICE IN 102 COMPANIES. Management Survey Report, no. 1. London: British Institute of Management, 1971. 43 p. Tables. Paperback.

> The authors suggest twelve factors as being critical to computer usage, including concentration on the needs of the business, not rushing into computers, recruiting a first-class staff, keeping systems simple, and laying down adequate standards.

1190 Bright, James R. AUTOMATION AND MANAGEMENT. Boston: Harvard University Graduate School of Business Administration, Division of Research, 1958. xv, 270 p. Illustrations, diagrams, forms, tables.

> This research study considers the evolution of automation and

its implications for management, including a review of thirteen
automation programs. Part three covers some critical areas of
automation, particularly its impact on personnel and sales.

1191 Brink, Victor Z. COMPUTERS AND MANAGEMENT: THE EXECUTIVE
      VIEWPOINT. Englewood Cliffs, N.J.: Prentice-Hall, 1971. xii, 172 p.
      Diagrams, bibliography.

      Brink examines practices in more than 100 large companies,
      dealing with such matters as the impact of computers on man-
      agement practice and on organizational policy and the man-
      agement of computer activities. Appendixes consider the
      changing dimension of the management role brought about by
      computers and the nature and capabilities of computers. An-
      notated bibliography, pp. 165-68.

1192 Buckingham, Walter. AUTOMATION: ITS IMPACT ON BUSINESS AND
      PEOPLE. New York: Harper, 1961. 196 p. Paperback ed. New York:
      New American Library, 1963.

      Buckingham uses many case studies to consider the impact of
      automation on industrial organization and structure, small busi-
      nesses, working conditions, employment, prices, and economic
      growth, as well as its implications for education, leisure, and
      culture.

1193 Dearden, John, and Nolan, Richard L. "How to Control the Computer
      Resource." HARVARD BUSINESS REVIEW 51 (November-December 1973):
      68-78. Diagrams.

      The authors note various mechanisms which are necessary for
      effective management control of the EDP function, including
      adequate accounting, planning, and auditing; steering commit-
      tees; and project management.

1194 Foy, Nancy. COMPUTER MANAGEMENT: A COMMON SENSE AP-
      PROACH. Philadelphia: Auerbach; London: Longman, 1972. xiv, 210 p.
      Diagrams, tables, bibliographies.

      The British edition is entitled COMPUTERS AND COMMON-
      SENSE. A readable guide to the management of computer sys-
      tems, with chapters on dealing with computer makers, working
      with consultants, leasing versus buying, use of service bureaus,
      communication of data, and selection and training of computer
      personnel.

1195 Grindley, Kit, and Humble, John W. THE EFFECTIVE COMPUTER: A
      MANAGEMENT BY OBJECTIVES APPROACH. New York: American
      Management Association; London: McGraw-Hill, 1973. xiii, 187 p.
      Diagrams, tables, bibliography.

      This book helps to analyze why the average computer installation is less effective than anticipated. The prevention and correction of defects in the system are also discussed.

1196 Harold, Frederick G. A HANDBOOK FOR ORIENTING THE MANAGER TO THE COMPUTER. Princeton, N.J.: Auerbach, 1971. 247 p. Diagrams, tables.

Harold offers a guide for trainers in computer orientation courses and seminars for managers.

1197 Hertz, David B. NEW POWER FOR MANAGEMENT: COMPUTER SYSTEMS AND MANAGEMENT SCIENCES. New York: McGraw-Hill, 1969. xiii, 208 p. Diagrams, tables, bibliography.

This is a guide by a director of the McKinsey Organization to the application of the tools of management science to such problems as long-range planning, capital investment analysis, production-distribution-marketing analysis, organization structure, and management control. Annotated reading list, pp. 198-202.

1198 Heyel, Carl. JOHN DIEBOLD ON MANAGEMENT. Foreword by Richard M. Cyert. Englewood Cliffs, N.J.: Prentice-Hall, 1972. 282 p. Illustrations, diagrams, portraits, tables, bibliography.

This collection, with commentaries, includes writings and speeches of a management expert who was one of the first to recognize the implications of the computer for management and society. The writings cover a wide range of management topics with the computer and technological change as the central themes.

1199 Higginson, M. Valliant. MANAGING WITH EDP: A LOOK AT THE STATE OF THE ART. AMA Research Study, no. 71. New York: American Management Association, 1965. 111 p. Diagrams, tables, bibliography.

Practices in twenty-six companies are considered. Annotated bibliography, pp. 107-8. Indexes of subjects and company names.

1200 International Labour Office. LABOUR AND AUTOMATION. 7 vols. Geneva: 1964-68. Paperback.

This important study consists of seven bulletins dealing with the impact of automation on industrial societies in various stages of development. Only bulletin no. 5 is indexed.

Bulletin no. 1: AUTOMATION: A DISCUSSION OF RESEARCH METHODS, 1964. 276 p. Forms.

Bulletin no. 2: A TABULATION OF CASE STUDIES ON TECH-

NOLOGICAL CHANGE: ECONOMIC AND SOCIAL PROB-
LEMS REVIEWED IN 160 CASE STUDIES, 1965. 87 p. Tables.

Bulletin no. 3: TECHNOLOGICAL CHANGE AND MAN-
POWER IN A CENTRALLY PLANNED ECONOMY: A STUDY
BASED ON SOVIET LITERATURE DEALING WITH THE METAL-
WORKING INDUSTRY IN THE U.S.S.R., 1966. 92 p. Dia-
grams, tables, bibliography.

Bulletin no. 4: MANPOWER ADJUSTMENT PROGRAMMES.
1: FRANCE, FEDERAL REPUBLIC OF GERMANY, UNITED
KINGDOM, 1967. 207 p.

Bulletin no. 5: AUTOMATION AND NON-MANUAL WORK-
ERS, 1967. 113 p. Bibliography.

Bulletin no. 6: MANPOWER ADJUSTMENT PROGRAMMES.
2: SWEDEN, U.S.S.R., UNITED STATES, 1967. 190 p.
Tables.

Bulletin no. 7: MANPOWER ADJUSTMENT PROGRAMMES.
3: CANADA, ITALY, JAPAN, 1968. 165 p. Tables.

1201 Mathes, Sorrell M. EDP AND THE SMALLER COMPANY. Managing
the Moderate-sized Company, Report no. 4. New York: Conference
Board, 1967. 31 p. Paperback.

Mathes summarizes the experiences of 160 U.S. and Canadian
manufacturing, mining, construction, and wholesaling organizations, most of which have fewer than 2,000 employees.
Topics covered include the use of EDP equipment and computers, computer service bureaus, benefits and problems of
EDP, and appraisal and justification of EDP.

1202 Maynard, Jeff. COMPUTER PROGRAMMING MANAGEMENT. London:
Butterworths, 1972. 99 p. Illustrations, tables.

This is a brief guide to management principles for the leader
of computer programming teams, written in the language of
programmers.

1203 O'Brien, James J. MANAGEMENT WITH COMPUTERS. New York:
Van Nostrand Reinhold, 1972. xiv, 302 p. Illustrations, diagrams,
tables.

O'Brien discusses the operations and management implications
of computers. Glossary, pp. 259-93.

1204 Rubin, Martin L., ed. HANDBOOK OF DATA PROCESSING MANAGE-
MENT. Vol. 6: DATA PROCESSING ADMINISTRATION. Princeton,
N.J.: Auerbach, 1971. xvii, 600 p. Illustrations, diagrams, tables,
bibliography.

This work includes chapters on data processing organization; data processing personnel policy; data processing education; data processing budget and cost control; data processing management audits; legal considerations in data processing; computer selection process; proposal evaluation; job accounting, maintenance, and emergency procedure; magnetic tape and disk operations; and computer time rental. Appendix of sample job descriptions, pp. 513-53. Glossary, pp. 565-76.

1205 Sanders, Donald H. COMPUTERS IN BUSINESS: AN INTRODUCTION. 3d ed. New York: McGraw-Hill, 1975. 608 p. Illustrations, diagrams, tables, bibliographies.

This review of the development, mechanics, and applications of computers has particularly valuable chapters on management and computers, planning for computers, organization and the computer, staffing and the computer, and control and the computer. Each concludes with a summary, discussion questions, and selected bibliographical references. There is a glossary.

1206 _____. THE CORPORATE COMPUTER: HOW TO LIVE WITH AN ECO- LOGICAL INTRUSION. London: McGraw-Hill, 1973. xiii, 161 p. Illustrations, diagrams, tables.

This humorous and practical approach to computer management also has a glossary ("A quick dip into the jargon"), pp. 146- 57.

1207 Simmons, J.R.M. LEO AND THE MANAGERS. London: Macdonald, 1962. 174 p. Diagrams, forms.

This is an account of the Lyons Electronic Office, a computer brought into operation by J. Lyons and Company (caterers), with proposals for its effective use by management. Glossary, pp. 168-69.

1208 Simon, Herbert A. THE SHAPE OF AUTOMATION FOR MEN AND MANAGEMENT. New York: Harper & Row, 1965. xv, 111 p. Paperback.

This book contains three lectures on the impact of computers on management: "The Long-Range Economic Effects of Automation"; "Will the Corporation be Managed by Machine?"; and the well-known "New Science of Management Decision." No index.

1209 Smith, Paul T. COMPUTERS, SYSTEMS, AND PROFITS. New York: American Management Association, 1969. 200 p. Diagrams, tables.

This guide to the successful installation and application of computer systems features an extensive case study. Smith emphasizes the importance of systems design if a computer system is to reap benefits.

1210 _____ . HOW TO LIVE WITH YOUR COMPUTER: A NONTECHNICAL GUIDE FOR MANAGERS. New York: American Management Association, 1965. 207 p. Diagrams, tables.

> Part one discusses the management and application of data processing systems, with many examples. Part two consists of five chapters on the mechanics of computers. Glossary, pp. 197-205. No index.

1211 Stewart, Rosemary. HOW COMPUTERS AFFECT MANAGEMENT. London: Macmillan, 1971; New York: M.I.T. Press, 1972. 244 p. Tables.

> An important British study, this work discusses a research project on implications of computers for clerical procedures, production planning and control, and investment planning, as well as the relations between computer staff and user management and the general implications of computers for management. The author includes case studies of the British Oxygen Company Ltd., British Petroleum Ltd., the Gas Council, Hayward Tyler, Oxford University Press, the West Midlands Gas Board, as well as four unnamed companies.

1212 Sturt, Humphrey, and Yearsley, Ronald B., eds. COMPUTERS FOR MANAGEMENT. London: Heinemann, 1969; New York: American Elsevier, 1970. 199 p. Diagrams, tables.

> This book contains papers on the historical perspective; computer hardware and software; the use of the computer in production, finance, marketing, and planning; the economics of computer usage; the placement of the computer in the organization; and computer people.

1213 Thompson, T.R. MANAGEMENT AND COMPUTER CONTROL. London: Gee, 1973. xiii, 330 p. Illustrations, diagrams, forms, tables. (Distributed by Counting House Publishing Co., Thiensville, Wis.)

> This book is designed to provide the manager with sufficient knowledge of computers to allow him to direct a computer project. Glossary, pp. 303-24.

1214 Tomlin, Roger. MANAGING THE INTRODUCTION OF COMPUTER SYSTEMS. McGraw-Hill European Series in Management and Marketing. London: McGraw-Hill, 1970. 186 p. Illustrations, diagrams (1 folding), forms.

> This practical, nontechnical guide includes references to applications at International Computers Ltd. (ICL), Barclays Bank Ltd., Ross Group Ltd., and Hoover Ltd. The chapter on departmental control has been praised by reviewers for its clarity and originality.

1215 Whisler, Thomas L. THE IMPACT OF COMPUTERS ON ORGANIZA-
TIONS. New Directions in Management and Economics. New York:
Praeger, 1970. xiv, 188 p. Tables.

> Developed from a study of a number of companies in the life
> insurance business, this book includes chapters on the impact
> of computers on organizational structure, decision making,
> authority and control, and job satisfaction.

1216 Withington, Frederic G. THE ORGANIZATION OF THE DATA PROCES-
SING FUNCTION. Wiley Business Data Processing Library. New York:
Wiley, 1972. 99 p. Diagrams.

> This is a guide to the planning, implementation, and opera-
> tion of data processing centers and to the place of the data
> processing function within the organization. The book is
> based on the experiences of many organizations and has case
> studies.

1217 Wooldridge, Susan, and London, Keith. THE COMPUTER SURVIVAL
HANDBOOK: HOW TO TALK BACK TO YOUR COMPUTER. Newton
Abbot, Eng.: David and Charles; Boston: Gambit, 1973. 200 p. Il-
lustrations, diagrams.

> This light-hearted but valuable guide for the manager to the
> pitfalls of computers also discusses what to do about them.
> Glossary, pp. 185-95. No index.

1218 Yearsley, Ronald B., and Graham, G.M.R., eds. HANDBOOK OF
COMPUTER MANAGEMENT. Epping, Eng.: Gower Press; New York:
Halsted Press, 1973. xxvii, 328 p. Diagrams, forms, tables.

> Twenty-two contributions are presented in four sections: survey
> of computing systems; buying computer services; managing the
> data processing function; and applications of computers in busi-
> ness. Glossary, pp. 313-18.

Periodicals

1219 THE COMPUTER JOURNAL. London: British Computer Society, 1958- .
Quarterly.

> Mainly technical in approach, this journal includes some man-
> agement articles.

1220 COMPUTERS AND PEOPLE. Newtonville, Mass.: Berkeley Enterprises,
1951- . Monthly.

> This journal, formerly COMPUTERS AND AUTOMATION, con-
> tains brief articles and notes on "the design, applications and
> implications of information processing systems."

1221 DATAMATION. Barrington, Ill.: Technical Publishing Company, 1957- . Monthly.

> This publication contains articles on technical and management aspects of data processing, details of new equipment, and book notes.

1222 DATA PROCESSING: THE INTERNATIONAL JOURNAL FOR COMPUTER MANAGEMENT. London: IPC Electrical-Electronic Press, 1959- . Bimonthly.

> This contains brief articles on developments in computer technology and applications, with notes on new books and equipment.

1223 DATA SYSTEMS FOR MANAGEMENT DECISIONS. London: Embankment Press, 1969- . Monthly.

Bibliographies

1224 Gotterer, Malcolm H. KWIC INDEX: A BIBLIOGRAPHY OF COMPUTER MANAGEMENT. Philadelphia: Auerbach, 1970. 152 p. Paperback.

> This contains separate permuted title and author indexes.

1225 INTERNATIONAL COMPUTER BIBLIOGRAPHY: A GUIDE TO BOOKS ON THE USE, APPLICATION AND EFFECTS OF COMPUTERS IN SCIENTIFIC, COMMERCIAL, INDUSTRIAL AND SOCIAL ENVIRONMENTS. Manchester, Eng.: National Computing Centre, 1968. 399 p. Paperback.

> This classified listing contains nearly 6,000 English, French, and German books, with abstracts in the language of the original publication. It was compiled jointly by the National Computing Centre and the Studiecentrum voor Administratieve Automatisering, Amsterdam, Holland. Indexes of authors and keywords.

1226 INTERNATIONAL COMPUTER BIBLIOGRAPHY: A GUIDE TO BOOKS ON THE USE, APPLICATION AND EFFECTS OF COMPUTERS IN SCIENTIFIC, COMMERCIAL, INDUSTRIAL AND SOCIAL ENVIRONMENTS. Vol. 2. Edited by H.J. van der Aa. Amsterdam, Holland: Stichting Het Nederlands Studiecentrum voor Information; Manchester, Eng.: National Computing Centre, 1971. 191 p. Paperback. (Distributed by Science Associates International, New York.)

> This work supplements the previous item.

1227 Morrill, Chester, Jr. COMPUTERS AND DATA PROCESSING INFORMATION SOURCES: AN ANNOTATED GUIDE TO THE LITERATURE, AS-

SOCIATIONS AND INSTITUTIONS CONCERNED WITH INPUT, THROUGH-
PUT AND OUTPUT OF DATA. Management Information Guide, no. 15.
Detroit: Gale Research Co., 1969. 275 p.

This is a very thorough and useful guide, mainly to U.S.
sources. It has indexes of authors, titles, and subjects.

Abstracting and Indexing Services

1228 ACCOUNTING + DATA PROCESSING ABSTRACTS. London: Anbar Publications, 1971- . Eight issues yearly.

This is particularly useful in that all the articles abstracted
emphasize the management, rather than technical, aspects of
computers. For a full annotation see item 1785.

1229 COMPUTER ABSTRACTS. St. Helier, Channel Islands: Technical Information Co., 1957- . Monthly.

This listing covers books, U.S. government reports, patents,
conference papers, and periodical articles. Abstracts are arranged under nineteen subject headings, one of which deals
with management applications. Indexes of authors and patents
are in each issue, with annual author, subject, and patent indexes.

1230 COMPUTING JOURNAL ABSTRACTS. Manchester, Eng.: National Computing Centre, 1969- . Weekly.

Abstracts of articles on technical and managerial aspects are
arranged under broad subject headings, with six-monthly indexes.

1231 COMPUTING REVIEWS: REVIEW JOURNAL OF THE ASSOCIATION FOR
COMPUTING MACHINERY. New York: 1960- . Monthly.

This contains critical abstracts and reviews of books, papers,
films, and video tapes on all aspects of computing, technical
and managerial, systematically arranged.

1232 DATA PROCESSING DIGEST. Los Angeles, 1955- . Monthly.

The digest contains synopses of periodical articles, signed book
reviews, details of meetings, and other activities.

1233 NEW LITERATURE ON AUTOMATION. Amsterdam: Netherlands Center
for Informatics, 1960- . Monthly.

Included are systematically arranged abstracts of books and
articles from about 300 periodicals, with the emphasis on the
continent of Europe. Abstracts are in the language of the

original item. Technical and management aspects are covered, and a list of forthcoming conferences and meetings follows the abstracts. Each issue has an author index, with occasional cumulative indexes.

Dictionaries

1234 Buerger, Erich, and Schuppe, Wolfgang. TECHNICAL DICTIONARY OF DATA PROCESSING, COMPUTERS, OFFICE MACHINES. Oxford, Eng.: Pergamon Press, 1970. 1,463 p.

This work lists about 13,000 terms in English, French, German, and Russian. It was originally published by VEB Verlag Technik, Berlin, 1970.

1235 Camille, Claude, and Dihaine, Michel. DICTIONARY OF DATA PRO-CESSING. 2 vols. London: Harrap, 1970. (Distributed by International Publications Service, New York.)

Volume 1: English-French (278 p.); volume 2: French-English (248 p.).

1236 Chandor, Anthony; Graham, John; and Williamson, Robin. A DICTION-ARY OF COMPUTERS. Harmondsworth, Eng.: Penguin; Magnolia, Mass.: Peter Smith, 1970. 406 p. Bibliography. Paperback.

1237 Sippl, Charles J. COMPUTER DICTIONARY AND HANDBOOK. Indianapolis: Howard W. Sams & Co., 1966; Slough, Bucks, Eng.: Foulsham, 1967. 766 p. Illustrations, diagrams, tables, bibliography.

Definitions of terms are followed by twenty-six appendixes which cover computer systems personnel, management science topics, operations research, flowcharting, acronyms and abbreviations, and computer publications. The English edition includes a specially written chapter for the English reader by W. Oliver.

1238 Trollhann, Lilian, and Wittman, Alfred. DICTIONARY OF DATA PRO-CESSING. Amsterdam: Elsevier, 1964. 300 p.

Originally published by R. Oldenbourg Verlag, Munich and Vienna, 1964, this work lists terms in English, French, and German without definitions.

1239 U.S. Bureau of the Budget. AUTOMATIC DATA PROCESSING: GLOS-SARY. Washington, D.C.: Government Printing Office, 1962. 62 p. Paperback.

MANAGEMENT INFORMATION SYSTEMS (MIS)

MIS refers to the use of the computer to provide management with the information it needs for planning, decision making, and control.

1240 Albrecht, Leon K. ORGANIZATION AND MANAGEMENT OF INFOR-
MATION PROCESSING SYSTEMS. New York: Macmillan; London:
Collier-Macmillan, 1973. xiii, 383 p. Diagrams, tables.

Part one deals with the organization of information systems;
part two with planning, designing, and implementing information systems; and part three with the management of information systems organizations. Part three includes a detailed
case study of MIS in a finance company.

1241 Bocchino, William A. MANAGEMENT INFORMATION SYSTEMS: TOOLS
AND TECHNIQUES. Englewood Cliffs, N.J.: Prentice-Hall, 1972.
xii, 404 p. Illustrations, diagrams, tables, bibliographies.

Bocchino covers industrial engineering tools, computer-oriented
techniques, and operations research techniques. Each chapter
has review questions and an annotated bibliography. Glossary,
pp. 13-44.

1242 Coleman, Raymond J., and Riley, M.J., eds. MIS: MANAGEMENT
DIMENSIONS. San Francisco: Holden-Day, 1973. 690 p. (Distributed
outside the U.S. by McGraw-Hill.)

This anthology represents the current thinking on the managerial
problems of designing and implementing a management information system. The selections are in six sections: MIS perspectives; the systems approach to management; organizational impact of MIS; the management information system; implementation of MIS; and case studies in MIS application.

1243 Enger, Norman L. PUTTING MIS TO WORK: MANAGING THE MAN-
AGEMENT INFORMATION SYSTEM. New York: American Management
Association, 1969. 255 p. Diagrams, bibliography.

This work includes many case studies of systems failure and
suggested controls for avoiding such failure. Glossary, pp.
227-37.

1244 Gallagher, James D. MANAGEMENT INFORMATION SYSTEMS AND
THE COMPUTER. AMA Research Study, no. 51. New York: American
Management Association, 1961. 191 p. Diagrams.

This volume includes case studies of the American Airlines
Sabre System and Sylvania Electric Products, Inc. No index.

1245 INFORMATION SYSTEMS. New York: Time-Life Video.

Three videotapes describe the principles, terminology, and objectives of MIS. Part one (A NEW IDEA, 7 min.) illustrates the development of an information system. Part two (RESPONDING TO CHANGING MARKET DEMANDS, 7 1/2 min.) and part three (INCREASING PROFIT, 4 min.) deal with the practical application of the information acquired.

1246 Kanter, Jerome. MANAGEMENT-ORIENTED MANAGEMENT INFORMATION SYSTEMS. 2d ed. Englewood Cliffs, N.J.: Prentice-Hall, 1977. xxvi, 484 p. Diagrams, tables, bibliographies.

The purpose of this book is to show business managers what Management Information Systems can do and--equally important--cannot do. He provides a practical approach to the subject, using many case studies.

1247 Li, David H., ed. DESIGN AND MANAGEMENT OF INFORMATION SYSTEMS. Chicago: Science Research Associates, 1972. 312 p. Diagrams, tables.

This book contains twenty-two readings and nine case studies from the United States, United Kingdom, Australia, and Canada and is intended for a beginning course in information systems analysis and design. Li assumes some knowledge of computer concepts and programming and the fundamentals of business administration and accounting. He regards the systems function as an integral part of management and concludes with a discussion of systems education.

1248 MANAGEMENT DATAMATICS. Leyden, Holland: Noordhoff International Publishing, 1968- . Quarterly.

This is the official journal of the International Federation for Information Processing, Paulus Potterstraat 40, Amsterdam, Holland, and the Society for Management Information Systems, 221 N. La Salle, Chicago, Ill. 60601. Formerly MANAGEMENT INFORMATICS.

1249 Martino, R.L. INFORMATION MANAGEMENT: THE DYNAMICS OF MIS. New York: McGraw-Hill, 1970. xxviii, 163 p. Diagrams, tables.

This nontechnical account of the role of the computer in providing information for management lacks an index.

1250 Nanus, Burt. "Managing the Fifth Information Revolution." BUSINESS HORIZONS 15 (April 1972): 5-13.

The author believes that a fifth information revolution will result from the introduction of mass (or community) information utilities. He defines these as "massive complexes of computer hardware and software, information banks, and communications

equipment designed to provide a wide array of information
services to public, private, and individual users who are on-
line to the system in their own environments." Advice is
given on how to cope with this revolution. He notes that
the first four information revolutions were brought about by
the invention of language, the invention of printing, the introduction of mass media, and the invention of the computer.

1251 O'Brien, James J. MANAGEMENT INFORMATION SYSTEMS: CON-
CEPTS, TECHNIQUES AND APPLICATIONS. New York: Van Nostrand
Reinhold, 1970. 314 p. Illustrations, diagrams, tables, bibliography.

1252 Pokempner, Stanley J. INFORMATION SYSTEMS FOR SALES AND MAR-
KETING MANAGEMENT. Conference Board Report, n.s., no. 591.
New York: Conference Board, 1973. 81 p. Diagrams, forms, tables,
bibliography. Paperback.

Based on the experiences of nearly 200 companies, this work
describes the evolution of management information systems;
classification structures being used for different kinds of systems; principal data sources and information uses of present
day sales/marketing information systems; problems which companies have encountered in systems development; and the out-
look for further extensions of management information systems
within the marketing area. Included are detailed descriptions
of sales and marketing information systems in the Aluminum
Company of America, Merck Sharp & Dohme Division of Merck
& Co. Inc., Vulcan Material Company, the Pillsbury Company, and a large diversified manufacturer.

1253 Rappaport, Alfred, ed. INFORMATION FOR DECISION MAKING:
QUANTITATIVE AND BEHAVIORAL DIMENSIONS. Englewood Cliffs,
N.J.: Prentice-Hall, 1970. 447 p. Diagrams, tables, bibliographies.

This contains thirty-four readings presented in three parts:
background and approach; information for planning and control;
and behavioral aspects of information. Each chapter concludes with an editorial commentary and a list of bibliographical references. No index.

1254 WHAT EVERY MANAGER NEEDS TO KNOW ABOUT INFORMATION
SYSTEMS. Rockville, Md.: BNA Communications; London: EMI Special
Films Unit, 1973.

These are two 16-mm color films. Part one (THE MERITT
CASE, 18 min.) is a case study of a company bogged down
with reports, statistics, and general data, but with no access
to the information which is vital to achieve company objectives and contribute to the successful running of the organization. In part two (THE COMPUTER AND YOU, 33 min.)
Isaac L. Auerbach defines the information system and discusses

with John W. Humble ways to make it more effective.

1255 Wilkinson, Alan. INFORMATION FOR MANAGERS: A PRACTICAL APPROACH. London: Pitman, 1971. 156 p. Diagrams, tables, bibliography.

> A middle manager in one of Britain's major chemical companies discusses the kind of data needed from a management information system and the most effective means of providing it. Annotated bibliography, pp. 151-52.

Bibliography

1256 Tricker, R. Ian. MANAGEMENT INFORMATION SYSTEMS: AN ANNOTATED BIBLIOGRAPHY. London: Institute of Chartered Accountants in England and Wales, General Educational Trust, 1969. 127 p. Paperback.

> Tricker lists 196 books and 368 articles in two alphabetical author sequences, with classified subject index. He also lists journals and abstracting and bibliographical services.

Organizations

1257 Society for Management Information Systems, Suite 2026, 221 North La Salle Street, Chicago, Ill. 60670.

> This organization was founded in 1968 to serve as an exchange or marketplace for technical information about MIS.

1258 Society of Management Information Technology, 40 Tyndalls Park Road, Bristol, BS8 1PL, England.

> This body was founded in 1968.

CYBERNETICS

Cybernetics, the study of communication systems in machines and in the human brain, was pioneered by Norbert Wiener (see items 1265-66). See also item 1131.

1259 Ashby, W. Ross. AN INTRODUCTION TO CYBERNETICS. London: Chapman & Hall, 1956. 295 p. Diagrams, tables, bibliography. Reprint. Scranton, Pa.: Barnes & Noble, 1968.

> This standard work requires no knowledge of mathematics beyond elementary algebra.

1260 Beer, Stafford. BRAIN OF THE FIRM: THE MANAGERIAL CYBERNETICS OF ORGANIZATION. London: Allen Lane, The Penguin Press; New York: McGraw-Hill, 1972. 319 p. Diagrams, bibliography.

    Beer deals with the development of cybernetics and the application to management problems. Glossary of cybernetics terms, pp. 305-7. Annotated bibliography, pp. 308-14. Indexes of names, management topics, and cybernetics topics.

1261 _____. "Cybernetics: A Systems Approach to Management." PERSONNEL REVIEW 1 (Spring 1972): 28-39. Diagrams.

    Beer considers what cybernetics could contribute toward solving "uncontrollable" situations which exist in government and industry. He proposes a seven-step program of action to achieve results.

1262 _____. CYBERNETICS AND MANAGEMENT. London: English Universities Press, 1959. xviii, 214 p. Diagrams, tables, bibliography.

    This is a clear introduction to the subject.

1263 Mantell, Leroy H. "On the Use of Cybernetics in Management." MANAGEMENT INTERNATIONAL REVIEW 13 (1973): 33-41.

    Mantell examines the impact of cybernetics on planning and control systems and suggests that general system theory emphasizes that all organizations are basically self-controlling.

1264 Rose, J., ed. SURVEY OF CYBERNETICS: A TRIBUTE TO DR. NORBERT WIENER. London: Iliffe, 1969; New York: Gordon & Breach, 1970. 391 p. Diagrams, tables, bibliographies.

    This collection of nineteen papers honors the "father of cybernetics." They are presented in five sections: the nature of cybernetics, cybernetics and living systems, cybernetics and artifacts, cybernetics and industry, and cybernetics and society.

1265 Wiener, Norbert. CYBERNETICS; OR, CONTROL AND COMMUNICATION IN THE ANIMAL AND THE MACHINE. 2d ed. New York: Wiley & M.I.T. Press, 1961. xvi, 212 p. Diagrams.

    This is a pioneering statement of the implications of automation for society.

1266 _____. THE HUMAN USE OF HUMAN BEINGS: CYBERNETICS AND SOCIETY. Rev. ed. Garden City, N.Y.: Doubleday, 1954. 199 p.

    This is a classic study of the impact of machines on society.

Organization

1267 American Society for Cybernetics, 1025 Connecticut Avenue N.W., Suite 914, Washington, D.C. 20036.

    Founded in 1964, the society publishes a quarterly JOURNAL and a monthly NEWSLETTER.

Section 10

INDUSTRIAL ENGINEERING

According to a definition of the American Institute of Industrial Engineers, industrial engineering is concerned with the design, improvement and installation of integrated systems of men, materials, and equipment. The industrial engineer's tasks include work measurement and related techniques, as well as job evaluation (see section 19) and aspects of production management such as plant layout, materials handling, and quality control (see section 16).

Included in this section are items on work measurement, method study, motion and time study, and systems and procedures, concerned with the analysis of methods, activities, and times involved in performing particular operations with a view to improving efficiency by establishing standardized times and procedures. These predetermined motion times may be used in connection with incentive bonus schemes.

A generic term used in Great Britain for these related procedures is work study.

GENERAL STUDIES

1268 Currie, Russell M. WORK STUDY. 3d ed. Revised by Joseph E. Faraday. London: Pitman & Management Publications, 1972. xvi, 263 p. Diagrams, tables. Paperback.

> This is a standard British text, but it is less useful than the International Labour Office's INTRODUCTION TO WORK STUDY (item 1269).

1269 International Labour Office. INTRODUCTION TO WORK STUDY. 2d ed. Geneva: 1969. xix, 436 p. Diagrams (1 folding), tables, bibliography.

> Part one deals with productivity and work study, part two with method study, and part three with work measurement, especially the organization of a work study department. There are several useful appendixes including examples of courses in work study and productivity improvement techniques and a glossary (pp.

413-24). It is a pity that a work as important as this lacks an index.

1270 Ireson, W. Grant, and Grant, Eugene L., eds. HANDBOOK OF IN-
DUSTRIAL ENGINEERING AND MANAGEMENT. 2d ed. Englewood
Cliffs, N.J.: Prentice-Hall, 1971. 907 p. Diagrams, maps, tables,
bibliographies.

This is a comprehensive work in seventeen sections.

1271 Johnson, Stanley, and Ogilvie, Grant. WORK ANALYSIS. London:
Butterworths, 1972; Levittown, N.J.: Transatlantic Arts, 1973. 168 p.
Illustrations, diagrams, tables, bibliography.

A practical guide to the identification and removal of causes
of waste and inefficiency, this work uses diagnostic charts
and has sections on analysis techniques (including photographic
techniques), operator performance, preparation of time standards, organization and control of assignments, and remuneration and compensation.

1272 Maynard, Harold B., ed. INDUSTRIAL ENGINEERING HANDBOOK.
3d ed. New York: McGraw-Hill, 1971. Var. pag. Diagrams, tables,
bibliographies.

The first edition of this outstanding work of reference was published in 1956. It contains eighty-seven contributions in thirteen sections.

1273 Oakley, Stan. ABC OF WORK STUDY. London: Pitman, 1973. 83 p.
Illustrations, diagrams, tables. Paperback.

Glossary, pp. 80-82.

1274 Rathe, Alex W., and Gyrna, Frank M. APPLYING INDUSTRIAL EN-
GINEERING TO MANAGEMENT PROBLEMS. AMA Research Study, no.
97. New York: American Management Association, 1969. 272 p.
Diagrams, forms, tables.

This survey contains case studies of Kodak Park Works of Eastman Kodak Company, Procter and Gamble, TRW Inc., United
Air Lines, United California Bank, and thirty-four studies of
specific applications of industrial engineering. An index would
make this useful work even more valuable.

1275 Whitmore, Dennis A. WORK STUDY AND RELATED MANAGEMENT
SERVICES. 2d ed. Heinemann Accountancy and Administration Series.
London: Heinemann, 1970. xv, 336 p. Diagrams, tables, bibliography.

After defining productivity and its importance, the author deals
with work study, time study, predetermined motion time systems,

method study, value analysis, organization and methods, ergonomics, operations research, and critical path analysis. Several case studies are included.

Periodicals

1276 INDUSTRIAL ENGINEERING. Norcross, Ga.: American Institute of Industrial Engineers, 1950- . Monthly.

1277 MANAGEMENT SERVICES. London: Institute of Practitioners in Work
Study, Organisation and Methods, 1956- . Monthly.

> This journal was previously called WORK STUDY AND MAN-
> AGEMENT SERVICES.

1278 WORK STUDY. London: Sawell Publications, 1952- . Monthly.

> This is described as "a journal which promotes productivity
> through time and motion study, job evaluation, process control
> and related subjects." Previously it was entitled TIME AND
> MOTION STUDY.

Abstracting and Indexing Service

1279 WORK STUDY + O AND M ABSTRACTS. London: Anbar Publications,
1973- . Eight issues yearly.

> This work is one of the excellent Anbar series, dating original-
> ly from 1961. It is published in association with the Institute
> of Practitioners in Work Study, Organisation and Methods.
> Each issue contains 100-150 abstracts of articles selected from
> more than 200 journals. Critical comments are occasionally .
> included, and these are printed in italics to distinguish them
> from factual summaries. Annual index. These were incorpo-
> rated in ANBAR MANAGEMENT SERVICES ABSTRACTS 1961-
> 71.

Organizations

1280 American Institute of Industrial Engineers, 25 Technology Park, Norcross,
Ga. 30071.

> Founded in 1948, this organization publishes INDUSTRIAL EN-
> GINEERING (item 1276).

1281 Institute of Practitioners in Work Study, Organisation and Methods, 9/10
River Front, Enfield, Middlesex, EN1 3TE, England.

Formed in 1975 by the amalgamation of the Institute of Work Study Practitioners and the Organization and Methods Society, this group publishes MANAGEMENT SERVICES (item 1277) and sponsors WORK STUDY + O AND M ABSTRACTS (item 1279).

WORK MEASUREMENT

1282 Abruzzi, Adam. WORK, WORKERS AND WORK MEASUREMENT. New York: Columbia University Press, 1956. xvi, 318 p. Diagrams, tables, bibliography.

A classic study, this work gives a detailed analysis of work measurement procedures and means for estimating production rates. Abruzzi emphasizes that a worker's behavior is affected by activities outside the work place as well as at the work place and that these often conflicting activities need to be considered when developing theories of work measurement.

1283 Crossan, Richard M., and Nance, Harold W. MASTER STANDARD DATA: THE ECONOMIC APPROACH TO WORK MEASUREMENT. 2d ed. New York: McGraw-Hill, 1972. 259 p. Diagrams, tables.

The authors report on a technique developed at the Serge A. Birn Company for measuring, predicting, and controlling any job performance with a high degree of accuracy.

1284 Currie, Russell M. THE MEASUREMENT OF WORK: A MANUAL FOR THE PRACTITIONER. London: British Institute of Management, 1965. 416 p. Illustrations, diagrams, tables.

This very important British work, written originally for work study officers at Imperial Chemical Industries Ltd., would be more useful with an index.

1285 Dudley, Norman A. WORK MEASUREMENT: SOME RESEARCH STUDIES. Studies in Management. London: Macmillan; New York: St. Martin's Press, 1968. 139 p. Diagrams, tables, bibliography.

This contains a glossary, pp. 130-35, plus indexes of authors and subjects.

1286 Whitmore, Dennis A. MEASUREMENT AND CONTROL OF INDIRECT WORK. London: Heinemann, 1971. 275 p. Diagrams, forms, bibliography. (Distributed by International Publications Service, New York.)

Whitmore describes the application of work measurement techniques to indirect workers involved in such activities as clerical work, storekeeping, maintenance, transport, design, and research.

WORK SIMPLIFICATION

1287 Lehrer, Robert N. WORK SIMPLIFICATION: CREATIVE THINKING ABOUT WORK PROBLEMS. Englewood Cliffs, N.J.: Prentice-Hall, 1957. xiv, 394 p. Illustrations, diagrams, forms, tables.

This is a very readable and well-illustrated survey.

1288 Nadler, Gerald. WORK SIMPLIFICATION. New York: McGraw-Hill, 1957. 292 p. Illustrations, diagrams, tables (1 folding), bibliography.

This work contains a bibliography of books and periodicals, pp. 267-71, and an annotated motion picture bibliography, pp. 273-85.

1289 Zinck, W. Clements. DYNAMIC WORK SIMPLIFICATION. Reinhold Management Reference Series. New York: Reinhold; London: Chapman & Hall, 1962. xii, 237 p. Diagrams, forms, tables.

Parts one to three deal with management's stake in work simplification, the foreman's stake in work simplification, and the techniques of work simplification. The fourth part consists of three "how-to-do-it" chapters on how to make a process analysis, how to make a man-machine analysis, and how to make an operation analysis.

METHODS-TIME-MEASUREMENT (MTM)

1290 Karger, Delmar W., and Bayha, Franklin H. ENGINEERED WORK MEASUREMENT: THE PRINCIPLES, TECHNIQUES, AND DATA OF METHODS-TIME-MEASUREMENT, MODERN TIME AND MOTION STUDY, AND RELATED APPLICATIONS ENGINEERING DATA. 2d ed. New York: Industrial Press; Brighton, Eng.: Machinery Publishing Co., 1965. xiv, 722 p. Diagrams, tables, bibliography.

This detailed account of the development and application of MTM has a final thirty-four page chapter on the management aspects of work measurement. There is a useful bibliography, pp. 701-15.

1291 Maynard, Harold B.; Stegemerton, G.J.; and Schwab, John L. METHODS-TIME-MEASUREMENT. McGraw-Hill Industrial Organization and Management Series. New York: McGraw-Hill, 1948. 292 p. Illustrations, diagrams, portraits, tables.

This is the original presentation of the MTM procedure for determining the motions required to perform an operation, assigning predetermined time standards to each limiting motion, and thus ascertaining the production standard for each job.

Periodical

1292 MTM JOURNAL OF METHODS-TIME-MEASUREMENT. Fair Lawn, N.J.:
International MTM Directorate, 1955- . Five issues yearly.

> This is the official journal of the MTM Association for Stan-
> dards and Research, 9-10 Saddle River Front, Fair Lawn, New
> Jersey 07410. It was founded in 1951. It also publishes a
> series of research reports.

MOTION AND TIME STUDY

1293 Barnes, Ralph M. MOTION AND TIME STUDY: DESIGN AND MEA-
SUREMENT OF WORK. 6th ed. New York: Wiley, 1968. 799 p. Illustrations, diagrams, forms, tables, bibliography.

> This is a standard text, the first edition of which was published
> in 1937. It includes a specimen time study manual, pp. 715-
> 21, and a specimen wage incentive manual, pp. 722-31, as
> well as problems, pp. 733-67, and a bibliography, including
> six films, pp. 769-88.

1294 Carroll, Phil. TIME STUDY FUNDAMENTALS FOR FOREMEN. 3d ed.
New York: McGraw-Hill, 1972. xv, 229 p. Illustrations, diagrams,
forms, tables.

> This practical manual shows how to make a study, how to
> establish fair and accurate standards, and how to get the most
> out of a study in terms of improved output and better working
> methods.

1295 Currie, Russell M. SIMPLIFIED PMTS (PREDETERMINED MOTION TIME
SYSTEMS): A MANUAL FOR PRACTITIONERS AND TRAINERS. London:
British Institute of Management, 1963. xv, 202 p. Diagrams (2 folding),
tables (3 folding).

> Currie describes a simplified system used successfully in Impe-
> rial Chemical Industries Ltd. No index.

1296 Gomberg, William. A TRADE UNION ANALYSIS OF TIME STUDY. 2d
ed. Prentice-Hall Industrial Relations & Personnel Series. New York:
Prentice-Hall, 1955. 318 p. Diagrams, tables, bibliography.

> Gomberg presents a rational basis of time study, to counteract
> the many "cookbooks" on procedures. Part one examines the
> theoretical requirements for a science of time study; part two
> examines the extent to which systems in the 1950s measured up
> to this theory.

1297 Mundel, Marvin E. MOTION AND TIME STUDY: PRINCIPLES AND PRACTICES. 4th ed. Englewood Cliffs, N.J.: Prentice-Hall, 1970. xiv, 674 p. Illustrations, diagrams, forms, tables, bibliography.

This is a standard text, the first edition of which was published in 1950. Problem exercises are included.

1298 Niebel, Benjamin W. MOTION AND TIME STUDY. 5th ed. Irwin Series in Management. Homewood, Ill.: Irwin, 1972. xii, 709 p. Illustrations, diagrams, forms, tables, bibliography.

This is a standard text, the first edition of which was published in 1955. It includes a glossary of terms used in method study, time study, and wage payments.

1299 Quick, Joseph H.; Duncan, James H.; and Malcolm, James A., Jr. WORK-FACTOR TIME STANDARDS: MEASUREMENT OF MANUAL AND MENTAL WORK. New York: McGraw-Hill, 1962. xv, 458 p. Illustrations, diagrams, forms, tables.

The authors describe the work-factor system, developed to minimize the judgment factor in standards setting and to correct standards inconsistencies. They supply values for measuring the time required to perform the various movements and mental processes used by people in the performance of their work. The book includes many descriptions of the application of work-factor techniques.

1300 Shaw, Anne G. THE PURPOSE AND PRACTICE OF MOTION STUDY. 2d ed. Manchester: Columbine Press, 1960. xvi, 324 p. Illustrations, diagrams.

This useful, though dated, British text includes case studies of typical motion study applications, pp. 261-311.

METHOD STUDY

1301 Krick, Edward V. METHODS ENGINEERING: DESIGN AND MEASUREMENT OF WORK METHODS. New York: Wiley, 1962. xviii, 530 p. Illustrations (1 folding), diagrams, forms, tables.

This work has six sections dealing with the design process, introduction to methods engineering, methods design, work measurement, special methods engineering problems, and administration of the methods engineering function.

1302 Raybould, E.B., and Minter, A.L. PROBLEM SOLVING FOR MANAGEMENT: A NEW LOOK AT METHOD STUDY. London: Management Publications for the Institute of Work Study Practitioners, 1971. 281 p. Diagrams, tables, bibliographies.

The authors show how recently developed techniques of method study may be applied to a wide variety of problems. No index.

WORK SAMPLING

Work sampling is defined by Heiland (item 1304) as "a measurement technique for the quantitative analysis, in terms of time, of the activity of men, machines, or of any observable state or condition of operation. . . . A work sampling study consists of a large number of observations taken at random intervals."

1303 Barnes, Ralph M. WORK SAMPLING. 2d ed. New York: Wiley; London: Chapman & Hall, 1957. 283 p. Illustrations, diagrams, forms, tables, bibliography.

This book is very rich in case studies of the application of work sampling to different activities.

1304 Heiland, Robert E., and Richardson, Wallace J. WORK SAMPLING. New York: McGraw-Hill, 1957. 243 p. Diagrams, tables.

SYSTEMS AND PROCEDURES

Systems and procedures ("organization and methods" in British parlance) is concerned with the systematic review of an organization's management and methods with a view to increasing its efficiency and reducing unnecessary operations and expense.

Systems and procedures is often associated with office management, but works dealing specifically with systems and procedures in the office are listed in section 20.

Many more references on systems and procedures will be found in the bibliographies listed as items 1319 and 1320, including Chester Morrill, Jr.'s, excellent companion volume in this series.

1305 Bunker, Laurence H. "History of O & M in the U.K." O & M BULLE-TIN 23 (August 1968): 117-25.

1306 ENCYCLOPEDIC DICTIONARY OF SYSTEMS AND PROCEDURES. Englewood Cliffs, N.J.: Prentice-Hall, 1966. 673 p. Diagrams, tables.

This work defines, explains, and illustrates systems and procedures techniques in the following areas: accounting, budgets, charts, credit, electronic data processing, forms design and control, management audits, operations research, personnel, procedures programs, systems manuals and reports, work analysis, and measurement. Articles are arranged alphabetically with no index but with cross-references in the text.

1307 Gardner, C. James. THE ADMINISTRATION OF ORGANIZATION AND METHODS SERVICES. New York: United Nations, 1969. 121 p. Diagrams, forms, tables, bibliography. Paperback.

This introductory guide to the setting up and management of systems and procedures services was prepared at the invitation of the United Nations Department of Economic and Social Affairs. Included are comments from administrators and heads of O & M units in several countries. No index.

1308 Great Britain. Treasury. Management Services Division. THE PRACTICE OF O & M. 2d ed. London: H.M. Stationery Office, 1965. 108 p. Diagrams, tables.

This standard British work prepared by the forerunner of the Civil Service Department is based on the collective experience of practicing O & M officers in the civil service and elsewhere. Glossary, p. 7.

1309 Kelly, William F. MANAGEMENT THROUGH SYSTEMS AND PROCEDURES: THE TOTAL SYSTEMS CONCEPT. New York: Wiley-Interscience, 1969. 556 p. Illustrations, diagrams (3 folding), forms, tables.

Kelly covers the nature of systems and procedures, organization and appraisal of manpower and physical facilities, the systems study, information technology, automatic data processing, and the presentation and implementation of recommendations.

1310 Lazzaro, Victor, ed. SYSTEMS AND PROCEDURES: A HANDBOOK FOR BUSINESS AND INDUSTRY. 2d ed. Englewood Cliffs, N.J.: Prentice-Hall, 1968. xvi, 528 p. Illustrations, tables.

Each of this work's eighteen sections was written by a recognized authority. Topics covered include charting, the management audit, work simplification, work measurement, forms design and control, records management, company manuals, budgets and cost control, data processing, work sampling in the office, operations research, management informations systems, and network systems (PERT/CPM).

1311 Milward, G.E. LAUNCHING AND MANAGING O AND M. London: Macmillan; New York: St. Martin's Press, 1961. 95 p.

This is an early but still important British work on setting up an O & M department, managing O & M, the place of O & M within the organization, and the application of O & M. These are illustrated and have references to the practices of some fifty companies.

1312 _____. ORGANISATION AND METHODS: A SERVICE TO MANAGE-MENT. 2d ed. London: Macmillan; New York: St. Martin's Press, 1967. xxxiv, 414 p. Illustrations, diagrams, bibliography.

Milward covers form design, clerical aids, office machinery, and the organization and management of O & M, with brief comments on background subjects such as statistical sampling and management information.

1313 _____, ed. APPLICATIONS OF O AND M. For Organisation and Methods Training Council. London: Macdonald & Evans, 1964. xxi, 200 p. Diagrams, tables.

The book is based on the experiences of a number of companies. The applications include office management, personnel management, exporting, production management, accounting procedures, and sales routines. Glossary of export terms, pp. 84-96; glossary of production control, p. 107.

1314 Milward, G.E., and Wroe, P.H.S., eds. FURTHER APPLICATIONS OF O AND M. For Organisation and Methods Training Council. London: Macdonald & Evans, 1966. xix, 140 p. Diagrams, tables, bibliography.

Applications include forms control, communications, job classification, drawing offices, plant maintenance, transport, and printing departments. Other sections consider the use of computers, mathematics, and statistics.

1315 Neuschel, Richard F. MANAGEMENT BY SYSTEM. 2d ed. New York: McGraw-Hill, 1960. 359 p. Diagrams, forms.

A revision of STREAMLINING BUSINESS PROCEDURES (1950), this work presents a systems and procedures approach to management in four parts: the case for a systematic ordering of operations, the ingredients of a successful procedures improvements program, procedure analysis and improvement techniques, and cashing in on procedures improvement recommendations.

1316 Rogers, Derek. CREATIVE SYSTEMS DESIGN. London: Anbar Publications, 1970. 162 p. Illustrations, diagrams. (Distributed by International Publications Service, New York.)

This is a practical guide to the design, rather than the techniques, of management services, with chapters on such topics as getting the feel of an organization, defining the assignment, establishing facts, and making things happen.

1317 Webster, W.A.H. HANDBOOK OF O AND M ANALYSIS. London: Business Books, 1973. xv, 236 p. Diagrams, forms, tables, bibliography. (Distributed by Cahners Publishing Co., Boston.)

> The handbook includes, as appendixes, information on office machines, the Gantt chart, sampling, activity sampling, and typefaces suitable for forms design.

Periodical

1318 JOURNAL OF SYSTEMS MANAGEMENT. Cleveland: Association for Systems Management, 1950- . Monthly.

> This publication formerly was SYSTEMS AND PROCEDURES JOURNAL. Published by the Association for Systems Management (formerly Systems and Procedures Association), it was founded in 1947. Among the Association's other publications are IDEAS FOR MANAGEMENT, the proceedings of its annual systems meetings, and AN ANNOTATED BIBLIOGRAPHY FOR THE SYSTEMS PROFESSIONAL (item 1319).

Bibliographies

1319 Association for Systems Management. AN ANNOTATED BIBLIOGRAPHY FOR THE SYSTEMS PROFESSIONAL. 2d ed. Cleveland: 1970. 183 p.

> This lists articles published in JOURNAL OF SYSTEMS MANAGEMENT and IDEAS FOR MANAGEMENT between 1960 and 1969 and monographs from 1949 to 1966.

1320 Morrill, Chester, Jr. SYSTEMS AND PROCEDURES, INCLUDING OFFICE MANAGEMENT, INFORMATION SOURCES: A GUIDE TO LITERATURE AND BODIES CONCERNED WITH THE SYSTEMS AND PROCEDURES ASPECTS OF ORGANIZATION AND MANAGEMENT, INCLUDING OFFICE MANAGEMENT, WHETHER IN BUSINESS, INDUSTRY, OR GOVERNMENT. Management Information Guide, no. 12. Detroit: Gale Research Co., 1967. 374 p.

> This outstanding guide is arranged in ten sections: general orientation; plans, policy, and programs; organizing; personnel; equipment, supplies and facilities; communication and records; comptrollership; data processing; directing; and front office references.

HUMAN ENGINEERING

Human engineering ("ergonomics" in British parlance) is the relationship between the worker, his environment, and the equipment he uses.

1321 Chapanis, Alphonse. MAN-MACHINE ENGINEERING. Behavioral Science in Industry Series. Belmont, Calif.: Wadsworth, 1965. vii, 134 p. Illustrations, diagrams, tables, bibliography.

This is a nontechnical introduction.

1322 _____. RESEARCH TECHNIQUES IN HUMAN ENGINEERING. Baltimore, Md.: Johns Hopkins Press, 1959. xii, 316 p. Diagrams, forms, tables, bibliography. Paperback.

1323 McCormick, Ernest J. HUMAN FACTORS ENGINEERING. 3d ed. New York: McGraw-Hill, 1970. xii, 639 p. Illustrations, diagrams, tables, bibliography.

This general guide to the relationship between man and his engineering environment includes sections on work space and arrangement, illumination, atmospheric conditions, and noise. Indexes of names and subjects.

1324 Murrell, K.F.H. ERGONOMICS: MAN IN HIS WORKING ENVIRONMENT. London: Chapman & Hall; New York: Halsted Press, 1965. xix, 496 p. Illustrations, diagrams, tables, bibliography.

An important British work on the nature and application of human engineering, this book was originally published in the United States by Reinhold (New York) as HUMAN PERFORMANCE IN INDUSTRY, 1965. Glossary, p. 452. Indexes of authors and subjects.

1325 Woodson, Wesley E., and Conover, Donald W. HUMAN ENGINEERING GUIDE TO EQUIPMENT DESIGN. 2d ed. Berkeley and Los Angeles: University of California Press, 1965. Var. pag. Illustrations, diagrams, tables, bibliography.

The authors discuss design of equipment and work space, vision, audition, body measurement, and other factors in human engineering.

Periodicals

1326 APPLIED ERGONOMICS. Guildford, Eng.: IPC Science & Technology Press, 1969- . Quarterly.

This periodical is published in association with the Ergonomics Research Society. It includes selected abstracts from the collection held at the Ergonomics Information Analysis Centre, Department of Engineering Production, University of Birmingham.

1327 ERGONOMICS: HUMAN FACTORS IN WORK, MACHINE CONTROL AND EQUIPMENT DESIGN. London: Taylor & Francis, 1957- . Bi-monthly.

> Published in association with the Ergonomics Research Society, Nederlandse Vereniging voor Ergonomie, and the International Ergonomics Association, this publication includes abstracts selected from ERGONOMICS ABSTRACTS.

Abstracting and Indexing Service

1328 ERGONOMICS ABSTRACTS. London: Taylor & Francis, 1969- . Quarterly.

> This is published for the Ergonomics Information Analysis Centre, Department of Engineering Production, University of Birmingham, P.O. Box 363, Birmingham 15, England. It continues the series issued by the Warren Spring Laboratory between 1961 and 1967. It includes approximately 5,000 abstracts annually, arranged according to a specially developed classification scheme within the following outline: general references; man as a systems component; design of the man-machine interface; systems design and organization; and methods, techniques, and equipment in ergonomics. The abstracts also include book reviews.

Section 11

THE ENTERPRISE

Included in this section are works which emphasize the firm or organization it-self rather than management methods. The section also contains works on the management of small enterprises, management of growth, and management of large enterprises. The section is continued by sections 12 (International and Multinational Business), 13 (Social Responsibility of Business) and 14 (Management in Specialist Areas).

GENERAL STUDIES

1329 Chamberlain, John. THE ENTERPRISING AMERICANS: A BUSINESS HIS-TORY OF THE UNITED STATES. Rev. ed. New York: Harper & Row, 1974. xix, 282 p. Portraits, bibliography. Paperback.

Business history from the pre-Revolution era to "the modern world of enterprise" is traced.

1330 Chamberlain, Neil W. ENTERPRISE AND ENVIRONMENT: THE FIRM IN TIME AND PLACE. New York: McGraw-Hill, 1968. 223 p.

The interplay between the firm and the changing environment of which it forms a part is explored. Part one contains six chapters on decision making within the firm. Part two contains four chapters on the environment, one on the international firm, and a summary.

1331 Chandler, Alfred D., Jr. STRATEGY AND STRUCTURE: CHAPTERS IN THE HISTORY OF AMERICAN INDUSTRIAL ENTERPRISE. New York: Doubleday, 1966. xiv, 580 p. Paperback.

This was originally published in hardback, Cambridge, Mass.: M.I.T. Press, 1962. xiv, 463 p. It includes case studies of the Du Pont Company, General Motors, Standard Oil Company (New Jersey), and Sears, Roebuck and Company.

1332 Channon, Derek F. THE STRATEGY AND STRUCTURE OF BRITISH EN-TERPRISE. Boston: Harvard University Graduate School of Business Administration, Division of Research; London: Macmillan, 1973. xvii, 257 p. Diagrams, tables.

This research study by a member of the staff of Manchester Business School was presented for a doctorate at Harvard Business School. It was partly inspired by Alfred D. Chandler's STRATEGY AND STRUCTURE (item 1331) and similar works. The author traces the development of Britain's "top 100" firms during the period 1950-70, viewing each enterprise both as a totality and as a member of a population of British firms.

1333 Edwards, Ronald S., and Townsend, Harry, eds. BUSINESS ENTERPRISE: ITS GROWTH AND ORGANISATION. London: Macmillan; New York: St. Martin's Press, 1958. xvii, 607 p. Tables. Hardcover and paperback.

1334 _____. BUSINESS GROWTH. London: Macmillan; New York: St. Martin's Press, 1966. xxiv, 409 p. Diagrams (some folding), maps, tables.

Developed from a series of seminars on Problems of Industrial Administration held at the London School of Economics, items 1333-35 contain case studies of many major British companies.

1335 _____. STUDIES IN BUSINESS ORGANISATION: A SUPPLEMENT TO BUSINESS ENTERPRISE. London: Macmillan; New York: St. Martin's Press, 1961. xxiii, 160 p. Diagrams. Hardcover and paperback.

1336 Eells, Richard, and Walton, Clarence. CONCEPTUAL FOUNDATIONS OF BUSINESS. Rev. ed. Irwin Series in Management. Homewood, Ill.: Irwin, 1969. 648 p. Bibliographies.

This is a detailed text developed from a course at Columbia University Graduate School of Business on the legal, philosophical, and historical foundations of the institution of business in the United States.

1337 Gilbert, M., ed. THE MODERN BUSINESS ENTERPRISE: SELECTED READINGS. Penguin Interdisciplinary Readings. Harmondsworth, Eng.: Penguin, 1972. Bibliography. Paperback.

This work contains twenty readings in five sections: perspectives, control of the enterprise, corporate goals and policies, decision making and organizational processes, and the impact of the modern business enterprise.

1338 Golightly, Henry O. "What Makes a Company Successful?" BUSINESS HORIZONS 14 (June 1971): 11-18.

The views of the presidents of seven companies are presented.

1339 Musselman, Vernon A., and Hughes, Eugene H. INTRODUCTION TO
MODERN BUSINESS ANALYSIS AND INTERPRETATION. 6th ed. Englewood Cliffs, N.J.: Prentice-Hall, 1973. xv, 656 p. Illustrations,
diagrams, tables, bibliography.

> This comprehensive text is presented in six sections: business
> and its environment, organization and management of the en-
> terprise, operating problems of the enterprise, financial man-
> agement and risk functions, quantitative controls for decision
> making, and marketing functions. The book includes several
> case studies. Glossary, pp. 636-44.

1340 Price, Karl E., and Walker, James W. ISSUES IN BUSINESS: AN IN-
TRODUCTION TO AMERICAN ENTERPRISE. 2d ed. New York: Wiley,
1974. 584 p. Illustrations, diagrams, maps, tables. Paperback.

> This textbook for students is presented in the popular style of
> a newspaper, with perforated sheets and tear-out worksheets
> containing review questions. Many case studies and definitions
> are included. Chapters deal with the enterprise system, plan-
> ning and the environment, supply and demand, marketing, ad-
> vertising, consumerism, manufacturing, money and banking,
> finance, growth of companies, international business, insurance,
> computers and business, managing, human resources in business,
> careers, labor relations and employment, minorities and women
> in business, and future of business. Glossary ("Superwhazzit"),
> pp. 573-78.

SMALL COMPANIES

1341 Allen, Louis L. STARTING AND SUCCEEDING IN YOUR OWN SMALL
BUSINESS. New York: Grosset & Dunlap; Geneva: Dirmas S.A.,
Management Editions Europe, 1968. xxi, 156 p.

> Six chapters deal with concerns of a small businessman, includ-
> ing raising money, getting customers, selecting products, man-
> aging, and understanding the philosophy of a venture capitalist.
> No index.

1342 American Society of Mechanical Engineers. Management Division. SMALL
PLANT MANAGEMENT: A GUIDE TO PRACTICAL, KNOW-HOW MAN-
AGEMENT. 2d ed. Revised by W.A. MacCrehan, Jr. New York:
McGraw-Hill, 1960. xv, 563 p. Diagrams, forms, tables, bibliography.

> The first edition was edited by Edward H. Hempel in 1950.
> The second edition contains twenty-one contributions, based
> on a systematic study of small plant activities by ASME's Small
> Plant Committee. Part one deals with the economic aspects of
> small plants, including government interest. Part two covers
> the management tasks of planning, organizing, operating, super-

vising, and controlling. Part three discusses legal problems, human relations, union relations, productivity, research, and financial matters. Part four covers the future of small plants, quality control, and a management checklist.

1343 Banks, Russell, ed. MANAGING THE SMALLER COMPANY. New York: American Management Association, 1969. 341 p. Tables.

Sixteen contributions make up this volume.

1344 Boswell, Jonathan. THE RISE AND DECLINE OF SMALL FIRMS. London: Allen & Unwin, 1973. 272 p. Tables, bibliography.

Based on a survey of sixty-four small firms in engineering, hosiery, and knitwear, this book analyzes the differences in economic performance and management attitudes in dynamic and stagnant firms. It suggests ways of countering company decline and encouraging entrepreneurship in small businesses. A chapter is included on the problem of takeovers.

1345 Broom, H.N., and Longenecker, Justin G. SMALL BUSINESS MANAGEMENT. 3d ed. Cincinnati: South-Western Publishing Co., 1971. 734 p. Diagrams, tables.

This comprehensive manual is divided into six sections: environment and management of the small enterprise, problems in initiating the business, financial and administrative control, marketing programs and policies, management of business operations, and legal and governmental relationships. The book includes many case studies and problems.

1346 Great Britain. Committee of Enquiry on Small Firms. SMALL FIRMS: REPORT OF THE COMMITTEE OF INQUIRY ON SMALL FIRMS. London: H.M. Stationery Office, 1971. xx, 435 p. Forms, tables.

This important British government report, known as the Bolton Report because of its chairman, J.E. Bolton, examines the role of small firms in the national economy, the facilities available to them, and the problems confronting them. It is supported by eighteen research reports which focus on problems of small firms in particular industries and such aspects as scientific and engineering manpower in small firms (J.G. Cox. Research Report No. 2. 24 p. Diagrams, tables. Paperback); financial facilities for small firms (The Economists Advisory Group directed by Dennis Lees. Research Report No. 4. 241 p. Form, tables. Paperback); the role of small firms in innovation in the United Kingdom since 1945 (C. Freeman. Research Report No. 6. 43 p. Forms, tables. Paperback); attitude and motivation (C.W. Golby and G. Johns. Research Report No. 7. 53 p. Paperback); and the relative efficiency of small and large firms. (Douglas Todd. Research Report No. 18.

39 p. Diagrams, tables, bibliography. Paperback).

1347 GUIDELINES FOR THE SMALLER BUSINESS. London: British Institute of Management, 1969- .

This is a series of concise publications (4-12 pages each), which are published irregularly. Titles have included "Planning in the Small Firm" (GUIDELINES FOR THE SMALLER BUSINESS, No. 2, March 1969, 4 p.), "Cost Reduction and Expenditure Control" (No. 8, March 1970, 4 p.), and "Making a Small Business Grow" (No. 12, June 1972, 12 p.). Most GUIDELINES conclude with a reading list.

1348 Hazel, Arthur Curwen, and Reid, Alan Scott. MANAGING THE SURVIVAL OF SMALLER COMPANIES. London: Business Books, 1973. 159 p. (Distributed by Cahners Publishing Co., Boston.)

Part one deals with the symptoms and causes of company decline and part two with prevention and cure. The authors suggest nine ways in which a company can rapidly be put back on a sound footing, and the book ends with stories of recovery of three small firms, from the brink of possible failure.

1349 Hosmer, W. Arnold; Tucker, Frank L.; and Cooper, Arnold C. SMALL BUSINESS MANAGEMENT: A CASEBOOK. Homewood, Ill.: Irwin, 1966. xii, 605 p. Illustrations, tables.

This work contains thirty-three cases and eight readings. No index.

1350 JOURNAL OF SMALL BUSINESS MANAGEMENT. Milwaukee, Wis.: National Council for Small Business Management Development, 1963- . Quarterly.

The journal is published jointly by the National Council and the Bureau of Business Research, College of Business and Economics, West Virginia University. Each issue of the journal deals with a particular theme--e.g., volume 12 (January 1974) deals with management assistance.

1351 Kelley, Pearce C.; Lawyer, Kenneth; and Baumback, Clifford M. HOW TO ORGANIZE AND OPERATE A SMALL BUSINESS. 4th ed. Englewood Cliffs, N.J.: Prentice-Hall, 1968. xvi, 624 p. Diagrams, forms, tables, bibliography.

1352 Klatt, Lawrence A., ed. MANAGING THE DYNAMIC SMALL FIRM: READINGS. Belmont, Calif.: Wadsworth, 1971. 359 p. Diagrams, tables, bibliographies. Paperback.

This work contains thirty-five readings in five sections: the foundations of the small enterprise, managerial aspects of the small business, operating the business, resources for decision making, and the future. No index.

1353 Krentzman, Harvey C. MANAGING FOR PROFITS. Washington, D.C.: Small Business Administration, 1968. 170 p. Forms, tables, bibliographies. Paperback. (Distributed by the Government Printing Office.)

> Advice is given for the small businessman on marketing, production, systems and records, financial management, credit and collections, purchasing and inventory management, accounting and statistics, taxation, insurance, and legal aspects of business operation.

1354 Lasser, Jacob K. HOW TO RUN A SMALL BUSINESS. 3d ed. New York: McGraw-Hill, 1963. xii, 475 p. Tables.

> This practical guide contains twenty-one chapters in three sections: going into business, managing and operating your business, and managing special business phases.

1355 Marting, Elizabeth, ed. MANAGEMENT FOR THE SMALLER COMPANY. New York: American Management Association, 1959. 399 p. Diagrams, tables, bibliography.

> Contains thirty-three practical contributions aimed at companies with fewer than 1,000 employees. Annotated bibliography, pp. 385-94.

1356 Petrof, John V.; Carusone, Peter S.; and McDavid, John E. SMALL BUSINESS MANAGEMENT: CONCEPTS AND TECHNIQUES FOR IMPROVING DECISIONS. McGraw-Hill Series in Management. New York: McGraw-Hill, 1970. 410 p. Diagrams, forms, tables.

> The authors emphasize the need for formalized management methods and the use of the marketing concept as a basis for planning, organizing, and controlling all the small firm's activities. They include problems and case studies.

1357 Rotch, William. MANAGEMENT OF SMALL ENTERPRISES: CASES AND READINGS. 2d ed. Charlottesville: University Press of Virginia, 1967. 262 p. Illustrations, tables. Paperback.

> Readings on the challenge of small enterprises, marketing, and financing are complemented by ten cases on new business and five cases on growing enterprises. No index.

1358 Stanworth, M.J.K., and Curran, J. MANAGEMENT MOTIVATION IN THE SMALLER BUSINESS. Epping, Eng.: Gower Press, 1973. 195 p. Diagrams, tables, bibliographies.

This work contains case studies of four electronics firms--Elecsonics Ltd., Control Engineering Ltd., Instrument Electronics Ltd., and James Stanley Ltd.--and four printing firms--Modern Offset Ltd., Leadprint Ltd., G.S. Gridley & Co. Ltd., and Printed Cartons & Co. Ltd.

1359 Steinhoff, Dan. SMALL BUSINESS MANAGEMENT FUNDAMENTALS. New York: McGraw-Hill, 1974. xix, 299 p. Illustrations, bibliography.

A practical guide, this work is designed to be used as a textbook for students and as a reference work for small business entrepreneurs. An introductory chapter explaining the small business situation is followed by sections dealing with planning, financing, form and structure of the firm, merchandising and sales, and financial management and control.

Bibliography

1360 Salond, Josephine I., comp. SMALL BUSINESS: A BIBLIOGRAPHY. SUPPLEMENT 1969-1973. Birmingham, Eng.: University of Aston in Birmingham Library, Gosta Green, Birmingham, B4 7ET, 1973. 49 p.

This work supplements a bibliography with a similar title compiled by the University of Aston Library and the Small Business Centre in 1969 (58 p.).

Organizations

1361 National Council for Small Business Management Development, c/o Robert O. Bauer, UW-Extension, 929 North Sixth Street, Milwaukee, Wis. 53203.

1362 Small Business Administration, 1441 L Street N.W., Washington, D.C. 20416.

This government department provides advice and protects the interests of small business. It attempts to improve the management skills of small business owners, potential owners, and managers and it publishes a number of series, including MANAGEMENT AIDS FOR SMALL MANUFACTURERS, SMALL BUSINESS BIBLIOGRAPHIES, MANAGEMENT RESEARCH SUMMARIES, and SMALL BUSINESS MANAGEMENT SERIES. Its development and work has been described in Addison W. Parris, THE SMALL BUSINESS ADMINISTRATION, Praeger Library of U.S. Government Departments and Agencies. New York: Praeger, 1968. xii, 292 p. Tables, bibliography.

1363 The Smaller Business Unit, British Institute of Management, Management House, Parker Street, London, WC2B 5PT, England.

This specialist unit of BIM was set up in 1972.

LARGE COMPANIES

1364 Bannock, Graham. THE JUGGERNAUTS: THE AGE OF THE BIG COR-PORATION. London: Weidenfeld & Nicolson; Indianapolis: Bobbs-Merrill Co., 1971. xii, 363 p. Illustrations, diagrams, tables, bibliography.

Bannock offers a warning about the coming domination of all Western economies by the super-corporations. He suggests that the ideology of size has captured the minds of businessmen, governments, and social scientists. He also discusses four corporate cliches--scientific management, the technological explosion, the marketing revolution, and progressive personnel policies.

1365 Lorsch, Jay W., and Allen, Stephen A. III. MANAGING DIVERSITY AND INTERDEPENDENCE: AN ORGANIZATIONAL STUDY OF MULTI-DIVISIONAL FIRMS. Boston: Harvard University Graduate School of Business Administration, Division of Research, 1973. xiii, 265 p. Diagrams, tables, bibliography.

The authors use a behavioral science approach to the organizational issues faced by managers of multidivisional firms. They show how such firms develop organizational arrangements which enable them to diversify while retaining effective corporate-divisional and interdivisional coordination.

1366 Sayles, Leonard R., and Chandler, Margaret K. MANAGING LARGE SYSTEMS: ORGANIZATIONS FOR THE FUTURE. New York: Harper & Row, 1971. xiv, 332 p. Diagrams, tables.

The authors review the traditional management functions--planning, organizing, staffing, directing, and controlling--in the context of complex systems, with particular reference to management methods at the National Aeronautics and Space Administration (NASA). They stress the role of the scientist in management, the project engineer, systems management, and management of research and development.

GROWTH OF COMPANIES

1367 Broadway, Frank. THE MANAGEMENT PROBLEMS OF EXPANSION. London: Business Publications, 1966. 220 p. Diagrams, tables, bibliography.

This book includes a checklist on expansion projects and twenty expansion case histories.

1368 Clifford, Donald K., Jr. "Growth Pains of the Threshold Company." HARVARD BUSINESS REVIEW 51 (September–October 1973): 143–54. Diagrams, tables.

Clifford suggests that there are two main problems to be faced by a company moving from medium to large size: lack of financial resources and lack of management skills. He recommends a series of organization, staffing, and management changes to ease the passage over the threshold.

1369 Dudick, Thomas S. "A Backward Look at Forward Planning." MANAGEMENT ADVISER 9 (January–February 1972): 15–19.

Dudick argues against the pursuit of growth for its own sake and presents "ten commandments for expansion." Based on the experience of the Durard Plastics Company.

1370 Hazel, Arthur Curwen, and Reid, Alan Scott. ENJOYING A PROFITABLE BUSINESS: A PRACTICAL GUIDE TO SUCCESSFUL GROWTH TECHNIQUES FOR SMALL COMPANIES. London: Business Books, 1971. xvi, 251 p. Diagrams, forms, tables, bibliography.

Part one (narrative) encourages the reader to think about his business and where he wants it to go. Part two (techniques) provides advice and checklists on management methods with guides to further reading and British sources of information.

1371 McGuire, E. Patrick, and Bailey, Earl L. SOURCES OF CORPORATE GROWTH: A SURVEY. Experiences in Marketing Management, no. 24. New York: Conference Board, 1970. 28 p. Tables. Paperback.

In this summary of the views of managers in 152 companies, the authors suggest that there are five key growth areas in practice, although few companies rely solely on any one source of growth: increased market demand, increased market penetration, new products and services, creation of new markets, and mergers and acquisitions.

1372 Mathes, Sorrell M. "Handling Company Growth." Managing the Moderate Sized Company, no. 5. New York: Conference Board, 1967. 28 p. Paperback.

This study queried managers of 129 companies. Most respondents believed that growth is essential to the continued success of their companies, but relatively few felt that planning had made a significant contribution to their recent growth.

1373 Stemp, Isay, ed. CORPORATE GROWTH STRATEGIES. New York: American Management Association, 1970. 445 p. Diagrams, tables.

> Included are eleven essays, aimed at the top management team, on the need for growth, planning for growth, conditions for growth, the people factor in corporate growth strategies, compensation for the management team, the marketing factor, growth through technological innovation, corporate financial strategy, international financing of corporate growth, and mergers and acquisitions.

GROWTH THROUGH MERGER AND ACQUISITION

1374 Albers, William W., and Segal, Joel E., eds. THE CORPORATE MERGER. University of Chicago Graduate School of Business, Studies in Business. Chicago: University of Chicago Press, 1966. xviii, 287 p. Diagrams, tables.

> These proceedings of a seminar held in 1963 contain eleven papers on growth as a policy of the firm, the evaluation of proposed mergers, and managerial problems of a merger. No index.

1375 Buckley, A.A. "Some Guidelines for Acquisitions." ACCOUNTING AND BUSINESS RESEARCH, no. 3 (Summer 1971), pp. 215-32. Tables, bibliography.

> Buckley examines the reasons for the failure of mergers and suggests four guidelines for successful acquisition based on formulation of acquisition objectives, planning for integration of activities, financing of acquisitions, and adequate control systems.

1376 Cook, P. Lesley, et al. EFFECTS OF MERGERS: SIX STUDIES. Cambridge Studies in Industry. London: Allen & Unwin; New York: Fernhill House, 1958. 458 p. Tables.

> These are historical and analytical studies of mergers in the British cement and calico print industries (by P. Lesley Cook), soap industry (by Ruth Cohen), flat-glass industry (by Cook), motor industry (by George Maxcy), and brewing industry (by George Vaizey).

1377 Gratwick, John. "Mergers, Takeovers, and Social Responsibility." JOURNAL OF GENERAL MANAGEMENT 1 (Autumn 1973): 73-80. Tables.

> Gratwick examines the reasons for takeovers and mergers against a background of increased public concern about their effects.

1378 Hackett, J.T. "Corporate Growth Revisited." BUSINESS HORIZONS 17 (February 1974): 25-31.

Hackett discusses the managerial problems presented by mergers and acquisitions and suggests greater decentralization or the division of large organizations into smaller, independent units.

1379 Harvey, John L., and Newgarden, Albert, eds. MANAGEMENT GUIDES TO MERGERS AND ACQUISITIONS. New York: Wiley-Interscience, 1969. xii, 319 p. Tables.

Twenty-four contributions consider planning and fact-finding, legal and accounting considerations, tax considerations, personnel considerations, postmerger integration, acquisition abroad, and three "how not to" contributions (how not to sell your company, how to succeed in business without really buying, and a sure guide to unsuccessful mergers).

1380 Hennessy, J.H., Jr. ACQUIRING AND MERGING BUSINESSES. Englewood Cliffs, N.J.: Prentice-Hall, 1966. xii, 274 p. Tables.

Hennessy emphasizes financial and legal aspects but also includes two case studies of motives for merging and a chapter on public and employee relations.

1381 Hovers, John. EXPANSION THROUGH ACQUISITION: EXPANSION STRATEGY BASED ON EXPERIENCE WITH A LARGE EUROPEAN COMPANY. London: Business Books, 1973. 178 p. Diagrams, forms, tables, bibliography. (Distributed by Cahners Publishing Co., Boston.)

Originally published by Samson Uitgeveru, Alphen aan den Rijn, Holland, in 1972 as EXPANSIE DOOR OVERNAME, this book won the 1973 prize of the Association of European Management Publishers. It was based partly on the author's experience as an employee of the Dutch reprographic firm Océ van der Grinten NV with the practical side of the takeover problem. He explains the usefulness of the strategic game theory, using some mathematics, and includes several checklists for procedures in the various phases of a takeover.

1382 Jones, Robert, and Marriott, Oliver. ANATOMY OF A MERGER: A HISTORY OF G.E.C., A.E.I. AND ENGLISH ELECTRIC. London: Cape, 1970; Mystic, Conn.: Verry, Lawrence Inc., 1971. 346 p. Illustrations, bibliography.

The background to the merger of the "big three" companies in the British electrical engineering industry is traced.

1383 Linowes, David F. MANAGING GROWTH THROUGH ACQUISITION. New York: American Management Association, 1968. 192 p. Bibliography.

Linowes argues that the need for growth is constant and dis-
putes C. Northcote Parkinson's maxim that "growth means complexity." He provides practical advice on such matters as
planning for growth, internal growth versus growth by acquisition, financial problems, negotiation, and integration.

1384 Mace, Myles L., and Montgomery, George G., Jr. MANAGEMENT
PROBLEMS OF CORPORATE ACQUISITIONS. Boston: Harvard University Graduate School of Business Administration, Division of Research,
1962. 276 p. Tables.

This work is concerned with the internal management problems
arising at each stage of the acquisition process, and it includes
many case studies. No index.

1385 MERGERS AND ACQUISITIONS: THE JOURNAL OF CORPORATE VEN-
TURE. McLean, Va.: 1965- . Quarterly.

1386 Moon, Ronald W. BUSINESS MERGERS AND TAKE-OVER BIDS: A
STUDY OF THE POST-WAR PATTERN OF AMALGAMATIONS AND RE-
CONSTRUCTIONS OF COMPANIES. 4th ed. London: Gee, 1971.
236 p. Tables.

This standard British text emphasizes financial and legal aspects.

1387 Reid, Samuel Richardson. MERGERS, MANAGERS AND THE ECONOMY.
New York: McGraw-Hill, 1968. xix, 302 p. Diagrams, tables. Hardcover and paperback.

Part one deals with merger waves, merger facets and a merger
mosaic. Part two concerns mergers, growth, and profitability.
Part three covers public policy considerations.

1388 Vice, Anthony. THE STRATEGY OF TAKEOVERS: A CASEBOOK OF
INTERNATIONAL PRACTICE. McGraw-Hill European Series in Management. London: McGraw-Hill, 1971. xvii, 137 p.

This work contains in-depth case studies of nine major mergers:
Slater Walker-Forestal, GEC-AEI-English Electric, British Ley-
land, International Publishing Corporation, Cadbury-Schweppes,
EMI, Boussois-Souchon-Neuvesel (BSN) and Saint-Gobin
(France), Chemical Bank, and Badische Anilin-und Soda-Fabrik
AG and Wintershall AG. No index.

1389 Wainwright, Jane. "The Human Side of Mergers." INDUSTRIAL SO-
CIETY 54 (December 1972): 7-8, 12.

The authors stress the importance of early, adequate communication to employees and unions of the facts regarding proposed

mergers and the avoidance of rumor and conjecture.

Bibliography

1390 Sperry, Robert, comp. MERGERS AND ACQUISITIONS: A COMPRE-
HENSIVE BIBLIOGRAPHY. Washington, D.C.: Mergers and Acquisitions,
the Journal of Corporate Venture, 1972. 223 p. Paperback.

> This has a classified arrangement, with indexes of countries
> and industries, but no author index. It does not include an-
> notations.

Section 12

INTERNATIONAL AND MULTINATIONAL BUSINESS

The crossing of national barriers is increasingly important in today's business environment, but internationalism presents its own problems. Apart from the political and social problems imposed by the need to adjust to foreign environments and government regulations, there are many management and organizational problems, such as the possible need to adopt new management styles and to handle staff from many different countries.

GENERAL STUDIES

1391 Blake, David H., ed. "The Multinational Corporation." ANNALS OF THE AMERICAN ACADEMY OF POLITICAL AND SOCIAL SCIENCE 403 (September 1972): 1-152. Diagrams, tables.

> Fourteen papers focus on the multinational corporation. Topics covered include multinational corporations in Western Europe and in the developing countries, their impact on labor unions and on foreign relations, and the international economic situation and multinational corporation.

1392 Bradley, Gene E., and Bursk, Edward C. "Multinationalism and the 29th Day." HARVARD BUSINESS REVIEW 50 (January-February 1972): 37-47.

> Interviews with the president of IBM World Trade and the chairman of General Electric center on the conflicts between economic internationalism and political nationalism, the relationship between corporate growth and the needs of society, and other matters.

1393 Brooke, Michael Z., and Remmers, H.L., eds. THE MULTINATIONAL COMPANY IN EUROPE: SOME KEY PROBLEMS. International Business Series. London: Longman, 1972. xv, 194 p. Diagrams, tables, bibliography.

> This book contains contributions by eight authors, including the editors, on growth and change in the international company;

financial strategy; accounting practices; the role of the national manager in a multinational company; the art of choosing an
American joint venture partner; organization of the multinational firm; decision making; communication, culture, and the
education of the multinational manager; and problems of resource allocation.

1394 _____. THE STRATEGY OF MULTI-NATIONAL ENTERPRISE: ORGANI-
SATION AND FINANCE. London: Longman; New York: American Elsevier, 1970. xiv, 388 p. Diagrams, tables, bibliography.

An introductory section on the role of the multinational company is followed by major sections on structure and relationships; financial policies and practices; and performance, motives,
and the environment. The book is based on material collected
by interviews with senior executives from more than eighty
companies.

1395 Business International S.A. and Centre d'Etudes Industrielles, Geneva.
MANAGING THE MULTINATIONALS: PREPARING FOR TOMORROW.
London: Allen & Unwin, 1972. 162 p. Tables, bibliography. (Distri-
buted by International Publications Service, New York.)

Inspired by the first European Management Symposium held in
Davos, Switzerland, on the occasion of the twenty-fifth anniversary of the Centre d'Etudes Industrielles, this book helps managers
of international companies to cope more effectively with the
changing environment. Part one forecasts the environmental
opportunities and challenges to be faced by business corporations during the next decade. Part two identifies four key
areas for management survival.

1396 Cullman, W. Arthur, and Knudson, Harry R. MANAGEMENT PROBLEMS
IN INTERNATIONAL ENVIRONMENTS. Prentice-Hall International Series
in Management. Englewood Cliffs, N.J.: Prentice-Hall, 1972. xxi,
455 p. Illustrations, diagrams, tables.

This work contains forty-five histories of multinational management developed at the IMEDE Management Development Institute, Lausanne, arranged under six broad subject headings:
financial management, management control, marketing management, production and operations management, organizational
behavior, and general management. Index of cases but no subject index.

1397 Dunning, John H., ed. THE MULTINATIONAL ENTERPRISE. London: Allen
& Unwin, 1971; New York: Praeger, 1972. 368 p.

Fourteen papers, originally given at a conference held at the
University of Reading, England, consider the general role of
the multinational enterprise, trade and the balance of payments,

direct foreign investment and the less developed countries, governments and the multinational enterprise, and the multinational company in Europe.

1398 Dymsza, William A. MULTINATIONAL BUSINESS STRATEGY. McGraw-Hill Series in International Business. New York: McGraw-Hill, 1972. xv, 253 p. Diagrams, bibliography. Hardcover and paperback.

This concise approach to international business strategy, organizational structure, and control arrangements, stresses the strategic planning process, objective setting, and formulation of international strategies. It includes comments on company practices during the period 1967 to 1969.

1399 Ettinger, Karl E., ed. THE INTERNATIONAL HANDBOOK OF MANAGEMENT. New York: McGraw-Hill, 1965. xv, 671 p. Diagrams, tables, bibliography.

Contained are fifty-nine contributions arranged in six sections: management principles and techniques, international corporate activities, problems in financing, special development problems, rural management problems, and training of managers. The book is particularly concerned with the problems of developing countries.

1400 Fayerweather, John. INTERNATIONAL BUSINESS MANAGEMENT: A CONCEPTUAL FRAMEWORK. McGraw-Hill Series in International Business. New York: McGraw-Hill, 1969. xii, 220 p. Diagrams, bibliography. Hardcover and paperback.

This book contains chapters on the international transmission of resources, relations with host societies, conflicts with nationalism and national interests, the global business strategy, and organization and administration of multinational enterprises.

1401 Kindleberger, Charles P., ed. THE INTERNATIONAL CORPORATION: A SYMPOSIUM. Cambridge, Mass.: M.I.T. Press, 1970. 415 p. Diagrams, tables.

These papers were given at a series of seminars at the Sloan School of Management, Massachusetts Institute of Technology, in 1969. Fifteen contributions deal with the theory of the international corporation; finance and technology; law and politics; the multinational corporation in petroleum, the automobile industry, and banking; the multinational corporation in Australia, Latin America, and Japan; and the future of the multinational enterprise.

1402 Kolde, Endel J. INTERNATIONAL BUSINESS ENTERPRISE. 2d ed. Englewood Cliffs, N.J.: Prentice-Hall, 1973. xv, 704 p. Diagrams, tables, bibliography.

This comprehensive textbook covers the background to international business, international trade, the multinational company, financial structures and processes of international business, marketing in a multinational context, international integration, and modernization of developing areas. Indexes of authors and subjects.

1403 Martyn, Howe. MULTINATIONAL BUSINESS MANAGEMENT. Studies in Business, Industry & Technology. Lexington, Mass.: Heath Lexington Books, 1970. xv, 221 p. Tables, bibliographies.

A professor of international business at the American University, Washington, D.C., believed to have introduced the first university course on the subject in 1961, describes this "new field of management." The early chapters trace the development of multinational companies, after which Howe deals with management methods, communication, job descriptions, finance, marketing, production and plant location, research and development, personnel problems, and business-government relations.

1404 MULTINATIONAL BUSINESS: AN EIU QUARTERLY REVIEW OF NEWS AND ANALYSIS. London: Economist Intelligence Unit, 1971- .

1405 Phatak, Arvind V. EVOLUTION OF WORLD ENTERPRISES. New York: American Management Association, 1971. 213 p. Diagrams, tables.

This is a study of twenty-six European and thirteen American companies.

1406 Robock, Stefan H., and Simmonds, Kenneth. INTERNATIONAL BUSINESS AND MULTINATIONAL ENTERPRISES. Irwin Series in Management. Homewood, Ill.: Irwin; London: Irwin-Dorsey International, 1973. xiii, 652 p. Diagrams, tables, bibliography.

Arranged in six parts, this book covers the nature and scope of international business, the framework of international transactions, international business and the nation state, assessing and forecasting the international business environment, managing the multinational enterprise, and cases and problems. Indexes of names and subjects.

1407 Salera, Virgil. MULTINATIONAL BUSINESS. Boston: Houghton Mifflin, 1969. xiii, 460 p. Diagrams, tables, bibliography.

A textbook for students, this work gives detailed consideration to the political and environmental factors affecting multinational business, as well as dealing with the operation and management of multinational enterprises.

1408 Sirota, David. "The Multinational Corporation: Management Myths."

PERSONNEL 49 (January–February 1972): 34–41.

Sirota attacks the "myth" that there are fundamental differences in the management philosophy of multinational firms. He suggests that the human problems encountered are very similar to those experienced by single-nation companies.

1409 Tugendhat, Christopher. THE MULTINATIONALS. London: Eyre & Spottiswoode, 1971; New York: Random House, 1972. xiii, 242 p. Diagrams, tables, bibliography.

Part one describes the growth of multinational business. Part two explains how multinationals such as SKF (Aktiebolaget Svenska Kullagerfabriken) and the IBM Corporation work today, with comments on such matters as planning, decision making, plant location, and trade union problems.

1410 Vernon, Raymond. MANAGER IN THE INTERNATIONAL ECONOMY. Prentice-Hall International Series in Management. Englewood Cliffs, N.J.: Prentice-Hall, 1972. xx, 460 p. Diagrams, tables.

This book focuses on the problems of crossing national boundaries and integrating business operations among national economies. Part two contains sixteen case studies and exercises.

1411 _____. SOVEREIGNTY AT BAY: THE MULTINATIONAL SPREAD OF U.S. ENTERPRISES. New York: Basic Books; London: Longman, 1971. 326 p. Tables.

Produced as part of Harvard University Graduate School of Business Administration's Multinational Enterprise Project, this book is concerned with the effect of multinationalism by U.S. enterprises on national economies and patterns.

1412 Wormald, Avison. INTERNATIONAL BUSINESS. Pan Management Series. London: Pan Books, 1973. 229 p. Diagrams, tables. Paperback.

Chapters deal with the mainsprings of international business, phases in the development of an international business, the nature of international business, and the problems of communication, complexity, and risk. Wormald concludes that international business is an exceptionally interesting activity in which many of the leading managers of tomorrow may win their spurs.

1413 Wriston, Walter B. "The World Corporation: New Weight in an Old Balance." SLOAN MANAGEMENT REVIEW 15 (1974): 25–33.

The author traces the development of multinational corporations and discusses the reasons for mistrust of them by home and host governments. He suggests that such corporations are the most

effective means of bringing a higher worldwide standard of living.

1414 Zenoff, David B. INTERNATIONAL BUSINESS MANAGEMENT: TEXT
AND CASES. New York: Macmillan; London: Collier-Macmillan, 1971.
xii, 320 p. Diagrams, tables, bibliographies.

> Covers the international business challenge, foreign market
> analysis, exporting, foreign licensing, international banking
> operations, analysis of the foreign environment, direct foreign
> investment, and managing an international company.

Bibliographies

1415 Bishop, Harvey P., and Lindfors, Grace V., eds. BIBLIOGRAPHY:
CASES AND OTHER MATERIALS FOR THE TEACHING OF MULTINATION-
AL BUSINESS. Boston: Harvard University Graduate School of Business
Administration, 1964. 283 p. Paperback.

> These annotated lists of cases (pp. 1-119), books and pam-
> phlets (pp. 121-84), and periodical articles (pp. 185-204) are
> not arranged in systematic order. Also included are lists of
> supplementary reference sources, educational institutions in
> countries other than the United States, and alphabetical in-
> dexes of authors and topics.

1416 Ewing, David W. "MNC's on Trial." HARVARD BUSINESS REVIEW 50
(May-June 1972): 130-43.

> This literature review has twenty-five bibliographical references.

1417 INTERNATIONAL EXECUTIVE. Hastings-on-Hudson, N.Y.: Foundation
for Advancement of International Business Administration, 1959- . Three
issues yearly.

> This reading service contains digests of books and articles on
> aspects of international management. It lacks indexes.

1418 Nehrt, Lee C.; Truitt, J. Frederick; and Wright, Richard W., comps.
INTERNATIONAL BUSINESS RESEARCH: PAST, PRESENT AND FUTURE.
International Business Research Series, no. 2. Bloomington: Indiana Univer-
sity Graduate School of Business, Bureau of Business Research, 1970. 362 p.
Diagrams, tables. Paperback.

> An introductory chapter is followed by an annotated bibliog-
> raphy of past research, an annotated bibliography of current
> research, and recommendations for future research. The rec-
> ommendations were developed using the DELPHI technique,
> and the appendixes include a note on the application of
> DELPHI. There is an author index, but no subject index.

1419 Peterson, Richard B. BIBLIOGRAPHY ON COMPARATIVE (INTERNA-
TIONAL) MANAGEMENT. Occasional Papers, no. 21. Seattle: University of Washington Graduate School of Business Administration, 1969. 20
leaves. Paperback.

> This is a classified, unannotated list of 278 books and articles.

1420 Stewart, Charles F., and Simmons, George B., comps. A BIBLIOGRAPHY
OF INTERNATIONAL BUSINESS. New York: Columbia University Press,
1964. xiii, 603 p.

> Arranged systematically under four broad headings, this bibliog-
> raphy covers comparative business systems, government and inter-
> national operations, the firm in international operations, and
> nations and regions. Books, reports, and articles are listed,
> but there are no indexes.

1421 Wheeler, Lora Jeanne. INTERNATIONAL BUSINESS AND FOREIGN
TRADE: INFORMATION SOURCES: A GUIDE TO LITERATURE AND
BODIES CONCERNED WITH THE PROCEDURES AND POLICIES OF CON-
DUCTING BUSINESS WITH OTHER COUNTRIES. Management Informa-
tion Guides, no. 14. Detroit: Gale Research Co., 1968. 221 p.

> This excellent classified and annotated guide has indexes of
> authors/titles/sources and a subject index. Sections of partic-
> ular interest include section 3, "Organizing for International
> Business," pp. 27-34; section 9, "Management of International
> Business," pp. 77-81; and section 10, "Attitudes, Management,
> Training, and Compensation of Personnel," pp. 85-89.

Organizations

1422 Academy of International Business, c/o James D. Goodnow, Roosevelt
University, 430 South Michigan Avenue, Chicago, Ill. 60605.

> This group publishes the AIB NEWSLETTER (5 issues yearly)
> and the JOURNAL OF INTERNATIONAL BUSINESS STUDIES
> (semiannually). The association has compiled an inventory of
> collegiate courses in international business. Founded in 1959
> as the Association for Education in International Business in
> 1972 it became the Academy of International Business.

1423 Center for Multinational Studies, 1625 Eye Street N.W., Suite 908, Washington, D.C. 20006.

> This was formed by the International Economic Planning Associa-
> tion to conduct research and to disseminate information on all
> aspects of multinational corporations. It maintains a library of
> research materials and publishes occasional papers.

ORGANIZATIONAL PROBLEMS OF MULTINATIONALS

1424 Alsegg, Robert J. "Reorganizing the International Operation." CON-
FERENCE BOARD RECORD 8 (December 1971): 52-64. Diagrams.

Alsegg suggests reasons for the frequent reorganization of international organization structures by U.S. companies and discusses the advantages and disadvantages of reorganization.

1425 Bodinat, Henri. "Multinational Decentralization: Doomed if You Do, Doomed
if You Don't." EUROPEAN BUSINESS, no. 41 (Summer 1974), pp. 64-70.

Bodinat contends that multinationals need decentralization for
control purposes but centralization for finance, marketing, and
production. He shows how some companies are attempting to
resolve this problem.

1426 Duerr, Michael G., and Roach, John M. ORGANIZATION AND CON-
TROL OF INTERNATIONAL OPERATIONS. Conference Board Report,
n.s., no. 597. New York: Conference Board, 1973. 151 p. Diagrams,
tables. Paperback.

The authors examine trends in the organization and control of
multinational companies since the mid-1960s, based largely on
information from personal interviews with executives in the
United States, Canada, Japan, and Western Europe. They include case studies of seventeen North American, fifteen European, and four Japanese companies.

1427 Hulme, Robert D., and Maydew, John C. "A View of the Top: A Study
of Collective Management Organization." BUSINESS HORIZONS 15
(October 1972): 19-30.

The authors report on research into top management organization, especially in large multinational corporations, with special reference to the trend towards the multiple top executive
or office of the president. A number of case studies are presented.

1428 Morris, Geoffrey. "Organization Development in a Multinational Company: A Case Study." EUROPEAN TRAINING 1 (Spring 1972): 78-87.
Diagrams.

Morris describes the introduction and evaluation of an organization development program, the stated aims of which were
"to develop the organization, and every manager in it, in
such a way as to ensure that individual efforts are effectively
integrated in the pursuit of company goals."

1429 Schollhammer, Hans. "Organization Structures of Multinational Corporations." ACADEMY OF MANAGEMENT JOURNAL 14 (September 1971):

345-65. Tables, bibliography.

Schollhammer analyzes similarities and differences in the organizational structures of multinational corporations based in the United States and four European countries.

1430 Siethoff, H.J. ten. "Organisational Development in a Large Multinational Organisation." EUROPEAN TRAINING 2 (1973): 228-38.

This review of a model for OD developed by a Dutch-based consultancy firm, NPI International, is quite technical in approach.

1431 Stanley, Alexander O. ORGANIZING FOR INTERNATIONAL OPERATIONS. AMA Research Study, no. 41. New York: American Management Association, 1960. 318 p. Diagrams, tables.

This book includes thirty case studies, more than fifty organization charts, and a description of methods used to define the international manager's job with 104 job descriptions.

1432 Stieglitz, Harold. ORGANIZATION STRUCTURES OF INTERNATIONAL COMPANIES. Studies in Personnel Policy, no. 198. New York: National Industrial Conference Board, 1965. 143 p. Diagrams, tables. Paperback.

Stieglitz provides organization charts of forty-two companies from various countries, together with several charts showing how the foreign operations of these companies are organized and integrated with the parent company. This material is preceded by a discussion of organizational patterns and the differences between U.S. companies and companies outside the United States.

1433 Stopford, John M., and Wells, Louis T., Jr. MANAGING THE MULTINATIONAL ENTERPRISE: ORGANIZATION OF THE FIRM AND OWNERSHIP OF THE SUBSIDIARIES. International Business Series. New York: Basic Books; London: Longman, 1972. xvi, 223 p. Diagrams, tables.

Produced as part of Harvard's Multinational Enterprise Project, this work deals in part one with the ways in which multinational companies have altered their structures as they have developed more complex strategies. Part two focuses on decisions about the inclusion of local partners in the foreign operations of the firm.

1434 Widing, J. William, Jr. "Re-organizing Your Worldwide Business." HARVARD BUSINESS REVIEW 51 (May-June 1973): 153-60. Tables.

Widing discusses such matters as how a corporation can identify the need to reorganize, the problems of integrating foreign and domestic operations, and the criteria for defining the best organizational structure.

MANAGERS IN MULTINATIONALS

See also items 761, 763, 765, 1830.

1435 Aitken, Thomas. THE MULTINATIONAL MAN: THE ROLE OF THE MANAGER ABROAD. London: Allen & Unwin; New York: Halsted Press, 1973. 176 p. Bibliography.

Aitken analyzes the functional responsibilities of the manager abroad in the light of his relationships with his home office and with his local environment. Several case studies are included.

1436 Business International Corporation. COMPENSATING INTERNATIONAL EXECUTIVES: HOW INTERNATIONAL COMPANIES SET SALARIES, INCENTIVES, BENEFITS. New York: Business International Corporation, 1970. 62 p. Forms, tables. Paperback.

This book, based on a survey of seventy companies, includes an introductory section on selecting and training international managers and a section on relocating international executives.

1437 Chorafas, Dimitris N. DEVELOPING THE INTERNATIONAL EXECUTIVE. AMA Research Study, no. 83. New York: American Management Association, 1967. 96 p. Bibliography. Paperback.

The book is based on information collected in interviews with more than 200 executives throughout the world.

1438 Franko, Lawrence G. "Who Manages Multinational Enterprises?" COLUMBIA JOURNAL OF WORLD BUSINESS 8 (Summer 1973): 30-42. Diagrams, tables.

Franko examines trends in management employment policies of multinational companies.

1439 Kuin, Pieter. "The Magic of Multinational Management." HARVARD BUSINESS REVIEW 50 (November-December 1972): 89-97.

Kuin discusses management development problems of multinational companies, particularly the need to weld together executives of different nationalities who have to cope with divided loyalties to their companies and countries. Using Unilever as an example, he shows how job rotation and career planning can help to overcome these problems. He also examines trends in executive remuneration and planning.

1440 Patrick, Stewart, and Kraus, David. "How to Pay Multinationally." MANAGEMENT TODAY, August 1974, pp. 83-86, 124. Tables.

The different national patterns of executive compensation, especially in Europe and the United States, and their implications for multinational companies are discussed.

1441 Reynolds, Calvin. "Career Paths and Compensation in the MNC's." COLUMBIA JOURNAL OF WORLD BUSINESS 7 (November-December 1972): 77-87. Tables.

Reynolds suggests that compensation policies can and should be geared towards organizational structures and corporate objectives.

1442 Shetty, Y.K. "Ownership, Size, Technology and Management Development: A Comparative Analysis." ACADEMY OF MANAGEMENT JOURNAL 14 (December 1971): 439-49. Tables.

This research study is concerned with the relationship between the management development programs of multinational firms, especially those with subsidiaries in developing countries, and such matters as patterns of ownership, size, type of technology, and product market characteristics.

PLANNING IN MULTINATIONALS

1443 Hussey, D.E. "Strategic Planning for International Business." LONG RANGE PLANNING 5 (June 1972): 16-20.

Hussey examines the decisions which remain within the province of the parent company when a multinational decides to decentralize, such as formulation of profit objectives and financial control. He also notes the parent/subsidiary conflict which may result.

1444 Schollhammer, Hans. "Long-Range Planning in Multinational Firms." COLUMBIA JOURNAL OF WORLD BUSINESS 6 (September-October 1971): 79-86.

The author describes the long-range planning systems used in two multinational firms, one with a centralized and one with a decentralized planning process. The firms are Avery Products Corporation, San Marino, California, and IBM World Trade Corporation, New York.

1445 Schwendiman, John Snow. STRATEGIC AND LONG-RANGE PLANNING FOR THE MULTINATIONAL CORPORATION. Praeger Special Studies in International Economics and Development. New York: Praeger, 1973. xii, 150 p. Diagrams, tables, bibliography.

This research, based on a doctoral dissertation, defines the key elements of international corporate planning and reports on the state of the art in major U.S. and European companies. The analysis is based on answers given by a selected sample of companies in the automobile, chemical, and electrical equipment industries to a series of questions on planning structure, company assessment, environmental assessment, strategy formulation, long- and intermediate-range plans, and implementation of plans. No index.

1446 Steiner, George A., and Cannon, Warren M., eds. MULTINATIONAL CORPORATE PLANNING. Studies of the Modern Corporation. New York: Macmillan; London: Collier-Macmillan, 1966. xiii, 330 p.

This book is based on a research seminar held in Fontainebleau in 1964. An introductory section by Steiner on the nature and significance of multinational corporate planning is followed by twenty contributions in three parts: organization for and practice of multinational corporate planning, the environment and multinational corporate planning, and comparison of multinational corporate planning amongst Western European and U.S. companies. Several references to the planning practices of major companies are included.

FINANCIAL MANAGEMENT IN MULTINATIONALS

1447 Chambers, John C., and Mullick, Satinder K. "Investment Decision-Making in a Multinational Enterprise." MANAGEMENT ACCOUNTING (New York) 53 (August 1971): 13-20. Diagrams, tables.

A description of the use by Corning Glass Works of a computer-assisted model to examine alternative investment opportunities, which resulted in revoking a decision (based on the availability of local tax subsidies) to build a new European plant.

1448 Dufey, Gunter, and Field, Judith J. FINANCIAL MANAGEMENT IN THE INTERNATIONAL CORPORATION: AN ANNOTATED BIBLIOGRAPHY. Ann Arbor: University of Michigan Graduate School of Business Administration, Institute for International Commerce, 1971. 95 p. Paperback.

This lists 323 items, arranged alphabetically by author with a subject index. It covers mainly material published in English between 1960 and 1970.

1449 Meister, Irene W. MANAGING THE INTERNATIONAL FINANCIAL FUNCTION. Studies in Business Policy, no. 133. New York: National Industrial Conference Board, 1970. 122 p. Tables. Paperback.

This is a study of the policies and practices of nearly 300 companies. Part one identifies three organizational patterns for the management of the international financial function. Part two deals with the assignment of functional responsibilities within the organization.

1450 Robbins, Sidney M., and Stobaugh, Robert B. MONEY IN THE MULTI-NATIONAL ENTERPRISE: A STUDY OF FINANCIAL POLICY. New York: Basic Books, 1973; London: Longman, 1974. xix, 231 p. Diagrams, tables.

One of the Harvard Business School's Multinational Enterprise Study series, this book deals thoroughly with the problems of financing overseas operations. It has an appendix on methods used in determining financial practices by U.S. multinational enterprises and also includes a simulation model of a multinational enterprise, constructed by Daniel M. Schydlowsky.

1451 Scott, George M. "Financial Control in Multinational Enterprises: The New Challenge to Accountants." INTERNATIONAL JOURNAL OF ACCOUNTING 7 (Spring 1972): 55-68.

This is a description of the impact of multinationals on accounting controls, with particular reference to such problems as the accountant's role in cash coordination and foreign exchange management and the basis for translating foreign currencies.

LABOR RELATIONS AND MULTINATIONALS

1452 Blake, David H. "Corporate Structure and International Unionism." COLUMBIA JOURNAL OF WORLD BUSINESS 7 (March-April 1972): 19-26.

Blake shows how national unions have cooperated to meet the challenge of the multinational corporation, identifies four types of multinational, and discusses the likely impact of each type on unions.

1453 Clutterbuck, David. "Have the International Unions Got Their Eyes on Your Company?" INTERNATIONAL MANAGEMENT 29 (August 1974): 30-34.

Many examples of union relations with multinational companies are discussed.

1454 Gennard, John. MULTINATIONAL CORPORATIONS AND BRITISH LABOUR: A REVIEW OF ATTITUDES AND RESPONSES. London: British-North American Committee, 12 Upper Belgrave Street, 1972. xv, 53 p. Tables. Paperback.

The British-North American Committee was established in 1969 to study and comment upon the developing relationships between Britain, the United States, and Canada. This report is in three parts: views of British labor on the multinational corporation, labor relations practices of foreign multinational companies in Britain, and British trade union responses to the multinational corporation.

1455 James, John Alan. "Multinational Trade Unions Muscle Their Strength." EUROPEAN BUSINESS 39 (Autumn 1973): 36-44. Diagram.

James suggests ways in which multinational management should adapt to the changing situation in industrial relations presented by the multinational trade union movement.

1456 Kamin, Alfred, ed. WESTERN EUROPEAN LABOR AND THE AMERICAN CORPORATION. Washington, D.C.: Bureau of National Affairs, 1970. xxvii, 546 p.

Twenty authorities evaluate the overseas labor relations policies of American companies conducting business in Western Europe, covering such topics as collective bargaining in Western Europe; labor relations and the law in Western Europe; manpower utilization, mobility, and training; wages and employment benefits; and U.S. investment and management in Western Europe. The book is based on a summer institute on business and law sponsored by Loyola University of Chicago in 1968 through its School of Law and School of Business Administration.

1457 Shaw, Robert d'A. "Foreign Investment and Global Labor." COLUMBIA JOURNAL OF WORLD BUSINESS 6 (July-August 1971): 52-62. Tables.

Shaw considers two major problems produced by the growth of multinational companies--complaints by unions that jobs, as well as capital and technology, are being exported and the possible distortion by foreign investment of the host country's plans for an even economic development.

Section 13

SOCIAL RESPONSIBILITY OF BUSINESS

Managers are becoming increasingly aware that they are responsible not only to their stockholders but also to their employees and to society at large. Included in a social responsibility audit are such matters as business ethics, management's attitudes to physically and socially disadvantaged people, the pollution problem, and the social problems imposed by technological change.

GENERAL STUDIES

1458 Ackerman, Robert W. "Putting Social Concern into Practice." EURO-PEAN BUSINESS, no. 40 (Winter-Spring 1974), pp. 31-35. Tables.

> Ackerman explains the difficulty of adopting a social responsibility policy, especially in divisionalized organizations, and notes the steps to be taken for the successful implementation of such a policy.

1459 Baker, Henry G. "Identity and Social Responsibility Policies: Six Large Companies Examined." BUSINESS HORIZONS 16 (April 1973): 23-28.

> Baker discusses the social responsibility policies of Ashland Oil and Refining Company, Standard Oil Company (Ohio), the General Electric Company, Procter and Gamble, Kroger, and Federated Department Stores.

1460 Bauer, Raymond A. "The Corporate Social Audit." CALIFORNIA MAN-AGEMENT REVIEW 16 (Fall 1973): 5-10.

> Bauer describes the characteristics of social audits as practiced in the United States and analyzes their advantages and short-comings.

1461 Brown, James K. SOCIAL RESPONSIBILITY AND THE SMALLER COM-PANY: SOME PERSPECTIVES. Conference Board Report, n.s., no. 568. New York: Conference Board, 1972. 21 p. Paperback.

This book examines the special difficulties which social responsibility programs impose on the smaller company and provides definitions of corporate social responsibility.

1462 BUSINESS AND SOCIETY REVIEW/INNOVATION: A QUARTERLY FORUM
ON THE ROLE OF BUSINESS IN SOCIETY. Boston: Warren, Gorham &
Lamont, 1972- .

1463 Butcher, Bernard L. "The Program Management Approach to the Corporate
Social Audit." CALIFORNIA MANAGEMENT REVIEW 16 (Fall 1973):
11-16.

An approach to social auditing used by the Bank of America
is described.

1464 Child, John. THE BUSINESS ENTERPRISE IN MODERN INDUSTRIAL
SOCIETY. Themes and Issues in Modern Sociology. New York: Macmillan; London: Collier-Macmillan, 1969. 152 p. Diagram, bibliography.

Child reviews the literature on sociological aspects of business.

1465 Committee for Economic Development. Research and Policy Committee.
SOCIAL RESPONSIBILITIES OF BUSINESS CORPORATIONS: A STATE-
MENT ON NATIONAL POLICY. New York: Committee for Economic
Development, 477 Madison Avenue, New York, 1971. 74 p. Paper-
back.

1466 Farmer, Richard N., and Hogue, W. Dickerson. CORPORATE SOCIAL
RESPONSIBILITY. Chicago: Science Research Associates, 1973. 225 p.
Illustrations, diagrams, tables, bibliography. Paperback.

The authors examine social responsibility from the points of
view of the managers, the employees, the stockholders, the
auditors, the trade, the consumers, government suppliers, and
the general public, with cases based on a fictitious but typical
large American conglomerate. No index.

1467 Fendrock, John J. MANAGING IN TIMES OF RADICAL CHANGE.
New York: American Management Association, 1971. 182 p.

Fendrock considers how managers can meet the new demands
being imposed on them by society in such areas as armaments,
product safety, pollution, and advertising.

1468 "The First Attempts at a Corporate 'Social Audit.'" BUSINESS WEEK, no.
2247 (September 23, 1972), pp. 88-92. Table.

This is a review of approaches by some U.S. companies to a
social audit, with a specimen social balance sheet from Abt
Associates Inc.

1469 Goyder, George. THE RESPONSIBLE COMPANY. Oxford, Eng.: Blackwell, 1961. 192 p.

Goyder analyzes the company's responsibilities to its employees and customers as well as to its shareholders.

1470 Hay, Robert, and Gray, Ed. "Social Responsibilities of Business Managers." ACADEMY OF MANAGEMENT JOURNAL 17 (March 1974): 135-43. Tables, bibliography.

The authors trace three historical phases through which the concept of business responsibility to society has passed: the profit maximizer style, the trusteeship style, and the quality-of-life style. They consider the management behavior patterns associated with each and their integration in the modern view of social responsibility. They predict increasing pressure for acceptance of the quality-of-life style. A useful comparative table of the managerial values associated with each style is included.

1471 Humble, John W. SOCIAL RESPONSIBILITY AUDIT: A MANAGEMENT TOOL FOR SURVIVAL. London: Foundation for Business Responsibilities, Room 18-11 Portland House, Stag Place, SW1E 5BS, 1973. 60 p. Forms, tables. Paperback.

Humble suggests key areas for scrutiny, such as community relations, consumer relations, pollution, packaging, and physical working conditions.

1472 McGuire, Joseph W. BUSINESS AND SOCIETY. New York: McGraw-Hill, 1963. 312 p. Hardcover and paperback.

McGuire examines the relationships between business and the social, political, and economic environment in the United States. The book was developed from a series of television programs.

1473 Packard, Vance. THE WASTE MAKERS. New York: McKay, 1960; London: Longman, 1961. 320 p. Paperback ed. New York: Pocket Books; Harmondsworth, Eng.: Penguin Books, 1963.

Packard criticizes various management practices, including the technique of planned obsolescence--deliberate production of equipment which will not last or will quickly go out of fashion.

1474 Peters, Lynn H., ed. MANAGEMENT AND SOCIETY. Dickenson Series on Contemporary Thought in Management. Belmont, Calif.: Dickenson, 1968. 150 p. Tables. Paperback.

This work contains fifteen contributions on business and the environment, business values, and business and civilization. No index.

1475 Petit, Thomas A. THE MORAL CRISIS IN MANAGEMENT. McGraw-Hill Series in Management. New York: McGraw-Hill, 1967. 180 p.

> Petit relates social responsibility to economic ideology, economic theory, decision making, and the status and function of corporation and manager.

1476 Quinn, Peter. "Management's Social Responsibility Role in the Post-Industrial Era." MANAGEMENT DECISION 10 (Winter 1972): 293-307. Bibliography.

> Quinn examines the place of the large corporation in society, suggesting that profit maximization is no longer a sufficient goal.

1477 Smith, George Albert, and Matthews, John Bowers. BUSINESS, SOCIETY AND THE INDIVIDUAL: PROBLEMS IN RESPONSIBLE LEADERSHIP OF PRIVATE ENTERPRISE ORGANIZATIONS OPERATING IN A FREE SOCIETY. CASES, ARTICLES AND RELATED MATERIALS. Rev. ed. Homewood, Ill.: Irwin, 1967. xxv, 745 p. Tables.

> The forty-one cases and readings in this volume concern such matters as the disclosure of information by firms; relations with unions and governments; prejudice and discrimination; mergers and takeovers; business ethics; industrial espionage; and responsibilities of the powerful and wealthy (individuals, firms, and countries) towards the weak, the poor, and the disadvantaged. No index.

1478 Steiner, George A. BUSINESS AND SOCIETY. New York: Random House, 1971. xiv, 610 p. Bibliography.

> Presented in five parts, this book covers the road to today's complex interrelationships, society-wide relationships (including business ideology, the social responsibilities of business, pollution, and business ethics), business and government, business and other major groups in society (labor unions, education, and consumers), and the future.

1479 _____. "Should Business Adopt the Social Audit? A Review of Some of the Considerations Which Must be in the Mind of Management." CONFERENCE BOARD RECORD 9 (May 1972): 7-10.

1480 Walton, Clarence. CORPORATE SOCIAL RESPONSIBILITIES. Problems in Business Society. Belmont, Calif.: Wadsworth, 1967. xiii, 177 p. Diagrams. Paperback.

> Walton examines two case studies: pricing policy and the public interest (Esso Standard Oil Company) and racial justice (U.S. Steel Corporation).

1481 Weissman, Jacob, ed. THE SOCIAL RESPONSIBILITIES OF CORPORATE
MANAGEMENT. Hofstra University Yearbook of Business, Series 3, vol.
2. Hempstead, N.Y.: Hofstra University, 1966. 328 p. Bibliographies.
Paperback.

> Fourteen papers evaluate the following hypothesis: "Corporate
> management is increasingly required to justify itself in terms
> of due process of law rather than by an approach to the mar-
> ket. The corporation in modern society evidences integration
> of the democratic processes hitherto reserved for politics with the
> private decisions hitherto reserved for private life." No index.

Organizations

1482 Center for New Corporate Priorities, 1516 Westwood Boulevard, Suite 202,
Los Angeles, Calif. 90024.

> This organization was formed in 1970 to allow an interchange
> of ideas between persons and organizations interested in social
> responsibility of corporations.

1483 Project on Corporate Responsibility, 1609 Connecticut Avenue N.W.,
Washington, D.C. 20009.

> Formed in 1970, the aim of this organization was to make
> corporations more responsive to public and social needs.
> Presently inactive.

THE POLLUTION PROBLEM

One particularly important aspect of social responsibility is the need to conquer
the pollution problem threatening today's world.

1484 Blumberg, Philip I. "Corporate Responsibility and the Environment."
CONFERENCE BOARD RECORD 8 (April 1971): 42-47.

> This is a brief review of the implications of environmental abuse
> and pollution arising from industrialization and technological
> change.

1485 Buggie, Frederick D., and Gurman, Richard. TOWARD EFFECTIVE AND
EQUITABLE POLLUTION CONTROL REGULATION. New York: American Management Association, 1972. 41 p. Diagrams, tables. Paperback.

> This is a survey of opinions based primarily on 262 question-
> naires completed by companies. It includes policy documents
> from Allied Chemical Corporation, Swift Fresh Meats Company,
> Dart Industries, and Allis-Chalmers. The book is printed on
> recycled paper--a demonstration of its points.

1486 Hopkinson, Richard A. CORPORATE ORGANIZATION FOR POLLUTION CONTROL. Conference Board Report, n.s., no. 507. New York: Conference Board, 1970. 72 p. Diagrams, tables. Paperback.

The author summarizes problems of policy formulation and implementation, with eight job descriptions and case studies of Abitibi Paper Co. Ltd., Allegheny Ludlum Steel Corporation, Allied Chemical Corporation, Aluminum Company of Canada Ltd., Boston Edison Company, Canadian Industries, Carborundum Company, Mobil Oil Corporation, Scott Paper Company, and Steel Company of Canada Ltd.

1487 Larderei, Jacqueline Aloisi, and Boutin, Anne-Marie. "How Do European (and American) Companies Really Manage Pollution?" EUROPEAN BUSINESS, no. 32 (Winter 1972), pp. 56-73. Diagrams, tables.

This is based on an international study of the literature and includes a tabular summary of government action in the United States, France, United Kingdom, West Germany, Sweden, Belgium, and the Netherlands.

1488 Marlin, John Teppler. "Accounting for Pollution." JOURNAL OF ACCOUNTANCY 135 (February 1973): 41-46. Tables.

Marlin suggests that accountants should work in the field of pollution performance reporting if only because "no other group has the necessary patience and insight that accountants can bring to the messy details of actually measuring performance."

1489 Mikhail, Azmi D. "Capital Budgeting for Pollution Control." JOURNAL OF GENERAL MANAGEMENT 1 (Autumn 1973): 32-44. Tables, bibliography.

A study of pollution control budgeting practices of a small sample of U.S. companies in four "polluting" industries (paper and pulp, steel, electric utility, and integrated oil-domestic).

1490 Sihler, William W., and Meiburg, Charles O. "The War on Pollution: Economic and Financial Impacts." BUSINESS HORIZONS 14 (August 1971): 19-30. Tables, bibliography.

The authors examine the probable implications for the U.S. economy of expenditure on pollution control over the next ten years.

1491 Smith, William J.J. ENVIRONMENTAL POLICY AND IMPACT ANALYSIS: ORIGINS, EVOLUTION, AND IMPLICATIONS FOR GOVERNMENT, BUSINESS AND THE COURTS. New York: Conference Board, 1973. 76 p. Tables. Paperback.

This is an assessment of the National Environment Policy Act of 1970 and its implications for industry.

1492 Varble, Dale L. "Social and Environmental Considerations in New Product Development." JOURNAL OF MARKETING 36 (October 1972): 11-15. Table, bibliography.

> Varble argues that new products should be a social success and that social responsibility need not be incompatible with profit. He points to the usefulness of new products which fight pollution.

1493 Wheelwright, Steven C. "Developing a Corporate Response to Pollution Control." EUROPEAN BUSINESS, no. 38 (Summer 1973), pp. 64-72.

1494 Wilts, Preston. "Dirty Water Swept Under the Bridge." INDUSTRIAL MANAGEMENT (London) 2 (September 1972): 29-30, 35-37. Illustrations.

> This report on the problem of industrial pollution in Britain concludes that the cost of pollution control could well outweigh the benefits.

Bibliography

1495 Heider, David A.; Coburn, Martha G.; Rosenbloom, Richard S., eds. BUSINESS AND THE URBAN ENVIRONMENT: A GUIDE TO CASES AND OTHER TEACHING MATERIALS. Boston: Harvard University Graduate School of Business Administration, 1969. 191 p. Paperback.

> This is an annotated guide to cases, readings, films, and tapes from the Intercollegiate Case Clearing House, Soldiers Field, Boston, Massachusetts 02163.

BUSINESS ETHICS

1496 Baumhart, Raymond. AN HONEST PROFIT: WHAT BUSINESSMEN SAY ABOUT ETHICS IN BUSINESS. New York: Holt, Rinehart & Winston, 1968. xiv, 248 p. Diagrams, table. Paperback ed. published as ETHICS IN BUSINESS.

> This is a summary by a Jesuit priest of the views of 1,800 U.S. businessmen.

1497 Eckel, Malcolm W. THE ETHICS OF DECISION-MAKING. New York: Morehouse-Barlow, 1968. 111 p. Bibliography. Paperback.

> This work contains twelve cases with a general summary and conclusions. It developed from a project initiated at St. Stephen's Episcopal Church, Pittsfield, Massachusetts.

1498 Fulmer, Robert M. "Business Ethics: Present and Future." PERSONNEL
ADMINISTRATION 34 (September-October 1971): 48-55.

1499 Garrett, Thomas M. ETHICS IN BUSINESS. New York: Sheed & Ward,
1966. 181 p. Bibliographies.

> A Jesuit priest gives his views on such matters as honesty in
> business, expense accounts, the ethics of personnel testing,
> computers and ethics, waste, and professional codes of ethics.
> The book includes two checklists but no index.

1500 Garrett, Thomas M.; Baumhart, Raymond C.; Purcell, Theodore V.; and
Roets, Perry. CASES IN BUSINESS ETHICS. Business Series. New York:
Appleton-Century-Crofts, 1968. 374 p. Tables. Paperback.

> The cases are grouped in twelve sections: personnel relations;
> hiring, firing, and promotion; industrial relations; production;
> pricing; advertising; dealers, agents, and suppliers; account-
> ing; finance and stockholders; government and community rela-
> tions; business policy and philosophy; and international busi-
> ness. No index.

1501 Ivens, Michael, ed. INDUSTRY AND VALUES: THE OBJECTIVES AND
RESPONSIBILITIES OF BUSINESS. London: Harrap, 1970. 222 p.

> This work contains seventeen contributions from businessmen,
> theologians, economists, sociologists, and others.

1502 Masterson, Thomas R., and Nunan, J. Carlton, eds. ETHICS IN BUSI-
NESS. New York: Pitman, 1969. xv, 218 p. Bibliography.

> The forty-three contributions in this work are grouped in five
> parts: development of the American economic system, should
> the economy be ethically oriented?, who should control the
> economy?, can industry control itself?, and current problems
> in business ethics. No index.

1503 Webley, Simon. "Business Policy and Business Ethics." JOURNAL OF
BUSINESS POLICY 3 (Spring 1973): 3-10. Tables, bibliography.

> Webley discusses attitudes to the private use of privileged in-
> formation, redundancy policies, gifts, and subsistence expenses
> and considers the need for a formal code of ethics.

Bibliography

1504 Christian, Portia, and Hicks, Richard. ETHICS IN BUSINESS CONDUCT:
SELECTED REFERENCES FROM THE RECORD--PROBLEMS, ATTEMPTED
SOLUTIONS, ETHICS IN BUSINESS EDUCATION. Management Informa-
tion Guide, no. 21. Detroit: Gale Research Co., 1970. 156 p.

Section 14

MANAGEMENT IN SPECIALIST AREAS

This section contains a selective list of items on the application of management techniques to specific industries or services.

BANKING AND FINANCIAL SERVICES

1505 C.F.A. Research Foundation. Seminar on Investment Company Portfolio Management, Charlottesville, Va., 1969. INVESTMENT COMPANY PORTFOLIO MANAGEMENT. Edited by Andrew P. Ferretti. C.F.A. Monograph Series, no. 4. Homewood, Ill.: Irwin, 1970. xv, 186 p. Bibliography.

    This work has no index.

1506 _____ . Seminar on Pension Fund Investment Management, Charlottesville, Va., 1968. PENSION FUND INVESTMENT MANAGEMENT. Edited by Esmond B. Gardner. C.F.A. Monograph Series, no. 3. Homewood, Ill.: Irwin, 1969. 141 p. Bibliography.

    This work covers the trust agreement, funding a pension plan, investing the pension fund, measuring investment performance, and ethics. No index.

1507 _____ . Seminar on Personal Trust Investment Management, Charlottesville, Va., 1967. PERSONAL TRUST INVESTMENT MANAGEMENT. C.F.A. Monograph Series, no. 2. Homewood, Ill.: Irwin, 1968. xxi, 260 p. Diagrams, bibliography.

    This work covers trust investment philosophy, the investment process, portfolio management, measurement of performance, and ethics. No index.

1508 Eilon, Samuel, and Fowkes, Terence R., eds. APPLICATIONS OF MANAGEMENT SCIENCE IN BANKING AND FINANCE. Epping, Eng.: Gower Press, 1972. 286 p. Diagrams, tables, bibliography.

    These seventeen papers cover such topics as discounted cash

flow, risk simulation and investment appraisal, corporate planning, management of insurance companies, capital budgeting,
and merger strategy.

AGRICULTURE

1509 Barnard, C.S., and Nix, J.S. FARM PLANNING AND CONTROL.
Cambridge, Eng.: Cambridge University Press, 1973. 549 p. Diagrams,
tables, bibliography.

This book's four sections consider the organization of resources,
the organization of enterprises, the combination of enterprises,
and the control of resources and enterprises.

1510 Great Britain. Ministry of Agriculture, Fisheries and Food. FARM
PLANNING BY COMPUTER. Technical Bulletin, no. 19. London: H.M.
Stationery Office, 1971. 132 p. Diagrams, forms, tables, plus linear
programming matrix in pocket, bibliography. Paperback.

COAL MINING

1511 Trist, E.L.; Higgin, G.W.; Murray, H.; and Pollock, A.B. ORGANIZA-
TIONAL CHOICE: CAPABILITIES OF GROUPS AT THE COAL FACE UN-
DER CHANGING TECHNOLOGIES. THE LOSS, REDISCOVERY AND
TRANSFORMATION OF A WORK TRADITION. London: Tavistock, 1963.
xv, 332 p. Diagrams, tables, bibliography. (Distributed by Barnes &
Noble, Scranton, Pa.)

This is a study of the effect of technological change in the
British mining industry on human relations. It particularly examines the ability of primary work groups of forty to fifty members to act as self-regulating, self-developing social organizations, able to maintain high productivity. The authors show
how alternative modes of work organization can be used with
the same technology. The book is based on research among
managers and workers, and is not so much a book about management in a particular industry as about a particular organizational problem.

ENGINEERING

1512 Burnham, T.H., and Hoskins, G.O. ELEMENTS OF INDUSTRIAL OR-
GANISATION. 8th ed. London: Pitman, 1971. 298 p. Tables. Hardcover and paperback.

This is a classic British guide to economics and management

for students of engineering, the first edition of which was published in 1929 as ENGINEERING ECONOMICS.

1513 Chironis, Nicholas P., comp. MANAGEMENT GUIDE FOR ENGINEERS AND TECHNICAL ADMINISTRATORS. New York: McGraw-Hill, 1969. 376 p. Illustrations, diagrams, tables.

Eighty experts discuss such issues as how to succeed as an administrator, organization charts, staff development, new product development, decision making, creativity, market research, consultancy, communication, salaries, job satisfaction, and ethics, as well as chapters on specialist aspects of engineering management. The contributions were originally published in various journals, especially PRODUCT ENGINEERING.

1514 DeGarmo, E. Paul, and Canada, John. ENGINEERING ECONOMY. 5th ed. New York: Macmillan; London: Collier-Macmillan, 1973. 572 p. Diagrams, tables, bibliography.

The first edition of this standard text was published by Macmillan in 1942 as INTRODUCTION TO ENGINEERING ECONOMY.

1515 Leech, D.J. MANAGEMENT OF ENGINEERING DESIGN. London: Wiley, 1972. 258 p. Diagrams, tables, bibliographies.

Developed from a course of lectures given to second-year students in a university engineering school, this work includes sections on the critical path method, linear programming, and brainstorming, with an appendix on value engineering.

1516 Lock, Dennis, ed. ENGINEER'S HANDBOOK OF MANAGEMENT TECHNIQUES. Epping, Eng.: Gower Press, 1973. xxix, 677 p. Diagrams, forms, tables, bibliographies. (Distributed by Cahners Publishing Co., Boston.)

This volume's thirty contributions cover financial management; marketing management; administration; personnel, human relations, and training; and production management.

1517 Roadstrum, W.H. EXCELLENCE IN ENGINEERING. New York: Wiley, 1967. xx, 247 p. Diagrams, bibliography.

Topics covered include the project and project team, quality control, human relations, marketing, creativity, and the engineering manager.

1518 Rubey, Harry; Logan, John A.; and Milner, Walker W. THE ENGINEER AND PROFESSIONAL MANAGEMENT. 3d ed. Ames: Iowa State University Press, 1970. 339 p. Illustrations, bibliography. Paperback.

1519 Semler, E.G., ed. MANAGEMENT FOR ENGINEERS. London: Institution of Mechanical Engineers, 1972. 184 p. Illustrations, diagrams,
tables.

> This collection of thirty-six articles, originally published in
> THE CHARTERED MECHANICAL ENGINEER between 1964 and
> 1971, is grouped under six headings: social aspects, manage-
> ment of men, organization and finance, production and quality
> control, commercial aspects, and innovation and research.

1520 Turner, Barry T. MANAGEMENT TRAINING FOR ENGINEERS. London:
Business Books, 1969. xviii, 401 p. Diagrams, tables. (Distributed by
Beekman, New York.)

> This work contains glossaries of commercial and legal terms,
> marketing terms, and stock exchange terms.

ELECTRONIC ENGINEERING

1521 IEEE TRANSACTIONS ON ENGINEERING MANAGEMENT. New York:
Institute of Electrical and Electronic Engineers, 1954- . Quarterly.

1522 International Symposium on Management and Economics in the Electronics
Industry, University of Edinburgh, 1970. PROCEEDINGS OF THE INTER-
NATIONAL SYMPOSIUM ON MANAGEMENT AND ECONOMICS IN
THE ELECTRONICS INDUSTRY, UNIVERSITY OF EDINBURGH, 17-20
MARCH 1970. IEE Conference Publication, no. 62. London: Institution
of Electrical Engineers, 1970. 445 p. Diagrams. Paperback.

> The symposium was organized by the Institution of Electrical
> Engineers in association with three other bodies and with the
> support of thirteen organizations. There is no index.

AUTOMOBILE ENGINEERING

1523 Sloan, Alfred P., Jr. MY YEARS WITH GENERAL MOTORS. Edited by
John McDonald with Catharine Stevens. New York: Doubleday, 1964;
London: Sidgwick & Jackson, 1965. xxix, 472 p. Illustrations, dia-
grams, tables.

> This is an important study of the "managerial revolution" at
> General Motors after the author's appointment in 1918. The
> emphasis is on diversification, coordination by committee,
> development of financial controls, and use of incentive schemes
> and fringe benefits to promote good labor relations.

CHEMICAL ENGINEERING

1524 Bauman, H. Carl. FUNDAMENTALS OF COST ENGINEERING IN THE
CHEMICAL INDUSTRY. New York: Reinhold; London: Chapman & Hall,
1964. xviii, 364 p. Diagrams, tables.

> This contains a glossary of cost estimating terms, as well as
> indexes of authors and subjects.

1525 Chilton, Cecil H., and the staff of CHEMICAL ENGINEERING, eds.
COST ENGINEERING IN THE PROCESS INDUSTRIES. New York:
McGraw-Hill, 1960. 475 p. Illustrations, diagrams, tables.

> This collection of articles from CHEMICAL ENGINEERING is
> grouped under seven headings: principles of cost estimation,
> process equipment costs, nonequipment capital costs, plant
> costs, manufacturing costs, profitability and economic analy-
> sis, and other areas in cost engineering. Indexes of authors
> and subjects.

1526 Popper, Herbert, and the staff of CHEMICAL ENGINEERING, eds.
MODERN TECHNICAL MANAGEMENT TECHNIQUES FOR ENGINEERS
IN MANAGEMENT AND FOR THOSE WHO WANT TO GET THERE.
New York: McGraw-Hill, 1971. 377 p. Illustrations, diagrams, tables.

> The contributions are arranged in six sections: careers and
> career-building in technical management; communications and
> information-gathering; appraisal, development, and rewarding
> of professional employees; the technical management aspects
> of business law; the techniques of economic analysis and oper-
> ations research; and tools specific to plant and project man-
> agement. Indexes of authors and subjects.

1527 Royal Institute of Chemistry. MANAGEMENT IN THE SCIENCE-BASED
INDUSTRIES: PAPERS DELIVERED AT A SYMPOSIUM HELD IN DUBLIN,
APRIL 1968. London: 1968. 117 p. Diagrams, maps, tables. Paper-
back.

> These eleven papers were given at a symposium at the joint
> annual conference of the Chemical Society and the Royal In-
> stitute of Chemistry. Subjects include management in large-
> scale science-based industries, management in the middle-range
> company, works management, personnel management, large-
> scale research management, financial control, design and lo-
> cation of plant, and opportunities for the chemist in manage-
> ment. An index and bibliographical references would have
> been useful.

TEXTILE INDUSTRY

1528 Textile Institute. MANAGEMENT IN THE TEXTILE INDUSTRY. London: Longman; Plainfield, N.J.: Textile Book Service, 1969. xvi, 557 p. Illustrations, diagrams, forms, tables.

> This work contains fifteen contributions on the structure and organization of the British textile industry, management and departmental organization, marketing, research and development, personnel, wage structures, raw-material purchasing, production, quality control, work study, plant maintenance, buildings, management accounting, data processing, operations research, and investment.

BUILDING AND CIVIL ENGINEERING

See also item 1182

1529 Antill, James M. CIVIL ENGINEERING MANAGEMENT. Sydney: Angus & Robertson; New York: American Elsevier, 1970. 339 p. Illustrations, diagrams, forms, tables.

> This book provides a comprehensive coverage for both the practicing engineer and the student.

1530 Atkinson, Ian. CONSTRUCTION MANAGEMENT. Amsterdam: Elsevier, 1971. 150 p. Diagrams, tables.

> This is a short introductory guide for the newcomer in construction management.

1531 Brech, E.F.L., ed. CONSTRUCTION MANAGEMENT IN PRINCIPLE AND PRACTICE. London: Longman, 1971. xx, 856 p. Illustrations, diagrams, forms, tables, bibliography.

> Fourteen contributions discuss management and the market, management of construction operations, and management services and aids. The aim is "to make the mark of the British construction industry in the management movement and its literature." The "underlying gospel of the three perennial P's-- performance, productivity, profitability" is stressed throughout.

1532 Calvert, R.E. INTRODUCTION TO BUILDING MANAGEMENT. 3d ed. London: Newnes-Butterworth, 1970; New York: Drake, 1971. 297 p. Diagrams, forms, tables, bibliographies.

1533 Clough, Richard H. CONSTRUCTION PROJECT MANAGEMENT. New York: Wiley-Interscience, 1972. 264 p. Diagrams (some folding), tables, bibliographies.

This comprehensive guide emphasizes time and cost control, with time control procedures based on the critical path method. An example project is used throughout to illustrate the workings of the management team.

1534 Deatherage, George E. CONSTRUCTION COMPANY ORGANIZATION AND MANAGEMENT. New York: McGraw-Hill, 1964. 316 p. Illustrations, diagrams, forms, tables.

The author wrote this book in an effort to make construction companies more conscious of the need to apply proven methods of organization and management in order to achieve success.

1535 Douglas, Clarence J., and Munger, Elmer L. CONSTRUCTION MANAGEMENT. Englewood Cliffs, N.J.: Prentice-Hall, 1969. xviii, 201 p. Illustrations, diagrams, bibliography.

This very practical introductory guide, intended for students of civil engineering, has an annotated bibliography on pp. 190-93.

1536 Dressel, Gerhard. ORGANIZATION AND MANAGEMENT OF A CONSTRUCTION COMPANY. Translated by A.B. Phillips. London: McLaren, 1968; New York: Gordon & Breach, 1969. 191 p. Diagrams, tables, bibliography.

This was originally published in German by Verlag Stocker-Schmid, Dietikon-Zurich, Switzerland, in 1965. No index.

1537 Foster, Charles. BUILDING WITH MEN: AN ANALYSIS OF GROUP BEHAVIOUR AND ORGANIZATION IN A BUILDING FIRM. London: Tavistock, 1969. xv, 220 p. Bibliography.

This work studies changing management attitudes in a small but rapidly growing London building firm in the late 1950s and early 1960s. An annotated bibliography, compiled by Charles Handy, is on pp. 212-17.

1538 Foxhall, William B. PROFESSIONAL CONSTRUCTION MANAGEMENT AND PROJECT ADMINISTRATION. New York: Architectural Record; Washington, D.C.: American Institute of Architects, 1972. 114 p. Diagrams, tables, bibliography. (Distributed by McGraw-Hill, New York and London, etc.)

1539 Gill, Paul G. SYSTEMS MANAGEMENT TECHNIQUES FOR BUILDERS AND CONTRACTORS. New York: McGraw-Hill, 1968. xiv, 210 p. Diagrams, forms, tables plus chart in pocket, bibliography.

Included is a case study involving a fifty-home project. Gill introduces a program control chart method, a noncomputer approach which he claims combines the best elements of bar charts, PERT, and CPM.

1540 O'Brien, James J., and Zilly, Robert G., eds. CONTRACTOR'S MANAGEMENT HANDBOOK. New York: McGraw-Hill, 1971. Var. pag. Illustrations, diagrams, forms, tables.

This work contains twenty-nine contributions on all aspects of construction management.

1541 Oppenheimer, Samuel P. DIRECTING CONSTRUCTION FOR PROFIT: BUSINESS ASPECTS OF CONTRACTING. New York: McGraw-Hill, 1971. xiii, 274 p. Diagrams, forms, bibliography.

1542 Parker, Henry W., and Oglesby, Clarkson H. METHODS IMPROVEMENT FOR CONSTRUCTION MANAGERS. New York: McGraw-Hill, 1972. 300 p. Illustrations, diagrams, tables.

This practical and systematic guide emphasizes the behavioral aspects of work improvement applications.

1543 Rubey, Harry, and Milner, Walker W. CONSTRUCTION AND PROFESSIONAL MANAGEMENT: AN INTRODUCTION. Macmillan Series in Civil Engineering. New York: Macmillan; London: Collier-Macmillan, 1966. xx, 306 p. Diagrams, tables, bibliography. Reprint. Norman: University of Oklahoma Press, 1971.

Topics covered include contracting, lease versus buy, personnel management, CPM and PERT, and computer applications. There are many case problems and questions. Annotated bibliography, pp. 289-94.

1544 Volpe, S. Peter. CONSTRUCTION MANAGEMENT PRACTICE. New York: Wiley-Interscience, 1972. 180 p. Diagrams, forms.

This is a practical guide to such matters as organization, labor relations, financial management, contracting, safety, and insurance. Glossary, pp. 175-78.

1545 Wass, Alonzo. CONSTRUCTION MANAGEMENT AND CONTRACTING. Englewood Cliffs, N.J.: Prentice-Hall, 1972. xiv, 298 p. Illustrations, diagrams, forms, tables.

This is a comprehensive and practical guide to establishing and running a contracting business including project management and labor-management relations.

NEWSPAPER PUBLISHING

1546 Rucker, Frank W., and Williams, Herbert Lee. NEWSPAPER ORGANI-

ZATION AND MANAGEMENT. 3d ed. Ames: Iowa State University
Press, 1969. xv, 579 p. Illustrations, diagrams, forms, tables, bibliography.

The first edition of this practical guide was published in 1955.

PROFESSIONAL SERVICES

1547 Sibson, Robert E. MANAGING PROFESSIONAL SERVICES ENTERPRISES:
THE NEGLECTED BUSINESS FRONTIER. New York: Pitman, 1971. 214 p.
Diagrams, tables.

This is a consultant's guide to the management of professional
services, defined as "any organization that essentially sells or
renders the knowledge of its people." It thus includes advertising agencies, consulting firms, and organizations in engineering, the creative arts, banking, law, medicine, accounting,
research and development laboratories, hospitals, educational
institutions, museums, religious organizations, social service
agencies, finance, insurance, real estate, transportation, public utilities, government, wholesale and retail trade, manufacturing, contracting, construction, mining, and agriculture.

HOSPITALS AND HEALTH SERVICES

1548 Barber, Barry, and Abbot, W. COMPUTING AND OPERATIONAL RE-
SEARCH AT THE LONDON HOSPITAL. Computers in Medicine Series.
London: Butterworths, 1972. 102 p. Illustrations, diagrams, bibliogra-
phy. Paperback.

This is an interesting case study of the introduction and use of
computers in a major London hospital.

1549 Ferrer, H.P., ed. THE HEALTH SERVICES: ADMINISTRATION, RE-
SEARCH AND MANAGEMENT. London: Butterworths, 1972. xii, 379 p.
Diagrams, tables, bibliography.

Although concerned with the British health service, this book
includes useful chapters on operations research, financial management, and organizational behavior.

1550 Rockart, John F. "An Approach to Productivity in Knowledge-Based Industries." SLOAN MANAGEMENT REVIEW 15 (Fall 1973): 23-33. Bibliography.

This is an analysis of productivity--or lack of it--in medicine
and education, which between them account for 10 percent of
the gross national product. Rockart suggests methods whereby
productivity may be improved, including automation and better
utilization of professional time by more effective scheduling.

1551 Rowbottom, Ralph; with Balle, Jeanne; Craig, Stephen; Dixon, Maureen; Packwood, Tim; and Tolliday, Heather. HOSPITAL ORGANIZATION: A PROGRESS REPORT ON THE BRUNEL HEALTH SERVICES ORGANIZATION PROJECT. London: Heinemann, 1973. 314 p. Diagrams, tables, bibliography.

> This review of research into hospital organization and management was prepared by the Health Services Organization Research Unit at Brunel University, London. Glossary, pp. 261-75.

EDUCATION

See also item 1550.

1552 Bennis, Warren G., with Biederman, Patricia Ward. THE LEANING IVORY TOWER. San Francisco: Jossey-Bass, 1973. 154 p.

> This stimulating critique of management in the area of education is based particularly on Bennis's own experiences at the State University of New York at Buffalo.

1553 Centre for Educational Research and Innovation, University of Copenhagen. DECISION, PLANNING AND BUDGETING. Project leader, Arne Jensen. Studies in Institutional Management and Higher Education. Paris: Organisation for Economic Cooperation and Development, 1972. 207 p. Diagrams, tables. Paperback.

1554 Fielden, J., and Lockwood, G. PLANNING AND MANAGEMENT IN UNIVERSITIES: A STUDY OF BRITISH UNIVERSITIES. London: Chatto & Windus for the University of Sussex, 1973. 352 p. Diagrams (3 folding), tables, bibliography. Hardcover and paperback.

> This is the report of the Planning and Management in Universities Project conducted jointly by members of the staffs of the University of Sussex and Peat, Marwick, Mitchell & Co., management consultants. They sought to examine the existing planning, management, and budgeting systems in a sample of British universities and produce recommendations in the form of a handbook for universities. This has been done well with some admitted limitations, such as their limiting of their attention to universities with between 5,000 and 7,500 students. A review of organizations, recent research, and bibliography, prepared by Alfred Morris and Michael Puckford, is on pp. 327-48.

1555 Jellema, William W., ed. EFFICIENT COLLEGE MANAGEMENT. Jossey-Bass Series in Higher Education. San Francisco: Jossey-Bass, 1972. xviii, 156 p.

These fourteen papers, originally given at an annual meeting of the Association of American Colleges, are on the application of management techniques to academic institutions. The collection includes papers on program budgeting, costs of student services, and cooperation.

GOVERNMENT

1556 Bray, Jeremy. DECISION IN GOVERNMENT. London: Gollancz, 1970. 320 p. Diagrams, tables, bibliography. (Distributed by International Publications Service, New York.)

This is a guide to the decision-making process in government, based on the author's experiences as a British minister between 1966 and 1969.

1557 Keeling, Desmond. MANAGEMENT IN GOVERNMENT. London: Allen & Unwin for the Royal Institute of Public Administration, 1972. 210 p. Bibliography. Hardcover and paperback.

Keeling surveys the development of the management process in government and its implications, with particular reference to British experience and prospects and to the role of accountable management, program budgeting, and analysis.

1558 Millett, John D. ORGANIZATION FOR THE PUBLIC SERVICE. New Perspectives in Political Science Series. New York: Van Nostrand Reinhold, 1966. xiii, 159 p. Paperback.

These five lectures cover the institutional context of organization for public service, organization as a political problem, organization as a technical problem, organization as a problem in human relations, and the art of organization. The book is based on the author's seventeen years experience in the U.S. government service.

Periodicals

1559 MANAGEMENT SERVICES IN GOVERNMENT, INCORPORATING THE O & M BULLETIN. London: Civil Service Department, 1945- . Quarterly.

This contains articles on the application of management services techniques in the British government service, with book reviews. Occasional special supplements are issued. It was formerly called O & M BULLETIN.

1560 PUBLIC ADMINISTRATION: JOURNAL OF THE ROYAL INSTITUTE OF PUBLIC ADMINISTRATION. London: 1923- . Quarterly.

1561 PUBLIC ADMINISTRATION REVIEW. Washington, D.C.: American Society for Public Administration, 1940- . Bimonthly.

LOCAL GOVERNMENT

1562 Eddison, Terry. LOCAL GOVERNMENT: MANAGEMENT AND CORPORATE PLANNING. 2d ed. London: Leonard Hill, 1975. xiv, 225 p. Tables.

> Although concerned primarily with management for the reorganization of local government in the United Kingdom, this book contains valuable material on planning, decision making, management by objectives, and the introduction of change in local government.

1563 Glendinning, J.W., and Bullock, R.E.H. MANAGEMENT BY OBJECTIVES IN LOCAL GOVERNMENT. London: Charles Knight, 1973. 255 p. Tables.

> This work includes an introductory section on the essentials of MBO, a description of the background to and implications of an MBO project initiated by the Local Government Training Board, and detailed case histories, compiled by the Local Government Training Board, of the application of MBO in West Riding (office of the county architect), Manchester (town clerk's department), and Somerset (education department). Glossary, pp. 249-52.

1564 "Local Government Management." PUBLIC MANAGEMENT 55 (September 1973): 4-35.

> Five reports by policy committees of the International City Management Association explore the management of growth in local government, the management of human resources, the achievement of high quality and productivity in local government, regionalism and municipal management, and the federal block grant and community development.

1565 LOGA: LOCAL GOVERNMENT ANNOTATIONS SERVICE. Romford, Eng.: London Borough of Havering Central Library, 1966- . Monthly.

> Brief abstracts of articles on local government, including management aspects, are published by the Advisory Body of Librarians, London Borough Association, in cooperation with nine public libraries in London.

1566 "Managing the Small City." PUBLIC MANAGEMENT 54 (September 1972): 1-21.

> Seven short articles examine aspects of small city management in the United States.

1567 PUBLIC MANAGEMENT. Washington, D.C.: International City Management Association, 1919- . Monthly.

1568 Stewart, J.D. MANAGEMENT IN LOCAL GOVERNMENT: A VIEWPOINT. London: Charles Knight, 1971. xv, 197 p. Tables.

This is geared to British practice, but it includes useful comments on MBO, PPBS (program budgeting), and corporate planning.

Section 15

MARKETING MANAGEMENT

As stated in the introduction, the sections on the management functions are particularly selective. The aim has been to list major handbooks and other works of reference, including guides to further sources of information, together with other titles which have made a special contribution to the particular subject.

Included in this section are works on selling (including the sales staff), international marketing, marketing research, developing and launching new products, advertising, and distribution.

GENERAL STUDIES

1569 Buell, Victor P., and Heyel, Carl, eds. HANDBOOK OF MODERN MARKETING. New York: McGraw-Hill, 1970. Var. pag. Diagrams, tables, bibliographies.

> These 120 contributions cover every facet of marketing management.

1570 DECISION MAKING IN MARKETING: A COLLOQUIUM. Conference Board Report, n.s., no. 525. New York: Conference Board, 1971. 103 p. Diagrams, tables, bibliography. Paperback.

> Part one deals with making marketing decisions, including a list of sixteen inhibitors of sound decision making. Part two describes some new tools for decision making.

1571 Frey, Albert Wesley, and Albaum, Gerald, eds. MARKETING HANDBOOK. 2d ed. New York: Ronald Press, 1965. Var. pag. Diagrams, forms, tables, bibliography.

> Although dated, this remains a useful handbook. It includes a 17-page list of books, periodicals, reports, and other sources of information.

1572 Holloway, Robert J., and Hancock, Robert S. MARKETING IN A
CHANGING ENVIRONMENT. 2d ed. New York: Wiley, 1973. xvi,
716 p. Diagrams, tables, bibliography.

> This comprehensive text has a useful glossary, pp. 679-91,
> and twelve pages of bibliographical references, pp. 693-704.
> Indexes of names and subjects.

1573 Kotler, Philip. MARKETING MANAGEMENT: ANALYSIS, PLANNING
AND CONTROL. 3d ed. Englewood Cliffs, N.J.: Prentice-Hall,
1976. 529 p. Illustrations, diagrams, tables.

> Kotler provides a summary and questions at the end of each
> chapter, as well as indexes of names and subjects.

1574 Levitt, Theodore. INNOVATION IN MARKETING: NEW PERSPECTIVES
FOR PROFIT AND GROWTH. McGraw-Hill Series in Marketing and Advertising. New York: McGraw-Hill, 1962. 253 p.

1575 _____. THE MARKETING MODE: PATHWAYS TO CORPORATE GROWTH.
New York: McGraw-Hill, 1969. xiii, 354 p.

> In these two books Levitt urges that more attention be paid to
> marketing as a vital function in the management process. He
> argues that marketing is not "just for marketing specialists"
> but also for presidents and other senior executives.

1576 McKay, Edward S. THE MARKETING MYSTIQUE. New York: American
Management Association, 1972. 258 p. Diagrams.

> A marketing consultant attempts to remove the mystical aura
> surrounding the marketing function and to contribute toward
> constructive codification of the positive and useful mystique
> that characterizes marketing philosophy, practice, and per-
> formance.

1577 Meloan, Taylor W.; Smith, Samuel V.; and Wheatley, John J., eds.
MANAGERIAL MARKETING POLICIES AND DECISIONS. Boston: Houghton Mifflin, 1970. 575 p. Diagrams, tables. Paperback.

> This work contains forty-five readings on various aspects of
> marketing. No index.

1578 Miller, Ernest C. OBJECTIVES AND STANDARDS OF PERFORMANCE
IN MARKETING MANAGEMENT. AMA Research Study, no. 85. New
York: American Management Association, 1967. 110 p. Bibliography.
Paperback.

> Miller presents a number of case studies, including the Green
> Giant Company, Calumet & Hecla Inc., American Standard,
> Univis Inc., Western Company, Rockwell Manufacturing Com-

pany, Standard Oil Company (Ohio), and B.F. Goodrill Co. Annotated bibliography, pp. 109-10. No index.

1579 Riso, Ovid, ed. THE DARTNELL SALES MANAGER'S HANDBOOK. Created by John Cameron Aspley. 11th ed. Chicago: Dartnell, 1968. 960 p. Illustrations, diagrams, forms, bibliography.

This standard, comprehensive manual contains many case studies and gives descriptions of the sales training programs of twelve companies. Glossary of marketing terms, pp. 767-97.

1580 Seibert, Joseph C. CONCEPTS OF MARKETING MANAGEMENT. Marketing Management Series. New York: Harper & Row, 1973. 566 p. Illustrations, diagrams, tables, bibliographies. Paperback.

This modern, comprehensive manual is presented in three broad sections: the background for marketing objectives; marketing plans to reach marketing objectives; and environmental constraints on marketing plans. Indexes of names and subjects.

1581 Staudt, Thomas A., and Taylor, Donald A. A MANAGERIAL INTRO-DUCTION TO MARKETING. 2d ed. Englewood Cliffs, N.J.: Prentice-Hall, 1970. xvi, 618 p. Diagrams, tables.

A comprehensive text, this book has questions and problems in each chapter.

Periodicals

1582 DARTNELL SALES AND MARKETING SERVICE. Chicago: Dartnell. Monthly.

This is a monthly service of reports, case histories, new techniques, recruitment and training, salesmen, sales meetings, sales manuals, compensation of salesmen, sales contests, sales promotion, sales bulletin material, marketing control, and marketing policy.

1583 EUROPEAN JOURNAL OF MARKETING. Bradford: MCB (European Marketing & Consumer Studies) Ltd., 1967- . Three issues yearly.

This was originally entitled BRITISH JOURNAL OF MARKETING.

1584 JOURNAL OF MARKETING. Chicago: American Marketing Association, 1936- . Quarterly.

The most outstanding marketing journal, this publication has long articles, briefer notes, a regular section on legal developments, signed book reviews, and a regular section of abstracts of journal articles and reports.

1585 MARKETING. Cookham, Eng.: Institute of Marketing, 1931- . Monthly.

1586 SALES AND MARKETING MANAGEMENT. New York: 1918- . Twice
monthly.

   This journal was previously called SALES MANAGEMENT.

Bibliographies

1587 American Marketing Association. AN ANNOTATED INDEX TO THE PRO-
CEEDINGS OF THE AMERICAN MARKETING ASSOCIATION CONFER-
ENCES '66/'71. Compiled and edited by Robert L. King. Bibliography
Series, no. 20. Chicago: 1973. 150 p. Paperback.

   This supplements the INDEX TO PROCEEDINGS '55/'65 (1966).

1588 Berman, Linda, and Berman, Barry. CASE STUDIES IN MARKETING:
AN ANNOTATED BIBLIOGRAPHY AND INDEX. Metuchen, N.J.:
Scarecrow Press, 1971. 211 p.

   A classified list of cases taken from twenty-eight American
   books, this work has a detailed subject index.

1589 Buzzell, Robert D., comp. A BASIC BIBLIOGRAPHY ON MATHEMATI-
CAL METHODS IN MARKETING. American Marketing Association Bibliography Series, no. 7. Chicago: American Marketing Association,
1962. 62 p. Paperback.

   This bibliography is classified and annotated, with an author
   index.

1590 Kelley, Eugene J.; Lazo, Hector; Corbin, Arnold; and Kahn, Edward,
comps. MARKETING MANAGEMENT: AN ANNOTATED BIBLIOGRAPHY.
American Marketing Association Bibliography Series, no. 8. Chicago:
American Marketing Association, 1963. xiv, 71 p. Paperback.

   A classified and annotated list of periodical articles is followed by an unannotated list of books. No index.

1591 Massy, William F. PLANNING IN MARKETING: A SELECTED BIBLIOG-
RAPHY. Cambridge, Mass.: M.I.T. Press, 1962. 56 p. Paperback.

   This is classified and annotated, but has no indexes.

1592 Pennington, Allan L., and Peterson, Robert A. REFERENCE GUIDE TO
MARKETING LITERATURE. Braintree, Mass.: D.H. Mark Publishing
Co., 1970. Unpaged.

   Lists 3,007 items alphabetically by author, with a subject index.

1593 Sandeau, Georges, comp. THE INTERNATIONAL BIBLIOGRAPHY OF MARKETING AND DISTRIBUTION. 4th ed. New York: Bowker; London: Staples Press, 1972. Var. pag. Paperback.

This major classified list covers books and periodical articles published in 1969 and 1970, with indexes of authors, subjects, and places. It supplements bibliographies published in 1966 and 1967 by the European Institute of Business Administration (INSEAD), Fontainebleau, France, and in 1970 by Editions d'Organisations, 5 rue Rousselet, Paris.

1594 Sheparovych, Zenon B.; Alexis, Marcus; and Simon, Leonard S., eds. and comps. A SELECTED ANNOTATED BIBLIOGRAPHY ON QUANTI-TATIVE METHODS IN MARKETING. American Marketing Association Bibliography Series, no. 15. Chicago: American Marketing Association, 1968. 86 p. Paperback.

This is a classified list with author and subject indexes.

1595 Thompson, Ralph B. A SELECTED AND ANNOTATED BIBLIOGRAPHY OF MARKETING THEORY. Bibliography Series, no. 14, revised. Austin: University of Texas Bureau of Business Research, 1970. 79 p. Paperback.

Classified list with no indexes.

Abstracting and Indexing Services

1596 MARKETING ABSTRACTS. Chicago: American Marketing Association. Bimonthly.

This is part of the JOURNAL OF MARKETING (item 1584).

1597 MARKETING + DISTRIBUTION ABSTRACTS. London: Anbar Publications, 1971- . Eight issues yearly.

One of the excellent Anbar series of abstracting journals, this is published in association with the Institute of Marketing. Each issue contains 100-150 abstracts of articles selected from more than 200 journals. Critical comments are occasionally included, these being distinguished from the factual summaries by being printed in italics. Annual index. The service was incorporated in ANBAR MANAGEMENT SERVICES ABSTRACTS from 1961 to 1971.

1598 MARKETING INFORMATION GUIDE. Garden City, N.Y.: Hoke Communications, 1954- . Monthly.

Each issue contains abstracts of books, articles, and papers.

The arrangement is systematic, and there are twice yearly cumulative indexes. The journal was originally issued by the U.S. Department of Commerce.

1599 WHAT'S NEW IN ADVERTISING AND MARKETING. New York: Special Libraries Association, Advertising & Marketing Division, 1945- . Ten issues yearly.

This is a mimeographed list of new publications.

Dictionaries

1600 Graham, Irvin. ENCYCLOPEDIA OF ADVERTISING. 2d ed. New York: Fairchild, 1969. xiii, 494 p. Illustrations.

In spite of its title, this covers much more than advertising. It contains more than 1,100 entries relating to advertising, marketing, publishing, law, research, public relations, publicity, and the graphic arts.

1601 Strand, Stanley. MARKETING DICTIONARY. New York: Philosophical Library, 1962. 810 p.

This includes information about organizations, as well as definitions of terms and concepts.

Organizations

1602 American Marketing Association, 222 South Riverside Plaza, Suite 606, Chicago, Ill. 60606.

Formed in 1915, this major organization is dedicated to the advancement of science in marketing.

1603 Institute of Marketing, Moor Hall, Cookham, Berkshire, SL6 9QH, England.

This organization was founded in 1911 as the Incorporated Sales Managers Association.

1604 Sales and Marketing Executives-International, 380 Lexington Avenue, New York, N.Y. 10017.

Founded in 1936, this is an association for executives concerned with sales and marketing management, research, training, and other managerial aspects of distribution.

INDUSTRIAL MARKETING

1605 INDUSTRIAL MARKETING MANAGEMENT: AN INTERNATIONAL JOUR-
NAL OF INDUSTRIAL MARKETING AND MARKETING RESEARCH. Amsterdam: European Association for Industrial Marketing Research (EVAF)
and Elsevier Scientific Publishing Co., 1971- . Quarterly.

1606 Risley, George. MODERN INDUSTRIAL MARKETING. New York:
McGraw-Hill, 1972. xv, 363 p. Diagrams, tables.

1607 Staudt, Thomas A., and Lazer, William, eds. A BASIC BIBLIOGRAPHY
ON INDUSTRIAL MARKETING. American Marketing Association Bibliography Series, no. 4. Chicago: American Marketing Association, 1958.
233 p.

THE MARKETING MANAGER AND HIS STAFF

1608 Dartnell Corporation. HOW TO RECRUIT, SELECT AND PLACE SALES-
MEN WHO CAN AND WILL SELL. Chicago: Dartnell, 1962.

> This multimedia kit consists of a 200-page looseleaf manual,
> three cassette tapes, practice forms, two case problems, and
> a tape player/recorder.

1609 Hopkins, David S., and Bailey, Earl L. THE CHIEF MARKETING EXEC-
UTIVE. Conference Board Report, n.s., no. 511. New York: Conference Board, 1971. 62 p. Diagrams, tables. Paperback.

> The authors examine the role of the chief marketing executive
> in 131 companies, with eleven job descriptions.

1610 Marting, Elizabeth, ed. THE MARKETING JOB: RESPONSIBILITIES OF
THE TOP MAN AND HIS STAFF. New York: American Management
Association, 1961. 448 p. Diagrams, tables.

> Contributions from forty-seven specialists are contained.

1611 Newgarden, Albert, ed. THE FIELD SALES MANAGER: A MANUAL OF
PRACTICE. AMA Management Report, no. 48. New York: American
Management Association, 1960. 380 p. Forms, maps, tables, bibliog-
raphy.

> This work contains twenty-four contributions on the management
> job; planning, organization, and control; leadership; communi-
> cating and reporting; recruitment and selection; and training
> and development. There is a sales representative's job de-
> scription from Merck & Co., Inc., Chemical Division, pp.
> 278-81. Annotated bibliography, pp. 365-72. Guide to
> audiovisual aids, pp. 373-74.

1612 O'Shaughnessy, J. EVALUATE YOUR SALES FORCE. London: Management Publications, 1971. 265 p. Diagrams, tables.

> This is a revised edition of WORK STUDY APPLIED TO A SALES FORCE, published by the British Institute of Management in 1965.

1613 THE SALES GRID. Rockville, Md.: BNA Communications, 1974.

> Two thirty-minute, 16-mm color films demonstrate the application of the managerial grid developed by Blake and Mouton (see items 521-27) to salesmen.

1614 Weeks, David A. COMPENSATING SALESMEN AND SALES EXECUTIVES. Conference Board Report, n.s., no. 579. New York: Conference Board, 1972. 57 p. Tables. Paperback.

> Weeks covers basic salaries, incentive bonuses, commissions, and indirect compensation of each level of the sales hierarchy from vice president of marketing to field salesmen in 341 companies.

1615 _____. INCENTIVE PLANS FOR SALESMEN. Studies in Personnel Policy, no. 217. New York: National Industrial Conference Board, 1970. 98 p. Form, tables, bibliography. Paperback.

> Incentive plans in 100 companies are examined.

INTERNATIONAL MARKETING

1616 Keegan, Warren J. MULTINATIONAL MARKETING MANAGEMENT. Englewood Cliffs, N.J.: Prentice-Hall, 1974. xiv, 593 p. Illustrations, diagrams, forms, tables, bibliographies.

> This comprehensive text has many case studies. Appendixes include an annotated guide to documentary sources of information, pp. 559-72.

1617 Terpstra, Vern. INTERNATIONAL MARKETING. Holt, Rinehart & Winston Marketing Series. New York: Holt, Rinehart & Winston, 1972. xxiv, 517 p. Diagrams, forms, tables, bibliography.

> Part one deals with the international environment, part two with international marketing management, and part three with the coordination of international marketing through planning, organization, and control. There are indexes of authors, companies, and subjects.

Bibliographies

1618 Bromley, David W. WHAT TO READ ON EXPORTING. 3d ed. Special Subject List, no. 42. London: Library Association, 1970. 95 p. Paperback.

1619 Goldstucker, Jae L., and Torre, Jose R. de la, comps. INTERNATIONAL MARKETING. American Marketing Association Bibliography Series, no. 19. Chicago: American Marketing Association, 1972. 117 p. Paperback.

MARKETING RESEARCH MANAGEMENT

1620 Blankenship, A.B., and Doyle, J.B. MARKETING RESEARCH MANAGEMENT. New York: American Management Association, 1965. xiii, 370 p. Diagrams, tables.

After an introductory chapter on the growth of marketing research, the authors place particular emphasis on the role of the research manager rather than techniques or applications of research.

1621 Boyd, Harper W., Jr., and Westfall, Ralph. MARKETING RESEARCH: TEXT AND CASES. 3d ed. Homewood, Ill.: Irwin, 1972. xv, 813 p. Diagrams, forms, tables.

This work includes sixty-six case studies and many textual references to information sources.

1622 Cox, Keith M., and Enis, Ben M. THE MARKETING RESEARCH PROCESS: A MANAGERIAL APPROACH TO PURCHASING RELEVANT INFORMATION FOR DECISION MAKING. Pacific Palisades, Calif.: Goodyear, 1972. xiv, 622 p. Diagrams, tables, bibliographies.

Each chapter begins with a brief summary and concludes with an annotated guide to further reading. Several case studies are included. Indexes of names and subjects.

1623 Ferber, Robert; Blankertz, Donald F.; and Hollander, Sidney. MARKETING RESEARCH. New York: Ronald Press, 1964. 679 p. Diagrams, tables.

The final section on management responsibilities is particularly relevant. Glossary, pp. 651-63.

1624 Luck, David J.; Wales, Hugh G.; and Taylor, Donald A. MARKETING RESEARCH. Englewood Cliffs, N.J.: Prentice-Hall, 1970. 645 p. Illustrations, diagrams, forms, tables, bibliography.

This includes thirty-nine case studies and an annotated bibliography, pp. 618-32.

Periodicals

1625 JOURNAL OF MARKETING RESEARCH. Chicago: American Marketing Association, 1964- . Quarterly.

1626 JOURNAL OF THE MARKET RESEARCH SOCIETY. London: Market Research Society, 1959- . Quarterly.

Bibliographies

1627 Carpenter, Robert N. GUIDELIST FOR MARKETING RESEARCH AND ECONOMIC FORECASTING. Rev. ed. AMA Research Study, no. 73. New York: American Management Association, 1966. 112 p. Paperback.

   Carpenter lists 374 items, classified and annotated, with an author index.

1628 Ferber, Robert; Cousineau, Alain; Crask, Millard; and Wales, Hugh G., comps. A BASIC BIBLIOGRAPHY ON MARKETING RESEARCH. 3d ed. American Marketing Association Bibliography Series, no. 7. Chicago: American Marketing Association, 1974. 299 p.

   This is a revision of the second edition (1963) by Hugh G. Wales and Robert Ferber. A classified and annotated list of books and articles and an author index are included.

1629 Frank, Nathalie D. DATA SOURCES FOR BUSINESS AND MARKET ANALYSIS. 2d ed. Metuchen, N.J.: Scarecrow Press, 1969. 361 p.

   This is a revision of MARKET ANALYSIS: A HANDBOOK OF CURRENT DATA SOURCES (1964).

1630 Tupper, Elizabeth, and Wills, Gordon, comps. SOURCES OF UK MARKETING INFORMATION. 2d ed. London: Benn, 1975. 156 p. Spiral binding.

   Sponsored by the Market Research Society, this is a guide to publications and organizations. The first edition was published by Nelson (London) in 1969.

Abstracting and Indexing Service

1631 MARKET RESEARCH ABSTRACTS. London: Market Research Society,

1960- . Twice yearly.

This highly selective service abstracts about 200 articles each year under broad subject headings, with author and subject indexes.

STATISTICS FOR MARKETING RESEARCH

1632 Harvey, Joan M., comp. STATISTICS AFRICA: SOURCES FOR MARKET RESEARCH. Beckenham, Eng.: CBD Research, 1970. 175 p. Bibliography. Paperback. (Distributed by International Publications Service, New York.)

1633 _____. STATISTICS AMERICA: SOURCES FOR MARKET RESEARCH (NORTH, CENTRAL AND SOUTH AMERICA). Beckenham, Eng.: CBD Research, 1973. 225 p. Bibliography. Paperback. (Distributed by International Publications Service, New York.)

1634 _____. STATISTICS ASIA AND AUSTRALIA: SOURCES FOR MARKET RESEARCH. Beckenham, Eng.: CBD Research, 1974. xii, 238 p. Bibliography. Paperback. (Distributed by International Publications Service, New York.)

1635 _____. STATISTICS EUROPE: SOURCES FOR MARKET RESEARCH. 3d ed. Beckenham, Eng.: CBD Research, 1976. 467 p. Bibliography. Paperback. (Distributed by International Publications Service, New York.)

1636 Wasserman, Paul, and Paskar, Joanne, eds. STATISTICS SOURCES: A SUBJECT GUIDE TO DATA ON INDUSTRIAL, BUSINESS, SOCIAL, EDUCATIONAL, FINANCIAL AND OTHER TOPICS FOR THE UNITED STATES AND INTERNATIONALLY. 4th ed. Detroit: Gale Research Co., 1974. 891 p.

NEW PRODUCT PLANNING

An important part of the marketing function is the evaluation and development of products to be placed on the market.

1637 Gisser, Philip. LAUNCHING THE NEW INDUSTRIAL PRODUCT. New York: American Management Association, 1972. 183 p. Diagrams.

This work lacks an index.

1638 Gorle, Peter, and Long, James. ESSENTIALS OF PRODUCT PLANNING. McGraw-Hill Management Manuals. London: McGraw-Hill, 1973. 100 p. Diagrams, tables, bibliography.

This includes a summary checklist on p. 90 and a glossary on pp. 91-94.

1639 Jolson, Marvin A. "New Product Planning in an Age of Future Consciousness." CALIFORNIA MANAGEMENT REVIEW 16 (Fall 1973): 25-33. Diagrams, tables, bibliography.

Jolson examines the need for, and limitations of, current methods of new product planning, with a discussion of techniques for collecting, processing, and analyzing information, including the Delphi method.

1640 McGuire, E. Patrick. EVALUATING NEW-PRODUCT PROPOSALS. Conference Board Report, n.s., no. 604. New York: Conference Board, 1973. 108 p. Diagrams, forms, tables, bibliography. Paperback.

The author describes methods used by management to judge new product proposals, based primarily on the practices of 203 manufacturing and service firms with active systems of product and service development.

1641 _____. GENERATING NEW-PRODUCT IDEAS. Conference Board Report, n.s., no. 546. New York: Conference Board, 1972. 70 p. Illustrations, diagrams, tables. Paperback.

This is a summary of the experiences of 154 manufacturing and service firms.

1642 Marting, Elizabeth, ed. NEW PRODUCTS/NEW PROFITS: COMPANY EXPERIENCES IN NEW PRODUCT PLANNING. New York: American Management Association, 1964. 303 p. Diagrams.

This work's thirty contributions summarize the experiences of twenty-four companies which have been outstandingly successful in new product planning and development.

1643 Marvin, Philip. PRODUCT PLANNING SIMPLIFIED. New York: American Management Association, 1972. xviii, 221 p. Tables.

This practical guide, based on actual experiences, is presented in four parts: finding and screening, funding and auditing, organizing, and staffing.

1644 THE PRODUCT MANAGER SYSTEM: A SYMPOSIUM. Experiences in Marketing Management, no. 8. New York: National Industrial Conference Board, 1965. 126 p. Diagrams. Paperback.

Seventeen senior marketing executives made contributions to this volume. There are selected position guides, pp. 75-104, and selected organization charts, pp. 106-23.

1645 Uman, David B. NEW PRODUCT PROGRAMS: THEIR PLANNING AND CONTROL. New York: American Management Association, 1969. 159 p. Diagrams, tables, bibliography.

> Uman proposes a new system designed to cut risk, lead time, and cost while also reducing failure rate.

Bibliography

1646 Megathlin, Donald E., and Schaeffer, Winnifred E., comps. A BIBLIOG-RAPHY ON NEW PRODUCT PLANNING. American Marketing Association Bibliography Series, no. 5. 2d ed. Chicago: American Marketing Association, 1966. 62 p. Paperback.

ADVERTISING

1647 Barton, Roger, ed. HANDBOOK OF ADVERTISING MANAGEMENT. New York: McGraw-Hill, 1970. Var. pag. Illustrations, diagrams, tables.

> This book has a 57-page glossary of advertising terms, which covers computers and descriptions of selected advertising organizations.

1648 Obermeyer, Henry. SUCCESSFUL ADVERTISING MANAGEMENT. New York: McGraw-Hill, 1969. xiv, 241 p.

> This is based in part on a survey in which 108 advertising managers gave their views on organizing for effective advertising, the role of the advertising manager, and the advertisers' relationships within the company and with external organizations, such as advertising agencies.

1649 Riso, Ovid. ADVERTISING COST CONTROL HANDBOOK. New York: Van Nostrand Reinhold, 1973. xx, 387 p. Illustrations, forms, tables, bibliography.

> This book contains major sections on management responsibilities, the creators and producers, the media, legal and international aspects, and evaluation and control. There is a directory of advertising industry associations, p. 379, and a select list of journals, p. 380.

Periodicals

1650 ADVERTISING QUARTERLY: A CRITICAL AND PROFESSIONAL REVIEW. London: Advertising Association, 1964- .

1651 JOURNAL OF ADVERTISING RESEARCH. New York: Advertising Research Foundation, 1960- . Bimonthly.

CHANNELS OF DISTRIBUTION

Works on the management of wholesaling and retailing.

1652 Davidson, William R., and Doody, Alton F. RETAILING MANAGEMENT. 3d ed. New York: Ronald Press, 1966. 905 p. Diagrams, forms, tables, bibliography.

> This comprehensive text has many cases and problems. There is an annotated bibliography, pp. 876-81. Indexes of cases, names, and subjects are also included.

1653 JOURNAL OF RETAILING. New York: New York University Institute of Retail Management, 1925- . Quarterly.

1654 Stacey, Nicholas A.H., and Wilson, Aubrey. THE CHANGING PATTERN OF DISTRIBUTION. 2d ed. Oxford: Pergamon Press, 1965. xiii, 427 p. Tables, bibliography.

> This is a survey of every selling method from department stores to automatic vending. Glossary, pp. 417-18.

1655 Will, R. Ted, and Hasty, Ronald W. RETAILING: A MID-MANAGEMENT APPROACH. San Francisco: Canfield Press; London: Harper & Row, 1973. xiii, 386 p. Illustrations, tables, bibliographies.

> This book contains a bibliography, discussion questions, and case studies at the end of each chapter. There is a selected and annotated list of information sources on retailing, pp. 369-72, and a glossary of retailing terms, pp. 373-82.

1656 Wingate, John W.; Schaller, Elmer D.; and Miller, F. Leonard. RETAIL MERCHANDISE MANAGEMENT. Englewood Cliffs, N.J.: Prentice-Hall, 1972. xiii, 386 p. Illustrations, diagrams, forms, tables, bibliography.

> Arranged in five sections, this work covers the basis for successful store operation, pricing, inventory, planning and control in dollars, and planning and control in units.

Bibliography

1657 Chute, A. Hamilton. A SELECTED AND ANNOTATED BIBLIOGRAPHY OF RETAILING. Rev. ed. Bibliography Series, no. 5, rev. Austin: University of Texas Bureau of Business Research, 1964. 112 p. Paperback.

PHYSICAL DISTRIBUTION MANAGEMENT

The organization and coordination of the various functions associated with the physical distribution of goods, such as packaging, warehousing, and transport, has aroused interest and generated much literature in recent years.

1658 American Management Association. PHYSICAL DISTRIBUTION MANAGE-MENT: THE TOTAL SYSTEMS ROUTE TO NEW PROFITS. PRIME 100 Series. New York: American Management Association, 1967. Var. pag.

A programmed guide scheduled to last for ten study hours, this publication shows how to integrate transportation, inventory, warehousing, packaging, and materials handling to achieve significant cost reduction.

1659 Arbury, James N.; Armstrong, Robert M.; Grossman, Charles L.; Lind, Carl T.; Lodge, David W.; Schubach, John J.; Shea, Daniel L.; Shumka, Donald M.; and Weinberg, Charles B. A NEW APPROACH TO PHYSI-CAL DISTRIBUTION. New York: American Management Association, 1967. 127 p. Diagrams, tables, bibliography.

This book describes a total systems approach being applied to PDM by a number of companies. No index.

1660 INTERNATIONAL JOURNAL OF PHYSICAL DISTRIBUTION. Bradford, Eng.: MCB (Physical Distribution Management), 1970- . Three issues yearly.

1661 Joubert, William H. PROFIT POTENTIALS OF PHYSICAL DISTRIBUTION. New York: American Management Association, 1972. 180 p. Tables, bibliographies.

Several case studies are covered.

1662 Smykay, Edward W. PHYSICAL DISTRIBUTION MANAGEMENT. Contribution by Ward A. Fredericks. 3d ed. New York: Macmillan, 1973. xv, 425 p. Illustrations, bibliography.

The first edition of this, now a standard work, was published in 1961.

1663 Wentworth, Felix R.L., ed. HANDBOOK OF PHYSICAL DISTRIBUTION MANAGEMENT. London: Gower Press, 1976. 543 p. Illustrations, diagrams, forms, maps, tables, bibliography. (Distributed by Cahners Publishing Co., Boston.)

Part one of this major handbook deals with the essential aspects of physical distribution management. The remaining four sections cover warehousing, bulk freight transport, delivery transport, and fleet management.

Bibliographies

1664 British Institute of Management. PHYSICAL DISTRIBUTION MANAGE-
MENT BIBLIOGRAPHY. London, 1970. 11 p. Paperback.

> This selective list of books, articles, and films was compiled
> by P. Fereday and members of the BIM library staff on behalf
> of the Centre for Physical Distribution Management. It lacks
> annotations.

1665 Marks, Norton E., and Taylor, Robert M., comps. PHYSICAL DISTRI-
BUTION AND MARKETING LOGISTICS: AN ANNOTATED BIBLIOG-
RAPHY. American Marketing Association Bibliography Series, no. 11.
Chicago: American Marketing Association, 1966. xii, 125 p. Paper-
back.

> This classified list of books and articles is followed by a list
> of bibliographies and directories and indexes of authors and
> periodicals.

1666 Smykay, Edward W., and La Londe, Bernard L. BIBLIOGRAPHY ON
PHYSICAL DISTRIBUTION MANAGEMENT. Washington, D.C.: Marketing Publications, National Press Building, 1967. Supplements.

> This classified and annotated looseleaf bibliography has indexes
> of authors and titles but no subject index. It was financed
> by the National Council of Physical Distribution Management.

Organizations

1667 Centre for Physical Distribution Management, British Institute of Management, Management House, Parker Street, London, WC2B 5PT, England.

> This center was set up within BIM in 1970 to cater to the
> growth of interest in Physical Distribution Management.

1668 National Council of Physical Distribution Management, 222 West Adams
Street, Chicago, Ill. 60606.

> This organization was founded in 1963.

Section 16

PRODUCTION MANAGEMENT

Included in this section are works on the production manager and his staff, including the foreman, and works on some of the activities contributing to the smooth running of the factory, production planning and control, scheduling, purchasing and materials management, quality control, value analysis and value engineering, plant layout, and maintenance management.

GENERAL STUDIES

1669 Bowman, Edward H., and Fetter, Robert B. ANALYSIS FOR PRODUCTION AND OPERATIONS MANAGEMENT. 3d ed. Irwin Series in Quantitative Analysis for Business. Homewood, Ill.: Irwin, 1967. xiii, 870 p. Diagrams, forms, tables.

   This is a combined revision of two earlier books by these authors, also published by Irwin: ANALYSIS FOR PRODUCTION MANAGEMENT (2d ed. 1961) and ANALYSES OF INDUSTRIAL OPERATIONS (1959). Sixteen case studies are included and there is a glossary of symbols on pp. 819-22.

1670 Buffa, Elwood S. MODERN PRODUCTION MANAGEMENT. 4th ed. Wiley Series in Management and Administration. New York: Wiley, 1973. xiii, 704 p. Diagrams, tables, bibliographies.

   This comprehensive text has many case problems. An abridged version is available as BASIC PRODUCTION MANAGEMENT. New York: Wiley, 1971. xii, 629 p. Illustrations, diagrams, tables, bibliographies.

1671 _____. OPERATIONS MANAGEMENT: PROBLEMS AND MODELS. 3d ed. Wiley Series in Management and Administration. New York: Wiley, 1972. xiii, 762 p. Diagrams (3 folding), tables, bibliographies.

   This standard work takes an analytical approach to production and operations management. Each chapter concludes with review questions, problems, and bibliographical references. A teacher's manual is also available.

1672 Maynard, Harold B., ed. HANDBOOK OF MODERN MANUFACTURING MANAGEMENT. New York: McGraw-Hill, 1970. Var. pag. Illustrations, diagrams, tables, bibliographies.

> This contains eighty-one contributions by eighty-six specialists on all aspects of the production management function, with the emphasis on the human, technical, and financial aspects and on procedures developed since midcentury.

1673 Miller, Ernest C. OBJECTIVES AND STANDARDS OF PERFORMANCE IN PRODUCTION MANAGEMENT. AMA Research Study, no. 84. New York: American Management Association, 1967. 112 p. Tables, bibliography. Paperback.

> A number of case studies, including Calumet & Hecla Inc., Donaldson Company Inc., Rockwell Manufacturing Company, Aluminum Company of Canada Ltd., Whirlpool Corporation, and ABC Company, are discussed. Annotated select reading list, pp. 111-12. No index.

1674 Moore, Franklin G. PRODUCTION MANAGEMENT. 6th ed. Irwin Series in Management. Homewood, Ill.: Irwin, 1973. xvi, 720 p. Diagrams, forms, tables, bibliographies.

> Standard work, comprehensive in approach. Previous editions entitled FACTORY MANAGEMENT.

1675 PRODUCTION HANDBOOK. Gordon B. Carson, Harold A. Bolz, and Hewitt H. Young, editorial consultants. 3d ed. New York: Ronald Press, 1972. Var. pag. Illustrations, diagrams, tables, bibliographies.

> The most important handbook in the field, this work was first published in 1944, edited by Leon Pratt Alford and John R. Bangs.

1676 Roscoe, Edwin Scott. ORGANIZATION FOR PRODUCTION: AN INTRODUCTION TO INDUSTRIAL MANAGEMENT. 5th ed. Irwin Series in Management. Homewood, Ill.: Irwin, 1971. xvi, 568 p. Illustrations, diagrams, portraits, tables, bibliography.

> Case problems and glossaries are found in this comprehensive text.

1677 Starr, Martin K. PRODUCTION MANAGEMENT: SYSTEMS AND SYNTHESIS. 2d ed. Englewood Cliffs, N.J.: Prentice-Hall, 1972. xv, 525 p. Diagrams, tables, bibliographies.

> Starr emphasizes planning the production system, implementing the production system design (especially using PERT), controlling operations, and synthesizing production management decisions with financial management and marketing.

Periodicals

1678 INTERNATIONAL JOURNAL OF PRODUCTION RESEARCH. London: Taylor & Francis, 1961/62- . Bimonthly.

> Sponsored by the American Institute of Industrial Engineers, Institution of Production Engineers, and Society of Manufacturing Engineers, this journal is concerned with research on efficient utilization of technical, economic, and human resources in industry.

1679 PRODUCTION AND INVENTORY MANAGEMENT. Chicago: American Production and Inventory Control Society, 1960- . Quarterly.

> This was originally entitled APICS QUARTERLY BULLETIN.

1680 THE PRODUCTION ENGINEER: JOURNAL OF THE INSTITUTION OF PRODUCTION ENGINEERS. London: 1921- . Monthly.

Dictionary

1681 ENCYCLOPEDIC DICTIONARY OF PRODUCTION AND PRODUCTION CONTROL. Englewood Cliffs, N.J.: Prentice-Hall, 1964. 569 p. Diagrams, tables.

Organizations

1682 American Production and Inventory Control Society (APICS), Watergate Building, Suite 504, 2600 Virginia Avenue N.W., Washington, D.C. 20037.

> This society was formed in 1957 with the primary aim of developing efficiency through the application of scientific principles and methods to production and inventory control.

1683 American Society of Mechanical Engineers, 345 East 47th Street, New York, N.Y. 10017.

> This group has a management section.

1684 Institution of Production Engineers, 66 Little Ealing Lane, London, W5 4XX, England.

> This organization, formed in 1921, is concerned with both the technical and management aspects of the production function.

THE PRODUCTION MANAGER AND HIS STAFF

1685 Finley, Robert E., and Ziobro, Henry, eds. THE MANUFACTURING
MAN AND HIS JOB. New York: American Management Association,
1966. 478 p. Diagrams, forms, tables.

> More than forty specialists contributed to this volume.

1686 Weinshall, Theodore D., and Twiss, Brian C. ORGANIZATIONAL PROB-
LEMS IN EUROPEAN MANUFACTURE. 2 vols. London: Longman, 1973.
Diagrams, maps, tables. Vol. 1, part 1: PRODUCTION IN THE TOTAL
SYSTEM. Vol. 2, part 2: PRODUCTION IN THE FUNCTIONAL SYSTEM;
part 3: PRODUCTION IN THE HUMAN RESOURCES SYSTEM.

> This work is concerned with the organizational problems arising
> from the relationships between production managers and other
> functions and the cultural influences which affect their decision
> making in different European countries. Included are forty case
> studies from Britain, France, Germany, Israel, Norway, and
> Spain.

THE FOREMAN

The foreman is sometimes regarded as a neglected member of the management
team (see, for example, item 1688).

1687 Busse, Frank A. THREE-DIMENSIONAL FOREMANSHIP. New York:
American Management Association, 1969. 239 p. Illustrations, tables.

> This work analyzes the role of the foreman as supervisor, man-
> ager, and instructor and emphasizes his importance to the in-
> dustrial community.

1688 Patten, Thomas H., Jr. THE FOREMAN: FORGOTTEN MAN OF MAN-
AGEMENT. New York: American Management Association, 1968. 191 p.
Bibliography. Paperback.

> This is a research study of the role and responsibilities of the
> foreman in U.S. industry. It includes an extensive bibliog-
> raphy but has no index.

1689 Wikstrom, Walter S. MANAGING AT THE FOREMAN'S LEVEL. Studies
in Personnel Policy, no. 205. New York: National Industrial Conference Board, 1967. 59 p. Diagrams, tables. Paperback.

> A review of the role of the foreman in management is followed
> by detailed case studies of four companies: Kimberly-Clark
> Corporation, Pillsbury Company, Air Preheater Company, and
> Arbogast and Bastian Inc.

PRODUCTION PLANNING AND CONTROL

The determination, execution, and control of manufacturing programs fall under this category.

1690 Burbidge, John L. THE PRINCIPLES OF PRODUCTION CONTROL. 3d
      ed. London: Macdonald & Evans, 1971. xxiv, 536 p. Diagrams,
      forms, tables.

> This is a standard British text. Glossary, pp. 489-527.

1691 Eilon, Samuel. ELEMENTS OF PRODUCTION PLANNING AND CON-
      TROL. New York: Macmillan; London: Collier-Macmillan, 1962.
      587 p. Diagrams, tables.

> Eilon also discusses problems in design, marketing, plant lay-
> out, and quality control. The text is often highly mathemati-
> cal, but the author has noted sections which may be omitted
> by readers with a limited knowledge of mathematics.

1692 Greene, James H., ed. PRODUCTION AND INVENTORY CONTROL
      HANDBOOK. New York: McGraw-Hill, 1970. Var. pag. Illustra-
      tions, diagrams, tables.

> Prepared under the supervision of the Handbook Editorial Board
> of the American Production and Inventory Control Society,
> this book contains thirty contributions on all aspects of pro-
> duction and inventory control. A final section summarizes
> American company practices as revealed in a survey of 5,408
> APICS members, conducted in collaboration with the magazine
> FACTORY.

Bibliography

1693 American Production and Inventory Control Society. BIBLIOGRAPHY OF
      ARTICLES, BOOKS AND FILMS ON PRODUCTION AND INVENTORY
      CONTROL AND RELATED SUBJECTS, 1968-71. Compiled and edited by
      Robert G. Ames. 4th ed. Washington, D.C.: 1972. 65 p. Paper-
      back.

> This annotated list is systematically arranged with an author
> index but no subject index. It supplements the third edition,
> compiled by George W. Plossl and published in 1968.

SCHEDULING

The planning of time and resources involved in the production process is referred to as scheduling.

1694 O'Brien, James J. SCHEDULING HANDBOOK. New York: McGraw-Hill, 1969. 605 p. Illustrations, diagrams, forms, tables.

> This comprehensive manual covers traditional and computerized methods. O'Brien emphasizes the scheduling of time but also covers the scheduling of manpower, equipment, and capital.

1695 Eilon, Samuel, and King, John R., comps. INDUSTRIAL SCHEDULING ABSTRACTS (1950-1966). Edinburgh: Oliver & Boyd, 1967. 231 p. (Distributed by Hafner Service Agency, New York.)

> This book contains abstracts of 462 papers arranged in author order with a classified index.

PURCHASING AND MATERIALS MANAGEMENT

The purchasing or materials manager is responsible for the procurement and management of materials, including such key decisions as whether to buy or make equipment and whether to buy or lease equipment.

1696 Aljian, George W., ed. PURCHASING HANDBOOK: STANDARD REFERENCE BOOK ON POLICIES, PRACTICES AND PROCEDURES UTILIZED IN DEPARTMENTS RESPONSIBLE FOR PURCHASING MANAGEMENT OR MATERIALS MANAGEMENT. 3d ed. New York: McGraw-Hill, 1973. Var. pag. Illustrations, diagrams, forms, tables, bibliographies.

> This major handbook contains contributions by 150 specialists presented in thirty-two sections, including three new sections on functions now delegated to purchasing managers: stores management, buying of capital equipment, and contracting for services. There are many bibliographical references, including a "Library" section. There is a 39-page glossary and a 36-page guide to professional purchasing associations.

1697 Ballott, Robert B. MATERIALS MANAGEMENT: A RESULTS APPROACH. New York: American Management Association, 1971. 309 p. Bibliography.

> Ballott shows the interrelationships of various functions of materials management and the interaction of this sector with other operating divisions.

1698 England, Wilbur B. MODERN PROCUREMENT MANAGEMENT: PRINCIPLES AND CASES. 5th ed. Homewood, Ill.: Irwin, 1970. 904 p. Diagrams, forms, tables.

> This comprehensive work has separate indexes to topics and cases.

1699 Heinritz, Stuart F., and Farrell, Paul V. PURCHASING: PRINCIPLES AND APPLICATIONS. 5th ed. Englewood Cliffs, N.J.: Prentice-Hall, 1971. xvii, 460 p. Illustrations, diagrams, forms, tables, bibliography.

> This standard work, the first edition of which was published in 1947, includes many case studies.

1700 JOURNAL OF PURCHASING AND MATERIALS MANAGEMENT. New York: National Association of Purchasing Management, 1965- . Quarterly.

Purchasing in the Smaller Company

1701 Hedrick, Floyd D. PURCHASING MANAGEMENT IN THE SMALLER COMPANY. New York: American Management Association, 1971. 190 p. Diagrams, forms. Paperback.

1702 Pegram, Roger M. PURCHASING PRACTICES IN THE SMALLER COMPANY. Conference Board Report, n.s., no. 553. New York: Conference Board, 1972. 34 p. Tables. Paperback.

Organizations

1703 Institute of Purchasing and Supply, 199 Westminster Bridge Road, London S.E.1, England.

> This body was founded in 1931 as the Purchasing Officers Association.

1704 International Material Management Society, Monroe Complex, 2520 Mosside Boulevard, Monroeville, Pa. 15146.

> This professional society of engineers, educators, and executives was founded in 1949.

1705 National Association of Purchasing Management, 11 Park Place, New York, N.Y. 10007.

> Originally the National Association of Purchasing Agents, this organization was formed in 1915.

QUALITY CONTROL

It is important to ensure that products reach the required quality and that obstacles to the attainment of this quality are removed.

1706 Hagan, John T. A MANAGEMENT ROLE FOR QUALITY CONTROL. New York: American Management Association, 1968. 248 p.

> This is a practical guide to the planning, organization, and execution of quality control procedures.

1707 Juran, Joseph M.; Gryna, Frank M.; and Bingham, Richard S., Jr., eds. QUALITY CONTROL HANDBOOK. 3d ed. New York: McGraw-Hill, 1974. Var. pag. Illustrations, diagrams, tables, bibliography.

> The third edition of this major handbook includes new sections on quality and income, quality costs, motivation, upper management and quality, support operation, and service industries.

Dictionary

1708 European Organisation for Quality Control. GLOSSARY OF TERMS USED IN QUALITY CONTROL. 2d ed. Rotterdam 3, Netherlands: Weena 700, 1969. 202 p. Paperback.

> Contains brief definitions in English with equivalent terms in German, French, Italian, Dutch, Norwegian, Polish, Romanian, Russian, Czech, Spanish, and Swedish.

Periodicals

1709 JOURNAL OF QUALITY TECHNOLOGY: A QUARTERLY JOURNAL OF METHODS, APPLICATIONS AND RELATED TOPICS. Milwaukee, Wis.: American Society for Quality Control, 1969- .

1710 QUALITY. Rotterdam: European Organisation for Quality Control, 1958- . Quarterly.

1711 QUALITY ASSURANCE: JOURNAL OF THE INSTITUTE OF QUALITY ASSURANCE. London: 1935- . Monthly.

1712 QUALITY PROGRESS: THE MONTHLY NEWS MAGAZINE OF THE AMERICAN SOCIETY FOR QUALITY CONTROL. Milwaukee, Wis.: 1944- .

Abstracting and Indexing Service

1713 QUALITY CONTROL AND APPLIED STATISTICS. Whippany, N.J.: Executive Sciences Institute, 1956- . Monthly.

> This looseleaf service of informative abstracts has annual author and subject indexes.

Organizations

1714 American Society for Quality Control, 161 West Wisconsin Avenue, Milwaukee, Wis. 53203.

> This professional association of quality control engineers and managers was founded in 1946.

1715 Institute of Quality Assurance, 54 Princes Gate, London SW7 2PG, England.

> This organization was founded in 1972.

VALUE ANALYSIS AND VALUE ENGINEERING

Value analysis involves the comparison of the cost of products with the value obtained from them, with the aim of obtaining an equally satisfactory performance from a product or service at lower cost. In value engineering value analysis is applied at an earlier stage, when capital expenditure is being planned. The technique was first used by Lawrence D. Miles in the General Electric Company (see item 1716).

1716 Miles, Lawrence D. TECHNIQUES OF VALUE ANALYSIS AND ENGINEERING. 2d ed. New York: McGraw-Hill, 1972. xviii, 366 p. Illustrations, diagrams, tables.

> The pioneer work by the man who introduced the technique into the General Electric Company, this volume includes many case studies.

1717 Mudge, Arthur E. VALUE ENGINEERING: A SYSTEMATIC APPROACH. New York: McGraw-Hill, 1971. xiv, 286 p. Illustrations, tables, bibliography.

> Part one outlines the fundamentals and theory of value engineering. Part two deals with applications to various management situations. Part three consists of twenty-five case studies. There is an annotated bibliography on creative thinking, p. 90.

1718 Ridge, Warren T. VALUE ANALYSIS FOR BETTER MANAGEMENT. New York: American Management Association, 1969. 206 p. Diagrams, forms, tables.

> Ridge gives an account of VAMP (Value Analysis of Management Practices), a combination of work simplication and value engineering intended to evaluate not only procedures but also the organizations that produce paperwork.

Bibliography

1719 Society of American Value Engineers. VALUE ENGINEERING/ANALYSIS BIBLIOGRAPHY. 2d ed. Smyrna, Ga.: 1969. xxviii, 198 p. Paperback.

>   This bibliography covers books, reports, articles, films, and government publications.

Organizations

1720 Institute of Value Management, c/o Williams & Glyn's Bank, 25 Millbank, London, SW1P 4RB, England.

>   This was founded in 1966 as the Value Engineering Association.

1721 Society of American Value Engineers, 2550 Hargrave Drive L-205, Smyrna, Ga. 30080.

>   This organization was founded in 1953.

PLANT LAYOUT

1722 Muther, Richard. PRACTICAL PLANT LAYOUT. New York: McGraw-Hill, 1955. xiii, 363 p. Illustrations, diagrams, tables.

1723 _____. SYSTEMATIC LAYOUT PLANNING. 2d ed. Boston: Cahners Publishing Co., 1973. Var. pag. Illustrations, diagrams, forms, tables. Paperback.

>   This practical guide consists of a framework of phases through which each layout project passes (as developed in Muther's PRACTICAL PLANT LAYOUT), a pattern of procedures for step-by-step planning, and a set of conventions for identifying, visualizing, and rating the various activities, relationships, and alternatives involved in a layout project.

MAINTENANCE MANAGEMENT

It is important to ensure that plant and equipment are examined at regular intervals so that any faults can be discovered and rectified.

1724 Cooling, W. Colebrook. LOW-COST MAINTENANCE CONTROL. New York: American Management Association, 1973. 62 p. Illustrations. Paperback.

1725 Corder, C.G. ORGANIZING MAINTENANCE. London: British Institute of Management, 1963. 44 p. Diagrams. Paperback.

1726 Morrow, L.C., ed. MAINTENANCE ENGINEERING HANDBOOK. New York: McGraw-Hill, 1966. Var. pag. Illustrations, diagrams, tables.

> Although this work stresses the technical aspects, many of the 108 contributions in this major handbook also deal with management problems. The problems include organization and administration of the maintenance force (nine chapters), maintenance personnel administration (five chapters), planning and scheduling maintenance work (eleven chapters, including one on the critical path method), project control (two chapters), and costs and budgets for maintenance operations (five chapters).

Organizations

1727 American Institute of Maintenance, 710 West Wilson Avenue, Glendale, Calif. 91209.

> This organization was founded in 1958.

1728 British Council of Maintenance Associations, c/o Instron, Coronation Road, High Wycombe, Bucks., HB12 3SY, England.

> This body was founded in 1968.

1729 International Maintenance Institute, P.O. Box 26695, Houston, Tex. 77207.

> This organization for senior maintenance executives was founded in 1961.

Section 17

RESEARCH AND DEVELOPMENT MANAGEMENT

Among the problems of research and development management (R & D) are the selection and evaluation of research projects, the extent to which outside research organizations should be used, the development of patents, the costing and evaluation of research results, the application of modern management techniques to the research process, and the management and motivation of creative personnel.

GENERAL STUDIES

1730 Bright, James R. RESEARCH, DEVELOPMENT AND TECHNICAL INNO-
VATION: AN INTRODUCTION. Homewood, Ill.: Irwin, 1964. xvii,
783 p. Illustrations, diagrams, forms, tables, bibliography.

> Five sections deal with the process of technological innovation;
> case studies in research, development, and technological in-
> novation; location and evaluation of significant technological
> opportunities; the use of advanced technology (mainly case
> studies); and technological planning and forecasting. Annotat-
> ed bibliography, pp. 773-77. There is an index to cases (by
> company) and readings (by author), but no subject index.

1731 Burns, Tom, and Stalker, G.M. THE MANAGEMENT OF INNOVA-
TION. London: Tavistock, 1961. 269 p. Bibliography. (Distributed
by Barnes & Noble, Scranton, Pa.)

> This is a classic British review of attempts, successful and un-
> successful, by twenty organizations (mainly in the field of
> electronics) to exploit new scientific information. The third
> section contains three chapters on the role of the managing
> director and the implications of new technologies for the in-
> dividual manager.

1732 Cetron, Marvin J., and Goldhar, Joel D., eds. THE SCIENCE OF
MANAGING ORGANIZED TECHNOLOGY. 4 vols. New York: Gordon & Breach, 1970. Diagrams, tables, bibliography.

A collection of readings aiming to provide a comprehensive survey of R & D management problems. A selection of book reviews appears in volume 4. No index.

1733 Dean, Burton V. EVALUATING, SELECTING AND CONTROLLING R & D PROJECTS. AMA Research Study, no. 89. New York: American Management Association, 1968. 128 p. Diagrams, tables, bibliography. Paperback.

Methods used by member companies of AMA, investigated through questionnaires, surveys, and an invitation seminar form the basis for this book. Dean also reviews the literature. Several case studies are included. There is an index of companies but no subject index.

1734 Fujita, Tsuneo, and Karger, Delmar W. "Managing R & D in Japan." MANAGEMENT INTERNATIONAL REVIEW 12, no. 1 (1972): 65-73. Tables, bibliography.

Findings from a survey of R & D budgeting, organization, and evaluation in 785 firms are discussed.

1735 Gerstenfeld, Arthur. EFFECTIVE MANAGEMENT OF RESEARCH AND DEVELOPMENT. Technical Management Series. Reading, Mass.: Addison-Wesley, 1970. 150 p. Diagrams, tables, bibliographies.

Gerstenfeld believes that management techniques can be applied more effectively to R & D projects, and he is concerned because more than 50 percent of project failures appear to be for nontechnical reasons. He synthesizes his findings from a survey of 170 R & D managers to compare present policies, investigate the relationship between marketing and R & D, and collect information relating to technological forecasting in 162 companies.

1736 Heyel, Carl, ed. HANDBOOK OF INDUSTRIAL RESEARCH MANAGEMENT. 2d ed. New York: Reinhold, 1968. xiv, 562 p. Diagrams, tables.

This major handbook contains twenty-four contributions grouped in six sections: management perspectives; research perspectives; departmental operation; accounting, control, and evaluation; personnel administration in research; and research for governmental agencies.

1737 Laserson, Gregory L., and Sperling, JoAnn. THE SURVIVAL OF R & D IN AMERICAN INDUSTRY. New York: American Management Association, 1972. 32 p. Diagrams, tables. Paperback.

The authors survey R & D practices in 242 companies. They suggest that communication of the importance of R & D to other branches of corporate management needs to be improved, as do the efficiency and effectiveness of R & D itself.

1738 McLoughlin, William G. THE FUNDAMENTALS OF RESEARCH MANAGEMENT. New York: American Management Association, 1970. 245 p. Diagrams, forms, tables, bibliography.

Specimen job descriptions and procedures and a sample patent are included.

1739 MANAGING ADVANCED TECHNOLOGY. Edited by the staff of INNO-VATION. 2 vols. New York: American Management Association, 1972. Diagrams, tables. Vol. 1: STRATEGIES AND TACTICS OF PRODUCT INNOVATION. 245 p. Vol. 2: CREATING AN ACTION TEAM IN R & D. 177 p.

The entire work contains thirty contributions, including several case studies. There is an index in each volume.

1740 Mayhall, William. CORPORATE R & D ADMINISTRATION. AMA Research Study, no. 102. New York: American Management Association, 1970. 63 p. Diagrams, tables. Paperback.

This book covers the factors influencing research management and administration, such as type of research, company size, and type of industry; the research director's job; and administrative research activities, such as budgeting and financial administration, capital equipment decisions, and initiation of projects. There is a case study of R & D administration in the Systems Group of TRW Inc., pp. 53-58.

1741 Miller, Ben. MANAGING INNOVATION FOR GROWTH AND PROFIT. Homewood, Ill.: Dow Jones-Irwin, 1970. 274 p. Diagrams, tables.

This book is designed to "develop a greater awareness among executives--in business, hospitals, and colleges--of the threat as well as the opportunity presented by an accelerating rate of change in our society," according to the author. The book deals with conflicting pressures on innovation and their implications for managers; development and implementation of company innovations; and the human problems of innovation. It includes two case studies.

1742 Morton, J.A. ORGANIZATION FOR INNOVATION: A SYSTEMS APPROACH TO TECHNICAL MANAGEMENT. New York: McGraw-Hill, 1971. xviii, 171 p. Illustrations, tables.

Practices at the Bell Telephone Laboratories, of which company the author is vice-president of electronics technology, are analyzed.

351

1743 Orth, Charles D.; Bailey, Joseph C.; and Wolek, Francis W. ADMIN-
ISTERING RESEARCH AND DEVELOPMENT: THE BEHAVIOR OF SCIEN-
TISTS IN ORGANIZATIONS. Homewood, Ill.: Irwin, 1964; London:
Tavistock, 1965. 585 p. Diagrams, tables.

> Includes introductions on the case method and R & D manage-
> ment, perception and motivation in R & D management, reports
> of seven research studies, seven conceptual readings, and
> several case studies. There are indexes to cases and readings,
> but no subject index.

1744 R & D MANAGEMENT SERIES: REPRINTS FROM HARVARD BUSINESS
REVIEW. 2 vols. Boston: Harvard University Graduate School of Business Administration, 1973. Diagrams, tables. Paperback.

> These twenty-five articles were published in HARVARD BUSI-
> NESS REVIEW during the 1960s.

Periodicals

1745 R & D MANAGEMENT. Oxford, Eng.: Blackwell, 1970- . Three issues yearly.

1746 RESEARCH MANAGEMENT. Westport, Conn.: Technomic Publishing Co.
for Industrial Research Institute, 1958- . Bimonthly.

Bibliographies

1747 Glueck, William F., and Thorp, Cary D., Jr. THE MANAGEMENT OF
SCIENTIFIC RESEARCH: AN ANNOTATED BIBLIOGRAPHY AND SYNOP-
SIS. Columbia: University of Missouri School of Business and Public Ad-
ministration, Research Center, 1971. xvi, 522 p. Diagrams, forms.
Paperback.

> This is part of a research study on the administration of scien-
> tific research. A classified list, it has extensive annotations
> and an author index.

1748 Goslin, Lewis N. A SELECTED ANNOTATED BIBLIOGRAPHY ON R &
D MANAGEMENT. Indiana Business Information Bulletin, no. 56. Bloomington: Indiana University Graduate School of Business, Bureau of Business Research, 1966. xiv, 204 p. Paperback.

> This is a classified list with indexes of authors and titles.

THE QUANTITATIVE APPROACH TO R & D

1749 Beattie, C.J., and Reader, R.D. QUANTITATIVE MANAGEMENT IN

R & D. London: Chapman & Hall; New York: Halsted Press, 1971.
347 p. Diagrams, tables, bibliographies.

The authors discuss for R & D managers at all levels the quantitative methods that have been developed for the more efficient management of R & D. Appendixes include a twenty-page
review of technological forecasting, a fifty-five-page review
of network planning methods, a nine-page account of discounted
cash flow, and a twenty-page discussion of the analysis of uncertainty in research project selection.

1750 Cetron, Marvin J.; Isenson, Raymond; Johnson, Jacob N.; Nutt, Ambrose
B.; and Wells, Howard A. TECHNICAL RESOURCE MANAGEMENT:
QUANTITATIVE METHODS. Cambridge, Mass.: M.I.T. Press, 1969.
236 p. Diagrams, tables, bibliography.

Believing that "technological resource management is too important to be handled with the traditional methods still in use
today in a majority of companies and government agencies,"
the authors review the newer quantitative methods now available for resource allocation.

1751 Ritchie, E. "Planning and Control of R & D Activities." OPERATIONAL
RESEARCH QUARTERLY 23 (1972): 477-90. Diagrams, bibliography.

Ritchie considers the possibilities for the application of network planning techniques to R & D.

1752 Seiler, Robert E. IMPROVING THE EFFECTIVENESS OF RESEARCH AND
DEVELOPMENT. New York: McGraw-Hill, 1965. 210 p. Diagrams,
forms, tables.

Seiler is particularly concerned with the use of quantitative
methods, budgetary control, and project selection. He includes the results of an R & D management control survey involving 116 companies.

1753 Wilson, Ira G., and Wilson, Marthann E. MANAGEMENT, INNOVA-
TION, AND SYSTEM DESIGN. Philadelphia: Auerbach, 1971. 175 p.
Diagrams, bibliography.

The authors, who regard innovation as "today's challenge to
management," consider its effect on management philosophies,
processes, and techniques, including the use of computers.

R & D PERSONNEL

1754 Allison, David, ed. THE R & D GAME: TECHNICAL MEN, TECHNICAL
MANAGERS, AND RESEARCH PRODUCTIVITY. Cambridge, Mass.: M.I.T.
Press, 1969. 322 p. Illustrations, diagrams, bibliography. Hardcover
and paperback.

Fifteen authors discuss the activities of research scientists, the research environment, and the internal organizational problems of research. There is a literature review, pp. 301-11.

1755 Kipp, Robert M. PEOPLE ASPECTS: ATTRACTING AND RETAINING R & D PERSONNEL. New York: Gordon & Breach, 1970. 104 p. Bibliography.

Kipp discusses the setting up of a job situation which the individual scientist will regard as challenging, attractive, and rewarding. No index.

Section 18

FINANCIAL MANAGEMENT

Knowing where to obtain money and the adequate management of it are vital to the success of any organization. The financial manager must be able to provide and interpret, at short notice, essential information concerning the financial state of the enterprise. He must advise on the practicability of new projects and ensure adequate budgeting and the use of modern accounting methods in order to exercise satisfactory control over the financial resources available. See also items 1447-51 for financial management in multinationals.

GENERAL STUDIES

1756 Bogen, Jules I., and Shipman, Samuel S., eds. FINANCIAL HANDBOOK. 4th ed. New York: Ronald Press, 1964. Var. pag. Illustrations, tables.

> This detailed handbook is arranged in twenty-seven sections, each with its own editor. There is a 10-page list of sources.

1757 FINANCIAL MANAGEMENT HANDBOOK. Epping, Eng.: Gower Press, 1972. xxiii, 397 p. Diagrams, tables. (Distributed by Beekman Publishers, New York.)

> This work contains eighteen contributions on financial planning, costing and budgetary control, and the financial environment.

1758 Hunt, Pearson, and Andrews, Victor L. FINANCIAL MANAGEMENT: CASES AND READINGS. Homewood, Ill.: Irwin, 1968. 936 p. Diagrams, tables.

> This book contains twenty-four readings and forty-five cases. No index.

1759 Hunt, Pearson; Williams, Charles M.; and Donaldson, Gordon. BASIC BUSINESS FINANCE: TEXT AND CASES. 4th ed. Homewood, Ill.: Irwin, 1971. xxiv, 957 p. Diagrams, tables.

> Thirty-nine case studies are included in this volume.

1760 Kent, Raymond P. CORPORATE FINANCIAL MANAGEMENT. 3d ed.

Homewood, Ill.: Irwin, 1969. xviii, 918 p. Tables.

> This revision of a work first published in 1960 places greater
> emphasis on the theory and techniques of capital budgeting
> and includes a new chapter on the cost of capital.

1761 Miller, Ernest C. OBJECTIVES AND STANDARDS OF PERFORMANCE
IN FINANCIAL MANAGEMENT. AMA Research Study, no. 87. New
York: American Management Association, 1968. 109 p. Bibliography.

> This book includes case studies of the Standard Oil Company
> (Ohio), Univis Inc., the Western Company, the Pillsbury Com-
> pany, Rockwell Manufacturing Company, Calumet & Hecla
> Inc., and a large diversified manufacturer of consumer and
> industrial products. There is an annotated reading list, pp.
> 107-9. No index.

1762 Serraino, William J.; Singhvi, Surendra S.; and Soldovsky, Robert M.,
eds. FRONTIERS OF FINANCIAL MANAGEMENT: SELECTED READ-
INGS. Cincinnati: South-Western Publishing Co., 1971. 462 p. Diagrams, tables. Paperback.

> This work contains thirty-four readings with an author index
> but no subject index.

1763 Symonds, Curtis W. BASIC FINANCIAL MANAGEMENT. New York:
American Management Association, 1969. 160 p. Diagrams, tables.

> The essentials of financial management are presented in a con-
> cise form.

1764 Van Horne, James Carter. FINANCIAL MANAGEMENT AND POLICY.
4th ed. Englewood Cliffs, N.J.: Prentice-Hall, 1977. 756 p.
Diagrams, tables.

> The author attempts to develop an understanding of financial
> theory in an organized manner, to explain the application of
> analytical techniques to a wide range of problems, and to ex-
> pose the reader to the institutional materials necessary for a
> thorough understanding of the environment in which financial
> decisions are made.

1765 _____. FUNDAMENTALS OF FINANCIAL MANAGEMENT. 3d ed.
Englewood Cliffs, N.J.: Prentice-Hall, 1977. 622 p. Diagrams,
tables, bibliographies.

Periodicals

1766 ACCOUNTANCY: THE JOURNAL OF THE INSTITUTE OF CHARTERED

ACCOUNTANTS IN ENGLAND AND WALES. London: 1889- . Monthly.

1767 THE ACCOUNTANT. London: 1874- . Weekly.

1768 ACCOUNTING AND BUSINESS RESEARCH. London: Institute of Chartered Accountants in England and Wales, 1970- . Quarterly.

1769 THE ACCOUNTING REVIEW. Sarasota, Fla.: American Accounting Association, 1926- . Quarterly.

1770 FINANCIAL EXECUTIVE. New York: Financial Executives Institute, 1932- . Monthly.

1771 FINANCIAL MANAGEMENT: THE OFFICIAL JOURNAL OF THE FINANCIAL MANAGEMENT ASSOCIATION. Albany, N.Y.: 1972- . Quarterly.

1772 INTERNATIONAL REGISTER OF RESEARCH IN ACCOUNTING AND FINANCE. Lancaster, Eng.: International Centre for Research in Accounting, 1974- . Twice yearly.

1773 JOURNAL OF ACCOUNTANCY. New York: 1905- . Monthly.

1774 JOURNAL OF ACCOUNTING RESEARCH. Chicago: University of Chicago Graduate School of Business, Institute of Professional Accounting, 1963- . Twice yearly.

1775 JOURNAL OF BUSINESS FINANCE AND ACCOUNTING. Oxford, Eng.: Blackwell, 1974- . Three issues yearly.

This is edited at the University of Warwick, England.

1776 JOURNAL OF FINANCE. New York: American Finance Association, 1946- . Five issues yearly.

1777 JOURNAL UEC (EUROPEAN JOURNAL OF ACCOUNTANCY). Duesseldorf: IdW-Verlag GmbH, 1966- . Quarterly.

Published for the Union Européenne des Experts Comptables' Economiques et Financiers. Includes articles in French, English, and German.

1778 MANAGEMENT ACCOUNTING. New York: National Association of Accountants, 1919- . Monthly.

1779 MANAGEMENT ACCOUNTING: JOURNAL OF THE INSTITUTE OF COST AND MANAGEMENT ACCOUNTANTS. London: 1921- . Monthly.

Bibliographies

1780 ACCOUNTANTS' INDEX. New York, N.Y. 10036: American Institute of Certified Public Accountants, 1211 Avenue of the Americas, 1921- .

> This consists of a basic bibliography (1921) listing books in print in 1912 and material published between 1913 and 1920. Supplementary volumes are issued at intervals; the twentieth supplement, covering material published between January and December 1971, was published in 1972. It attempts to cover all material published in the English language and includes many references to sections of books and to articles appearing in journals not specifically concerned with accounting.

1781 Brealey, R.A., and Pyle, C., comps. A BIBLIOGRAPHY ON FINANCE AND INVESTMENT. London: Elek; Cambridge, Mass.: M.I.T. Press, 1973. 361 p.

> This classified list has an author index but no annotations.

1782 Demarest, Rosemary R. ACCOUNTING INFORMATION SOURCES: AN ANNOTATED GUIDE TO THE LITERATURE, ASSOCIATIONS AND FEDERAL AGENCIES CONCERNED WITH ACCOUNTANCY. Management Information Guide, no. 18. Detroit: Gale Research Co., 1970. 420 p.

> This comprehensive bibliography is well annotated and well indexed.

1783 Donaldson, Gordon, and Stubbs, Carolyn, comps. CORPORATE AND BUSINESS FINANCE: A CLASSIFIED BIBLIOGRAPHY OF RECENT LITERATURE. Reference List, no. 22. Boston: Harvard University Graduate School of Business Administration, Baker Library, 1964. 85 p. Paperback.

> This classified list of books and articles has references to book reviews in the AMERICAN ECONOMIC REVIEW, the JOURNAL OF BUSINESS, and the JOURNAL OF FINANCE. It includes an author index, but has no annotations.

See also item 58.

Abstracting and Indexing Services

1784 ACCOUNTING ARTICLES. New York: Commerce Clearing House, 1963- .

This looseleaf service covers periodical articles, books, and
pamphlets. It has a classified arrangement, under eight broad
subject headings: accounting principles and practices, statements and reports, cost accounting, budgeting, auditing, management services, public accounting practice, and accounting
education. There are indexes of topics and authors.

1785 ACCOUNTING + DATA PROCESSING ABSTRACTS. London: Anbar Publications, 1970- . Eight issues yearly.

This is one of the excellent Anbar series, published in association with the Institute of Chartered Accountants in England
and Wales. Each issue contains 100-150 abstracts of articles
selected from more than 200 journals. Critical comments are
occasionally included, these being distinguished from the factual summaries by being printed in italics. Annual index.
This was incorporated in ANBAR MANAGEMENT SERVICES
ABSTRACTS 1961-71.

Dictionary

1786 ENCYCLOPEDIC DICTIONARY OF BUSINESS FINANCE. Englewood
Cliffs, N.J.: Prentice-Hall, 1960. 658 p. Diagrams, forms, tables.

Organizations

1787 American Accounting Association, 653 South Orange Avenue, Sarasota, Fla.
33577.

This association was established in 1916.

1788 American Institute of Certified Public Accountants, 1211 Avenue of the
Americas, New York, N.Y. 10036.

This institute was established in 1887 as the American Institute
of Accountants.

1789 Association of Certified Accountants, 22 Bedford Square, London, WC1B
3HS, England.

This body incorporates the Corporation of Accountants, founded
in 1891, and the Institute of Certified Public Accountants,
formed in 1903.

1790 Financial Executives Institute, 633 Third Avenue, New York, N.Y.
10017.

Established in 1931 as the Controllers Institute of America, this is now the recognized association for top financial executives in the United States and Canada.

1791 Financial Executives Research Foundation, 633 Third Avenue, New York, N.Y. 10017.

This body was established by the Financial Executives Institute in 1944 to conduct fundamental research in business management with particular emphasis on the principles and practice of financial management.

1792 Institute of Chartered Accountants in England and Wales, Chartered Accountants Hall, Moorgate Place, London EC2R 6EQ, England.

This is the leading body of accountants in England, incorporated by Royal Charter in 1880.

1793 Institute of Cost and Management Accountants, 63 Portland Place, London, W1N 4AB, England.

This organization was formed in 1919 as the Institute of Cost and Works Accountants.

1794 National Association of Accountants, 919 Third Avenue, New York, N.Y. 10022.

Founded in 1919, this body now has members from more than seventy countries.

THE FINANCIAL MANAGER

1795 Bacon, Jeremy, and Walsh, Francis J. DUTIES AND PROBLEMS OF CHIEF FINANCIAL EXECUTIVES. Managing the Financial Function Report, no. 1. New York: National Industrial Conference Board, 1968. 34 p. Tables. Paperback.

A survey of 163 chief financial executives forms the basis for this work.

1796 Harkins, Edwin P. ORGANIZING AND MANAGING THE CORPORATE FINANCIAL FUNCTION. Studies in Business Policy, no. 129. New York: National Industrial Conference Board, 1969. 56 p. Diagrams, tables. Paperback.

Based on an analysis of the financial management functions of 325 companies. Includes several organization charts and job specifications.

1797 Marting, Elizabeth, and Finley, Robert E., eds. THE FINANCIAL MAN-
AGER'S JOB. New York: American Management Association, 1964.
464 p. Diagrams, forms, tables.

Contributions from forty-one executives reflect the current financial policies of many American companies.

CAPITAL INVESTMENT

1798 Bierman, Harold, Jr., and Smidt, Seymour. THE CAPITAL BUDGETING
DECISION: ECONOMIC ANALYSIS AND FINANCING OF INVEST-
MENT PROJECTS. 3d ed. New York: Macmillan; London: Collier-
Macmillan, 1971. 482 p. Diagrams, tables, bibliography.

The authors emphasize the value of the present-value method
of evaluating the economic worth of investments, a modifica-
tion of the discounted cash flow method (see items 1802-3).

1799 Harrison, Ian W. CAPITAL INVESTMENT APPRAISAL. London: McGraw-
Hill, 1973. 91 p. Diagrams, tables, bibliography. Paperback.

Harrison tries to provide the nonspecialist manager with an understanding of the problems of capital investment appraisal and
the techniques used to solve these problems. Annotated bibliography, pp. 88-89.

1800 Magee, John F. "How to Use Decision Trees in Capital Investment."
HARVARD BUSINESS REVIEW 42 (September-October 1964): 79-96. Diagrams, tables.

1801 Merrett, A.J., and Sykes, Allen. THE FINANCE AND ANALYSIS OF
CAPITAL PROJECTS. 2d ed. London: Longman; New York: Halsted
Press, 1973. xxiv, 573 p. Diagrams, tables, bibliography.

This is a very comprehensive text.

DISCOUNTED CASH FLOW

This is a method of investment appraisal involving the application of a suitable
discount to estimated profits and depreciation to allow for the fact that a dollar
cannot begin to earn interest until it is received and that a dollar to be spent
in the future can be earning interest until then. The method is used particularly to evaluate alternative investment proposals.

1802 Alfred, A.M., and Evans, J.B. APPRAISAL OF INVESTMENT PROJECTS
BY DISCOUNTED CASH FLOW PRINCIPLES AND SOME SHORT CUT
TECHNIQUES. 3d ed. London: Chapman & Hall, 1971. 71 p. Dia-
grams, forms, bibliography. Paperback.

This excellent introduction includes comments on the use of discounted cash flow at Courtaulds Ltd.

1803 Wright, M.G. DISCOUNTED CASH FLOW. 2d ed. London: McGraw-Hill, 1973. 167 p. Tables.

This work includes a useful checklist for the capital investment decision process, problems, and solutions.

ACCOUNTING

1804 ACCOUNTANTS' ENCYCLOPEDIA. 4 vols. Englewood Cliffs, N.J.: Prentice-Hall, 1962. Diagrams, forms, tables.

The encyclopedia is arranged systematically with a subject index in volume 4.

1805 ACCOUNTANTS' HANDBOOK. Rufus Wixon, Walter G. Kell, and Norton M. Bedford, editorial consultants. 5th ed. New York: Ronald Press, 1970. Var. pag. Diagrams, forms, tables.

The first edition of this well indexed standard reference work was published in 1923.

1806 Bierman, Harold, and Drebin, Allan R. FINANCIAL ACCOUNTING: AN INTRODUCTION. 2d ed. New York: Macmillan; London: Collier-Macmillan, 1972. 470 p. Forms, tables.

The authors discuss the reporting of financial results of operations to investors, managers, and other interested parties. This work complements the same authors' MANAGERIAL ACCOUNTING: AN INTRODUCTION (item 1814).

1807 Davidson, Sidney, ed. HANDBOOK OF MODERN ACCOUNTING. New York: McGraw-Hill, 1970. Var. pag. Diagrams, forms, tables.

This thorough handbook contains forty-nine contributions.

1808 Kohler, Eric L. A DICTIONARY FOR ACCOUNTANTS. 4th ed. Englewood Cliffs, N.J.: Prentice-Hall, 1970. 455 p. Diagrams, tables.

1809 Lasser, Jacob K., ed. HANDBOOK OF ACCOUNTING METHODS. Edited by the J.K. Lasser Institute: Lee Gray, Bernard Greisman, T.R. Lasser. 3d ed. New York: Van Nostrand Reinhold, 1964. 970 p. Forms, tables.

Part one is concerned with data processing and includes descriptions of four specific applications. Part two considers accounting systems used in sixty-six specific industries.

1810 McNeill, James H., ed. ACCOUNTING PRACTICE MANAGEMENT
HANDBOOK. New York: American Institute of Certified Public Accountants, 1962. xiv, 952 p. Diagrams, forms, tables.

> The 109 contributions are supplemented by a detailed subject
> index. A revised edition would be useful.

1811 Sweeny, Allen. ACCOUNTING FUNDAMENTALS FOR NON-FINANCIAL
EXECUTIVES. New York: American Management Association, 1972.
147 p. Diagrams, tables.

> Sweeny stresses concepts essential to understanding accounting
> information and principles.

MANAGEMENT ACCOUNTING

This section covers the provision and interpretation of accounting and statistical
information to management to assist in the efficient operation of the organization.

1812 Anthony, Robert N. MANAGEMENT ACCOUNTING: TEXT AND CASES.
4th ed. Willard J. Graham Series in Accounting. Homewood, Ill.: Irwin,
1970. xxvii, 790 p. Diagrams, tables, bibliographies.

> Anthony includes nearly 100 cases. Some of the bibliographi-
> cal references are annotated.

1813 _____. MANAGEMENT ACCOUNTING PRINCIPLES. Rev. ed. Willard
J. Graham Series in Accounting; Irwin Series in Management. Homewood,
Ill.: Irwin, 1970. xvi, 490 p. Diagrams, tables.

> Anthony shows how accounting information can be used by all
> levels of management for management control and decision
> making. The book essentially consists of the text of the
> fourth edition of the author's MANAGEMENT ACCOUNTING:
> TEXT AND CASES (item 1812), with the addition of some il-
> lustrative material.

1814 Bierman, Harold, and Drebin, Allan R. MANAGERIAL ACCOUNTING:
AN INTRODUCTION. 2d ed. New York: Macmillan; London: Collier-
Macmillan, 1972. 426 p. Diagrams, tables.

> This work is designed to be read after FINANCIAL ACCOUNT-
> ING: AN INTRODUCTION (item 1806). It focuses on four
> essential aspects of reporting accounting data for management:
> cost determination, cost control, performance evaluation, and
> financial information for planning and special decisions.

1815 Caplan, Edwin H. "The Behavioral Implications of Management Accounting." MANAGEMENT INTERNATIONAL REVIEW 13, nos. 2, 3 (1973):
21-31.

Caplan suggests that management accountants must become
more aware of the behavioral implications if accounting systems
which are fully consistent with modern organization theory are
to be developed.

1816 _____. MANAGEMENT ACCOUNTING AND BEHAVIORAL SCIENCE.
Addison-Wesley Series in Accounting. Reading, Mass.: Addison-Wesley,
1971. 134 p. Tables, bibliography. Paperback.

Caplan compares classical and modern views of accounting and
provides behavioral views of cost accounting, budgeting, and
performance measurement and evaluation.

1817 Horngren, Charles Thomas. ACCOUNTING FOR MANAGEMENT CON-
TROL: AN INTRODUCTION. 3d ed. Englewood Cliffs, N.J.: Prentice-
Hall, 1974. 619 p. Diagrams, tables, bibliography.

This work includes many case problems and a glossary, pp.
603-11.

1818 STUDIES IN MANAGEMENT INFORMATION. London: Institute of Chartered Accountants in England and Wales, General Educational Trust, 1969.
767 p. Diagrams, tables, bibliographies.

This useful manual was originally issued in 1966-68 as eight
separate pamphlets: BUSINESS PLANNING AND CONTROL,
by S.V. Bishop; RESEARCH AND DEVELOPMENT: THE KEY
TO FUTURE PROFITABILITY, by J. Bullock and F. Clive de
Paula; THE CASE FOR MARGINAL COSTING, by Stanley
Dixon; THE USE OF RATIOS IN THE STUDY OF BUSINESS
FLUCTUATIONS AND TRENDS, by K.W. Bevan; THE PREPA-
RATION OF INTERIM ACCOUNTS FOR MANAGEMENT IN
THE SMALLER MANUFACTURING CONCERN, by A.B. Snow;
MANAGEMENT INFORMATION AND STATISTICAL METHOD,
by C.W. Shaw; IMPROVING THE EFFICIENCY OF ADMINIS-
TRATION OF ACCOUNTING DEPARTMENTS, by A.P. Raven-
hill; and THE COMPUTER AS AN AID TO MANAGEMENT by
Dudley W. Hooper. There is a detailed general index.

BUDGETING AND BUDGETARY CONTROL

The following items review the allocation of financial limits to sections of an
organization, within which a manager is expected to plan his activities.

1819 Bacon, Jeremy. MANAGING THE BUDGET FUNCTION. Studies in
Business Policy, no. 131. New York: National Industrial Conference
Board, 1970. 88 p. Diagrams, tables, bibliography. Paperback.

Based on a survey of practices in more than 400 companies,
this work has an annotated bibliography, p. 84.

1820 British Institute of Management. BUDGETARY CONTROL FOR THE SMALL-ER COMPANY. Management Guide, no. 4. London: 1972. 31 p. Tables, bibliography. Paperback.

> This has a glossary of budget terminology, p. 18, and a case study of integrated budgetary control, pp. 19–27. There is a summary of a 1966 BIM survey on budgetary control in the small- and medium-sized company, pp. 28–30.

1821 Hofstede, G.H. THE GAME OF BUDGET CONTROL. Technology and Democratic Society Series. London: Tavistock, 1968. 363 p. Diagrams, tables, bibliography. (Distributed by Barnes & Noble, Scranton, Pa.)

> Hofstede presents the findings of a Dutch research project which investigated what effect, if any, budgetary control had on managerial motivation. He offers advice on the improvement of budgetary systems and on how executives at all levels can learn to work effectively with budgets and budgetary standards. Indexes of names and subjects.

1822 Jones, Reginald L., and Trentin, H. George. BUDGETING: KEY TO PLANNING AND CONTROL. PRACTICAL GUIDELINES FOR MAN-AGERS. New York: American Management Association, 1971. xii, 308 p. Illustrations, diagrams, forms, tables.

> The authors show nonfinancial executives when and how to use budgets to achieve their objectives.

1823 Scott, J.A. BUDGETARY CONTROL AND STANDARD COSTS. 6th ed. London: Pitman, 1970. 324 p. Diagrams, tables, bibliography.

> This standard British text presents a practical approach to budgeting, costing, and financial control. It has a section on long-range planning and decision problems.

COST REDUCTION

1824 American Management Association. COST CONTROL AND REDUCTION. PRIME 10. New York: American Management Association, 1970. Var. pag.

> This programmed text, scheduled to last twenty study hours, shows how to strike the optimum balance between economy and efficiency.

1825 Radke, Magnus. MANUAL OF COST-REDUCTION TECHNIQUES. Translated by B.P. Peters. McGraw-Hill European Professional and Business Books Series. London: McGraw-Hill, 1972. 259 p. Forms, tables.

> Radke outlines fifteen steps for the reduction of costs in pur-

chasing, warehousing, materials utilization, manufacturing, fixed assets, development, administration, distribution, and publicity.

1826 Walsh, Francis J. ADMINISTRATION OF COST REDUCTION PROGRAMS. Studies in Business Policy, no. 117. New York: National Industrial Conference Board, 1965. 76 p. Illustrations, diagrams, forms, tables, bibliography. Paperback.

Walsh shows, through the experiences of 204 companies, how profit margins can be improved through the elimination of all forms of waste in both factory and office. Annotated bibliography, pp. 73-74.

FINANCIAL MANUALS

1827 Davey, Patrick J. FINANCIAL MANUALS. Conference Board Report, n.s., no. 510. New York: Conference Board, 1971. 76 p. Illustrations, diagrams, forms, tables. Paperback.

Davey examines the purposes, preparation, maintenance, contents, and physical production of financial manuals based on a study of 295 manuals from ninety companies.

Section 19

PERSONNEL MANAGEMENT

No organization can function satisfactorily without people, and hence personnel management is important. It is vital to know how to plan one's manpower, how to select and recruit staff of the right caliber, how to promote good working conditions and to institute and administer proper wage and salary payment systems, how to train effectively, and how to maintain good labor relations.

The literature of personnel management is prolific, and this section is perhaps the most selective in this entire guide.

GENERAL STUDIES

1828 Beach, Dale S. PERSONNEL: THE MANAGEMENT OF PEOPLE AT WORK. 2d ed. New York: Macmillan; London: Collier-Macmillan, 1970. xvi, 844 p. Diagrams, forms, tables.

This standard text contains twenty-nine chapters in six sections: management, employees, unions, and organization; employment and development of people; understanding and managing people; financial compensation; security; and perspectives. There are indexes of names and subjects.

1829 _____, comp. MANAGING PEOPLE AT WORK: READINGS IN PERSONNEL. New York: Macmillan; London: Collier-Macmillan, 1971. 515 p. Tables. Paperback.

This work contains forty-five readings in nine sections: perspectives on managing people at work, the personnel function, organization, employment and development of people, motivation and management of people, financial composition, health and safety, collective bargaining, and ethics and social responsibility. No index.

1830 Chruden, Herbert J., and Sherman, Arthur W., Jr. PERSONNEL PRACTICES OF AMERICAN COMPANIES IN EUROPE. New York: American Management Association, 1972. 148 p. Illustrations, tables, bibliographies.

The authors analyze the personnel practices of selected American companies with subsidiaries in two or more European
countries, after interviewing sixty-four persons representing
forty organizations in Belgium, Denmark, England, France,
Italy, Scotland, Sweden, Switzerland, and West Germany.

1831 Exton, William, Jr. THE AGE OF SYSTEMS: THE HUMAN DILEMMA.
New York: American Management Association, 1972. xxiii, 261 p.

Exton traces the evolution of the systems approach to management and its advantages and disadvantages, particularly for the
human being operating the system. He suggests ways of reducing the harmful effects of systems which have led to frustration, aggression, and alienation.

1832 Famularo, Joseph J., ed. HANDBOOK OF MODERN PERSONNEL AD-
MINISTRATION. New York: McGraw-Hill, 1972. Var. pag. Diagrams, forms, tables.

Eighty-one contributions are contained.

1833 Flippo, Edwin B. PRINCIPLES OF PERSONNEL MANAGEMENT. 3d ed.
McGraw-Hill Series in Management. New York: McGraw-Hill, 1971.
xiv, 585 p. Diagrams, tables, bibliographies.

New features of this edition are a chapter on the personnel
manager's responsibility to advise top management on organization design and more attention to the role of the computer in
the recruitment process. There are twenty-two case studies,
and discussion questions are given at the end of each chapter.
Indexes of names and subjects.

1834 French, Wendell L. THE PERSONNEL MANAGEMENT PROCESS: HU-
MAN RESOURCES ADMINISTRATION. 3d ed. Boston: Houghton Mifflin, 1974. 756 p. Illustrations, bibliography.

In the third edition of his standard work, French gives attention to organization development, management by objectives,
and other modern trends, including the systems approach.

1835 Gellerman, Saul. EFFECTIVE SUPERVISION. Rockville, Md.: BNA
Communications.

Three thirty-minute 16-mm color films are MANAGING IN A
CRISIS, in which Richard Beckhard works with a frustrated
work group and shows them how to channel their energies into
constructive problem solving; WORKING WITH TROUBLED EM-
PLOYEES, in which Gellerman interviews Harry Levinson,
president of the Levinson Institute, Cambridge, Mass., on how
to deal with employees who exhibit extreme forms of nonpro-
ductive behavior; and CONTROLLING ABSENTEEISM, in which

Gellerman illustrates five kinds of absentees, explains their motivation, and suggests ways of overcoming the problem.

1836 Jucius, Michael J. PERSONNEL MANAGEMENT. 7th ed. Irwin Series in Management. Homewood, Ill.: Irwin, 1971. xiii, 587 p. Illustrations, diagrams, forms, tables, bibliography.

This comprehensive text was first published in 1947. It includes forty case problems.

1837 National Industrial Conference Board. Division of Personnel Administration. PERSONNEL PRACTICES IN FACTORY AND OFFICE: MANUFACTURING. Studies in Personnel Policy, no. 194. New York: 1964. 152 p. Tables. Paperback.

This survey covers practices in 1,834 companies, all with 250 or more employees.

1838 Odiorne, George S. PERSONNEL ADMINISTRATION BY OBJECTIVES. Irwin Series in Management. Homewood, Ill.: Irwin, 1971. xiv, 470 p. Diagrams, tables.

This guide to the application of management by objectives to the personnel function includes many case studies.

1839 Pigors, Paul, and Myers, Charles A. PERSONNEL ADMINISTRATION: A POINT OF VIEW AND A METHOD. 8th ed. New York: McGraw-Hill, 1977. 546 p. Bibliographies.

This standard text presents a point of view of personnel administration at policy level and detailed practical advice on methodology for implementing policy. It includes many case studies and pays special attention to recent trends. Indexes of names and subjects are included.

1840 Pigors, Paul; Myers, Charles A.; and Malm, F.T. MANAGEMENT OF HUMAN RESOURCES: READINGS IN PERSONNEL ADMINISTRATION. 3d ed. New York: McGraw-Hill, 1973. xii, 589 p. Diagrams, tables. Hardcover and paperback.

Pigors's work contains forty-three readings with no index.

1841 Rowntree, B. Seebohm. THE HUMAN FACTOR IN BUSINESS: FURTHER EXPERIMENTS IN INDUSTRIAL DEMOCRACY. 3d ed. London: Longman, 1938. xx, 244 p. Illustrations, tables.

This classic British study is based on the author's experiences in introducing welfare services into the Rowntree Company at York.

1842 Scheer, Wilbert E., ed. THE DARTNELL PERSONNEL DIRECTOR'S HANDBOOK. Chicago: Dartnell, 1969. 960 p. Illustrations, diagrams, forms, tables.

> This is a comprehensive guide to personnel management, employment, education, training, health and safety, employee services, wage and salary administration, benefits, labor relations, administration, policy, and personnel statesmanship.

1843 Strauss, George, and Sayles, Leonard R. PERSONNEL: THE HUMAN PROBLEMS OF MANAGEMENT. 3d ed. Englewood Cliffs, N.J.: Prentice-Hall, 1972. xvii, 684 p. Diagrams, tables, bibliographies.

> A social and behavioral sciences approach to personnel administration, this work uses many case problems. Indexes of names and subjects.

1844 Yoder, Dale. PERSONNEL MANAGEMENT AND INDUSTRIAL RELATIONS. 6th ed. Englewood Cliffs, N.J.: Prentice-Hall, 1970. xiii, 784 p. Diagrams, tables, bibliographies.

> A standard text, this was first published in 1938 as PERSONNEL AND LABOR RELATIONS. It includes several case studies and discussion problems, as well as indexes of names and subjects.

Periodicals

1845 HUMAN RESOURCE MANAGEMENT. Ann Arbor: University of Michigan Graduate School of Business Administration, Division of Management Education, 1961- . Quarterly.

> This formerly was MANAGEMENT OF PERSONNEL QUARTERLY.

1846 PERSONNEL: THE MANAGEMENT OF PEOPLE AT WORK. New York: AMACOM, 1919- . Bimonthly.

1847 THE PERSONNEL ADMINISTRATOR: THE MAGAZINE OF PEOPLE AT WORK. Berea, Ohio: American Society for Personnel Administration, 1956- . Eight issues yearly.

1848 PERSONNEL AND TRAINING MANAGEMENT YEARBOOK AND DIRECTORY. London: Kogan Page, 1972- .

> This was originally entitled INDUSTRIAL TRAINING YEARBOOK.

1849 PERSONNEL JOURNAL: THE MAGAZINE OF INDUSTRIAL RELATIONS
AND PERSONNEL MANAGEMENT. Swarthmore, Pa.: 1922- . Monthly.

1850 PERSONNEL MANAGEMENT: THE JOURNAL OF THE INSTITUTE OF
PERSONNEL MANAGEMENT. London: Mercury House Business Publications, 1920- . Monthly.

1851 PERSONNEL REVIEW. London: Gower Press for the Institute of Personnel Management, 1971- . Quarterly.

>   This is described as a "professional journal reporting new de-
>   velopments in research, theory and practice of personnel man-
>   agement."

1852 PUBLIC PERSONNEL MANAGEMENT: JOURNAL OF THE INTERNA-
TIONAL PERSONNEL MANAGEMENT ASSOCIATION. Chicago: 1940- .
Quarterly.

1853 SUPERVISORY MANAGEMENT. New York: AMACOM, 1955- . Monthly.

1854 WORK AND PEOPLE. Canberra: Australian Government Publishing
Service, 1945- . Quarterly.

>   The bulletin is prepared by the Personnel Practice section of
>   the Australian Department of Labour. Formerly PERSONNEL
>   PRACTICE BULLETIN.

Bibliographies

1855 Institute of Personnel Management. Information Department. IPM BIB-
LIOGRAPHY. Rev. ed. Part 1. London: 1973. Unpaged. Paperback.

>   This very useful list of 122 books, classified according to THE
>   LONDON CLASSIFICATION OF BUSINESS STUDIES and an-
>   notated, has an author index but no subject index. Part one
>   deals with management and the enterprise and personnel man-
>   agement in general. Further parts will cover manpower studies
>   and labor economics; education, training and development; pay
>   and employment conditions; industrial relations; and the be-
>   havioral sciences.

1856 Moore, Larry F. GUIDELINES FOR MANPOWER MANAGERS: A SE-
LECTED ANNOTATED BIBLIOGRAPHY. University of British Columbia
Monograph Series, no. 3. Vancouver: University of British Columbia,
Faculty of Commerce and Business Administration, 1969. 83 p. Paperback.

>   This classified list of periodical articles has no indexes.

1857 U.S. Civil Service Commission Library. THE PERSONNEL MANAGE-
MENT FUNCTION. Personnel Bibliography Series, no. 42. Washington,
D.C.: 1971. 55 p. Paperback.

> This classified and annotated list of books and articles has no
> indexes. A revision of lists was issued in 1960 and 1968.

Abstracting and Indexing Services

1858 PERSONNEL + TRAINING ABSTRACTS. London: Anbar Publications,
1971- . Eight issues yearly.

> This publication is one of the excellent Anbar series, published
> in association with the Institute of Personnel Management.
> Each issue contains 100-150 abstracts of articles selected from
> more than 200 journals. Critical comments are occasionally
> included, and these are distinguished from the factual sum-
> maries by being printed in italics. Annual index. These were
> incorporated in ANBAR MANAGEMENT SERVICES ABSTRACTS
> 1961-71.

1859 PERSONNEL LITERATURE. Washington, D.C.: Government Printing Office, 1942- . Monthly.

> These are abstracts of selected books, pamphlets, articles, dis-
> sertations and micromaterials received in the library of the
> U.S. Civil Service Commission, arranged under subject head-
> ings. There are annual author and subject indexes.

1860 PERSONNEL MANAGEMENT ABSTRACTS. Ann Arbor: University of
Michigan Graduate School of Business Administration, Bureau of Industrial
Relations, 1955- . Quarterly.

> Books and periodical articles are covered in separate sequences.
> Abstracts of articles are arranged under alphabetical subject
> headings with indexes of authors and titles in each issue. Book
> reviews are occasionally included.

Dictionaries

1861 Hopke, William E., ed. DICTIONARY OF PERSONNEL AND GUIDANCE
TERMS, INCLUDING PROFESSIONAL AGENCIES AND ASSOCIATIONS.
Chicago: J.G. Ferguson Publishing Co., 1968. xix, 464 p. Bibliog-
raphy.

> The main part of this work consists of an alphabetical list of
> terms with definitions. This is followed by a bibliography of
> sources; a list of associations, agencies, and professional or-
> ganizations; and a classification of terms by categories.

1862 Torrington, Derek P., ed. ENCYCLOPEDIA OF PERSONNEL MANAGE-
MENT. Epping, Eng.: Gower Press, 1974. 474 p. Diagrams, tables,
bibliography.

> This work contains brief articles by twenty-five contributors,
> alphabetically arranged. There is no index, but there are
> cross-references in the text.

Organizations

1863 American Association of Industrial Management, 7425 Old York Road,
Melrose Park, Pa. 19216.

> An old established organization, dating from 1899, this group
> is particularly concerned with personnel administration and in-
> dustrial relations.

1864 American Society for Personnel Administration, 19 Church Street, Berea,
Ohio 44017.

> This professional organization of personnel and industrial rela-
> tions administrators was founded in 1948.

1865 Institute of Personnel Management, Central House, Upper Woburn Place,
London, W.C.1, England.

> This major British body was founded in 1913.

1866 International Personnel Management Association, 1313 East 60th Street,
Chicago, Ill. 60637.

> This organization, founded in 1973 by a merger of the Society
> of Personnel Administration and the Public Personnel Associa-
> tion, is particularly concerned with improving personnel prac-
> tices in government.

THE PERSONNEL MANAGER

1867 Finley, Robert E., ed. THE PERSONNEL MAN AND HIS JOB. New
York: American Management Association, 1962. 448 p. Diagrams,
tables.

> This book contains contributions from forty-seven personnel
> managers and specialists on their responsibilities and functions.

1868 Ritzer, George, and Trice, Harrison M. AN OCCUPATION IN CON-
FLICT: A STUDY OF THE PERSONNEL MANAGER. Ithaca, N.Y.:
Cornell University, New York State School of Industrial and Labor Rela-
tions, 1969. 127 p. Forms, tables.

Reported are results of a research study carried out by questionnaire and personal interviews with members of the American Society for Personnel Administration, particularly concerned with establishing how professional and committed are personnel managers, how they behave in conflict situations, and what their occupational images are. No index.

MANPOWER PLANNING

There is a vast amount of literature on manpower planning, or ensuring that the right people are available for the right jobs. Some of this literature is concerned with manpower planning within the firm, some deals with the wider national or international implications, and some covers both. Only items concerned with manpower planning within the organization are listed here.

1869 "Enterprise Manpower Management." PERSONNEL PRACTICE BULLETIN 29 (September 1973): 175-233.

Eight articles consider manpower planning in Australia.

1870 Geisler, Edwin B. MANPOWER PLANNING: AN EMERGING STAFF FUNCTION. AMA Management Bulletin. New York: American Management Association, 1967. 32 p. Diagrams, tables, bibliography. Paperback.

1871 Institute of Personnel Management. COMPANY PRACTICES IN MANPOWER PLANNING. London, 1972. 134 p. Diagrams, tables, bibliography. Paperback.

This report was compiled by Jenny Dorling, after a working seminar arranged by the National Committee on Organization and Planning. It includes case studies of manpower planning in International Computers Ltd. (ICL), the Royal Air Force, British Petroleum Ltd., and the Ford Motor Company.

1872 McBeath, Gordon. ORGANIZATION AND MANPOWER PLANNING. 3d ed. London: Business Books, 1974. 266 p. Diagrams, forms, tables.

This British work, whose first edition was published in 1966, stresses the need for manpower planning to be integrated with overall company planning.

1873 Margerison, Charles J., and Ashton, David, eds. PLANNING FOR HUMAN RESOURCES. Business Strategy and Planning Series. London: Longman, 1974. xiv, 205 p. Diagrams, tables.

This work contains thirteen contributions on manpower planning, organizational change, and personnel policy, with many case studies from British industry.

1874 Timperley, Stuart. "Towards a Behavioral View of Manpower Planning."
PERSONNEL REVIEW 1 (Summer 1972): 4-6, 8-13.

> Timperley forecasts a growing complexity of interrelations be-
> tween individual abilities, motivation, and organizational fac-
> tors affecting manpower management.

1875 Vetter, Eric W. MANPOWER PLANNING FOR HIGH TALENT PERSON-
NEL. Ann Arbor: University of Michigan Graduate School of Business
Studies, Bureau of Industrial Relations, 1967. 222 p. Diagrams, tables,
bibliography.

> Vetter presents analytical approaches by which an organization
> can study its manpower situation and identify "high talent"
> personnel. He suggests, with case studies, objectives for re-
> cruiting, selecting, training, and developing such personnel.
> No index.

1876 Walker, James W. "Manpower Planning: How Is It Really Applied?"
EUROPEAN BUSINESS, no. 36 (Winter 1973), pp. 72-78. Diagrams,
table.

> This is a description of U.S. research and application.

1877 Wikstrom, Walter S. MANPOWER PLANNING: EVOLVING SYSTEMS.
Conference Board Report, n.s., no. 521. New York: National Industrial Conference Board, 1971. 74 p. Diagrams, tables. Paperback.

> This study of manpower planning activities in eighty-four com-
> panies has detailed case studies of Standard Oil Company (New
> Jersey), Union Oil Company of California, and Lockheed Air-
> craft Corporation and briefer accounts of the Hewlett-Packard
> Company, 3M Company, Bell Telephone System, Scott Paper
> System, and IBM Corporation.

Bibliographies

1878 Lewis, C.G., et al., eds. MANPOWER PLANNING: A BIBLIOGRAPHY.
London: English Universities Press, 1969; New York: American Elsevier,
1970. 96 p.

> This bibliography lists 706 books and periodical articles alpha-
> betically by author with no annotations but with introductory
> comments in three chapters: "Manpower Planning at the Na-
> tional Level," by C.S. Leicester; "Manpower Planning at In-
> dustry Level," by G.A. Yewdall; and "Manpower Planning at
> the Level of the Firm," by D.J. Bell, W.R. Hawes, C.G.
> Lewis, and C.J. Purkiss.

1879 Sinha, Nageshwar P., and Herman, Georgiana. MANPOWER PLANNING: A RESEARCH BIBLIOGRAPHY. University of Minnesota Industrial Relations Center, Bulletin no. 52. Minneapolis: University of Minnesota, 1970. 59 p. Paperback.

   This classified list has an author index but no annotations.

1880 U.S. Civil Service Commission Library. MANPOWER PLANNING AND UTILIZATION. Personnel Bibliography Series, no. 39. Washington, D.C.: 1971. 58 p. Paperback.

   This classified and annotated list, including a section on job redesign, supplements an earlier list (1968) on manpower planning.

PERSONNEL RECORDS

1881 Bassett, Glenn A., and Weatherbee, Harvard Y. PERSONNEL SYSTEMS AND DATA MANAGEMENT. New York: American Management Association, 1971. 241 p. Diagrams, tables.

   The authors discuss the application of the systems approach and computer management to activities of the personnel function, including manpower planning, personnel research, and skills inventories.

1882 Industrial Society. DESIGN OF PERSONNEL SYSTEMS AND RECORDS. Compiled by Gerard Tavernier. 2d ed. Epping, Eng.: Gower Press, 1973. xvi, 210 p. Forms, tables, bibliography. (Distributed by Beekman Publishers, New York.)

   This work describes the purposes and requirements of a personnel system and contains many specimen forms.

1883 Marting, Elizabeth, ed. AMA BOOK OF EMPLOYMENT FORMS. New York: American Management Association, 1967. 702 p. Illustrations, forms.

   Marting presents forms from sixty-six companies in eight sections, each section beginning with an essay by an appropriate specialist. There are indexes of subjects and companies.

1884 Morrison, Edward J. DEVELOPING COMPUTER-BASED EMPLOYEE INFORMATION SYSTEMS. AMA Research Study, no. 99. New York: American Management Association, 1969. 80 p. Diagrams, tables. Paperback.

   Morrison reviews the experiences of 408 companies in the use of computers to process personnel information.

1885 National Industrial Conference Board. FORMS AND RECORDS IN PER-
SONNEL ADMINISTRATION. Studies in Personnel Policy, no. 175.
New York, 1960. 384 p. Forms.

> More than 150 forms used by ninety-two companies are clas-
> sified under nineteen subject headings. The book contains an
> index of companies.

RECRUITMENT AND SELECTION

1886 Jackson, Matthew J. RECRUITING, INTERVIEWING AND SELECTING:
A MANUAL FOR LINE MANAGERS. McGraw-Hill European Management
Series. London: McGraw-Hill, 1972. 158 p. Illustrations, diagrams,
forms, tables.

> Examples of recruitment advertisements, forms, and letters are
> given.

1887 McMurry, Robert N. TESTED TECHNIQUES FOR PERSONNEL SELEC-
TION. Chicago: Dartnell, 1966. 250 p. Forms, looseleaf.

1888 Ungerson, Bernard, ed. RECRUITMENT HANDBOOK. Epping, Eng.:
Gower Press, 1970. xviii, 285 p. Diagrams, tables, bibliographies.

> Twenty contributions are arranged in two parts. Part one is a
> general guide to recruitment methods, and part two deals with
> the recruitment of specific categories of personnel.

INTERVIEWING

1889 Bassett, Glenn A. PRACTICAL INTERVIEWING: A HANDBOOK FOR
MANAGERS. New York: American Management Association, 1965.
160 p.

> No index.

1890 Drake, John D. INTERVIEWING FOR MANAGERS: SIZING UP PEOPLE.
New York: American Management Association, 1972. xii, 194 p. Diagrams, tables, bibliography.

> Drake includes a list of tested questions and an interviewer's
> feedback checklist.

1891 Fletcher, John. THE INTERVIEW AT WORK. London: Duckworth, 1973.
96 p. Hardcover and paperback.

> This includes several checklists and covers appraisal and other
> interviews as well as recruitment interviews.

1892 Kahn, Robert L., and Cannell, Charles F. THE DYNAMICS OF INTER-
VIEWING: THEORY, TECHNIQUE AND CASES. New York: Wiley,
1957. 368 p. Diagrams, bibliography.

> A highly praised book, this work is particularly concerned with
> interviewing to obtain information. Part two contains a series
> of transcripts of recorded interviews with comments from the
> authors.

1893 Peskin, Dean B. HUMAN BEHAVIOR AND EMPLOYMENT INTERVIEW-
ING. New York: American Management Association, 1971. 250 p.
Diagrams, bibliography.

> Peskin uses the findings of behavioral scientists and psycholog-
> ical and sociological knowledge to examine a wide range of
> interviewing problems.

1894 Rodger, Alec. THE SEVEN-POINT PLAN. 3d ed. London: National
Institute of Industrial Psychology, 1970. 19 p. Paperback.

> Rodger describes a plan widely used in British industry, which
> consists of a series of questions under seven headings usable to
> assess a candidate's possibilities.

1895 Sidney, Elizabeth, and Brown, Margaret. THE SKILLS OF INTERVIEW-
ING. London: Tavistock, 1961. xii, 396 p. Form, tables.

> Part one outlines the basic concepts of the interview and of-
> fers advice on preparing and conducting interviews with special
> reference to the seven-point plan (see item 1894). Part two
> includes an analysis of different types of personnel interviews.
> A personnel particulars form used by Imperical Chemical Indus-
> tries Ltd. is reproduced.

JOB ENRICHMENT

An attempt to give greater satisfaction to employees by increasing the responsibility of their jobs, job enrichment has been the subject of much literature during recent years. See also items 438, 543, 551, 575, 579.

1896 Fein, M. "Job Enrichment: A Re-Evaluation." SLOAN MANAGEMENT
REVIEW 15 (Winter 1974): 69-88.

> Fein suggests that many of the "successes" of job enrichment
> actually result from common sense. He discusses constraints on
> its use and suggests that it does not have the support of either
> managers or workers.

1897 Ford, Robert N. "Job Enrichment Lessons from A.T. & T." HARVARD
BUSINESS REVIEW 51 (January-February 1973): 96-106. Diagrams.

This is a case study of a job enrichment program in the American Telephone & Telegraph Company (A.T. & T.).

1898 _____. MOTIVATION THROUGH THE WORK ITSELF. New York: American Management Association, 1969. 267 p. Diagrams, forms, tables.

A fuller, but older, account of job enrichment experiments at the American Telephone & Telegraph Company (A.T. & T.).

1899 Grote, Richard C. "Implementing Job Enrichment." CALIFORNIA MANAGEMENT REVIEW 15 (Fall 1972): 16-21. Illustrations, diagrams, tables.

This step-by-step program for implementing an experimental job enrichment project is based on the experiences of United Air Lines.

1900 Herzberg, Frederick. JOB ENRICHMENT IN ACTION. Rockville, Md.: BNA Communications; New York: Time-Life Video; Peterborough, Eng.: Guild Sound & Vision, 1969.

This is available in a twenty-five-minute 16-mm color film (BNA Communications and Guild Sound & Vision) or videotape (Time-Life Video) as part of Herzberg's Motivation to Work series.

1901 _____. MOTIVATION THROUGH JOB ENRICHMENT. Rockville, Md.: BNA Communications; New York: Time-Life Video; Peterborough, Eng.: Guild Sound & Vision, 1967.

This is available as a twenty-eight-minute 16-mm color film (BNA communications and Guild Sound & Vision) or videotape (Time-Life Video).

1902 Paul, William J., Jr., and Robertson, Keith B. JOB ENRICHMENT AND EMPLOYEE MOTIVATION. Epping, Eng.: Gower Press, 1970. 119 p. Diagrams, tables. (Distributed by Cahners Publishing Co., Boston.)

Attitudes about job enrichment at Imperial Chemical Industries Ltd. are studied.

1903 Paul, William J., Jr.; Robertson, Keith B.; and Herzberg, Frederick. "Job Enrichment Pays Off." HARVARD BUSINESS REVIEW 47 (March-April 1969): 61-78. Diagrams.

This is a report of studies in the Imperial Chemical Industries Ltd. and four other British companies. The authors describe its application to laboratory technicians, sales representatives, design engineers, and factory supervisors and give details of motivational results.

1904 Rush, Harold M.F. JOB DESIGN FOR MOTIVATION: EXPERIMENTS
IN JOB ENLARGEMENT AND JOB ENRICHMENT. Conference Board Report, n.s., no. 515. New York, 1971. 83 p. Diagrams, forms, tables,
bibliography. Paperback.

> This work includes case studies of Arapahoe Chemicals, Texas
> Instruments, Inc., the U.S. Internal Revenue Service, Weyer-
> haeuser Company, Valley National Bank, PPG Industries, and
> Monsanto Company.

1905 Schappe, Robert H. "Twenty-two Arguments Against Job Enrichment."
PERSONNEL JOURNAL 53 (February 1974): 116-23. Bibliography.

> Schappe presents a checklist of arguments against job enrich-
> ment and discusses how to answer them. A concluding section
> is entitled "Toward Effective Job Enrichment."

1906 Taylor, Lynda King. NOT FOR BREAD ALONE: AN APPRECIATION
OF JOB ENRICHMENT. London: Business Books, 1972. xiv, 141 p.
Illustrations, diagrams, tables, bibliography. (Distributed by Cahners
Publishing Co., Boston.)

> Taylor includes several case studies and provides a classified
> bibliography, pp. 123-35.

FLEXIBLE WORKING HOURS

Flexible Working Hours, or flextime, whereby employees choose their starting
and finishing times while still working a specified number of hours each day,
has been widely applied in Britain and on the continent of Europe.

1907 Baum, Stephen J., and Young, W. McEwan. A PRACTICAL GUIDE TO
FLEXIBLE WORKING HOURS. London: Kogan Page, 1973. 186 p.
Illustrations, diagrams, forms, tables.

> The work includes flextime rules from Riker Laboratories, the
> Cascelloid Division of Bakelite Xylonite Ltd., Legal and Gen-
> eral Assurance Society Ltd., and the Essex River Authority;
> an agreement between the London and Manchester Assurance
> Company Ltd. and the Association of Scientific, Technical,
> and Managerial Staffs; and a list of U.K. manufacturers of
> flexible time recording equipment.

1908 Bolton, J. Harvey. FLEXIBLE WORKING HOURS. London: Anbar Publications, 1971. 55 p. Illustrations, tables, bibliography. (Distributed
by International Publications Service, New York.)

> Bolton discusses case studies of Messerschmidt-Bolkow-Blohm
> GmbH and J. Walter Thompson GmbH (Frankfurt), with a table
> giving information about the use of flexible working hours in
> thirteen German companies.

1909 Elbing, Alvar O.; Gaden, Herman; and Gordon, John R.M. "Flexible Working Hours: It's About Time." HARVARD BUSINESS REVIEW 52 (January-February 1974): 18-33, 154-55.

> The authors trace the development of flexible working hours in Europe and suggests that the system may replace the shorter working week in North America as a method of varying hours of work.

1910 Gordon, John R.M., and Elbing, Alvar O. "The 'Flexible Hours' Work Week: European Trend is Growing." BUSINESS QUARTERLY 36 (Winter 1971): 66-72. Diagrams.

> The authors suggest that the flexible working hours system has much to offer North American industry.

1911 Institute of Personnel Management. Information Department. FLEXIBLE WORKING HOURS. Information Reports, n.s., no. 12. London: 1972. 65 p. Tables, bibliography. Paperback.

> This is a review of experiences in six British companies (Allen & Hanburys Ltd., Lufthansa German Airlines, Imperial Chemical Industries Ltd., Patcel Convertors Ltd., Pilkington Brothers Ltd., Wiggins Teape Ltd.), two West German companies (Messerschmidt-Boelkow-Blohm GmbH and Vickers Zimmer AG), two French companies (CATRAL and Bergerat-Monnyeaur), and one Swiss company (Sandoz Products Ltd.).

1912 Rousham, Sally. FLEXIBLE WORKING HOURS TODAY: PRACTICE AND EXPERIENCES OF OVER FIFTY BRITISH ORGANISATIONS. Management Survey Report, no. 17. London: British Institute of Management, 1973. 58 p. Illustrations, diagrams, forms, tables. Paperback.

> This book includes descriptions of applications in Esso Petroleum Company, local government, and the civil service. Appendixes include the Essex River Authority rules, Inland Revenue District Office rules, Bosch Limited rules, and an agreement between the London and Manchester Assurance Company and the Association of Scientific, Technical, and Material Staffs.

1913 Summers, Derek. FLEXIBLE WORKING HOURS: A CASE STUDY. London: Institute of Personnel Management, 1974. 51 p. Diagrams, forms, tables.

> This review of experiences in the Essex River Authority, England, includes comments from management, staff, and unions.

1914 Wade, Michael. FLEXIBLE WORKING HOURS IN PRACTICE. Epping, Eng.: Gower Press, 1973. 112 p. Illustrations, diagrams, forms.

> This work includes many case studies, notably J. Walter Thomp-

son GmbH, Wiggins Teape Ltd., Pilkington Brothers Ltd., and
Schreiber Wood Industries Ltd. There is a planning and implementation checklist and a list of fifty leading British organizations which use flexible working hours.

WAGE AND SALARY ADMINISTRATION

1915 COMPENSATION REVIEW. New York: AMACOM, 1969- . Quarterly.

This journal reviews trends in salaries and fringe benefits, and
includes original articles, digests of articles from other journals,
abstracts, and book reviews.

1916 Cothliff, J.S. SALARY ADMINISTRATION: A SURVEY OF 216 COM-
PANIES. Management Survey Reports, no. 16. London: British Institute
of Management, 1973. 42 p. Diagrams, forms, tables, bibliography.
Paperback.

1917 Dunn, J.D., and Rachel, Frank M. WAGE AND SALARY ADMINISTRA-
TION: TOTAL COMPENSATION SYSTEMS. McGraw-Hill Series in Management. New York: McGraw-Hill, 1971. xii, 468 p. Diagrams,
tables.

This book includes twenty case problems and five major case
studies.

1918 Jaques, Elliott. EQUITABLE PAYMENT: A GENERAL THEORY OF
WORK, DIFFERENTIAL PAYMENT AND INDIVIDUAL PROGRESS. Gla-
cier Project Series. London: Heinemann; Carbondale, Ill.: Southern
Illinois University Press, 1961. 336 p. Diagrams, tables, bibliography.

1919 _____. PROGRESSION HANDBOOK: HOW TO USE EARNINGS PRO-
GRESSION DATA SHEETS FOR ASSESSING INDIVIDUAL CAPACITY FOR
PROGRESSION AND FOR MANPOWER PLANNING AND DEVELOP-
MENT. Glacier Project Series. London: Heinemann; Carbondale, Ill.:
Southern Illinois University Press, 1968. 72 p. Diagrams (8 folding),
tables, bibliography.

1920 _____. TIME-SPAN HANDBOOK: THE USE OF TIME-SPAN OF DIS-
CRETION TO MEASURE THE LEVEL OF WORK IN EMPLOYMENT ROLES
AND TO ARRANGE AN EQUITABLE PAYMENT STRUCTURE. Glacier
Project Series. London: Heinemann; Carbondale, Ill.: Southern Illinois
University Press, 1964. 133 p. Diagrams, tables, bibliography.

Three works from the Glacier Project (see items 563-68) are
concerned specifically with the development of an equitable
wage payment system.

1921 McBeath, Gordon, and Rands, D.N. SALARY ADMINISTRATION. 2d ed. London: Business Books, 1969. xiii, 283 p. Diagrams, tables.

This is a practical British guide.

1922 Management Centre Europe. SALARY ADMINISTRATION AND CONTROL: A HANDBOOK ON GUIDELINES. Brussels: 1972. 151 p. Diagrams, forms, tables. Paperback.

This includes sections on budgeting and budgetary control, as well as the computer and salary administration. Glossary, pp. 40-42.

1923 Rock, Milton L., ed. HANDBOOK OF WAGE AND SALARY ADMINISTRATION. New York: McGraw-Hill, 1972. 666 p. Diagrams, forms, tables.

Contributions from sixty-four authorities are contained.

INCENTIVE PAYMENT SYSTEMS

A controversial area of wage and salary administration is the question of incentive payments or payment according to a worker's productivity.

1924 Brown, Wilfred. PIECEWORK ABANDONED: THE EFFECT OF WAGE INCENTIVE SYSTEMS ON MANAGERIAL AUTHORITY. Glacier Project Series. London: Heinemann; Carbondale, Ill.: Southern Illinois University Press, 1962. 119 p. Bibliography.

Brown has written an essay on methods of paying operators in the engineering industry. He describes the abandonment of incentive schemes at the Glacier Metal Company.

1925 Currie, Russell M. FINANCIAL INCENTIVES BASED ON WORK MEASUREMENT. 2d ed. Revised by Joseph E. Faraday. London: Management Publications, 1971. 175 p. Diagrams, tables.

This useful textbook would have been even more useful with an index.

1926 Mangum, Garth L. WAGE INCENTIVE SYSTEMS. Berkeley: University of California Institute of Industrial Relations, 1964. 83 p. Diagrams, tables, bibliography. Paperback.

Mangum discusses the attitudes of unions, employees, and managers towards incentives, and examines the effect of automation on incentives. No index.

1927 Marriott, R. INCENTIVE PAYMENT SYSTEMS: A REVIEW OF RESEARCH

AND OPINION. 4th ed. London: Staples Press, 1971. 317 p.
Tables, bibliography.

Marriott describes various types of incentive schemes, analyzes
their advantages and disadvantages, and includes many case
studies. A 1968 postscript by Sylvia Shimmin provides a review of the literature carried out in 1968 after the publication
of the third edition in that year.

1928 Von Kaas, H.K., and Lindemann, A.J. MAKING WAGE INCENTIVES
WORK. New York: American Management Association, 1971. 195 p.
Diagrams, tables.

The authors explain thirteen types of incentive plans and their
suitability for various applications, techniques for evaluating
the performance of existing plans, and computer-based approaches for generating and maintaining satisfactory time al-
lowances.

1929 Whyte, William Foote, et al. MONEY AND MOTIVATION: AN
ANALYSIS OF INCENTIVES IN INDUSTRY. New York: Harper & Row,
1955. xii, 268 p. Diagrams.

This is a classic study of the effect of incentives on human
performance, productivity, and group relations. The authors
draw attention to the difficulties of applying incentive schemes
and the need for managers to be aware of these difficulties.
The collaborating authors are Melville Dalton, Donald Roy,
Leonard R. Sayles, Orvis Collins, Frank Miller, George Strauss,
Friedrich Fuerstenberg, and Alex Bavalar.

JOB EVALUATION

Job evaluation is determining, for wage and salary purposes, the relative value
of jobs within an organization.

1930 British Institute of Management. JOB EVALUATION: A PRACTICAL
GUIDE FOR MANAGERS. London: Management Publications, 1970.
xii, 109 p. Illustrations, diagrams (1 folding), tables, bibliography.

Prepared by a panel of eight persons, this is a brief introduction. It includes case studies of Texas Instruments Inc. and
the British Broadcasting Corporation. There is a glossary of
job evaluation terms, pp. 107-8.

1931 International Labour Office. JOB EVALUATION. Studies and Reports,
n.s., no. 56. Geneva, 1960. 146 p. Tables.

This work defines job evaluation, describes various methods,

summarizes experiences in various U.S. and Canadian companies and in the West German steel industry, and analyzes
its advantages and disadvantages. The major features of job
evaluation schemes in Australia, Belgium, France, the German
Democratic Republic, the German Federal Republic, India,
the Netherlands, Sweden, United Kingdom, and United States
are outlined in appendix C. No index.

1932 Lytle, Charles Walter. JOB EVALUATION METHODS. 2d ed. New
York: Ronald Press, 1954. 507 p. Diagrams, forms, tables.

This is a comprehensive, though now dated, guide with many
case studies.

1933 Morris, James Walker. PRINCIPLES AND PRACTICE OF JOB EVALUA-
TION. London: Heinemann, 1973. 194 p. Diagrams, forms, tables,
bibliography.

This is a review of procedures and their applications, with
comments on their limitations and suggestions for further research.

1934 Paterson, Thomas Thomson. JOB EVALUATION. 2 vols. London: Business Books, 1972. Diagrams, forms, tables, bibliography. (Distributed
by Cahners Publishing Co., Boston.)

Volume one discusses seven methods of job evaluation and their
limitations before proposing the "Paterson Method" which, the
author claims, can be applied to all job levels from board
room to shop floor and throughout a nation, thus making possible a national pay policy. Volume two provides a manual
for the Paterson Method.

EMPLOYEE BENEFITS

1935 Hart, Carole S., and Wells, Robert, eds. SOURCEBOOK ON INTER-
NATIONAL INSURANCE AND EMPLOYEE BENEFIT MANAGEMENT. 2
vols. AMA Research Studies, nos. 80 and 88. New York: American
Management Association, 1967-68. Bibliographies. Paperback.

This is a survey of systems in ninety-three countries. Volume
one (EUROPE, edited by Carole S. Hart, Research Study no.
80) covers fourteen countries and volume two (SELECTED
COUNTRIES OF THE WORLD, edited by Robert Wells, Research
Study no. 88) covers seventy-nine countries.

1936 Hymans, Clifford, ed. HANDBOOK ON PENSIONS AND EMPLOYEE
BENEFITS: THEIR PROVISION AND ADMINISTRATION. London: Kluwer-
Harrap, 1973. Var. pag. Tables.

This comprehensive survey of the British situation has been kept up to date by amendments.

1937 McCaffery, Robert M. MANAGING THE EMPLOYEE BENEFITS PRO-GRAM. New York: American Management Association, 1972. 198 p. Forms, tables, bibliography.

McCaffery stresses the financial aspects and includes case studies and many forms used by companies. There is a bibliography and guide to associations and service organizations, pp. 189-90.

1938 Meyer, Mitchell, and Fox, Harland. PROFILE OF EMPLOYEE BENE-FITS. Conference Board Report, n.s., no. 645. New York: Conference Board, 1974. 103 p. Diagrams. Paperback.

Practices in 1,800 firms are summarized with regard to employee benefits in health insurance, disability benefits, retirement income and capital accumulation, death benefits, unemployment pay, and time off with pay.

1939 Moonman, Jane. THE EFFECTIVENESS OF FRINGE BENEFITS IN INDUS-TRY: INCLUDING A SURVEY OF CURRENT PRACTICE UNDERTAKEN BY AN INDEPENDENT STUDY GROUP. Epping, Eng.: Gower Press, 1973. xii, 222 p. Tables, bibliography.

Fringe benefits covered include annual holidays, sick pay, pensions and life insurance, insurance against accidents, redundancy payments, housing schemes and moving expenses, company cars, profit sharing and share option schemes. There are special chapters dealing with executive fringe benefits, the cost of fringe benefits, and trade unions and fringe benefits.

Bibliography

1940 U.S. Civil Service Commission Library. EMPLOYMENT BENEFITS AND SERVICES. Personnel Bibliography Series, no. 33. Washington, D.C.: 1970. 150 p. Paperback.

This classified and annotated list supplements two earlier lists issued in 1964. No index.

TRAINING

1941 Barber, John W., ed. INDUSTRIAL TRAINING HANDBOOK. London: Iliffe; Reading, Mass.: A.S. Barnes & Co., 1968. 412 p. Diagrams, tables, bibliographies.

This work contains forty contributions on all aspects of training, with accounts of nine British organizations concerned with training.

1942 Campbell, John P. "Personnel Training and Development." ANNUAL REVIEW OF PSYCHOLOGY 22 (1971): 565-602. Bibliography.

This is a review of 213 training and development studies published over a period of twenty years. The author suggests that training and development literature is "voluminous, nonempirical, nontheoretical, poorly written, and dull."

1943 Craig, Robert L., ed. TRAINING AND DEVELOPMENT HANDBOOK. 2d ed. New York: McGraw-Hill, 1976. Var. pag. Illustrations, diagrams, tables, bibliographies.

An authoritative work, sponsored by the American Society for Training and Development, this volume includes forty-seven contributions on training policy and techniques.

1944 Marting, Elizabeth, ed. ENCYCLOPEDIA OF SUPERVISORY TRAINING: BASIC MATERIAL FROM SUCCESSFUL COMPANY PROGRAMS. New York: American Management Association, 1961. 451 p. Illustrations.

This encyclopedia includes a 96-page supplement on "The Supervisor and Audio-Visual Aids."

1945 Otto, Calvin P., and Glaser, Rollin O. THE MANAGEMENT OF TRAINING: A HANDBOOK FOR TRAINING AND DEVELOPMENT PERSONNEL. Reading, Mass.: Addison-Wesley, 1970. 410 p. Illustrations, diagrams, tables, bibliographies.

This comprehensive guide has several appendixes listing selected books for the training director's shelf, motion picture film directories, training consultants, useful periodicals, guides to products and services, audiotape directories, training seminars, and professional associations.

1946 Tracey, William R. DESIGNING TRAINING AND DEVELOPMENT SYSTEMS. New York: American Management Association, 1971. xii, 432 p. Illustrations, forms, tables, bibliographies.

1947 _____. MANAGING TRAINING AND DEVELOPMENT SYSTEMS. New York: American Management Association, 1974. 480 p. Illustrations, tables, bibliography.

The above two works are practical and complementary. See also Tracey's EVALUATING TRAINING AND DEVELOPMENT SYSTEMS (item 745).

Periodicals

See also item 704.

1948 EUROPEAN TRAINING. Bradford, Yorkshire, Eng.: MCB (European Training) Ltd., 1972- . Three issues yearly.

1949 INDUSTRIAL AND COMMERCIAL TRAINING. Northampton, Eng.: Wellens Publishing, 1969- . Monthly.

1950 INDUSTRIAL TRAINING INTERNATIONAL: A REVIEW FOR INDUSTRY AND COMMERCE, TECHNICAL AND FURTHER EDUCATION. London: MGS Publications, 1966- . Monthly.

Bibliographies

1951 Mesics, Emil A. EDUCATION AND TRAINING FOR EFFECTIVE MAN-POWER UTILIZATION: AN ANNOTATED BIBLIOGRAPHY ON EDUCA-TION AND TRAINING IN WORK ORGANIZATIONS. Bibliography Series, no. 9. Ithaca, N.Y.: Cornell University New York State School of Industrial and Labor Relations, 1969. 157 p. Paperback.

This classified list of 728 books and articles has an author index but no subject index.

1952 U.S. Civil Service Commission Library. PLANNING, ORGANIZING AND EVALUATING TRAINING PROGRAMS. Personnel Bibliography Series, no. 41. Washington, D.C.: 1971. 140 p. Paperback.

A classified and annotated list with no indexes, this work is a revision of a list issued in 1968.

Abstracting and Indexing Services

1953 C.I.R.F. ABSTRACTS. Geneva: International Labour Office, C.I.R.F. Publications, 1961- .

This well-organized looseleaf service produces about 300 abstracts yearly from periodicals, books, pamphlets, and reports.

1954 TRAINING ABSTRACTS SERVICE. Liverpool, Eng.: Information for Education, 1967-75.

This service was begun by the British Department of Employment. Abstracts from books, reports, and about seventy periodicals were dispatched monthly on 6 by 4 inch cards.

Dictionary

1955 Great Britain. Department of Employment. GLOSSARY OF TRAINING
TERMS. 2d ed. London: H.M. Stationery Office, 1971. 43 p. Bibliography. Paperback.

> The glossary defines nearly 300 terms used in industrial train-
> ing, including many management terms and "management" it-
> self.

Organizations

1956 American Society for Training and Development, P.O. Box 5307, Madison, Wis. 53705.

> This professional society of persons engaged in the training
> and development of business, industrial, and government per-
> sonnel was founded in 1944.

1957 Institution of Training Officers, 5 Baring Road, Beaconsfield, Buckinghamshire, HP9 2NX, England.

> This organization was founded in 1964 to promote the develop-
> ment of training in industry, the armed services, and govern-
> ment.

TRAINING TECHNIQUES

1958 Zoll, Allen A. III. DYNAMIC MANAGEMENT EDUCATION. Reading, Mass.: Addison-Wesley, 1969. 502 p. Diagrams, forms, tables,
bibliographies.

> This is a comprehensive review of modern training techniques,
> with many examples and annotated bibliographical references.
> No index.

SENSITIVITY TRAINING (T-GROUPS)

Sensitivity training (also called laboratory training, group dynamics training,
group relations training, and T-Group training) is a generic term used to describe a number of related techniques in which groups of up to about twelve
members meet without any formal structure or agenda. Each member tries to
improve his relationships with his colleagues by making them more aware of
his personal behavior.

1959 Berger, M.L., and Berger, P.J., eds. GROUP TRAINING TECH-
NIQUES: CASES, APPLICATIONS AND RESEARCH. Epping, Eng.:

Gower Press, 1972; New York: Halsted Press, 1973. xvi, 191 p. Diagrams, tables, bibliographies.

This work includes sections on the use of managerial grid training in ICI Pharmaceuticals Division, group training and consultancy approaches in IBM (UK) Ltd., and the outcome of a group training course for the Ford Motor Credit Company. Glossary, pp. 175-80.

1960 Bradford, Leland P.; Gibb, Jack R.; and Benne, Kenneth D., eds. T-GROUP THEORY AND LABORATORY METHOD: INNOVATION IN RE-EDUCATION. New York: Wiley, 1964. xii, 498 p. Tables.

Case studies and contributions by nine T-Group trainers focus on use of the method.

1961 Cooper, C.L., and Mangham, I.L., eds. T-GROUPS: A SURVEY OF RESEARCH. London: Wiley-Interscience, 1971. xvii, 283 p. Diagrams, tables, bibliography.

Each of these readings, grouped in seven parts, has an introductory section by the editors.

1962 THE T-GROUP EXPERIENCE. Rockville, Md.: BNA Communications.

These four thirty-minute, 16-mm color films have commentaries by Chris Argyris, Warren G. Bennis, and Alfred J. Marrow.

1963 Weschler, Irving R., with Reisel, Jerome. INSIDE A SENSITIVITY TRAINING GROUP. Industrial Relations Monographs, no. 4. Los Angeles: University of California Institute of Industrial Relations, 1960. 133 p. Tables, bibliography.

Weschler describes and analyzes the relationships between a trainer and the members of one of his training groups over a period of thirty days. Annotated bibliography, pp. 129-33. No index.

1964 Whitaker, Galvin, ed. T-GROUP TRAINING: GROUP DYNAMICS IN MANAGEMENT EDUCATION. A.T.M. Occasional Papers. Oxford, Eng.: Blackwell, 1965. 82 p. Bibliographies. Paperback.

This work has a glossary, pp. 78-82, but no index.

MANAGEMENT GAMES

Management games are exercises in which teams of students are presented with a simulation of actual business conditions and are asked to make appropriate decisions.

1965 Abt, Clark C. "Playtime in the Boardroom." EUROPEAN BUSINESS, no. 30 (Summer 1971), pp. 54-63. Table.

> Explores the state of the art of management games with some brief examples of games for specific management situations. Emphasizes the cheapness and effectiveness of games as a training process and also explains their limitations. A useful table compares the value of games with programmed instruction, the case method, and T-groups.

1966 Belch, Jean, comp. CONTEMPORARY GAMES: A DIRECTORY AND BIBLIOGRAPHY COVERING PLAY SITUATIONS OR SIMULATIONS USED FOR INSTRUCTION AND TRAINING BY SCHOOLS, COLLEGES AND UNIVERSITIES, GOVERNMENT, BUSINESS AND MANAGEMENT. 2 vols. Detroit: Gale Research Co., 1973.

> Volume one provides a directory of management games, and volume two provides an annotated bibliography of management games.

1967 Graham, Robert G., and Gray, Clifford F., eds. BUSINESS GAMES HANDBOOK. New York: American Management Association, 1969. 480 p. Illustrations, tables, bibliography.

> Contains brief abstracts of more than 200 available games, preceded by fifteen papers on the use of business games.

THE CASE STUDY

The case study is a technique popularized by the Harvard Business School, in which real situations are presented to trainees for their analysis and suggestions for possible action.

1968 McNair, Malcolm P., and Hersum, Anita C., eds. THE CASE METHOD AT THE HARVARD BUSINESS SCHOOL: PAPERS BY PRESENT AND PAST MEMBERS OF THE FACULTY AND STAFF. New York: McGraw-Hill, 1954. xvi, 292 p. Tables, bibliography.

> This contains twenty-six contributions with a list of some printed and mimeographed collections of Harvard Business School cases. No index.

1969 Simmons, Donald D. NOTES ON THE CASE STUDY. Cranfield, Eng.: Cranfield Institute of Technology, Case Clearinghouse of Great Britain and Ireland, 1974. Diagrams, tables. Paperback.

> The author's experiences in Britain and Canada are recounted.

PROGRAMMED INSTRUCTION

With this technique the subject to be taught is broken down into consecutive steps and the student questions himself on the facts he has assimilated at each step. He receives feedback about the correctness of his responses before he proceeds to the next step.

1970 Ofiesh, Gabriel D. PROGRAMMED INSTRUCTION: A GUIDE FOR MANAGEMENT. With chapters by Joseph A. Tucker, Jr., and Jerome P. Lysaught. New York: American Management Association, 1965. 416 p. Diagrams, tables.

> Part one covers the development and application of training systems based on programmed instruction. Part two contains case histories of programmed instruction in thirty-five organizations.

1971 PROGRAMMED LEARNING. Rockville, Md.: BNA Communications.

> This thirty-one-minute 16-mm color film introduces the subject.

INDUSTRIAL SAFETY

1972 Handley, William, ed. INDUSTRIAL SAFETY HANDBOOK. London: McGraw-Hill, 1969. 475 p. Illustrations, diagrams, tables, bibliographies.

> Contributions from forty-three experts are included.

1973 International Labour Office. ENCYCLOPEDIA OF OCCUPATIONAL HEALTH AND SAFETY. 2 vols. Geneva, 1971. Illustrations, diagrams, tables, bibliographies.

> The encyclopedia has signed articles, arranged alphabetically by topic, with a subject index in volume two.

Abstracting and Indexing Service

1974 C.I.S. ABSTRACTS. Geneva, Switzerland: International Occupational Safety and Health Information Centre (C.I.S.), 1963- . Eight issues yearly.

> This classified abstracting bulletin is available in English, French, Italian, Russian, and Spanish. There is a subject index in each issue with annual computer-produced subject and author indexes. This continues OCCUPATIONAL SAFETY AND HEALTH ABSTRACTS.

PROTECTION AGAINST BOMBING

An important aspect of industrial safety today is the need to protect personnel and property against bombing by various political and other militant groups.

1975 Cramer, William M., Jr. "Mr. Jones, A Bomb Will Go Off in Seven Minutes." AMS PROFESSIONAL MANAGEMENT BULLETINS 12 (August 1971): 11-20. Form.

This includes a bomb threat checklist.

1976 McGuire, E. Patrick. "When Bombing Threatens: What to Do Before the Clock Starts Ticking." CONFERENCE BOARD RECORD 8 (September 1971): 57-63. Diagrams.

McGuire suggests ways of detecting and apprehending bombers. He recommends a code of practice for searching for the bomb and advises about what to do when it is found.

1977 Wackenhuf, G.R. "Business is the Target of Bombings and Bomb Hoaxes." THE OFFICE 74 (September 1971): 14-20. Illustrations, tables.

Gives statistics on the "urban guerilla warfare" in the United States since 1970 and advice on how to be prepared.

LABOR RELATIONS

Maintaining good relations with his work force and with the unions is a major-- and sometimes difficult--task of the personnel manager. See also items 1452-57 for labor relations in multinationals.

1978 Curtin, Edward R. WHITE-COLLAR UNIONIZATION. Studies in Personnel Policy, no. 220. New York: National Industrial Conference Board, 1970. 70 p. Diagrams, forms, tables. Paperback.

A survey of 140 companies is discussed.

1979 Dore, Ronald. BRITISH FACTORY--JAPANESE FACTORY: THE ORIGINS OF NATIONAL DIVERSITY IN INDUSTRIAL RELATIONS. London: Allen & Unwin; Berkeley and Los Angeles: University of California Press, 1973. 432 p. Diagrams, tables. Hardcover and paperback.

Dore compares two English Electric factories (Bradford and Liverpool) with two factories of the Hitachi Company (Furusato and Taga), examining workers, wages, unions, industrial relations, and employment systems.

1980 Marting, Elizabeth, ed. UNDERSTANDING COLLECTIVE BARGAINING:

THE EXECUTIVE'S GUIDE. New York: American Management Association, 1958. 415 p. Diagrams, forms, tables, bibliography.

This is a study of the collective bargaining process with references to company practices and examples of company documents.

1981 Selekman, Benjamin M.; Fuller, Stephen H.; Kennedy, Thomas; and Baitsell, John M. PROBLEMS IN LABOR RELATIONS. 3d ed. New York: McGraw-Hill, 1964. xiii, 754 p. Tables.

The author examines several case studies of labor relations in the United States plus a few in Britain, France, Germany, and Italy. There is an index to cases by company but no subject index.

1982 Sloane, Arthur A., and Witney, Fred. LABOR RELATIONS. 2d ed. Englewood Cliffs, N.J. London: Prentice-Hall, 1972. xiii, 544 p.

This standard text covers union structure, the historical and legal framework, and the collective bargaining process.

1983 Wilson, Vivian. LABOR RELATIONS HANDBOOK. 2 vols. Princeton, N.J.: Auerbach, 1972. 116 p.

Part one (looseleaf) contains basic facts on labor contracts, management policy, unions, the law, current trends in labor relations, and important supervisory practices. Part two is a self-instructional text.

Periodicals

1984 BRITISH JOURNAL OF INDUSTRIAL RELATIONS. London: London School of Economics and Political Science, 1963- . Three issues yearly.

1985 I.I.L.S. BULLETIN. Geneva, Switzerland: International Institute for Labour Studies, 1966- . Issued irregularly.

1986 INDUSTRIAL AND LABOR RELATIONS REVIEW. Ithaca, N.Y.: Cornell University, New York State School of Industrial and Labor Relations, 1948- . Quarterly.

1987 INDUSTRIAL RELATIONS: A JOURNAL OF ECONOMY AND SOCIETY. Berkeley: University of California Institute of Industrial Relations, 1962- . Three issues yearly.

1988 INDUSTRIAL RELATIONS JOURNAL. London: Mercury House Business

Publications, 1970- . Quarterly.

The journal is edited at the University of Nottingham Department of Adult Education, Industrial Relations Unit.

1989 INTERNATIONAL LABOUR REVIEW. Geneva, Switzerland: International
Labour Office, 1921- . Monthly.

1990 LABOR LAW JOURNAL. Chicago: Commerce Clearing House, 1949- .
Monthly.

1991 MONTHLY LABOR REVIEW. Washington, D.C.: Government Printing
Office, 1915- .

This is edited at the Bureau of Labor Statistics, U.S. Department of Labor. Each issue contains articles on industrial and
labor relations, summaries of research, labor law cases and
labor statistics, book reviews and notes, and lists of journal
articles.

Bibliography

1992 U.S. Civil Service Commission Library. LABOR MANAGEMENT RELA-
TIONS IN THE PUBLIC SERVICE. Personnel Bibliography Series, no. 44.
Washington, D.C.: 1972. 74 p. Paperback.

This is a classified and annotated list of books and articles,
supplementing lists issued in 1962, 1967, and 1970. No index.

Abstracting and Indexing Services

1993 INTERNATIONAL LABOUR DOCUMENTATION. Geneva, Switzerland: -
International Labour Office, 1957- . Fortnightly.

This is a computer-produced list of books, papers, reports,
and articles added to the Central Library of the International
Labour Office, with full catalog entries and brief abstracts.
The abstracts are arranged in random order with a subject
index in each volume, and there has been a full cumulation
for the period 1965-69 (8 vols.) and a cumulated subject index
for 1957-64 (2 vols.).

1994 WORK RELATIONS ABSTRACTS. Detroit: Information Co-ordinators,
1950- . Monthly.

Formerly LABOR-PERSONNEL INDEX, and then EMPLOYMENT
RELATIONS ABSTRACTS, this publication has a classified ar-
rangement with an index in each issue which cumulates in the
December issue.

Dictionaries

1995 Doherty, Robert E., and De Marchi, Gerard. INDUSTRIAL AND LABOR
RELATIONS TERMS: A GLOSSARY FOR STUDENTS AND TEACHERS.
2d ed. Bulletin no. 44. Ithaca, N.Y.: Cornell University, New York
State School of Industrial and Labor Relations, 1971. 37 p. Paperback.

1996 Marsh, A.I., and Evans, E.O. THE DICTIONARY OF INDUSTRIAL RE-
LATIONS. London: Hutchinson, 1973. 415 p. Bibliography.

1997 Roberts, Harold S. ROBERTS' DICTIONARY OF INDUSTRIAL RELATIONS.
Rev. ed. Washington, D.C.: Bureau of National Affairs, 1971. xv,
599 p. Bibliography.

The previous edition (1963) was entitled DICTIONARY OF
LABOR-MANAGEMENT RELATIONS.

Section 20

OFFICE MANAGEMENT

An efficiently organized office is a vital part of a good management system. The office manager must have a broad knowledge of all aspects of management, and he has a particular responsibility to receive, record, and store information coming into the organization and to transmit information as required. Thus there are close links between office management and communication, dealt with in section 21, and also with public relations--covered in the same section as communication--since an organization is judged by the material sent by its office.

GENERAL STUDIES

1998 Aspley, John Cameron, ed. THE DARTNELL OFFICE MANAGER'S HAND-BOOK. 3d ed. Chicago: Dartnell, 1965. 1,022 p. Illustrations, diagrams, forms, tables.

This comprehensive manual has many case studies.

1999 Batty, J., ed. DEVELOPMENTS IN OFFICE MANAGEMENT. London: Heinemann; New York: Crane, Russak & Co., 1972. xii, 302 p. Illustrations, tables, bibliography.

Published in collaboration with the Institute of Office (now Administrative) Management, this work contains articles on various aspects of office management, many of them originally published in the journal OFFICE MANAGEMENT.

2000 Heyel, Carl, ed. HANDBOOK OF MODERN OFFICE MANAGEMENT AND ADMINISTRATIVE SERVICES. New York: McGraw-Hill, 1972. Var. pag. Illustrations, diagrams, forms, tables, bibliography.

Contributions by eighty-one experts cover all aspects of office management.

2001 Johnson, H. Webster, and Savage, William G. ADMINISTRATIVE OF-

FICE MANAGEMENT. Reading, Mass.: Addison-Wesley, 1968. 628 p. Illustrations, diagrams, forms, tables.

Many case problems and review questions are included.

2002 Leffingwell, William Henry. TEXTBOOK OF OFFICE MANAGEMENT. 3d ed. By Edwin M. Robinson. New York: McGraw-Hill, 1950. xiv, 649 p. Illustrations, forms, diagrams, tables.

This is a classic text, the first edition of which was published in 1932.

2003 Mills, Geoffrey, and Standingford, Oliver, eds. OFFICE ORGANIZA- TION AND METHOD: A MANUAL OF ADMINISTRATIVE METHOD. 5th ed. London: Pitman, 1972. 440 p. Illustrations, diagrams, tables, bibliography. Hardcover and paperback.

The authors intend this as a compact reference work for com- pany accountants, cost accountants, and managers, and as a textbook for students.

2004 Neuner, John J.W., and Keeling, Lewis S. ADMINISTRATIVE OFFICE MANAGEMENT. 5th ed. Cincinnati: South-Western Publishing Co.; London: Edward Arnold, 1966. 775 p. Illustrations, diagrams, forms, tables.

This work includes cases, discussions, and review questions at the end of each chapter and a comprehensive case study of the Wescott Packing Company. There is also a section of problems.

2005 OFFICE PRACTICE. Brooklyn, N.Y.: Business Education Films, 1972.

These three 16-mm films are: MANNERS AND CUSTOMS (13 1/2 min.); YOUR ATTITUDE (11 min.); and WORKING WITH OTHERS (13 1/2 min.).

2006 Symes, Mark. OFFICE PROCEDURES AND MANAGEMENT. Heinemann Accountancy and Administration Series. London: Heinemann, 1969. xvi, 478 p. Illustrations, diagrams, forms, bibliography.

2007 Terry, George R. OFFICE MANAGEMENT AND CONTROL: THE AD- MINISTRATIVE MANAGING OF INFORMATION. 6th ed. Homewood, Ill.: Irwin, 1970. xvii, 817 p. Illustrations, diagrams, forms, tables.

This comprehensive text includes many case problems and re- view questions.

2008 Wylie, Harry L., ed. OFFICE MANAGEMENT HANDBOOK. 2d ed. New York: Ronald Press, 1958. Var. pag. Diagrams, forms, tables.

Contributions by thirty-one authorities are included. The book is now outdated, and a revised edition would be welcome.

Periodicals

2009 ADMINISTRATIVE MANAGEMENT. Beckenham, Eng.: Institute of Administrative Management, 1947- . Quarterly.

Formerly this was entitled OFFICE MANAGEMENT.

2010 ADMINISTRATIVE MANAGEMENT: THE MAGAZINE OF BUSINESS SYSTEMS, EQUIPMENT AND PERSONNEL. New York: Geyer-McAllister Publications, 1940- . Monthly.

This journal is published for the Administrative Management Society.

2011 MANAGEMENT WORLD. Willow Grove, Pa.: Administrative Management Society, 1960- . Monthly.

This publication now incorporates AMS PROFESSIONAL MANAGEMENT BULLETINS.

2012 THE OFFICE: MAGAZINE OF MANAGEMENT, EQUIPMENT, AUTOMATION. Stamford, Conn.: Office Publications, 1935- . Monthly.

Organizations

2013 Administrative Management Society, World Headquarters, Willow Grove, Pa. 19090.

Originally the National Office Management Association, this society was founded in 1919.

2014 Institute of Administrative Management, 205 High Street, Beckenham, Kent, BR3 1BA, England.

This organization was formed in 1915 as the Office Management Association and later became the Institute of Office Management.

OFFICE STAFF

2015 Finley, Robert E., ed. LEADERSHIP IN THE OFFICE: GUIDELINES FOR OFFICE SUPERVISORS. New York: American Management Association, 1963. 287 p. Illustrations, tables.

Contributions by thirty-seven individuals and organizations make up this volume, which has no index.

2016 Mandell, Milton M. RECRUITING AND SELECTING OFFICE EM-PLOYEES. AMA Research Report, no. 27. New York: American Management Association, 1956. 175 p. Forms, tables.

This survey of practices in 320 organizations has examples of job description forms, application forms, interview rating forms, tests, reference inquiry forms, performance follow-up forms, and merit rating forms. No index.

2017 National Industrial Conference Board. Division of Personnel Administration. OFFICE PERSONNEL PRACTICES: NON-MANUFACTURING. Studies in Personnel Policy, no. 197. New York: 1965. 196 p. 511 tables. Paperback.

Practices in insurance, banking, gas and electric utilities, retail trade, and wholesale trade, are surveyed. The book covers employment procedures; hours of work and pay; communications, training, and education; company services; time off with pay; employee benefit plans; health and safety; and miscellaneous work rules.

2018 Scott, K.L., and Smith, H.J. OFFICE HOURS AND PAYMENT PRACTICES. Beckenham, Eng.: Institute of Administrative Management, 1973. 52 p. Tables. Paperback.

This review of practices in Britain is superseded, for salaries, by OFFICE SALARIES ANALYSIS 1974, Institute of Administrative Management, 1974. 132 p. Paperback.

OFFICE LANDSCAPING

Office landscaping refers to a system of office planning in which all activities and employees are grouped, often on a whole floor without dividing partitions, to achieve a smooth work flow and to minimize loss of working space. Any necessary divisions are achieved by the strategic placing of cabinets and other furniture and equipment.

2019 Duffy, Frank. OFFICE LANDSCAPING: A NEW APPROACH TO OFFICE PLANNING. Anbar Monograph, no. 9. London: Anbar Publications, 1969. 30 p. Illustrations, diagrams, bibliography.

Duffy explains the principles of office landscaping and examines landscaped offices from the point of view of the office worker and the employer. The bibliography consists mainly of abstracts of periodical articles. This publication is bound with LAYOUT PLANNING IN THE LANDSCAPED OFFICE, item 2020.

2020 Wankum, A. LAYOUT PLANNING IN THE LANDSCAPED OFFICE.
London: Anbar Publications, 1969. 42 p. Illustrations, diagrams, tables.

Wankum offers a simple set of rules for planning the layout of
a landscaped office with a table of symbols for layout planning and many plans adapted from MOBILARORDNUNG IN
DER BUEROLANDSCHAFT (Quickbon, West Germany: Verlag
Schnelle, 1968).

COST REDUCTION IN THE OFFICE

2021 American Management Association. PAPERWORK MANAGEMENT MANU-
AL. New York: 1966. 104 p. Paperback.

This is a programmed text.

2022 Birn, Serge A.; Crossan, Richard M.; and Eastwood, Ralph W. MEA-
SUREMENT AND CONTROL OF OFFICE COSTS: MASTER CLERICAL
DATA. New York: McGraw-Hill, 1961. 318 p. Illustrations, dia-
grams, tables.

The authors first define scientific management and then show how
office costs can be measured and controlled by using methods-
time-measurement. The appendix gives time measurement units
for various office processes.

2023 British Institute of Management. AN INTRODUCTION TO CLERICAL
WORK MEASUREMENT TECHNIQUES. Information Note, no. 67. London: 1970. 12 p. Bibliography. Paperback.

This book summarizes the available techniques for measuring
and controlling clerical activities, such as work sampling,
predetermined motion time systems such as master clerical data,
group capacity assessment, variable factor programming, and
short interval scheduling.

2024 Cemach, Harry P. A FAREWELL TO TYPISTS. London: Anbar Publications, 1974. 85 p. Diagrams, tables.

Cemach suggests ways in which business organizations can reduce their typing load.

2025 _____. WORK STUDY IN THE OFFICE. 5th ed. London: Anbar
Publications, 1977. 196 p. Illustrations, diagrams, tables, bibliography.
Paperback.

This is a standard British guide to the achievement of high
productivity in the office through work study, method study,
and work measurement.

2026 Longman, Harold H. HOW TO CUT OFFICE COSTS. London: Anbar

Publications, 1967. 300 p. Illustrations, diagrams, tables. (Distributed by International Publications Service, New York.)

This practical guide has many case histories on pp. 244-81.

2027 Nance, Harold W., and Nolan, Robert E. OFFICE WORK MEASUREMENT. New York: McGraw-Hill, 1971. 184 p. Diagrams, forms, tables.

These guidelines to cost reduction in the office use the master clerical data (MCD) concept evolved in 1958. The results claimed for MCD include better employee relations, improved performance, and more effective organization.

2028 Strong, Earl P. INCREASING OFFICE PRODUCTIVITY: A SEVEN-STEP PROGRAM. NOMA Series in Office Management. New York: McGraw-Hill, 1962. 287 p. Diagrams, forms, tables.

The seven steps are presented in two sections: (1) office work study (work management), including making position analyses, improving work methods, and setting performance standards; and (2) office employee study (man management), including selecting qualified employees, training effective employees, applying work incentives, and improving supervision.

2029 Terry, George R. OFFICE SYSTEMS AND PROCEDURES. Homewood, Ill.: Dow Jones-Irwin, 1966. 175 p. Illustrations, diagrams, forms, tables.

This is a useful text, but it lacks an index.

Section 21

COMMUNICATION

Included in this section are works on all aspects of communication: oral and written communication, formal and informal, within the company; communication through a formal information service; unwanted communication of information and ideas through industrial espionage; and communication of information about the company to the outside world (public relations). See also item 982.

GENERAL STUDIES

2030 Aurner, Robert Ray, and Wolf, Morris Philip. EFFECTIVE COMMUNI-
CATION IN BUSINESS WITH MANAGEMENT EMPHASIS. 5th ed. Cincinnati: South-Western Publishing Co.; London: Edward Arnold, 1967.
644 p. Illustrations, diagrams, forms.

This work contains sections on written communication; oral communication; functional types of communication; employment applications; successful sales through effective communication; successful adjustment, credit, and collection communication; effective oral and written reports; and a final reference division on locating of information, efficient reading, and letter writing. Each chapter concludes with a summary, discussion questions, and problems.

2031 Bassett, Glenn A. THE NEW FACE OF COMMUNICATION. New York:
American Management Association, 1968. 204 p. Tables.

Bassett discusses the elements of communication, man/manager communication, and the organization as communicator. He pays special attention to the impact of new technology on communication.

2032 Lillico, T.M. MANAGERIAL COMMUNICATION. Oxford, Eng.: Pergamon Press, 1972. xii, 160 p. Illustrations, diagrams, tables, bibliography.

This work is based partly on research carried out among man-

agers in the Scottish electronics industry. Appendixes include
an illustrated guide to status differentials and a glossary. Indexes of authors and subjects.

2033 McLaughlin, Ted J.; Blum, Lawrence P.; and Robinson, David M.: CASES
AND PROJECTS IN COMMUNICATION. Columbus: Merrill, 1965.
117 p. Diagrams, tables. Paperback.

This study guide is divided into three parts: foundations of
communication; person-to-person communication through speech
and letters; and group communication through speech and business reports. No index.

2034 _____. COMMUNICATION. Columbus: Merrill, 1964. 499 p. Tables.

This is a total approach to management communication with
sections on person-to-person communication (letters, conferences, interviews, etc.), group communication (including report writing), and communication with outside groups (including public speaking and communicating with organized labor).

2035 Marting, Elizabeth; Finley, Robert E.; and Ward, Ann, eds. EFFECTIVE
COMMUNICATION ON THE JOB: A GUIDE FOR SUPERVISORS AND
EXECUTIVES. Rev. ed. New York: American Management Association,
1963. 304 p. Tables.

Thirty-four writers consider face-to-face communication, introduction of the new employee, training, safety, motivation,
the giving of orders, discipline, appraisal interviewing, the
handling of grievances, and written communication through
job descriptions, reports, and letters. The original edition
(1956) was edited by M. Joseph Dooher and Vivienne Marquis.

2036 Seybould, Geneva. EMPLOYEE COMMUNICATION: POLICY AND
TOOLS. Studies in Personnel Policy, no. 200. New York: National
Industrial Conference Board, 1966. 91 p. Forms, tables. Paperback.

Seybould includes a detailed checklist of more than 100 media
which can be used as a means of communicating with employees.

2037 Vardaman, George T. EFFECTIVE COMMUNICATION OF IDEAS. Effective Communications Series. New York: Van Nostrand Reinhold,
1970. 255 p. Diagrams, forms, tables, bibliography.

Vardaman emphasizes oral presentation but also discusses written communication. He includes twenty specimens of oral pre-
sentations.

2038 Vardaman, George T.; Halterman, Carroll C.; and Vardaman, Patricia
Black. CUTTING COMMUNICATIONS COSTS AND INCREASING IM-

PACTS: DIAGNOSING AND IMPROVING THE COMPANY'S WRITTEN DOCUMENTS. Wiley Series on Human Communication. New York: Wiley, 1970. 281 p. Diagrams, forms, tables, bibliography.

Part one is a general critical review of methods currently used to communicate; part two advises on costing and assessing the company's communication technique; and part three makes recommendations for designing improved company communications.

2039 Vardaman, George T., and Vardaman, Patricia Black. COMMUNICATION IN MODERN ORGANIZATIONS. Wiley Series in Management and Administration. New York: Wiley, 1973. xvi, 516 p. Diagrams, forms, tables, bibliography.

This comprehensive guide to all forms of written and oral communication has many exercises and case problems. There are specimens of letters, memoranda, etc., pp. 393-502.

Audiovisual Materials

2040 Bassett, Glenn A. COMMUNICATING BOTH WAYS. New York: American Management Association, 1968.

This tape cassette, reel-to-reel tape, or record lasts approximately forty-five minutes and focuses on the techniques of negotiation. It reproduces typical exchanges with a skeptical customer, a dissatisfied employee, and a critical fellow manager.

2041 Berlo, David. EFFECTIVE COMMUNICATION. Rockville, Md.: BNA Communications; Peterborough, Eng.: Guild Sound and Vision.

Five twenty-four-minute 16-mm color films deal with avoidance of a communication breakdown, the problem of different interpretations of verbal messages, feedback, change of attitudes through communication, and the point of view of the communicating management.

2042 COMMUNICATING FILM SERIES. Peterborough, Eng.: Guild Sound & Vision; Rockville, Md.: BNA Communications, 1973.

These three twenty-three-minute 16-mm color films are A QUESTION OF MAY, which revolves around a communication mixup between sales and production over a vital order; ONE-SIDED TRIANGLE, which deals with group communication; and BLOWING HOT AND COLD, which continues the theme of group communication by illustrating a conflict between design, sales, and production.

2043 COMMUNICATING SUCCESSFULLY. New York: Time-Life Video.

A multimedia program consisting of three twenty-five-minute videotapes or 16-mm color films on making a more effective speech, giving a more persuasive presentation, and conducting a more productive meeting.

Periodicals

2044 JOURNAL OF BUSINESS COMMUNICATION. Urbana, Ill.: American Business Communication Association, 1963- . Quarterly.

2045 JOURNAL OF COMMUNICATION. Philadelphia, Pa.: University of Pennsylvania, Annenberg School of Communications, 1951- . Quarterly.

Bibliographies

2046 Carter, Robert M. COMMUNICATION IN ORGANIZATIONS: AN AN-NOTATED BIBLIOGRAPHY AND SOURCEBOOK. Management Information Guide, no. 25. Detroit: Gale Research Co., 1972. 286 p.

2047 Walsh, Ruth M., et al. "Business Communications: A Selected Annotated Bibliography." JOURNAL OF BUSINESS COMMUNICATION 11 (Fall 1973): 65-112.

Prepared by students at the University of Florida, this list covers books and articles, with the emphasis on business writing.

MEETINGS PROCEDURE

2048 Anstey, Edgar. COMMITTEES: HOW THEY WORK AND HOW TO WORK THEM. London: Allen & Unwin, 1962. 116 p.

Anstey provides practical advice on a major management activity.

2049 Barber, James David. POWER IN COMMITTEES: AN EXPERIMENT IN THE GOVERNMENTAL PROCESS. American Politics Research Series. Chicago: Rand McNally, 1966. xii, 189 p. Tables.

Barber analyzes the exercise of power in government committees through a study of twelve local government committees which met and made decisions in the small group laboratory at Yale University.

2050 Hegarty, Edward J. HOW TO RUN BETTER MEETINGS. New York: McGraw-Hill, 1957. xiv, 312 p.

Although not concerned specifically with management meetings, this contains much useful information on the management of meetings.

2051 TAKE THE CHAIR. Peterborough, Eng.: Guild Sound & Vision, 1973.

A multimedia program consisting of a twenty-six-minute 16-mm color film, a forty-eight-page book, and a sixteen-minute record, this presents amusing and practical advice on meetings procedure from five managers.

PUBLIC SPEAKING

2052 THE FLOOR IS YOURS. Peterborough, Eng.: Guild Sound & Vision; Rockville, Md.: BNA Communications, 1973.

This multimedia program consists of a twenty-six-minute 16-mm color film, a sixty-four-page book and a sixteen-minute record. It advises on planning the talk, rehearsal, delivery, and the use of audiovisual aids.

2053 Jay, Antony. THE NEW ORATORY. New York: American Management Association, 1971. 133 p. British ed. published as EFFECTIVE PRESENTATION: THE COMMUNICATION OF IDEAS BY WORDS AND VISUAL AIDS. London: Management Publications, 1970. 113 p.

This guide also includes sections on commissioning a film and writing film commentary, together with a useful checklist. No index.

2054 Powell, Joe. UNACCUSTOMED AS THEY ARE. Rockville, Md.: BNA Communications; Peterborough, Eng.: Guild Sound & Vision, 1972.

A thirty-minute 16-mm color film.

BUSINESS INTELLIGENCE AND INFORMATION SERVICES

This section covers collecting, storing, and communicating information by means of an organized library or information service. This legitimate activity should not be confused with the illegal transmission or acquisition of information by spies (industrial espionage), although at least two books (items 2058 and 2061) cover both topics.

2055 Aguilar, Francis Joseph. SCANNING THE BUSINESS ENVIRONMENT. Studies of the Modern Corporation. New York: Macmillan; London: Collier-Macmillan, 1967. xiii, 239 p. Diagrams, tables, bibliography.

Aguilar gives an account of research carried out in the United

States and six European countries into the information which
managers obtain about the outside environment for the purposes
of determining strategy, the sources used to obtain this information, the ways in which they acquire it, and the reasons
that they scan the environment. The sample consisted of 137
managers in forty-one companies, mainly chemical, and publications were found to be a major source of information.
This is an important study. Originally written as a dissertation for the Harvard Business School, it was awarded the 1966
doctoral dissertation prize by the Program for Studies for the
Modern Corporation, Graduate School of Business, Columbia
University.

2056 Bakewell, K.G.B., ed. LIBRARY AND INFORMATION SERVICES FOR
MANAGEMENT. London: Bingley, 1968. 130 p. Bibliographies.

This book contains ten papers given at a short course organized
by the School of Library and Information Studies, Liverpool,
England.

2057 Dews, J.D. THE USE OF INFORMATION SOURCES BY TEACHERS AND
RESEARCH WORKERS IN THE FIELD OF BUSINESS STUDIES: REPORT
TO THE OFFICE FOR SCIENTIFIC AND TECHNICAL INFORMATION
ON PROJECT SI/25/228. Manchester, Eng.: Manchester Business School,
1970. 127 leaves and appendixes. Diagrams, tables, bibliographies.

This is a report on the information-gathering habits of 443
academics in sixty-four British institutions. The report might
well be called Non-use of information sources: the highest
proportion of respondents to use any abstracting service, for
example, was 12 percent of the sample.

2058 Greene, Richard M., Jr., ed. BUSINESS INTELLIGENCE AND ESPI-
ONAGE. Homewood, Ill.: Dow Jones-Irwin, 1966. 312 p. Illustrations, diagrams, forms, tables, bibliography.

Most of this book consists of contributions on legitimate business intelligence, but there are also chapters on the ethics
of business intelligence, the use of and countermeasures for
electronic eavesdropping or bugging, and an appendix on industrial espionage by Edward F. Furash. Another chapter
deals with the use of business intelligence to build through
mergers and acquisitions.

2059 Keegan, Warren J. "Acquisition of Global Business Information." CO-
LUMBIA JOURNAL OF WORLD BUSINESS 3 (March-April 1968): 35-41.
Diagrams.

This is a summary of a thesis submitted in partial fulfillment
of the requirements for the degree of Doctor of Business Administration, reporting the results of interviews with fifty top

managers in thirteen international companies aimed at discovering how they acquire business information. The reading patterns of most management groups was found to be wasteful, with many managers often reading the same item. Keegan recommends a regular audit of reading activity but neglects the role which the librarian/information officer could play in reducing the reading load.

2060 Meltzer, Morton F. THE INFORMATION IMPERATIVE. New York: American Management Association, 1971. 210 p. Diagrams, tables, bibliography.

The manager of a large information center writes on the importance of information to the management and development of an organization. He discusses ways to control the information flood through indexing, microform storage systems, computer-based storage systems, etc. There is a select list of government-supported information analysis centers; a select list of professional organizations; a select list of abstracting and indexing services; plus a glossary and a bibliography.

2061 Smith, Paul I. Slee. INDUSTRIAL ESPIONAGE AND INTELLIGENCE. London: Business Books, 1970. xii, 173 p. Bibliography.

Part one deals with the ethical and legal approach to business intelligence, including setting up a unit and sources of information. Part two covers industrial espionage and methods for countering it.

2062 Symonds, Curtis W. A DESIGN FOR BUSINESS INTELLIGENCE. New York: American Management Association, 1971. 168 p. Tables.

Symonds deals with the need to gear an information system to corporate objectives, the importance of planning and control, and the applications of the computer.

CLASSIFICATION AND INDEXING

2063 Blagden, John. MANAGEMENT INFORMATION RETRIEVAL: A NEW INDEXING LANGUAGE. Rev. ed. London: Management Publications, 1971. 227 p. Diagrams, tables, bibliography. (Distributed by International Publications Service, New York.)

This thesaurus for indexing the literature of management has an introduction which outlines the indexing problem. There is a list of glossaries of management terms, pp. 225-27.

2064 Harvard University Graduate School of Business Administration. Baker Library. A CLASSIFICATION OF BUSINESS LITERATURE. Rev. ed.

Hamden, Conn.: Shoe String Press, 1960. xviii, 256 p.

This is the classification scheme formerly used in the Baker Library and still used in a number of business libraries. The first edition was published in 1937.

2065 Vernon, K.D.C., and Lang, Valerie. THE LONDON CLASSIFICATION OF BUSINESS STUDIES. London: London Graduate School of Business Studies, Sussex Place, Regents Park, London, NW1 4SA, 1970. 132 p. Bibliography. Paperback.

This is a faceted classification scheme developed at the London Graduate School of Business Studies, England, and now used in more than fifty libraries throughout the world. It is also used, with several amendments, as the basis of the arrangement of this guide. Kept up to date by amendments bulletins, it is currently undergoing revision.

INDUSTRIAL ESPIONAGE

See also items 2058 and 2061.

2066 Engberg, Edward. THE SPY IN THE CORPORATE STRUCTURE. Cleveland: World Publishing Company, 1967. 274 p. Diagrams.

This is an account of the methods and devices used by the industrial espionage agent, with a final chapter on proposals for fighting industrial espionage. Unfortunately, it lacks an index.

2067 Walsh, Timothy J., and Healy, Richard J. PROTECTING YOUR BUSINESS AGAINST ESPIONAGE. New York: AMACOM, 1973. Bibliographies.

This book includes chapters on bugging and wiretapping, the computer and espionage, and the ethics of information collection. A model policy statement on the protection of sensitive data is given as an appendix.

PUBLIC RELATIONS

2068 Blumenthal, L. Roy. THE PRACTICE OF PUBLIC RELATIONS. New York: Macmillan; London: Collier-Macmillan, 1972. xvi, 278 p. Diagrams, tables, bibliographies.

Although written as a textbook with exercises at the end of each chapter, this also provides the executive with useful guidance on the practice of public relations, including press relations, preparation of annual reports and other documentation, television, and ethics. There are thirty-one case exercises, a specimen annual report, a specimen press release, and specimen public relations programs.

2069 Cutlip, Scott M., and Center, Allen H. EFFECTIVE PUBLIC RELATIONS. 4th ed. Englewood Cliffs, N.J.: Prentice-Hall, 1971. xvii, 701 p. Diagrams, tables, bibliographies.

This is a standard text, the first edition of which was published in 1952. Each chapter concludes with a case problem and reading list. A final chapter covers the profession of public relations, ethics, professional organizations, literature, and education.

2070 Kemp, Graham. THE COMPANY SPEAKS: COMMUNICATION IN MODERN BUSINESS MANAGEMENT. London: Longman, 1973. xiv, 262 p. Tables, bibliographies.

Kemp summarizes the traditional view of public relations to draw attention to many opportunities for the enlargement of company activities. He argues that organizations must become more articulate, more communicative, and more aware of their responsibilities to their customers and to society.

2071 Markham, Vic. PLANNING THE CORPORATE REPUTATION. Unwin Professional Management Library. London: Allen & Unwin; Beverly Hills, Calif.: Davlin Publications, 1972. 204 p. Diagrams, tables.

Markham argues that public relations--the establishment of a favorable and identifiable corporate reputation--is essential for any enterprise.

2072 Marquis, Harold H. THE CHANGING CORPORATE IMAGE. New York: American Management Association, 1970. 231 p. Illustrations, diagrams, tables.

This guide to modern techniques in image building and public relations has case studies of Kaiser Aluminum and Chemical Corporation, Crown Zellerback Corporation, and Montgomery Ward Container Corporation of America.

2073 Stephenson, Howard, ed. HANDBOOK OF PUBLIC RELATIONS: THE STANDARD GUIDE TO PUBLIC AFFAIRS AND COMMUNICATIONS. 2d ed. New York: McGraw-Hill, 1971. xx, 836 p. Bibliographies.

This work contains thirty-one contributions presented in four sections: the principles of public relations, PR in public affairs, PR in private enterprise, and communication methods.

Periodicals

2074 PUBLIC RELATIONS. London: Institute of Public Relations, 1948- . Monthly.

2075 PUBLIC RELATIONS JOURNAL. New York: Public Relations Society of America, 1945- . Monthly.

2076 PUBLIC RELATIONS QUARTERLY. New York, 1957- .

Bibliographies

2077 Cutlip, Scott M., comp. A PUBLIC RELATIONS BIBLIOGRAPHY. 2d ed. Madison: University of Wisconsin Press, 1965. xiv, 305 p.

This work was prepared with the support of the Public Relations Society of America. It has an annotated list of 5,947 books and papers, classified under thirty-seven headings, with an author index.

2078 Norton, Alice. PUBLIC RELATIONS INFORMATION SOURCES. Management Information Guide, no. 22. Detroit: Gale Research Co., 1971. 153 p.

This well-annotated and well-indexed guide covers general sources, special fields, public relations tools, public relations in the United States, careers in public relations, and international public relations.

Appendix A

DIRECTORY OF ORGANIZATIONS

The number in parentheses refers to the item number in the text at which the organization is listed and, in some cases, briefly described.

Academy of International Business, c/o James D. Goodnow, Roosevelt University, 430 South Michigan Ave., Chicago, Ill. 60605 (1422)

Academy of Management, c/o Rosemary Pledger, Secretary-Treasurer, University of Houston at Clear Lake City, 2700 Bay Area Blvd., Houston, Tex. 77058 (298)

Administrative Management Society, World Headquarters, Willow Grove, Pa. 19090 (2013)

American Accounting Association, 653 South Orange Ave., Sarasota, Fla. 33577 (1787)

American Association of Industrial Management, 7425 Old York Rd., Melrose Park, Pa. 19216 (1863)

American Foundation for Management Research (299). See American Management Association

American Institute for Decision Sciences, University Plaza, Atlanta, Ga. 30303 (1127)

American Institute of Certified Public Accountants, 1211 Ave. of the Americas, New York, N.Y. 10036 (1788)

American Institute of Industrial Engineers, 25 Technology Park, Norcross, Ga. 30071 (1280)

American Institute of Maintenance, 710 West Wilson Ave., Glendale, Calif. 91209 (1727)

American Institute of Management, 125 East 38th St., New York, N.Y. 10016 (348)

American Management Association, 135 West 50th St., New York, N.Y. 10020 (300)

American Marketing Association, 222 South Riverside Plaza, Suite 606, Chicago, Ill. 60606 (1602)

American Production and Inventory Control Society (APICS), Watergate Bldg., Suite 504, 2600 Virginia Ave., N.W., Washington, D.C. 20037 (1682)

American Society for Cybernetics, 1025 Connecticut Ave., N.W., Suite 914, Washington, D.C. 20036 (1267)

American Society for Personnel Administration, 19 Church St., Berea, Ohio 44017 (1864)

American Society for Quality Control, 161 West Wisconsin Ave., Milwaukee, Wis. 53203 (1714)

American Society for Training and Development, P.O. Box 5307, Madison, Wis. 53705 (1956)

American Society of Mechanical Engineers, 345 East 47th St., New York, N.Y. 10017 (1683)

Association for Systems Management, 24587 Bagley Rd., Cleveland, Ohio 44138 (1318)

Association of Certified Accountants, 22 Bedford Square, London, WC1B 3HS, England (1789)

Association of Consulting Management Engineers, 347 Madison Ave., New York, N.Y. 10017 (878)

Association of Internal Management Consultants, c/o Albert Aiello, Jr., Sperry and Hutchinson Co., 330 Madison Ave., New York, N.Y. 10017 (349)

Association of Management Consultants, 811 East Wisconsin Ave., Milwaukee, Wis. 53202 (879)

British Council of Maintenance Associations, c/o Instron, Coronation Rd., High Wycombe, Bucks., HP12 35Y, England (1728)

British Institute of Management (BIM), Management House, Parker St., London, WC2B 5PT, England (301)

Canadian Institute of Management, 51 Eglinton St. E., Toronto, Ontario, Canada (302)

Canadian Management Centre of the American Management Association, CIL House, Suite 1635, 630 Dorchester Blvd. W., Montreal, Quebec, Canada (303)

Center for Multinational Studies, 1625 Eye St., N.W., Suite 908, Washington, D.C. 20006 (1423)

Center for New Corporate Priorities, 1516 Westwood Blvd., Suite 202, Los Angeles, Calif. 90024 (1482)

Centre for Physical Distribution Management, British Institute of Management, Management House, Parker St., London, WC2B 5PT, England (1667)

CIOS - World Council of Management, 1 rue de Varembé, CH-1211 Geneva 20, Switzerland (304)

The Conference Board, 845 Third Ave., New York, N.Y. 10022 (305)

The Conference Board in Canada, 615 Dorchester Blvd. W., Montreal, Quebec, Canada (306)

Council for International Progress in Management, 135 West 50th St., New York, N.Y. 10020 (307)

European Association of Management Training Centres, rue de la Concorde 53, 1050 Brussels, Belgium (718)

European Institute for Advanced Studies in Management, Place Stéphanie 20, B-1050 Brussels, Belgium (73)

Financial Executives Institute, 633 Third Ave., New York, N.Y. 10017 (1790)

Financial Executives Research Foundation, 633 Third Ave., New York, N.Y. 10017 (1791)

Industrial Management Society, 570 Northwest Highway, Des Plaines, Ill. 60016 (308)

The Industrial Society, Robert Hyde House, 48 Bryanston Sq., London, W1H 1BQ, England (309)

Institute for Operational Research, 56-60 Hallam St., London, WIN 5LH, England (1158)

Institute of Administrative Management, 205 High St., Beckenham, Kent, BR3 1BA, England (2014)

Institute of Chartered Accountants in England and Wales, Chartered Accountants Hall, Moorgate Place, London, EC2R 6EQ, England (1792)

Institute of Cost and Management Accountants, 63 Portland Place, London, WIN 4AB, England (1793)

Institute of Directors, 10 Belgrave Sq., London, SW1X 8PW, England (310)

Institute of Internal Auditors, 5500 Diplomat Circle, Suite 104, Orlando, Fla. 32810 (350)

The Institute of Management Sciences (TIMS), 146 Westminster St., Providence, R.I. 02903 (1128)

Institute of Marketing, Moor Hall, Cookham, Berkshire, SL6 9QH, England (1603)

Institute of Personnel Management, Central House, Upper Woburn Place, London, W.C.1, England (1865)

Institute of Practitioners in Work Study, Organisation and Methods, 9/10 River Front, Enfield, Middlesex, EN1 3TE, England (1281)

Institute of Purchasing and Supply, 199 Westminster Bridge Rd., London, S.E.1, England (1703)

Institute of Quality Assurance, 54 Princes Gate, London, SW7 2PG, England (1715)

Institute of Scientific Business, 200 Keighley Rd., Bradford, Yorkshire, BD9 4JZ, England (311)

Institute of Value Management, c/o William & Glyn's Bank, 25 Millbank, London, SW1P 4RB, England (1720)

Institution of Production Engineers, 66 Little Ealing Lane, London, W5 4XX, England (1684)

Institution of Training Officers, 5 Baring Rd., Beaconsfield, Buckinghamshire, HP9 2NX, England (1957)

International Academy of Management, 100 Pacific Hwy., North Sydney, N.S.W. 2060, Australia (312)

International Maintenance Institute, P.O. Box 26695, Houston, Tex. 77207 (1729)

International Management Association, 135 West 50th St., New York, N.Y. 10020 (313)

International Material Management Society, Monroe Complex, 2520 Mosside Blvd., Monroeville, Pa. 15146 (1704)

International Personnel Management Association, 1313 East 60th St., Chicago, Ill. 60637 (1866)

Management Centre Europe, avenue des Arts 3/4, Brussels, Belgium (314)

Management Consultants Association, 23/24 Cromwell Place, London, SW7 2LG, England (880)

Management Consulting Services Information Bureau, British Institute of Management, Management House, Parker St., London, WC2B 5PT, England (881)

MTM Association for Standards and Research, 9-10 Saddle River Front, Fair Lawn, N.J. 07410 (1292)

National Association of Accountants, 919 Third Ave., New York, N.Y. 10020 (1794)

National Association of Purchasing Management, 11 Park Place, New York, N.Y. 10007 (1705)

National Council for Small Business Management Development, c/o Robert O. Bauer, UW-Extension, 929 North Sixth St., Milwaukee, Wis. 53203 (1361)

National Council of Physical Distribution Management, 222 West Adams St., Chicago, Ill. 60606 (1668)

National Management Association, 2210 Arbor Blvd., Dayton, Ohio 45439 (315)

North American Society for Corporate Planning, P.O. Box 3114, Grand Central Station, New York, N.Y. 10017 (938)

Operational Research Society, 6th Floor, Neville House, Waterloo St., Birmingham, B2 5TX, England (1159)

Operations Research Society of America, 428 East Preston St., Baltimore, Md. 21202 (1160)

Planning Executives Institute, 5500 College Corner Pike, Oxford, Ohio 45056 (939)

Project Management Institute, P.O. Box 43, Drexel Hill, Pa. 19026 (1085)

Sales and Marketing Executives-International, 380 Lexington Ave., New York, N.Y. 10017 (1604)

Small Business Administration, 1441 L St., N.W., Washington, D.C. 20416 (1362)

The Smaller Business Unit, British Institute of Management, Management House, Parker St., London, WC2B 5PT, England (1363)

Society for Long Range Planning, 8th Floor, Terminal House, Grosvenor Gardens, London, SW1W OAR, England (940)

Society for Management Information Systems, Suite 2026, 221 North La Salle, Chicago, Ill. 60670 (1257)

Society for the Advancement of Management (SAM), 135 West 50th St., New York, N.Y. 10020 (316)

Society of American Value Engineers, 2550 Hargrave Drive L-205, Smyrna, Ga. 30080 (1721)

Society of Management Information Technology, 40 Tyndalls Park Rd., Bristol, BS8 1PL, England (1258)

Society of Professional Management Consultants, 205 West 89th St., New York, N.Y. 10024 (882)

Appendix B

DIRECTORY OF PERIODICALS

A.A.C.S.B. BULLETIN. American Assembly of Collegiate Schools of Business, 760 Office Parkway, Suite 50, St. Louis, Mo. 63141

ACADEMY OF MANAGEMENT JOURNAL. P.O. Drawer KZ, Mississippi State University, State College, Miss. 39762

ACADEMY OF MANAGEMENT PROCEEDINGS. P.O. Drawer KZ, Mississippi State University, State College, Miss. 39762

ACCOUNTANCY. Institute of Chartered Accountants in England and Wales, Chartered Accountants Hall, Moorgate Place, London, EC2R 6EQ, England

THE ACCOUNTANT. 151 Strand, London, WC2R 1JJ, England

ACCOUNTANTS' DIGEST. Institute of Chartered Accountants in England and Wales, Chartered Accountants Hall, Moorgate Place, London, EC2R 6EQ, England

ACCOUNTING AND BUSINESS RESEARCH. 56-66 Goswell Rd., London, EC1M 7AB, England

ACCOUNTING + DATA PROCESSING ABSTRACTS. Anbar Publications, P.O. Box 23, Wembley, HA9 8DJ, England

ACCOUNTING ARTICLES. Commerce Clearing House, 420 Lexington Ave., New York, N.Y. 10017

THE ACCOUNTING REVIEW. American Accounting Association, 653 South Orange Ave., Sarasota, Fla. 33577

ACROSS THE BOARD. The Conference Board, 845 Third Ave., New York, N.Y. 10022

ADMINISTRATIVE MANAGEMENT. Institute of Administrative Management, 205 High St., Beckenham, Kent, BR3 1BA, England

ADMINISTRATIVE MANAGEMENT: THE MAGAZINE OF BUSINESS SYSTEMS, EQUIPMENT AND PERSONNEL. Geyer-McAllister Publications, 51 Madison Ave., New York, N.Y. 10010

ADMINISTRATIVE SCIENCE QUARTERLY. Malott Hall, Cornell University, Ithaca, N.Y. 14850

THE ADVERTISING QUARTERLY, Advertising Association, Abford House, 15 Wilton Rd., London, SW1V 1NJ, England

AMERICAN BEHAVIORAL SCIENTIST. Sage Publications, P.O. Box 776, Beverly Hills, Calif. 90213

A.M.S. PROFESSIONAL MANAGEMENT BULLETINS. Now incorporated in MANAGEMENT WORLD

ANBAR MANAGEMENT SERVICES BIBLIOGRAPHY. Anbar Publications, P.O. Box 23, Wembley, HA9 8DJ, England

ANBAR MANAGEMENT SERVICES JOINT INDEX. Anbar Publications, P.O. Box 23, Wembley, HA9 8DJ, England

ANNALS OF THE AMERICAN ACADEMY OF POLITICAL AND SOCIAL SCIENCE. American Academy of Political and Social Science, 3937 Chestnut St., Philadelphia, Pa. 19104

ANNUAL REVIEW OF PSYCHOLOGY. Annual Reviews, 4139 el Camino Way, Palo Alto, Calif. 94306

APPLIED ERGONOMICS. Chapman & Hall, 11 New Fetter Lane, London, EC4P 4EE, England

BELL JOURNAL OF ECONOMICS AND MANAGEMENT SCIENCE. American Telephone and Telegraph Co., 195 Broadway, Room 01-1940, New York, N.Y. 10007

BRITISH JOURNAL OF INDUSTRIAL RELATIONS. London School of Economics and Political Science, Houghton St., Aldwych, London, W.C.2, England

BRITISH MANAGEMENT REVIEW. No longer published

BULLETIN OF THE OPERATIONS RESEARCH SOCIETY OF AMERICA. Operations Research Society of America, 428 East Preston St., Baltimore, Md. 21202

BUSINESS AND SOCIETY REVIEW. Warren, Gorham & Lamont, 870 Seventh Ave., New York, N.Y. 10019

BUSINESS GRADUATE. Business Graduates Association, 87 Jermyn Street, London, SW1Y 7JD, England

BUSINESS HISTORY. Frank Cass & Co., Gainsborough House, Gainsborough Rd., London, E11 1RS, England

BUSINESS HISTORY REVIEW. Harvard Graduate School of Business Administration, Baker Library, Soldiers Field, Boston, Mass. 02163

BUSINESS HORIZONS. Graduate School of Business, Indiana University, Bloomington, Ind. 47401

BUSINESS PERIODICALS INDEX. H.W. Wilson Co., 950 University Ave., Bronx, N.Y. 10452

BUSINESS QUARTERLY. School of Business Administration, University of Western Ontario, London, Ontario, Canada

BUSINESS SERVICE CHECKLIST. U.S. Government Printing Office, Washington, D.C. 20402

BUSINESS WEEK. McGraw-Hill, McGraw-Hill Building, 1221 Ave. of the Americas, New York, N.Y. 10020

CALIFORNIA MANAGEMENT REVIEW. Graduate School of Business Administration, University of California, Berkeley, Calif. 94720

C.I.R.F. ABSTRACTS. C.I.R.F. Publications, International Labour Office, CH-1211 Geneva 22, Switzerland

C.I.S. ABSTRACTS. International Occupational Safety and Health Information Centre (C.I.S.), International Labour Office, CH-1211 Geneva 22, Switzerland

COLUMBIA JOURNAL OF WORLD BUSINESS. Columbia University Graduate School of Business Administration, 408 Uris, Columbia University, New York, N.Y. 10027

COMPENSATION REVIEW. AMACOM, Box 319, Saranac Lake, N.Y. 12983

COMPUTER ABSTRACTS. Technical Information Co., Martins Bank Chambers, P.O. Box 59, St. Helier, Jersey, Channel Islands

COMPUTER BULLETIN. No longer published

THE COMPUTER JOURNAL. British Computer Society, 29 Portland Place, London, W1N 4AP, England

COMPUTERS AND PEOPLE. Berkeley Enterprises, 815 Washington St., Newtonville, Mass. 02160

COMPUTING JOURNAL ABSTRACTS. National Computing Centre, Oxford Rd., Manchester, M1 7ED, England

COMPUTING REVIEWS. Association for Computing Machinery, 1133 Ave. of the Americas, New York, N.Y. 10036

CONFERENCE BOARD RECORD. Title changed. See ACROSS THE BOARD

CONTENTS PAGES IN MANAGEMENT. Manchester Business School, Booth St. W., Manchester, M15 6BP, England

CURRENT CONTENTS: BEHAVIORAL, SOCIAL AND MANAGEMENT SCIENCES. Institute for Scientific Information, 325 Chestnut St., Philadelphia, Pa. 19106

DARTNELL SALES AND MARKETING SERVICE. Dartnell Corp., 4660 Ravenswood Ave., Chicago, Ill. 60640

DATAMATION. Technical Publishing Co., 1301 South Grove Ave., Barrington, Ill. 60010

DATA PROCESSING. IPC Electrical-Electronic Press, Dorset House, Stamford St., London, SE1 9LU, England

DATA PROCESSING DIGEST. 6820 La Tijera Blvd., Los Angeles, Calif. 90045

DATA SYSTEMS FOR MANAGEMENT DECISIONS. Embankment Press, Building 59, GEC Estate, East Lane, Wembley, Middlesex, England

DECISION SCIENCES. American Institute for Decision Sciences, University Plaza, Atlanta, Ga. 30303

DISSERTATION ABSTRACTS INTERNATIONAL: A. THE HUMANITIES AND SOCIAL SCIENCES. University Microfilms Xerox Corp., 300 North Zeeb Rd., Ann Arbor, Mich. 48106

DUN'S REVIEW. Dun & Bradstreet Publications Corp., 666 Fifth Ave., New York, N.Y. 10019; 7 Wallgrave Terrace, London, S.W.5, England

ECONOMIC ABSTRACTS. Martinus Nijhoff, 9-11 Lange Voorhout, P.O. Box 269, The Hague, Netherlands

EMPLOYMENT RELATIONS ABSTRACTS. Title changed. See WORK RELATED ABSTRACTS

ERGONOMICS. Taylor & Francis, 10-14 Macklin St., London, WC2B 5NF, England

ERGONOMICS ABSTRACTS. Taylor & Francis, 10-14 Macklin St., London, WC2B 5NF, England

EUROPEAN BUSINESS. Société Européenne d'Edition et de Diffusion (SEED), 73 rue de Turbigo, 75003 Paris, France

EUROPEAN COMMUNITY. 2100 M St., N.W., Washington, D.C. 20037; 20 Kensington Palace Gardens, London, W8 4QQ, England

EUROPEAN JOURNAL OF MARKETING. MCB (European Marketing & Consumer Studies), 200 Keighley Rd., Bradford, Yorkshire, BD9 4JZ, England

EUROPEAN TRAINING. MCB (European Training), 200 Keighley Rd., Bradford, Yorkshire, BD9 4JZ, England

FINANCIAL EXECUTIVE. Financial Executives Institute, 633 Third Ave., New York, N.Y. 10017

FINANCIAL MANAGEMENT. Financial Management Association, c/o University of Wisconsin Press, P.O. Box 1379, Madison, Wis. 53701

FORBES. Forbes, 60 Fifth Ave., New York, N.Y. 10011

FORTUNE. Time, 531 North Fairbanks Court, Chicago, Ill. 60611

FUTURES: THE JOURNAL OF FORECASTING AND PLANNING. IPC Science & Technology Press, IPC House, 32 High St., Guildford, Surrey, GU1 3EW, England; IPC (America), 205 East 42nd St., New York, N.Y. 10017

GUIDELINES FOR THE SMALLER BUSINESS. British Institute of Management, Management House, Parker St., London, WC2B 5PT, England

HARVARD BUSINESS REVIEW. Harvard University, Graduate School of Business Administration, Soldiers Field, Boston, Mass. 02163

HUMAN RELATIONS. Plenum Press, 4a Lower John St., London, W1R 3PD, England; 227 West 17th St., New York, N.Y. 10011

HUMAN RESOURCE MANAGEMENT. Division of Management Education, Graduate School of Business Administration, University of Michigan, Ann Arbor, Mich. 48104

IEEE TRANSACTIONS ON ENGINEERING MANAGEMENT. Institute of Electrical and Electronic Engineers, 345 East 47th St., New York, N.Y. 10017

I.I.L.S. BULLETIN. International Institute for Labour Studies, 154 route de Lausanne, CH-1211 Geneva 22, Switzerland

INDUSTRIAL AND COMMERCIAL TRAINING. Wellens Publishing, Guilsborough, Northampton, NN6 8PY, England

INDUSTRIAL AND LABOR RELATIONS REVIEW. Cornell University, Ithaca, N.Y. 14853

INDUSTRIAL ENGINEERING. American Institute of Industrial Engineers, 25 Technology Park/Atlanta, Norcross, Ga. 30092

INDUSTRIAL MANAGEMENT. Embankment Press, Building 59, GEC Estate, East Lane, Wembley, Middlesex, HA9 7PG, England

INDUSTRIAL MARKETING MANAGEMENT. European Association for Marketing Research (EVAF) and Elsevier Scientific Publishing Co., Box 211, Amsterdam, Netherlands

INDUSTRIAL PARTICIPATION. Industrial Participation Association, 25/28 Buckingham Gate, London, SW1E 6LP, England

INDUSTRIAL RELATIONS. Institute of Industrial Relations, University of California, Berkeley, Calif. 94720

INDUSTRIAL RELATIONS JOURNAL. Mercury House Business Publications, Mercury House, Waterloo Rd., London, SE1 8UL, England

INDUSTRIAL SOCIETY. The Industrial Society, 48 Bryanston Sq., London, W1H 1BQ, England

INDUSTRIAL TRAINING INTERNATIONAL. MGS Publications, 17 Crouch Hill, Finsbury Park, London, N4 4AP, England

INFOR: CANADIAN JOURNAL OF OPERATIONAL RESEARCH AND INFORMATION PROCESSING. P.O. Box 2225, Station D, Ottawa, Canada

THE INTERNAL AUDITOR. Institute of Internal Auditors, 5500 Diplomat Circle, Suite 104, Orlando, Fla. 32810

INTERNATIONAL ABSTRACTS IN OPERATIONS RESEARCH. Elsevier/North-Holland Journal Division, P.O. Box 211, Amsterdam, Netherlands

INTERNATIONAL EXECUTIVE. Foundation for the Advancement of International Business Administration, 64 Ferndale Drive, Hastings-on-Hudson, N.Y. 10706

INTERNATIONAL JOURNAL OF PHYSICAL DISTRIBUTION. MCB (Physical Distribution Management), 200 Keighley Rd., Bradford, Yorkshire, BD9 4JZ, England

INTERNATIONAL JOURNAL OF PRODUCTION RESEARCH. Taylor & Francis, 10-14 Macklin St., London, WC2B 5NF, England

INTERNATIONAL LABOUR DOCUMENTATION. International Labour Office, Central Library and Documentation Branch, CH-1211, Geneva 22, Switzerland

INTERNATIONAL LABOUR REVIEW. International Labour Office, CH-1211 Geneva 22, Switzerland

INTERNATIONAL MANAGEMENT. McGraw-Hill Publishing Co., 1221 Ave. of the Americas, New York, N.Y. 10020; McGraw-Hill House, Maidenhead, Berkshire, SL6 2QL, England

INTERNATIONAL MANAGEMENT INFORMATION, EDITION B. AB Information, Parkgatan 42, S-24200, Hoerby, Sweden

INTERNATIONAL REGISTER OF RESEARCH IN ACCOUNTING AND FINANCE. International Centre for Research in Accounting, Furness College, Bailrigg, Lancaster, LA1 4YG, England

INTERNATIONAL REVIEW OF ADMINISTRATIVE SCIENCES. rue de la Charite 25, B-1040 Brussels, Belgium

INTERNATIONAL REVIEW OF APPLIED PSYCHOLOGY. Liverpool University Press, 123 Grove St., Liverpool, L7 7AF, England

JOURNAL OF ACCOUNTANCY. 1211 Ave. of the Americas, New York, N.Y. 10036

JOURNAL OF ACCOUNTING RESEARCH. Graduate School of Business, University of Chicago, Chicago, Ill. 60637

JOURNAL OF ADVERTISING RESEARCH. Advertising Research Foundation, 3 East 54th St., New York, N.Y. 10022

JOURNAL OF APPLIED BEHAVIORAL SCIENCE. NTL Institute for Applied Behavioral Science, P.O. Box 9155, Rosslyn Station, Arlington, Va. 22209

JOURNAL OF APPLIED PSYCHOLOGY. American Psychological Association, 1200 17th St., N.W., Washington, D.C. 20036

JOURNAL OF BUSINESS. University of Chicago Press, 5801 Ellis Ave., Chicago, Ill. 60637

JOURNAL OF BUSINESS ADMINISTRATION. Faculty of Commerce and Business Administration, University of British Columbia, Vancouver, B.C., V6T 1W5, Canada

JOURNAL OF BUSINESS COMMUNICATION. American Business Communication, 317-B David Kinley Hall, University of Illinois, Urbana, Ill. 61801

JOURNAL OF BUSINESS FINANCE AND ACCOUNTING. Basil Blackwell, 5 Alfred St., Oxford, OX1 4HB, England

JOURNAL OF BUSINESS POLICY. Mercury House Business Publications, Mercury House, Waterloo Rd., London, SE1 8UL, England

JOURNAL OF BUSINESS RESEARCH. Fred D. Reynolds, College of Business Administration, University of Georgia, Athens, Ga. 30602

JOURNAL OF COMMUNICATION. Annenberg School of Communication, University of Pennsylvania, P.O. Box 13358, Philadelphia, Pa. 19101

JOURNAL OF CONTEMPORARY BUSINESS. Graduate School of Business Administration, University of Washington, Seattle, Wash. 98195

JOURNAL OF ECONOMIC LITERATURE. American Economic Association, Readings Fels, 1313 21st Ave. S., Nashville, Tenn. 37212

JOURNAL OF FINANCE. American Finance Association, 100 Trinity Place, New York, N.Y. 10006

JOURNAL OF GENERAL MANAGEMENT. Mercury House Business Publications, Mercury House, Waterloo Rd., London, SE1 8UL, England

JOURNAL OF MANAGEMENT STUDIES. Basil Blackwell, 5 Alfred St., Oxford, OX1 4HB, England

JOURNAL OF MARKETING. American Marketing Association, 222 South Riverside Plaza, Chicago, Ill. 60606

JOURNAL OF MARKETING RESEARCH. American Marketing Association, 222 South Riverside Plaza, Chicago, Ill. 60606

JOURNAL OF PERSONALITY AND SOCIAL PSYCHOLOGY. American Psychological Association, 1200 17th St., N.W., Washington, D.C. 20036

JOURNAL OF PURCHASING AND MATERIALS MANAGEMENT. National Association of Purchasing Management, 11 Park Place, New York, N.Y. 10007

JOURNAL OF QUALITY TECHNOLOGY. American Society for Quality Control, Plankinton Bldg., 161 West Wisconsin Ave., Milwaukee, Wis. 53203

JOURNAL OF RETAILING. New York University, 202 Tisch Hall, Washington Sq., New York, N.Y. 10003

JOURNAL OF SMALL BUSINESS MANAGEMENT. National Council for Small Business Management Development, UW-Extension, 929 North Sixth St., Milwaukee, Wis. 53203

JOURNAL OF SYSTEMS MANAGEMENT. Association for Systems Management, 24587 Bagley Rd., Cleveland, Ohio 44138

JOURNAL OF THE MARKET RESEARCH SOCIETY. 15 Belgrave Sq., London, SW1X 8PF, England

JOURNAL UEC (EUROPEAN JOURNAL OF ACCOUNTANCY). IdW-Verlag GmbH, D4 Duesseldorf, Cecilienallee 36, Postfach 10 226, West Germany

LABOR LAW JOURNAL. Commerce Clearinghouse, 4025 West Peterson Ave., Chicago, Ill. 60646

LIBRARY JOURNAL. R.R. Bowker Co., 1180 Ave. of the Americas, New York, N.Y. 10036

LOGA: LOCAL GOVERNMENT ANNOTATIONS SERVICE. London Borough of Havering, Central Library, Romford, England

LONDON BUSINESS SCHOOL JOURNAL. London Graduate School of Business Studies, Sussex Place, Regent's Park, London, NW1 4SA, England

LONG RANGE PLANNING. Pergamon Press, Journals Division, Headington Hill Hall, Oxford, OX3 OBW, England; Pergamon Press, Maxwell House, Fairview Park, Elmsford, N.Y. 10523

McKINSEY QUARTERLY. McKinsey & Co., 245 Park Ave., New York, N.Y. 10017

MANAGEMENT ACCOUNTING. National Association of Accountants, 919 Third Ave., New York, N.Y. 10022

MANAGEMENT ACCOUNTING: JOURNAL OF THE INSTITUTE OF COST AND MANAGEMENT ACCOUNTANTS. 63 Portland Place, London, W1N 4AB, England

MANAGEMENT ADVISER. No longer published

MANAGEMENT AND PRODUCTIVITY. International Labour Office, Management Development Branch, CH-1211 Geneva 22, Switzerland

THE MANAGEMENT AUDIT. American Institute of Management, 125 East 38th St., New York, N.Y. 10016

MANAGEMENT BY OBJECTIVES. Classified Media, P.O. Box 356, Addlestone, Weybridge, Surrey, England

MANAGEMENT CHECKLISTS. British Institute of Management, Management House, Parker St., London, WC2B 5PT

MANAGEMENT DATAMATICS. Noordhoff International Publishing, P.O. Box 26, Leyden, Holland

MANAGEMENT DECISION. MCB (Management Decision), 200 Keighley Rd., Bradford, Yorkshire, BD9 4JZ, England

MANAGEMENT EDUCATION AND DEVELOPMENT. Association of Teachers of Management. M. Greatorex, c/o Dept. of Management Studies, Polytechnic of Central London, 35 Marylebone Rd., London, NW1 5LS, England

MANAGEMENT IN ACTION. No longer published

MANAGEMENT INFORMATICS. Title changed. See MANAGEMENT DATAMATICS

MANAGEMENT INFORMATION SHEETS. British Institute of Management, Management House, Parker St., London, WC2B 5PT, England

MANAGEMENT INTERNATIONAL REVIEW. Betriebswirtschaftlicher Verlag Dr. Th. Gabler SmbH, 6200 Wiesbaden, West Germany

MANAGEMENT OF PERSONNEL QUARTERLY. Now HUMAN RESOURCE MANAGEMENT

MANAGEMENT REVIEW. AMACOM, Saranac Lake, N.Y. 12983

MANAGEMENT REVIEW AND DIGEST. British Institute of Management, Management House, Parker St., London, WC2B 5PT, England

MANAGEMENT SCIENCE. The Institute of Management Sciences (TIMS), 146 Westminster St., Providence, R.I. 02903

MANAGEMENT SERVICES. Institute of Practitioners in Work Study, Organisation and Methods, 9/10 River Front, Enfield, EN1 3TE, England

MANAGEMENT SERVICES IN GOVERNMENT. Civil Service Department, Whitehall, London, SW1A 2AZ, England

MANAGEMENT TODAY. Haymarket Publishing, Craven House, 34 Foubert's Place, London, W.1, England

MANAGEMENT WORLD. Administrative Management Society, AMS Building, Maryland Rd., Willow Grove, Pa. 19090

MANAGERIAL PLANNING. Planning Executives Institute, P.O. Box 70, Oxford, Ohio 45056

MARKETING. Institute of Marketing, Moor Hall, Cookham, Berkshire, SL6 9QH, England

MARKETING ABSTRACTS. Incorporated in JOURNAL OF MARKETING

MARKETING + DISTRIBUTION ABSTRACTS. Anbar Publications, P.O. Box 23, Wembley, HA9 8DJ, Middlesex, England

MARKETING INFORMATION GUIDE. Hoke Communications, 224 Seventh St., Garden City, N.Y. 11530

MARKET RESEARCH ABSTRACTS. Market Research Society, 51 Charles St., London, W1X 7PA, England

MERGERS AND ACQUISITIONS. Box 36, McLean, Va. 22101

MICHIGAN BUSINESS REVIEW. Graduate School of Business Administration, University of Michigan, Ann Arbor, Mich. 48104

M.S.U. BUSINESS TOPICS. Graduate School of Business Administration, Berkey Hall, Michigan State University, East Lansing, Mich. 48824

MTM JOURNAL. International MTM Directorate (IMD), MTM Association for

Standards and Research, 9-10 Saddle River Front, Fair Lawn, N.J. 07410

MULTINATIONAL BUSINESS. Economist Intelligence Unit, Spencer House, 27 St. James's Place, London, SW1A 1NT, England

NEW BOOKS IN BUSINESS AND ECONOMICS. Baker Library, Harvard University Graduate School of Business Administration, Boston, Mass. 02163

NEW LITERATURE ON AUTOMATION. Netherlands Centre for Informatics, 6 Stadhouderskade, Amsterdam 1013, Netherlands

O & M BULLETIN. Now MANAGEMENT SERVICES IN GOVERNMENT

OCCUPATIONAL PSYCHOLOGY. British Psychological Society, 18-19 Albemarle St., London, W1X 4DN, England

THE OFFICE. Office Publications, 1200 Summer St., Stamford, Conn. 06904

OMEGA: THE INTERNATIONAL JOURNAL OF MANAGEMENT SCIENCE. Pergamon Press, Journals Division, Headington Hill Hall, Oxford, OX3 OBW, England; Pergamon Press, Maxwell House, Fairview Park, Elmsford, N.Y. 10523

OPERATIONAL RESEARCH QUARTERLY. Pergamon Press, Journals Division, Headington Hill Hall, Oxford, OX3 OBW, England; Pergamon Press, Maxwell House, Fairview Park, Elmsford, N.Y. 10523

OPERATIONS RESEARCH. Operations Research Society of America, 428 East Preston St., Baltimore, Md. 21202

OPERATIONS RESEARCH/MANAGEMENT SCIENCE. Executive Sciences Institute, P.O. Drawer M, Whippany, N.J. 07981

ORGANIZATIONAL BEHAVIOR AND HUMAN PERFORMANCE. Academic Press, 111 Fifth Ave., New York, N.Y. 10003; 24/28 Oval Rd., London, N.W.1, England

ORGANIZATIONAL DYNAMICS. AMACOM, Box 319, Saranac Lake, N.Y. 12983

PERSONNEL. AMACOM, Box 319, Saranac Lake, N.Y. 12983

THE PERSONNEL ADMINISTRATOR. American Society for Personnel Administration, 19 Church St., Berea, Ohio 44017

PERSONNEL + TRAINING ABSTRACTS. Anbar Publications, P.O. Box 23, Wembley, HA9 8DJ, England

PERSONNEL JOURNAL. 1131 Olympic Blvd., Santa Monica, Calif. 90404

PERSONNEL LITERATURE. Government Printing Office, North Capitol and H Streets, N.W., Washington, D.C. 20401

PERSONNEL MANAGEMENT. Mercury House Business Publications, 110 Fleet St., London, E.C.4, England

PERSONNEL MANAGEMENT ABSTRACTS. Graduate School of Business Administration, University of Michigan, Ann Arbor, Mich. 48104

PERSONNEL PRACTICE BULLETIN. Title Changed. See WORK AND PEOPLE

PERSONNEL PSYCHOLOGY. 3121 Cheek Rd., Durham, N.C. 27704

PERSONNEL REVIEW. Gower Press, P.O. Box 5, Epping, Essex, CM16 4B, England

PRODUCTION AND INVENTORY MANAGEMENT. American Production and Inventory Control Society, Watergate Bldg., Suite 504, 2600 Virginia Ave., N.W., Washington, D.C. 20037

THE PRODUCTION ENGINEER. Institution of Production Engineers, 66 Little Ealing Lane, London, W5 4XX, England

PSYCHOLOGICAL ABSTRACTS. American Psychological Association, 1200 17th St., N.W., Washington, D.C. 20036

PUBLIC ADMINISTRATION. Royal Institute of Public Administration, Hamilton House, Mabledon Place, London, WC1H 9BD, England

PUBLIC ADMINISTRATION REVIEW. American Society for Public Administration, 1225 Connecticut Ave., N.W., Washington, D.C. 20036

PUBLIC AFFAIRS INFORMATION SERVICE BULLETIN. Public Affairs Information Service, 11 West 40th St., New York, N.Y. 10018

PUBLIC MANAGEMENT. International City Management Association, 1140 Connecticut Ave., N.W., Washington, D.C. 20036

PUBLIC PERSONNEL MANAGEMENT. International Personnel Management Association, Room 240, 1313 East 60th St., Chicago, Ill. 60637

PUBLIC RELATIONS. Institute of Public Relations, 1 Great James St., London, WC1N 3DA, England

PUBLIC RELATIONS JOURNAL. Public Relations Society of America, 845 Third Ave., New York, N.Y. 10022

PUBLIC RELATIONS QUARTERLY. 44 West Market St., Rhinebeck, N.Y. 12572

QUALITY. European Organization for Quality Control, P.O. Box 1976, Weena 734, Rotterdam 3003, Netherlands

QUALITY ASSURANCE. Institute of Quality Assurance, 54 Princes Gate, London, 2PG, England

QUALITY CONTROL AND APPLIED STATISTICS. Executive Sciences Institute, Whippany, N.J. 07981

QUALITY PROGRESS. American Society for Quality Control, 161 West Wisconsin Ave., Milwaukee, Wis. 53203

R & D MANAGEMENT. Basil Blackwell, 108 Cowley Rd., Oxford, OX4 1JF, England

RESEARCH INDEX. Business Surveys, P.O. Box 21, Dorking, Surrey, RH5 4EE, England

RESEARCH MANAGEMENT. Industrial Research Institute at Technomic Publishing Co., 265 Post Rd. W., Westport, Conn. 06880

RYDGE'S. Rydge Publications Pty., 74 Clarence St., Sydney 2000, Australia

SALES AND MARKETING MANAGEMENT. 633 Third Ave., New York, N.Y. 10017

S.A.M. ADVANCED MANAGEMENT JOURNAL. Society for the Advancement of Management, 135 West 50th St., New York, N.Y. 10020

SCIENCE AND TECHNOLOGY. International Communications, 114 Manhattan St., Stamford, Conn. 06904

SELECTED RAND ABSTRACTS. Rand Corp., 1700 Main St., Santa Monica, Calif. 90406

SLOAN MANAGEMENT REVIEW. Massachusetts Institute of Technology, Cambridge, Mass. 02139

SOCIAL SCIENCES CITATION INDEX. Institute for Scientific Information, 325 Chestnut St., Philadelphia, Pa. 19106; 132 High St., Uxbridge, UB8 1DP, England

SOCIOLOGICAL ABSTRACTS. P.O. Box 22206, San Diego, Calif. 92122

STANFORD BUSINESS SCHOOL ALUMNI BULLETIN. Stanford Business School Alumni Association, Stanford University, Stanford, Calif. 94305

SUPERVISORY MANAGEMENT. AMACOM, Saranac Lake, N.Y. 12983

TOP MANAGEMENT ABSTRACTS. Anbar Publications, P.O. Box 23, Wembley, HA9 8DJ, England

TRAINING ABSTRACTS SERVICE. Ceased publication 1975

TRAINING AND DEVELOPMENT JOURNAL. American Society for Training and Development, P.O. Box 5307, Madison, Wis. 53705

WHAT'S NEW IN ADVERTISING AND MARKETING. Advertising & Marketing Division, Special Libraries Association, c/o Research Library, Foote, Cone & Belding, 200 Park Ave., New York, N.Y. 10017

WORK AND PEOPLE. Australian Government Publishing Service, P.O. Box 84, Canberra, A.C.T. 2600

WORK RELATED ABSTRACTS. Information Co-ordinators, 1435-7 Randolph St., Detroit, Mich. 48226

WORK STUDY. Sawell Publications, 127 Stanstead Rd., London, SE23 1JE, England

WORK STUDY + O AND M ABSTRACTS. Anbar Publications, P.O. Box 23, Wembley, HA9 8DJ, England

Appendix C

DIRECTORY OF PUBLISHERS AND DISTRIBUTORS

ABELARD-SCHUMAN, 666 Fifth Ave., New York, N.Y. 10019; 450 Edgware Rd., London, W2 1EG, England

ACADEMIC PRESS, 111 Fifth Ave., New York, N.Y. 10003; 24-8 Oval Rd., Camden Town, London, NW1 7DX, England

ADDISON-WESLEY PUBLISHING CO., Jacob Way, Reading, Mass. 01867; West End House, 11 Hills Place, London, W1R 2LR, England

ALDINE PUBLISHING CO., 529 South Wabash Ave., Chicago, Ill. 60605

ALLEN & UNWIN, 40 Museum St., London, WC1A 1LU, England

ALLEN LANE, THE PENGUIN PRESS, 17 Grosvenor Gardens, London, SW1W 0BD, England

ALLYN & BACON, 470 Atlantic Ave., Boston, Mass. 02210

AMACOM, 135 West 50th St., New York, N.Y. 10020

AMERICAN ELSEVIER PUBLISHING CO., 52 Vanderbilt Ave., New York, N.Y. 10017

AMERICAN FOUNDATION FOR MANAGEMENT RESEARCH, 135 West 50 St., New York, N.Y. 10020

AMERICAN INSTITUTE OF CERTIFIED PUBLIC ACCOUNTANTS, 1211 Ave. of the Americas, New York, N.Y. 10036

AMERICAN LIBRARY ASSOCIATION, 50 East Huron St., Chicago, Ill. 60611

AMERICAN MANAGEMENT ASSOCIATION. See AMACOM

AMERICAN MARKETING ASSOCIATION, 222 South Riverside Plaza, Suite 606, Chicago, Ill. 60606

AMERICAN PRODUCTION & INVENTORY CONTROL SOCIETY, Watergate Bldg., Suite 504, 2600 Virginia Ave., N.W., Washington, D.C. 20037

AMERICAN SOCIETY OF CORPORATE SECRETARIES, 1 Rockefeller Plaza, New York, N.Y. 10020

AMERICAN SOCIETY OF MECHANICAL ENGINEERS, 345 East 47th St., New York, N.Y. 10017

ANBAR PUBLICATIONS, P.O. Box 23, Wembley, HA9 8DJ, England

ANGUS & ROBERTSON, 221 George St., Sydney, N.S.W. 2000, Australia; 2 Mount Place, Lewes, E. Sussex, BN7 1YH, England

EDWARD ARNOLD (PUBLISHERS), 25 Hill St., London, W1X 8LL, England

ASLIB, 3 Belgrave Square, London, SW1X 8PL, England

ASSOCIATION FOR SYSTEMS MANAGEMENT, 24587 Bagley Rd., Cleveland, Ohio 44138

AUERBACH PUBLISHERS, c/o Mason & Lipscomb, 384 Fifth Ave., New York, N.Y. 10018; Spectrum House, Alderton Cresc., London, NW4 3XX, England

AVON BOOKS, 959 Eighth Ave., New York, N.Y. 10019

A.S. BARNES & CO., P.O. Box 421, Cranbury, N.J. 08512

BARNES & NOBLE, Division of Harper & Row Publishers, 10 East 53rd St., New York, N.Y. 10022

BARRIE & JENKINS, 24 Highbury Crescent, London, N5 1RX, England

BASIC BOOKS, 10 East 53 St., New York, N.Y. 10022

BATH UNIVERSITY PRESS, Claverton Down, Bath, BA2 7AY, England

BEEKMAN PUBLISHERS, 38 Hicks St., Brooklyn Heights, N.Y. 11201

BETRIEBSWIRTSCHAFTLICHER VERLAG DR. TH. GABLER, 6200 Wiesbaden, Taumusstrasse 25, West Germany

CLIVE BINGLEY, 16 Pembridge Rd., London, W.11, England

B.H. BLACKWELL, Broad St., Oxford, England

BNA COMMUNICATIONS, 5615 Fishers Lane, Rockville, Md. 20852

BOBBS-MERRILL CO., 4 West 58 St., New York, N.Y. 10019

R.R. BOWKER CO., 1180 Ave. of the Americas, New York, N.Y. 10036

BRANDON SYSTEMS PRESS. See AUERBACH PUBLISHERS

BRITISH BOOK CENTER, 153 East 78th St., New York, N.Y. 10021

BRITISH INSTITUTE OF MANAGEMENT, Management House, Parker St., London, WC2B 5PT, England

BROOKS/COLE PUBLISHING CO., 555 Abrego St., Monterey, Calif. 94606

BUSINESS BOOKS, 24 Highbury Cresc., London, N5 1RX, England

BUSINESS EDUCATION FILMS, 5113 16 Ave., Brooklyn, N.Y. 11204

BUSINESS PUBLICATIONS, 1818 Ridge Rd., Homewood, Ill. 60430

BUSINESS PUBLICATIONS (U.K.). See BUSINESS BOOKS

BUTTERWORTH & CO. (PUBLISHERS), 88 Kingsway, London, WC2B 6AB, England; 19 Cummings Park, Woburn, Mass. 01801

CAHNERS PUBLISHING CO., 221 Columbus Ave., Boston, Mass. 02116

CAMBRIDGE UNIVERSITY PRESS, Bentley House, P.O. Box 92, 200 Euston Rd., London, NW1 2DB, England; 32 East 57 St., New York, N.Y. 10022

CANFIELD PRESS, 850 Montgomery St., San Francisco, Calif. 94133

JONATHAN CAPE, 30 Bedford Square, London, WC1B 3EL, England

FRANK CASS & CO., 10 Woburn Walk, London, WC1, England

CASSELL & CO., 35 Red Lion Square, London, WC1R 4SG, England

CBD RESEARCH, 154 High St., Beckenham, Kent, BR3 1EA, England

CHANDLER PUBLISHING CO., 257 Park Ave. S., New York, N.Y. 10010

CHAPMAN & HALL, 11 New Fetter Lane, London, EC4P 4EE, England

CHATTO & WINDUS, 40-42 William IV St., London, WC2N 4DF, England

CIOS. 1 rue de Varembé, CH-1211 Geneva 20, Switzerland

COLLIER-MACMILLAN PUBLISHERS, 35 Red Lion Square, London, WC1R 4SG, England

COLUMBIA UNIVERSITY PRESS, 562 West 113 St., New York, N.Y. 10025

COLUMBINE PRESS (PUBLISHERS), The School House, 12 Market St., Buxton, SK17 6LD, England

CONFERENCE BOARD, 845 Third Ave., New York, N.Y. 10022

CONSTABLE & CO., 10 Orange St., Leicester Square, London, WC2H 7EG, England

CORNELL UNIVERSITY PRESS, 124 Roberts Place, Ithaca, N.Y. 14850

CRANE, RUSSAK & CO., 347 Madison Ave., New York, N.Y. 10017

CROOM HELM, 2-10 St. John's Rd., London, S.W.11, England

CROSBY LOCKWOOD STAPLES, c/o Granada Publishing, P.O. Box 9, 29 Frogmore St., St. Albans, Herts., England

THOMAS Y. CROWELL CO., 666 Fifth Ave., New York, N.Y. 10019

DARTNELL CORP., 4660 Ravenswood Ave., Chicago, Ill. 60640

DAVID & CHARLES, P.O. Box 4, South Devon House, Railway Station, Newton Abbott, Devon, England; P.O. Box 57, North Pomfret, Vt. 05031

DAVLIN PUBLICATIONS, 13521 Alondra Blvd., Santa Fe Springs, Calif. 90670

DICKENSON PUBLISHING CO., 16250 Ventura Blvd., Encinco, Calif. 91436

DOUBLEDAY & CO., 245 Park Ave., New York, N.Y. 10017

DOW JONES-IRWIN, 1818 Ridge Rd., Homewood, Ill. 60430

DRAKE PUBLICATIONS, 801 Second Ave., New York, N.Y. 10017

GERALD DUCKWORTH & CO., The Old Piano Factory, 43 Gloucester Cresc., London, NW1 7DY, England

DUNELLEN PUBLISHING CO., 90 South Bayles Ave., Port Washington, N.Y. 10050

ELEK BOOKS, 54-8 Caledonian Rd., London, N1 9RN, England

ELSEVIER PUBLISHING CO., P.O. Box 211, 335 Jan Van Galenstraat, Amsterdam, Netherlands. See also AMERICAN ELSEVIER PUBLISHING CO.

EMI SPECIAL FILMS UNIT, Dean House, 7 Soho Square, London, W1V 5FA, England

ENGLISH UNIVERSITIES PRESS. See HODDER & STOUGHTON EDUCATIONAL

EYRE & SPOTTISWOODE (PUBLISHERS), 11 New Fetter Lane, London, EC4P 4EE, England

FABER & FABER, 3 Queen Square, London, WC1N 3AV, England

FAIRCHILD PUBLISHERS, 7 East 12th St., New York, N.Y. 10003

FAWCETT WORLD LIBRARY, 1515 Broadway, New York, N.Y. 10036

FERNHILL HOUSE, c/o Humanities Press, Atlantic Highland, N.J. 07716

W. FOULSHAM & CO., Yeovil Rd., Slough, Bucks., SL1 4JH, England

FUNK & WAGNALLS CO., c/o Thomas Y. Crowell Co., 666 Fifth Ave., New York, N.Y. 10019

GALE RESEARCH CO., Book Tower, Detroit, Mich. 48226

GAMBIT, 306 Dartmouth, Boston, Mass. 02116

GEE & CO. (PUBLISHERS), The City Library, 151 Strand, London, WC2R 1JJ, England

GENERAL LEARNING CORP., 250 James St., Morristown, N.J. 07960

GOETEBORG GRADUATE SCHOOL OF ECONOMICS AND BUSINESS ADMIN-ISTRATION, BAS et foer, Vasegaten 3, 411 24 Goeteborg, Sweden

VICTOR GOLLANCZ, 14 Henrietta St., Covent Garden, London, WC2E 8QJ, England

GOODYEAR PUBLISHING CO., 1640 Fifth St., Santa Monica, Calif. 90401

GORDON & BREACH SCIENCE PUBLISHERS, 1 Park Ave., New York, N.Y. 10016

GOVERNMENT PRINTING OFFICE, Washington, D.C. 20402

GOWER PRESS, P.O. Box 5, Epping, Essex, CM16 4BU, England

GREENWOOD PRESS, 51 Riverside Ave., Westport, Conn. 06880

GROSSET & DUNLAP, 51 Madison Ave., New York, N.Y. 10010

GUILD SOUND & VISION, Training & Education Division, 85-129 Oundle Rd., Peterborough, PE2 9PY, England

GULF PUBLISHING CO., P.O. Box 2608, Houston, Tex. 77001

HAFNER SERVICE AGENCY, 866 Third Ave., New York, N.Y. 10022

G.K. HALL & CO., 70 Lincoln St., Boston, Mass. 02111

HALSTED PRESS, 605 Third Ave., New York, N.Y. 10016

H.M. STATIONERY OFFICE, Atlantic House, Holborn Viaduct, London, EC1P 1BN, England

HARCOURT BRACE JOVANOVICH, 757 Third Ave., New York, N.Y. 10017

HARPER & ROW PUBLISHERS, 10 East 53rd St., New York, N.Y. 10022; 28 Tavistock St., London, WC2E 7PN, England

GEORGE G. HARRAP & CO., 182-4 High Holborn, London, WC1V 7AX, England

HARVARD UNIVERSITY, GRADUATE SCHOOL OF BUSINESS ADMINISTRA-TION, Soldiers Field, Boston, Mass. 02163

HARVARD UNIVERSITY PRESS, 79 Garden St., Cambridge, Mass. 02138

HASTINGS HOUSE PUBLISHERS, 10 East 40th St., New York, N.Y. 10016

HAWTHORN BOOKS, 260 Madison Ave., New York, N.Y. 10016

HEATH LEXINGTON BOOKS, D.C. Heath & Co., 125 Spring St., Lexington, Mass. 02173

WILLIAM HEINEMANN, 15-16 Queen St., London, W1X 8BE, England

WILLIAM S. HEINMAN, 1966 Broadway, New York, N.Y. 10023

LEONARD HILL BOOKS, c/o International Textbook Co., 450 Edgware Rd., London, W2 1EG, England

HIVE PUBLISHING CO., P.O. Box 1004, Easton, Pa. 18042

HODDER & STOUGHTON, St. Paul's House, Warwick Lane, London, EC4P 4AH, England

HODDER & STOUGHTON EDUCATIONAL, P.O. Box 702, Mill Rd., Dunton Green, Sevenoaks, Kent, TN13 2YD, England

HOFSTRA UNIVERSITY, Hempstead, N.Y. 11550

HOLDEN-DAY, 500 Sansome St., San Francisco, Calif. 94111

HOLT, RINEHART & WINSTON, 383 Madison Ave., New York, N.Y. 10017

HOUGHTON MIFFLIN CO., 2 Park St., Boston, Mass. 02107; Kershaw House, 3 Henrietta St., London, WC2 8LU, England

HUMANITIES PRESS, Atlantic Highlands, N.J. 07716

HUTCHINSON PUBLISHING GROUP, 3 Fitzroy Square, London, W1P 6JD, England

ILIFFE. See BUTTERWORTH & CO.

INDUSTRIAL PRESS, 200 Madison Ave., New York, N.Y. 10016

INSTITUTE OF ADMINISTRATIVE MANAGEMENT, 205 High St., Beckenham, Kent, BR3 1BA, England

INSTITUTE OF CHARTERED ACCOUNTANTS IN ENGLAND AND WALES, Chartered Accountants Hall, Moorgate Place, London, EC2R 6EQ, England

INSTITUTE OF PERSONNEL MANAGEMENT, Central House, Upper Woburn Place, London, W.C.1, England

INSTITUTE OF PUBLIC ADMINISTRATION, 55 West 44th St., New York, N.Y. 10036

INSTITUTION OF ELECTRICAL ENGINEERS, P.O. Box 8, Southgate House, Stevenage, Herts., SG1 1HQ, England

INSTITUTION OF MECHANICAL ENGINEERS, 1 Birdcage Walk, Westminster, London, SW1H 9JJ, England

INSTITUT POUR L'ETUDE DES METHODES DE DIRECTION DE L'ENTREPRISE (IMEDE), 23 Chemin de Bellerive, CH-1007, Lausanne, Switzerland

INTERNATIONAL COUNCIL FOR SCIENTIFIC MANAGEMENT. See CIOS

INTERNATIONAL LABOUR OFFICE, CH-1211 Geneva 22, Switzerland

INTERNATIONAL PUBLICATIONS SERVICE, 114 East 22nd St., New York, N.Y. 10016

INTERNATIONAL TEXTBOOK COMPANY. See INTEXT EDUCATIONAL PUBLISHERS

INTERNATIONAL UNIVERSITIES PRESS, 239 Park Ave., New York, N.Y. 10003

INTEXT EDUCATIONAL PUBLISHERS, 257 Park Ave. S., New York, N.Y. 10010

IOWA STATE UNIVERSITY PRESS, Press Building, Ames, Iowa 50010

RICHARD D. IRWIN, 1818 Ridge Rd., Homewood, Ill. 60430

IRWIN-DORSEY, 8 High St., Arundel, W. Sussex, BN18 9AB, England

JOHNS HOPKINS PRESS, Baltimore, Md. 21218

JORDAN & SONS, P.O. Box 260, 15 Pembroke Rd., Bristol, BS99 7DX, England

JOSSEY-BASS, 615 Montgomery St., San Francisco, Calif. 94111

AUGUSTUS M. KELLEY, 305 Allwood Rd., Clifton, N.J. 07012

KLUWER-HARRAP HANDBOOKS, 539 London Rd., Isleworth, TW7 4DA, England

FRITZ KNAPP VERLAG, 6000 Frankfurt am Main 1, Neuer Mainzer Strasse 60, West Germany

CHARLES KNIGHT & CO., c/o Ernest Benn-Benn Brothers, Sovereign Way, Tonbridge, Kent, TN9 1RW, England

ALFRED A. KNOPF, 201 East 50th St., New York, N.Y. 10022

KOGAN PAGE, 116A Pentonville Rd., London, N1 9JN, England

LEVIATHAN HOUSE, 80 East St., Epsom, Surrey, England; distr. by Hippocrene Books, P.O. Box 978, Edison, N.J. 08817

LEXINGTON BOOKS, c/o D.C. Heath, 125 Spring St., Lexington, Mass. 02173

LIBRARY ASSOCIATION, 7 Ridgmount St., Store St., London, WC1E 7AE, England

LONDON GRADUATE SCHOOL OF BUSINESS STUDIES, Sussex Place, Regent's Park, London, NW1 4SA, England

LONDON SCHOOL OF ECONOMICS AND POLITICAL SCIENCE, Houghton St., Aldwych, London, WC2A 2AE, England

LONGMAN GROUP, Longman House, Burnt Mill, Harlow, Essex, CM20 2JE, England; Longman, 19 West 44th St., Suite 1012, New York, N.Y. 10036

MACDONALD & EVANS, 8 John St., London, WC1N 2HY, England

MACDONALD EDUCATIONAL, St. Giles House, 49 Poland St., London, W1A 2LG, England

McGRAW-HILL INTERNATIONAL BOOK CO., 1221 Ave. of the Americas, New York, N.Y. 10020; McGraw-Hill Book Co. (U.K.), Shoppenhangers Rd., Maidenhead, Berkshire, England

MACHINERY PUBLISHING CO., New England House, New England St., Brighton, BN1 4HN, England

MACMILLAN PUBLISHERS, Little Essex St., London, WC2R 3LF, England

MACMILLAN PUBLISHING CO., 866 Third Ave., New York, N.Y. 10022

MANAGEMENT CENTRE EUROPE, avenue des Arts 3/4, Brussels, Belgium; 27 Albemarle St., London, W.1, England

MANAGEMENT PUBLICATIONS. See BRITISH INSTITUTE OF MANAGEMENT

MANAGEMENT TRAINING, Guild House, Upper St. Martin's Lane, London, WC2H 9EL, England

MANCHESTER BUSINESS SCHOOL, Booth St. W., Manchester, M15 6PB, England

MANSELL INFORMATION/PUBLISHING, 3 Bloomsbury Place, London, WC1A 2QA, England

MARKHAM PUBLISHING CO., P.O. Box 7600, Chicago, Ill. 60680

CHARLES E. MERRILL, 1300 Alum Creek Dr., Columbus, Ohio 43216

MICHIGAN STATE UNIVERSITY, GRADUATE SCHOOL OF BUSINESS ADMIN-ISTRATION, East Lansing, Mich. 48823

M.I.T. PRESS, 28 Carleton St., Cambridge, Mass. 02142; 126 Buckingham Palace Rd., London, SW1W 9SD, England

MOREHOUSE-BARLOW CO., 78 Danbury Rd., Wilton, Conn. 06897

WILLIAM MORROW & CO., 105 Madison Ave., New York, N.Y. 10016

JOHN MURRAY PUBLISHERS, 50 Albemarle St., London, W1X 4BD, England

NATIONAL COMPUTING CENTRE, Oxford Rd., Manchester, M1 7ED, England

NATIONAL COUNCIL FOR EDUCATIONAL TECHNOLOGY (now COUNCIL FOR EDUCATIONAL TECHNOLOGY IN THE UNITED KINGDOM), 160 Great Portland St., London, W1N 5TB, England

NATIONAL INDUSTRIAL CONFERENCE BOARD. See CONFERENCE BOARD

THOMAS NELSON & SONS, Lincoln Way, Windmill Rd., Sunbury-on-Thames, Middlesex, TW16 7HP, England; 30 East 42nd St., New York, N.Y. 10017

NEW AMERICAN LIBRARY, 1301 Ave. of the Americas, New York, N.Y. 10019

NEW ENGLISH LIBRARY, Barnard's Inn, Holborn, London, EC1N 2JR, England

NEWMAN NEAME, c/o PERGAMON PRESS (see below)

NEWNES (now NEWNES-BUTTERWORTH), 88 Kingsway, London, WC2B 6AB, England

NEW YORK UNIVERSITY PRESS, 21 West Fourth St., New York, N.Y. 10003

W.W. NORTON & CO., 500 Fifth Ave., New York, N.Y. 10012

OHIO STATE UNIVERSITY PRESS, Hitchcock Hall, Room 316, 2070 Neil Ave., Columbus, Ohio 43210

OLIVER & BOYD, Croythorn House, 23 Ravelston Terrace, Edinburgh, EH4 3TJ, Scotland

ORGANIZATION FOR ECONOMIC CO-OPERATION AND DEVELOPMENT, 1750 Pennsylvania Ave., N.W., Washington, D.C. 20006; 2 rue Andre-Pascal, Paris, 16^e, France

OXFORD UNIVERSITY PRESS, Ely House, 37 Dover St., London, W1X 4AH, England; 200 Madison Ave., New York, N.Y. 10016

PACIFIC BOOKS, P.O. Box 558, Palo Alto, Calif. 94302

PAN BOOKS, 18-21 Cavaye Place, London, SW10 9PG, England

PENGUIN BOOKS, Harmondsworth, Middlesex, England; 625 Madison Ave., New York, N.Y. 10022

PERGAMON PRESS, Headington Hill Hall, Oxford, OX3 OBW, England; Maxwell House, Fairview Park, Elmsford, N.Y. 10523

PHILOSOPHICAL LIBRARY, 15 East 40th St., New York, N.Y. 10016

SIR ISAAC PITMAN & SONS, Pitman House, Parker St., Kingsway, London, WC2B 5PB, England; Pitman Publishing, 6 Davis Drive, Belmont, Calif. 94002

PLANNING EXECUTIVES INSTITUTE, 5500 College Corner Pike, Oxford, Ohio 45056

PLAYBOY PRESS, 919 North Michigan Ave., Chicago, Ill. 60611

POCKET BOOKS, 630 Fifth Ave., New York, N.Y. 10020

POLITICAL AND ECONOMIC PLANNING, 12 Upper Belgrave St., London, SW1X 8BB, England

PRAEGER, 111 Fourth Ave., New York, N.Y. 10003

PRENTICE-HALL, Englewood Cliffs, N.J. 07632; Prentice-Hall International, 66 Wood Lane End, Hemel Hempstead, Hertfordshire, HP2 4RG, England

PUTNAM & CO., 9 Bow St., London, WC2E 7AL, England

RAND McNALLY & CO., Box 7600, Chicago, Ill. 60680; 3 Henrietta St., London, WL2E 8LU, England

RANDOM HOUSE, 201 East 50th St., New York, N.Y. 10022

RANK AUDIO VISUAL, P.O. Box 70, Great West Rd., Brentford, Middlesex, England

D. REIDEL PUBLISHING CO., 38 Papeterspad, P.O.B. 17, Dordrecht, Netherlands; 160 Old Derby St., Hingham, Mass. 02043

REINHOLD. See VAN NOSTRAND REINHOLD

RESTON PUBLISHING CO., c/o Prentice-Hall, Englewood Cliffs, N.Y. 07632

RONALD PRESS CO., 79 Madison Ave., New York, N.Y. 10016

ROTTERDAM UNIVERSITY PRESS, Heemraadssingel 112, Rotterdam 3, Netherlands

ROUTLEDGE & KEGAN PAUL, Broadway House, Reading Rd., Henley-on-Thames, Oxon., RS9 1EN, England; 9 Park St., Boston, Mass. 02108

ROWMAN & LITTLEFIELD, 81 Adams Drive, Totowa, N.J. 07512

ROYAL INSTITUTE OF CHEMISTRY, Blackhorse Rd., Letchworth, Herts., SG6 1HN, England

RUTGERS UNIVERSITY, New Brunswick, N.J. 08903

ST. MARTIN'S PRESS, 175 Fifth Ave., New York, N.Y. 10010

SALES AND MARKETING EXECUTIVES INTERNATIONAL, 380 Lexington Ave., New York, N.Y. 10017

HOWARD W. SAMS & CO., 4300 West 62nd St., Indianapolis, Ind. 46268

SCARECROW PRESS, 52 Liberty St., Box 656, Metuchen, N.J. 08840

SCHOCKEN BOOKS, 200 Madison Ave., New York, N.Y. 10016

SCIENCE RESEARCH ASSOCIATES, 1540 Page Mill Rd., Palo Alto, Calif. 94304; Newtown Rd., Henley-on-Thames, Oxon., RG9 1EW, England

SCIENTIFIC METHODS, 1201 West 24th St., Austin, Tex. 78705

CHARLES SCRIBNER'S SONS, 597 Fifth Ave., New York, N.Y. 10017

SHEED & WARD, 6 Blenheim St., London, W1Y 0SA, England; 64 University Place, New York, N.Y. 10003

SHOE STRING PRESS, 995 Sherman Ave., Hamden, Conn. 06514

SIDGWICK & JACKSON, 1 Tavistock Chambers, Bloomsbury Way, London, WC1A 2SG, England

SIMON & SCHUSTER, 630 Fifth Ave., New York, N.Y. 10020

PETER SMITH, 6 Lexington Ave., Gloucester, Mass. 01930

SOCIETY OF AMERICAN VALUE ENGINEERS, 2550 Hargrave Drive, L-205, Smyrna, Ga. 30080

SOUTHERN ILLINOIS UNIVERSITY PRESS, Carbondale, Ill. 62901

SOUTH-WESTERN PUBLISHING CO., 5101 Madison Rd., Cincinnati, Ohio 45227

SPECIAL LIBRARIES ASSOCIATION, 235 Park Ave. S., New York, N.Y. 10003

E. & F.N. SPON, 11 New Fetter Lane, London, EC4P 4EE, England

STANFORD UNIVERSITY PRESS, Stanford, Calif. 94305

STAPLES PRESS. See CROSBY LOCKWOOD STAPLES

TAPLINGER PUBLISHING CO., 200 Park Ave. S., New York, N.Y. 10003

TAVISTOCK PUBLICATIONS, 11 New Fetter Lane, London, EC4P 4EE, England

TIME-LIFE VIDEO, Department 32-27, Time-Life Building, New York, N.Y. 10020

TRANSATLANTIC ARTS, North Village Green, Levittown, N.Y. 11756

UNITED NATIONS, Sales Section, Publishing Science, New York, N.Y. 10017

U.S. CIVIL SERVICE COMMISSION, 1900 E St., N.W., Washington, D.C. 20415

U.S. DEPARTMENT OF COMMERCE, 14th St. between Constitution Ave. and E St., N.W., Washington, D.C. 20230

UNIVERSAL PUBLISHING & DISTRIBUTION CORP., 235 East 45th St., New York, N.Y. 10017

UNIVERSAL REFERENCE SYSTEM, 720 Sequoia Dr., Sunnyvale, Calif. 94036

UNIVERSITY MICROFILM & XEROX CORPORATION, 300 North Zeeb Rd., Ann Arbor, Mich. 48106

UNIVERSITY OF ALABAMA PRESS, Drawer 2877, University, Ala. 35486

UNIVERSITY OF ASTON IN BIRMINGHAM, Gosta Green, Birmingham, B4 7ET, England

UNIVERSITY OF BRADFORD, MANAGEMENT CENTRE, Emm Lane, Bradford 9, Yorkshire, England

UNIVERSITY OF BRITISH COLUMBIA, FACULTY OF COMMERCE & BUSINESS ADMINISTRATION, Vancouver, V62 1W5, Canada

UNIVERSITY OF CALIFORNIA PRESS, 2233 Fulton St., Berkeley, Calif. 94720

UNIVERSITY OF CHICAGO PRESS, 5801 Ellis Ave., Chicago, Ill. 60637

UNIVERSITY OF MICHIGAN, GRADUATE SCHOOL OF BUSINESS ADMINIS-TRATION, Ann Arbor, Mich. 48104

UNIVERSITY OF MICHIGAN, INSTITUTE FOR SOCIAL RESEARCH, P.O. Box 1248, 426 Thompson St., Ann Arbor, Mich. 48106

UNIVERSITY OF WASHINGTON, GRADUATE SCHOOL OF BUSINESS, Mac-kenzie Hall, DJ-10, Seattle, Wash. 98195

UNIVERSITY OF WISCONSIN PRESS, Box 1379, Madison, Wis. 53701

UNIVERSITY PRESS OF VIRGINIA, Box 3608, University Station, Charlottes-ville, Va. 22903

VAN NOSTRAND-REINHOLD CO., 450 West 33rd St., New York, N.Y. 10001; Molly Millar's Lane, Wokingham, Berks., England

VERRY, LAWRENCE, 16 Holmes St., Mystic, Conn. 06355

WADSWORTH PUBLISHING CO., 10 Davis Drive, Belmont, Calif. 94002

WEIDENFELD & NICHOLSON, 11 St. John's Hill, London, SW11 1XA, England

JOHN WILEY & SONS, 605 Third Ave., New York, N.Y. 10016; Baffins Lane, Chichester, Sussex, PO19 1UD, England

WORLD PUBLISHING CO., 110 East 59th St., New York, N.Y. 10022; 2080 West 117th St., Cleveland, Ohio 44102

PROPER NAME INDEX

Included in this index are the names of persons and corporate bodies mentioned as authors or subjects of the works listed. The index does not refer to entries describing management organizations, which are listed in appendix A. References are to ITEM NUMBERS, not page numbers. Alphabetization is letter by letter.

A

Aa, H.J. van der 1226
Abbot, W. 1548
A.B.C. Co. 1673
Abruzzi, Adam 1282
Abt, Clark C. 1965
Abt Associates Inc. 1468
Abtibi Paper Co. 1486
Academy of Management 237
Ackerman, Robert W. 929, 1458
Ackoff, Russell L. 883, 1130, 1142
ACME Aircraft Corp. 1164
ACME Brass Mfg. Co. 330
Adair, John 528-29
Adelman, Harvey M. 971
Adler, Nancy 921
Administrative Staff College, Henley-on-Thames 696
Advisory Panel on Management Education 722
A.E.I. Ltd. 1382, 1388
Aguilar, Francis Joseph 249, 2055
Ahmedabad Mfg. and Calico Printing Co. 474
Aigner, Dennis J. 1086
Air Preheater Co. 1689
Aitken, Hugh G.J. 1
Aitken, Thomas 1435
Aktiebolaget Svenska Kullagerfabriken 1409

Albaum, Gerald 1571
Albers, Henry H. 139-40
Albers, William W. 1374
Albrecht, Leon K. 1240
Albrook, Robert C. 569
Alcan Aluminum 802
Alexander Hamilton Institute 108
Alexis, Marcus 992, 1594
Alford, Leon Pratt 22, 27, 1675
Alfred, A.M. 1802
Alfred Herbert Ltd. 249
Aljian, George W. 1696
Allegheny Ludlum Steel Corp. 1486
Allen, A.J. 671
Allen, David E., Jr. 34
Allen, Eleanor B. 54
Allen, Isobel 671
Allen, Louis A. 141-42, 557, 598
Allen, Louis L. 1341
Allen, Stephen A. 1365
Allen & Hanburys Ltd. 1911
Allied Chemical Corp. 1485-86
Allis-Chalmers Co. 1485
Allison, David 1754
Alsegg, Robert I. 1424
Aluminum Co. of America 1252
Aluminum Co. of Canada 1486, 1673
Amado-Fischgrund, G. 644
American Airlines 178, 416, 1244

American Association of Collegiate
Schools of Business 707
American Enka Corp. 785
American Institute of Consulting
Engineers 874
American Management Association 35,
209, 738, 740–41, 848, 1188,
1658, 1824, 2021
American Marketing Association 1587
American Production and Inventory
Control Society 1692–93
American Society of Mechanical
Engineers 2, 12, 22, 39, 1342
American Standard Co. 1578
American Telephone & Telegraph Co.
682, 1897–98
Ames, Robert G. 1693
Amey, Lloyd R. 993
Anbar 36, 90, 105, 1279, 1597,
1785, 1858
Anderla, Georges 131
Anderson, I.G. 106
Andrews, Kenneth R. 884, 914
Andrews, Robert 760
Andrews, Victor L. 1758
Ansoff, H. Igor 885
Anstey, Edgar 2048
Anthony, Robert N. 886, 974,
1812–13
Antill, James M. 1529
Appleby, Robert C. 143
Applewhite, Philip B. 409
Appley, Lawrence 212–13, 672
Appleyard, J.R. 570
Arapahoe Chemicals 1904
Arbogast & Bastian Inc. 1689
Arbury, James N. 1659
Archibald, Russell D. 1170
Argenti, John 109–10, 144, 887–88
Argyle, Michael 484
Argyris, Chris 351–55, 371, 395,
416, 444, 530, 537, 551, 558,
849, 1962
Armand, Richard 866
Armco Steel Corp. 717
Armstrong, Robert M. 1659
Armstrong Cork Co. 416
Arnstein, William E. 317
Ashby, W. Ross 1259
Ashland Oil & Refining Co. 1459

Ashton, David 966, 1873
Aspley, John Cameron 1579, 1998
Associated Electrical Industries 1382,
1388
Association for Systems Management
1319
Association of Certified Accountants
58
Association of Scientific, Technical
and Managerial Staffs 1907, 1912
Association of Teachers of Accounting
in the United Kingdom 993
Aston University Library 1360
Astra Group 925
A.T. & T. 682, 1897–98
Athos, Anthony G. 356
Atkinson, Ian 1530
Atlantic Refining Co. 786
Atlas Electronics Corp. 1164
Atwater, Franklin S. 149
Auerbach, Isaac L. 1254
Aurner, Robert Ray 2030
Autometics 576
Auto Supply Co. 550
Avery Products Corp. 1444
Avis Rent-a-Car Corp. 208
Avon Rubber Co. 575
Avots, Ivars 1073
A. Wander Ltd. 925

B

B.F. Goodrill Co. 1578
Babbage, Charles 7, 13, 27
Babcock, George D. 14
Bach, George R. 555
Bacon, Jeremy 828–30, 850, 868,
889, 1795, 1819
Badische Anilin- und Soda-Fabrik AG
1388
Bagley, J.G. 944
Bailey, Earl L. 1371, 1609
Bailey, Joseph C. 1743
Baitsell, John M. 1981
Bakelite Xylonite Ltd. 1907
Baker, Henry G. 1459
Baker, John K. 318
Baker Library, Harvard Business School
55–57, 84, 2064
Bakewell, K.G.B. 37, 53, 2056

Eastman Kodak Co. 717, 1274
Eastwood, Ralph W. 2022
Eccles, A.J. 997
Eckel, Malcolm W. 1497
Economists Advisory Group 1346
Eddison, R.T. 1135, 1137
Eddison, Terry 1562
Edwards, Ronald S. 133-35
Eells, Richard 1336
Egerton, Henry C. 868, 899
Eichborn, Reinhardt von 133
Eilon, Samuel 245, 977, 1508,
    1691, 1695
Eisen, H. 322
Eisenberg, Joseph 328
Elbing, Alvar O. 1909-10
Elbourne, Edward Tregaskiss 7, 18
Elecsonics Ltd. 1358
Elliott-Jones, M.F. 900
Emerson, Harrington 19, 27
Emery, David A. 636
Emery, F.E. 580
E.M.I. Co. 1388
Emory, William 1098
Enell, John W. 785
Engberg, Edward 2066
Enger, Norman L. 1243
England, Wilbur B. 1698
English Electric Co. 1382, 1388,
    1979
Enis, Ben M. 1622
Enrick, Norbert Lloyd 1136
E.N.V. Co. 575
Equitable Life Assurance Society of
    the United States 717
Essex River Authority 1907, 1912-13
Esso Petroleum Co. 1912
Esso Standard Oil Co. 1480
Ethyl Corp. 785
Ettinger, Karl E. 1399
European Association of Management
    Training Centres 718
European Association of National
    Productivity Centres 582
European Centre for Permanent Educa-
    tion (CEDEP) 721
European Community Commission 592
European Federation of Management
    Consultants Associations 874
European Foundation for Management
    Development 51, 79

European Institute for Advanced
    Studies in Management 73
European Institute for Business Admin-
    istration (INSEAD) 79, 721
European Organization for Quality
    Control 1708
Evans, E.O. 1996
Evans, Gordon H. 756
Evans, J.B. 1802
Everard, Kenneth E. 201
Ewing, David W. 637, 902, 1416
E.W. Walton Co. 330
Exton, William 1831
Exxon Co. 476
Eyring, Henry B. 389

F

Fabricant, Solomon 121
Falk, Sir Roger 164
Famularo, Joseph J. 607, 1832
Faraday, Joseph E. 1268, 1925
Farmer, Richard N. 1466
Farrell, Paul V. 1699
Fatchett, D.J. 577
Faucett, Philip M. 329
Faure, R. 1138
Fayerweather, John 1400
Fayol, Henry 5, 7, 15, 20, 24, 27,
    32, 196
Federal Electric Corp. 209
Federated Department Stores 1459
Feigenbaum, E.A. 362
Fein, M. 1896
Feinberg, Mortimer R. 638
Fendrock, John J. 817, 1467
Ferber, Robert 1623, 1628
Fereday, P. 1664
Ferrell, Robert W. 903
Ferrer, H.P. 1549
Ferretti, Andrew P. 1505
Fetter, Robert B. 1669
Fiddes, D.W. 114
Fidelity Radio 863
Field, Judith J. 1448
Fielden, J. 1554
Fielden, John S. 801
Finkle, Robert B. 711
Finley, Robert E. 1685, 1797,
    1867, 2015, 2035

First National Bank of Denver 668
First National City Bank 682
Fischgrund, G. Amado- 644
Fish, Lounsberry 173
Fisher, Dalmar 751
Fisk, Margaret 107
Fisons Ltd. 528
Fitzgerald, Ardra F. 1161
Fitzgerald, John M. 1161
Flaherty, John E. 215
Flaster, Stephen 870
Fletcher, John 52, 1891
Flippo, Edwin B. 365, 1833
Fogarty, Michael P. 671, 860
Fogg, A.H. 600
Follett, Mary Parker 5, 7, 21, 24, 27, 32
Foote, George H. 775
Ford, Henry 221
Ford, Monica M. 85
Ford, Robert N. 1897-98
Ford Motor Co. 160, 847, 1091, 1871
Ford Motor Credit Co. 1959
Fordyce, Jack K. 453
Forest, Joseph R., Jr. 190
Forestal Co. 1388
Forest Products Laboratory 1054
Forrest, Andrew 986
Forrester, Jay W. 1099
Foster, Charles 1537
Foster, Douglas W. 165
Foster, Eric 833
Foster, Richard N. 969
Fowkes, Terence R. 1508
Fox, Alan 511
Fox, Elliot M. 21
Fox, Harland 766, 776, 1938
Foxhall, William B. 1538
Foy, Nancy 1194
Frank, H. Eric 366
Frank, Nathalie D. 1629
Frank, W.F. 176
Franklin, Jerome L. 482
Franklin Mfg. Co. 14
Franko, Lawrence G. 1438
Fraser, John Munro 487
Fredericks, Ward A. 1662
Freeman, C. 1346

Freminville, Charles de 7
French, Richard W. 1162
French, Wendell L. 454, 1834
Frey, Albert Wesley 1571
Froehlich, John C. 1162
Frohman, Mark A. 483
Fromkin, Joseph N. 121
Fuerstenberg, Friedrich 1929
Fujita, Tsuneo 1734
Fuller, Stephen H. 1981
Fulmer, Robert M. 905, 1498
Furash, Edward F. 2058
Fusfield, Alan R. 969
Fyffes Group 925

G

Gabriel, H.W. 1025
Gaden, Herman 1909
Galbraith, Jay 455
Gallagher, James D. 1244
Gantt, Henry Laurence 7, 17, 22, 27
Gardner, C. James 1307
Gardner, Esmond B. 1506
Garmo, E. Paul De 1514
Garrett, Ray, Jr. 834
Garrett, Thomas M. 1499-1500
Gas Council 1211
Gebhard, Charles N. 78
Gee, Kenneth P. 53, 976
Geigy Ltd. (U.K.) 925
Geisler, Edwin B. 1870
Gellerman, Saul W. 260, 438, 488, 536-38, 551, 1835
Gemmill, Gary R. 1084
General Aniline & Film Corp. 847
General Dynamics Corp. 847
General Electric Co. (U.K.) 1382, 1388
General Electric Co. (U.S.A.) 786, 924, 1029, 1091, 1459, 1716
General Mills Inc. 1072
General Motors Corp. 158, 475, 603, 952, 1029, 1331, 1523
Genesco 372, 416
Gennard, John 1454
George, Claude S., Jr. 4, 166
George Washington University 958

Gregg, Lee W. 489
Greiner, Larry E. 451, 581
Greisman, Bernard 125, 1809
Gridley (G.S.) & Co. 1358
Grindley, Kit 1195
Grosset, Serge 252
Grossman, Charles L. 1659
Grote, Richard C. 1899
Grunberg, E. 362
Gryna, Frank M. 1707
G.S. Gridley & Co. 1358
Guetzkow, Harold 399
Guilford, Joan S. 540
Gulick, Luther 24
Gullett, C. Ray 172, 1078
Gunston, C.A. 134
Gurman, Richard 816, 1485
Guth, William D. 914
Guzzardi, Walter 642
Gyrna, Frank M. 1274

H

Haas, Frederick C. 804
Haas, George H. 785
Hackamack, Laurence C. 666
Hackett, J.T. 1378
Hacon, Richard 370
Haeri, F.H. 1034
Hagan, John T. 1706
Haimann, Theo 167
Haire, Mason 371-72, 490, 643, 689
Hake, Bruno 908
Haley, K. Brian 1102
Halff, John F. 181
Hall, David 644
Hall, Elizabeth 258
Hall, James L. 585
Hall, Roger I. 245
Halterman, Carroll C. 982, 2038
Hamburger, Edward 117
Hammond, William Rogers 190
Hampton, David R. 223
Hancock, Robert S. 1572
Hand, Herbert H. 734
Handley, William 1972
Handy, Charles 1537
Haney, William V. 601
Hanika, F. de P. 660, 1163

Hanken, A.F.G. 463
Hansberger, Robert V. 258
Harkins, Edwin P. 1796
Harold, Frederick G. 1196
Harper, Edwin L. 948
Harper, Shirley F. 1038
Harrison, Ian W. 1799
Harrison, Roger 353, 805
Hart, Carole S. 1935
Hartmann, Heinz 667
Harvard Business School Association 777, 985
Harvard University Graduate School of Business Administration 1968
Baker Library 55-57, 84, 2064
Harvey, Joan M. 1632-35
Harvey, John L. 1379
Harvey, M.G.J. 58
Harwood Companies 438, 589
Hasty, Ronald W. 1655
Hausman, Warren H. 1087
Hawes, W.R. 1878
Hawkins, Kevin 928
Hay, Robert 1470
Hayden, Spencer 491
Hayes, James L. 261
Hayes, John J. 397
Haynes, W. Warren 168
Hayward Tyler Co. 1211
Hazel, Arthur Curwen 1348, 1370
Hazen, N. William 229
Heald, Gordon 373
Healey, James H. 623
Healy, Richard J. 2067
Hedrick, Floyd D. 1701
Hegarty, Edward J. 2050
Heider, David A. 1495
Heiland, Robert E. 1304
Hein, Leonard W. 1103
Heinritz, Stuart F. 1699
Heller, Frank A. 1000
Heller, Milton F., Jr. 836
Heller, Robert 169
Hempel, Edward H. 1342
Hemphill, John K. 757
Henderson, L.J. 24
Hennessy, J.H. 1380
Herbert (Alfred) Ltd. 249
Herbst, Robert 135
Herman, Georgiana 1879

457

Margerison, Charles J. 468, 1873
Margolis, Sarah R. 54
Margulies, Newton 469-70
Maria, Alfred T. de 816
Markham, Vic 2071
Marks, Norton E. 1665
Markwell, D.S. 694
Marlin, John Teppler 1488
Marquis, Harold H. 2072
Marquis, Vivienne 2035
Marriott, Oliver 1382
Marriott, R. 1927
Marrow, Alfred J. 438, 589, 1962
Marschak, Jacob 371
Marsh, A.I. 1996
Marsh, J.G. 371
Martin, Michael J.C. 1140
Martindell, Jackson 338
Marting, C.H. 1143
Marting, Elizabeth 675, 1355, 1610,
    1642, 1797, 1883, 1944, 1980,
    2035
Martino, Joseph P. 964
Martino, R.L. 1178-79, 1249
Martyn, Howe 1403
Marvin, Philip 187, 1007, 1643
Marx, Karl 406
Maslow, Abraham H. 400, 416, 549
Massachusetts Institute of Technology
    1401
Massarik, Fred 555
Massie, Joseph L. 168, 188-89, 229
Massy, William F. 1591
Masterson, Thomas R. 1502
Mathes, Sorrell M. 1201, 1372
Matthews, John Bowers 1477
Matthews (Bernard) Ltd. 863
Mausner, Bernard 542
Maxcy, George 1376
Maydew, John C. 609, 1427
Mayhall, William 1740
Maynard, Harold B. 127-28, 1272,
    1291, 1672
Maynard, Jeff 1202
Mayo, Elton 5, 24, 27, 401-2,
    537, 572
Maytag Co. 372
Meat & Cannery Workers' Union 1038
Megathlin, Donald E. 1646

Meiburg, Charles O. 1490
Meister, Irene W. 1449
Melesse, Jacques 1137
Melman, Seymour 1008
Meloan, Taylor W. 1577
Meltzer, Morton F. 2060
Merck & Co. 1252, 1611
Merewitz, Leonard 951
Merrett, A.J. 778, 1801
Merrill, Harwood F. 27
Mescon, Michael H. 190
Mesics, Emil A. 1951
Messerschmidt-Belkow-Blohm GmbH
    1908, 1911
Metcalfe, Henry 27
Metz, C.K.C. 336
Meyer, Mitchell 1938
Mezack, M. 733
Michael, Stephen R. 339
Michelon, L.C. 156, 191
Michels, Robert 406
Michigan University Institute for
    Social Research 483
Mikhail, Azmi D. 1489
Miles, Lawrence D. 1716
Miller, Ben 1741
Miller, David W. 1112
Miller, E.J. 403
Miller, Ernest C. 917, 1059, 1578,
    1673, 1761
Miller, Ernest G. 950
Miller, F. Leonard 1656
Miller, Frank 1929
Miller, Martin R. 750
Miller, Robert B. 489
Miller, Robert W. 1180
Millett, John D. 1558
Mills, Geoffrey 2003
Mills, John K., Jr. 668
Milner, Walker W. 1518, 1543
Milward, G.E. 1311-14
Miner, John B. 404, 679, 695
Minnesota Mining & Mfg. Co. (now
    3-M Co.) 599, 1072, 1877
Minter, A.L. 1302
Mintzberg, Henry 651
Misshauk, Michael J. 409
Mitchell, Don G. 854

Robbins, Sidney M. 1450
Roberts, B.C. 577
Roberts, Harold S. 1997
Roberts, T.J. 694
Robertson, Andrew B. 123
Robertson, Keith B. 1902-3
Robinson, David M. 2033-34
Robinson, Edwin M. 2002
Robock, Stefan H. 1406
Rock, Milton L. 1923
Rockart, John F. 1550
Rockware Glass Ltd. 925
Rockwell Mfg. Co. 1578, 1673, 1761
Rodger, Alec 1894
Roeber, Richard J.C. 475
Roethlisberger, F.J. 414-15
Roets, Perry 1500
Rogers, Derek 1316
Rope, Crispin 110
Roscoe, Edwin Scott 1676
Rose, Harold B. 729
Rose, J. 1264
Rose, T.G. 340, 981
Rosen, Ned A. 552
Rosenbloom, Richard S. 1495
Rosenblum, John W. 929
Rosenthal, Robert A. 382
Rosenzweig, James E. 177, 1164
Ross Group Ltd. 1214
Rotch, William 1357
Rouse, Andrew M. 948
Rousham, Sally 1912
Rowbottom, R.W. 568
Rowbottom, Ralph 1551
Rowland, Virgil K. 791
Rowntree, B. Seebohm 5, 7, 1841
Rowntree Co. 1841
Roy, Donald 1929
Royal Air Force 1871
Royal Institute of Chemistry 1527
Royal Navy 1047, 1052
Royster, Vermont 258
Rubey, Harry 1518, 1543
Rubin, Martin L. 1204
Rucker, Frank W. 1546
Rue, Leslie W. 905, 922
Rugby Portland Cement Co. 249
Rush, Harold M.F. 416, 476, 591, 1904
Ryans Tourist Holdings 863

S

Saga Administrative Corp. 476
Saint-Gobin Co. 1388
St. Regis Paper Co. 1072
Salera, Virgil 1407
Salond, Josephine I. 1360
Salter, Malcolm S. 772
Sampson, Robert C. 518
Sandeau, Georges 1593
Sanders, Donald H. 1205-6
Sandoz Products Ltd. 1911
Sands, Edith 681
Santocki, J. 341
Sarabhai Industries 474
Sashkin, Marshall 483
Sasieni, Maurice W. 1130
Sauer, Robert L. 758
Savage, William G. 2001
Saville, John 29
Sayles, Leonard R. 417-18, 431, 496, 535, 655, 1366, 1843, 1929
Scanlan, Burt K. 200, 744
Scantlebury, D.L. 342
Schaeffer, Winnifred E. 1646
Schaffer, Robert H. 318
Schaffir, Walter B. 923
Schaller, Elmer D. 1656
Schappe, Robert H. 1905
Schaupp, D. 584
Scheer, Wilbert E. 1842
Schein, Edgar H. 477, 497, 548
Scheinfeld, Aaron 753
Schellenberger, Robert E. 1116
Schick, Allen 957, 959
Schkade, Lawrence L. 1095
Schlaifer, Robert 1117
Schleh, Edward C. 990
Schmidt, Warren H. 554
Schmidt-Anderla, Georgette 131
Schmieder, Frank J. 780
Schnee, Jerome E. 226
Schollhammer, Hans 1429, 1444
Schonfeld, Hanns-Martin 137
Schoonmaker, Alan N. 754, 826
Schreiber Wood Industries 1914
Schroeter, Louis C. 419
Schubach, John J. 1659
Schuppe, Wolfgang 1234
Schuster, Fred E. 1066

Walton, Clarence 1336, 1480
Walton, Richard E. 480
Walton (E.W.) Co. 330
Wander (A.) Ltd. 925
Wankum, A. 2020
Ward, Ann 2035
Warr, Peter B. 502, 746
Warren, E. Kirby 196, 226
Warren Lamb Associates 855
Warren Spring Laboratory 1328
Washington (George) University 958
Wass, Alonzo 1545
Wasserman, Paul 50, 69, 876-77, 1031, 1040, 1636
Watertown Arsenal 1
Watling, T.F. 202, 1082-83
Weatherbee, Harvard Y. 1881
Webber, Ross A. 663
Weber, C. Edward 1020
Weber, Max 406
Webley, Simon 1503
Webster, W.A.H. 1317
Weeks, David A. 1614-15
Wegner, Robert E.C. 431
Weick, Karl E. 631
Weiher, Ronald L. 38
Weil, Raymond 453
Weinberg, Charles B. 1659
Weinshall, Theodore D. 1686
Weir, E.T. 603
Weisselberg, Robert C. 1121
Weissman, Jacob 1481
Weldon Mfg. Co. 589
Wells, Howard A. 1750
Wells, Louis T. 1433
Wells, Robert 1935
Wells, Theodore 669
Welsch, Lawrence A. 1096
Wentworth, Felix R.L. 1663
Weschler, Irving R. 555, 1963
Wescott Packing Co. 2004
West, Jude P. 716
Western Co. 1578, 1761
Westfall, Ralph 1621
Westinghouse Electric Corp. 603
West Midlands Gas Board 1211
West Riding County Council 1563
Weyerhaeuser Co. 1164, 1904
Wheatcroft, Mildred 730
Wheatley, John J. 1577

Wheeler, Lora Jeanne 1421
Wheelwright, Steven C. 1493
Whirlpool Corp. 1673
Whisler, Thomas L. 1038, 1215
Whitaker, D. 942
Whitaker, Galvin 1964
White, Carl M. 70
White, K.K. 620
White, M.R.M. 778
White, William L. 767
Whitehead, T.N. 24
Whitelaw, Matt 747
Whiting, Charles S. 1029
Whitmore, Dennis A. 1275, 1286
Whitworth, Brian 174
Whyte, William Foote 371, 432, 537, 1929
Whyte, William H., Jr. 819-20
Wickert, Frederic R. 793
Widing, J. William 1434
Wiener, Norbert 1265-66
Wiest, J.D. 1122
Wiggins Teape Ltd. 1911, 1914
Wikstrom, Walter S. 699, 717, 1072, 1689, 1877
Wilcock, Stephen 481
Wild, Ray 235
Wilde, Frazer B. 346
Wilkerson, C. David 619
Wilkinson, Alan 1255
Will, R. Ted 1655
Williams, A.P.O. 527
Williams, Charles M. 1759
Williams, Herbert Lee 1546
Williams, M.R. 794
Williams, R. 748
Williamson, Oliver E. 362, 433
Williamson, Robin 1236
Wills, Gordon 5, 236, 248, 966, 973, 1630
Willsmore, A.Q. 975
Wilson, Aubrey 1654
Wilson, B. 467
Wilson, Charles Z. 992
Wilson, Ira G. 1753
Wilson, Marthann E. 1753
Wilson, Sidney R. 783-84
Wilson, Vivian 1039, 1983
Wilts, Preston 1494
Winchell, Constance M. 71

TITLE INDEX

This index is alphabetized letter by letter. References are to ITEM NUMBERS, not page numbers. Titles of periodical articles are not included.

A

AACSB Bulletin 700
ABC of Work Study 1273
Abstracting Services 86
Academy of Management Journal 263
Academy of Management Proceedings 237
Accountancy 1766
Accountant, The 1767
Accountants' Encyclopedia 1804
Accountants' Handbook 1805
Accountants' Index 1780
Accounting and Business Research 1768
Accounting + Data Processing Abstracts 1228, 1785
Accounting Articles 1784
Accounting for Management Control 1817
Accounting Fundamentals for Non-Financial Executives 1811
Accounting Information Sources 1782
Accounting Practice Management Handbook 1810
Accounting Review, The 1769
Achieving Computer Profitability 1189
Acquiring and Merging Businesses 1380
Across the Board 264
Action-Centred Leadership 528
Administering Research and Development 1743
Administration and Management: A Selected and Annotated Bibliography 47
Administration of Cost Reduction Programs 1826
Administration of Organization and Methods Services, The 1307
Administrative Action 195
Administrative Behavior 1017
Administrative Decision-Making 999
Administrative Management 2009
Administrative Management: The Magazine of Business, Systems, Equipment and Personnel 2010
Administrative Office Management (Johnson & Savage) 2001
Administrative Office Management (Neuner & Keeling) 2004
Administrative Revolution, The 357
Administrative Science Quarterly 265
Advanced Techniques for Strategic Planning 917
Advertising Cost Control Handbook 1649
Advertising Quarterly 1650
Age of Systems, The 1831
AMA Book of Employment Forms 1883
AMA Management Handbook 129
American Association of Collegiate Schools of Business, 1916-1966, The 707
American Behavioral Scientist 439

O

SUBJECT INDEX

This index does not include the names of persons or corporate bodies as subjects, which are listed in the Proper Name Index. Although names of countries are included here, the United States and Great Britain are not listed since so many of the items listed deal with these two countries. References are to ITEM NUMBERS, not page numbers. Alphabetization is letter by letter.

A

Absenteeism 402, 1835
Abstracting and indexing services
  advertising 1599
  bibliographies of 85-86
  computers 1228-33
  financial management 1784-85
  human engineering 1328
  industrial engineering 1279
  industrial psychology 508
  international management 1417
  labor relations 1993-94
  local government 1565
  management in general 90-105
  marketing 1596-99
  marketing research 1631
  operations research 1156-57
  personnel management 1858-60
  quality control 1713
  safety 1974
  training 1953-54
Accounting 1804-18
  applications of operations research
    1155
  bibliographies 1780-85
  organizations 1787-89, 1792-94
  periodicals 1766-69, 1772-75,
    1777-79

pollution control and 1488-89
systems and procedures 1306, 1313.
  See also Budgeting; Costing;
  Financial management
Acquisition of companies. See
  Mergers and acquisitions
Action profile method of assessment
  855
A.D.P. See Computers
Advertising 1340, 1599-1600,
  1647-51
  agencies 1547
  ethics 1467, 1500
Africa 229, 250, 1632
Aging 492, 502
Agriculture 1509-10, 1547
Airline management 403, 913
Alcoholics in industry 821-22
Alternatives and Differences Approach
  450
Applications for employment 1882-86,
  2030
Appraisal
  employee 404, 501, 509, 538,
    546, 560, 565, 1032-40, 1078
  management methods 317-50
  managers 536, 686, 698, 715,
    764, 769, 771, 785-94

C

Calico print industry 1376
Canada 586-87, 945, 953, 1054, 1247
Capital investment 998, 1798-1803
Career planning 259, 499, 689, 694, 749-54, 1439
Car industry 1376, 1401, 1445, 1523
Case studies 244-49
as training technique 1965, 1968-69
bibliographies 75-82, 1415, 1495
use in decision making 1014
Cassettes. See Audiovisual materials
Cement industry 1376
Change, problems of 363, 409, 432, 435, 446, 448, 451-52, 458, 464, 471, 474, 479, 537, 1511. See also Organization design/development
Channels of distribution 1652-57
Charting 1161, 1306, 1310. See also Bar charts; Gantt chart; Organization charts
Chemical industry 249, 368, 1445, 1524-27
Chief executive 848-58, 899, 1011. See also Top managers
Chile 699
Civil engineering 1529-45
Civil service 671. See also Government; Public administration
Classics of management 12-33
Classification and indexing 2060, 2063-65
Clerical work measurement 2022-23, 2025-29
Coal mining 1511
Collective bargaining 1829, 1980, 1982. See also Labor relations; Labor unions
Collective management 609
Colleges, management of 1552-55
Columbus, Ohio, managers in 649
Command Group Training 370
Committees 565, 853, 1523, 2048-49
Communication 161, 259, 380, 383, 398, 409, 428, 485, 488, 490, 531, 533, 541, 650, 653, 661, 687, 982, 1083, 1314, 1393, 1403, 1412, 2017, 2030-78
Community relations 1471, 1500
Companies. See Corporations
Comparative management 250-52
Compensation. See Remuneration
Computers 156, 328, 642, 1188-1258, 1306, 1310, 1314, 1340, 1785, 1809
applications to
advertising 1647
building management 1543
farm planning 1510
financial management 943, 1212, 1447
hospital management 1548
libraries and information services 2060, 1447
personnel records 1881, 1884
planning 915, 941-43, 1212
project management 1083
cybernetics and 1131, 1259-67
decision making and 362, 502, 866, 1012, 1095, 1101, 1103, 1106, 1215
ethics and 1499
industrial espionage and 2067
management consultancy and 866
operations research and 1133
organization structure and 604, 1198, 1215
recruitment and 1833
systems analysis and 1165-66
See also Automation; Management information systems; Network planning
Confectionery industry 600
Conferences
as communication media 2034
in decision making 1005
organization of 661
Conflict in organizations 381, 388, 397, 399, 464, 479-80, 486, 509
Construction industry 403, 844, 1182, 1529-45, 1547
Consultants 866-82, 1547
internal 317-50
role in organization development 452, 454

Management and society 7, 16, 22.
See also Social responsibility of
business
Management appraisal. See Appraisal
Management as a profession 141-42
Management audit 317-50, 1306,
1310
Management by exception 32, 983
Management by objectives 128, 156,
160, 395, 1041-72
applications to
appraisal of managers 788, 794
decision making 1013
government 1044, 1047, 1054,
1071, 1562-63, 1568
management development and
training 686, 697-98
personnel management 1834, 1838
computers and 1196
managerial grid and 526
organization development and 449,
454, 461, 1043, 1060
Management by objectives and results
1043, 1061
Management by results 988, 990
Management consultants. See
Consultants
Management control. See Control,
managerial
Management development and training
185, 251, 259, 328, 449, 486,
502, 509, 517, 560, 602, 631,
650, 684-754
multinationals 1399, 1436-37,
1439, 1442
See also Appraisal--managers
Management games 1163, 1965-67
Management information systems 373,
460, 977, 1101, 1143, 1174,
1240-58, 1310, 1312
Management organization structure.
See Organization structure
Management ratios 1090, 1818
Management sciences 1011,
1086-1328. See also Quantitative methods; names of specific
tools and techniques, e.g.,
Computers, Operations research
Management services 317-50, 1316,
1784. See also Industrial

engineering; Systems and procedures; names of specific techniques, e.g., Operations research
Management styles 380, 423, 509-27,
554, 642, 687, 865, 1000. See
also Managerial grid; Participative management; Theory X and
theory Y; Three-dimensional
management style
Managerial grid 321, 395, 483,
521-27, 1068, 1613, 1959
Managerial matrix 525
Managerial obsolescence 486, 799,
803-4
Managerial psychology 21, 23, 384,
484-508
Managers 251-52, 261, 384, 423,
438, 606, 615, 627-882
biographies 7, 12, 22, 26, 28, 33,
672-74
financial department 1795-97
fringe benefits 769, 771, 1939
marketing department 1608-15
multinational 1431, 1435-42
personnel department 1867-68
production department 1685-86
recruitment and selection 384,
404, 509, 537, 675-83, 698,
1436
remuneration 251, 328, 404, 678,
698, 760-84, 1436
society and 815-20, 823
use of time 259, 606, 634-35,
660-63, 856
women as 243, 260, 664-71, 685
See also Management styles
Manpower planning 373, 698, 711,
936, 1078, 1869-81, 1919
Marginal costing 1818
Marketing management 258, 367,
600, 926, 1092, 1340, 1520,
1569-1668, 1691, 2030
management by objectives 1052
management information systems
1252
multinationals 1396, 1402-3,
1616-19
operations research 1144, 1155
production management and 1677
research and development and 1735

local government 1562, 1568
marketing 1591
multinationals 928, 1398, 1409,
1443-46
production 943, 1211, 1690-93
quantitative methods use 917-18,
928, 1093, 1132, 1143-44,
1155, 1508
top management's role 852, 858,
899
See also Network planning
Planning-programming-budgeting
system 944-59, 1555, 1557,
1568
Plant layout 1691, 1722-23
Plant maintenance 492, 1314,
1724-29
PMTS 1275, 1295, 2023
Poland 597
Political parties, organization of 398
Pollution 258, 1467, 1471, 1478,
1484-95. See also Environment
and management
PPBS 944-59, 1555, 1557, 1568
Predetermined motion time systems
1275, 1295, 2023
Present-value method 1798
Presidents. See Top managers
Press relations 404, 2068-78
Pricing 245, 897, 998, 1090, 1480,
1656
ethics 1500
Printing departments 1314
Printing industry 1358
Prisons, organization of 398
Procurement of materials 1155,
1696-1705, 1825
Product development 600, 915, 926,
964, 1093, 1492, 1637-46
Production control 943, 1211,
1690-93
Production management 245, 367,
1313, 1669-1729
engineering 1516, 1519
ethics 1473
multinationals 1396, 1403
quantitative methods for 1090,
1092, 1144, 1212, 1669, 1671
Production managers 1685-86
Production planning 943, 1211,
1690-93

Productivity 37, 490, 517, 537,
556, 1008, 1269, 1275, 1550
Professional organizations. See
Organizations, trade and professional
Professional services management 1547
Profits, improving company 1050
Program budgeting 944-59, 1555,
1557, 1568
Program evaluation and review technique. See PERT
Programmed instruction 1965, 1970-77
Programmed texts
computers 1188
cost control 1824
employee appraisal 1039
management in general 209-11
motivation 540
office management 2021
physical distribution management
1658
Project management 1073-85, 1517,
1526, 1533
large company 1366
management development tool 715
network planning 1075, 1172,
1174, 1177, 1179, 1181,
1186-87
research and development 893
Promotion of staff 488, 560, 678,
680, 682, 771, 823
Psychological problems of managers
822-27
Psychology in industry 21, 23, 384,
484-508
Public administration 398, 944-59,
1168. See also Civil service;
Government management; Local
government management
Public relations 404, 2068-78
Public speaking 2034, 2043, 2052-54
Public utilities management 1547
Purchasing 1155, 1696-1705, 1825

Q

Quality control 1517, 1519, 1691,
1706-15
Quantitative methods
management in general 376,
1086-1267

marketing 1589, 1594
production management 1090,
1092, 1144, 1212, 1669, 1671
research and development management 1749-53
See also Decision making; Planning

R

Racial problems 1480
Readings
behavioral sciences 356, 359, 363,
367-9, 373, 384, 396, 409,
420-21, 428, 430
corporate planning 891, 907
decision making 992-93, 1019
enterprises 1337
executive career planning 749
financial management 1758, 1762
industrial psychology 492, 494
leadership and motivation 370,
409, 502, 534-5, 553
management audit 330
management by objectives 1043,
1052
management control 974, 980, 982
management information systems
1247, 1253
management in general 212-36
management science 1092, 1096,
1101, 1109
marketing 1577
mergers and acquisitions 1379
operations research 1135, 1139
organization theory 366, 370-72,
398, 410, 411, 448, 451, 465,
478-79
personnel management 1829, 1840
program budgeting 949-50
research and development management 1732, 1743
small companies 1349, 1352, 1357
social responsibility of business
1477
T-group training 1961
Real estate management 1547
Records management 1310
Recruitment and selection 352, 380,
485, 488, 497, 501-2, 536-38,
681, 1833, 1886-95

managers 384, 404, 509, 537,
675-83, 698, 1436
multinationals 1436
office staff 2016
salesmen 1608, 1611
Redundancy 798, 800-802, 805-9,
811
ethical aspects 1503
payments 1939
Religious organizations management
1547
Remuneration 438, 490, 560, 579,
1915-34, 1979
administration of 560, 1078,
1915-23
directors 828
managers 251, 328, 404, 678,
698, 760-84
multinationals 1436, 1440-41
office staff 2017-18
sales staff 1614-15
Report writing 1001, 1161, 2030, 2035
Reprographic firms management 1381
Research and development management
376-77, 403, 1366, 1547,
1730-55
engineering and 1519
management by objectives 1052
multinationals 1403
operations research 1132
planning 893, 915, 926, 961,
964, 968, 1751
Research audit 929
Retailing 1547, 1652-57, 2017
Retirement 498, 805, 1938
Romania 229
Rural management 1399
Russia 240, 251, 519, 777

S

Sabbaticals 796-97
Safety 1829, 1972-77, 2017, 2035
Salaries. See Remuneration
Sales forecasting 943
Sales staff 1608-15
Sampling 1117, 1136, 1312, 1317
Scalar process 32
Scandinavia 718. See also:
Denmark; Norway; Sweden